DATE DUE

MY 1 4 '10			

DEMCO 38-296

TORTS AND PERSONAL INJURY LAW

Paralegal Titles from Delmar Publishers

Legal Writing, 2nd ed., Steve Barber, 1997
Administration of Wills, Trusts, and Estates, 2nd ed., Gordon W. Brown, 1997
Basics of Legal Document Preparation, Robert R. Cummins, 1997
Constitutional Law: Cases and Commentary, Daniel E. Hall, 1997
Criminal Procedure and the Constitution, Daniel E. Hall, 1997
Survey of Criminal Law, 2nd ed., Daniel E. Hall, 1997
California Estate Administration, Zella Mack, 1997
Torts and Personal Injury Law, 2nd ed., William R. Buckley, Cathy J. Okrent, 1997
The Law of Corporations, Partnerships, and Sole Proprietorships, 2nd ed.,
    Angela Schneeman, 1997
Texas Legal Research, 2nd ed., Pamela R. Tepper, Peggy N. Kerley, 1997

Legal Research, Steve Barber, Mark A. McCormick, 1996
Wills, Estates, and Trusts, Jay H. Gingrich, 1996
Criminal Law and Procedure, 2nd ed., Daniel E. Hall, 1996
Introduction to Environmental Law, Harold Hickok, 1996
Civil Litigation, 2nd ed., Peggy N. Kerley, Joanne Banker Hames, Paul A. Sukys, 1996
Client Accounting for the Law Firm, Elaine M. Langston, 1996
Law Office Management, 2nd ed., Jonathan S. Lynton, Terri Mick Lyndall,
    Donna Masinter, 1996
Foundations of Law: Cases, Commentary, and Ethics, 2nd ed., Ransford C. Pyle, 1996
Administrative Law and Procedure, Elizabeth C. Richardson, 1996
Legal Research and Writing, David J. Smith, 1996

Legal Research and Writing, Carol M. Bast, 1995
Federal Taxation, Susan G. Covins, 1995
Everything You Need to Know About Being a Legal Assistant, Chere B. Estrin, 1995
Paralegals in New York Law, Eric M. Gansberg, 1995
Ballentine's Legal Dictionary and Thesaurus, Jonathan S. Lynton, 1995
Legal Terminology with Flashcards, Cathy J. Okrent, 1995
Wills, Trusts, and Estate Administration for Paralegals, Mark A. Stewart, 1995
The Law of Contracts and the Uniform Commercial Code, Pamela R. Tepper, 1995
Life Outside the Law Firm: Non-Traditional Careers for Paralegals, Karen Treffinger, 1995

An Introduction to Paralegal Studies, David G. Cooper, Michael J. Gibson, 1994
Administrative Law, Daniel E. Hall, 1994
Ballentine's Law Dictionary: Legal Assistant Edition, Jack G. Handler, 1994
The Law of Real Property, Michael P. Kearns, 1994
Ballentine's Thesaurus for Legal Research and Writing, Jonathan S. Lynton, 1994
Legal Ethics and Professional Responsibility, Jonathan S. Lynton, Terri Mick Lyndall, 1994
Criminal Law for Paralegals, Daniel J. Markey, Jr., Mary Queen Donnelly, 1994
Family Law, Ransford C. Pyle, 1994
Paralegals in American Law: Introduction to Paralegalism, Angela Schneeman, 1994
Intellectual Property, Richard Stim, 1994

TORTS AND PERSONAL INJURY LAW

SECOND EDITION

William R. Buckley
Cathy J. Okrent

Delmar Publishers

an International Thomson Publishing company I

Albany · Bonn · Boston · Cincinnati · Detroit · London · Madrid
Melbourne · Mexico City · New York · Pacific Grove · Paris · San Francisco
Singapore · Tokyo · Toronto · Washington

NOTICE TO THE READER

f the products described herein or perform any independent analysis in con-
ntained herein. Publisher does not assume, and expressly disclaims, any obli-
than that provided to it by the manufacturer.

The reader is expressly warned to consider and adopt all safety precautions that might be indicated by the activities herein and to avoid all potential hazards. By following the instructions contained herein, the reader willingly assumes all risks in connection with such instructions.

The publisher makes no representations or warranties of any kind, including but not limited to, the warranties of fitness for particular purpose or merchantability, nor are any such representations implied with respect to the material set forth herein, and the publisher takes no responsibility with respect to such material. The publisher shall not be liable for any special, consequential, or exemplary damages resulting, in whole or in part, from the reader's use of, or reliance upon, this material.

Cover Design: Linda C. DeMasi
Background by: Jennifer McGlaughlin

Delmar Staff:

Acquisitions Editor: Christopher Anzalone
Editorial Assistant: Judy A. Roberts
Developmental Editor: Jeffrey D. Litton

Project Editor: Eugenia L. Orlandi
Production Coordinator: Linda J. Helfrich
Art & Design Coordinator: Douglas J. Hyldelund

COPYRIGHT © 1997
by West Publishing
an imprint of Delmar Publishers
a division of International Thomson Publishing
The ITP logo is a trademark under license.
Printed in the United States of America

For more information, contact:
Delmar Publishers
3 Columbia Circle, Box 15015
Albany, New York 12212-5015
International Thomson Publishing–Europe
Berkshire House
168-173 High Holborn
London WC1V 7AA
England

Thomas Nelson Australia
102 Dodds Street
South Melbourne, 3205
Victoria, Australia

Nelson Canada
1120 Birchmount Road
Scarborough, Ontario
Canada, M1K 5G4

International Thomson Editores
Campos Eliseos 385, Piso 7
Col Polanco
11560 Mexico D F Mexico

International Thomson Publishing GmbH
Königswinterer Strasse 418
53227 Bonn
Germany

International Thomson Publishing Asia
221 Henderson Road
#05 - 10 Henderson Building
Singapore 0315

International Thomson Publishing–Japan
Hirakawacho Kyowa Building, 3F
2-2-1 Hirakawacho
Chiyoda-ku, Tokyo 102
Japan

1 2 3 4 5 6 7 8 9 10 XXX 02 01 00 99 98 97 96

Library of Congress Cataloging-in-Publication Data

Buckley, William R. 1958–
    Torts and personal injury law.—2nd ed. / William R. Buckley,
Cathy J. Okrent.
        p. cm.
    Rev. ed. of: Torts and personal injury law / William R. Buckley. c 1993
    Includes bibliographical references and index.
    ISBN 0-8273-7572-7
    1. Torts—United States. 2. Personal injuries—United States.
3. Legal assistants—United States—Handbooks, manuals, etc.
I. Okrent, Cathy J. II. Buckley, William, 1958– Torts and personal
injury law. III. Title.
KF1250.Z9B83 1997
346.7303—dc20   96-20067
[347.3063]   CIP

DEDICATION

This book is dedicated to Jay and our children, Diana and Lisa. Without their support and encouragement, I would never have attempted or completed this project.

Cathy J. Okrent

CONTENTS

IIII CHAPTER 2:   Introduction to Torts and Legal Analysis   44

IIII CHAPTER 3:   Negligence   60

IIII CHAPTER 4:   Special Negligence Actions   108

▇ CHAPTER 5:   Defenses to Negligence   150

▇ CHAPTER 6:   Intentional Torts: Injuries to Persons   174

IIII **CHAPTER 8:** Defenses to Intentional Torts   276

IIII CHAPTER 11: Special Tort Actions   382

IIII CHAPTER 12: Tort Immunities   422

IIII CHAPTER 13: Paralegal Ethics   442

IIII Appendices

DELMAR PUBLISHERS INC.

 AND

LAWYERS COOPERATIVE PUBLISHING

ARE PLEASED TO ANNOUNCE THEIR PARTNERSHIP TO CO-PUBLISH COLLEGE TEXTBOOKS FOR PARALEGAL EDUCATION.

DELMAR, WITH OFFICES AT ALBANY, NEW YORK, IS A PROFESSIONAL EDUCATION PUBLISHER. DELMAR PUBLISHES QUALITY EDUCATIONAL TEXTBOOKS TO PREPARE AND SUPPORT INDIVIDUALS FOR LIFE SKILLS AND SPECIFIC OCCUPATIONS.

LAWYERS COOPERATIVE PUBLISHING (LCP), WITH OFFICES AT ROCHESTER, NEW YORK, HAS BEEN THE LEADING PUBLISHER OF ANALYTICAL LEGAL INFORMATION FOR OVER 100 YEARS. IT IS THE PUBLISHER OF SUCH REKNOWNED LEGAL ENCYCLOPEDIAS AS **AMERICAN LAW REPORTS, AMERICAN JURISPRUDENCE, UNITED STATES CODE SERVICE, LAWYERS EDITION,** AS WELL AS OTHER MATERIAL, AND FEDERAL- AND STATE-SPECIFIC PUBLICATIONS. THESE PUBLICATIONS HAVE BEEN DESIGNED TO WORK TOGETHER IN THE DAY-TO-DAY PRACTICE OF LAW AS AN INTEGRATED SYSTEM IN WHAT IS CALLED THE "TOTAL CLIENT-SERVICE LIBRARY®" (TCSL®). EACH LCP PUBLICATION IS COMPLETE WITHIN ITSELF AS TO SUBJECT COVERAGE, YET ALL HAVE COMMON FEATURES AND EXTENSIVE CROSS-REFERENCING TO PROVIDE LINKAGE FOR HIGHLY EFFICIENT LEGAL RESEARCH INTO VIRTUALLY ANY MATTER AN ATTORNEY MIGHT BE CALLED UPON TO HANDLE.

INFORMATION IN ALL PUBLICATIONS IS CAREFULLY AND CONSTANTLY MONITORED TO KEEP PACE WITH AND REFLECT EVENTS IN THE LAW AND IN SOCIETY. UPDATING AND SUPPLEMENTAL INFORMATION IS TIMELY AND PROVIDED CONVENIENTLY.

FOR FURTHER REFERENCE, SEE:

AMERICAN JURISPRUDENCE 2D: AN ENCYCLOPEDIC TEXT COVERAGE OF THE COMPLETE BODY OF STATE AND FEDERAL LAW.

AM JUR LEGAL FORMS 2D: A COMPILATION OF BUSINESS AND LEGAL FORMS DEALING WITH A VARIETY OF SUBJECT MATTERS.

AM JUR PLEADING AND PRACTICE FORMS, REV: MODEL PRACTICE FORMS FOR EVERY STAGE OF A LEGAL PROCEEDING.

AM JUR PROOF OF FACTS: A SERIES OF ARTICLES THAT GUIDE THE READER IN DETERMINING WHICH FACTS ARE ESSENTIAL TO A CASE AND HOW TO PROVE THEM.

AM JUR TRIALS: A SERIES OF ARTICLES DISCUSSING EVERY ASPECT OF PARTICULAR SETTLEMENTS AND TRIALS WRITTEN BY 180 CONSULTING SPECIALISTS.

UNITED STATES CODE SERVICE: A COMPLETE AND AUTHORITATIVE ANNOTATED FEDERAL CODE THAT FOLLOWS THE EXACT LANGUAGE OF THE STATUTES AT LARGE AND DIRECTS YOU TO THE COURT AND AGENCY DECISIONS CONSTRUING EACH PROVISION.

ALR AND ALR FEDERAL: SERIES OF ANNOTATIONS PROVIDING IN-DEPTH ANALYSES OF ALL THE CASE LAW ON PARTICULAR LEGAL ISSUES.

U.S. SUPREME COURT REPORTS, L ED 2D: EVERY REPORTED U.S. SUPREME COURT DECISION PLUS IN-DEPTH DISCUSSIONS OF LEADING ISSUES.

FEDERAL PROCEDURE, L ED: A COMPREHENSIVE, A-Z TREATISE ON FEDERAL PROCEDURE—CIVIL, CRIMINAL, AND ADMINISTRATIVE.

FEDERAL PROCEDURAL FORMS, L ED: STEP-BY-STEP GUIDANCE FOR DRAFTING FORMS FOR FEDERAL COURT OR FEDERAL AGENCY PROCEEDINGS.

FEDERAL RULES SERVICE, 2D AND 3D: REPORTS DECISIONS FROM ALL LEVELS OF THE FEDERAL SYSTEM INTERPRETING THE FEDERAL RULES OF CIVIL PROCEDURE AND THE FEDERAL RULES OF APPELLATE PROCEDURE.

FEDERAL RULES DIGEST, 3D: ORGANIZES HEADNOTES FOR THE DECISIONS REPORTED IN FEDERAL RULES SERVICE ACCORDING TO THE NUMBERING SYSTEMS OF THE FEDERAL RULES OF CIVIL PROCEDURE AND THE FEDERAL RULES OF APPELLATE PROCEDURE.

FEDERAL RULES OF EVIDENCE SERVICE: REPORTS DECISIONS FROM ALL LEVELS OF THE FEDERAL SYSTEM INTERPRETING THE FEDERAL RULES OF EVIDENCE.

FEDERAL RULES OF EVIDENCE NEWS

FEDERAL PROCEDURE RULES SERVICE

FEDERAL TRIAL HANDBOOK, 2D

FORM DRAFTING CHECKLISTS: AM JUR PRACTICE GUIDE

GOVERNMENT CONTRACTS: PROCEDURES AND FORMS

HOW TO GO DIRECTLY INTO YOUR OWN COMPUTERIZED SOLO PRACTICE WITHOUT MISSING A MEAL (OR A BYTE)

JONES ON EVIDENCE, CIVIL AND CRIMINAL, 7TH

LITIGATION CHECKLISTS: AM JUR PRACTICE GUIDE

MEDICAL LIBRARY, LAWYERS EDITION

MEDICAL MALPRACTICE—ALR CASES AND ANNOTATIONS

MODERN APPELLATE PRACTICE: FEDERAL AND STATE CIVIL APPEALS

MODERN CONSTITUTIONAL LAW

NEGOTIATION AND SETTLEMENT

PATTERN DEPOSITION CHECKLISTS, 2D

QUALITY OF LIFE DAMAGES: CRITICAL ISSUES AND PROOFS

SHEPARD'S CITATIONS FOR ALR

SUCCESSFUL TECHNIQUES FOR CIVIL TRIALS, 2D

STORIES ET CETERA—A COUNTRY LAWYER LOOKS AT LIFE AND THE LAW

SUMMARY OF AMERICAN LAW

THE TRIAL LAWYER'S BOOK: PREPARING AND WINNING CASES

TRIAL PRACTICE CHECKLISTS

2000 CLASSIC LEGAL QUOTATIONS

WILLISTON ON CONTRACTS, 3D AND 4TH

FEDERAL RULES OF EVIDENCE DIGEST: ORGANIZES HEAD-NOTES FOR THE DECISIONS REPORTED IN FEDERAL RULES OF EVIDENCE SERVICE ACCORDING TO THE NUMBERING SYSTEM OF THE FEDERAL RULES OF EVIDENCE.

ADMINISTRATIVE LAW: PRACTICE AND PROCEDURE

AGE DISCRIMINATION: CRITICAL ISSUES AND PROOFS

ALR CRITICAL ISSUES: DRUNK DRIVING PROSECUTIONS

ALR CRITICAL ISSUES: FREEDOM OF INFORMATION ACTS

ALR CRITICAL ISSUES: TRADEMARKS

ALR CRITICAL ISSUES: WRONGFUL DEATH

AMERICANS WITH DISABILITIES: PRACTICE AND COMPLI-
ANCE MANUAL

ATTORNEYS' FEES

BALLENTINE'S LAW DICTIONARY

CONSTITUTIONAL LAW DESKBOOK

CONSUMER AND BORROWER PROTECTION: AM JUR PRAC-
TICE GUIDE

CONSUMER CREDIT: ALR ANNOTATIONS

DAMAGES: ALR ANNOTATIONS

EMPLOYEE DISMISSAL: CRITICAL ISSUES AND PROOFS

ENVIRONMENTAL LAW: ALR ANNOTATIONS

EXPERT WITNESS CHECKLISTS

EXPERT WITNESSES IN CIVIL TRIALS

FORFEITURES: ALR ANNOTATIONS

FEDERAL LOCAL COURT RULES

FEDERAL LOCAL COURT FORMS

FEDERAL CRIMINAL LAW AND PROCEDURE: ALR ANNOTA-
TIONS

FEDERAL EVIDENCE

FEDERAL LITIGATION DESK SET: FORMS AND ANALYSIS

PREFACE

Focus

Welcome to the exciting and dynamic field of tort law. The immediacy of the issues dealt with in this text is reflected in the headline cases and human interest pieces that appear throughout the book. These will particularly appeal to the personal injury paralegal.

Overview

This text is an overview of tort law for the personal injury paralegal. Each chapter includes a professional profile highlighting some of the everyday tasks a paralegal might handle in various office settings in bringing or defending tort actions. Chapter 1 introduces the reader to the role of the paralegal in tort investigation and litigation. Chapter 2 discusses tort law generally and historically. Chapter 3 summarizes negligence. Chapter 4 discusses special negligence actions, including premises liability, bailments, vicarious liability, and negligent infliction of emotional distress. Chapter 5 focuses on the defenses to negligence actions. Chapter 6 considers intentional torts and injuries to persons. Chapter 7 is devoted to intentional torts and injuries to property. Chapter 8 addresses defenses to intentional torts. Chapter 9 covers strict, or absolute, liability. Chapter 10 illustrates product liability cases. Chapter 11 features special tort actions. Chapter 12 discusses tort immunities. Chapter 13 reviews paralegal ethics.

Chapter Features

Chapters begin with an outline summary. Each chapter ends with a summary, review questions, and projects.

The running glossary features standard definitions from *Ballentine's Legal Dictionary and Thesaurus*. Students can, at a glance, learn or refresh their memories regarding these general terms. The *Ballentine's* definitions are supplemented by more subject-specific material supplied by the author (author definitions are marked with a dagger).

The text combines theoretical and practical applications. Accompanying each tort topic are hypothetical examples to illustrate how the abstract rules pertain to real life. Illustrative cases are included to portray the actual application of legal principles in appellate court opinions, legal encyclopedia summaries, and the *Restatement (Second) of Torts*.

All cases included are for educational purposes, as examples. The cases have been heavily edited, and citations omitted, so as to include as many cases in the text as possible. The reader should always refer to original sources and verify that there have been no recent changes in the law in a particular jurisdiction. Sample letters, forms, and reports are included for illustrative purposes. The people named in the exhibits and hypotheticals are all fictional; any resemblance to known people is purely coincidental.

Acknowledgments

Torts and Personal Injury Law could not have been produced without the dedication of many people. I thank my editors at Delmar (in particular, Chris Anzalone), Graphics West, and Brooke Graves of Graves Editorial Service; and the American Law Institute, the National Law Journal, and the *Rutgers Computer & Technology Law Journal,* for allowing use of reprinted portions of their materials.

Additionally, I would like to acknowledge the contributions of the following reviewers:

Kenneth Archambault
California State University
    at Hayward
Hayward, CA

James Bullock
Pitt Community College
Greenville, NC

Janet Cox
Northeast Mississippi
    Community College
Booneville, MS

James Hodge
International College
Naples, FL

Norman W. Holt II
Daytona Beach
    Community College
Daytona, FL

Peggy Nickerson
William Woods University
Fulton, MO

Edwards O'Boyle
Gwinnett Business College
Lilburn, GA

DeShaunta Stewart
San Jacinto College North
Houston, TX

Jo Ann Tresco
Central Pennsylvania
Business School
Summerdale, PA

Kathleen Urban
Laramie County
Community College
Cheyenne, WY

TABLE OF CASES

||||

CHAPTER 1

THE PERSONAL INJURY PARALEGAL AND TORT CASE INVESTIGATION

§ 1.1 Personal Injury Paralegals in Tort Litigation

Approximately 10 percent of the paralegals in the United States specialize in personal injury litigation. Many more paralegals work on personal injury cases from time to time as one of the many areas of law that are routinely handled by general practice firms.

Some of the many tasks a personal injury paralegal performs are:

- Interviewing clients to elicit the particular facts of their cases

- Obtaining witness statements

- Investigating the accident, condition, or occurrence

- Assisting in the preparation of legal documents, such as summons, complaint, answer, or reply

- Preparing settlement summaries

- Preparing discovery requests, tracking and monitoring responses to discovery requests, and summarizing deposition transcripts

- Researching legal issues and assisting in preparing motions

- Scheduling witnesses and experts for trial

- Preparing exhibits for trial

- Organizing evidence for trial

- Preparing cases for arbitration

- Preparing subpoenas for trial and arranging for service of process

- Aiding in preparing clients for testifying at trial

- Being present at trial to assist the attorney

- Assisting in the preparation and research of appellate briefs.

§ 1.2 Introduction to Investigation

Investigating the facts and circumstances surrounding tortious injury or death offers many challenges. Every tort case presents the following fundamental questions, which journalists use every day in a reporting context: *Who? What? Where? When? Why? How?* In tort cases, the paralegal queries: Who injured the victim (plaintiff)? What injuries happened? How did the victim (plaintiff) get hurt? Where and when did the injuries occur? Why did the victim (plaintiff) incur injuries (that is, did the defendant(s) cause the victim's/plaintiff's injuries)? How did the injuries occur?

This chapter examines the procedures paralegals use to investigate tort cases. These techniques are then illustrated in the context of specific types of tort cases.

§ 1.3 The Importance of Tort Case Investigation

Key facts must be ascertained if a law firm is to properly handle a personal injury or property damage lawsuit. This entails an **investigation**.

Paralegals and Investigators

Each attorney or law firm has its own specialized methods for conducting investigations. Some have in-house investigators; others hire outside investigators or investigation services. Some attorneys hire specialists for specific aspects of a tort case. Some rely on law clerks, paralegals, or other staff members to perform certain aspects of investigations.

Even if the paralegal is not required to conduct investigations, it is essential that he or she know what is needed for each type of case in order to supervise or monitor the investigation. Paralegals need to know when a particular piece of information may lead to something else and therefore merits additional investigation. Conversely, paralegals should develop a

---

TERMS

investigation 1. An inquiry, either judicial, legislative, or administrative, for the discovery and collection of facts concerning a particular matter or matters. 2. Inquiry; looking into something; research.

IIII   PROFESSIONAL PROFILE   IIII

Jean Scott, a paralegal in a small personal injury law firm, particularly enjoys investigating the facts and circumstances surrounding an injury or death case. It is one part of her work where she feels completely in control of what she does, and where her input is always welcomed and needed.

There are many ways to go about investigating a case. Each case always has a unique set of facts that can be handled from a variety of angles. Jean always likes to begin at the scene of the accident, seeing things from the client's perspective. Many things come to mind when viewing the site of an accident that would not be apparent when merely discussing the case in an office conference room. If the client has sufficiently recovered from his or her injuries, Jean appreciates his or her company and assistance in locating the precise area of the occurrence. Jean may return to the scene several times thereafter, but the client's presence may not be needed in these followup visits.

At the scene, Jean sees things that the client did not necessarily notice or remember. Jean wonders aloud how the client was able to see through a rather large tree to scan the intersection. The question prods the client into remembering that she did not just stop once at the intersection, but that she stopped 100 feet before the intersection (because of the obstructed view), and then inched her way toward the stop sign and then into the intersection. Skid marks that Jean notices prompt the client to recall yet another aspect of the occurrence that the client forgot to mention.

Jean always likes to make a sketch of the scene so that she will be perfectly clear about the compass directions in respect to the accident scene. This sketch is always useful later when the allegations of a plaintiff's claim are incorporated into the complaint. Jean likes to be sure of the plaintiff's path of travel. While sketching the area, Jean jots down the best vantage point for future photographs. Jean also notes the presence of several smashed mailboxes. Perhaps this section of road has inherent design problems and an engineer should be engaged to study the scene.

Upon returning to the office, Jean discusses her findings with the senior partner. The partner is pleased to have the additional information in support of the client's case. The partner concurs with Jean's recommendations and sends both a photographer and an engineer to the scene to investigate further.

---

sense of what items of information are not useful or relevant. One must be able to review the investigation, make sure it has been done properly and completely, and ascertain whether further research is needed.

Many paralegals handle particular aspects of investigation, either in the stages of case evaluation and development or in the course of case management. This is especially true when the trial team is determining potential defendants and ascertaining the basic facts of what happened and why. At times, a knowledgeable paralegal will spot legal issues early on that have a significant bearing on the case investigation. For example, the paralegal might learn of the existence of photographs taken by a rescue squad which show details about the condition of an accident scene.

Customizing the Investigation

The tort trial team will want to adapt the investigation to fit the case. Investigations can be quite simple or highly complex and technical. Factors such as the severity of the injury involved and resources available often control the scope of the investigation. "Resources available" are such factors as the client's ability to pay, the attorney's ability to advance the costs of investigation, the financial condition of prospective defendants, and the existence of insurance, all of which must be considered.

Details, Details, Details!

In litigation, details are very important. An overlooked detail could make a real difference in the outcome of the case. Investigations must be customized, with more than a little creativity. For example, suppose that you are investigating an automobile accident. You cannot understand why the driver of the vehicle did not stop for the pedestrian in the crosswalk. A witness tells you that she noticed the driver was wearing glasses, but this should *not* be enough proof for you to automatically conclude that the driver could see properly. It is possible that the driver was only wearing reading glasses when distance glasses were needed. It is also possible that the driver was wearing an old pair of glasses and never bothered to get a new prescription. Little details like these can make or break a case.

Goals of Tort Case Investigation

Factual investigation is designed to shed light on liability and damages. Information is gathered in terms of what happened to the injured party, who may or may not have been responsible for the injuries, and any act or omission by the injured party that contributed to the accident.

If all else fails, it may be necessary to turn over the investigation, or portions of it, to a professional investigator who has access to automated databases and other resources. However, this is not practical in a small case or in a case where the firm's client has limited financial resources.

§ 1.4 Witness Interview Techniques and Questions

Witnesses will explain their account of the circumstances before and after the accident, how the accident occurred, and the damages or injuries received by the people involved. Some firms prefer that such interviews be electronically recorded, or written and signed by the witness for future reference or use. Witnesses sometimes forget or change their testimony. It is important to interview witnesses as soon as possible; they will be easier to locate, and their recollections will be clearer. Figure 1-1 shows a sample witness statement.

WITNESS STATEMENT

14 Fern Dr.   Albany   N.Y.   5/03/96
LOCATION   CITY   STATE   DATE

1. My name is Kris J. McGrail. I reside at 14 Fern Drive,
2. Albany, NY. I am employed by the Albany Police
3. Department. My date of birth is 10/10/59. On 4/28/96
4. I witnessed an accident on Sand Creek Road east
5. of Wolf Road. I was sitting on my motorcycle at
6. the Hess Station on Sand Creek and Wolf Road. I
7. was just finished getting gas and was getting
8. ready to leave when I witnessed an accident. I was
9. just about to leave the gas station when I noticed
10. a motorcycle heading across Wolf Road going east-
11. bound. This motorcycle had a green light as it
12. crossed Wolf Road on Sand Creek Road. I noticed
13. the motorcycle because the driver was wearing a
14. T-shirt and I thought he was brave because
15. although it was nice out it wasn't that warm.
16. There was a gold-toned vehicle behind me at the pumps
17. at the Hess Station facing north. This vehicle, which
18. I later learned was driven by Deborah Lawrence,
19. pulled around me at the pump and began to exit
20. from the Hess Station. Ms. Lawrence used the exit
21. of the Hess Station going onto Sand Creek Road. Ms.
22. Lawrence came to a gliding stop and exited the
23. driveway going westbound. Ms. Lawrence never
24. brought her car to a full stop as she exited the
25. driveway. Ms. Lawrence did not have the directional
26.
27. Wit: Cathy Okrent   Kris McGrail

◄■■■■■■ **DO NOT WRITE BELOW THIS LINE** ■■■■■■►

FIGURE 1-1
Sample witness statement

Client Interview Techniques

Personal injury paralegals are often involved in interviewing clients and witnesses. Some firms will have the client fill out an initial information questionnaire that is specifically geared to garner the information needed to handle a personal injury case. (See the client information questionnaire in Appendix A.) Other firms might desire a more informal

FIGURE 1-1
(continued)

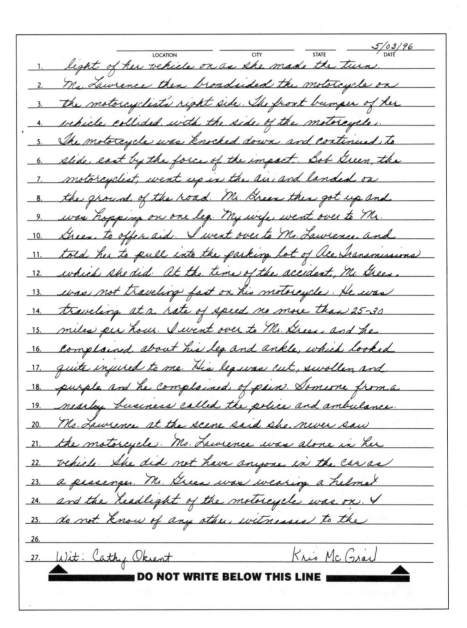

```
                    LOCATION        CITY        STATE        5/03/96
                                                             DATE
 1.  light of her vehicle on as she made the turn.
 2.  Ms. Lawrence then broadsided the motorcycle on
 3.  the motorcyclist's right side. The front bumper of her
 4.  vehicle collided with the side of the motorcycle.
 5.  The motorcycle was knocked down and continued to
 6.  slide east by the force of the impact. Bob Green, the
 7.  motorcyclist, went up in the air and landed on
 8.  the ground of the road. Mr. Green then got up and
 9.  was hopping on one leg. My wife went over to Mr.
10.  Green to offer aid. I went over to Ms. Lawrence and
11.  told her to pull into the parking lot of Ace Transmissions
12.  which she did. At the time of the accident, Mr. Green
13.  was not traveling fast on his motorcycle. He was
14.  traveling at a rate of speed no more than 25-30
15.  miles per hour. I went over to Mr. Green and he
16.  complained about his leg and ankle, which looked
17.  quite injured to me. His leg was cut, swollen and
18.  purple and he complained of pain. Someone from a
19.  nearby business called the police and ambulance.
20.  Ms. Lawrence at the scene said she never saw
21.  the motorcycle. Ms. Lawrence was alone in her
22.  vehicle. She did not have anyone in the car as
23.  a passenger. Mr. Green was wearing a helmet
24.  and the headlight of the motorcycle was on. I
25.  do not know of any other witnesses to the
26.
27.  Wit: Cathy Okrent                    Kris McGrail
     ▲ ══════ DO NOT WRITE BELOW THIS LINE ══════ ▲
```

initial contact with clients, and prefer that a paralegal or attorney greet the clients and interview them.

It is always important to put the client at ease. Be sure the client is comfortable with you and the law office surroundings before getting down to details. Small talk of a general nature helps. When the client sees that you care about him or her as a person, rather than as the next slip-and-fall

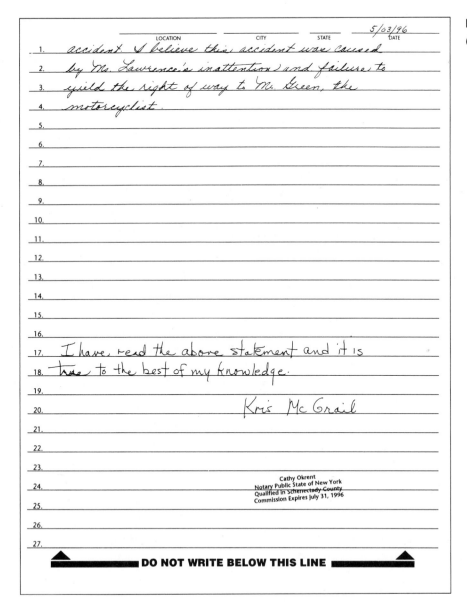

FIGURE 1-1
(continued)

case, he or she will be more apt to confide in you and provide you with the information needed for the best possible representation.

It is important to remember that, for many clients, this injury claim represents the first time that they have been to an attorney's office. For some clients, an appointment with an attorney is a very intimidating experience, particularly when the attorney hastily greets them and then must excuse himself or herself to go to court at the last minute. The clients are thus left feeling that the attorney was too busy to see them. The paralegal then becomes an invaluable bridge between the attorney and the client. Eventually, the client will see that the paralegal often has more time to speak with the client and is more readily accessible by telephone or for office conferences than the trial attorney. Some clients prefer to speak with the paralegal working on their case for this very reason. You might even notice that clients will tell you things that they are reluctant to tell the attorney. Some clients are hesitant to take up the attorney's time, or feel that the attorney will think less of them, or will not want to represent them if they tell the attorney all the details of the case.

This is one reason why the role of the paralegal is so important. A paralegal who encourages the client to talk and thoroughly interviews the client about the accident provides a wealth of information for the attorney and other members of the litigation team who might later work on the file.

Depending on your jurisdiction, it could take anywhere from months to four or five years for a personal injury case to reach the trial date. At the time of trial, your client's only recollection of the accident may be that which previously was told to you and recorded in the file. The same is true of witnesses. The importance of a thorough interview, and possible followup interviews, at the outset of a case cannot be emphasized enough. In time, each paralegal develops his or her own method of interviewing. Some think of an interview like a tree. You proceed up the main trunk, but at any time, your client might say something that causes you to branch off to focus on specific facts or issues. Then it is up to you to determine if you need to return to your main series of questions, or if perhaps the new information obtained should be pursued first.

§ 1.5 Determining and Locating Defendants

Besides the client, the most critical participant in any tort litigation is the potential defendant(s). If a plaintiff's attorney cannot find someone to sue successfully, then the client's tort case comes to a halt. A paralegal may be asked to locate all prospective defendants. In most tort cases, determining defendants to sue is done through in-house investigation, although occasionally it will be necessary for an investigator with more extensive resources to locate a defendant or research information (for example, regarding the principals of a defunct partnership or corporation).

It is sometimes difficult to identify and locate defendants. This is particularly true if a business operating under a trade name has been dissolved or has otherwise "vanished" since the tort was committed. Even individuals can "disappear," as debt collectors and skip-tracers become acutely aware when searching for fleeing debtors. Some tortfeasors lie low to avoid service of process and liability. Some businesses create dummy corporations or partnerships to "front" for shareholders, who may be individuals, other corporations, or partnerships that hope to remain hidden from potential tort plaintiffs. In the law of business organizations, courts speak of **piercing the corporate veil** to reach the true company owners who have violated an injured party's legal rights. In some instances, the client may simply be unaware of the defendant's correct corporate name. Knowledge of business and corporate law is beneficial in such a search.

Using Discovery to Locate Defendants

Discovery is the phase in a lawsuit when information is exchanged between the parties and the issues for trial are narrowed. Occasionally, discovery will be served upon known defendants to uncover information about unknown defendants or ones that cannot be located. The paralegal should check the rules of civil procedure and discovery in his or her jurisdiction to see if prelitigation discovery is allowed, and if a court order is needed. If not, discovery will have to be conducted after the lawsuit

---

TERMS

piercing the corporate veil Ignoring the corporate entity to reach or to proceed legally against the corporation's directors, officers, or managers directly and personally. Although a corporation's officers and directors are not normally liable for the acts of the corporation, the courts will hold them responsible for corporate acts if the purpose of organizing the corporation was to perpetrate fraud or if the corporation was a mere shell without substantial assets or capital. This judicial process is known as "piercing the corporate veil."

discovery A means for providing a party, in advance of trial, with access to facts that are within the knowledge of the other side, to enable the party to better try his or her case. A motion to compel discovery is the procedural means for compelling the adverse party to reveal such facts or to produce documents, books, and other things within his or her possession or control.

commences. An example of this is California Civil Code § 2025, which puts a hold on discovery for ten days after the summons and complaint are served.

Study Documents Carefully

Every piece of paper a paralegal obtains regarding a client's tort case is a prospective source of information regarding potential defendants. Police accident reports are an obvious example in personal injury cases, but there are many others. Letters, invoices, leases, articles in newspapers, ambulance reports, witnesses' statements, and other documents often contain vital leads to find defendants. Any document connected to the parties and the circumstances involved in the tort might contain information a paralegal could use to locate defendants. (See Figure 1-2.) Frequently one finds a clue about the accident through which one may determine a defendant's name, address, or parent company name—perhaps from the fine print in the document.

Use Caution When Naming Defendants

Paralegals must be certain to have the correct defendants before a tort lawsuit is filed. If one files notice, sues the wrong defendant, or fails to name a proper defendant, serious problems may arise. For instance, the attorney or law firm may be subject to legal action and/or disciplinary proceedings for filing a frivolous lawsuit against the innocent defendant. Additionally, the statute of limitations or a notice requirement may run on a client's lawsuit without the correct defendant(s) having been notified or sued. Mistakes in this area may even result in a claim of malpractice by the client against the attorney.

The paralegal should check all available resources to ensure that the correct individual or business entity is being identified as the defendant. Investigatory novices might be satisfied by pulling a company or individual's name out of the telephone directory, but this practice can be disastrous if the purported defendant turns out to be an innocent "same-name" person or business.

Using the Telephone as a Research Tool

Modern telecommunication has made pounding the pavement an obsolete method of obtaining some case information. Telephone calls are usually faster in uncovering details concerning defendants, particularly when the person called is cooperative and talkative. If a shopping center, apartment complex, or similar business or building is involved,

FIGURE 1-2
Sample discovery documents

chances are that someone at the office will tell a paralegal over the phone who the owners are or will reveal the name of the management company. Oral communication skills are at a premium here. A good investigative paralegal, like a good journalist, knows how to get information without giving away any secrets or motives. In general, information should flow *to* the paralegal from nonclient witnesses; the paralegal should be wary of giving out information.

FIGURE 1-2
(continued)

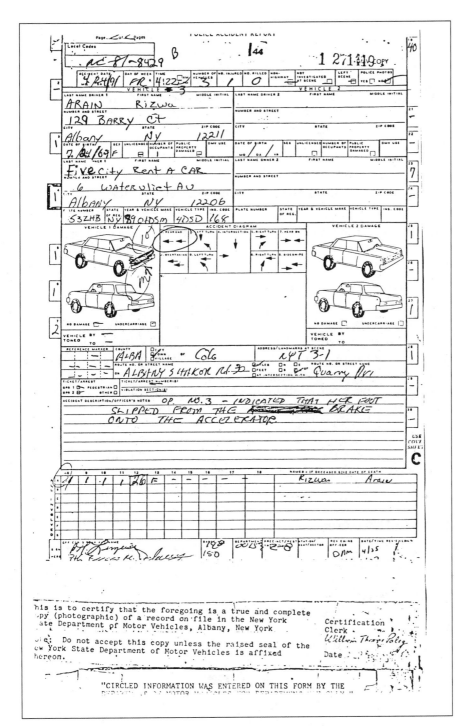

FIGURE 1-2
(continued)

With facsimile machines, an avalanche of documents can be secured without ever leaving one's law office, if one knows the correct contact person. With governmental agencies, however, one usually must still visit the appropriate offices to obtain documents, as there are usually photocopying fees associated with any governmental record, and governmental clerks are instructed not to release documents to someone making a nameless, faceless fax inquiry.

Obtaining Information About Corporations

Most jurisdictions require corporations to be registered with the state in which they were incorporated, created, or are doing business.

Secretaries of State Offices

To locate a corporation, a paralegal should first contact the state agency that is responsible for keeping business organizational records. This is usually the secretary of state's corporate division for each state. Through a series of telephone calls, a paralegal may determine the correct names, addresses, officers, directors, and contact persons for service of process upon a corporation operating in a particular state. One may also discover the name of a parent corporation by searching the secretary of state's records. (See Figure 1-3.)

For a minimal fee, in most states the secretary of state's office will furnish other written documentation, such as a corporation's articles of incorporation, that has been filed with the governmental agency.

Business Directories

Business directories are another excellent source of information about business defendants. **Business directories** list corporations and other business organizations according to name, geographic location, product or service, brand name, advertising, and other subject headings. Most public or university libraries have these reference texts on reserve. Various private services, such as Dun & Bradstreet, Inc., also provide this information, in print or on-line.

═══════════════◄ TERMS ►═══════════════

business directory   A listing (whether print or online) of corporations and other business organizations according to name, geographic location, product or service, brand name, advertising, and the like.

VAN & LIAL, P.C.
10 Church Street, New York, N.Y. 10007
Telephone (212) 732-9000

FIGURE 1-3
Sample
request to
Secretary of
State's office

November 12, 1997

Department of State
Corporation Division
Albany, New York

Re: Koche v. Patrick

Gentlemen:

Kindly advise whether you have any filing for the following corporation:
D. B. Associates, Inc., doing business out of Albany, New York.
Please indicate whether the above corporation is a New York
corporation, and if so, when it was incorporated, where its principal office
is, and whether the above designation is correct.
If it is not a New York corporation, kindly advise us in what state it was
incorporated and if it is authorized to do business in the State of New York.
Thank you for a prompt reply to the undersigned.

Very truly yours,

VAN & LIAL, P.C.

By:_____
Donald Bronte, paralegal

DB/kn

Public Business Records

Other potential sources of information about business defendants
include:

- Company annual reports
- The state attorney general's office
- The state or federal Departments of Commerce
- The Securities and Exchange Commission (SEC)
- Online services

SEC reports are surprisingly fertile sources of corporate information. The reports that companies are required to file with the SEC typically contain much more detailed information than is found in annual reports to stockholders. Also, SEC reports have the advantage of being more accessible than shareholder reports, which companies often consider rather confidential.

Obtaining Information About Partnerships

Partnerships can be more elusive than corporations. Investors sometimes form partnerships for specific projects, such as shopping centers or housing developments, and then disband them after the project is complete. Some jurisdictions require that partnerships be registered, in which case they can be located through the partnership section of the Secretary of State's offices. However, there are fewer requirements for partnership registration than there are for corporations in some states. Most jurisdictions allow service of process upon any partner as notice to the partnership. **Process service** is the delivery of the summons to the defendant as a means of notifying the defendant of a pending action and compelling the defendant to appear in court.

Obtaining the Names of Sole Proprietors and Partners

Many jurisdictions require that partnerships and individuals doing business under a trade name or assumed, **fictitious name** file a *doing business as (d/b/a)* certificate or affidavit with an appropriate governmental agency. Many local governments require sole proprietors and partnerships doing business in the county or city to file d/b/a certificates and affidavits with the local recorder's office.

Ambulance Services and Fire Departments as Defendants

Even the people called upon for assistance can end up being defendants in a lawsuit. If the fire department or ambulance service is called,

---

TERMS

service of process (process service) Delivery of a summons, writ, complaint, or other process to the opposite party, or other person entitled to receive it, in such manner as the law prescribes, whether by leaving a copy at his or her residence, by mailing a copy to [the opposite party] or his or her attorney, or by publication.

fictitious name An artificial name that a person or a corporation adopts for business or professional purposes.

and there is an unusual delay in their arrival, or if they do not have standard and appropriate equipment, the department may be liable. If equipment is not working properly, personnel are not properly trained to use it, or personnel are not supervised adequately, they may be potential defendants.

Usually the agency for which the offending individuals, firefighters, or ambulance service persons are working is added to the lawsuit for failure to supervise, failure to adequately train, or failure to provide appropriate and functional equipment. Of course, the theories of liability would depend upon the circumstances.

A fire department or ambulance service is often owned or supervised by a governmental agency, such as the city, county, or town. However, there may be a volunteer organization in a small town or a rural or unincorporated area. If so, its contract with the cities or counties in the service area should be reviewed, if possible. **Sunshine laws** in each state usually provide for the disclosure of such information from governmental entities. (Figure 1-4 shows a typical request for information.) Some local governments contract out ambulance services to private companies. Ambulances may also be owned and operated by hospitals and funeral homes.

Paralegals should carefully follow statutes or procedural rules for special notice requirements when suing governmental agencies. Some municipalities and governmental entities require prior notice of a condition or defect before a suit is permitted.

When handling reports about situations in which negligence may be a factor, a paralegal should study the documents not only to determine the *facts* of what happened, but also to identify *who* was responsible.

Practical Applications

Investigating Licensed or Regulated Businesses

Most states have a central department or agency that oversees licensed and regulated businesses. For example, in Texas this agency is the Texas Department of Licensing and Regulation. To uncover additional information about a licensed or regulated business, a paralegal should consult the state governmental listings in the telephone directory in the state in which the business is located.

◀ TERMS ▶

---

sunshine law   State and federal statutes requiring that meetings of administrative agencies be open to the public.

FIGURE 1-4
Sample request for information to government agency

EVANS AND MYERS, P.C.
12 State Street, Albany, New York
(518) 474-3691

January 25, 1998

Hon. Guy D. Paquin
Albany County Clerk
Office of the County Clerk
Albany, New York 12207

Re: FREEDOM OF INFORMATION REQUEST
of January 11, 1998
Airplane Crash of December 1, 1997
in the Town of Knox, County of Albany,
New York

Dear Mr. Paquin:

Thank you for your letter dated January 16, 1998 and the investigative report of the Albany County Sheriff's Department with respect to the above airplane crash.

On Page 3 of said report, the third paragraph mentions that photographs were taken by I.D. Officer George Dinell. If possible, this office would like copies of the prints of said photographs pursuant to the Freedom of Information Act.

Would you please be so kind as to inform the undersigned, in writing, of the necessary procedures to procure said photographs, and the fee for obtaining same.

Again, I thank you for your assistance and your fine efforts, and I look forward to hearing from your office soon with respect to the above mentioned photographs.

Very truly yours,

By: _____
Anna Lee Chin, Attorney at Law

AC/km

Agencies can also provide listings of all state licensing requirements. By checking with the state agency, one may discover whether a potential business defendant's license, certification, or insurance has lapsed or is not in good standing. Also, information might be available about the defendant's proper name, address, and telephone number.

One typically must complete a request form to gain access to the information on file for a particular business at the state licensing agency. These documents will range from the business's initial application for the license to a copy of its insurance certificate.

If the defendant is local, the paralegal should check the display advertisements in the telephone directory. Many businesses include their business license number in the advertisement or post it for inspection at the place of business. Having this information available may speed up one's request for information.

Practical
Applications

Sample Defendant Search

Consider the following hypothetical defendant search. The accident report lists Axtco Construction as the owner of a truck that struck the client's vehicle. The accident report will also have Axtco's address.

If Axtco is listed in the local telephone directory, the paralegal could first call to obtain the name of the president, owner, or chief executive officer. If the address on the accident report is out-of-town, obtain the number from directory assistance for that area code.

The paralegal should be prepared to reach an uncooperative Axtco employee who will not divulge any of this information without first knowing the reason. One should be extremely cautious regarding how much information to disclose during such a direct telephone contact with a potential business defendant. Recall also that there are ethical considerations involved in such direct contact. The paralegal should consult with his or her supervising attorney to decide how much to tell the company personnel to obtain the names and addresses of the company chief executive officer, president, or other officer who can be sent a notice letter or demand letter and, subsequently, service of process. Usually, it is best to reveal as little as possible, and to truthfully downplay any legal implications for which the information is being requested. Also, business directories (often found in reference sections of libraries) can be consulted for information about a business, as can online resources.

Assuming that the direct contact approach yields little or no useful information regarding Axtco, the paralegal could next consult the Secretary of State's corporate or partnership divisions to see if Axtco is a corporation or partnership authorized to conduct business in the state. If not, the paralegal could next contact the city or county governmental agency in which assumed or trade names are registered (e.g., the county recorder's office). The agency to consult will be located in the city or county in which Axtco's business offices are found. Then the paralegal could look up Axtco's trade or assumed name certificate or affidavit on file with the agency. Also, online resources might contain the needed information.

In case the accident report is unavailable or contains incomplete information about Axtco, the paralegal should look at any photographs of the vehicle from the accident scene. Do the company's name and address appear on the truck's doors or body? If not, the information may be available from the state's Department of Motor Vehicles.

Knowing who and where the defendants are is an important initial stage in every tort investigation. Another critical investigatory aspect involves the circumstances surrounding the victim/plaintiff's injuries. Section 1.6 considers how paralegals document tort accident scenes.

§ 1.6 Documenting the Scene

Although legal staff are almost never on the scene when a tort actually occurs, it is critical to document the scene of a tort injury as soon as possible.

Obtaining Visual Documentation, Measurements, and Other Details

Paralegals may take photographs or videotape recordings of accident scenes. Also, paralegals take measurements and describe physical conditions at the location itself. Documenting the scene should be done as soon as possible, because valuable evidence is often lost as conditions change over time. Accident scenes can alter naturally due to environmental changes, or, more frequently, people might deliberately modify conditions to prevent others from being harmed or to conceal possible liability.

Practical Applications

The scene of an accident should be documented as soon as possible. The paralegal should keep in mind that places and situations change, sometimes rapidly. Weather conditions can change streets and roads, construction projects may start or end, streetlights may be installed, or lighting that was on at the time of an accident may go out. A place of business may put up warnings or fences; a pool may be covered or drained. One may safely presume that potential defendants, if they are aware of their possible liabilities, will act quickly to have the cause of an accident repaired to prevent others from being injured.

Paralegals should be exceedingly thorough when documenting the scene of an accident or other tort. What seems insignificant at the time may be found to be important after more is known about the accident itself. For example, the distance between steps on a stairway, and whether the stairs were tiled or carpeted, could be vitally important in a slip-and-fall case. Also, it is meaningful, when reconstructing an accident, to have as much information about the actual scene at the time of the accident as possible. (See Figure 1-5.) You might want to consider bringing a portable cassette tape recorder with you to supplement your investigatory notes.

Knowing the Evidentiary Rules for One's Jurisdiction

Every state has rules of evidence that regulate the admissibility of evidence. Not all evidence will automatically be admitted into evidence at the time of the trial. Sometimes the evidence must be in a specific form. You may have to obtain original records rather than photocopies.

As the tort investigation is conducted, the paralegal should put each item to be used at trial in admissible form. Rules of evidence from your jurisdiction should be consulted. Even evidence that will be used only for in-house purposes, or for settlement brochures or mediation packages, should be maintained in a form that could be admitted at trial if necessary. Documents that the trial team plans to use for evidence at trial *must* be suitable to present at trial. Otherwise, a paralegal may find himself or herself tracking down these documents at the last minute, having to put them into admissible form (such as certified copies, which also usually requires another fee), and generally wasting time that could have been better spent on other aspects of trial preparation. Sometimes opposing counsel will cooperate in stipulating to the admissibility of certain documents; sometimes not.

Using Proper Evidentiary Form

Looking ahead to trial, paralegals should consult the relevant state, local, or federal procedural and evidentiary rules to determine the form in which evidence must be submitted into the trial record and what type of documentation is required. For instance:

- Does the court require supporting affidavits for admission of medical records and bills into evidence?

- Is there a certain form or language for business records? If not, how are they proved in court? Are original records necessary, or will copies suffice?

- Can documents or pleadings (the formal statements of the parties, such as the complaint and the answer) from other cases be used as evidence in one's case? If so, must they be certified by a court clerk or someone else?

```
                    National Transportation Safety Board
                            Washington, D.C. 20594

                              Brief of Accident

File No. -  265    12/01/93   ALTAMONT,NY          A/C Reg. No. N3034U        Time (Lcl) - 1615 EST

---Basic Information---
Type Operating Certificate-NONE (GENERAL AVIATION)          Injuries
                                   Aircraft Damage        Fatal  Serious  Minor  None
Type of Operation         -PERSONAL       SUBSTANTIAL  Crew   0      0       0     1
Flight Conducted Under    -14 CFR 91      Fire         Pass   0      0       0     2
Accident Occurred During  -LANDING        NONE

---Aircraft Information---
Make/Model    - BEECH 35              Eng Make/Model  - CONTINENTAL E-225   ELT Installed/Activated - YES/YES
Landing Gear  - TRICYCLE-RETRACTABLE  Number Engines  - 1                   Stall Warning System - YES
Max Gross Wt  - 1600                  Engine Type     - RECIPROCATING-CARBURETOR
No. of Seats  - 4                     Rated Power     - 225 HP

---Environment/Operations Information---
Weather Data                       Itinerary                            Airport Proximity
Wx Briefing    - NO RECORD OF BRIEFING   Last Departure Point              OFF AIRPORT/STRIP
Method         - N/A                       DUNESBURG,NY
Completeness   - N/A                     Destination                      Airport Data
Basic Weather  - VMC                       LOCAL
Wind Dir/Speed - CALM                                                       Runway Ident    - N/A
Visibility     - 30.0   SM               ATC/Airspace                       Runway Lth/Wid  - N/A
Lowest Sky/Clouds -     CLEAR            Type of Flight Plan - NONE         Runway Surface  - N/A
Lowest Ceiling    - NONE                 Type of Clearance   - NONE        Runway Status   - N/A
Obstructions to Vision- NONE             Type of Apch/Lnds   - NONE
Precipitation     - NONE
Condition of Light - DAYLIGHT

---Personnel Information---
                               Age - 31                Medical Certificate - VALID MEDICAL-NO WAIVERS/LIMIT
Pilot-In-Command              Biennial Flight Review          Flight Time (Hours)
Certificate(s)/Rating(s)        Current       - YES     Total      -  733      Last 24 Hrs-   0
  COMMERCIAL                     Months Since  - 7       Make/Model -  388      Last 30 Days- UNK/NR
  SE LAND                        Aircraft Type - UNK/NR  Instrument -  110      Last 90 Days-  32

Instrument Rating(s)  - AIRPLANE

---Narrative---
THE ENG STARTED RUNNING ROUGH SHORTLY AFTER TAKE OFF & THE PLT MADE A FORCED LANDING IN A SNOW COVERED FIELD.
```

FIGURE 1-5 Sample accident report

```
                              Brief of Accident (Continued)

     File No. -  265     12/ 1/93   ALTAMONT,NY        A/C Reg. No. N3034U        Time (Lcl) - 1615 EST
------------------------------------------------------------------------------------------------------------

Occurrence #1       LOSS OF POWER
Phase of Operation  CRUISE - NORMAL

Finding(s)
   1. UNDETERMINED
------------------------------------------------------------------------------------------------------------

Occurrence #2       FORCED LANDING
Phase of Operation  LANDING - FLARE/TOUCHDOWN

Occurrence #3       IN FLIGHT COLLISION WITH TERRAIN
Phase of Operation  LANDING - FLARE/TOUCHDOWN

Finding(s)
   2. TERRAIN CONDITION - SNOW COVERED
----Probable Cause----

The National Transportation Safety Board determines that the Probable Cause(s) of this accident
is/are finding(s) 1

Factor(s) relating to this accident is/are finding(s) 2
```

FIGURE 1-5 *(continued)*

Hearsay Problems

Hearsay is an out-of-court statement offered as evidence to prove the fact contained in the statement. Statements may be verbal, written, or even gestural.

Some documents may not be admissible because they are considered hearsay. At times, only portions of documents may be admissible. For example, all or part of a police or ambulance report may be considered hearsay because the police officer and/or ambulance attendant who wrote the report did not actually see the accident. This person's report will contain information from someone else, such as the injured party or a witness. Hearsay is not admissible, but there are numerous exceptions to this rule.

The trial team will want to review the documents and the evidence rules. They may want to offer the reports into evidence simply as business records (an exception to the hearsay rule), or use them to refresh the memory of a testifying police officer or paramedic, without offering them as evidence.

Video and Computer Technologies

The use of video and computer animation technologies is a fast-growing practice in tort law. Videotape and computer animation are routinely used in accident reconstruction, "day-in-the-life" documentaries, and settlement brochures. Even video news footage is being utilized in the courtroom. Paralegals should know how to document the authenticity of this type of evidence so that it can be used during trial.

§ 1.7 Public and Private Sector Resources

Governmental agencies and private entities are sources of a variety of information that may be germane to the paralegal's tort case investigation. Online computer networks may be the information superhighway, but there are many more information side streets available to the paralegal in charge of investigating a tort case. Much of this information is stored the old-fashioned way—on paper, microfilm, microfiche, or

────────────────── **TERMS** ──────────────────

hearsay The testimony of a witness as to a statement made to him or her outside of court, or made to someone else who told him or her what was said, that is offered in court to prove the truth of the matter contained in the statement.

other archival media—and paralegals need only know where to look to uncover this treasure-trove of material.

Local Governmental Agencies

Governmental agencies are literal stockpiles of information that the paralegal will find invaluable in tort case investigation. Sunshine laws provide for governmental disclosure of most contracts. Archives contain vital statistics, marriage licenses, civil suit records, and probate and estate records. One can obtain information from automobile license tag records, such as the name and current address of the owner of a vehicle involved in an accident. Also, information can be obtained from driver's license records, deeds, and liens. The tax assessor's office can provide property ownership information by name or address of the property.

Newspapers

Newspapers and newspaper personnel can be good sources of information. For instance, an article about the tort incident might quote a witness about whom the paralegal did not know. There could also be helpful information about how the accident happened or who was involved. The paralegal should find out if a newspaper reporter took any photographs of the scene, even if none were printed in the newspaper.

There may be information about one's client, or a potential defendant, in the archives of the newspaper. The paralegal should look beyond articles about the tort incident for photographs or profiles of people involved. There may be information to document a client's activities before an accident or to aid in service on an individual or business.

Television and Radio News Reports

If the accident that is the basis of the tort lawsuit was reported on the news, one may want to get an audiotape, videotape, or transcript of what was reported to the public. It may be useful if a jury trial is anticipated, because prior publicity may affect jurors and even the venue of the case.

Additionally, if video news footage was taken, the paralegal should obtain a copy. It may have scene footage that is not obtainable from any other source. This footage may also have been taken closer in time to the actual incident than later documentary efforts by the law firm. The trial team may be glad to have this footage when preparing a video settlement brochure or video recreation of the accident for trial. If the television station will not cooperate, consult your rules of discovery; it may be possible to subpoena the footage.

Paralegals should also give some thought to any local conditions that might have contributed to the accident. If a fire or storm occurred at the time, and was significant, it is possible that it was reported on the local news. For example, a client's case might involve a storm-damaged building that was not repaired. The client was later injured at that business when a portion of the roof caved in. In this case, it would be a good idea to check local television stations for any news footage that might have been taken of the storm or wind shears on the day the building was believed to have been originally damaged. If found, this footage would dramatically help document not only when the building was damaged, but also that the owner or manager of the building knew, or reasonably should have known, that the building needed repair, well in advance of the injury occurring. Official weather statistics are frequently obtained from the National Oceanic and Atmospheric Administration (NOAA), which is part of the United States Commerce Department. These statistics can be found at major airports. For local information, the department of meteorology at a local university or television station will have weather statistics. Such statistics are frequently used in arbitration and litigation.

Databases

There are many types of computerized databases and networks, each holding a wealth of information. Different jurisdictions have rules and requirements about how much information is accessible to the public or admissible at trial. Even with these restrictions, it is surprising what can be learned. Databases can be used to uncover:

- Driving records
- Driver's licenses, which provide a history of residences
- Vehicle registration
- Credit reports
- Criminal history
- Public record filings, such as deeds and liens
- Business filings, such as assumed names, corporate filings, partnership filings, bankruptcy, and company officers and incorporators
- Civil lawsuits, including divorces
- Asset and other financial information.

Additional Information Regarding Criminal Acts

If the incident that is the basis of the tort lawsuit also involves a criminal act, such as a shooting or other type of assault or battery, there will be a criminal investigation, and additional information resources may be available to the trial team. (See Figure 1-6.) The paralegal will want to review and possibly obtain copies of the following:

- Police report

- Criminal record of the perpetrator

- Trial transcript of any criminal trial, conviction, or judgment

- Exhibits used at criminal trial

- 911 or other emergency telephone call audiotapes and/or transcripts

- Floor plans or diagrams of incident location

- Map of the area

- Crime statistics of the specific law enforcement jurisdiction

Most tort cases involve damages, insurance coverage, and other elements that must be researched. Section 1.8 investigates these considerations.

§ 1.8 Additional Areas to Investigate

Tort damages present a variety of details to investigate. These items include degree and permanence of the injury, employment and lost wages, injury expenses, insurance coverage, prior tort claims, preexisting injuries, past criminal records, and driving history, to name but a few.

Employment and Lost Wages

The plaintiff's damages may be based in part on the dollar amount of wages lost due to injuries. Another factor that is often considered is impairment of future earning capacity. The paralegal needs this earnings information for in-house evaluation, but the defendants will also be entitled to obtain certain information regarding wages.

FIGURE 1-6
Sample sheriff's
report

The plaintiff's income must be documented. It is not sufficient for a client to simply testify, "I could have made $175,000 this year if it weren't for this injury." Income and income potential must be substantiated by independent evidence.

Tax returns and affidavits from the client's employer are commonly used to document lost wages and the client's wage-earning capacity. The paralegal will also want to gather information from the client's W-2

FIGURE 1-6
(continued)

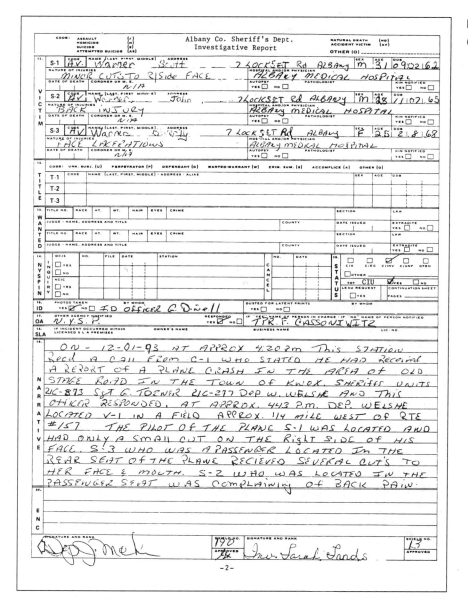

forms, pay stubs for hourly or salaried workers, and, in some instances, documentation of employment contracts or fringe benefits.

The trial team may plan to have an economist, actuary, or account-ant prepare an evaluation of economic damages. Most economic experts will request tax returns for at least three years preceding the date of in-jury, to make a determination as to future economic loss, when there has been impairment of future earning capacity.

Expenses Related to the Injury

The client should provide documentation of all expenses paid in relation to the injury and medical treatment. This includes receipts for equipment and supplies, such as:

- Canes and braces
- Heating pads or ice packs
- Hospital bills
- Doctor bills
- Physical therapy bills
- Bandages
- Prescription medicines
- Over-the-counter medicines
- Special mattresses or recuperative furniture or equipment
- Bills from housekeeper, cook, visiting nurses, or other helpers needed during recuperation

The client should also document mileage and parking fees for trips to the doctor, hospital, and for any other therapy sessions. The paralegal should follow up to make sure the client is keeping records of this information.

Insurance Coverage and Other Benefits

The trial team will need to know how much of the client's medical and related expenses were paid by insurance policies, workers' compensation benefits, or through other sources. The paralegal should also find out if the client is covered by or receiving any assistance from Social Security, Medicare, Medicaid, or any other governmental or private program.

The client should provide the paralegal with copies of any documentation about insurance coverage or possible assistance through governmental agencies. If the client is unable to produce such documentation, it may be necessary for the paralegal to contact the various agencies and request the information. The defendants may also be entitled to some information regarding the insurance payments and government or other benefits, even if such information is not admissible at trial. Depending on your jurisdiction, the fact that some of your bills have been paid may affect the defendant's responsibility to reimburse for expenses.

Previous Claims or Lawsuits of Plaintiff

*Practical
Applications*

Some people are "professional plaintiffs"; that is, they sue people for a living for injuries that are contrived or exaggerated. These people are not usually honest with their attorneys. Other clients are just injury-prone and seem to incur more than their share of injuries. A thorough interview and study of current and past medical records often help to determine whether a client's claims ring true. Note that the occasional malingerer is the exception and not the rule!

It is necessary to know about any previous claims or lawsuits in which the client has been involved and how they were resolved. The trial team will determine the information to which the defendant is entitled if defense counsel inquires about this subject matter during discovery. Defendants usually ask for this type of information so as to use it against the plaintiff, to discredit the plaintiff, or to reduce the amount of damages in a lawsuit.

Clients will not always be able or willing to provide all the information concerning prior claims or lawsuits in which they have been involved. Some clients discard legal documents once a legal action is completed. The paralegal may have to visit the court clerk's offices to obtain the relevant documents concerning any past lawsuits.

Previous Injuries to Plaintiff

As a general rule, "one takes the victim (plaintiff) as one finds him." However, it is important to determine if the part of the plaintiff's body that was injured in the accident and is the basis of the current lawsuit was ever injured in the past. It is vital to review the medical record carefully to determine whether there are any references to similar injuries or other problems relating to the same part of the body, or whether there is evidence of any preexisting injuries.

For instance, if a plaintiff who has a stiff back, from an earlier car accident, slips and falls on a slippery floor at the grocery store and reinjures her back, the injured plaintiff may only bring a claim against the grocery store for the injuries and expenses that result from aggravation of the existing condition. There can be no recovery against the grocery store for the stiff back that the plaintiff already had. The plaintiff's claim might be that her back is stiff more often, or that it gives her more pain than she previously experienced. An award against the grocery store for aggravation of an existing condition may be much less than the award for the preexisting stiff back condition.

In this example, the paralegal should be sure to have all the medical information to evaluate and let trial team members know that there was more than one injury to the plaintiff's back. The trial team will probably want to follow up with additional questions to the client regarding the previous back problem to ascertain if it is related to the pain attributed to the slip and fall. One's trial team may also want to follow up with the client's doctor.

The Parties' Criminal Histories

Information on the parties' criminal histories is relevant for both defendants and plaintiffs in some cases. The trial team needs to know anything regarding the parties' arrests, convictions, and/or time spent in jail or prison, although this data might not be admissible at trial in your particular case.

Driving Records

Driving records may be particularly relevant in the investigation of an automobile accident, and can also be utilized to determine other information regarding the parties, such as alcohol use. If any party has been ticketed or arrested for an offense such as driving under the influence of alcohol or drugs, the trial team will want to know about it.

Having considered various investigatory techniques, it would be useful to apply these methods to specific types of tort cases. These applications are discussed in § 1.9.

§ 1.9 Investigating Different Types of Tort Cases

Various types of tort cases require specialized methods of investigation. Paralegals and attorneys learn the "right" techniques primarily through experience. This section provides some basic guidelines for investigating some typical tort cases encountered in private law practice.

Automobile Accident Cases

An automobile accident causing injury usually entails a relatively straightforward investigation. The trial team needs to know who and what caused the accident and what damages the plaintiff has suffered. A typical general investigation includes the following steps:

- The client is interviewed for information as to how the accident happened, injuries, who was at fault, and any witnesses.

- Police accident reports are obtained for information such as:
  —Witness names and addresses
  —The exact location of the accident
  —The disposition of each party to the accident and each vehicle (i.e., what parties were taken to which hospital, what vehicles had to be towed and where they were taken)
  —Injury and property damage to vehicle and contents
  —Any tickets issued by police at the scene
  —Any comments in the report as to fault or factors that contributed to the accident (such as eating, drinking, falling asleep, or other activities).

- Photographs should be taken of the vehicle or vehicles and the parties' injuries, if necessary.

- Medical records should be ordered and particular attention paid to any tests for alcohol or drugs.

- If there is a question regarding a mechanical malfunction, an expert may be called in to inspect the vehicle or vehicles involved.

- If there are allegations of dangerous street design or street conditions, additional investigation may be required.

In addition to the preceding, when the trial team represents the defendant, it will be interested in investigating the following:

- Names of other possible defendants

- Defenses to the plaintiff's claims

- Acts of the plaintiff that contributed to the accident

- Prior lawsuits by the plaintiff

- Preexisting injuries of the plaintiff

- The plaintiff's prior accidents or claims

- Reputation and standing of the plaintiff's treating physician (who may be relied on by the plaintiff as an expert at trial).

Mechanical Malfunction

If there is a question about possible mechanical malfunction, the trial team probably will find itself going beyond a simple investigation and into the more extensive inquiry necessary in a products liability case. The client should be consulted regarding projected future expenses for which the client would be responsible before the investigation proceeds.

Dangerous Street Conditions

If there are indications of dangerous street conditions, the paralegal should watch for scenarios such as:

- Debris that fell from a truck or other vehicle that might have contributed to the accident

- Vegetation affecting visibility

- A street being repaired or under construction or allegations that lanes were not properly marked, equipment or machinery were left in the street, visibility was obscured, and so on

- A dangerous intersection or design of the street itself

- A street sign, such as a stop sign or one-way sign, that is obscured or missing

- Possible involvement of a municipality, and whether it is entitled by law to notice of the condition claimed before suit can be brought.

Construction Sites

If the site of the accident was under construction or repair at the time of the incident, an inquiry as to the conditions may be undertaken. Likewise, if there are allegations of debris on the road, that should be followed up, as any of these scenarios may indicate additional defendants.

Other Complexities

At this point, if one's case seems to be more than a simple "fender-bender" accident, the investigation will probably progress into more complex areas. It may be necessary to find out about other accidents that were reported for that same location to determine if there have been an unusual number of accidents at that spot.

Medical Negligence Cases

If a paralegal has a case involving possible medical negligence or malpractice, investigation can be quite complex. Consider a hypothetical but not unrealistic example. A patient goes into a hospital to have his appendix removed. The doctor fails to remove a clamp from the patient before suturing him up. One week after being discharged from the hospital, the patient experiences severe pain and a high fever. The patient goes to the emergency room and is admitted for emergency exploratory surgery. The clamp is found and removed. Potential areas of investigation in such a case would include:

- What was the cause of injury or death?
  —Was it a result of medical treatment or lack thereof?
  —Was it a result of negligence on the part of the hospital staff or doctors?
  —Was it a result of something that was done or not done prior to admission to the facility?

- What do the medical records or autopsy records indicate as the cause of injury or death? (See Figures 1-7, 1-8, and 1-9.)

- What was the plaintiff's condition upon arriving at the emergency room?

- What diagnosis had been rendered during the previous hospital admission? (See Figure 1-7.)

- What types of consent forms and releases for treatment were signed, and who signed them (the victim, his or her guardian, etc.)?

FIGURE 1-7 Sample medical report (radiology)

FIGURE 1-8
Sample
medical report
(doctor's
evaluation)

DON ACOMB, M.D., P.C.
STAN HOFF, M.D., D.M.D., P.C.
65 Western Avenue, Albany, New York 12203
Telephone 438-4400

March 12, 1997

Cathy J. Okrent, Esq.
Washington Square
Box 1501
Albany, New York 12212

Re: Scott Powers
d/a: 5/2/96

Dear Ms. Okrent:

Scott Powers was in the office on March 12, 1997 concerning scars of the
right lower leg. According to the history on May 2, 1996 he was
apparently attacked by four dogs, receiving bites on the right lower leg.
One bite required three sutures and one puncture wound required one
suture. The wounds healed without infection.

Examination disclosed a white, soft scar 3 × 1.5 cms. on the lateral part of
the mid calf of the right lower leg. This scar is permanent and no
treatment is indicated. There are two puncture scars, each measuring 0.6
cms., on the upper and lower lateral leg. These scars are permanent and
no treatment is indicated.

If I can be of any further help to you please do not hesitate to let me
know.

Sincerely,

_____
DON ACOMB, M.D.

DA: mk

If the initial evaluation indicates a potential case, additional investigation
will be warranted. Paralegals will want to find out about any doctors
involved, their qualifications and training, and whether they have been
the subject of previous lawsuits or complaints. One will also want to
find out the same information about the hospital and its personnel.

FIGURE 1-9
Sample medical report (discharge form)

Obtaining Information About Health Care Providers

Health care facilities, such as hospitals, nursing homes, retirement centers, and rehabilitation hospitals, are overseen by various governmental and private agencies and licensing organizations. For instance, if a

FIGURE 1-9
(continued)

3. Course in hospital, continued:

V. LIMIT OF DISABILITY:

Patient may return to work: ☐ YES   ☒ NO
Patient is essentially home bound: ☒ YES   ☐ NO

VI. PAP SMEAR INFORMATION FOR FEMALE PATIENTS:

Pap Smear done during this admission   ☐ YES ☐ NO ☐ WITHIN LAST 3 YEARS
☐ REFUSED BY PATIENT

VII. PATIENT OR RESPONSIBLE OTHER VERBALIZES, DEMONSTRATES, OR EXHIBITS KNOWLEDGE OF:

		Completed by

1. Nature of Illness   ☒ YES ☐ NO ☐ N/A   ☐ M.D. ☐ RN
☐ Other _____
(Sign & Date)

2. Diet   ☐ YES ☐ NO ☒ N/A   ☐ M.D. ☐ RN
☐ Other _____
(Sign & Date)

3. Wound care   ☐ YES ☐ NO ☒ N/A   ☐ M.D. ☐ RN
☐ Other _____
(Sign & Date)

4. Medications   ☒ YES ☐ NO ☐ N/A   ☐ M.D. ☐ RN
☐ Other _____
(Sign & Date)

5. Special health teaching   ☒ YES ☐ NO ☐ N/A   ☐ M.D. ☐ RN
(colostomy care, casts,   ☐ Other _____
diabetic care, etc.)   (Sign & Date)

6. Activity   ☒ YES ☐ NO ☐ N/A   ☐ M.D. ☐ RN
☐ Other _____
(Sign & Date)

7. Follow-up appointments   ☒ YES ☐ NO ☐ N/A   ☐ M.D. ☐ RN
and referrals   ☐ Other _____
(Sign & Date)

COMMENTS _____

VIII. SIGNATURE OF PHYSICIAN RESPONSIBLE FOR DISCHARGE OF PATIENT:

_____ M.D.   ☐ Intern ☒ Resident
☐ Acting Intern
☐ Fellow ☐ Attending

TO BE COMPLETED BY THE NURSING DIVISION AT THE TIME THE PATIENT LEAVES THE HOSPITAL:

Date __/5__ Time __11:10__ Mode: ☒ Wheelchair ☐ Stretcher ☐ Walked out

Discharge to: ☐ Nursing Home of Extended Care Facility
☒ Home
☐ Other (Specify) _____

Belongings to _____ Accompanied by _____
Signature   ☒ Floor Clerk ☐ Nurse ☐ Other

paralegal has a case involving someone who contracted a disease from a blood transfusion, he or she should know that all blood banks are overseen by the American Association of Blood Banks. The Association sets out standards and requirements, as well as inspection criteria.

Various specifications and standards for health care providers are set by governmental agencies, professional organizations, and licensing boards. They keep records regarding:

- Current addresses

- Schools attended and grades earned

- Professional credentials

- Honors and awards

- Continuing education requirements

- Licensure status and board certification

- Past and present complaints

Therefore, these organizations are excellent resources for gathering information on defendant doctors, nurses, and other health care professionals. This information can also be utilized to evaluate health care professionals who have been designated as expert witnesses by defendants and those one might want to use as experts.

If the health care professional is a specialist, the paralegal should keep in mind that there are additional qualifications for each specialty area. A separate licensing board or organization typically oversees each specialty. For example, a surgeon might be certified to operate by the American Board of Surgery.

Practical
Applications

Health Care Facilities That Receive Governmental Funding

If a health care facility receives government funds (such as Medicare), it is inspected by the state health department for compliance with regulations. Such state inspections, along with any compliance and deficiency reports, are public records. As such, they can be obtained for review under the Freedom of Information Act and through discovery.

Summary

Fact gathering is a significant paralegal role in tort investigations. Paralegals investigate and document the tort scene and interview the client, eyewitnesses, and other persons with pertinent information. Attorneys and law firms often have specialized techniques for conducting investigations. Some use in-house personnel; others hire outside investigative services. Paralegals should customize their investigations to fit the type and size of tort case involved. Details are critical. In part, factual investigations are designed to determine liability and damages. It is important to interview witnesses as soon as possible to obtain the best recollected information. Witnesses explain how the tort occurred according to their observational perspectives.

Defendants are usually determined in-house. It may be difficult to identify or locate potential defendants, especially if they are business entities or transient individuals. One should exercise extreme caution when naming defendants in lawsuits. The client and/or attorney or law firm could be liable or disciplined for suing the wrong business or person. Potential defendants can be identified in many ways: scrutinizing documents to glean names, addresses, and telephone numbers; making telephone calls to businesses or individuals involved; checking with the Secretary of State's corporation or partnership divisions or the county or city offices in which assumed names of businesses are registered; searching company records and documents. Special difficulties arise with ambulance and fire departments as defendants. These entities are often owned or supervised by local governmental agencies, or they may be volunteer services working under governmental contract. Information concerning licensed or regulated businesses can be obtained through the federal or state regulatory agencies.

Paralegals use photographs, videos, and traditional pencil-and-paper methods of documenting tort scenes. The events in a tort case and their sequence are documented and reconstructed under the same conditions in which the tort originally occurred. Paralegals must know their jurisdiction's evidentiary rules if they are to recognize the types of evidence that will be useful in the tort case. It is important to collect evidence in the proper evidentiary form so that it may be used at trial. Hearsay problems should be anticipated and overcome. Most litigation firms now use computer and video technologies to assist in documenting and reconstructing tort cases.

Local governmental agencies may possess a wealth of information concerning some parties involved in the tort case. Archives contain vital statistics, marriage licenses, property ownership records, police records, and civil suit or criminal records. Newspapers, television, and radio can also provide valuable information about the events that occurred when the tort happened. Databases can also furnish considerable information about the persons or businesses involved in the case.

Paralegals investigate employment and lost wages to help determine the client's damages. Tax, wage, and income records should be obtained. Injury expenses are carefully documented and investigated. It is important to know whether the injured party has received insurance or governmental benefits as a result of the tort. It is also necessary to know whether the plaintiff has previously been involved in claims or lawsuits, as well as preexisting injuries, involving the same factual circumstances as the present tort case. The parties' driving or criminal records may be critical to the current case.

Investigations are tailored to fit the specific aspects of each tort case. Cases involving automobile accidents or medical negligence and health care providers each require specialized questions that paralegals use to gather the information necessary for the trial team to successful conclude the case.

Review Questions

1. What are the basic components of a tort case investigation? Who conducts these investigations? How are investigations customized? What types of questions are witnesses asked in tort investigations?

2. Why is it important to identify the correct defendant(s) in a tort case? What could happen if incorrect persons or businesses are sued as defendants?

3. How can a client's documents and the telephone help locate potential defendants? Who should a paralegal contact to obtain information about corporations, partnerships, or sole proprietorships that are prospective defendants?

4. What special problems are associated with ambulance and fire departments that are defendants?

5. Who should a paralegal contact to investigate licensed or regulated businesses?

6. How should a paralegal document an accident scene? What conditions should be prevalent when the scene is investigated? What items should be included on the investigation checklist?

7. Why is it important to tort investigations to know the evidentiary rules from one's jurisdiction?

8. How can local governmental agencies, newspapers, television, radio, and computer databases be helpful in researching a tort case?

9. Why are criminal and driving records pertinent to tort investigations? What can this information reveal about the case being investigated?

10. What additional areas should a tort paralegal investigate?

Project

Divide your class into small groups to investigate the following hypothetical tort cases. Develop question lists, checklists, and other tools that will assist in your work. Group members should role-play the client, witnesses, or other interested persons. This can be done within a group, or groups in class could assume these various roles.

Case #1:   *English v. Sidcup College*

Sharon B. English, an audiology and speech pathology student at Sidcup College, slipped and fell down stairs leading from the first floor to the basement of the Student Memorial Union. She suffered substantial physical injury as a result of the fall.

Case #2:   *Watermark v. Ootheca Convalescence Center*

Terry D. Watermark is a patient at the Ootheca Convalescence Center, a medical facility devoted to the treatment and rehabilitation of physical injuries. Terry's knees were damaged during a motorcycling accident. During whirlpool treatment, an occupational therapist working for the Rehabilitative Services Corporation, which owned the Center, failed to check the thermostat on the water heating unit affixed to the whirlpool system. Near-boiling water filled the whirlpool, severely scalding Terry's entire body.

Case #3:   *Joist v. Mason Dixon Poultry Company*

Samantha K. Joist was driving her automobile along State Highway 144 when a truck, driven by Elliot R. Daniel, ran a stop sign and collided with Samantha's vehicle. Both Elliot and Samantha were injured in the crash. Elliot, who was conscious following the collision, told a paramedic that his brakes had failed suddenly. The truck had the name "Mason Dixon Poultry Company" painted on the sides, along with a telephone number.

CHAPTER 2

INTRODUCTION TO TORTS AND LEGAL ANALYSIS

The law often allows what honor forbids.
——— ***Bernard Joseph Saurin***

§ 2.1 Introduction

This chapter covers the definition of a tort, the three broad categories of torts, the history of tort law, the public policy objectives behind tort law, and analytical processes used to understand appellate court opinions and to solve hypothetical problems.

This chapter includes:

- Definitions of torts

- An initial description of negligence

- The elements of strict (absolute) liability

- The historical roots of tort law

- The public policy objectives of tort law in terms of compensating injured parties, holding wrongdoers liable, and allocating losses across society

- Development of an analytical framework to understand appellate court opinions

- Construction of an analytical formula to solve hypothetical problems by applying the legal principles to the facts of the case

- Assembly of an analytical formula that allows any tort law problem or question to be continuously narrowed to reveal the answer

- Demonstration of how tort law analysis goes from the general to the specific.

§ 2.2 Torts Defined

A **tort** is a wrongful injury to a person or his or her property. The person inflicting the harm is called the **tortfeasor** (*feasor* meaning "doer"). The word *tort* is French, taken from the Latin *torquere* (meaning "to twist") to characterize behavior that warps or bends society's rules about avoiding harm to others. The French phrase *de son tort demesne* (meaning "in his own wrong") was used to describe grievous misconduct between individuals and to assign blame to the responsible party.

Sources of Tort Law

Tort law is derived both from common and statutory law. Legislatures often enact statutes to supplement, modify, or supersede common law tort principles. For example, at common law, the government was exempt from tort liability under the doctrine of **sovereign immunity**. Today many state legislatures have passed statutes to abolish sovereign immunity for most tort claims against the government. Courts may turn the tables on the legislature by issuing new common law rulings interpreting the meaning of statutes. In this way, the law matures, with both courts and legislatures adjusting the law to meet the changing needs of society.

Broad Categories of Tort Law

Tort law considers the rights and remedies available to persons injured through other people's carelessness or intentional misconduct. Tort law also holds persons in certain circumstances responsible for other people's injuries regardless of blame. Torts are commonly subdivided into three

---

◖ TERMS ◗

tort A wrong involving a breach of duty and resulting in an injury to the person or property of another. A tort is distinguished from a breach of contract in that a tort is a violation of a duty established by law, whereas a breach of contract results from a failure to meet an obligation created by the agreement of the parties. Although the same act may be both a crime and a tort, the crime is an offense against the public which is prosecuted by the state in a criminal action; the tort is a private wrong that must be pursued by the injured party in a civil action.

tortfeasor A person who commits a tort.

sovereign immunity The principle that the government—specifically, the United States or any state of the United States—is immune from suit except when it consents to be sued.

|||| PROFESSIONAL PROFILE ||||

"The most rewarding aspect of my work is the knowledge that I have used all my talents, education, and skills to help our local community hospital stay open. To see an account proceed from 30 to 60 to 90 days overdue, to payment in full, and knowing that your hard work and diligence made it happen, is truly rewarding," says Stephanie Wong.

Married, with four teenage children, Wong has long been employed by her neighborhood hospital near Los Angeles, California. In 1982, she originally applied for a clerical position to supplement the family income. At that time, being a paralegal was the furthest thing from her mind. "I am not sure I really understood what a paralegal actually did," she says. After two years as a supervisor of the billing department an opportunity to join the hospital's legal office became available. "I applied, was accepted, and loved the job immediately. I soon enrolled in college, and have attended evening paralegal classes for the past year," Wong explains.

Wong's paralegal training has been a combination of on-the-job training, by staff attorneys and supervisory personnel, and formal education received in the paralegal program at college. Her on-the-job training has helped her to see the material learned in class applied to practice every day.

"The patient record states volumes," Wong says. Wong now has a greater appreciation for the work the physicians, nurses, and other support staff perform each day. Now she is involved in training and educating employees to avoid lawsuits. What is said—or even what is not said—in the patient record can be pivotal when suit is brought against the hospital and staff. Wong is now looking at the daily activities that occur at the hospital from a new perspective: risk management. Not only must hospital procedure be strictly maintained, authorizations for surgery and other procedures be obtained in advance, but there must be full disclosure of the potential risks and danger to the patient.

Wong's advice to those embarking on a paralegal career is to research the avenues of possible employment, get a good educational base, and then pursue the area of the law that is personally interesting. "Be aware that there are endless opportunities to learn and that none should be missed," Wong concludes.

---

broad categories: negligence, intentional torts, and strict (or absolute) liability.

Negligence

Negligence is the failure to exercise reasonable care to avoid injuring others. It is distinguishable from intentional torts in that negligence

TERMS

negligence The failure to do something that a reasonable person would do in the same circumstances, or the doing of something a reasonable person would not do. Negligence is a wrong generally characterized by carelessness, inattentiveness, and neglectfulness rather than by a positive intent to cause injury.

does not require the *intent* to commit a wrongful action; instead, the wrongful action itself is sufficient to constitute negligence. Intentional torts, as the name indicates, require the tortfeasor to intend to commit the wrongful act. What makes misconduct negligent is that the behavior was not reasonably careful and someone was injured as a result of this unreasonable carelessness, such as failing to watch the road ahead when driving a car.

Intentional Torts

Intentional torts are actions designed to injure another person or that person's property. The tortfeasor intends a particular harm to result from the misconduct. There are several specific types of intentional torts: battery, assault, false imprisonment, infliction of emotional distress, fraud, misrepresentation, malicious prosecution, abuse of process, invasion of privacy, defamation (libel and slander), trespass, conversion, slander of title, disparagement of goods, and defamation by computer. Each of these is discussed in detail in later chapters. For now, a brief summary will provide a guide for later chapters.

Specific Intentional Torts: Brief Definitions   **Battery** occurs when a tortfeasor touches another person without consent. **Assault** is an attempted battery. **False imprisonment** happens when an individual is intentionally confined against his or her will. **Infliction of emotional distress** results from someone's outrageous conduct that is designed to cause

---

TERMS

intentional injury (tort)   An injury inflicted by positive, willful, and aggressive conduct, or by design, as opposed to an injury caused by negligence or resulting from an accident.

battery   The unconsented-to touching or striking of one person by another, or by an object put in motion by [that other], with the intention of doing harm or giving offense. Battery is both a crime and a tort.

assault   An act of force or threat of force intended to inflict harm upon a person or to put the person in fear that such harm is imminent; an attempt to commit a battery. The perpetrator must have, or appear to have, the present ability to carry out the act.

false imprisonment   The unlawful restraint by one person of the physical liberty of another. Like false arrest, to which it is closely related, it is both a tort and a crime.

infliction of emotional distress   Results from someone's outrageous conduct which is designed to cause another to suffer anxiety, fright, or anguish.

another to suffer anxiety, fright, or anguish. **Fraud** occurs when the tort-feasor intentionally makes false statements to entice someone to give up something of value to the tortfeasor. **Misrepresentation** exists when one person makes a false statement (or behaves so as) to deceive another individual. **Malicious prosecution** happens when a prosecutor purpose-fully and in bad faith files groundless criminal charges against a defen-dant. **Abuse of process** exists when a plaintiff maliciously uses the court system against a defendant to achieve some unlawful objective. **Invasion of privacy** occurs when someone publicly exploits another's private af-fairs in an unreasonably intrusive manner. **Defamation** is an injury to one's reputation in the community and may be inflicted by *libel,* which is written defamation, or *slander,* which is oral defamation. **Trespass** is un-lawful or unreasonable interference with the use of someone's property. **Conversion** is wrongfully taking personal property from its rightful owner, either permanently or for an indefinite period of time. **Slander of title** happens when someone falsely and maliciously disparages the own-ership rights that a legal owner has in his or her property. **Commercial disparagement** occurs when one makes a false or misleading statement

---

TERMS

fraud   Deceit, deception, or trickery that is intended to induce, and does induce, another to part with anything of value or surrender some legal right.

misrepresentation   The statement of an untruth; a misstatement of fact designed to lead one to believe that something is other than it is; a false statement of fact designed to deceive.

malicious prosecution   A criminal prosecution or civil suit commenced mali-ciously and without probable cause. After the termination of such a prose-cution or suit in the defendant's favor, the defendant has the right to bring an action against the original plaintiff for the tort of "malicious prosecution."

abuse of process   The use of legal process in a manner not contemplated by the law to achieve a purpose not intended by the law.

invasion of privacy   A violation of the right of privacy.

defamation   Libel or slander; the written or oral publication, falsely and intentionally, of anything that is injurious to the good name or reputation of another person.

trespass   An unauthorized entry or intrusion on the real property of an-other.

conversion   Control over another person's personal property which is wrongfully exercised; control applied in a manner that violates that person's title to or rights in the property. Conversion is both a tort and a crime.

slander of title   A false or malicious statement, oral or written, that brings into question a person's right or title to real or personal property, causing him or her damage.

commercial disparagement   When one makes a false or misleading state-ment about a business to discourage the public from patronizing the business.

about a business to discourage the public from patronizing that business. **Defamation by computer** exists when personal information about an individual that is kept in a computer system is misused or is incorrect and results in injury to that person's reputation or ability to obtain credit.

Strict, or Absolute, Liability

Strict (or **absolute**) **liability** is the tortfeasor's responsibility for injuring another regardless of intent, negligence, or fault. The most important type of strict liability is *products liability,* a theory under which the manufacturer or other seller of an unreasonably dangerous or defective product is held liable for injuries the product causes. Strict liability is different from intentional torts in that intent to commit an absolute liability tort is irrelevant. Likewise, strict liability is distinguishable from negligence, because the tortfeasor is responsible under absolute liability regardless of how careful he or she might have been.

These concepts are presented here only to establish basic terminology. Subsequent chapters explore each of these topics in greater detail.

The Unique Elements of Each Tort

Each type of tort contains its own unique elements. For instance, battery may be readily distinguished from defamation because it carries its own definition and rules that separate it from other intentional torts. Likewise, the elements of negligence are different from strict liability's components, and so on. The key to understanding tort law is to identify the type of broad tort category involved in the case. Ask whether the problem contains intentional torts (and, if so, which particular one(s)), negligence, or strict liability. Next, apply the appropriate rules of law to the specific facts of the case.

Like all forms of law, torts have undergone a long and interesting period of growth and development. Section 2.3 briefly examines the history of tort law.

TERMS

defamation by computer When personal information about an individual that is kept in a computer system is misused or is incorrect and results in injury to that person's reputation or ability to obtain credit.

strict (absolute) liability Liability for an injury whether or not there is fault or negligence; absolute liability. The law imposes strict liability in product liability cases.

§ 2.3 History of Tort Law

Tort law, like all American law, traces its origins to English and Western European history. After the Norman conquest of England in 1066, William the Conqueror brought Norman law (which itself was heavily influenced by Roman law) to intermingle with Anglo-Saxon and Celtic legal traditions. The result was the common law, which at the time consisted of the underlying legal principles and social attitudes gleaned from generations of judicial decisions by local tribunals. Even today, the bulk of tort law has been derived from our common law heritage.

The King's Writs

During the Middle Ages, much of this common law was passed on orally, although substantial portions were written down by scriveners, who were mostly monks or church clerics. Thus, common law often varied widely among localities, even those separated by only a few miles. To unify these divergent legal ideas, the king eventually established formal procedures by which crown subjects could petition the king's courts for redress. These formal processes were called the *king's writs*.

Evolution to Modern Tort Law

During the eighteenth and nineteenth centuries, English tort law began to shift from the old writs system to torts involving intent and fault, which are known today as intentional torts and negligence. This evolution was copied in the United States. Gradually, the common law grew to include the modern torts discussed throughout this text. Today's tort law is a combination of English and American common law plus statutory law.

What does tort law seek to accomplish? Section 2.4 examines the social and economic purposes that influence, and are influenced by, tort law.

§ 2.4 Public Policy Objectives in Tort Law

Like every aspect of our legal system, there are several purposes underlying tort principles. These include (1) protecting persons and property from unjust injury by providing legally enforceable rights; (2) compensating victims by holding accountable those persons responsible for causing such harms; (3) encouraging minimum standards of social conduct among society's members; (4) deterring violations of those standards of conduct; and (5) allocating losses among different participants in the social arena.

Protecting Persons and Property: Accountability

Like the king's writs, modern tort law strives to prevent unjustified harm to innocent victims. Tort law enables private citizens to use the legal system to resolve disputes in which one party claims that the other has acted improperly, resulting in harm. The system compels the tortfeasor to compensate the injured party for his or her losses. This *accountability* (or *culpability*) factor is crucial to our legal sense of fair play and equity. People should be held responsible for their actions, especially when they wreak havoc on others. Redress should be available for innocent victims of carelessness, recklessness, or intentional injury.

Minimum Standards of Social Conduct: Deterrence

To function meaningfully in American society, citizens must understand society's norms and values. One extremely important norm encourages the public to behave so as to avoid hurting others or their belongings. Tort law is largely composed of *minimum standards of conduct,* and persons functioning below such thresholds are defined as tortfeasors, whereas individuals acting at or above such criteria are acceptable to the community. However, the intention is not to ensure conformity; rather, the ideal is to inspire people to respect the dignity and integrity each individual possesses. Persons should not infringe heedlessly upon others' activities unless society is willing to accept such interference with its members' lives. Tort law discourages abuses by establishing a clear system of legal rights and remedies enforceable in court proceedings. We know that we can go to court when someone strikes us, invades our privacy, creates a nuisance, or acts negligently toward us. Likewise, we know that we might be hauled into court if we do these things to others. By establishing minimum standards of conduct, tort law sets the rules for living—those "rules of thumb" by which we try to get along with other people.

Allocating Losses among Different Individuals or Groups

It is easy to grasp the idea that an individual tortfeasor should compensate the victim for the tortfeasor's wrongdoing. However, in modern society there are often many different participants in virtually any activity, and it is less clear who should be labeled as tortfeasor or victim. For example, at the time of the American Revolution, most Americans were fairly self-sufficient and dealt directly with other individuals for goods or services. If a colonist bought a broken plow or a poorly shod horse from the local blacksmith, he or she knew who to take to task. However, as the United States became more industrialized, commercial transactions ceased to be one-on-one interactions. Today, people buy canned fruit from a local grocery that bought it from a wholesaler that bought it from a manufacturer that bought it from a grower. If the fruit is spoiled, perhaps the purchaser's spouse or child, rather than the purchaser, will suffer the injury. The culpability lines become less clear as the producer of the defective item becomes more removed from the ultimate user. Tort law has evolved *products liability* to determine who is in the best position to bear the costs of defective products—the innocent user or the sellers and manufacturers. It is an economic decision that courts and legislatures have made in stating that industry can best afford the costs of injuries caused by dangerously made goods. In other words, the burden of shouldering the economic loss is placed upon commercial business instead of the individual suffering the harm. Thus, tort law can be used to assign the expenses associated with misfortune, even when fault is hazy at best. More commonly, though, a single tortfeasor can be identified and saddled with the financial obligation.

§ 2.5 Analyzing Hypothetical Problems

This book poses many hypothetical fact problems (or, simply, hypotheticals) to help develop analytical talents. Perhaps the most popular analytical framework for hypotheticals is discussed here.

Analytical Framework for Hypotheticals

This framework sequentially investigates four general elements of a problem: issue, rules of law, application of the rules to the facts, and conclusions. With this approach, legal principles are applied to specific factual scenarios. When analyzing a hypothetical, first decide which *issues* are presented. To accomplish this, one must identify the general area of law involved in the problem. For instance, if John takes Peter's bicycle without permission, then John has committed some type of tort. This identifies the broad area of law (torts). Next, the different parts of the general legal area must be explored to see which specific tort applies.

The particular tort John appears to have engaged in is called conversion. So the issue would be whether or not John converted Peter's property. This question can be answered by referring to the appropriate *rule of law*. To generalize, the rule of law for conversion defines it as the wrongful deprivation of another's property without consent. This rule must now be *applied* to the facts. John took Peter's property without permission. This means John wrongfully deprived Peter of the use and enjoyment of his property. This constitutes conversion. The *conclusion* would be that Peter may successfully sue John to recover possession of the bicycle, plus damages, because these legal remedies are appropriate for conversion (as an upcoming chapter explains).

This analytical formula is a useful tool in applying abstract legal principles to different fact situations.

HYPOTHETICAL

Delroy Magnus visited the Gym Dandy Fitness Center to use its weight and steam rooms. As he walked from the locker room into the weight room, he slipped and fell on a puddle of water on the floor. The puddle was caused by leaking water pipes along the wall leading to the steam room. Delroy broke his left arm as a result of the fall. Mary Perrington, another patron, mentioned that she had seen the puddle when she first arrived at the center approximately two hours before Delroy's accident.

Legal Analysis in Action

Would Delroy's negligence lawsuit against Gym Dandy Fitness Center succeed? Applying the rules of law established in other negligence cases, Delroy (the plaintiff) must prove that Gym Dandy (the defendant) either created the hazardous condition or had actual or constructive notice of the danger. The puddle was caused by Gym Dandy's leaking water pipes, so Gym Dandy created the danger that hurt Delroy. Further, Mary testified that the puddle had been visible on the floor for two hours. That was sufficient time for Gym Dandy's employees to observe and correct the problem. Thus, Gym Dandy had constructive notice of the puddle and the danger it posed to customers. The conclusion: Gym Dandy was negligent in creating the puddle upon which Delroy fell and was injured. Accordingly, Delroy's negligence lawsuit against Gym Dandy should be successful.

Factual Distinctions Result in Different Conclusions

A rule of law may be applied to various factual situations to reach different results. This is exactly what appellate courts do when deciding cases dealing with similar legal issues. It is also what attorneys and paralegals do when applying rules of law to the particular facts of a client's case.

§ 2.6 Solving Tort Problems

Another approach to tort problem solving is moving from broad subject areas to specific types of torts. This method identifies the exact issues, rules of law, and conclusions in a problem by helping the reader to narrow the analytical focus.

Tort Analysis: From General to Specific

Tort analysis should go from the general to the specific. For example, how can one tell if infliction of emotional distress has occurred unless one is aware that some type of tort law was involved in the problem? Experienced paralegals may appear to strike the analytical nail directly on the head, such as the paralegal who immediately recognizes assumption of risk in a negligence case. In reality, that paralegal has streamlined the analytical process, but still has moved from the general to the specific. (See Figure 2-1.) Implicitly, that paralegal recognized a general negligence problem and then narrowed it to a specific defense—assumption of risk—necessary to excuse the negligent conduct.

Hypotheticals

Two hypotheticals should more clearly illustrate tort analysis.

HYPOTHETICAL 1: FRAUD AND MISREPRESENTATION

In an effort to sell his 1966 Ford automobile to Della, Roger claims that the vehicle's total mileage is 20,000 miles when, in reality, it is 520,000 miles. This sounds like an intentional tort, but which type of intentional tort might apply? When one person misinforms another, as Roger has done to Della, it is most likely fraud, deceit, or misrepresentation. One must now construct the issues in terms of the facts: When Roger sold Della a 1966 Ford and told her it had been driven only 20,000 miles when, in fact, it had been driven 520,000 miles, has Roger committed fraud or misrepresentation? The elements of fraud and misrepresentation, respectively, are intentionally making a false statement to entice someone to give up something of value to the defrauder, and making a false statement to deceive another. One applies the rules to the facts. Roger intentionally distorted the truth about his automobile's mileage to encourage Della to give up something valuable to him (namely, her money to buy it). Roger's false statement about the mileage also deceived Della. The conclusion is clear: Roger has committed fraud and misrepresentation against Della, who may now sue Roger to recover damages.

FIGURE 2-1

Sequence of tort analysis: from general to specific

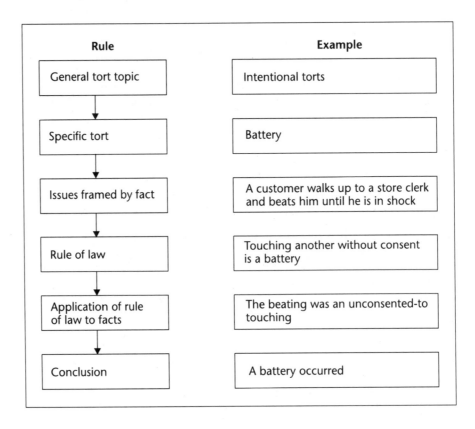

Rule	Example
General tort topic	Intentional torts
Specific tort	Battery
Issues framed by fact	A customer walks up to a store clerk and beats him until he is in shock
Rule of law	Touching another without consent is a battery
Application of rule of law to facts	The beating was an unconsented-to touching
Conclusion	A battery occurred

HYPOTHETICAL 2: TRESPASS

Jerry lives next to a vacant lot owned by Steven. Jerry dumps his grass clippings onto Steven's lot after mowing his lawn. Eventually, these grass clippings begin to smell and attract rats. Steven never gave Jerry permission to dump grass (or anything else) on Steven's lot. What legal rights does Steven have, if any?

Jerry's actions appear to fall within the intentional torts category, as Jerry is deliberately discarding his grass clippings onto Steven's lot. A quick glance among the summarized definitions in § 2.2 of this chapter reveals that Jerry may have committed trespass against Steven. The framed issue is: Did Jerry trespass against Steven by dumping grass on Steven's lot without permission? The elements of trespass are, generally, unlawful interference with another person's use of his or her property. Applying this rule to the facts, Jerry's actions (1) were unlawful, in that he did not have Steven's permission to dump grass onto Steven's lot, and (2) interfered with Steven's use of his property, because Steven could not use his lot freely without having to contend with the grass and vermin. The conclusion: Jerry is liable to Steven for the intentional tort of trespass.

Summary

Tort law involves the study of wrongful conduct. Torts are wrongful injury to another's person or property. The wrongdoer is called the tortfeasor, and tort law provides the injured party with legal rights and remedies that may be enforced in a court of law. Torts may be divided into three general categories: negligence, intentional torts, and strict (absolute) liability. Negligence is the failure to exercise reasonable care to avoid injuring others. Intentional torts consist of misconduct designed to injure another person or that person's property. Strict (absolute) liability holds the tortfeasor liable for injuring another regardless of intent, negligence, or fault.

Much of tort law comes from ancient English and early American court decisions. In medieval England, there were primarily two torts. These were breaches of the king's peace. Today, there are many more tort actions, because society is much more complicated today than during the Middle Ages, and tort law has become more sophisticated to deal with modern legal problems.

Tort law seeks to accomplish several goals. First, it serves to protect innocent persons and their property from careless or intentional injury at the hands of tortfeasors. It also attempts to hold tortfeasors responsible for their misconduct. Second, tort law encourages minimum standards of conduct among the public to avoid injuring others through heedless, reckless, or intentional behavior. It also deters persons from injuring other people and their property by holding tortfeasors liable for such mischief. Third, tort law allocates losses among different groups or individuals, based upon society's decision (as expressed through its legislatures and courts) as to who is best able to bear such misfortunes.

To apply the rules of law to different hypothetical problems, one method breaks down the factual scenario in terms of the issues, rules of law that must then be applied to each case's specific facts, and the conclusions regarding the probable outcome of the hypothetical case. When analyzing tort law problems, decide on the general tort topic area, the specific tort involved, the issues framed by the facts, rules of law for the particular tort involved, and how to apply those rules of law to the facts. Then draw the conclusions to the hypothetical or problem.

Review Questions

1. How is a tort best defined? What are the three broad categories of torts? How might you define each variety?

2. What is negligence? How might you distinguish it from intentional torts? From strict (absolute) liability?

3. What are intentional torts? What are the specific types of intentional torts? How might you broadly define them?

4. How might you define strict, or absolute, liability? How might you distinguish it from intentional torts? From negligence?

5. Discuss the historical roots of tort law. From what country or countries did torts originate? How have torts changed since their inception?

6. What are the purposes that tort law attempts to accomplish? Do these objectives sometimes conflict? Do they sometimes complement one another?

7. Suggest an analytical formula you might use to answer a hypothetical fact problem. In what order are these steps taken? Why do you think this order is appropriate? Is each step of the technique necessary to reach the next phase?

8. What method might you use to analyze tort problems? How does this approach help you reach your answers? Do you see any similarities between this method and those discussed in the text? Any differences?

9. Does tort analysis move from the specific to the general, or vice versa? Why is the correct approach best suited to answering tort hypotheticals?

Project

Read the case of *Frankel v. Warwick Hotel* in Appendix C. Was Adam Frankel's dismissal from the hotel a wrongful discharge? Was the plaintiff successful with his claim for intentional infliction of emotional distress? Explain. Did Frankel's acts constitute an invasion of privacy? Do you agree with the court's decision?

IIII

CHAPTER 3

NEGLIGENCE

§ 3.1 Introduction

The field of negligence is the most complex of the torts. What makes negligence enigmatic is its conceptual ambiguity. The elements of negligence appear to be so broadly defined that it is difficult to discern clear lines for negligent behavior. But negligence is not a mathematical equation. Instead, negligence resembles probability theory, in which specific conduct is more likely than not to be considered negligent under a particular set of circumstances. In this chapter, the following aspects of negligence are discussed:

- The elements of negligence

- The tortfeasor's duty of reasonable care

- The scope of duty, reasonable care, and the reasonable person standard

- Cause-in-fact, but-for causation, substantial factor analysis, and joint and several liability

- Proximate cause and reasonable foreseeability

- Damages available in negligence actions

- Burdens of proof and rejoinder in negligence cases

- Res ipsa loquitur.

§ 3.2 Negligence

Most people equate negligence with carelessness. The phrase conjures up images of actions that are slovenly, haphazard, heedless, or foolhardy. As a legal concept, negligence is much more precise, but it embodies all of these characteristics.

Negligence Defined: Reasonable Care

Negligence may be broadly defined as the failure to exercise reasonable care to avoid injuring others or their property. Reasonable care depends upon the exact circumstances of each case. This is the "shifting sands" aspect of negligence with which legal students—and the legal system—struggle. The key term is *reasonableness.* In any tort case in which negligence might exist, ask the threshold question: Did the tortfeasor act unreasonably under the circumstances? This is essentially all that negligence entails.

Acts or Omissions

The tortfeasor can be negligent either by doing or not doing something. When courts speak of *negligent acts or omissions* by the tortfeasor, they mean that the tortfeasor behaved unreasonably either by doing a specific careless activity or by failing to do something that the tortfeasor should have done.

Negligent actions are positive events; something is done. For instance, if Roger lit a fire in high winds that carried sparks onto a neighbor's roof and set the house ablaze, Roger's action (heedless burning) would be deemed unreasonable. Negligent omissions are usually phrased negatively; the tortfeasor failed to do a reasonable act. For example, suppose Marie's front porch has a rotten step that she has failed to repair. A salesperson visiting her home falls through the step and breaks a leg. Marie's omission (failure to repair the step) would be considered unreasonable.

Like all areas of law, negligence has developed discernible elements that may be enumerated and outlined more clearly. Section 3.3 outlines the elements of negligence.

§ 3.3 Elements of Negligence

Negligence may be specifically defined as the tortfeasor's failure to exercise reasonable care which causes a foreseeable injury to another person or that person's property. Negligence includes the following elements:

TERMS

negligence The failure to do something that a reasonable person would do in the same circumstances, or the doing of something a reasonable person would not do. Negligence is a wrong generally characterized by carelessness, inattentiveness, and neglectfulness rather than by a positive intent to cause injury.

IIII   PROFESSIONAL PROFILE   **IIII**

Maria Alvaraez started out her career as an emergency room nurse in a major metropolitan hospital. After eight years she wanted a change. She was still interested in medicine, but wanted to do something different. No matter what she selected, she still wanted a job where she could feel that she was helping people. Maria enrolled in her local community college. After two years of full-time day classes, she earned an associate's degree in Paralegal.

Maria was concerned that her lack of office experience would be a problem in her job search. She did not realize that her prior medical experience and knowledge would be such an asset. A law firm that specialized in medical malpractice cases was looking for a nurse paralegal. Even though the attorneys were knowledgeable about medical issues, and knew the basic terminology, they needed someone with a medical background who could evaluate the medical records and reports for each case. In the past, the law firm had sent each case out of the office for an independent medical evaluation. However, this was very cumbersome and time-consuming.

The fact that a relative dies in a hospital, or that a patient does not have the particular medical result he or she would have liked does not necessarily mean that there was malpractice. For malpractice, a doctor or hospital must deviate from accepted standard procedure. For each case, it is Maria's responsibility to make an initial evaluation of the medical records and reports and state if there are potential legal issues. As the cases progress, Maria summarizes new medical reports as they are received and notes her impressions in the file. When a clamp or needle shows up on a client's x-ray, there is a good possibility that there was malpractice. However, when a patient ends up paralyzed following spinal surgery, the undesirable result is not proof of malpractice; something more must be shown.

Maria also uses her medical expertise to draft proposed complaints and detailed bills of particulars outlining the client's injuries and treatment. Sometimes the attorneys ask Maria for suggestions when they are preparing for depositions of physicians. Maria suggests particular areas to cover, such as hospital policy and procedure. Maria also drafts proposed questions for depositions for cases involving complex medical issues. As a case progresses, the law firm usually obtains its own medical expert who may have to testify should the case go to trial. Maria then acts as an intermediary working with the doctor and the attorneys to develop the case.

1. Duty of reasonable care and scope of duty (foreseeability of victim)
2. Breach of the duty by the tortfeasor
3. Causation of injury to the victim (cause-in-fact or substantial factor)
4. Proximate cause (foreseeability of injury)
5. Damages to the victim (recovery).

Each of these elements is required for negligence to exist, so each element is a threshold question. If "no" answers any single element, negligence does not exist. For example, the first question is: Did the tortfeasor owe a duty of reasonable care to the injured party? If not, then the analysis stops, with the conclusion that no negligence has occurred. If yes, then:

The Case of the Quarter-Sized Puddle

One of the more common negligence actions you will encounter is the slip-and-fall case. If the plaintiff is to be successful, causation must be established.

ADGER

v.

DILLARD DEPARTMENT STORES
Court of Appeal of Louisiana
662 So. 2d 864 (La. Ct. App. 1995)
November 1, 1995
Williams, Judge

On the evening of May 11, 1993, the plaintiff and a companion, Beverly Franklin, visited Dillard's Department Store at Pierre Bossier Mall. ... Ms. Franklin was walking slightly ahead of the plaintiff and did not see her slip, but turned and saw her falling to the floor.

Margaret P. Stinson, area sales manager for Dillard's, was notified of the incident. When Ms. Stinson arrived at the young-men's section, plaintiff was standing with Ms. Franklin and David Piazza, a security guard. They helped plaintiff walk to a nearby chair. The security officer questioned the plaintiff and filled out an accident report.

* * *

[P]laintiff testified that she did not know what caused her fall and had not noticed anything on the floor before or immediately after she fell. She apparently did not examine her clothing for dampness or staining, which would have indicated that she slipped in liquid. She testified that her foot slid along the floor, but defense counsel pointed out that plaintiff had not made that claim during a prior deposition.

Ms. Franklin also testified that she did not notice any water on the floor before plaintiff fell, or immediately after the fall, when her attention centered on helping the plaintiff. Ms. Franklin asserted that a short time later, she returned to the place where the plaintiff fell and found a quarter size puddle of water. Ms. Franklin maintained that she told someone standing nearby that plaintiff had slipped in water. However, Ms. Stinson testified that she inspected the area where the accident occurred and found the floor clean and dry.

* * *

Here, the plaintiff has failed to establish that her fall was caused by the quarter-sized puddle of water observed by Ms. Franklin. Moreover, another witness contested the presence of any water in the area of the accident. Even if we were to assume that the small puddle of water was present at the time of the accident, there is no evidence, other than Ms. Franklin's hypothesis, that the water contributed to the plaintiff's fall. After reviewing the record and the trial transcript, we cannot find that the trial court was clearly wrong in granting the defendant's motion for involuntary dismissal.

* * *

AFFIRMED.

Case Questions

1. Do you think the trial court believed the plaintiff's version of the facts? Explain.
2. What kinds of facts would have had to be presented to hold the defendant department store liable for the slip and fall?

Did the tortfeasor breach the duty of reasonable care? If not, the inquiry is finished, and once again the analyst surmises that there was no negligence. If yes, then one continues querying through causation, proximate cause, and injury. Each element must be satisfied for negligence to arise.

Each of the elements of negligence receives detailed treatment in the following sections.

§ 3.4 Scope of Duty and Standards of Reasonable Care

Negligence analysis begins with the duty of reasonable care. First, the scope of the duty must be determined. This focuses on the foreseeability of the victim.

Duty Defined

Duty in tort law is the obligation either to do or not to do something. In negligence, the duty of **reasonable care** is the responsibility to act reasonably so as to avoid injuring others. This may also be stated negatively: the duty of reasonable care is the obligation *not* to behave *un*reasonably so as to avoid injuring others.

For example, motor vehicle operators owe a duty of reasonable care to drive carefully and avoid injuring other drivers, their vehicles, or pedestrians. Suppose Parker is driving on a four-lane highway and chooses to pass the truck in front of him. He fails to look in the rear-view mirror before pulling into the left lane. Unbeknownst to Parker, another vehicle is attempting to pass him, and he pulls directly in front of that driver. This action forces that driver to swerve and collide with a telephone pole. Did Parker violate any duty of reasonable care?

In analyzing this duty hypothetical, the first question is: Did Parker owe the other driver a duty of reasonable care? Parker owed anyone driving or walking upon the street a duty to drive safely. By failing to check his rear-view mirror to see if any traffic was approaching from behind in the left lane, Parker breached his duty to the other driver. He acted imprudently by not looking for other traffic before he switched lanes. He failed to see that which was there to be seen.

TERMS

duty 1. A legal obligation, whether imposed by the common law, statute, court order, or contract. A tort is committed only when there has been a breach of duty resulting in injury. 2. Any obligation or responsibility.

due (reasonable) care That degree of care which a person of ordinary prudence would exercise in similar circumstances. Same as ordinary care or reasonable care.

Scope of Duty

Clearly, one does not owe a duty of reasonable care to everyone else in the universe. **Scope of duty** is a limitation on the persons to whom one owes the duty.

For example, while driving on the four-lane highway in her city, Janet owes no duty of reasonable care to someone driving in another city hundreds of miles away. Janet's actions (i.e., driving her car) could not possibly have any effect on such a person. Janet's scope of duty does not extend to individuals who cannot be affected by her carelessness. Scope of duty is often described in terms of reasonable foreseeability.

Foreseeability

Foreseeability in tort law is the notion that a specific action, under particular circumstances, would produce an anticipated result. If an injury were foreseeable, then one could take precautions to avoid the behavior that might be expected to cause harm. If a tortfeasor failed to take such precautions, he or she breached the duty of reasonable care.

For instance, in the preceding driving example, Parker did not check his rear-view mirror before attempting to pass on a four-lane highway. Is it foreseeable that another vehicle might be passing Parker in the lane he was trying to enter, and that his failure to look behind him could result in a collision? This consequence is clearly foreseeable. Suppose, however, that it is late at night, and that the other driver trying to pass Parker did not have headlights on. Thus, Parker could not see the car approaching as he moved into the left lane to pass the truck. Was it reasonably foreseeable that another driver would come up from behind

---

TERMS

scope of duty[†]   In negligence law, defined in terms of those individuals who might foreseeably be injured as a result of the tortfeasor's actions. This is called *reasonable foreseeability.* The scope of duty includes all those foreseeable plaintiffs who could have been hurt because of the tortfeasor's conduct. This is called *foreseeability of the victim.*

foreseeability[†]   The notion that a specific action, under particular circumstances, would produce an anticipated result. In negligence law, if it were reasonably foreseeable that the plaintiff would be harmed by the defendant's actions, then the scope of duty includes the plaintiff. Foreseeability of injury is another aspect of negligence theory, which falls within proximate cause. Foreseeability is defined in terms of reasonableness.

without headlights? No. So the result (the other driver swerving to avoid hitting Parker's car) was not foreseeable under these facts. A slight difference in the circumstances changes the answer.

Foreseeable Plaintiffs Theory

Foreseeability limits the scope, or extent, of the duty owed to others. One asks the threshold question: Was it reasonably foreseeable that the person injured would be harmed as a consequence of the tortfeasor's actions? If so, the scope of the duty of reasonable care includes the individual hurt. This is sometimes called the **foreseeable plaintiffs theory**, because it was reasonably foreseeable that the plaintiff (who is suing the tortfeasor for negligence) would be damaged because of the tortious conduct. It is the foreseeability of injury or damage that is of concern, not the degree or amount of injury or damage involved.

Persons outside this range of duty are considered **unforeseeable plaintiffs**, because the tortfeasor could not reasonably have anticipated that they would be harmed by the tortfeasor's actions. People driving several hundred feet in front of Parker would not likely be influenced by either Parker or the swerving other driver. They would be beyond Parker's scope of duty, and so he would not be required to exercise reasonable care toward them. However, persons driving close behind Parker and the swerving driver could reasonably be expected to become involved in the accident. These individuals would be within Parker's scope of duty. His failure to use reasonable care (by not looking in the rear-view mirror, which caused him to cut off the swerving driver) violated his duty to them as well as to the swerving driver.

Figure 3-1 outlines scope of duty and the foreseeable plaintiffs theory.

TERMS

---

foreseeable plaintiffs theory[†] A theory used in analyzing negligence cases. Under this theory, if it were reasonably foreseeable that the injured victim would be harmed as a consequence of the tortfeasor's actions, then the tortfeasor's scope of duty includes the victim. The victim is said to be a *foreseeable plaintiff.* Unforeseeable plaintiffs fall outside the defendant's scope of duty, because their injuries could not have been reasonably anticipated as a result of the defendant's conduct. The theory is also used in products liability analysis.

unforeseeable plaintiffs[†] Persons whose injuries the tort feasor could not reasonably have anticipated as a result of the tortfeasor's actions.

Scope of Duty	Foreseeable Plaintiffs Theory
The tortfeasor owes a duty of reasonable care to avoid injuring others or their property.	The plaintiff may recover from the defendant only if it were reasonably foreseeable that the defendant's actions would injure the plaintiff.
Duty includes persons for whom it is reasonably foreseeable that injury will occur as a result of the tortfeasor's actions.	Persons outside the defendant's scope of duty are considered unforeseeable plaintiffs.

FIGURE 3-1   Scope of duty of reasonable care and foreseeable plaintiffs theory

Standards of Reasonable Care

Reasonable care is a most elusive concept in negligence law. It depends upon the particular facts of each problem. Still, tort law has developed an abstract measure of reasonable care, called the **reasonable person standard**.

The Reasonable Person Standard

The *reasonable person* is an imaginary individual who is expected to behave reasonably under a given set of circumstances to avoid harming others. The tortfeasor is alleged to have done something, or have failed to do something, that was unreasonable and that caused the victim's injuries. The tortfeasor's conduct is measured under the reasonable person standard in this fashion: In the same or similar circumstances, would the reasonable person have acted as the tortfeasor behaved? If so, then the tortfeasor did not violate his or her duty of reasonable care. If not, then the tortfeasor breached the duty.

In our previous driving hypothetical, would the reasonable person have looked in his or her rear-view mirror before entering the left lane to pass a truck on a four-lane highway, when it was reasonably foreseeable that another vehicle might already be occupying that lane while attempting to pass the reasonable person's car? Checking the rear-view

---

TERMS

reasonable man (person) test (standard)   A standard for determining negligence, which asks: "What would a reasonable person have done in the same circumstances?" In short, it measures the failure to do that which a person of ordinary intelligence and judgment would have done in the circumstances, or the doing of that which a person of ordinary intelligence and judgment would not have done.

The Case of Drunken Duty

In negligence litigation, an injured plaintiff always argues that the defendant's scope of duty extends to the injured party. The contention sometimes reaches absurdity. Plaintiffs may attempt to avoid personal responsibility for their own injuries by claiming that a defendant breached some supposed duty of care. In the following case, an intoxicated driver injured himself and then sought damages against the tavern owner for having served alcohol to the plaintiff when he was already visibly drunk. As the Oklahoma Supreme Court observed, negligence law will not assist careless persons in avoiding personal responsibility for their apparent stupidity.

OHIO CASUALTY INSURANCE CO.

v.

TODD

Supreme Court of Oklahoma

813 P.2d 508 (Okla. 1991)

June 11, 1991

Summers, Justice

The question certified for our resolution calls upon us to decide whether *Brigance v. Velvet Dove Restaurant, Inc.* [citation omitted], should be extended to create a common law cause of action against a tavern owner for an adult who voluntarily becomes intoxicated and is injured as a result of his own inability to drive a vehicle properly. We decline to extend *Brigance* to this situation, following the reasoning used by a majority of jurisdictions.

* * *

On November 6, 1986, Rick Robertson was injured in a one-car accident after having been served alcohol in Todd's Tavern. ...

Robertson [alleged] that the employees of Todd's Tavern served him alcoholic beverages when he was noticeably intoxicated in violation of [Okla. Stat. tit. 37,] § 537 [1981], and that for this reason Todd is liable for [Robertson's] injuries. Todd moved to dismiss ... .

All agree that the pertinent case is *Brigance* ... . Robertson urges that *Brigance* should be extended to cover the situation at bar. Todd, however, asserts that *Brigance* creates a cause of action for innocent third parties, and should not be stretched to include a situation wherein the inebriate sues for his own injuries.

In *Brigance* we recognized for the first time a common law "dram shop" action; a third party who was injured in an intoxicated driver's auto accident may now state a cause of action against the restaurant that served liquor to the driver. At common law, such an action was not possible. ...

In changing the common law rule and creating this cause of action, we acknowledged that legal duty and liability are matters of public policy and are therefore subject to the changing attitudes and needs of society. We pointed out that protection must be afforded to the innocent bystander ... .

The creation of this cause of action, therein limited to third parties, served to protect the innocent by allowing liability to be placed not only on the intoxicate drivers but concurrently on those parties who continued to serve alcohol to their customers already noticeably intoxicated.

Left open by *Brigance* was the question of whether the consumer-inebriate would have a cause of action against the vendor for on-premises consumption. ...

The elements of negligence are "(1) the existence of a duty on [the] part of defendant to protect plaintiff from injury; (2) a violation of that duty; and (3) injury proximately resulting therefrom." All three of these elements must exist before the plaintiff has a valid cause of action. Robertson, relying on [Okla. Stat. tit. 37,] § 537(A)(2) [Supp. 1985], urges that a duty exists on the part of a tavern keeper to refrain from serving alcoholic beverages to an adult customer who is noticeably intoxicated. Section 537(A)(2) states in relevant part that no person shall "[s]ell, deliver or knowingly furnish alcoholic beverages to an intoxicated person."

... Because we find that the duty of the tavern owner does not extend to an adult customer who voluntarily consumes intoxicants and is injured, we need not address the question of proximate cause.

* * *

Several states have considered the question. See Annot., 98 A.L.R.3d 1230 (1980). A majority of them have refused to create a cause of action for an adult who voluntarily drinks to the point of intoxication and is thereby injured. These jurisdictions have generally concluded that as a matter of public policy drunken persons who harm themselves are responsible for their condition, and should not prevail either under a common law or statutory basis. Focusing on the "duty" concept, these courts hold the view that no duty should be imposed "upon the tavernkeeper, and protection should not be extended, because the adult voluntarily created the vulnerability that is the problem."

* * *

If this Court were to create a cause of action against the tavern owner, the inebriate could be rewarded for his own immoderation. Such was not the intent of *Brigance,* nor will we allow such a reward. ...

Then there are the practical consequences of recognizing such suits. "Pause, if you will and contemplate the vast number of claims that may be urged by drunks, if they were entitled to every expense and injury that are natural concomitants of their intoxication." In a world where alcohol is readily available for consumption by adults the ultimate accountability should rest on the adult consumer, absent unusual circumstances or injury to an innocent third party. ...

Here, the question is simply whether the intoxicated adult must bear the responsibility for his own injury which occurred due to his voluntary consumption of an excessive amount of alcohol. ...

Accordingly, under the facts as presented to us we find that the tavern owner has no liability to the intoxicated adult who voluntarily consumes alcoholic beverages to excess and sustains injuries as a result of his intoxication.

Case Questions

1. What was the court's public policy justification for its decision? Do you agree or disagree? Explain.
2. Suppose a passenger in Robertson's vehicle had been injured. Would the passenger have a cause of action against the tavern owner under the common law and statute? Explain.

mirror when changing lanes seems reasonable, and so the reasonable person could be expected to do so under these conditions. Parker did not, however. Therefore, Parker acted unreasonably in this case. He violated his duty of care to the swerving driver because he did not act as the reasonable person would have behaved in the same situation.

The mythical reasonable person may seem too intangible to compare to real-life persons. Nevertheless, American and English courts have relied on the concept in over 200 years of court decisions (though older opinions refer to the *reasonable man*).

Who Decides How the Reasonable Person Would Have Acted

The trier-of-fact in a negligence lawsuit determines whether the defendant did not act as the reasonable person would have behaved in a specific case. This is usually a jury, but it could be the judge in a bench trial. In effect, the jurors decide what was reasonable by investigating how they, and others they know, would have behaved. Suddenly, the reasonable person standard becomes clear: it is what the jurors conclude was reasonable under the circumstances. This settles the question of whether the defendant breached the duty of reasonable care to the plaintiff.

At first glance, the reasonable person standard seems arbitrary, as each juror determines the defendant's negligence based upon his or her own personal, gut-level response. However, sociologists would remind us that this is precisely how each individual views the world—through the eyes of his or her own experience. The judicial system safeguards against one capricious definition of reasonableness by offering the option of a jury trial, which forces several persons to agree upon an appropriate measure of due care. Although a judge in a bench trial is the sole trier-of-fact, the judge's legal training is presumed to compensate for any bias in defining reasonableness.

Matching Skills and Handicaps

The reasonable person is supposed to resemble the defendant as closely as possible in terms of special abilities. This enables the trier-of-fact to assess reasonableness more precisely in a specific case. For example, if the defendant were a plumber and was alleged to have negligently installed a leaking water line, the reasonable person would also possess the same training and knowledge as plumbers employed in the defendant's geographical area. This is sometimes called the **professional community standard of care**, which is based on the custom and practice among professionals working in the defendant's community. This measure is determined through expert testimony from members of the defendant's profession. Physicians, attorneys, accountants, veterinarians, electricians, beauticians—those in virtually every professional activity—are evaluated in negligence lawsuits by this standard of care.

The defendant's limitations are also important in shaping the reasonable person standard. For instance, if the defendant were physically handicapped, then the reasonable person would likewise share identical handicaps. One could hardly decide how a blind defendant should have behaved by comparison with a reasonable person who has normal vision. This forces the trier-of-fact to empathize with the defendant's situation to understand more clearly how the defendant acted. In effect, the jury must conceptualize how the reasonable person would have

---

TERMS

professional community standard of care [†] The standard of reasonable care used in negligence cases involving defendants with special skills and knowledge.

behaved in a wheelchair, with impaired hearing, or without certain limbs. The outcome of this empathy should be a more accurate reasonableness definition that best fits the defendant and the circumstances of the case. The result, ideally, is a just and equitable outcome in the litigation.

Figure 3-2 summarizes the reasonable person standard.

FIGURE 3-2
Reasonable
person
standard

1. Ask: Would the reasonable person have acted as the defendant did, under the same or similar circumstances?
2. Match the skills or abilities of the reasonable person to those of the defendant (e.g., physician, attorney, plumber, rodeo rider) if these abilities were involved in the alleged negligent actions (professional community standard).
3. Trier-of-fact decides how the reasonable person would have acted in a particular situation.

Professional Malpractice

A professional's negligent failure to observe the appropriate standard of care in providing services to a client or patient, or misconduct while engaging in the practice of a profession, is considered malpractice. Failure to exercise the degree of care and skill reasonably required of like professionals in similar circumstances, if that failure causes damage or injury, is malpractice. Originally, the precise degree of skill used to judge a professional's actions was the care and skill of other professionals practicing in the same community. Many jurisdictions have now expanded this to include the same community or similar locality. Likewise, a specialist must possess the degree of skill and competence that a specialist in the same or similar community would exercise. Many jurisdictions have taken this a step further and hold specialists to a national standard, without regard to their location. Some jurisdictions are applying the national standard to general practitioners as well. Professional malpractice cases have been brought against doctors, lawyers, accountants, travel agents, and even priests, depending on the jurisdiction.

Medical Malpractice

To prove a medical malpractice case, generally one or more expert witnesses will be needed for trial. This major expense prevents attorneys from bringing suit for anything but serious and permanent injury cases.

The Case of the Late Diagnosis

A physician's negligent failure to observe the appropriate standard of care in providing services to a patient is malpractice. In this case, a medical malpractice action was brought against a gynecologist for failure to diagnose breast cancer.

MEZRAH v. BEVIS
District Court of Appeal of Florida,
Second District
593 So. 2d 1215
(Fla. Dist. Ct. App. 1992)
February 21, 1992
Lehan, Acting Chief Judge

In this medical malpractice action the defendants, a gynecologist and his professional association, appeal a final judgment entered on a jury verdict finding them liable to plaintiff for failing to diagnose breast cancer. We affirm.

As to defendants' first argument that the trial court erred in allowing expert testimony from a pathologist that defendants breached the standard of care, we conclude that there was no error. Also, there was additional competent testimony from another expert to that effect.

As to defendants' second argument, we do not agree that the evidence on the issue of causation was merely speculative. There was competent expert testimony which, as we have said, was not improperly allowed that had defendants not breached the standard of care, plaintiff's breast cancer "more likely than not" would have been completely cured.

Noor v. Continental Casualty Co., in which this court affirmed a judgment for defendants in a medical malpractice case based upon the alleged failure to timely diagnose breast cancer, is distinguishable. Damages were sought in that case on the alleged basis that Mrs. Noor's life expectancy had been shortened due to a delay of several months in failing to diagnose her cancer. This court pointed out that her life expectancy had been shortened as a result of the disease even if the disease had been correctly diagnosed by defendant doctor at the first opportunity. The plaintiffs in that case did not prove causation because they did not produce any "nonspeculative evidence as to what extent, if any, [defendant doctor's] failure to immediately diagnose her disease added to Mrs. Noor's decreased life expectancy." On the other hand, plaintiff in this case apparently sought damages on a different basis, i.e., that had the breast cancer been timely diagnosed, she more likely than not would have been cured. As noted above, she produced sufficient evidence in that regard.

Affirmed.

Case Questions

1. How is the *Noor* case distinguishable from the instant case?
2. Can you put a dollar value on a patient's claim of having lost the chance to be cured?

Practical Applications

As a practical note, it is important to remember that the mere fact that there is an injury, or the occurrence of a bad result in medicine, does not necessarily mean that there has been malpractice.

Typically, medical malpractice cases involve one or more of the following:

- Abandonment (failure to attend to a patient)
- Improper diagnosis
- Medical instruments, sponges, needles, or other foreign objects dropped and left in surgical field
- Lack of informed consent
- Errors in prenatal diagnostic testing
- Failure of hospital to supervise employees
- Failure to diagnose
- Failure to advise of diagnosis
- Medication errors.

The next hypothetical examines another situation in which the standard of care is at issue. Note how scope of duty, foreseeability and the reasonable person standard are established.

HYPOTHETICAL

John makes an appointment to see his family physician. John's throat has been hurting him for the past week. The doctor takes a throat culture. John has strep throat, a condition that requires antibiotics. John's doctor calls John with the results and advises that he will call the pharmacy and order medication. Unbeknownst to John, the drug that the doctor orders is one in a category of drugs to which John is highly allergic and should never take. The doctor failed to check John's chart for known allergies before ordering the prescription. Because the drug has a different name than the drug John previously had a reaction to, John assumes that the drug is a different drug that is safe for him to take. Minutes after taking the prescription, John goes into shock and dies. Did the doctor owe John a duty of reasonable care? If so, did the doctor breach that duty?

To establish negligence by a physician, it must be shown that the injury complained of was caused by the physician's failing to act as a family physician would have acted under like circumstances. Failing to check a chart for allergies falls below the standard of care that a family physician of ordinary skill would have used under similar circumstances. The physician did not follow professional practices and failed to comply with the reasonable standard of care owed to John. It was foreseeable that John would be hurt.

The Case of Restraint

A patient enters a hospital and leaves in a worse condition than when admitted. Malpractice does not always involve problems with the actual surgery or medication; it could also involve issues such as failure to order appropriate restraints or to properly monitor the patient following surgery.

DOUGLAS
v.
GIBSON
Supreme Court, Appellate Division,
Third Department
630 N.Y.S.2d 401 (App. Div. 1995)
August 3, 1995
Cardona, Presiding Justice

On December 1, 1988, defendant Mark D. Gibson surgically removed a previously placed fixation device from plaintiff's left hip. Following the surgery, plaintiff was placed in a vest restraint. Although no doctor ordered that plaintiff be restrained, his wife requested restraints during plaintiff's admission procedures because he had become confused in the past after surgery. Plaintiff was 64 years old at the time and suffering from Parkinson's disease. On the day after the surgery, plaintiff was examined by Gibson's partner, defendant William C. Bishop, who found him to be in stable condition. In the early morning hours of December 3, 1988, it was discovered that plaintiff had fallen between the side rails of his bed and suffered a fracture of his left distal femur.

Plaintiff commenced this medical malpractice action against Gibson and Bishop (hereinafter collectively referred to as defendants) alleging, *inter alia,* that they were negligent in failing to order that plaintiff be appropriately restrained, in failing to provide him with an adequate restraint and in failing to adequately monitor him. The bill of particulars further alleged that defendants failed to properly supervise staff personnel. Following joinder of issue and examinations before trial, defendants moved for summary judgment

dismissing the complaint against them. Supreme Court granted the motion and plaintiff now appeals.

Initially, we are of the view that defendants made a prima facie showing that no material issues of fact exist as to the alleged malpractice asserted against them in the complaint as amplified by the bill of particulars. In support of their motion, defendants submitted, *inter alia,* their own affidavits, the affidavits of their attorney and Donald Douglas, a physician, as well as hospital records and transcripts of examinations before trial of staff personnel. Through this and other evidence in the record, defendants established that although they did not order plaintiff to be restrained, the vest restraint placed on him was appropriate and would have been the same devise they would have ordered postoperatively. Douglas averred that the vest restraint used was the standard restraint and was not a departure from accepted medical standards of care. Defendants also established that no additional or further restraint prior to the incident was medically indicated. Finally, defendants sufficiently rebutted plaintiff's claim of improper supervision.

Given this evidence, the burden shifted to plaintiff to come forward with evidentiary proof sufficient to raise a question of fact. His evidence, in opposition to defendants' motion, consisted of the affidavits of Patricia Newland, a registered nurse, and Miles St. John, a surgeon. These averments, however, lacked the requisite level of proof necessary to defeat defendants' motion. These affidavits state that based on plaintiff's prior medical history, he was a "high risk" patient who needed more secure restraints than those provided and that defendants' failure to do so constituted a deviation from accepted medical practice. They claim that on previous occasions plaintiff had attempted to get out of bed and had fallen or injured himself. Notably absent from the record, however, is any evidence of any such prior incidents to support these allegations. Therefore, the allegations are conclusory, unsupported by competent evidence and fail to raise a question of fact. The affidavits also claim malpractice due to the lack of a physician's order to use a restraint. Defendants, however, averred that, had they ordered a restraining device, it would have been the vest restraint actually used. Thus, insofar as a restraint was in fact used and was the same one that would have been ordered, the failure to so order does not raise an issue of fact.

Plaintiff also failed to offer any competent proof that another physician would have ordered anything other than a vest restraint. Although Newland's affidavit claimed that a more secure device was required, she was giving her professional opinion as to what a physician should have ordered which, in our view, went beyond her professional and educational experience and cannot be considered "competent medical opinion" on this issue. As to St. John's averment that a more secure restraint was warranted, this was based only on his unsupported assertion that plaintiff was a high risk patient. ... There were no medical records submitted to support the specifically disputed factual assertion that there were prior falls, which was the basis for St. John's conclusion that plaintiff was a high risk patient.

We also note that plaintiff failed to offer any proof that the type of security restraint he claims should have been used would have prevented him from failing. He thus failed to establish the requisite nexus between the alleged malpractice and his injury. Finally, plaintiff submitted no adequate proof on the issue of sufficient oversight of plaintiff's case or of staff personnel. We therefore conclude that summary judgment was properly awarded to defendants. Plaintiff's remaining arguments are rejected as unpersuasive.

Case Questions

1. What was the court's reason for denying the plaintiff's medical malpractice claim?
2. What specific kinds of proof did Justice Cardona suggest could have been introduced at trial to prove malpractice, which were not offered as proof by this plaintiff's attorneys?
3. If you were the plaintiff in this case, how would you feel upon reading an appellate decision in which numerous suggestions are made to counsel as what could have been offered at trial?

§ 3.5 Causation of Injury

Even if the defendant breaches his or her duty of care owed to the plaintiff, the defendant will not be legally negligent, nor liable for the plaintiff's injuries, unless the defendant's actions proximately caused the harm.

Cause-in-Fact

Causation is a critical component of negligence. To be liable, the tortfeasor must have caused the victim's injuries. *Causation of injury* relates to the tortfeasor's actions that result in harm to the injured party. Courts frequently refer to this as **cause-in-fact**, meaning that, in negligence litigation, the defendant's misconduct produced the plaintiff's injuries.

Causation may be direct or indirect. **Direct causation** is often called **but-for causation**, a term often applied in the common law. The formula is straightforward: but for the tortfeasor's (defendant's) actions, the victim (plaintiff) would not have been harmed. But-for, or direct, causation is straight-lined, that is, the tortfeasor's behavior is usually the immediate, direct, and dominant cause of the victim's misfortune. For example, if Samantha spills a beverage on a stairway and does not clean it up, and Daniel slips on the slick spot and falls down the stairs, Samantha has caused Daniel's injuries. The causation is direct: but for Samantha's failure to clean the drink spill on the stairs, Daniel would not have slipped and fallen.

Consider another illustration. Suppose an automobile mechanic changes the tires on Quinn's car but neglects to tighten the lug nuts properly. While the vehicle is moving, the left rear tire comes loose and flies off. The car skids out of control and crashes into a telephone pole, hurting Quinn. Again, there is direct causation: but for the mechanic's failure to tighten the nuts sufficiently, the tire would not have come off and Quinn would not have collided with the pole.

Indirect causation occurs when several forces combine to produce injuries. For example, in the loose tire example, suppose the tire had not come completely off the automobile but was wobbling loosely. However, as Quinn was driving, he encountered broken glass on the highway, which punctured his left rear tire. Because of the flat tire and the looseness of

---

TERMS

cause-in-fact [†]   Cause of injury in negligence cases. If the tortfeasor's actions resulted in the victim's injuries, then the tortfeasor was the cause-in-fact of the victim's harm. Cause-in-fact includes direct, or but-for, causation as well as indirect causation.

direct (but-for) causation [†]   A form of causation of injury in negligence cases. The formula is applied as a question: But for the defendant's actions, would the plaintiff have been harmed? If not, then the defendant directly caused the plaintiff's injuries.

indirect causation [†]   A form of causation of injury in negligence cases. The most common test is substantial factor analysis.

all the tires, Quinn lost control of the car and crashed. Here, two factors resulted in Quinn's injuries: the glass that ruptured his tire and the loose nuts that lessened his control of the vehicle. In this version of the facts, the but-for test does not provide a clear-cut answer. Could one now say that, but for the mechanic's failure to tighten the nuts, Quinn would not have driven into the pole? Did not the flat tire also cause him to lose control of the car? Would the punctured tire alone have caused him to lose control and crash? To resolve this causation dilemma, the but-for test serves poorly. Instead, one needs a formula that satisfactorily accounts for the multiple factors that produced the injuries. For indirect causation, there is substantial factor analysis.

Substantial Factor Analysis

Substantial factor analysis states that the tortfeasor is liable for injuries to the victim when the tortfeasor's misconduct was a *substantial factor* in producing the harm. In the preceding tire illustration, the broken glass flattened Quinn's tire and made the car difficult to handle. However, had the lug nuts not also been loose, the tires would not have been wobbling. Quinn probably would have been able to control the vehicle better and might not have crashed at all. The mechanic's failure to tighten the nuts was a substantial factor in Quinn's losing control and colliding with the pole. Thus, the mechanic would be liable, even though the broken glass and punctured tire also influenced the accident.

A classic substantial factor analysis case is *Summers v. Tice*, 33 Cal. 2d 80, 199 P.2d 1 (1948). In this case, the plaintiff was hunting quail with two defendants. When the birds were flushed out, the defendants aimed and fired their shotguns in the plaintiff's direction, striking the plaintiff and causing severe physical injuries. It was unclear which defendant's shot hit the plaintiff, because both defendants used the same gauge shotgun and size of shot. The California Supreme Court applied the substantial factor test in determining causation and liability. Although it could not be conclusively established which defendant's weapon caused the plaintiff's injuries, either defendant's action was sufficient to produce the resulting harm. Quoting a Mississippi Supreme Court case, Justice Carter stated: "We think that ... each is liable for the resulting injury ... , although no one can say definitely who actually shot [the plaintiff]. To hold otherwise would be to exonerate both from liability, although each was negligent, and the injury resulted from such negligence."

TERMS

substantial factor analysis [†] A test for indirect causation in negligence cases. The tortfeasor is liable for injuries to the victim when the tortfeasor's conduct was a substantial factor in producing the harm.

Summers v. Tice resembles another type of case in which multiple forces combine to produce harm. When two or more defendants act together to produce the plaintiff's injury, the courts consider them to have *acted in concert*. All defendants are held liable for their combined conduct in such cases. This is called **joint and several liability,** another form of causation.

Joint and Several Liability

Multiple tortfeasors are each held individually accountable to the victim for the combined negligent behavior of all the tortfeasors. For instance, suppose that a surgical team, composed of two surgeons, three nurses, and an anesthesiologist, loses count of surgical sponges and leaves one in the patient's abdomen. The patient contracts peritonitis as a consequence. Because all of the medical personnel acted together in the operation, they are said to have functioned in concert. Their collective conduct produced harm to the patient. Thus, each individual would be personally liable for the patient's injuries. In other words, all of the personnel would be jointly and severally liable.

Multiple tortfeasors may injure a victim by acting in sequence, rather than simultaneously as in the medical malpractice example. The sequence of combined events produces the harmful results. For example, assume that a shipping company does not refrigerate a shipment of perishable food. As a result, the items spoil in transit. The shipment arrives at a supermarket, which fails to notice the spoiled condition of the products and stocks them on its shelves. Carla's roommate buys some of the goods but does not check them for freshness, despite obvious odors and discoloration. After her roommate cooks dinner, Carla eats the bad food and becomes seriously ill.

Who does Carla sue? Several tortfeasors combined negligent behavior to produce her injury. First the shipper failed to refrigerate the food, and it turned rotten. Next the grocery store failed to notice the spoiled food and stocked it. Then Carla's roommate failed to notice the spoilage and prepared the food for her to eat. All these tortfeasors—the shipping company, the supermarket, and Carla's roommate—contributed to a sequence of events that resulted in her illness. Carla would not have become sick had any of these tortfeasors identified the threat (spoiled food) and taken reasonable precautions to avoid injuring customers. But for the concerted conduct of these tortfeasors, Carla would not

TERMS

joint and several liability   The liability of two or more persons who jointly commit a tort (joint tortfeasors).

have been hurt. Therefore, they are all jointly and severally liable to her for the harm caused.

Figure 3-3 outlines the three types of causation-of-injury theories.

Cause-in-Fact (Direct) (But-For Causation)	*Cause-in-Fact (Indirect) Substantial Factor Analysis*	*Joint and Several Liability*
But for the defendant's actions, the plaintiff's injury would not have happened.	When multiple defendants combine to injure the plaintiff, a single defendant is liable if his or her actions were a substantial factor in producing the harm.	When multiple defendants act together to injure the plaintiff, all defendants are liable for the harm.

Contribution

Contribution is another issue that comes up when multiple defendants are involved in a negligence action. Most jurisdictions permit one tortfeasor to seek contribution from the others. **Contribution** means that one tortfeasor pays all or part of the liability for a wrong and is then allowed to get back all or part of this amount from the other tortfeasors. Some jurisdictions allow parties to seek contribution only when there was no concert of action, when the wrong was not an intentional one, or when the person seeking contribution was not primarily liable. For example, Marie sues Adam, Bobby, and Cindy and is awarded a judgment for $12,000. Each defendant's share is one-third of $12,000, or $4,000. If Adam pays the entire $12,000 judgment, he can seek contribution of $4,000 from Bobby and $4,000 from Cindy.

Courts Blur the Distinctions

American Jurisprudence 2d, a legal encyclopedia, provides an excellent and accurate summary of legal principles gleaned from multitudes of

TERMS

contribution   1. A payment of his share of a debt or judgment by a person who is jointly liable. 2. The right of a person who has satisfied a shared indebtedness to have those with whom she shared it contribute in defraying its cost.

court opinions. As the quoted discussion hints, courts blur the distinctions between direct and indirect causation, but-for and substantial factor causation, and proximate cause. There is an almost endless variety of definitions of these terms in the common law. Despite the confusion, concepts surface that are essentially identical to those discussed in this chapter. The excerpt is included here to reflect the different analytical approaches to the causation query.

57A AMERICAN JURISPRUDENCE 2D *Negligence*
§§ 431, 434, 436, 464, 471, 474–75, 478
(1989)
[All footnotes omitted.]

[§ 431] Cause in fact as an element of proximate cause means that the wrongful act was a substantial factor in bringing about the injury and without which no harm would been incurred. ...

[§ 434] There are two steps in analyzing a defendant's tort liability. The first is determining whether he breached his duty of care, the second whether the breach was at least a cause of the accident. Liability for negligence is predicated upon a causal connection between the negligence alleged as the wrong and the injury of which complaint is made, and the common law refers the injury to the proximate, not the remote, cause, and establishes as an essential element of liability for negligence what has traditionally been referred to as proximate cause, or, as it is now frequently denominated, legal cause. ...

[§ 436] The Restatement of Torts 2d says that, in order for a negligent actor to be found liable for another's harm, it is necessary not only that the actor's conduct be negligent toward the other, but also that the negligence of the actor be a legal cause of the other's harm. The Restatement further points out that the conduct of a negligent actor need not be the predominant cause of the harm. The wrongful conduct of a number of third persons may also be a cause of the harm, so that such third persons may be liable for it, concurrently with the actor. ...

[§ 464] It has been recognized that the issue of "causation in fact" is regarded as an aspect of "proximate cause" ... . Traditionally, courts have used the term "proximate cause" as descriptive of the actual "cause in fact" relation which must exist between a defendant's conduct and a plaintiff's injury before there may be liability. Additionally, the courts have used the same term as a shorthand description of various complex legal concepts and principles which have nothing to do with the fact of actual causation, but which define and control the existence and extent of liability ... .

In all cases where proximate cause is in issue, the first step is to determine whether the defendant's conduct, in point of fact, was a factor in causing plaintiff's damage. ... If the inquiry as to cause in fact shows that the defendant's conduct, in point of fact, was not a factor in causing plaintiff's damage, the matter ends there, but if it shows that his conduct was a factor in causing such damage, then the further question is whether

his conduct played such a part in causing the damage as makes him the author of such damage and liable therefor in the eyes of the law. ...
[§ 471] Most jurisdictions have historically followed this so-called "but-for" causation-in-fact test. It has proven to be a fair, easily understood and serviceable test of actual causation in negligence actions ... . Where the "but for["] test is recognized, it has been said to be useful and generally adequate for the purpose of determining whether specific conduct actually caused the harmful result in question, but that it cannot be indiscriminately used as an unqualified measure of the defendant's liability ... .
[§ 474] The "but-for" test, while it explains the greater number of cases, does not in all instances serve as an adequate test. If two causes concur to bring about an event, and either one of them, operating alone, would have been sufficient to cause the identical result, some other test is needed. ... The response of many courts to this problem has been to apply the "substantial factor" test, either in addition to or in place of the "but for" test. ...
[§ 475] The substantial factor test ... makes the question of proximate or legal cause depend upon the answer to the question, "was defendant's conduct a substantial factor in producing plaintiff's injuries?"

As pronounced in the Restatement, Torts 2d, the test is as follows: The actor's negligent conduct is a legal cause of harm to another if (a) his conduct is a substantial factor in bringing about the harm, and (b) there is no rule of law relieving the actor from liability because of the manner in which his negligence has resulted in the harm. ...
[§ 478] Many courts lump the "but for" and the "substantial factor" tests together and apply them both, with some taking the view that the "but for" standard is only one element of the "substantial factor" standard, and a few holding that in the great majority of cases the two tests amount to the same thing ... .

Causation becomes clearer through an example. The following illustration should lend substance to the analytical formula.

HYPOTHETICAL

Cindy runs a beauty salon. Aspen is one of her regular customers. Cindy received a shipment of hair coloring products in unlabeled bottles. Rather than return the shipment, Cindy placed the bottles in a storeroom for future use. She applied one bottle to Aspen's hair without carefully checking its contents beforehand. Because of unusually high pH levels in Aspen's hair, the product turned Aspen's hair bright blue. Did Cindy cause Aspen's injury?

But for Cindy's failure to inspect the bottle's contents prior to treating Aspen's hair, Aspen would not have suffered hair discoloration. Direct causation functions easily and clearly to conclude that Cindy caused Aspen's injury.

Suppose instead that Angie, one of Cindy's employees, had taken the bottle from the storeroom and applied it to Aspen. Would both Cindy and Angie be liable for Aspen's harm and damage? Cindy failed to identify the unlabeled bottles before storing them. Angie failed to check the bottle's contents before applying them to Aspen's hair. Both combined in their unreasonable actions to produce the harmful result. Accordingly, Cindy and Angie are jointly and severally liable to Aspen.

Suppose the bottles had been mislabeled by the manufacturer. Cindy unknowingly stocked the bottles, assuming the labels to be correct. Angie then applied the contents of one bottle to Aspen's hair without observing that the contents were the wrong color and texture (a point that an experienced beautician should reasonably have known). The but-for test does not produce clear results in this case. One cannot say that, but for the manufacturer's mislabeling, Aspen would not have been hurt, because Angie actually misapplied the product to Aspen's hair. Neither may one contend that, but for Angie's use of the improperly labelled product, Aspen would not have been harmed, because Angie was not responsible for the mislabeling. Substantial factor analysis, however, helps to reach an acceptable answer. Angie's failure to inspect the bottle's contents and determine the error before applying the mixture to Aspen's hair was a substantial factor in producing Aspen's injury. Accordingly, Angie would be liable to Aspen.

§ 3.6   Proximate Cause

Joint and several liability is simple to discern when the chain of negligent events is relatively short and direct, such as in the preceding bad food or hair discoloration hypotheticals. However, when the sequence of activity is long, drawn-out, and complicated by peculiar twists and unexpected occurrences, then the three types of causation analysis (cause-in-fact, substantial factor analysis, and joint and several liability) become unreliable for determining whether the tortfeasor is liable to the victim. Another analytical tool must be applied to establish negligence in such circumstances. This approach is called proximate cause.

Foreseeability of Injury

Proximate cause, or *legal cause* as it is sometimes called, exists when the tortfeasor's actions cause a foreseeable injury to the victim. Court opinions often refer to the plaintiff's injuries as the natural and

---

TERMS

proximate cause   As an element of liability in a tort case, that cause which, unbroken by any intervening cause, produced the injury, and without which the result would not have occurred; the primary cause; the efficient cause. Note that the proximate cause of an injury is not necessarily the final cause or the act or omission nearest in time to the injury.

probable consequence of the defendant's misconduct. The key to proximate cause is foreseeable injury. Was the victim's injury the reasonably foreseeable result of what the tortfeasor did? If so, then the tortfeasor's actions proximately caused the plaintiff's harm. If not, then proximate cause did not exist, and the defendant will not be liable to the plaintiff under negligence theory.

Proximate cause is distinguishable from causation. The term *proximate cause* is unfortunate because it is a constant source of confusion with causation. *Causation* is the chain of events linking the tortfeasor's conduct to the victim's injury. *Proximate cause* is the zone within which the plaintiff's injury was reasonably foreseeable as a consequence of the defendant's behavior. Think of proximate cause as a circle. Actions inside the circle cause foreseeable injuries to victims. Actions outside the circle are beyond the zone of danger. Figure 3-4 illustrates this concept.

Consider a hypothetical. Patrick is building an additional garage and workshop in his backyard. As he is excavating to install the foundation, he hits an underground natural gas pipeline that services his neighborhood. The pipe ruptures and disrupts gas supplies to the other houses in the area. As a result, those houses with gas heat cannot use their furnaces. It is January, and outside temperatures fall well below freezing at night. With no heat, the water pipes in the neighbors' homes freeze and burst, causing substantial water damage to the structures and furnishings. Did Patrick proximately cause the harm to the neighbors' houses?

It was reasonably foreseeable that an underground utility line might be severed. If this line were carrying a heating source, such as natural

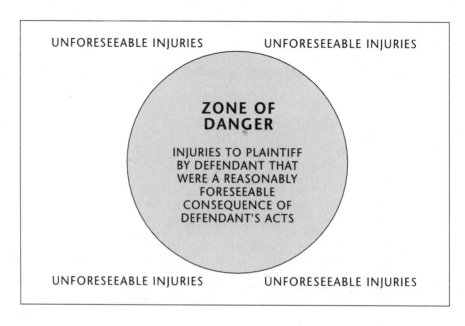

FIGURE 3-4 Proximate cause zone of danger (entire shaded area)

The Case of the Scale That Shook Tort Law

In this landmark case, a man waiting for a train was carrying a package wrapped in newspaper with fireworks inside. The railroad guards were unaware of the contents of the parcel and helped the man board the moving train. As the guards tried to help, the package was dislodged, fell to the tracks, and exploded. This caused the platform to shake, which in turn caused a scale to fall. The scale seriously injured Helen Palsgraf, who was waiting on the platform. Were the plaintiff's injuries the proximate result of the defendant's negligence? Where does one draw the line?

PALSGRAF
v.
LONG ISLAND RAILROAD
Court of Appeals of New York
162 N.E. 99 (N.Y. Ct. App. 1928)
May 29, 1928
Cardozo, C.J.

Plaintiff was standing on a platform of defendant's railroad after buying a ticket to go to Rockaway Beach. A train stopped at the station, bound for another place. Two men ran forward to catch it. One of the men reached the platform of the car without mishap, though the train was already moving. The other man, carrying a package, jumped aboard the car, but seemed unsteady as if about to fall. A guard on the car, who had held the door open, reached forward to help him in, and another guard on the platform pushed him from behind. In this act, the package was dislodged, and fell upon the rails. It was a package of small size, about fifteen inches long, and was covered by a newspaper. In fact it contained fireworks, but there was nothing in its appearance to give notice of its contents. The fireworks when they fell exploded. The shock of the explosion threw down some scales at the other end of the platform many feet away. The scales struck the plaintiff, causing injuries for which she sues.

The conduct of the defendant's guard, if a wrong in its relation to the holder of the package, was not a wrong in its relation to the plaintiff, standing far away. Relatively to her it was not negligence at all. Nothing in the situation gave notice that the falling package had in it the potency of peril to persons thus removed. Negligence is not actionable unless it involves the invasion of a legally protected interest, the violation of a right. "Proof of negligence in the air, so to speak, will not do." "Negligence is the absence of care, according to the circumstances." ... If no hazard was apparent to the eye of ordinary vigilance, an act innocent and harmless, at least to outward seeming, with reference to her, did not take to itself the quality of a tort because it happened to be a wrong, though apparently not one involving the risk of bodily insecurity, with reference to some one else.

* * *

One who jostles one's neighbor in a crowd does not invade the rights of others standing at the outer fringe when the unintended contact casts a bomb upon the ground. The wrongdoer as to them is the man who carries the bomb, not the one who explodes it without suspicion of the danger. ... What the plaintiff must show is "a wrong" to herself; i.e., a violation of her own right, and not merely a wrong to some one else, nor conduct "wrongful" because unsocial, but not "a wrong" to any one. ... The risk reasonably to be perceived defines the duty to be obeyed, and risk imports relation; it is risk to another or to others within the range of apprehension. This does not mean, of course, that one who launches a destructive force is always relieved of liability, if the force, though known to be destructive, pursues an unexpected path. "It was not necessary that the defendant should have had notice of the particular method in which an accident would occur, if the possibility of an accident was clear to the ordinarily prudent eye." Some acts, such as shooting as so imminently dangerous to any one who may come within reach of the missile however unexpectedly, as to impose a duty of prevision not far from that of an insurer. Even today, and much oftener in earlier stages of the law, one acts sometimes at one's peril. Under this head, it may be, fall certain cases of what is known as transferred intent, an act willfully dangerous to A resulting in injury to B. These cases aside, wrong is defined in terms of the natural or probable, at least when unintentional. The range of reasonable apprehension is at times a question for the court, and at times, if varying inferences are possible, a question for the jury. Here, by concession, there was nothing in the situation to suggest to the most cautious mind that the parcel wrapped in newspaper would spread wreakage through the station. If the guard had thrown it down knowingly and willfully, he would not have threatened the plaintiff's safety, so far as appearances could warn him. His conduct would not have involved, even then, an unreasonable probability of invasion of her bodily security. Liability can be no greater where the act is inadvertent.

* * *

One who seeks redress at law does not make out a cause of action by showing without more that there has been damage to his person. If the harm was not willful, he must show that the act as to him had possibilities of danger so many and apparent as to entitle him to be protected against the doing of it though the harm was unintended.

* * *

The law of causation, remote or proximate, is thus foreign to the case before us. The question of liability is always anterior to the question of the measure of the consequences that go with liability. If there is no tort to be redressed, there is no occasion to consider what damage might be recovered if there were a finding of a tort. We may assume, without deciding, that negligence, not at large or in the abstract, but in relation to the plaintiff, would entail liability for any and all consequences, however novel or extraordinary. There is room for argument that a distinction is to be drawn according to the diversity of interests invaded by the act, as where conduct

negligent in that it threatens an insignificant invasion of an interest in property results in an unforeseeable invasion of an interest of another order, as, e.g., one of bodily security. Perhaps other distinctions may be necessary. We do not go into the question now. The consequences to be followed must first be rooted in a wrong.

The judgment of the Appellate Division and that of the Trial Term should be reversed, and the complaint dismissed, with costs in all courts.

ANDREWS, J. (dissenting). Assisting a passenger to board a train, the defendant's servant negligently knocked a package from his arms. It fell between the platform and the cars. Of its contents the servant knew and could know nothing. A violent explosion followed. The concussion broke some scales standing a considerable distance away. In falling, they injured the plaintiff, an intending passenger.

Upon these facts, may she recover the damages she has suffered in an action brought against the master? The result we shall reach depends upon our theory as to the nature of negligence. Is it a relative concept—the breach of some duty owing to a particular person or to particular persons? Or, where there is an act which unreasonably threatens the safety of others, is the doer liable for all its proximate consequences, even where they result in injury to one who would generally be thought to be outside the radius of danger?

* * *

Negligence may be defined roughly as an act or omission which unreasonably does or may affect the rights of others, or which unreasonably fails to protect one's self from the dangers resulting from such acts.

* * *

Where there is the unreasonable act, and some right that may be affected there is negligence whether damage does or does not result. That is immaterial.

* * *

The proposition is this: Every one owes to the world at large the duty of refraining from those acts that may unreasonably threaten the safety of others. Such an act occurs. Not only is he wronged to whom harm might reasonably be expected to result, but he also who is in fact injured, even if he be outside what would generally be thought the danger zone.

* * *

But, when injuries do result from our unlawful act, we are liable for the consequences. It does not matter that they are unusual, unexpected, unforeseen, and unforeseeable. But there is one limitation. The damages must be so connected with the negligence that the latter may be said to be the proximate cause of the former.

* * *

The proximate cause, involved as it may be with many other causes, must be, at the least, something without which the event would not happen. The court must ask itself whether there was a natural and continuous sequence between cause and effect. Was the one a substantial factor in producing the other? Was there a direct connection between them, without too many intervening causes?

* * *

When a lantern is overturned, the firing of a shed is a fairly direct consequence. Many things contribute to the spread of the conflagration— the force of the wind, the direction and width of streets, the character of intervening structures, other factors. We draw an uncertain and wavering line, but draw it we must as best we can.

* * *

The act upon which defendant's liability rests is knocking an apparently harmless package onto the platform. The act was negligent. For its proximate consequences the defendant is liable.

Case Questions

1. What did Justice Cardozo mean by referring to the following statement in his decision: "Proof of negligence in the air, so to speak, will not do"?
2. Was it foreseeable that Helen Palsgraf would be injured as a result of the guards' attempt to assist the man with the package?
3. How does the dissenting opinion differ from the majority opinion?

gas, it would likewise be reasonably foreseeable that neighboring homes would lose their heat service. Because it was winter, it was also reasonably foreseeable that temperatures could go below freezing and cause water pipes in unheated buildings to freeze and burst. Water damage to structures and furnishings is a natural and inevitable consequence of broken pipes. Clearly, Patrick's actions proximately caused the injury to his neighbors' homes, because the harm was reasonably foreseeable as a result of Patrick's breaking the natural gas pipeline.

Proximate Cause and Scope of Duty Combined

Some legal scholars have included scope of duty as an aspect of proximate cause. This seems logical, as both include the element of foreseeability, but there is a subtle distinction. Scope of duty examines whether it was reasonably foreseeable that the plaintiff would be injured as a result of the defendant's actions. Proximate cause focuses upon whether the injury itself was reasonably foreseeable.

Thus, it is possible for the tortfeasor to owe a duty of reasonable care to the victim but not proximately cause the injury if the harm was unforesee-able. For instance, suppose that Shannon, who manages a shoe store, gave away free helium balloons to families as a promotional gim-mick. One of her customers, Addison, suffered from a rare allergy to helium, but was unaware of this condition. Addison inhaled some he-lium from the balloon to make himself talk in a high-pitched, funny voice, which is a common side effect of helium inhalation. Instead, Ad-dison went into anaphylactic shock, suffered cardiac arrest, and died. Did Shannon proximately cause Addison's death?

Definitely, Shannon owed a duty of reasonable care to all of her pa-trons to maintain reasonably safe premises. But Addison's uncommon sensitivity to helium (of which even he was unaware) was not some-thing that Shannon could reasonably have been expected to anticipate. The injury simply was not reasonably foreseeable. The vast majority of the population (say, 98 percent) would not possess this allergy and would suffer no ill effects. Accordingly, Shannon did not proximately cause Addison's injury.

"Taking the Victim as You Find Him"

Nonetheless, many appellate courts decide this issue differently. These opinions speak of a tortfeasor's **"taking the victim as you find him."** This means that peculiar health conditions are considered to be reasonably foreseeable, as one must always assume that a victim could suffer from an odd affliction such as helium allergy. Most of these cases, however, involve more deliberate actions (such as striking the head of a person with an "eggshell skull" and killing him or her). Such cases involve more intentional torts than negligence (battery, in the eggshell-skull cases), as is typical with the taking-the-victim cases. Still, taking-the-victim analysis surfaces in pure negligence cases as well.

Taking-the-victim cases make almost any physical injury reasonably foreseeable. This raises proximate cause to the point at which the tort-feasor becomes an insurer of the victim's safety. Such reasoning removes the cases from the realm of negligence and deposits them in the field of strict liability, which is discussed later in this text.

The range of the zone of danger is further explored in the next example.

TERMS

"taking the victim as you find him" [†]   A theory of negligence cases which states that the victim's injuries were reasonably foreseeable even if the tort-feasor was unaware of the victim's peculiar physical, health, or other preexisting conditions. In effect, the tortfeasor takes the victim as the tort-feasor finds him, and thus proximately causes the harm.

The Case of the Burning Candle

An owner of land generally knows more about the parcel of land than strangers coming upon the land. Accordingly, an owner must remedy any dangerous condition that might cause foreseeable harm. However, the owner of land has no duty to remedy a condition that presents an obvious risk. This case discusses whether a burning candle presents an obvious risk to a child of four years.

SAMPSON

v.

ZIMMERMAN

Appellate Court of Illinois,
Second District
502 N.E.2d 846 (Ill. App. Ct. 1986)
December 31, 1986
Reinhard, Justice

Plaintiff, Paige Sampson, a minor, by her father and closest friend, Randy S. Sampson, appeals from the order of the circuit court of DuPage County which granted summary judgment for defendants, Dennis L. Zimmerman and Linda C. Zimmerman, upon finding that defendants owed no duty to plaintiff as a matter of law.

The issues plaintiff raises on appeal are: (1) whether summary judgment is a proper and appropriate remedy where factual questions concerning foreseeability and appreciation of danger were for the jury; (2) whether a 4-year-old who cannot be held responsible for her own negligence can be held to have "assumed" the risk presented by fire; and (3) whether the trial court erred in failing to ascertain plaintiff's competency to testify as a witness.

The complaint alleges that on December 4, 1983, plaintiff, then four years and four months old, came in contact with a dangerous condition, that being a lighted and unprotected candle on a bathroom counter shelf, while visiting at defendants' home causing her clothes to catch fire and injuring her; that defendants knew or should have known of this dangerous condition; that defendants were negligent because they failed to warn plaintiff of the dangerous condition, failed to extinguish the lighted candle, and failed to provide a protective cover or other safety device for the candle; and that as a direct and proximate result of these acts plaintiff was injured.

After filing an answer, defendants filed a motion for summary judgment stating that they owed no duty as a matter of law to plaintiff to protect her from an obvious danger. They further asserted that a landowner is never an insurer of a child's safety and has no legal duty to protect against obvious dangers, that fire is an obvious danger recognized by case law as one which any child could be expected to appreciate and avoid, that plaintiff understood, as evidenced by deposition testimony, a lighted candle to be fire which was hot and could injure her, and that the child was of above-average intelligence and knew enough to avoid fire. Attached to the summary judgment motion were excerpts of plaintiff's deposition testimony in which she acknowledged that she knew fire could hurt her and that she could be burned by fire, that she had seen birthday candles before and knew fire was on top of the candle, that she had seen the candle enclosed in glass on the counter on the day in question, and that she climbed onto the bathroom counter before she got hurt. ...

Plaintiff responded to the motion arguing that this case does not involve a situation where she was engaged in an activity or conduct directly involving the obvious danger, but was merely sitting on the bathroom counter unaware that the candle posed a danger to her, that whether fire was an obvious danger to plaintiff is a question of fact, that any obvious danger should have been recognized by an adult and remedied, that the candle was not such an extreme condition as to allow defendants to not protect against an injury to a child, and that the duty owed to plaintiff is for the jury to decide. Plaintiff, however, did not attach any documents to contradict the deposition excerpts accompanying defendants' motion for summary judgment.

The trial court granted the motion for summary judgment. Thereafter, plaintiff filed a motion for rehearing asserting therein that the trial court improperly granted summary judgment without the entire deposition testimony of plaintiff, that plaintiff's deposition testimony demonstrates that she was confused and upset during the deposition proceedings, and that there were insufficient questions presented during the deposition to establish plaintiff's ability "to appreciate on [sic] oath" which can only be judged in person by the trial court.

* * *

In considering whether defendants owed a duty to plaintiff under the circumstances of this case, the customary principles of ordinary negligence must be applied to determine the liability of owners of premises upon which a child is injured. The common law categories of trespasser, licensee and invitee, as they pertain to an injured child's status, however, are no longer relevant in determining liability. The duty which would be imposed under ordinary negligence is that the law impels an owner or occupier of land to remedy any dangerous condition on the premises where that person in possession or control of the premises knows or should know that children frequent the premises, as harm to the children caused by the dangerous condition is sufficiently foreseeable. A dangerous condition is defined as one which is likely to cause injury to children generally who, by reason of their age and immaturity, would not be expected to comprehend and avoid the attendant risks; however, if the condition complained of presents an obvious risk which under ordinary conditions may reasonably be expected to be fully understood, appreciated and avoided by any child of an age to be allowed at large, there is no duty to remedy that condition as children are expected to avoid dangers which are obvious, negating any reasonably foreseeable risk of harm.

Illinois has acknowledged that fire is a danger which under ordinary conditions may reasonable be expected to be fully understood and appreciated by any child of an age to be allowed at large. Additionally, fire has been found to be an obvious danger. See *Jackson v. City of Biloxi* (a 5-year-old boy was found to be mature and intelligent enough to appreciate the obvious danger of an open fire).

Essentially, plaintiff maintains on appeal that the issues of foreseeability of this injury and plaintiff's appreciation of the danger are questions of fact which should not have been decided by summary judgment. We disagree. The material facts on this record are not in dispute, and the issue before us is whether there is a legal duty owed by defendants under the pleadings and depositions filed.

As our supreme court has acknowledged that a danger such as fire under ordinary circumstances may reasonably be expected to be fully understood by any child of an age to be allowed at large we conclude that the danger of fire from a burning candle is similarly one to be understood and appreciated by a child of an age to be allowed at large. The record shows that plaintiff is of above-average intelligence for her age and has been taught by her mother of the danger of fire and that fire burns at the end of a candle. Plaintiff, too, stated in her deposition that she knew fire could hurt her, that fire burned, and that fire was on top of a candle. Plaintiff saw the candle and no issue is raised in the pleadings that defendants were negligent in where they placed the candle. As there can be no recovery for injury caused by a danger found to be obvious, we hold that defendants owed no duty to plaintiff under these facts as a matter of law.

Although plaintiff appears to argue that the trial judge's decision suggests that plaintiff assumed the risk, it is clear that the court below analyzed the duty issue properly in terms of appreciation of the risk rather than assumption of the risk. There also is no merit to plaintiff's contention that the trial court erred in failing to ascertain whether she, as a 5-year-old at the time of her deposition, was competent to appreciate an oath and give testimony as a witness. No objection was made to her competency during the taking of the deposition or at the time the excerpts were submitted in support of the motion for summary judgment. Any objection was therefore waived. ...

For the foregoing reasons, the judgment of the circuit court of DuPage County is affirmed. AFFIRMED.

Case Questions

1. Do you agree with the court that a burning candle presents an obvious risk, even to a four-year-old child?
2. Would the plaintiffs have been more successful had they argued that the defendants were negligent in where they placed the candle? Explain.

McDonald's Coffee, A Burning Issue

In Albuquerque, New Mexico, in August 1994, a jury awarded Stella Liebeck $2.7 million in punitive damages and $200,000 in compensatory damages (to be reduced for the plaintiff's being 20 percent at fault) against McDonald's Corporation. Liebeck was riding as a passenger in her grandson's car when she bought a cup of coffee at McDonald's. She tried to hold the cup between her knees when she removed the lid, but the cup tipped over and caused third-degree burns.

This case caused a sensation when the jury award was first reported. Few people were privy to all the facts. Most people were aware that a woman was burnt while drinking coffee from McDonald's, but few could understand why the woman was suing McDonald's if it was she who spilled the coffee. More puzzling was why a jury would award almost $3 million in punitive damages against McDonald's when the plaintiff was either careless enough or foolish enough to be drinking hot coffee in a car.

The details put a different slant on the case. As a company policy, McDonald's sold coffee at between 180 and 190 degrees Fahrenheit. It takes two to seven seconds for coffee at this temperature to cause third-degree burns, which require skin grafts and debridement. The burns can leave a person in pain and disabled for many months or years, and can result in permanent and disfiguring injuries. Liebeck ended up in the hospital for a week and was disabled for more than two years.

During trial, McDonald's acknowledged having been aware of the risk of serious burn injuries from its coffee for over 10 years. In fact, more than 700 people reported being burnt by McDonald's steaming coffee prior to Liebeck's incident. Witnesses who appeared for McDonald's admitted that consumers were unaware of the risk of serious burns from the coffee and that customers were never warned. Most incredible, witnesses for McDonald's stated that the company had no plans to reduce the temperature of the coffee sold, despite the fact that the coffee was "not fit for consumption" when sold because it could cause scalding burns.

Case Questions

1. Taking the case from McDonald's perspective, are there any possible reasons for selling such hot coffee?
2. Balancing McDonald's need to sell hot coffee versus the possible risk of serious injury posed, could there be any reason that McDonald's did not have a plan to reduce the coffee's temperature in the future, despite the prior incidents?

The Case of the Shocking Church Fair

In this case, a church rented beer-dispensing trailers to sell beer at a church fair. When a patron was shocked, who should be responsible? Is it the church, as owner of the property; the manufacturer of the trailer; or the company that leased to the church the trailer that caused the incident? This case shows how a trial court apportions liability among multiple defendants.

BERTHELOT

v.

AETNA CASUALTY & SURETY CO.
Court of Appeals of Louisiana
623 So. 2d 14 (La. Ct. App. 1993)
July 2, 1993
Whipple, Judge

On the weekend of June 2, 3, and 4, 1989, St. Joan of Arc Catholic Church (St. Joan of Arc) held its annual church fair in Bayou Pigeon, Louisiana. The church had rented beer dispensing trailers to sell beer to fair patrons. The Miller Lite beer trailer was owned by B. Olinde and manufactured by Waymatic, Inc.

Because of a lack of sufficient electrical outlets near the fair grounds, church volunteers had run temporary electrical lines to the grounds for the beer dispensing trailers and a daiquiri machine. The lines were connected to three-hole sockets, but only two wires were used instead of three. A third wire, for grounding, was not used. The Miller Lite trailer was plugged into one of these lines.

Plaintiff attended the fair on Saturday evening, June 3, 1989. Because of rainy weather on Friday evening and Saturday morning, the ground was very wet. Plaintiff purchased a cup of beer at the Miller Lite trailer and then walked over to the Budweiser trailer to speak with relatives. It became apparent that the Budweiser trailer was shocking patrons, and thus, plaintiff suggested to her relatives that they walk over to the Miller Lite trailer which had not shocked her when she purchased her beer.

Plaintiff's brother ordered a round of beers at the Miller Lite trailer. As plaintiff reached to pick up her beer from the metal counter of the trailer, her finger touched the counter, and she received an electrical shock. According to plaintiff, she experienced blurred vision, started shaking and felt

like she was "glued to the ground". The force of the shock then caused her to fall to the ground. Plaintiff's relatives helped her up, and she left the fair to change her clothes.

* * *

Over the next few days, plaintiff became very nervous and apprehensive of electrical appliances in her house, including light switches. She developed trouble with her memory and concentration. Plaintiff began to experience episodes of weakness and shaky limbs and was eventually diagnosed as suffering from post-traumatic stress disorder.

On October 4, 1989, plaintiff filed suit against B. Olinde and its insurer, Aetna; and St. Joan of Arc and its insurer, Catholic Mutual Relief Society. St. Joan of Arc and Catholic Mutual Relief Society answered the petition and filed a cross-claim against B. Olinde and Aetna, and a third party demand against Waymatic, Inc., as a manufacturer of the beer trailer. Plaintiff then amended her petition to name Waymatic, Inc. as a defendant. Subsequently, St. Joan of Arc and its insurer cross claimed against Waymatic.

Prior to trial, plaintiff settled her claims against St. Joan of Arc, Catholic Mutual Relief Society, and Waymatic and the case proceeded to trial against B. Olinde and Aetna. In written reasons for judgment dated September 30, 1991, the trial stated that plaintiff had suffered damages in the amount of $204,072.00, consisting of $28,340.00 in past loss of wages; $118,121.00 for future loss of wages; $7,611.00 in medical expenses; and $50,000.00 in general damages. Fault was apportioned to B. Olinde in the amount of 33% with the remaining fault apportioned to Waymatic and St. Joan of Arc, the parties dismissed prior to trial.

Accordingly, on January 3, 1992, the trial court rendered judgment in favor of plaintiff and against B. Olinde and Aetna for damages in the amount of $67,343.76 plus $3,530.00 for expert witness fees. B. Olinde and Aetna appeal this judgment ... .

After carefully considering the record, we find no error in the trial court's finding of fault on the part of each of these alleged tortfeasors or in its apportionment of fault.

As stated in written reasons for judgment, the trial court found that the volunteer electrician who installed the electrical lines for the church was negligent in improperly connecting the wires. The court further found that other church volunteers were negligent in installing metal poles in the ground which were wired to the beer trailer in an attempt to ground the trailer after it became apparent that patrons were being shocked. The trial court concluded that St. Joan of Arc was responsible for the negligence of its volunteers.

Plaintiff challenges this finding, alleging there was no showing made that the church knew or should have known that a grounded connection would be required; and that the church can not be held vicariously liable for the acts of its volunteers. We find that both of these arguments lack merit and conclude St. Joan of Arc was at fault as the owner or entity having custody of immovable property with an unreasonably dangerous condition or defect.

* * *

It is undisputed that the church fair was sponsored on church premises. The record also supports the finding that the electrical lines installed for the purpose of supplying electricity to the beer trailers presented an unreasonable risk of harm to fair patrons. Huey Hebert, an electrician and member of the St. Joan of Arc church parish, testified that the electrical outlets on the fair grounds were not appropriately wired and that any electrician should have understood the need for a ground wire.

* * *

We conclude that such a risk of harm to patrons was an unreasonable risk.

Finally, it is clear from the record that this defect in the premises, i.e. faulty wiring which resulted in an unreasonable risk that fair patrons would be shocked, was a cause-in-fact of plaintiff's injury. St. Joan of Arc was at fault under the theory of strict liability of [state statute]. Because we find that St. Joan of Arc was properly found at fault under a theory of strict liability, we need not address the issue of whether it was negligent or could be held vicariously liable for the acts of its volunteers.

The lower court also concluded that Waymatic was at fault for manufacturing a defective thing. The court found the trailer to be defective because no adequate warning was given concerning grounding and electrical shock and because the trailer did not have a circuit interrupter which would stop the current to the appliance when dangerous voltage was emitted.

* * *

Moreover, the written information furnished with the trailer did not provide any instruction or warning with respect to the risk of leakage current or adequate warning of the risk of electrical shock and the need to properly ground the appliance.

* * *

The trial court also concluded that B. Olinde was at fault for its ownership of a defective thing and for its negligence in renting the trailer without proper warning or installation. B. Olinde challenges this finding. ...

B. Olinde is in the business of renting large refrigerated appliances. Part of its responsibility in renting the beer dispensing trailers is to set up the trailer and ascertain that it is operating properly.

* * *

Because of B. Olinde's failure: (1) to properly install the beer dispensing trailer, (2) to inspect the outlet used and (3) to properly train its employees, we also conclude that B. Olinde was negligent and breached the duty owed to plaintiff and other patrons of the St. Joan of Arc fair.

* * *

The parties to the appeal challenged the trial court's apportionment of fault at 33% to B. Olinde and the remaining fault apportioned to St. Joan of Arc and Waymatic.

* * *

Clearly, the fault of each of these parties contributed to plaintiff's accident. Moreover, a comparison of the respective degrees of duty and the respective breach of duty by the parties leads us to conclude that the trial court was not manifestly erroneous in apportioning fault to B. Olinde in the amount of 33% or in apportioning the remaining fault to St. Joan of Arc and Waymatic.

* * *

The trial court found that plaintiff suffers from post-traumatic stress disorder induced by the electrical shock she received from the Miller Lite trailer at the fair and awarded $50,000.00 in general damages. ...

Although the electrical shock experienced by plaintiff was characterized by the two electrical engineer experts as probably being mild, plaintiff perceived this event as a life threatening experience.

* * *

Plaintiff's family physician, Dr. William Gatow, testified that since the accident plaintiff has been extremely apprehensive and frightened. As a result of this disorder, plaintiff's tolerance for anxiety or stress in daily activities is very limited. Whenever plaintiff is faced with a stressful event in her life, she reverts back to a debilitating state.

Considering the record in its entirety, we find no abuse of discretion in the trial court's award of $50,000.00 for general damages.

Loss or impairment of earning capacity is determined by subtracting plaintiff's earning ability after the injury from earning ability immediately prior to the injury. The focus in not on actual earnings per se. ...

Prior to the incident in question, plaintiff was employed as a dredge boat cook, earning $6.50 per hour, working twelve hours a day in fourteen day shifts, followed by seven days off. Plaintiff has not been able to work since the accident.

Dr. Bolter opined that at the time of trial, plaintiff was psychologically disabled from returning to work. Although he stated that "hopefully" plaintiff would not be disabled forever, he believed that plaintiff was going to encounter serious problems in returning to work ... .

Dr. G. Randolph Rice, an expert economist, calculated plaintiff's future loss of earnings based on her work history and wages as a dredge cook, with no allowance for overtime. Dr. Rice noted that plaintiff was fifty-three years old with less than a high school education. He calculated her work life expectancy as 6.95 years, taking into account the possibility of times of layoff, illness and voluntary decision not to work. Based on all of these factors, Dr. Rice calculated the present value of plaintiff's future loss of earnings as $118,121.00.

Considering the circumstances of this case, including the uncertainty that plaintiff will ever be able to return to the work force, we find no abuse of discretion in the award made by the trial court for plaintiff's loss of future wages and earning capacity.

AFFIRMED.

Case Questions

1. What special problems might a trial attorney encounter in bringing a claim against a church before a jury?
2. Do you think the church could have done anything to prevent the incident? Explain.

HYPOTHETICAL

Colleen operates a laundromat. Geoffrey often washes and dries his clothes there. One day, while Geoffrey was loading his laundry into the washer, the machine unexpectedly began agitating and injured his arms and hands. Did Colleen proximately cause Geoffrey's injuries?

Foreseeability of injury is the starting point. Was it reasonably foreseeable that the washer Geoffrey used would short-circuit and suddenly begin operating while Geoffrey was loading his clothes? It is not uncommon for electrical, mechanical devices to jump to life by themselves unexpectedly. This often occurs when electrical wiring short-circuits after the wires' insulation has frayed. Because people must insert their hands and arms inside the washing machine drum to load clothing, it is reasonably foreseeable that a shorted machine might start itself while a patron's arms were inside. Thus, Geoffrey's injuries were reasonably foreseeable and Colleen proximately caused the harm suffered.

Suppose, however, that Geoffrey's arms and hands were not trapped inside the machine when it suddenly began agitating. Suppose, instead, that the surprise simply frightened Geoffrey, who was unusually susceptible to sudden, loud noises and suffered a heart attack as a consequence of the shock. Could Colleen have reasonably anticipated this tragedy? Most courts would reverse the reasonable person standard (applying it to the plaintiff) and say that a reasonable person would not be so easily alarmed (to the point of heart failure) by an upstart washing machine. However, a few courts would employ taking-the-victim analysis and say that even this remote and unexpected injury was foreseeable.

Figure 3-5 summarizes the elements of proximate cause.

1. Was the plaintiff's injury a reasonably foreseeable result of the defendant's actions?	**FIGURE 3-5** Proximate cause elements
2. Did the defendant's duty of reasonable care include the plaintiff?	
3. Does the case involve special circumstances, in which the plaintiff has peculiar physical or emotional characteristics (such as brittle bones, mental illness, or sensitivity to noise) so that the defendant must take the victim as he finds him?	

§ 3.7 Damages

Damages are the injury that the plaintiff suffered as a result of the defendant's tortious conduct. As in all torts, damages must be proven for negligence. Courts will not compensate a victim unless some documentable harm has been done.

TERMS
---

damages   The sum of money that may be recovered in the courts as financial reparation for an injury or wrong suffered as a result of breach of contract or a tortious act.

With certain intentional torts, such as battery, assault, or trespass, no physical harm is required. With a technical trespass, it is sufficient that the tortfeasor engaged in the unauthorized act. Battery can be achieved merely by unconsented touching. In negligence law, however, some determinable injury must be proven for the tortfeasor to be held liable to the injured party. Normally, this involves monetary losses as a result of harm to a person or the person's property. For instance, if someone loses muscular control in the legs after an automobile accident with a careless driver, then the injured party could demonstrate economic loss as a consequence of the harm. The plaintiff could quantify the losses sustained through lost wages, inability to continue an occupation, loss of bodily function, emotional impairment, and related damages.

This vital element of liability is often glossed over by legal scholars and courts. Following such reasoning, damage is often assumed from the fact that the plaintiff sued the defendant for negligence. Of course, it is always a mistake to assume anything in legal study. The plaintiff must prove actual injury to recover in a negligence action. This harm may be physical or emotional or both, but it must exist.

Compensatory Damages

Compensatory damages are most common in negligence cases. As the name suggests, **compensatory damages** are designed to compensate the victim for the tortfeasor's negligence. Normally, the plaintiff proves monetary losses, such as out-of-pocket expenses (e.g., medical, property repair), lost income, pain and suffering, loss of property value, or loss of bodily function.

Nominal Damages

Nominal damages are not recoverable in actions for ordinary negligence when damages are an element of the cause of action. Nominal damages are awarded in situations in which no actual damages have

---

TERMS

compensatory damages Damages recoverable in a lawsuit for loss or injury suffered by the plaintiff as a result of the defendant's conduct. Also called actual damages, they may include expenses, loss of time, reduced earning capacity, bodily injury, and mental anguish.

nominal damages Damages awarded to a plaintiff in a very small or merely symbolic amount. Such damages are appropriate in a situation where: (1) although a legal right has been violated, no actual damages have been incurred, but the law recognizes the need to vindicate the plaintiff; or occurred, or the amount of injury has not been proven even though a right has been violated in an intentional tort action. The court might then award a dollar to a winning party as a symbolic gesture.

Punitive Damages

Punitive or **exemplary damages**, which are often awarded for intentional torts such as fraud or intentional infliction of emotional distress, are almost nonexistent in negligence cases, because negligence involves carelessness rather than wanton or intentionally tortious behavior. The punishment component of punitive damages would be excessive in most negligence cases, although exemplary damages are occasionally used in gross negligence cases. **Gross negligence** involves carelessness that exceeds ordinary, reasonable care standards and approaches willful and wanton misconduct. If the negligence is sufficiently excessive, the court might allow punitive damages for the injured party. For instance, if a surgeon left a scalpel inside a patient during an operation, this might be considered gross negligence by the medical community. Such misconduct exceeds that degree of reasonable care ordinarily expected of doctors. Physicians simply are expected to avoid such slipshod surgical efforts.

Figure 3-6 summarizes damages in negligence actions.

Plaintiff must suffer actual loss as a result of injury.
Loss is usually gauged in monetary terms.
Compensatory damages provide the plaintiff with recovery for losses that resulted from the defendant's actions (out-of-pocket expenses, pain and suffering, lost income, lost property value, loss of bodily function).

FIGURE 3-6
Damages in negligence cases

==={ TERMS }===

(2) some compensable injury has been shown, but the amount of that injury has not been proven.

punitive damages Damages that are awarded over and above compensatory damages or actual damages because of the wanton, reckless, or malicious nature of the wrong done by the plaintiff. Such damages bear no relation to the plaintiff's actual loss and are often called exemplary damages, because their purpose is to make an example of the plaintiff to discourage others from engaging in the same kind of conduct in the future.

gross negligence Willfully and intentionally acting, or failing to act, with a deliberate indifference to how others may be affected.

§ 3.8 Proving Negligence

Proof is an essential aspect of all litigation. A cynic might suggest that what is true or false is irrelevant; rather, what can be proven during a lawsuit is all that matters. Negligence claims are normally proven through the typical evidentiary processes. These include oral testimony, written transcripts of discovery depositions, documentary evidence, and demonstrative evidence (such as photographs or computer simulations).

Affirmative defenses must be alleged or proven by the defendant. Unless alleged and proven, the law will presume that no defense exists. These defenses are covered in Chapter 5.

Burdens of Proof and Rejoinder

The plaintiff has the burden of proving that the defendant was negligent. This forces the plaintiff to prove by a **preponderance of the evidence** that all negligence elements existed (duty, breach, causation, proximate cause, and injury). The evidence must establish that the defendant's actions were negligent and caused the plaintiff's injuries.

Once the plaintiff has made a **prima facie case** (meaning that proof has been established by or beyond a preponderance), the burden shifts to the defendant, who must then counter the plaintiff's evidence with proof of his or her own. This is sometimes called the defendant's **burden**

TERMS

preponderance of the evidence The degree of proof required in most civil actions. It means "more likely than not"; that the greater weight and value of the credible evidence, taken as a whole, belongs to one side in a lawsuit rather than to the other side. In other words, the party whose evidence is more convincing has a "preponderance of the evidence" on its side and must, as a matter of law, prevail in the lawsuit because it has met its burden of proof. The expression "preponderance of the evidence" has nothing to do with the number of witnesses a party presents, only with the credibility and value of their testimony.

prima facie case A cause of action or defense that is sufficiently established by a party's evidence to justify a verdict in his or her favor, provided the other party does not rebut that evidence; a case supported by sufficient evidence to justify its submission to the trier of fact and the rendition of a compatible verdict.

burden of rejoinder (rebuttal)[†] The defendant's burden of proof to refute the plaintiff's evidence in a lawsuit.

of rejoinder or **rebuttal**. The defendant must refute the plaintiff's case against him or her.

In some cases, however, the burden of proof is different. What if the plaintiff cannot prove the defendant's negligence? Consider an example. Suppose a patient was unconscious during an operation. Suppose the surgical nurse failed to remove all the sponges from the patient, and later the patient contracted peritonitis. How could the plaintiff prove that the defendants (nurse, surgeon, and hospital) were negligent in leaving the sponge inside the plaintiff? What witnesses could the plaintiff call to testify, other than the surgical team? The plaintiff was unconscious and unaware of the entire procedure. How could the plaintiff meet the burden of proof in such circumstances? Such unusual cases require a special burden of proof, which is called *res ipsa loquitur.*

Res Ipsa Loquitur

Res ipsa loquitur is Latin meaning "the thing [*res*] speaks [*loquitur*] for itself [*ipsa*]." It is used in negligence cases in which the plaintiff is in a disadvantaged position for proving the defendant's negligence, because the evidence is unavailable to the plaintiff, but is or should be available to the defendant. Under the doctrine of res ipsa loquitur, the defendant's negligence is presumed as a result of his or her actions. This shifts the burden of proof to the defendant. In other words, the defendant must disprove his or her negligence from the outset of litigation. The plaintiff's burden of proof is converted into the defendant's burden of rejoinder.

Elements of Res Ipsa Loquitur

The plaintiff must prove only certain essential facts, such as what injury occurred, what the defendant was doing, and how the defendant's action (or inaction) related to the plaintiff's harm. To use res ipsa loquitur, whatever occurred must not ordinarily occur without someone acting negligently. Court opinions often quote the following elements:

TERMS

res ipsa loquitur [Latin for] "the thing speaks for itself." When an instrumentality (i.e., a thing) causes injury, an inference or rebuttable presumption arises that the injury was caused by the defendant's negligence, if the thing or instrumentality was under the exclusive control or management of the defendant and the occurrence was such as in the ordinary course of events would not have happened if the defendant had used reasonable care.

1. The defendant (or his or her employee[s]) must have been in exclusive control of the object or action that produced the plaintiff's injury.

2. The plaintiff's injury must be of a type that ordinarily would not have happened unless negligence were involved.

3. The defendant must be in a better position to prove his or her lack of negligence than the plaintiff is to prove the defendant's negligence.

Certain courts and legal scholars add a fourth element, which states that the plaintiff cannot have contributed to his or her own injuries. This, however, simply states contributory and comparative negligence, which are two similar defenses to negligence.

Defendant's Exclusive Control

For res ipsa loquitur to apply, the events that led to the plaintiff's injury must have been under the defendant's exclusive control. This includes the defendant's employees. For example, suppose the plaintiff was walking through the defendant's warehouse. Suppose the defendant's employees had stacked many crates of merchandise, and the stacks rose thirty feet high. If a top crate fell upon and injured the plaintiff, but nobody except the plaintiff was present in that part of the building, who could the plaintiff point the finger toward as having been negligent? Using res ipsa loquitur, the plaintiff would shift the burden of proof to the defendant (warehouse owner) to show that the crates had been safely stowed. Because the crates were under the defendant's exclusive control, and one crate fell and hurt the plaintiff, the first element of res ipsa loquitur would be satisfied.

Presumption of Negligence

Res ipsa loquitur insists that the plaintiff's injury be one that normally would not have happened unless negligence were involved. Consider the preceding illustration. Crates usually do not fall over in warehouses unless they are improperly stacked. Negligence may be presumed in this case because the box indeed fell. This would not normally occur if ordinary, reasonable care were used to store the crates. Because the box did fall on the plaintiff, then the defendant must not have exercised reasonable care in stacking the crates. At least the court will make this presumption and allow the defendant to refute it by proving that reasonable care was used when storing the boxes.

The Case of the Airplane That Fell from the Sky

Normally, airplanes do not fall from the sky. In the following case, the court allowed the plaintiff's estate to prove the defendant's negligence by using the doctrine of res ipsa loquitur. The defendant's negligence was presumed and the defendant airline had to disprove its negligence.

COX

v.

NORTHWEST AIRLINES, INC.
United States Court of Appeals,
Seventh Circuit
379 F.2d 893 (7th Cir. 1967)
August 28, 1967
Castle, Circuit Judge

The appellant, Northwest Airlines, Inc., prosecutes this appeal from a judgment entered against it in an admiralty action instituted in the District Court by the libellant-appellee, Irene Cox, administratix. [The plaintiff in a suit in admiralty is called the libellant.] Libellant sought recovery of damages under the Death on the High Seas Act for the death of her husband. The action was tried to the court without a jury. The court made and entered findings of fact and conclusions of law, and awarded judgment against the appellant for $329,956.59.

The record discloses that the libellant's decedent, her husband, Randall S. Cox, a Captain in the United States Army, 29 years of age, was a passenger on appellant's Douglas DC-7C airplane N290, flight 293, which crashed in the Pacific Ocean on June 3, 1963 during a flight from McChord Air Force Base, near Seattle, Washington, to Elmendorf, Alaska, at approximately 11:12 A.M. at a point about one hundred sixteen miles west-southwest of Annette Island off the west coast of Canada. The flight had taken off from McChord at about 8:32 A.M. after having been briefed on the weather by both its dispatch office at the Seattle Airport and by a U.S. Air Force weather specialist at McChord, and having followed the usual procedures in preparation for flight. The crew reported by radio at 11:07 A.M.

that it had been over Domestic Annette at 11:06 at an altitude of 14,000 feet and requested clearance to climb to 18,000 feet. No reason for the requested change in altitude was given. Domestic Annette is a fix-point at which directional radio bearings are obtained along the air route from McChord to Elmendorf. This was the last known transmission made by the crew of the aircraft. On the following day, June 4, 1963, floating debris was sighted in the Pacific Ocean about 35 nautical miles west of Domestic Annette. Approximately 1,500 pounds of wreckage identified as being from the aircraft, including life vests still encased in their plastic containers and extremely deformed seat frames, was recovered. The bodies of none of the crew or passengers were ever recovered.

The District Court made a number of findings with respect to facts and circumstances concerning the flight. But none of these subsidiary findings afford, or were relied upon by the court as affording, a basis for finding and concluding that any specific conduct attributable to the appellant constituted negligence and was a proximate cause of the crash. The court's conclusion that the negligence of appellant was the proximate cause of decedent's death is predicated upon the court's finding that:

"[A]s a result of the occurrence Randall S. Cox met his death. The instrumentality which produced the death of Randall S. Cox was under the exclusive control and management of the [appellant] and that the occurrence in question was such as does not ordinarily occur in the absence of negligence, and, further, that there is no possibility of contributing conduct which would make Randall S. Cox responsible; that the facts herein justify a finding of negligence."

The appellant recognizes that the doctrine of res ipsa loquitur may properly have application in actions involving airline accidents. But the appellant contends that in the instant case it was error to apply that doctrine in resolving the issue of liability because there is substantial proof of the exercise of due care by the appellant and no countervailing evidence of specific negligence or even of unusual circumstances. ...

The evidence of due care to which appellant alludes concerns its maintenance records and procedures with respect to the aircraft involved; the qualified and certified status, and the competence, of the operating personnel of the aircraft and of the dispatcher; the safety training received by the crew; and the evidence that the flight was properly dispatched and the weather normal.

There is no evidence as to the cause of the aircraft's crash into the ocean or concerning what happened to affect the operation of the aircraft during the period following 11:07 A.M. and prior to the crash. In the absence of such evidence, the probative value of appellant's general evidence of due care is not of substantial import. ...

We perceive nothing in appellant's due care evidence which precludes an application of the res ipsa loquitur doctrine or conditions such application upon the libellant's responding with evidence to support some specific negligent act or omission on the part of the appellant. Here the cause of the crash which resulted in the death of Randall S. Cox is wholly unexplained. ...

We are of the opinion that the court properly applied the doctrine of res ipsa loquitur and that its finding of negligence was a permissible one—

warranted though not compelled—and that the court's conclusion on the issue of appellant's liability is thus supported by the evidence and the application of correct legal criteria.

We turn to consideration of appellant's contentions that the District Court erred in its computation of the amounts of certain of the specific elements of damage it included in the $329,956.59 award it made.

* * *

[T]he court erred in two respects. ... No reduction was made for income tax the decedent would have paid on the earnings and income ... .

We agree with the rationale of the United States Court of Appeals for the Second Circuit ... , and conclude that the income level here attributed to the twenty-year period commencing with 1979 is such that a reduction for income tax is required to be made from the annual gross income during that period. ...

The damages award also embraces an item of loss of inheritance to the widow ... . The court's failure to discount this amount to its present value was error.

* * *

The judgment of the District Court is affirmed insofar as it adjudicates the issue of the liability of the appellant, Northwest Airlines, Inc., to the libellant, and the cause is remanded to the District Court with directions that the court modify the judgment by reducing the amount of damages awarded therein to conform with the views herein expressed.

Case Questions

1. Why was the plaintiff's estate permitted to use the doctrine of res ipsa loquitur in this case?
2. Is it possible that an airplane could crash without any negligence whatsoever on the part of the airline? Explain.
3. Do you think it is fair for the courts to allow use of the res ipsa loquitur doctrine in certain negligence cases? Explain.

Defendant's Superior Proof Position

Under res ipsa loquitur, the defendant must be in a better position to prove that he or she was not negligent than the plaintiff is to establish the defendant's negligence. In the warehouse example, the plaintiff did not see how the crate fell. None of the defendant's employees were present or nearby when the accident occurred. No witnesses actually saw why the crate fell. But the defendant originally stacked the crates. This makes it easier for the defendant to prove that reasonable care was used in stacking the boxes. The plaintiff is at a disadvantage to prove the defendant's negligence. However, the defendant can more easily show that safeguards were used in stacking the crates (such as ropes tied to support beams and crates, or walls and doors surrounding the stacked boxes). In this fashion, the defendant could prove that reasonable care was used when stacking the crates and therefore no negligence occurred.

Res ipsa loquitur cases often involve medical malpractice, particularly surgery. The doctrine is not restricted to such negligence cases, however, as the following hypothetical illustrates.

HYPOTHETICAL

Eugene supervises a road repair crew employed by Pavement Plus, Inc. The county contracts road construction and renovation to Pavement Plus. Eugene's crew was filling potholes on Elm Avenue one spring day. One of Eugene's employees, Everest, improperly mixed the asphalt so that it would not harden adequately. This bad asphalt was used to fill the Elm Avenue holes. Rutherford, who lives on Elm Avenue, drove over the patched potholes a few days later. The asphalt collapsed and the front right tire of Rutherford's automobile wedged in a hole, bending the front axle. Rutherford discovered that Pavement Plus had repaired the street, but had kept no record of the asphalt mixtures used.

Could Rutherford use res ipsa loquitur to shift the burden of proof? Evaluate the elements under these facts. Pavement Plus's foreman, Eugene, and an employee were under exclusive control of the weak asphalt used to fix the street. Asphalt does not normally collapse under vehicular weight unless it is improperly prepared or applied. The defendant is in the best position to prove that the mixture was suitable, as its employees prepared and applied the asphalt. Thus, res ipsa loquitur applies in this case, and the plaintiff need only prove what happened (i.e., his car was damaged when it fell through an asphalted hole that the defendant repaired). The defendant must now establish that its employees used reasonable care in preparing and applying the asphalt. As an aside, this problem also illustrates the value of retaining written records (in this case, of asphalt mixture) to document reasonable care.

Figure 3-7 summarizes proof of negligence and res ipsa loquitur.

Burdens of Proof and Rejoinder (Rebuttal)	Res Ipsa Loquitur
Plaintiff must generally prove the defendant's negligence beyond a preponderance of the evidence.	"The thing speaks for itself." This doctrine shifts the burden of proof to the defendant, who must disprove the presumed negligence.
	Elements: (1) the defendant's exclusive control over acts or objects that injured the plaintiff; (2) the plaintiff's injury must be one that ordinarily does not occur without negligence; and (3) the defendant is in best position to prove that he or she was not negligent.

FIGURE 3-7   Burden of proof, burden of rejoinder (rebuttal), and res ipsa loquitur

Summary

Negligence is the failure to use reasonable care to avoid injuring others or their property. Reasonable care is dependent upon the particular facts of each case. The key is the reasonableness or unreasonableness of the tortfeasor's actions under the circumstances.

There are five elements of negligence: duty of reasonable care, breach of duty, causation, proximate cause, and injury. The elements are considered sequentially. If any one is missing, then no negligence occurred.

The duty of reasonable care is the tortfeasor's obligation to act reasonably to avoid injuring others. The tortfeasor does not owe this duty to everyone in the world, however; the injured party must fall within the scope of the tortfeasor's duty. This means that it must have been reasonably foreseeable that the plaintiff would be harmed as a consequence of the defendant's actions. This is called the reasonable plaintiffs theory. Only foreseeable plaintiffs (who were actually injured as a result of the defendant's conduct) may recover damages in a negligence lawsuit. Reasonable care is defined by the standard of the mythical reasonable person. Would a reasonable person have acted in the same way the defendant did, under the same or similar circumstances? The trier-of-fact decides how the reasonable person would have behaved. The reasonable person standard is adjusted to reflect the defendant's special skills or limitations.

In professional malpractice actions, professionals such as physicians are held to exercise the degree of care and skill reasonably required of like professionals in similar circumstances. Depending on the jurisdiction, the professional will be judged by the skills of professionals in the same community, a similar locality, or (as is the trend) nationally.

The tortfeasor's actions must cause the victim's injuries. Causation under negligence is usually shown through cause-in-fact. Cause-in-fact states that but for the defendant's misconduct, the plaintiff would not have been harmed. When multiple tortfeasors are involved in producing the victim's injuries, however, but-for causation does not function well. An alternative causation theory, substantial factor analysis, states that each defendant is liable for the plaintiff's injuries if that defendant was a substantial factor in producing the harm. Joint and several liability holds multiple defendants liable for a plaintiff's injuries when those defendants combine to create the harm.

Proximate cause is different from causation. Proximate cause declares the line at which injuries are reasonably foreseeable. Inside the boundary are tortfeasors' actions that could reasonably have been anticipated to produce the victim's harm. Outside the perimeter are injuries that were not reasonably foreseeable as a consequence of the tortfeasor's behavior. This circle is sometimes called the zone of danger. Some courts speak of proximate cause in terms of foreseeability and scope of duty. Other courts state that tortfeasors take their victims as they find them, which means that the particular injury the plaintiff suffered (usually due to some peculiar physical condition) is always considered foreseeable.

Damages must be proven in every negligence case. The plaintiff must prove that he or she suffered some actual loss as a result of the defendant's actions, whether physical injury, emotional injury, or harm to property. This loss is normally quantified in monetary terms as consequential damages.

Most often, the plaintiff must prove that the defendant was negligent in causing the plaintiff's injuries. This burden of proof calls for a preponderance of the evidence. Once established, the defendant has the burden of rejoinder, or rebuttal, to counter the plaintiff's prima facie case. In certain cases, however, the plaintiff is at a disadvantage in proving the defendant's negligence. Res ipsa loquitur allows the plaintiff to shift the burden of proof to the defendant. Thus, the defendant must disprove the plaintiff's allegations of negligence. Res ipsa loquitur applies in cases in which the defendant exclusively controlled the object or action that hurt the plaintiff; that the plaintiff's injury was one that ordinarily would not happen without negligence; and the defendant is in the better position to prove that he or she was not negligent.

Review Questions

1. Provide a broad definition of negligence. What key factors are involved in analyzing negligence problems?

2. List the elements of negligence. How do they fit together? How do you apply each part to a particular problem?

3. What is duty? How does it relate to reasonable care? How do you define the scope of duty? What role does foreseeability play in scope of duty? What is the foreseeable plaintiffs theory? What is reasonable care? Who is the reasonable person, and why is he or she important in negligence analysis? Who defines this standard and how? How does the standard vary in different cases?

4. Define causation. What is cause-in-fact? But-for causation? How do direct and indirect causation differ? What is substantial factor analysis, and when is it used? How does it differ from joint and several liability? How is it similar?

5. Define proximate cause. What role does foreseeability play? What is the zone of danger? How is scope of duty involved? What is taking the victim as you find him? How is it applied?

6. How are damages determined in negligence cases? What are consequential damages?

7. How is negligence normally proven? Who generally bears the burden of proof? The burden of rejoinder or rebuttal? When is negligence presumed? What Latin phrase is used to describe this presumption? What are this doctrine's elements, and how are they used?

8. What is medical malpractice? If a needle is left in a patient after surgery, can the doctrine of res ipsa loquitur be used to prove the plaintiff's case? Explain your answer.

Projects

1. Find a recent court opinion in your state that defines the elements of negligence. Do these elements differ from those discussed in this chapter? If so, in what ways?

2. In class or study groups, create your own hypotheticals using the negligence formula in this chapter. Then change the facts to alter the outcomes of the cases.

3. An argument has been made that large malpractice awards are driving up the price of health care. Should all jurisdictions impose a cap or ceiling limiting the amount awarded in malpractice cases for pain and suffering, as some jurisdictions already do? Explain.

4. Read the case of *Russell v. Archer Building Centers, Inc.* in Appendix C. Was the store owner negligent? Explain.

5. Read the case of *Stander v. Orentreich* in Appendix C. What difference would it make if the physician's acts were treated as simple negligence rather than malpractice?

‖‖

CHAPTER 4

SPECIAL NEGLIGENCE ACTIONS

> *To succeed in the other trades, capacity must be shown; in the law, concealment of it will do.*
> — **Mark Twain**

§ 4.1 Introduction

Negligence theory has evolved special legal concepts to apply, in certain circumstances, to particular types of activities.

Special negligence actions are cases involving certain well-defined activities. Special rules of negligence apply in these instances. The most common special negligence actions involve property ownership, employer/employee activities, and motor vehicle use. Theories of vicarious liability, in which someone is held accountable for the negligence of another person, and negligent infliction of emotional distress add unique and recognizable elements to the study of torts.

The basic negligence formula applies to all special actions discussed in this chapter. Negligence includes the following elements: duty of reasonable care, breach of duty, causation, proximate cause, and damages. Always keep this approach in mind when examining any negligence problem. However, each special action has its own peculiar analytical twists and turns that distinguish these from the other torts. This chapter covers the following:

- Premises liability

- Distinctions between trespassers, licensees, and invitees

- Attractive nuisance

- Bailment liability

- Vicarious liability and respondeat superior

- Negligent infliction of emotional distress.

§ 4.2 Premises Liability

Special negligence rules apply to owners and occupiers of land. **Occupiers** include individuals who do not own but who do use real estate, including tenants (lessees). For simplicity's sake, we will speak in terms of the owner. The term *occupier* may always be substituted for *owner,* because negligence theories apply to both.

Land Owner's Different Duties of Reasonable Care

As negligence law developed in the late nineteenth and early twentieth centuries, American courts devised different standards of reasonable care for land owners or land users. The distinctions depended upon who the injured party (plaintiff) was, in terms of the victim's purpose for being on the land where the owner's negligence was alleged to have occurred.

Victim's Status on Land Defines Scope of Duty

For example, under old common law, the land owner owed a different duty of reasonable care to the injured party depending upon whether the victim was a trespasser, a licensee, or an invitee. (These terms are explained later in this section.) Thus, the plaintiff's status as a trespasser, licensee, or invitee determined the scope of duty that the owner owed. These distinctions affect the balance of risk of injury from the tort in question, versus the possible benefits that might be received. Intentional torts involve intentional acts, and as such carry a high degree of risk and usually a low degree of social benefit. That is, the risk greatly outweighs the benefit. Therefore, the duty not to intentionally injure someone or something is great.

Modern Judicial Trends

Courts and legal scholars for decades have complained that this three-tier analytical approach is arbitrary and unnecessary. After all, ordinary negligence theory appears adequately equipped to establish the land owner's duty of reasonable care. If an owner acted unreasonably in

---

TERMS

occupier † An individual who does not own, but who uses, real estate, including tenants (lessees).

PROFESSIONAL PROFILE

John Sherman just started working for a single practitioner who limits her legal practice to personal injury cases and real estate transactions. The attorney had stated to John that personal injury was her favorite area of practice. When John inquired why the attorney did not exclusively handle personal injury cases, she reminded John of something that he had known but had forgotten: most negligence cases undergo a two- to six-year wait before a trial is scheduled. At the same time, there are many overhead expenses in preparing cases for trial and they require a steady cash flow. Hence, the need for a second area of practice.

John was always interested in the business aspects of running a law firm. He was determined to make the practice the best possible. John attended a seminar given by the local bar association on law office management. The need for management in a large office with many employees is readily apparent, but John learned that good management is equally important even in smaller firms.

It took more than a year before John's efforts really paid off. John looked at every aspect of the practice. The office was centrally located, with plenty of parking available, but there was one big problem. The attorney's advertisements were all directed toward seriously injured clients, yet the office was located on the second story of an office building that had stairs but no elevator! When the first-floor office suite became vacant, John negotiated with the landlord to move the practice downstairs, to enable access by almost all injured clients.

Another of John's ideas paid off almost instantly. He started purchasing office supplies in bulk. Office supplies had previously been purchased by the secretaries as needed, on the way to or from work. Though this was convenient, it was not very economical. Bulk purchasing required more advance planning, but the savings were significant, particularly for computer paper and file folders.

John is most proud of his latest project. He designed a brochure highlighting the attorney's credentials, as well as his own. Also included in the brochure are a brief description of personal injury cases, the firm's policy of maintaining client contact throughout all stages of a lawsuit, and the fact that Spanish is spoken by the entire staff.

maintaining his or her realty, and as a result a victim was harmed, then the owner should be liable. Regular negligence theory works well to produce a just result, say these critics.

Many courts have in fact abolished the three-tier land owner standards of care. The landmark case was *Rowland v. Christian*, 69 Cal. 2d 108, 443 P.2d 561, 70 Cal. Rptr. 97 (1968) (superseded by statute, as explained in *Perez v. Southern Pacific Transport Co.*, 218 Cal. App. 3d 462, 267 Cal. Rptr. 100 (1990)), in which the distinctions were ousted in favor of traditional negligence theory. For instance, in states such as New York, the three-tier approach has been discarded by the courts in favor of a traditional negligence approach, whereby all who come upon property must be treated with the same degree of reasonable care. There is no longer a distinction as to the status of a person, such as guest or invitee, and the reason for which they are upon the land. Many states have followed the California Supreme Court's lead. Still, many courts continue to apply the three-tier system.

Land Owner's "Zero Duty" Toward Trespassers

Land owners owe no duty of reasonable care toward trespassers. The risk to a trespasser should be essentially nonexistent compared to the benefit of keeping the trespasser away. Owners may not intentionally injure trespassers upon their real estate, but they need not search their realty and safeguard it for trespassers' unauthorized uses. Courts favoring this policy reason that a land owner should not be required to exercise ordinary reasonable care to protect a tortfeasor (i.e., trespasser) from harm. Because the trespasser is committing an intentional tort, negligence law insists only that real estate owners avoid intentionally injuring trespassers. Otherwise, the trespasser *assumes the risk* of entering someone else's land without permission.

Special Rule for Trespassing Children: Attractive Nuisance

Land owners owe a higher duty of reasonable care to trespassing children, however. The reasoning behind this special rule states that children, especially when young, are so inexperienced and naive that they may not fully appreciate dangers lurking upon the land. Therefore, owners must exercise ordinary, reasonable care to safeguard their realty for trespassing children who are enticed onto the land to investigate the dangerous condition that injured them. Young children are often attracted, out of curiosity, to investigate dangerous conditions on realty, such as abandoned wells, railroad tracks, swimming pools, or unused machinery. These alluring items are often hazardous, a fact that the trespassing child may not understand. The attraction element has given this special rule its name of **attraction theory** or, more commonly, **attractive nuisance**.

```
==================【 TERMS 】==================
```

attractive nuisance doctrine (attraction theory)   The principle in the law of negligence that a person who maintains an attractive nuisance on his or her property must exercise reasonable care to protect young children against its dangers, or be held responsible for any injury that occurs, even though the injured child trespassed upon [the] property or was otherwise at fault.

attractive nuisance   An unusual mechanism, apparatus, or condition that is dangerous to young children but is so interesting and alluring as to attract them to the premises on which it is kept.

The Case of the Nuisance Ladder

Special care is taken to protect children under the law. What is clearly dangerous or foolhardy to an adult might seem like the perfect opportunity for fun and
entertainment to a child. Must homeowners survey their homes and remove every
loose item or structure that can be transformed into a dangerous instrumentality in
the hands of a child? What are the ground rules?

WIEGERS v. FITZPATRICK
Missouri Court of Appeals, Western District
766 S.W.2d 126 (Mo. Ct. App. 1989)
February 28, 1989
Fenner, Judge

John and Jan Fitzpatrick appeal from a jury
verdict and judgment entered thereon in favor of
Shawn Wiegers and his mother, Raylene Evans
(now Raylene Sharp), upon Wiegers' and Evans'
suit to recover damages for injuries to Wiegers
occasioned by the Fitzpatricks' negligence. ...

[S]ometime before January 8, 1986, appellant,
John Fitzpatrick, was informed that a warehouse
near where he worked had discarded some shelving. He went to the warehouse and salvaged
some of the parts of the shelving which he reconstructed on the back porch of his home. He
also found and brought home two metal ladder
structures that he assumed had been used to access the tops of the shelves. These ladders had
very rough and sharp edges and appeared as if
they had been either torched or hacksawed so
that they might be severed from another metal
structure.

After the ladders were brought home they were
generally stored on the Fitzpatricks' back porch. ...

Mr. Fitzpatrick testified that on only one occasion had he seen the ladders other than on the
back porch. On that one occasion Fitzpatrick noticed one of the ladders leaning up against the
back fence at the rear of his back yard. He asked
his children, a son, age 15 and a daughter, age
10, why the ladder was there and was told that
the ladder had been used to climb over the
fence. The children were told to put the ladder
back on the porch and they were told not to use
the ladders.

Jan Fitzpatrick testified that prior to January 7,
1986, she was unaware that the metal ladders

had been acquired. The first time she saw the ladders was on the evening of January 7, 1986. ...
She got out of her car, picked the ladder up out
of the yard and leaned the ladder up against the
side of the house.

Respondent, Shawn Wiegers, went to the Fitzpatrick home on the morning of January 8, 1986, and
asked if Jennie, the Fitzpatricks' daughter [,] could
come out and play. Jennie came out, took her
books to the bus stop and the two children proceeded to the yard where they were going to slide
down an incline in the Fitzpatricks' yard. ...

Jennie testified at trial that she got the ladder
leaning on the side of the house and stuck it into
the ground so that she and Shawn could slide
down the hill then climb back up with the aid of
the ladder and that she had used the ladder for this
purpose before the day of the accident that occurred herein. Shawn testified that the ladder was
frozen in the ground when they began playing.

The children agreed that they began playing,
Jennie first sliding and climbing up the ladder
with Shawn following suit. After the second or
third time Shawn had slid down the hill he fell
on the ladder and lacerated his leg on the ladder's rough edges. After hearing Shawn scream,
Jennie ran to tell her mother.

... Shawn's mother, Raylene, filed suit on behalf of herself and her minor child to recover
damages caused by appellants' negligence.

* * *

Both parties agree that this is essentially a
negligence action governed by § 339 of the Restatement (Second) of Torts. ...

§ 339. Artificial Conditions Highly Dangerous
to Trespassing Children
A possessor of land is subject to liability for
physical harm to children trespassing thereon
caused by an artificial condition upon the land if

(a) the place where the condition exists is one upon which the possessor knows or has reason to know that children are likely to trespass, and
(b) the condition is one of which the possessor knows or has reason to know and which he realizes or should realize will involve an unreasonable risk of death or serious bodily harm to such children, and
(c) the children because of their youth do not discover the condition or realize the risk involved in intermeddling with it or in coming within the area made dangerous by it, and
(d) the utility to the possessor of maintaining the condition and the burden of eliminating the danger are slight as compared with the risk to children involved, and
(e) the possessor fails to exercise reasonable care to eliminate the danger or otherwise to protect the children.

Initially the parties dispute what constitutes an "artificial condition" upon the land. The Fitzpatricks take the position that the metal ladder structure was an ordinary physical object, as opposed to a fixture attached to the land or other classic conditions.

* * *

Respondents, however, note that few courts have defined what constitutes an artificial condition and cite a South Dakota Supreme Court case wherein that court defined the terms to mean "a condition on the land created by the action of man." Borrowing that definition and applying it to the present factual situation, it is clear that the metal ladder structure obtained by Mr. Fitzpatrick was an "artificial condition" which he placed on his land.

The next inquiry pursuant to § 339 is whether the condition is one which the Fitzpatricks did realize or should have realized would involve an unreasonable risk of death or serious bodily injury to a child.

The Fitzpatricks argue that a ladder cannot, in and of itself, be considered an inherently dangerous object. ...

What appears to be overlooked by the Fitzpatricks is the fact that the ladder on which Shawn Wiegers was injured was not an ordinary ladder. Rather, the metal device had rough and sharp edges, thus distinguishing it from an ordinary ladder structure. Because of the condition of its edges, the structure herein involved was transformed from an innocuous instrument. Furthermore, the Fitzpatricks acknowledged on more than one occasion an appreciation for the danger that may be involved as is illustrated by the testimony at trial. Mr. Fitzpatrick testified that he kept the ladders on his back porch but on one occasion he noticed that one of the ladders was leaning on the back fence of his yard. He questioned his children as to what the ladder was doing there and his children told him they had used the ladder to climb over the fence. In response to questions at trial concerning this incident, the following colloquy took place on cross-examination:

Q. And were you concerned about their use for climbing over the fence?
A. Yes.
Q. What was your concern about climbing over the fence?
A. Because of the—being these type of ladders that they are, that they could fall off of the ladder or they could fall on to the ladder and get hurt.

* * *

Contrary to the Fitzpatricks assertion, there was sufficient evidence from which a submissible case was made and from which the jury could find in favor of Shawn Wiegers, that is, viewing the evidence in the light most favorable to Wiegers. Clearly the record indicates that the Fitzpatricks appreciated the danger presented by these ladders and appreciated they were dangerous to children. Therefore, the requirement of § 339(b), regarding foreseeability was sufficiently shown so as to overcome a motion for directed verdict.

* * *

Because no error is found to exist in the trial court's denial of the motions for directed verdict and judgment notwithstanding the verdict, the judgment for plaintiffs is affirmed.

All concur.

Case Questions

1. Was it foreseeable that children might be hurt by the ladders on the Fitzpatricks' property?
2. What conditions must be found for the court to hold that an attractive nuisance exists?
3. Would the case have been decided differently if the ladder had been new, with smooth edges?

A four-part test is employed to hold the land owner liable under the attractive nuisance doctrine:

1. The owner must know or have reason to know of the dangerous condition on the premises.
2. The structure, instrumentality, or condition must be alluring to children and endanger them.
3. The presence of children must reasonably have been anticipated.
4. The danger posed to the children outweighs the cost of making the condition safe.

If a trespassing child is injured as a result of having been enticed onto the land to investigate some dangerous condition, then the land owner is liable for such harm.

Restatement (Second) of Torts § 339

Many courts now follow § 339 of the *Restatement (Second) of Torts* and hence have discarded the attraction element to the theory. For these courts, it is sufficient that (1) the injury to the trespassing child was reasonably foreseeable; (2) the danger on the land presented an unreasonable risk of harm to trespassing children; (3) the danger on the land was artificial, meaning manmade rather than natural; (4) because of the child's youth, he or she could not appreciate the risks involved or did not discover (and understand) the threat; (5) the threatening condition was located at a place across which children were likely to trespass; and (6) the land owner failed to exercise reasonable care to protect trespassing children from the danger that caused the harm. Under this version of attractive nuisance, the danger did not have to entice the child onto the land. It is adequate that the child encountered and was hurt by a danger that he or she did not fully discern.

Beneath all its trimmings, *Restatement* § 339 is simply negligence theory applied to trespassing children. The basic negligence elements are there, and the reasoning is identical.

A number of jurisdictions depart from the *Restatement*'s artificial condition element. These courts would include natural dangers, such as streams, quicksand, or rock formations, as risks against which the land owner must take precautions to protect trespassing children.

HYPOTHETICAL

Maybelline is a student attending the local community college. She occasionally trespasses across Farmer Bob's cattle pasture when she walks from her apartment to campus. One day, while cutting across the land, Maybelline encountered Bob's prize bull, which was in a particularly agitated frame of mind. The bull charged and knocked Maybelline to the ground, injuring her. Is Bob liable?

Because Maybelline was a trespasser, Bob owed her no duty of reasonable care. Accordingly, she took her chances by walking across the pasture without permission. Bob would not be liable for her injuries.

Suppose that Maybelline were five years old and came upon Bob's farm to play on the swing set. The set is rickety and old. Attractive nuisance theory would hold Bob liable when Maybelline cuts her hand on a broken, jagged edge of the swing. Maybelline was enticed onto the realty by the swing set, which, due to her youth, she did not notice was old and in disrepair. Bob failed to exercise reasonable care to protect trespassing children such as Maybelline from the risk of being cut by a sharp edge on the swing. The threat of being hurt on the swing was unreasonable, as a child of Maybelline's age could not be expected to realize that the set was too old to be used safely. Young children are likely to be lured onto land to play on playground equipment. The dangerous condition was artificial because Bob installed the swing set on his property and then failed to repair the set or take it down. Any of the attractive nuisance theories discussed previously would hold Bob accountable under these facts.

Suppose, instead, that Maybelline were a cat burglar who was breaking into Bob's barn late one night. Unbeknownst to Maybelline, Bob had wired a shotgun to the windows inside the barn; anyone raising the window frame would instantly be shot. Maybelline tried to enter through the window and was seriously hurt by the gun blast. Would Bob be liable?

Although Bob owes Maybelline (who was trespassing) no duty of reasonable care, he may not set a lethal trap for would-be burglars. Land owners cannot create an unreasonable danger to injure trespassers. Bob would be liable for Maybelline's injuries in this factual scenario.

Licensees Defined

Licensees are persons who have permission to be upon another's land. They are distinguishable from trespassers in that the land owner has consented to their presence upon his or her realty. This consent may be expressed or implied. Examples of licensees include social guests, such as friends who gather at a person's house to study or neighbors

TERMS

licensee A person who enters upon the property of another for his own convenience, pleasure, or benefit, uninvited but tolerated by the owner. [N]ote that the distinction between a licensee and an invitee has been abandoned in some jurisdictions.

coming over to borrow tools; door-to-door salespersons or charitable solicitors (when the land owner has not prohibited their entry by posting warning signs); and frequent trespassers to whose incursions the land owner implicitly consents (such as when trespassers frequently use shortcuts that the land owner does not discourage through fencing or sign-posting).

Land Owner's Duty of Reasonable Care Toward Licensees

Owners owe licensees a duty of reasonable care in using the real estate, because the risk and the benefit are equal. This includes the owner's obligation to correct known dangers (both artificial and natural) on the land. In other words, if the owner knows (or reasonably should know) that a hazardous condition exists on the realty, then he or she must exercise reasonable care in safeguarding licensees from these risks. For example, if an abandoned well has not been covered, and a travelling salesperson visits and falls into the well (which cannot be seen because of overgrown grass), then the land owner has breached his or her duty of reasonable care to the salesperson, assuming that the owner knew (or should have known) that the well was there and could not be detected.

For licensees, the owner is not required to discover and correct unknown threats on the land. For invitees, however, the owner is obligated to do this, as we shall see later.

HYPOTHETICAL

Irving owns an apartment building. Fundraisers for a local charity frequently solicit contributions from his tenants. Irving does not object to this solicitation, although he does not encourage it. Sterling is one of the charity's fundraisers. While visiting Irving's apartment complex, Sterling broke his leg when he fell through a rotten wooden stairway. Sterling could not see the rotting from the top of the steps, but the damage was evident if one looked up from below the stairway. Is Irving liable to Sterling?

Sterling is a licensee, because Irving permitted him to come onto the apartment premises. The key in this case is whether the rotten steps were a known hazard. Perhaps Irving did not know that the steps were rotten. However, Irving reasonably should have known that his apartment steps were dangerous. A building owner is expected to be aware of such easily discoverable risks, as it is easily foreseeable that a stairway user might be hurt if rotten steps collapse. Thus, Irving would be liable for Sterling's injuries.

Suppose, instead, that Irving had posted signs clearly warning, "NO SOLICITORS ALLOWED! ALL TRESPASSERS WILL BE PROSECUTED!" Would he be liable for Sterling's injuries? In this version of the facts, Sterling would be a trespasser, and so

Irving would not owe a duty of reasonable care to Sterling. Accordingly, Irving would not be liable for the harm to Sterling.

Suppose that Irving had posted such signs but did nothing further to discourage solicitors from coming onto his premises. Suppose that door-to-door salespersons and charitable solicitors, including Sterling, regularly visited the apartments with impunity. Under this set of facts, Irving has implicitly consented to the solicitors' presence, including Sterling's. Thus, Sterling would be a licensee.

Invitees Defined

Invitees, or *business invitees* as older court opinions call them, are persons invited upon the land owner's premises. Originally, the common law restricted the term to individuals invited onto premises for business purposes, such as customers to a grocery, clothing store, amusement park, or tavern. Modern cases, however, state that an invitee need not be seeking any business-related purposes when he or she enters another's real estate. It is sufficient that the land owner encourage the invitee to visit.

Usually, invitees are persons coming onto the land for some purpose that the owner wishes to serve. Commonly, this includes any business, but could also include nonprofit organizations, such as churches, soup kitchens, charitable hospitals, or even colleges.

Land Owner's Highest Duty of Reasonable Care Toward Invitees

Land owners owe the highest duty of reasonable care to invitees, because the risk of injury is greater and the benefit is more personal than social. Owners must not only repair known dangers on the property but also must discover and correct unknown risks. This is a broader standard, requiring the land owner to take extra efforts to render his or her premises reasonably safe for invitees.

The logic underlying this stiffer standard of care suggests that owners who invite someone onto realty should be expected to exercise greater caution to ensure that the premises are reasonably danger-free. After all, the invitee would not be on the land to begin with had it not been for the owners' invitation.

─────────────── TERMS ───────────────

invitee A person who enters the premises of another at the latter's invitation, or for business purposes, or for their mutual advantage. [N]ote that the distinction between invitee and licensee has been abandoned in some jurisdictions.

Invitees and Licensees Distinguished

Invitee is a subcategory of *licensee,* yet the terms are distinguishable. All licensees have the owner's implied or expressed permission to be on the land, but the land owner does not have to invite or encourage licensees to visit; rather, the owner may just passively tolerate the licensees' presence. With invitees, however, the owner impliedly or expressly invites them onto the real estate. This reflects the owner's active role in getting the invitees onto his or her land. Usually, the owner seeks customers for business; hence, courts often speak of business invitees.

Implicit or Express Invitation

The land owner's invitation to others to enter the premises may be expressed (e.g., a welcome sign outside a church, or a business posting its hours on its door) or implied (e.g., a business leaving its doors open during business hours).

Limited Areas of Invitation

Obviously, most land owners do not invite people into every nook and cranny of their property. Certain regions are off-limits. For example, most businesses have storage rooms, manager's offices, or machinery rooms that patrons are specifically discouraged from entering. Virtually any business has door signs warning "private," "authorized personnel only," "keep out," and similar prohibitions. The owner's invitation to invitees does not include such areas. If an individual were injured while visiting an off-limits zone, then that person would be considered merely a licensee, or perhaps even a trespasser (depending upon how sternly the warning was phrased—such as "no trespassing—keep out!"), rather than an invitee.

From a plaintiff's standpoint, being included as an invitee spells maximum tort relief—at least in terms of monetary damages. The following examples explore invitee cases.

HYPOTHETICALS

Elvis operates a shelter for homeless persons. Anyone forced to live on the streets is welcome at the facility. Jo Ellen frequently visits the shelter for free meals and a bed for the night. While sleeping one evening, Jo Ellen was stabbed by a loose, rusty wire through the mattress upon which she was lying. She had to undergo precautionary medical treatment for tetanus. Would Elvis be liable for Jo Ellen's injury?

Jo Ellen was an invitee, because she was homeless and Elvis expressly encouraged persons such as her to use his premises. Jo Ellen was injured as a result of a hidden danger (the loose wire) that could have been discovered if Elvis had inspected the mattresses for wear and tear. Thus, Elvis failed to exercise reasonable care to make the shelter reasonably safe for his patrons. As a result, one of his customers, Jo Ellen, was harmed, so Elvis is liable to her.

■ ■ ■

Danielle manages a local appliance store. Wayne came in one day to look for a new washer and dryer. Danielle showed Wayne a popular model. Wayne wished to see the units operate, but there were no electrical outlets nearby. Danielle went to her office to get an extension cord. Meanwhile, Wayne wandered through a set of swinging doors labeled "warehouse—employees only," hoping that he might find another salesperson who could locate an extension cord. Instead, he found a fork-loading truck that swerved around a wall and knocked Wayne to the ground, severely injuring him. The truck driver did not expect anyone to be in the area. Is Danielle liable to Wayne?

Wayne was an invitee when he visited the store to look for new appliances. However, he ceased to be an invitee when he entered the restricted area (the warehouse) without permission. Because he had been invited into the store originally, most courts would say that Wayne became a licensee once he entered the storeroom, as it is reasonably foreseeable that customers might mistakenly trespass into such a limited-access area. Danielle owed Wayne a duty of reasonable care to discover and correct known dangers on the premises. In this case, the fork truck was not threatening in and of itself, as a rotten stairway or improperly stacked boxes would be. The danger would be considered unknown, as it was not reasonably foreseeable that a patron would be hurt by a truck moving around a restricted-access warehouse. Accordingly, Danielle would not be liable for Wayne's injury.

Arguably, though, the threat of the fork truck harming a wayward customer *was* foreseeable, because the truck driver reasonably should have anticipated that patrons might enter the warehouse from time to time, looking for salespersons or restrooms. This would make the risk known, and arguably, Danielle breached her duty of reasonable care when her employee failed to watch for patrons while driving the truck through the warehouse. This reasoning is equally sound and persuasive. This case points out the artificial distinctions in classifying people by the reason they are on land. The traditional negligence approach would be much simpler.

Using Traditional Negligence Theory in Land Owner Cases

As noted earlier, many courts have eliminated the trespasser/licensee/invitee approach in favor of regular negligence theory. Instead of forcing the injured party into one of these three categories, many courts simply ask the routine negligence questions: Was the injury reasonably foreseeable? Did the land owner's scope of duty include the victim? Did the owner cause the victim's injury? and so forth. Many courts, however, cling tenaciously to the older three-tier analysis. This demonstrates how entrenched precedent becomes; once a rule of law

The Case of the Free-Falling Flight Attendant

The outcomes of premises liability cases often hinge upon subtle factual distinctions that place participants within one of the three familiar categories. Courts adhering to the three-tier approach are hesitant to discard the formula, despite the difficulties in its application, as the following case demonstrates.

EGEDE-NISSEN
v.
CRYSTAL MOUNTAIN, INC.
Supreme Court of Washington
606 P.2d 1214 (Wash. 1980)
February 14, 1980
Hicks, Justice

This is an action for personal injuries sustained by petitioner A. E. Egede-Nissen, a Norwegian national, when she fell from a chairlift at Crystal Mountain ski area. A Pierce County Superior Court jury found Crystal Mountain, Inc., negligent, assessed total damages of $150,000, and found Egede-Nissen "contributorially negligent" to the extent of 55 percent.

Sidebar: Contributory negligence is one defense to negligence and is discussed in Chapter 5. The jury probably intended to find the petitioner *comparatively negligent* to the extent of 55 percent. Contributory negligence would completely bar the plaintiff's recovery. Presumably, Justice Hicks placed "contributorially negligent" in quotation marks to imply this misstatement.

Crystal Mountain appealed and the Court of Appeals, Division Two, reversed and remanded for a new trial. We agree with the Court of Appeals, although we base our conclusion on somewhat different grounds.

... Crystal Mountain, Inc., operates recreational ski facilities on public-owned land open to the public for recreational purposes. [On] April 25, 1973, plaintiff Egede-Nissen, a stewardess, and several members of her Scandinavian Airlines System (SAS) flight crew traveled to Crystal Mountain to picnic and sightsee. The ski lodge and chairlifts were not open for business, although the C-4 chairlift was running as an accommodation for three employees of a ski manufacturing company. No lift attendants were present.

From the loading area of the C-4 lift, the SAS group noted two or three skiers on the slopes above. Captain Hartvedt decided to ride the lift up to the skiers and look for and inquire about a picnic site. He boarded a moving chair and Egede-Nissen impulsively decided to accompany him. In her haste to board, she slipped and landed in a precarious position facing and grasping the chair with her lower torso and legs dangling below. Captain Hartvedt, occupying the same chair, attempted to stabilize her without himself falling from the chair.

Crystal Mountain employees working in the C-1 lift area had observed the foregoing situation develop and two of them immediately hastened to the C-4 lift, intending to assist Egede-Nissen. In the course of their efforts, one of the employees stopped the lift, restarted it and then stopped it a second time. The chairs on the lift swayed markedly at each stop. Following the second stop, Egede-Nissen's hold on the chair became insecure and she fell 30 feet to the ground, sustaining injuries.

Petitioner commenced this negligence action against Crystal Mountain in Pierce County Superior Court in June 1973. The case was not tried until November 1976, at which time it was vigorously, often heatedly, contested. A verdict was returned in favor of the plaintiff in the amount of $67,500.

A major legal question at trial was Egede-Nissen's status (invitee, licensee or trespasser) aboard the chairlift. Her status depended upon a factual determination whether Crystal Mountain had given adequate notice, by signs or barricades, that the C-4 lift was not in public operation. On that issue, the evidence was sharply in conflict.

* * *

We granted Egede-Nissen's petition for discretionary review to consider, *inter alia*, whether we should abandon the traditional common-law categories of entrants upon land and adopt a unified standard of reasonable care under the circumstances.

Petitioner Egede-Nissen and amicus curiae urge this court to discard the categorical approach to landowner liability. Although we have questioned the common-law classification scheme in the past, we are not ready at this time to totally abandon the traditional categories and adopt a unified standard. ...

There is no serious dispute that ... Egede-Nissen's status upon *entering* the Crystal Mountain area was that of a public invitee. Accordingly, as to her, Crystal Mountain's duty was to maintain its premises in a reasonably safe condition. This duty, however, extends only to the "area of invitation"—that portion of the premises arranged so as to lead an invitee to reasonably believe it is open to her.

Petitioner's status aboard the chairlift turned on the resolution of a factual dispute—whether Crystal Mountain had given adequate notice that the C-4 lift was closed to the public. Initially, Egede-Nissen's status was that of a public invitee, which status she would retain until adequately warned of limits to the area of her invitation. If, however, petitioner unreasonably strayed beyond the area of invitation, her status would change from that of invitee to a licensee or trespasser, with a corresponding change in the duty owed to her by Crystal Mountain.

In the instant case, it was Crystal Mountain's theory that Egede-Nissen was at best a licensee and more properly a trespasser aboard the C-4 lift, to whom it owed a duty only to refrain from willful or wanton misconduct. While there was substantial evidence to support the trespasser theory, as pointed out by the Court of Appeals, ... [a]s previously noted, her [Egede-Nissen's] status was dependent upon factual resolution.

The Court of Appeals also found [trial court jury] instruction No. 18 to be erroneous because it assumed petitioner to be an invitee as a matter of law. ...

Egede-Nissen's status aboard the lift was dependent upon the scope of the invitation extended to her by Crystal Mountain. The scope of the invitation was a contested matter to be resolved by the jury. As pointed out by the Court of Appeals, the trial court erred in giving instruction No. 18, which assumed that Egede-Nissen had the status of an "invitee." The resolution of that question was dependent upon facts to be found by the jury. We hold that the trial court was sufficiently apprised of the defect in instruction No. 18 and that the giving of the instruction constituted reversible error for which a new trial is required.

* * *

As modified herein, the Court of Appeals is affirmed.

* * *

Case Questions

1. In the Washington Court of Appeals' *Egede-Nissen* opinion, the lower court gave a detailed discussion of the "notice of lift closure" issue. As Acting Chief Judge Reed stated the majority opinion:

    > The major factual dispute in the case revolves around the extent of defendant's efforts to cordon off the loading area of the C-4 lift or warn away visitors. Plaintiff's witnesses, the other SAS crew members, testified that the loading area was not blocked and that there were no warning signs present. In fact, Tollef Bakke, the SAS copilot, testified that the only writing he noticed were two phrases written on a blackboard: "400 yards to go" and "You see what you get." Captain Hartvedt also stated that he read the phrase "You see what you get" on the blackboard. In contrast, defendant's witnesses, all employees of Crystal Mountain, stated that the area was surrounded by metal rope and fencing, and that a "Sorry Lift Closed" sign had been posted.

    Egede-Nissen v. Crystal Mountain, Inc., 21 Wash. App. 130, 584 P.2d 432 (1978). You can see how sharply the parties' witnesses disagree on this issue. Suppose you were a juror in the case. If you

believed the plaintiff's witnesses over the defendant's, what would be the outcome of the liability issue? What if you believed the defendant's witnesses instead? Would the outcome change? Explain.
2. What reversible error did the trial court commit in this case? How did it influence the jury's decision?
3. As you can see from the reprinted opinion, the Washington Supreme Court affirmed the court of appeals' decision to reverse and remand the case for a new trial. Given the facts as presented in the preceding excerpts, how would you decide the plaintiff's status issue? Do you think that Egede-Nissen was a trespasser, licensee, or invitee with regard to the lift chair? Support your conclusion using the legal elements discussed in the opinion and the concepts discussed in this chapter.

becomes settled, it is difficult to raze the monolith and renovate its concepts. The law changes at a snail's pace. More often than not, this provides valuable stability and predictability in legal problem solving. Nonetheless, it also makes legal principles slow to adapt to the rapid changes of our dynamic society. Figure 4-1 summarizes the special negligence analysis for land owners and occupiers.

Another type of property may be the object of negligence. This is personal property, or chattels, which are the subject of bailments, discussed in § 4.3.

§ 4.3 Bailments

A **chattel** is personal property. Personal property includes everything that is not land, which is real property. Chattels include this textbook, an automobile, a cat, a bicycle, and the chewing gum a classmate just borrowed from another student.

A **bailment** exists when the personal property owner, called the **bailor**, delivers possession of but not title to, his or her chattel to someone else, called the **bailee**, who keeps it until the bailor requests that the item be returned or delivered to someone else. Examples of bailments

TERMS

chattel   Personal property that is visible, tangible, and movable. Animals are included within the definition of chattel.

bailment   The entrusting of personal property by one person (the bailor) to another (the bailee) for a specific purpose, with the understanding that the property will be returned when the purpose is accomplished, the stated duration of the bailment is over, or the bailor reclaims it.

bailor   The person who entrusts property to another in a bailment.

bailee   The person to whom property is entrusted in a bailment.

Duty to Trespasser	Land owner/occupier owes no duty of reasonable care; is required only to avoid intentional (or willful and wanton) injury.
Duty to Licensee	Land owner/occupier owes duty of reasonable care to correct known dangers on premises.
Duty to Invitee	Land owner/occupier owes duty of reasonable care to discover and correct unknown dangers on premises.
Traditional Negligence Theory	Applies regular negligence standards to determine land owner/occupier liability.
Duty to Trespassing Children (Attractive Nuisance Theory)	Land owner/occupier owes duty of reasonable care to protect trespassing children from artificial dangers on premises, when (1) owner knows or has reason to know of the dangerous condition on the premises, (2) the structure, instrumentality, or condition is alluring to children and endangers them, (3) the presence of children can reasonably be anticipated, and (4) the danger posed to the children outweighs the cost of making the condition safe.

include attended pay parking garages, lockers at the college bookstore, dry cleaners, and commercial shippers. Any business in which the chattel owner transfers possession of the personal property to the bailee, who keeps it on the owner's behalf, creates a bailment relationship between owner and holder.

Bailee's Negligence Liability: Three-Tier Benefit Scheme

Historically, courts developed a three-tier approach to bailments, just as with land owners' negligence. First of all, the bailee must exercise reasonable care to safeguard the owner's personal property while the bailee possesses it. However, the standard of care differs depending upon who benefits from the bailment relationship.

Bailment Benefit Analysis

The bailor and the bailee often do not benefit equally in a bailment relationship. In some cases, only the bailor benefits. This is called a *bailment for the bailor's sole benefit* or a *gratuitous bailment*. For instance, suppose Ann asks Eleanor, her neighbor, to store Ann's automobile in

Eleanor's garage while Ann is away on vacation. Ann is the bailor, because she owns the property. Eleanor is the bailee, because Ann delivered possession of the car to her. No payment is exchanged for this bailment; it is simply a friendly arrangement between neighbors. Eleanor gets nothing from the deal. Ann, as bailor, derives all the benefits, because her car is being protected from weather and theft in her neighbor's garage.

What if only the bailee benefits? For example, suppose Eleanor borrows Ann's lawn mower to cut her grass. Eleanor does not offer to pay for borrowing the mower and Ann does not ask for anything in return. Ann, the bailor, receives no benefit. Eleanor, as bailee, gets to use the mower. This is *bailment for the bailee's sole benefit.*

Bailments that benefit only the bailor or bailee are often *gratuitous bailments.* This is because the nonbenefiting party does not receive any payment or compensation for his or her role in the bailment relationship. The foregoing illustrations are gratuitous bailments.

Most often, both bailor and bailee benefit. For instance, suppose Charles takes his overcoat to the dry cleaners. Charles, the bailor, owns the coat but delivers possession to the dry cleaners, the bailee, to clean the chattel. Charles will pay the bailee for dry cleaning, and in return he receives a clean overcoat. Both Charles and the dry cleaners profit from the bailment relationship. This is called a *mutual benefit bailment* and is typical of *bailments for hire,* in which the bailee is in the bailment business. Examples include pawn shops, attended pay parking lots, pay storage lockers, and commercial shippers.

Bailees' Different Standards of Care for Each Type of Bailment

When a bailment is for the sole benefit of the bailor, the bailee owes only a duty of slight care to safeguard the personal property from harm. **Slight care** is that degree of caution one uses when involved in relatively unimportant activities in which damage is not a concern.

With a mutual benefit bailment, the bailee owes a duty of ordinary, reasonable care to safeguard the chattel from damage.

When a bailment benefits only the bailee, the bailee owes a duty of great care to safeguard the personal property from injury. **Great care** is an extraordinary degree of caution one uses when involved in exceedingly

════════════ TERMS ════════════

slight care   A very minimal degree of care; the least degree of care.
great care   The degree of care a prudent person usually exercises concerning his or her own affairs of great importance.

The Case of the Stripped Car

Every bailee's nightmare is to have a chattel in his or her possession damaged or stolen. As the case excerpted here illustrates, sometimes a bailee can escape liability when the bailor fails to prove that the appropriate standard of care was violated. One wonders why this issue was not proven at trial.

HOBART

v.

P.J.'S AUTO VILLAGE, INC.
Supreme Court of Vermont
136 Vt. 287, 388 A.2d 419 (1978)
June 6, 1978
Daley, Justice

The plaintiff brought his vehicle to the defendant's place of business for certain repairs which the defendant undertook to perform. One night while the car was in a lot used by the defendant as a storage area for used cars and vehicles undergoing repair, some unknown person or persons jacked up the car and stole two wheels and tires. Damage occurred to the exhaust, suspension and brake systems when the car was lowered or fell to the ground unsupported by the missing wheels. The plaintiff brought suit claiming that his damages were proximately caused by the negligence of the defendant in failing to protect the vehicle from vandals. In a trial by court, the defendant was found liable. He now appeals claiming the judgment is not supported by the trial court's findings of fact and conclusions. We agree.

... In the case of a bailment for hire the bailee is liable for injury to the property bailed that results from his failure to exercise due care and diligence in its preservation. The burden was upon the plaintiff to prove that the defendant did not exercise such care and was negligent.

It is also the well-established law that negligence, to be actionable, must be the proximate cause of the injury for which compensation is sought.

The trial court found (1) that some automobiles awaiting service were stored outdoors overnight adjacent to that portion of the building containing the service department, (2) that the storage area was not enclosed by a fence or other structure, (3) that while the storage area was illuminated, it was not illuminated as brightly as another portion of the premises where other automobiles were stored, (4) that the business premises were unguarded at night except for routine police patrols at management's request, (5) that an L-shaped storage canopy effectively screened the storage area from the most likely direction of public view, ... because the canopy was more brightly illuminated and the dealer had a policy of always filling the canopy at the close of business with a row of closely parked automobiles, and (6) at least one car dealer in the Burlington area maintains a fenced area for cars parked outside awaiting repairs.

Apart from the isolated instance of fencing by one other dealer in the locality, the trial court did not address the question of what precautions a reasonable garagekeeper would have taken under circumstances where he had knowledge of occasional vandalism to automobiles stored on his premises overnight.

In short, the plaintiff's evidence and the trial court's findings do not support its apparent conclusion, not specifically stated, that the defendant failed to exercise the care required of it and that such failure constituted negligence. Even if we were to assume that it did, there is no finding that such negligence was the proximate cause of the plaintiff's loss. Our reading of the record convinces us that the plaintiff's evidence would not support a finding of proximate cause even if one had been made.

Under these circumstances, since there is no basis for the judgment as rendered, we will enter judgment for the defendant.

Reversed; judgment for the defendant.

Case Questions

1. Do you agree with the court that the plaintiff failed to prove a standard of care for garagekeepers? What about the one car dealer in the area who used fencing? Is that not sufficient proof, presuming the defendant did not counter with more persuasive evidence? Explain.
2. Do you agree with the court that the plaintiff failed to prove that the defendant's acts or omissions proximately caused the plaintiff's injuries? If you had been a juror at trial, how would you have decided this issue? Explain.

important activities in which extreme care should be used to avoid injury.

Modern Judicial Trends

In recent years, courts have begun to abandon the three-tier analysis for bailments, just as many have done for land owners' negligence liability. Instead, these modern courts apply regular negligence theory to decide if the bailee failed to exercise reasonable care in protecting the bailor's chattel from harm. This approach is easier to apply, because benefits analysis often is difficult to conceptualize. It is easier simply to ask whether the bailee used reasonable care in safeguarding the personal property.

Both bailment benefit analysis and regular negligence theory can be applied to the following hypotheticals.

HYPOTHETICALS

Amelia owns several airplane hangars at the local airport. Many pilots store their single- and double-engine airplanes in the hangars for a monthly fee. Theresa owns a single-engine Piper aircraft that she uses for commercial aerial photography. In December, Amelia decided to cut costs by disconnecting electrical service to the hangars. Consequently, none of the stored planes could use their engine block heaters (which plug into electrical outlets for power). Theresa came to fly her plane during this time and found the engine damaged because the heater had no electricity to function. Is Amelia liable to Theresa?

This is a bailment relationship, because Theresa (owner/bailor) delivered possession of her chattel (airplane) to Amelia (storer/bailee) to store in the hangar. It is a mutual benefit bailment, as Amelia received a monthly payment from Theresa for storage fees, and Theresa's plane was protected from weather and theft.

Did Amelia breach her duty of reasonable care in safeguarding the bailment property? Because airplane owners commonly use block heaters to keep engines warm during cold winter months, and because Amelia provided electrical outlets for plane owners to use for precisely that purpose, then it was reasonably foreseeable that engine damage would result if the electricity were discontinued. Amelia failed to use ordinary, reasonable care in protecting Theresa's plane's engine from such harm. Accordingly, Amelia breached her duty and would be liable to Theresa for damages.

■ ■ ■

Melvin borrowed Janet's lawn mower to mow his grass. Janet loaned the mower for free. While using the mower, Melvin ran over a large rock in his yard and broke the mower's blade. Melvin could not see the rock because of the tall grass. Would Melvin be liable to Janet for the loss?

Janet is the bailor (owner) who delivered possession of her personal property (lawn mower) to Melvin, who is the bailee (possessor). This is a bailment solely for the bailee's benefit, since Janet received nothing from the relationship, and Melvin derived all the benefit from using the mower free of charge. Accordingly, Melvin owed Janet a duty of great care to safeguard her lawn mower from damage. Accordingly, Melvin should have closely examined the tall grass to find any hidden threats, such as large rocks that could break the blade if mowed over. Ordinary, reasonable care requires such a search. Thus, Melvin breached his duty of great care and would be liable to Janet for damaging the mower blade.

■ ■ ■

Mark asked Nye to keep his pet parrot while he was out of town. No payment was discussed, but Nye agreed. Nye did not know exactly what type of food the bird ate, so he telephoned a veterinarian, who recommended a particular brand of parrot food available at local pet stores. Nye fed the parrot for several days. One morning, Nye discovered that the bird was seriously ill. He rushed it to the veterinarian, who diagnosed that the bird had had an allergic reaction to the feed Would Nye be liable to Mark for the veterinary expenses and injury to the parrot?

Nye (bailee/possessor) owed Mark (owner/bailor) a duty of slight care. This is because the bailment relationship was solely for Mark's benefit. Nye was not paid for his efforts. Mark benefited, though, because Nye watched over the bird in Mark's absence.

Did Nye fail to exercise slight care in feeding the bird? Nye telephoned a veterinarian to discover which type of food to use. A reasonable person, using slight care, would have done the same thing. Nye had every reason to believe the veterinarian's judgment, as veterinarians are professionals experienced in the care of animals such as parrots. Nye used slight care in feeding Mark's parrot, and accordingly Nye would not be liable to Mark for the bird's unfortunate injuries.

Figure 4-2 lists the special negligence analysis for bailments.

Bailment for Bailor's Sole Benefit	Bailee owes duty of slight care to safeguard chattel from harm.
Bailment for Mutual Benefit	Bailee owes duty of ordinary, reasonable care to protect chattel from injury.
Bailment for Bailee's Sole Benefit	Bailee owes duty of great care to guard personal property from damage.
Traditional Negligence Theory	Applies regular negligence elements to determine bailee's liability.

FIGURE 4-2
Bailee's negligence liability in bailment cases

§ 4.4 Vicarious Liability

Previous chapters have presented hypotheticals in which someone acting on behalf of the defendant actually caused harm to the plaintiff. These have been employees of defendant businesses, in most problems. This illustrates one aspect of vicarious liability.

Vicarious Liability Defined

Vicarious liability is the liability of one person, called the *principal,* for the tortious conduct of another, subordinate individual, called the *agent,* who was acting on the principal's behalf. In negligence law, principal/agent relationships most often involve employers and employees. The situation is simple. The principal is the employer, who hires the agent (employee) to work on the employer's behalf.

Employment Not Essential Element

The principal/agent relationship, however, need not be that of employer and employee. Nineteenth- and early twentieth-century cases

TERMS

vicarious liability   Liability imposed upon a person because of the act or omission of another.

spoke of *master and servant*. This older classification suggested that the servant could work for the master without being paid. Thus, whether the agent is compensated for acting upon the principal's behalf is largely irrelevant to the issue of vicarious liability. Instead, focus upon this inquiry: Was one person acting on behalf of another? If so, a principal/agent relationship is present, and vicarious liability could exist.

Respondeat Superior

The employer is responsible for the negligence (or, for that matter, any torts) that his or her employees commit while working. This doctrine of vicarious liability is called **respondeat superior**, a Latin phrase meaning, "Let the superior answer."

Liability Within Scope of Employment

Not every employee activity gives rise to the respondeat superior doctrine, however. An employer is responsible for an employee's actions that fall within the scope of employment. **Scope of employment** can be described as the range of conduct that the employer expects the employee to perform as part of his or her job. For example, a truck driver is expected to make deliveries and pickups for her employer; these actions fall within the scope of employment. But the driver is not expected to rob a liquor store while driving the company truck; this action falls outside the scope of employment.

TERMS

respondeat superior [Latin for] "let the master respond." The doctrine under which liability is imposed upon an employer for the acts of its employees committed in the course and scope of their employment. Similarly, respondeat superior makes a principal liable for a tort committed by his or her agent, and a master responsible for the negligence of his or her servant.

scope of employment A phrase referring to activities carried out by an employee in doing the work assigned to him or her by his or her employer. Under the doctrine of respondeat superior, an employer is not liable for injury inflicted by an employee acting outside of the "scope of his employment." However, an employee's acts which are merely incidental to his or her regular duties, but are of benefit to the employer, are generally deemed to fall within the scope of his or her employment.

Outside Scope of Employment: Examples

Employers are not liable for torts committed by employees that fall outside the scope of employment. Thus, in the preceding example, the employer would be responsible if the truck driver negligently crashed into another vehicle while making deliveries. However, the employer would not be accountable for the robbery (which actually involves criminal behavior but illustrates the scope concept).

Suppose the driver used the truck for personal purposes while not working, thereby going against company policy. Assume that the driver then negligently collided with another vehicle. Would the employer be responsible? No. The driver was acting outside the scope of her employment. She was using the truck not for the employer's business, but for unauthorized personal use.

Coming and Going Rule

Employers are usually not vicariously liable for the negligence of their employees while the employees are coming to or going from work. This is called the **coming and going rule**. The only situation in which an employer would be liable in such circumstances is if the employee were performing work-related activities while on the way to or from the job.

Frolic and Detour Rule

Employers are not vicariously liable for the negligence of their employees when employees go off on their own to handle personal matters, even though they might be performing work otherwise. For instance, suppose that, while making deliveries for her employer, the truck driver decided to drive 180 miles to stop by and visit her friend in the next state. The employer probably did not authorize this sidetrack from the employee's assigned duties. Visits to socialize with friends fall outside the employee's scope of employment. Thus, if the driver were negligent while pursuing activities unrelated to employment during ordinary

---

TERMS

coming and going rule [†] Rule used when employees commit torts while coming to or going from work. In respondeat superior cases, this rule helps decide whether an employee's actions fall outside the scope of employment.

The Case of Full Disclosure

Patients rely on the confidential relationship they establish with doctors and other health care workers. Disclosure of the most intimate details is made by a patient to ensure proper diagnosis and treatment. This case demonstrates what happens when the system fails.

JONES v. BAISCH
United States Court of Appeals, Eighth Circuit 40 F.3d 252 (8th Cir. 1994)
October 24, 1994
Per Curiam

In this diversity action, the District Court entered summary judgment in favor of defendants. Justin Jones appeals, and we affirm.

The parties agree on the material facts. Defendant Dr. Steven Baisch was the sole stockholder of Defendant Region West Pediatric Services (Region West). Nurse Joyce Hallgren and her daughter, Nurse's Assistant Jeni Hallgren, were employees of Region West. In 1989, Jones sought treatment at Region West because he had developed a blistering in his genital area. Baisch diagnosed him as suffering from genital herpes. Joyce learned of the diagnosis from another Region West employee. Thereafter, during a family discussion concerning sexuality, Joyce warned Jeni that Jones had genital herpes. After Jeni confirmed what her mother had told her by examining Jones's medical records, she informed her friends and some of Jones's friends that Jones had herpes. When Jones discovered that Jeni had disclosed his condition to others, he contacted Baisch, who in turn interviewed the Hallgrens. They admitted that they had breached the confidentiality of Jones's medical records in violation of Region West's employee handbook. Baisch then advised them about the harm they had caused and cautioned them about making further disclosures.

After Jones discovered that Jeni had continued to inform her friends about his condition, he filed suit in Nebraska District Court against Baisch and Region West. ...

* * *

We ... reject Jones's argument that, in these circumstances, the Nebraska Supreme Court would extend liability to defendants on the basis of respondeat superior for failure to maintain the confidentiality of Jones's medical records.

* * *

The uncontroverted evidence shows that the Hallgrens were not acting within the scope of their employment when they disclosed Jones's diagnosis. In their depositions, the Hallgrens testified that they were not authorized to reveal patients' medical records and that disclosure of Jones's condition did not occur substantially within the authorized work time and space limits. In fact, the employee handbook specifically forbade disclosures of patients' medical records, and, after learning of the disclosures, Baisch reprimanded the Hallgrens and warned them against further disclosures. Moreover, it is clear that the unauthorized disclosures made by the Hallgrens were not actuated in any way by a purpose to serve their employer. Because Jones failed to proffer any contradictory evidence, defendants were entitled to summary judgment as a matter of law on the respondeat-superior claim.

* * *

[O]nly when an employee is acting pursuant to a physician's direction will the employee's actions be imputed to the physician. [The] patient-physician testimonial privilege "extends not only to physicians but to their agents as well"; [the] law imputes to [a] principal responsibility for negligent acts of his agent performed in obedience to the principal's express orders or directions. ...

In light of the foregoing, we conclude that the District Court did not err by granting summary judgment in favor of the defendants and against Jones.

For the reasons stated above, the judgment of the District Court is affirmed.

Case Questions

1. Joyce and Jeni were named as defendants in the original trial court action. They consented to have a $50,000 judgment entered against them. Do you think this was sufficient compensation for Jones? Explain.
2. Why do you suppose Jones was continuing with the appeal against Baisch despite the entry of judgment against Joyce and Jeni?

working hours, this would be considered **frolic and detour**, and the employer would not be vicariously liable.

Independent Contractors

An **independent contractor** is someone who has entered into a contract with another person to perform a specific task. The independent contractor controls how he or she accomplishes the job. The individual hiring the independent contractor simply agrees to pay him or her for doing the chore. Independent contractors are distinguishable from employees in that the employer does not control how an independent contractor does the job. In contrast, employers do control how their employees perform their tasks. Adjunct college instructors are an example of independent contractors.

No Vicarious Liability for Independent Contractors

Persons hiring independent contractors are not vicariously liable for the independent contractors' negligence. The reasoning is that the independent contractor is engaging in his or her own work and should be responsible for his or her own negligence. The hirer is simply buying

TERMS

frolic of his own (frolic and detour rule)   The conduct of an employee or agent who has departed from the scope of employment (that is, from doing [the] employer's or principal's business) to do something for himself or herself. The principal or employer is not liable for injury to a third party caused by the negligence of an agent or employee who is on a "frolic of his own."

independent contractor   As distinguished from an employee, a person who contracts to do work for another person in his or her own way, controlling the means and method by which the work is done but not the end product. An independent contractor is the agent of the person with whom he or she contracts.

the independent contractor's finished service, and has nothing to do with how the independent contractor achieves the desired results.

For example, suppose Tom hires a plumber to install a new shower in his house. Tom has nothing to do with the actual job; in fact, he only lets the plumber in to go to work. The plumber negligently installs the water lines, so that the hot faucet is connected to the cold water line and vice versa. After the shower is completed, Tom's visiting friend is the first to use it and shockingly discovers the mistake, suffering severe burns. Is Tom vicariously liable to his friend for the plumber's negligence? No. The plumber was an independent contractor. Tom had no say in how the plumber completed the job. Tom merely paid the final price after the plumber did the work. Thus, Tom cannot be vicariously liable for the plumber's negligence. Instead of suing Tom, his friend should sue the plumber.

Motor Vehicle Vicarious Liability

Since the first half of the twentieth century, courts have ruled that passengers in automobiles could be held vicariously liable for the driver's negligence. Using this analysis, if the automobile occupants were involved in a joint enterprise, such as a family travelling to a single destination, then the driver's negligence could be imputed to the passengers. This outcome may seem unfair, because a passenger has no actual control over how the driver operates the vehicle. Legal commentators have long criticized this type of vicarious liability. The better principle, long employed by the courts, holds the vehicle owner vicariously liable for the negligence of a driver other than the owner. For instance, suppose Linda's younger brother is driving her car negligently. He crashes into a motorcyclist, injuring her. Under vicarious liability, Linda would be accountable for her brother's negligence, because he was carelessly using her vehicle and injured another person as a result.

Many state legislatures have enacted statutes imposing vicarious liability on owners for the negligence of others who drive their vehicles. These are sometimes called *motor vehicle consent statutes*. An example of this is California's Vehicle Code § 17150 *et seq.*

HYPOTHETICALS

Sarah is a physician. Her nurse's aide, Gladys, draws blood from patients as part of her responsibilities on the job. One day, Gladys used a contaminated needle and thus infected a patient when she drew blood for testing. Would Sarah be vicariously liable for Gladys's negligence?

Gladys was performing a specific job assignment on Sarah's behalf. Drawing blood falls within Gladys's scope of employment. Under respondeat superior, Sarah would be accountable for Gladys's negligent act of using a contaminated needle and infecting a patient.

Suppose Gladys worked for a blood bank that routinely did blood draws and tests for area physicians. Under this scenario, Sarah would not have control over how Gladys acted. Gladys's employer is the blood bank, which would be an independent contractor in relation to Sarah. Accordingly, Sarah would not be accountable for Gladys's negligence.

■ ■ ■

Fargo is a fast-food restaurant manager. Mitchell is one of his employees. Fargo asked Mitchell to drive across town to a soft drink supplier and pick up additional carbonated water. While on this errand, Mitchell stopped by the post office to check his mail. As he was leaving the post office parking lot, he failed to look both ways and collided with another vehicle. Would Fargo be vicariously liable for Mitchell's negligent driving?

Although Mitchell was running a business-related errand on Fargo's behalf, stopping by the post office to check personal mail falls outside Mitchell's scope of employment. However, as this is only a slight deviation, frolic and detour would not apply here. Thus Fargo would be responsible for Mitchell's negligent conduct.

Suppose Fargo had been a passenger in Mitchell's car during this incident. Fargo (as the boss) could have controlled his employee, Mitchell, and instructed him not to stop at the post office. By permitting Mitchell to check his mail, Fargo implicitly consented to Mitchell's detour. This would place the detour within the scope of Mitchell's employment. Assuming that no statutes stated differently, Fargo would be vicariously liable.

Figure 4-3 outlines vicarious liability.

§ 4.5 Negligent Infliction of Emotional Distress

Emotional distress consists of mental anguish caused by a tortfeasor. This condition includes fright, anxiety, shock, grief, mental suffering,

---

TERMS

emotional distress [†]   Mental anguish. In the intentional torts called *intentional* and *reckless infliction of emotional distress,* the mental anguish is caused by the tortfeasor's outrageous conduct.

FIGURE 4-3
Vicarious
liability
summary

Vicarious Liability	Liability of principal for negligent actions of agent serving on principal's behalf. Commonly involves employer/employee relationships.
Respondeat Superior	"Let the superior answer": Doctrine through which employers may be held vicariously liable for employees' negligent actions committed within the scope of employment.
Scope of Employment	Range of conduct that employer expects of employee during performance of assigned employment responsibilities.
Coming and Going Rule	Employers are not vicariously liable for employees' negligence while employees are coming to and going from work, unless employer has specifically requested employee to carry out a specific work-related task during such times.
Frolic and Detour Rule	Employers are not vicariously liable for employees' negligence when employees deviate from assigned tasks within scope of employment, unless the deviation is minor. Usually this involves employees going off on their own to pursue personal needs.
Independent Contractors	Employers are not liable for independent contractors' negligence, because ICs act independently and are responsible for their own conduct.
Motor Vehicle Vicarious Liability	Motor vehicle owners may be held vicariously liable for the driver's negligence. Liability may also be established in motor vehicle consent statutes.

shame, embarrassment, and emotional disturbance. The tort exists when the tortfeasor inflicts psychological injury on the victim. **Negligent infliction of emotional distress** consists of: (1) Conduct by the tortfeasor, which (2) the tortfeasor reasonably should have anticipated would produce (3) significant and reasonably foreseeable emotional injury to the victim; when (4) the tortfeasor breached his or her duty of reasonable care to avoid causing such emotional harm to the victim; and (5) the victim was a reasonably foreseeable plaintiff.

Extra Elements in the Common Law

These generalized elements of negligent infliction of emotional distress are synthesized from those of many jurisdictions. Different courts apply various special requirements to negligent infliction cases, and it is always wise to check the rules and cases of the particular jurisdiction in which your case lies.

Impact Rule

A minority of courts insist that some physical impact accompany the emotional injury. Thus, the tortfeasor must negligently do something that physically touches the victim if the victim is to recover damages for negligent infliction of emotional distress. This is often called the **impact rule**, and it has been severely criticized in the legal literature and judicial decisions.

The purpose of the impact requirement is to protect against false claims of emotional distress. Because mental anguish is largely invisible, courts at the turn of the century felt that the defendant had to make contact with the plaintiff to justify compensating something as easy to fake as mental harm. Modern courts utilizing the impact rule

---

TERMS

negligent infliction of emotional distress[†] Outrageous conduct by the tortfeasor which the tortfeasor reasonably should have anticipated would produce significant and reasonably foreseeable emotional injury to the victim. By his or her actions, the tortfeasor must breach the duty of reasonable care, and the victim must be a reasonably foreseeable plaintiff.

impact rule The rule, existing in only a few states, that for a plaintiff to recover damages for mental anguish in a negligence action, impact must have occurred, or at a minimum, there must have been physical contact.

The Case of the Unyielding Postal Carrier

Scope of employment can be a fuzzy line in some cases. Courts sometimes struggle to apply the coming and going rule, as this case reveals. Although the concurring opinion suggests that the rule can be effortlessly applied, the majority, in its reading of the facts, discerned more subtle employment-related activities for which vicarious liability could exist.

KONRADI v. UNITED STATES
U.S. Court of Appeals,
Seventh Circuit
919 F.2d 1207 (7th Cir. 1990)
November 29, 1990
Posner, Circuit Judge

While driving to work early one morning, Robert Farringer, a rural mailman, struck a car driven by the plaintiff's decedent, Glenn Konradi, killing him. The suit is against the United States under the Federal Tort Claims Act, 28 U.S.C. §§ 1346(b), 2671 et seq. ... The basis of [plaintiff's] claims is that Farringer's negligence in failing to yield the right of way to Konradi at an intersection was the cause of the accident. The district judge dismissed the suit on the government's motion for summary judgment. He ruled that the accident had not occurred within the scope of Farringer's employment by the Postal Service, which let off the Service ... .

The parties agree that the question whether the accident occurred within the scope of Farringer's employment is governed by Indiana law, that under Indiana law it is a question of fact, and therefore that the judge was right to dismiss the case on summary judgment only if no reasonable jury, presented with the evidence that was before the judge when he ruled, could have answered the question in the plaintiff's favor. ...

The general rule is that an employee is not within the scope of his employment when commuting to or from his job. As the Supreme Court of Indiana put it the last time it addressed the

issue, more than three decades ago, "an employee on his way to work is normally not in the employment of the corporation." The rub is "normally" ... . In State v. Gibbs, 166 Ind. App. 387, 336 N.E.2d 703 (1975), the employer furnished the employee with a car for use on the job but also allowed him to take it home at night. The accident occurred while he was driving home, and the employer was held liable. In Gibbs v. Miller, [152 Ind. App. 326, 283 N.E.2d 592 (1972)], the employer was held liable for an accident that occurred when its traveling salesman, who used his own car to make his rounds, was driving home for lunch from an appointment with a customer; he had other appointments scheduled for that afternoon. On the other hand, in City of Elkhart v. Jackson, 104 Ind. App. 136, 10 N.E.2d 418 (1937), which also involved an employee driving the company car at lunch time—this time he was returning to work after lunch when the accident occurred—the accident was held to be outside the scope of employment. ... In City of Crawfordsville v. Michael, 479 N.E.2d 102 (Ind. Ct. App. 1985), the employee was using the company car (actually truck) for personal business on his day off when the accident occurred; he too was held not to have been acting within the scope of his employment.

It is impossible to find the pattern in this carpet without a conception of what the law is trying to accomplish by making an employer liable for the torts of his employees committed within the scope of their employment and by excluding commuting from that scope—"normally." The

Indiana decisions are few and not articulate on these issues ... .

The liability of an employer for torts committed by its employees ... when they are acting within the scope of their employment [is] the liability that the law calls "respondeat superior." ...

But the law has to draw some lines for ease of administration, and a rough-and-ready one is between accidents on the job and accidents off the job—including accidents while commuting—in recognition of the fact that the employer's ability to prevent accidents by employees is normally much less when the employees are not at work. Indiana recognizes, however, that the line is indeed a rough one ... .

The Postal Service, Farringer's employer, requires its rural postal carriers to furnish their own vehicle (Farringer's was a pick-up truck) in making their rounds. The alternative would be for the Service to buy or lease mail trucks for these carriers to use. ... The Postal Service's rule pretty much guarantees that its mailmen will drive to and from work, and by doing this it increases the amount of driving ... . One cost of more driving is more accidents, and this cost can be made a cost to the Postal Service ... . Farringer's postmaster required the postal carriers to take the most direct route in driving to and from work, and hence not to divagate for personal business. Nor was the carrier to stop for such business, or give anyone a ride. ...

The rules of commuting that the postmaster has imposed upon his carriers may ... reflect a belief that the work of a rural deliveryman begins when he gets into his car in the morning and ends when he gets out of it in the evening. ... Of course the two *Gibbs* cases are factually different from our case—every case is factually different from every other case—but that is no warrant for refusing to follow them in this case unless the factual differences between them and this case are connected with a difference in principle.

... [T]he imposition of liability on the Postal Service [may] be consistent with most of the Indiana cases ... . By driving to and from work Farringer conferred a *benefit* on his employer because he was bringing an essential instrumentality of the employer's business. ... The employer exerted substantial *control* over the employee's commuting, as shown by the regulations discussed earlier. And finally the employee while commuting was in the *service* of the employer ... .

... [T]he district court acted prematurely in granting summary judgment. ... [T]he dismissal of the United States is reversed and the case remanded for further proceedings consistent with this opinion. ...

MANION, Circuit Judge, concurring.

* * *

Indiana law is clear that, with very limited exceptions, an employee is not within the scope of his employment while driving to and from work. ... Unless we have some exceptional circumstance, a rural postal worker driving to work is on his own and not within the scope of his employment. ... [T]here is virtually no evidence that Farringer was in the scope of his employment. Farringer was driving his own car to work, not the government's. He was not providing any benefit to the government while en route; his job did not begin until he reached the post office to sort and pick up his mail for delivery. He was not, as in *Gibbs v. Miller*, going home for lunch and to do some paperwork in between business appointments, while receiving payment for mileage incurred on the trip. He was not, as in *State v. Gibbs*, properly driving a state-owned vehicle home from work following the day's activities, while on call 24 hours a day. Rather, he was simply travelling to work. Until he is at work, Indiana does not impose his misdeeds on the employer.

... I do not agree with this court that the "employer exerted substantial control over the employee's commuting, as shown by the regulations discussed ... ."

have seen impact in almost any physical touching. Something as casual as putting one's hand on a classmate's shoulder would be considered sufficient contact to satisfy the impact rule. Hence, it would seem that, as a safeguard against faked claims of emotional distress, the physical impact requirement does little or nothing to ensure honesty and sincerity for allegations of mental hurt.

Physical Manifestations Rule

The majority of courts have abandoned the impact rule in favor of the **physical manifestations rule**. This requires that, in addition to mental suffering, the plaintiff must experience physical symptoms as a result of the emotional distress. This rule is also thought to protect against bogus claims of emotional injury. After all, if a victim experiences some physical malady associated with an emotional harm, such as an ulcer, hives, sleeplessness, weight loss, or bowel dysfunction, then the probability is that the emotional harm is genuine.

Zone of Danger Rule

What happens when the negligent action occurs to someone else, and the plaintiff is a bystander who witnesses a negligent injury to another person? Could the tortfeasor be liable to the bystander for negligent infliction of emotional distress? Consider an example. Suppose parents witnessed their child being struck by a negligent driver. Would the parents have a cause of action against the driver for negligent infliction of emotional distress?

──────────────── **TERMS** ────────────────

physical manifestations rule[†]   Doctrine applied in negligent infliction of emotional distress cases. Under this rule, the plaintiff may recover damages if he or she suffered physical symptoms accompanying the mental anguish.

No impact occurred to the parents, although they may suffer physical manifestations as a result of witnessing their child's injury. The proper question, however, may be phrased in ordinary negligence terms: Did the driver owe (and breach) a duty of reasonable care to the parents by injuring their child? Did the driver's actions cause the parents' emotional suffering? Does proximate cause exist? Were the parents injured?

Certainly, the driver could not reasonably anticipate that any bystander would suffer emotional distress as a result of the driver's negligent act of hitting a pedestrian. There must be some way to limit the scope of duty (and, hence, the range of foreseeable plaintiffs). Courts have attempted to establish such limits by creating the **zone of danger rule.** Under this rule, only bystanders who fall within the zone of danger can recover for negligent infliction of emotional distress. In other words, these individuals must have been threatened by the original negligent action (e.g., negligent driving of a vehicle) and have reasonably feared for their own safety, or have certain family relationships, as discussed later.

Family Relationships Rule

Other courts have restricted recovery in negligent infliction cases to bystander plaintiffs who are related to the victim whom they witnessed being injured. This may be called the **family relationships rule.**

Sensory Perception Rule

Still other courts have insisted that the bystander perceive the traumatic, negligent event directly through the senses (e.g., seeing the collision; hearing the child's screams; feeling the heat of the car exploding; smelling the burning clothing). This may be labelled the **sensory perception rule.**

◗ TERMS ◖

zone of danger rule [†] Doctrine used in negligent infliction of emotional distress cases. Under this rule, if a bystander witnesses substantial injury to another person, often a relative, then the bystander may recover damages for negligent infliction of emotional distress if he or she fell within the zone of danger created by the tortfeasor's conduct that hurt the other person.

family relationships rule [†] Doctrine used in negligent infliction of emotional distress cases. Under this rule, a bystander may recover damages if he or she witnesses a tortfeasor injuring one or more of the bystander's relatives.

sensory perception rule [†] Doctrine used in negligent infliction of emotional distress cases. Under this rule, a bystander may recover damages if he or she witnesses a tortfeasor injuring another person, so long as the bystander perceives the event directly through his or her own senses.

The Case of the Return of the Living Dead

In *Decker v. Princeton Packet, Inc.,* the New Jersey Supreme Court held that a false obituary was not defamatory per se, when published without malicious intent or additional defamatory information. The opinion also discussed intentional and negligent infliction of emotional distress.

DECKER
v.
PRINCETON PACKET, INC.
Supreme Court of New Jersey
116 N.J. 418, 561 A.2d 1122 (1989)
August 8, 1989

* * *

Finally, the [trial] court concluded that plaintiffs were not entitled to any recovery based on any claims for negligent or intentional infliction of emotional distress. It rejected plaintiffs' negligent-infliction-of-emotional-distress claim because New Jersey case law does not allow recovery for the negligent infliction of emotional distress outside the zone-of-risk and family-observation theories.

Plaintiffs appealed to the Appellate Division, which upheld the trial court's ruling ... .

... [P]laintiff alleged that the publication of the false obituary based on an unsigned death notice left at defendant's office without any attempt to ascertain its truth or falsity constituted negligence that caused her emotional distress. These injuries included the loss of her job in part due to the obituary ... and the aggravation of emotional distress.

The tort involving the negligent infliction of emotional distress can be understood as negligent conduct that is the proximate cause of emotional distress in a person to whom the actor owes a legal duty to exercise reasonable care. Thus, to establish liability for such a tort, a plaintiff must prove that defendant's conduct was negligent and proximately caused plaintiff's injuries. The negligence of defendant, however, depends on whether defendant owes a duty of care to the plaintiff, which is analyzed in terms of foreseeability. "[L]iability should depend on the defendant's foreseeing fright or shock severe enough to cause substantial injury in a person normally constituted."

While the foreseeability of injurious consequences is a constituent element in a tort action, foreseeability of injury is particularly important in the tort of negligent infliction of emotional harm. This reflects the concern over the genuineness of an injury consisting of emotional distress without consequent physical injury. In these situations, there must be "an especial likelihood of genuine and serious mental distress, arising from special circumstances, which serves as a guarantee that the claim is not spurious." In emotional distress cases, there has been "a constant concern about the genuineness of the claim."

The progression has been from denying recovery unless the emotional distress is accompanied by physical impact, to permitting recovery if the emotional distress results in physical injury. More recently, we have found a sufficient guarantee of genuineness, even in the absence of physical injury, if the plaintiff perceives an injury to another at the scene of the accident, the plaintiff and the victim are members of the same family, and the emotional distress is severe. Thus, recovery for negligent infliction of emotional harm requires that it must be reasonably foreseeable that the tortious conduct will cause genuine and substantial emotional distress or mental harm to average persons.

Unless a plaintiff's alleged distress is truly genuine and substantial, the tort of negligent infliction should not be broadened to permit recovery of damages. ... Thus, in the *Buckley* case, the Court observed that plaintiff's emotional distress "complaints amount to nothing more than aggravation, embarrassment, an unspecified number of headaches, and loss of sleep," and, as a matter of law, could not constitute severe mental distress sufficient to impose liability.

* * *

In this case, the emotional distress alleged by Marcy Decker resulting from the false report of her death, and, derivatively, the emotional distress assertedly experienced by Ms. Decker's son and mother, are not materially different from that described in cases like *Buckley*, in which the injury is not sufficiently palpable, severe, or enduring to justify the imposition of liability and the award of compensatory damages. Rather

the alleged emotional distress approximates the subjective reactions of ordinary persons who feel victimized by the false report of death, namely, annoyance, embarrassment, and irritation. ... [T]here is no suggestion in the record that any serious or substantial distress on the part of Ms. Decker and her family would be particularly foreseeable. These considerations dictate rejection of the claim for the negligent infliction of emotional distress under these circumstances as a matter of law.

Case Questions

1. Do you agree with the court that the plaintiff and family's emotional distress was not reasonably foreseeable? How would a newspaper reasonably expect a person and family to react to reading an erroneous obituary for which no attempt at verification was made?
2. How does the court's discussion of the elements of negligent infliction of emotional distress compare with this chapter's presentation?

California Approach

The California courts were first to produce a further evolutionary development in negligent infliction law. In *Dillon v. Legg,* 68 Cal. 2d 728, 441 P.2d 912, 69 Cal. Rptr. 72 (1968), the California Supreme Court jettisoned the zone of danger rule and focused upon pure foreseeability. The straightforward question was, simply: Was the emotional injury reasonably foreseeable, given the tortfeasor's actions? This analysis neatly handled bystanders as well as immediate victims of negligent conduct. The court produced the following guidelines to decide the foreseeability issue:

1. The bystander's closeness to the emotionally disturbing incident (*physical proximity*)
2. The bystander's relationship to the injured party (*family relationships rule*)
3. The bystander's personal perception of the emotionally distressing occurrence (*sensory perception rule*)
4. Physical manifestations arising from the emotional distress.

The *Dillon* approach has been both praised and debunked by other courts and legal scholars. It presents another twist in negligent infliction cases, in a continuing attempt to clarify the circumstances in which a plaintiff may hold a defendant liable for this type of negligent tort.

The diversity of negligent infliction of emotional distress formulas used in different jurisdictions makes analysis dependent upon a specific state's version. The following hypothetical considers the varieties discussed in this section.

HYPOTHETICAL

Heddison owns an apartment building. Skyler and Melville are brothers who share an apartment. One day, while barbecuing on their apartment balcony, Skyler stepped upon rotten floorboards, which collapsed. Heddison had known about this dangerous condition for months but did not correct it. Skyler fell through the balcony floor and hung upside down by one leg 30 feet above the ground. Meanwhile, Melville, who was waxing his car in the parking lot below, became very upset upon seeing this situation develop. As he ran upstairs to assist his brother, Skyler fell and suffered debilitating injuries. Subsequently, Melville began having horrible nightmares involving endless falling. He would awaken nightly in cold sweats. He lost weight, had little appetite, and developed a phobia about heights. This phobia made it extremely difficult for Melville to continue his occupation as a roofing installer. Heddison's liability to Skyler is an issue of land owner liability, which we discussed at the beginning of this chapter. Would Heddison be liable to Melville for negligent infliction of emotional distress?

Clearly, Melville suffered no physical impact as a result of Heddison's negligence. Melville did not come into contact with the rotten balcony when it gave way. In states following the impact rule, Melville could not recover damages against Heddison for negligent infliction.

In states following the zone of danger rule, Melville was not sufficiently close to the dangerous balcony to be threatened by its condition. He was not even below the point at which Skyler fell, which would have placed him at risk. Under the zone of danger test, Melville could not recover.

In jurisdictions following California's approach, it was reasonably foreseeable that Melville would be emotionally harmed by witnessing Skyler's life-threatening situation, which Skyler became involved in because of Heddison's negligent maintenance of the balcony. Melville is Skyler's brother, so the family relationship test is met. Melville saw Skyler dangling from the balcony and knew that he could fall and be killed. This satisfies the sensory perception rule. Melville was standing close to the accident site, and thus met the physical proximity standard. He also displayed physical symptoms resulting from his mental anguish. All of the *Dillon* criteria have been satisfied. Accordingly, Heddison would be liable to Melville for negligent infliction of emotional distress, under the California theory.

Figure 4-4 illustrates the various analytical approaches to negligent infliction of emotional distress.

Common Elements (applying standard negligence theory to emotionally distressing conduct)	(1) conduct by tortfeasor, when (2) tortfeasor reasonably should have anticipated that behavior would produce (3) significant and reasonably foreseeable injury in plaintiff, (4) tortfeasor breached duty of reasonable care, and (5) victim was foreseeable plaintiff.
Impact Rule	Plaintiff must experience physical impact from defendant's actions to recover for negligent infliction of emotional distress.
Physical Manifestations Rule	No physical impact is required, but plaintiff must experience physical symptoms associated with mental anguish that defendant caused.
Zone of Danger Rule	Bystander witnessing negligent injury to third party must have been immediately threatened by the negligent activity.
Family Relationships Rule	Bystander must be a family relative of the person injured by the tortfeasor's negligent act.
Sensory Perception Rule	Bystander must perceive with his or her senses (sight, hearing, smell, touch, taste) the injury to another person as a result of the tortfeasor's negligent act.

FIGURE 4-4   Elements of negligent infliction of emotional distress

Summary

In premises liability, owners and occupiers of land owe special duties of reasonable care to individuals who are injured while visiting the premises. Traditionally, courts have defined these duties differently, depending upon the injured party's status on the realty. There are three such distinctions: trespasser, licensee, and invitee. Land owners owe no duty of reasonable care to trespassers; they must simply refrain from intentionally injuring trespassers. Special rules, called attractive nuisance theory, apply to trespassing children. Licensees are persons that the owners permit to come onto their real estate. To licensees, land owners owe a duty to correct known dangers on the premises. Land owners owe a duty to discover and correct unknown risks on the premises for invitees, who have come onto the premises at the owners' expressed or implied invitation. The owner may limit the places on the land to which such invitation extends. Many courts have abandoned this three-tier analysis in favor of regular negligence theory.

Chattels are personal property. They are the subject of bailments. In a bailment relationship, the chattel owner (bailor) delivers possession of but not title to, the property to another person (bailee), who keeps the object until the bailor asks for its return or delivery to someone else. The bailee owes the bailor a duty of care to safeguard the bailment property from harm. This duty depends upon which party benefits from the bailment. This is called bailment benefits analysis. If the bailor alone benefits, then the bailee owes only a duty of slight care with regard to the chattel. If both bailor and bailee benefit, then the bailee owes a duty of ordinary, reasonable care. If only the bailee benefits, then the bailee owes a duty of great care. Recent court decisions have moved away from these distinctions toward regular negligence theory in bailment cases.

Vicarious liability is the liability of one person (principal) for the negligent actions of another (agent). Many vicarious liability situations involve employer/employee relationships. Under the doctrine of respondeat superior, the employer must answer to the injured party for the employee's negligence when the employee has acted within the scope of his or her employment. This normally involves assigned tasks during normal working hours. Special rules apply for employees coming to and going from work, and for employees who frolic and detour from assigned tasks to pursue personal pleasures. A person hiring independent contractors is not vicariously liable for their negligence. Many states have motor vehicle consent statutes holding a vehicle owner liable for another driver's negligence.

Negligent infliction of emotional distress occurs when the tortfeasor engages in conduct that produces a reasonably foreseeable mental injury in a reasonably foreseeable victim. Many states have different rules to decide negligent infliction cases. A few courts require that the tortfeasor cause some physical impact to the emotionally distressed victim. Many courts hold that mental anguish is recoverable when accompanied by physical manifestations or symptoms. Others allow bystanders to recover when they witness negligent injuries to other people when the bystanders fall within the zone of danger. Courts that follow California's reasoning base liability upon foreseeability, using physical manifestations, physical proximity, family connection, and whether the bystander witnessed the injury to determine the outcome of negligent infliction litigation.

Review Questions

1. Define the three classes of plaintiffs to whom land owners and occupiers owe duties of reasonable care.

2. Describe the land owner/occupier's duty of reasonable care to trespassers. Does the rule apply to all trespassers?

3. What is attractive nuisance? To which type of plaintiffs would the doctrine apply? Why is the land owner/occupier's duty of reasonable care different for these plaintiffs?

4. Discuss the land owner/occupier's duty of reasonable care to licensees. How do licensees differ from trespassers? From invitees?

5. What duty of reasonable care does the land owner/occupier owe to invitees? Why and how are invitees distinguishable from licensees and trespassers?

6. Explain how you might use traditional negligence theory to determine land owners'/occupiers' liability to persons injured on the real estate. Do you find this approach easier than the three-tier analysis discussed in problem 1? Why or why not?

7. What are bailments? Who is the bailor and the bailee? Which one owes the other a duty of reasonable care? Why?

8. What is bailment benefits analysis? How is it used to determine the standards of reasonable care? Would traditional negligence theory be easier to apply? Why or why not?

9. Define vicarious liability. What types of relationships involve this theory? What is respondeat superior? Explain scope of employment, the coming and going rule, and the frolic and detour rule. Why are these important to your analysis? How does vicarious liability relate to independent contractors? To motor vehicle owners or passengers?

10. Explain negligent infliction of emotional distress. What are its elements? In what types of factual situations would the tort apply? Describe the different analytical approaches to this tort. Define the impact rule, the physical

manifestations rule, the zone of danger rule, the family relationships rule, and the sensory perception rule. How have the California courts combined these concepts in negligent infliction cases?

Projects

1. Which special negligence actions discussed in this chapter are included in your state's common law? Are any controlled by statute? Has your state legislature enacted a motor vehicle consent statute?

2. Suppose a partner in your firm asks you to interview a potential client about an alleged negligent infliction of emotional distress claim. What issues will you need to cover to have sufficient information to state a cause of action for negligent infliction of emotional distress in your jurisdiction?

CHAPTER 5

DEFENSES TO NEGLIGENCE

The business of the law is to make sense of the confusion of what we call human life—to reduce it to order but at the same time to give it possibility, scope, even dignity.

— *Archibald Macleish*

§ 5.1 Introduction

Tort defenses are an important protection for defendants. They provide legal justification for the defendants' actions.

Defendants' defenses excuse negligent behavior. In effect, defenses provide defendants with a blame-shifting weapon. Negligence defenses examine any plaintiff misconduct that was involved in causing the plaintiff's injuries. Even though the tortfeasor was negligent toward the victim, the tortfeasor's mischief may be forgiven (totally or partially) because of the victim's participation in producing his or her injuries.

This chapter discusses:

- How negligence defenses are used

- Contributory negligence

- Last clear chance

- Comparative negligence

- Assumption of risk

- Statutes of limitations.

§ 5.2 How Negligence Defenses Are Used

Once the plaintiff has alleged a cause of action for negligence in the complaint, it is assumed that the defendant has no defense unless he or she pleads one (or more) in his or her answer. Always remember these basic analytical rules:

1. *Negligence defenses are used only by the defendant against the plaintiff.*

   Put more generally, these defenses are responses to negligence allegations. The party alleged to have been negligent can use defenses against the party alleging negligence. In cases involving counterclaims, in which the defendant counter-sues the plaintiff, remember that the defendant becomes a counter-plaintiff against the original plaintiff, who becomes a counter-defendant, at least as far as the counterclaim is concerned. The same holds true for third-party complaints and answers.

2. *Negligence defenses are applied only in response to the plaintiff's allegations that the defendant acted negligently, not to claims of intentional action.*

   Again, in counterclaims and third-party claims, remember who is the alleging party and who is the alleged wrongdoer. In a counterclaim, the defendant might allege that the plaintiff acted negligently toward the defendant. Retitle the parties to reflect their new roles toward each other with respect to the counterclaim. The counter-defendant (i.e., the plaintiff) would be entitled to use negligence defenses against the counter-plaintiff (i.e., the defendant).

   The same is true for third-party claims. Recall that defendants may become third-party plaintiffs, bringing third-party defendants who were not a part of the lawsuit, into the litigation through **impleader.** The scenario is this: A plaintiff sues a defendant, alleging that a tort has been committed. The defendant impleads a third-party defendant for that third party's participation in committing the tort. Negligence defenses are available to the third-party defendant against the third-party plaintiff's negligence claims.

3. *Ask who is alleging negligence and who is alleged to have been negligent.*

   The alleged tortfeasor, usually the defendant, is the person who may utilize defenses. A simple analogy might assist in remembering how negligence defenses are applied. Suppose Kelly throws a snowball at Mel. Mel blocks the snowball with a garbage can lid as a shield. Kelly (throwing the snowball) is the plaintiff, and the snowball itself is the accusation that Mel was negligent. Mel is the defendant, who allegedly committed the tort. Mel's shield is the negligence defenses discussed in this chapter. Mel avoids liability (i.e., being struck by the snowball) by using his shield to deflect the plaintiff's negligence allegations. Kelly, the snowball (accusation)

TERMS

impleader   A defendant's action in bringing into a lawsuit, as an additional defendant, a party whom the defendant asserts is responsible to the plaintiff for the damages or other remedy the plaintiff seeks.

thrower, does not use the shield, as she is doing the throwing. Only the intended recipient of the snowball (Mel, the defendant) needs to block the attack with the shield.

§ 5.3 Contributory Negligence and Last Clear Chance

With this fundamental approach in mind, it is time to examine contributory negligence.

Contributory Negligence Defined

Contributory negligence is the plaintiff's own negligence that contributed to his or her injuries. The elements of contributory negligence include:

1. The plaintiff's duty of reasonable care to himself or herself
2. The plaintiff's breach of that duty
3. The plaintiff's actions (or failures to act) that contributed to his or her injuries (causation, proximate cause)
4. Resulting injuries to the plaintiff.

Duty of Care to Oneself

One has a duty of reasonable care to protect oneself from injury. If a person breaches this duty by causing injury to himself, then he has been negligent toward himself. Suppose a tortfeasor (defendant) also participated in causing the harm. Nonetheless, the victim (plaintiff) contributed to the resulting injury. This is contributory negligence.

Consider this illustration. Suppose that Zelda is speeding while driving to school. Suppose that another driver runs a stop sign and the vehicles collide with one another. By failing to stop at the sign, the other driver breached the duty of reasonable care to other vehicle users such as Zelda. The other driver's negligence proximately caused injuries to Zelda and her vehicle. However, because Zelda was speeding, she contributed to her own injuries. Apply the contributory negligence formula: (1) Zelda breached her duty of reasonable care to herself by exceeding the speed limit; (2) but for Zelda's excessive speed, she would not have reached the intersection at precisely the time the other driver ran the stop sign; (3) Zelda's high speed proximately contributed to the collision with the other driver. Accordingly, Zelda was contributorily negligent.

Common Law Rule

At common law, contributory negligence barred the plaintiff from recovering any damages from the defendant. Even if the defendant were

---

TERMS

contributory negligence In the law of negligence, a failure by the plaintiff to exercise reasonable care which, in part at least, is the cause of an injury. Contributory negligence defeats a plaintiff's cause of action for negligence in states that have not adopted the doctrine of comparative negligence.

negligent in causing 99 percent of the plaintiff's harm, and the plaintiff were only 1 percent contributorily negligent, the courts ruled that the plaintiff could collect nothing against the defendant.

Last Clear Chance

When a defendant uses the contributory negligence defense against a plaintiff, the plaintiff has a responsive weapon to defeat this defense. This is called **last clear chance** and is a rebuttal to a contributory negligence defense. Last clear chance theory states that, although the plaintiff was contributorily negligent in causing his or her own injuries, the defendant had the last opportunity to avert harm but, because of the defendant's negligence, the defendant failed to take advantage of this "last clear chance" to avoid hurting the plaintiff.

Effect of Last Clear Chance

Last clear chance nullifies the contributory negligence defense. In other words, the defendant cannot escape liability for his or her negligence (by invoking the contributory negligence defense) if the defendant had the last clear chance to avoid the injury.

An example should clarify the concept. Consider the preceding speeding/stop sign hypothetical. Recall that the defendant (the other driver) was negligent in running the stop sign. However, Zelda (the plaintiff) was contributorily negligent in speeding. Nevertheless, the defendant had the last clear chance to avoid crashing into Zelda's vehicle—a reasonable person would have slowed while approaching the stop sign and seen Zelda's rapidly approaching vehicle. Because Zelda had the right-of-way, she was not as likely to anticipate oncoming traffic as was the other driver, as he or she approached the stop sign. The defendant should have been going slower than Zelda and should have been able to stop more quickly and easily than Zelda. This was the defendant's last clear chance to avert the collision.

TERMS

last clear chance doctrine   A rule of negligence law by which a negligent defendant is held liable to a plaintiff who has negligently placed himself or herself in peril, if the defendant had a later opportunity than the plaintiff to avoid the occurrence that resulted in injury. In some jurisdictions, the doctrine is referred to as the *discovered peril doctrine* and in others as the *humanitarian doctrine*.

HYPOTHETICAL

Alfred Peddlemore owns the Peddlemore Moving Company. Midge Hargrade packed several boxes of books. The boxes were marked "garden supplies" in clear, black block letters. Alfred arrived to load the boxes into the company van. Because of an estimation error, there was insufficient room in the van for all of Midge's furniture. Alfred decided to haul the remaining boxes in an open pickup truck. He selected items that would not be harmed if they got wet, including the boxes marked "garden supplies." He did not know that they actually contained books. While Alfred drove across town, a thunderstorm flooded the back of the pickup, destroying the texts.

Alfred was negligent in failing to safeguard all of Midge's property by moving it in an enclosed vehicle. He breached his duty of reasonable care to move the property safely. All of the elements of negligence appear to be satisfied. However, Alfred can use contributory negligence as a defense, because Midge mismarked the boxes, and this mistake misled Alfred into loading the books into an open truck exposed to the elements. Midge was contributorily negligent by using the mislabelled boxes, which resulted in rain damage to her books. Nevertheless, Alfred had the last clear chance to avoid disaster. As a professional mover, he should have double-checked the contents of each box that Midge had loaded. The reasonable person, as a professional mover, would have assumed that customers often do not correctly mark boxes they pack themselves. This last opportunity to identify the labelling error would have prevented the book damage. Because he failed to avail himself of this last clear chance, Alfred cannot successfully plead the contributory negligence defense. Accordingly, Alfred's negligence would render him liable to Midge for the book damage.

Figure 5-1 summarizes the elements of contributory negligence and last clear chance.

FIGURE 5-1
Contributory negligence and last clear chance

Contributory Negligence	Last Clear Chance
Plaintiff's duty of reasonable care to himself or herself	Although plaintiff was contributorily negligent, defendant had the last reasonable opportunity to avoid harming plaintiff (as a consequence of defendant's negligence)
Plaintiff breaches duty	Nullifies contributory negligence defense
Plaintiff acts, or fails to act, which contributes to his or her injuries (causation and proximate cause)	Plaintiff uses last clear chance to respond to defendant's use of contributory negligence defense
Plaintiff is injured	

The Case of the Un-Easy Rider

Negligence is contagious. Those around a careless person sometimes find themselves infected by carefree, irresponsible attitudes. As a result, it is occasionally difficult to determine the degree to which each party is at fault.

The old contributory negligence defense made no effort to apportion fault. It simply and arbitrarily torpedoed the plaintiff's action if he or she were the least bit at fault for his or her injuries. As § 5.4 discusses, comparative negligence attempts to resolve this unfairness. The following case discusses last clear chance and contributory and comparative negligence, as modified by Arizona statute.

DYKEMAN v. ENGLEBRECHT
Court of Appeals of Arizona
166 Ariz. 398, 803 P.2d 119 (1990)
August 16, 1990
Voss, Presiding Judge

Appellant/Plaintiff Heidi Leigh Dykeman appeals from a jury verdict finding her 60 percent at fault and apportioning damages accordingly. She raises the following issue on appeal:

Did the trial court err by refusing to instruct the jury on the last clear chance doctrine?

* * *

Plaintiff, a passenger on a motorcycle driven by defendant, was injured when the motorcycle hit a curb during a turn. Defendant contended that plaintiff jerked and improperly shifted her weight during the turn, causing the accident. Both plaintiff and defendant had been drinking alcoholic beverages. It is undisputed that plaintiff was very intoxicated at the time of the accident, and that defendant had a blood alcohol content of .128 two hours after the accident.

* * *

Plaintiff contends that the trial court erred by refusing to give the jury an instruction regarding the last clear chance doctrine. She argues that defendant had the last clear chance to avoid the accident when he allowed her to get on the motorcycle in an inebriated condition. Defendant asserts that last clear chance is not applicable, and, in any event the doctrine was effectively abolished by the enactment of [Ariz. Rev. Stat.] § 12-2505, the comparative negligence statute in Arizona.

Prior to the enactment of Arizona's comparative negligence statute, a contributory negligence defense could preclude a plaintiff, whose own negligence contributed in any degree to his injury, from recovering from a negligent defendant. The last clear chance doctrine was judicially created to alleviate the harshness of the contributory negligence rule. Arizona recognized this doctrine. The doctrine provides that a contributorily negligent plaintiff may recover from a negligent defendant if:

1) The plaintiff could not have avoided the injury after he negligently subjected himself to risk of harm;
2) The defendant knew or should have known of the plaintiff's perilous situation; and,
3) The defendant had the last clear chance to avoid the harm by the exercise of reasonable care and failed to do so.

The doctrine has been criticized because of the confusion it creates in the law of torts.

In 1984 our state legislature enacted the Uniform Contribution Among Tortfeasors Act. This legislation established comparative negligence in Arizona. The statute provides:

[Ariz. Rev. Stat.] § 12-2505
The defense of contributory negligence or of assumption of risk is in all cases a question of fact and shall at all times be left to the jury. If the jury applies either defense, the claimant's action is not barred, but the full damages shall be reduced in proportion to the relative degree of the claimant's fault which is a proximate cause of the injury or death, if any.

Under this statute a negligent plaintiff is not prohibited from recovering from a negligent defendant; instead his award is reduced by the percentage of his own fault.

Plaintiff asserts that last clear chance remains a viable doctrine despite Arizona's adoption of comparative negligence. We disagree and agree with the jurisdictions that have found that the last clear chance doctrine is superfluous in a comparative negligence system.

The last clear chance doctrine was specifically created to enable a negligent plaintiff to recover from a negligent defendant in a contributory negligence system. However, its application in a comparative negligence system would directly contravene the intent of the statute because [last clear chance] provides complete recovery to a negligent plaintiff rather than apportioning recovery based upon degrees of fault. An instruction on the doctrine, then, would misstate the law and confuse the jury. ...

Additionally, the doctrine is unnecessary in a comparative negligence system. By definition, comparative negligence avoids the harshness inherent in an all-or-nothing contributory negligence system because it "distribute[s] responsibility, in proportion to the degree of fault attributable to the parties who have negligently caused an injury." A comparative negligence system, then, accomplishes the same result as the last clear chance doctrine as it enables a negligent plaintiff to recover from a negligent defendant. The trial court correctly refused the instruction.

* * *

Affirmed.

Case Questions

1. Which do you consider the more just doctrines: (a) contributory negligence and last clear chance, or (b) comparative negligence? Do you agree with this court's opinion? Explain.
2. Has your state adopted a statute similar to the Arizona statute discussed here?

Unfairness of Contributory Negligence

Is the common law theory of contributory negligence fair and just? Even if the defendant was 99 percent responsible for the plaintiff's injury, the plaintiff's 1 percent of contributory negligence completely barred the plaintiff's claim. Would it not be more logical for the defendant's liability to reflect his or her share of responsibility for the injury?

Many legal scholars and judges criticized the common law rule for much of the twentieth century. It seemed unduly harsh to the plaintiff, who might have been only marginally involved in injuring himself or herself. Also, it allowed the defendant, who might have been significantly responsible for the plaintiff's harm, to completely avoid liability.

Courts and legislatures have modified the common law rule by adopting comparative negligence theory, which is discussed in § 5.4. This defense avoids the unjust outcome in contributory negligence cases.

§ 5.4 Comparative Negligence

The comparative negligence defense has replaced contributory negligence in most states' common law or statutes. Primarily since the 1960s, courts and legislatures have adopted the defense as an alternative to the rigid, unfair results that contributory negligence often produced. The defense of comparative negligence enables the defendant's liability to be adjusted according to the extent of the plaintiff's contribution to his or her own injuries. **Comparative negligence** may be defined as a measurement and comparison of the plaintiff's and the defendant's negligence in causing the plaintiff's injuries.

Elements

The comparative negligence defense has three elements:
1. The plaintiff was negligent in contributing to his or her own injuries.
2. Calculation of the percentage of the plaintiff's negligence that contributed to his or her injuries.
3. Calculation of the percentage of the defendant's negligence that produced the plaintiff's injuries.

In some jurisdictions, a fourth element is included: the defendant must have been more negligent than the plaintiff.

The Balancing Act

Comparative negligence balances the degrees of each party's negligence that produced the plaintiff's harm. In effect, the plaintiff's and defendant's negligence are compared to see which was more responsible for causing injury. This comparative negligence balancing is typically

TERMS

comparative negligence The doctrine adopted by most states that requires a comparison of the negligence of the defendant with the negligence of the plaintiff: the greater the negligence of the defendant, the lesser the level of care required of the plaintiff to permit him or her to recover. In other words, the plaintiff's negligence does not defeat his or her cause of action, but it does reduce the damages he or she is entitled to recover. Also called *comparative fault.*

measured in percentages of negligence. This is sometimes called **culpability factoring** or **liability apportionment.**

For instance, consider the speeding/stop sign example discussed earlier in this chapter. The defendant ran a stop sign. This is more negligent than merely speeding, as the plaintiff's speeding alone would not have produced the accident. It took the greater negligence of the defendant (i.e., failing to stop at the sign) to cause the damage. The defendant was more negligent than the plaintiff in that example. But what percentages of negligence would be assigned to the plaintiff (for contributing to the injuries) and the defendant (for negligently causing the harm)? Well, the defendant was more than half responsible, so the defendant's percentage must be higher than 50 percent. What percentages would be used? Defendant 75 percent, plaintiff 25 percent? 60/40? 90/10?

Readers may find this approach frustrating. What are the correct percentages? There is no exact formula. It depends upon the facts of each case. Whatever percentages are selected, readers and triers-of-fact probably rely on intuition and gut feeling as much as anything.

Who Decides the Percentages

The trier-of-fact decides the percentages in comparative negligence. Thus, the jury (or judge, in a bench trial) must closely examine the facts and assign negligence percentages to the plaintiff and the defendant.

Why Calculate Percentages

Comparative negligence is used to calculate the amount of the defendant's liability to the plaintiff. Assume that the following percentages were selected for the speeding/stop sign problem: defendant 75 percent negligent, plaintiff 25 percent negligent. What would be the outcome of the case? The defendant would be liable to the plaintiff for 75 percent of the amount plaintiff received in damages. If the plaintiff recovered judgment against the defendant, receiving a $100,000 damages award, under this percentage the defendant would be liable for

═══════════════ **TERMS** ═══════════════

culpability factoring (liability apportionment) [†]   A defense to negligence. When the plaintiff's negligence contributed to his or her injuries, comparative negligence calculates the percentages of the defendant's and the plaintiff's negligence and adjusts the plaintiff's damages according to the numbers. The trier-of-fact decides the percentages.

$75,000, with $25,000 having been subtracted out for the plaintiff's comparative negligence.

The advantages of comparative negligence are immediately apparent. Instead of completely barring the plaintiff's recovery (as common law contributory negligence would have done), culpability factoring enables the plaintiff to recover damages for the defendant's share of responsibility in causing the injuries. Liability apportionment also protects the defendant from paying for the plaintiff's share in harming himself or herself. The result is a just and equitable outcome to the litigation. It allows a plaintiff to bring an action even though he or she is somewhat at fault.

Criticism of Comparative Negligence

Comparative negligence has been criticized for its arbitrary and capricious approach to assigning percentages of negligence. Critics complain that liability apportionment is imprecise and based entirely upon the emotional attitudes of the jury or judge. Think back to the speeding/stop sign illustration. If one disapproved of running stop signs more than speeding, would one not be more likely to raise the defendant's percentage of liability? Of course, juries are composed of several people, a fact that is intended to balance out such personal biases. Still, disapproval of comparative negligence continues in the legal literature and court opinions.

This attack on the defense is simplistic. Juries always decide the facts of each case based on their personal feelings and attitudes. Which witness does the jury believe? Which exhibit is most persuasive? Which attorney makes the best case presentation? Which party seems the most honest? Has the plaintiff proven the case by a preponderance of the evidence (sometimes called the "51 percent line")? These are all intuitive, subjective decisions with which triers-of-fact have wrestled for centuries. Using percentages in culpability factoring is no more arbitrary than any other factfinding process that juries and judges use everyday. Further, comparative negligence decides the lawsuit more fairly than contributory negligence ever could. The plaintiff recovers the extent of damages that the defendant was responsible for causing. This comports with one's sense of fair play.

HYPOTHETICAL

Ikeda Osaka manages and owns a hotel. Frances Borgioni is a guest. The smoke detector in Frances's room has a dead battery and does not function. None of

Ikeda's employees has checked the detector recently, despite a management protocol instructing maintenance to check batteries every month. The customer staying in the room next to Frances's smoked in bed and started a fire. Smoke poured under the door adjoining the two rooms, but the malfunctioning detector did not awaken Frances before the room became filled with smoke. Frances awoke, coughing, and stumbled to the hallway door. He could not get the door open, however, because he had placed his own safety lock on the door, and that lock jammed as he was trying to escape. Frances passed out from smoke inhalation and suffered severe burns. Fortunately, the fire department rescued him.

Frances sued Ikeda for negligently failing to maintain an operative smoke detector in the room. Ikeda responded that Frances had contributed to his own injuries by placing his own lock on the door, so that he could not escape. May Ikeda invoke the defense of comparative negligence?

Was Ikeda negligent in failing to maintain a functioning smoke detector in Frances's room? Analyze the facts and apply the elements of negligence. If one decides that Ikeda was negligent (which is arguably the correct answer), then the comparative negligence defense should next be considered. Apply its elements. Was Frances negligent in contributing to his own injuries? Frances breached his duty of reasonable care to himself by placing a defective lock on the door, which prevented his escape during the fire. But for this act, Frances could have escaped before passing out from the smoke. Frances was negligent in harming himself. Next, decide if Ikeda's negligence exceeded Frances's. Would Frances have been endangered by the smoke at all if the smoke detector had activated? This would have given Frances more time to escape the room before the smoke thickened and knocked him unconscious. Ikeda's negligence exceeded Frances's. Now use liability apportionment. What percentages would be assigned? Ikeda's must be at least 51 percent. 60/40? 70/30? 80/20? There is no single correct answer here. A juror must use his or her best judgment based upon the facts.

Figure 5-2 lists the elements of comparative negligence.

FIGURE 5-2
Comparative
negligence

Elements of Comparative Negligence
Plaintiff was negligent in contributing to his or her own injuries (defendant was also negligent in causing plaintiff's injuries)
Culpability factoring (liability apportionment): Calculate each party's percentage of negligence [How much did plaintiff contribute to his or her own injuries?] [How much was defendant responsible for plaintiff's harm?]
In some jurisdictions, defendant's percentage of negligence must be greater than plaintiff's percentage of negligence

§ 5.5 Assumption of Risk

Assumption of risk is another defense to negligence. **Assumption of risk** means that the plaintiff assumed the risk of doing (or not doing) something that resulted in his or her injuries. Assumption of risk involves (1) the plaintiff's voluntary assumption of a known risk (2) with a full appreciation of the dangers involved in facing that risk.

Voluntary Assumption of Known Risk

For the assumption-of-risk defense to insulate the defendant from negligence liability, the plaintiff must have voluntarily decided to engage in an activity that the plaintiff knew (or reasonably should have known) was dangerous. In other words, the plaintiff must willfully face a known risk.

For instance, suppose Gilda's employer orders her to carry stacked boxes down a long flight of stairs. Her employer specifically instructs her to carry all the boxes in a single trip. To do this, however, Gilda must hold the boxes in front of her, blocking her forward vision. She knows that it is dangerous to descend stairs when she cannot see where she is going. Gilda slips and falls because her right foot misses a step. She sues her employer for negligence. The employer alleges that Gilda assumed the risk. Did she? No. Gilda did not voluntarily assume the dangerous activity. In fact, she was coerced into carrying all the boxes in one trip. She would not have done so but for her employer's command. Thus, Gilda did not voluntarily assume the risk of falling down the stairway.

Suppose that Brian slipped on some liquid somebody had spilled on the stairway. Brian thought the stairs were clean and dry, because he had walked up them just a few minutes earlier. He was unaware of the new danger that had appeared to threaten his safety. Brian did not assume a known risk.

─────────────────── TERMS ───────────────────

assumption of risk The legal principle that a person who knows and deliberately exposes himself or herself to a danger assumes responsibility for the risk, rather than the person who actually created the danger. Assumption of risk is often referred to as *voluntary assumption of risk*. It is a defense to negligence.

Suppose that Gilda was carrying the boxes into a storeroom instead of down a stairway. The room was pitch black, and she knew that the ceiling light bulb was burned out. Nevertheless, she carried the boxes into the room in which she could not clearly see. Gilda stumbled over a mop and broom on the floor, and the boxes fell upon and injured her. Again, she sues her employer for negligence in failing to replace the burned-out bulb. Her employer replies that Gilda voluntarily assumed a known risk—she knew the bulb was burned out. Further, she knew that the room was so dark that it would take her eyes several minutes to adjust. Still, she entered the room despite the obvious danger that she could fall over invisible objects. Gilda assumed the risk in this version of the facts.

Full Appreciation of Danger

The plaintiff must fully understand the dangerous nature of the activity that he or she voluntarily undertakes. Suppose that Brett visits a friend's woods. He comes across a cavern and decides to explore it. He has no way of knowing that, higher above him, on a nearby hill, a highway construction crew is preparing to detonate dynamite. They explode a powerful charge, which sends a shock wave through the ground and causes part of the cavern walls to collapse, trapping Brett inside the cave. He sues the highway company for negligence in detonating excessively powerful explosives. Run through the negligence formula to determine if the company was negligent toward Brett, closely examining foreseeability of the injury and foreseeable plaintiffs theory. Presuming that the company acted negligently, it responds with the defense of assumption of risk.

Did Brett voluntarily assume a known risk with a full appreciation of the dangers involved? He willfully entered the cave. He knew (or reasonably should have known) that cavern walls sometimes fall in. That risk was known, but he had no way to anticipate the additional danger created by a forceful explosion. He did not fully appreciate this aspect of the risk in entering the cave. Arguably, the dynamite was also an unknown risk to him. Thus, the company's defense would fail.

The Complete Defense

Assumption of risk is a complete defense to negligence in some jurisdictions. Like common law contributory negligence, it totally bars the plaintiff's recovery. If the plaintiff assumed the risk, the defendant cannot be liable for negligence.

Assumption of the risk is commonly raised in spectator sport situations. There is a known risk that if you attend a baseball game, you might get hit by a fly ball. Likewise, observers of speed car races or demolition derbies might get hit by a car or piece of equipment hurled into the air. A spectator assumes these risks with full appreciation of the dangers and thus is barred from bringing suit as a result of any injuries sustained. Contrast the situation in which bleachers collapse at a football stadium. Seats caving in is not a known or foreseeable risk, nor could the dangers be appreciated. Thus, in this case, assumption of the risk would not apply and suit would be allowed.

The Case of Treading on Thin Ice

When plaintiffs and defendants share a negligent experience, it is inevitable that the defendants will argue assumption of risk. Because the plaintiff volunteered to share the dangers, he or she should not recover, says the defendant. As the following case illustrates, this argument, like the litigants, sometimes treads upon thin ice.

THOMPSON v. HILL
Minnesota Court of Appeals
366 N.W.2d 628 (Minn. Ct. App. 1985)
April 23, 1985
Hierengarten, J.

Respondent Juli-Ann Thompson commenced suit against appellant Douglas Hill under Minn. Stat. § 573.02 for the wrongful death of her husband, Dennis Ray Thompson. The case was bifurcated with the issues of liability and damages tried separately. The jury first returned a verdict finding Hill 60% negligent and [Dennis Ray] Thompson (decedent) 40% negligent. The jury subsequently returned a verdict assessing Juli-Ann's damages at $318,000. As a surviving spouse, Juli-Ann received no-fault benefits totalling $27,500. The trial court deducted this sum from Thompson's recovery after reducing the jury award by the 40% [comparative] negligence attributed to decedent.

The trial court denied Hill's motion for judgment N.O.V., or, in the alternative, for a new trial. Judgment was entered on August 6, 1984. We affirm.

FACTS

Dennis Thompson drowned when the vehicle in which he and Douglas Hill were riding broke through the ice of the Mississippi River near Winona, Minnesota. Hill, a close friend and employee of the Thompsons, was driving an automobile owned by Thompson at the time of the accident.

Thompson and Hill had been friends for nearly three years prior to the accident. They had spent a lot of time together, including fishing on the Mississippi River.

During the morning of February 2, Hill and Thompson ran several errands when Thompson asked Hill to drive. The two then ran a few more errands before they headed back to the Thompson home.

As they passed Lake Winona, Hill spotted several fish houses and suggested that they take a closer look. There were several other vehicles on the lake so they proceeded to drive onto the ice. They spent no more than 15 minutes driving around before exiting the lake at the point at which they had entered.

Sometime later, Thompson commented that he wanted to go look at the boathouse located on the Mississippi. He told Hill to head towards the river and Hill selected the route. They proceeded onto the ice, which appeared the same as Lake Winona. Neither Hill nor Thompson made an effort to determine the thickness of the ice nor did they make a complete stop before proceeding.

They then headed diagonally upstream when they noticed steam rising from the river.

Thompson commented that steam meant open water and told Hill to turn around. Hill turned around and headed downstream. After travelling a short distance, Hill noticed that there were no other tracks on the river and that he "didn't like that" and "felt uncomfortable" so he suggested that they "should turn around." Before he could head towards shore, there was "a loud cracking or crumbling sound" and the front of the auto began to sink.

Hill escaped through the back tailgate of the jeepster and heard Thompson splashing behind him. Hill attempted to grab Thompson but he lost his hold and Thompson went under the ice.

ISSUES

1. Was there a primary assumption of the risk which would preclude a finding of negligence on the part of Hill?
2. Were Thompson and Hill engaged in a joint enterprise, thereby imputing Hill's negligence to Thompson?
3. Did the trial court err when it denied Hill's request for an instruction on the doctrine of secondary assumption of risk?
4. Did the trial court err when it deducted the no-fault benefits paid to Juli-Ann after it reduced the verdict by the percentage of negligence attributed to Thompson?

ANALYSIS

Hill argues he was entitled to judgment notwithstanding the verdict because the doctrine of primary assumption of risk precludes a finding of negligence on his part. Primary assumption of risk is an absolute bar to the plaintiff's recovery. "Primary assumption of the risk * * * indicates that the defendant did not even owe the plaintiff any duty of care." If Hill owed no duty to Thompson, there was no negligence.

The doctrine does not apply because Hill, as the driver, owed Thompson certain duties of reasonable care while driving on the river ice. Hill owed his passenger "the duty to operate the car with reasonable care so that the danger of riding in it is not increased or a new danger added to those assumed when the guest entered the car."

Although Thompson assumed certain risks when he and Hill proceeded onto the ice, Hill was not relieved of his duties as the driver to use reasonable care, including proper lookout for dangers incident to driving on river ice. The jury could reasonably have found Hill breached his duty. First, after they spotted the steam rising from the river, Hill was negligent in not immediately driving off of the ice towards shore. Second, the area in which they were travelling did not contain any tracks which, in itself, should warn a driver that the ice might be thin or unsafe.

The law is well settled in this jurisdiction that in examining a verdict on appeal the evidence must be considered in the light most favorable to the prevailing party and the verdict must be sustained if it is possible to do so on any reasonable theory of evidence. The verdict should not be disturbed unless it is manifestly and palpably contrary to the evidence. Based on all of the evidence, the jury could find that it was negligent for Hill to continue driving on the ice.

* * *

A passenger in a motor vehicle has a duty to use that care which a reasonable person riding as a passenger would use under like circumstances. It is the duty of the passenger to exercise reasonable care for his own safety. A passenger has a duty to take active measures to protect himself from danger only when it is apparent to him that he can no longer rely upon the driver for protection, as when the driver by his conduct shows that he is incompetent to drive or the driver is unmindful of or does not know of a danger known to the passenger, and then only if the passenger becomes aware of the danger at the time and under circumstances when he could have prevented the harm.

* * *

[S]econdary assumption of risk [is] defined ... as follows:

Assumption of risk is voluntarily placing (oneself) (one's property) in a position to chance known hazards. To find that a person assumed the risk you must find:

1. That he had knowledge of the risk.

2. That he appreciated the risk.
3. That he had a choice to avoid the risk or chance it and voluntarily chose to chance it.

In light of our comparative negligence statute, Minn. Stat. § 604.01, secondary assumption of risk is no longer a complete bar to the plaintiff's recovery. Instead, it is an aspect of contributory negligence. ... [C]ontributory negligence and secondary assumption of risk were merged.

[W]here a defendant has a duty to exercise ordinary care, that plaintiff's "secondary, express or implied" assumption of risk, as distinguished from "primary" assumption of risk, becomes part of the defense of contributory negligence and is to be measured under the comparative negligence statute, Minn. St[at.§] 604.01.

"Fault," as used in our comparative fault statute, "includes breach of warranty, unreasonable assumption of risk not constituting an express consent, misuse of a product and unreasonable failure to avoid an injury or to mitigate damages." Minn. Stat. § 604.01, subd. 1a (1982).

An instruction on assumption of risk would have focused the jury's attention on Thompson's comparative negligence and prejudiced plaintiff. The instruction would have also forced the jury to apportion fault to Thompson under both the general fault instruction and under the assumption of risk instruction. The jury would have been needlessly confused. Improper submission of secondary assumption of risk to the jury is reversible error. Based on the facts of this case, it would have been improper to submit the issue of assumption of risk to the jury.

* * *

DECISION
The doctrine of primary assumption of risk does not apply because the driver owed his passenger certain duties of reasonable care while driving on the ice of the Mississippi River.

* * *

A separate instruction on secondary assumption of risk would have needlessly confused the jury.

* * *

Affirmed.

Case Questions

1. In *Thompson*, the Minnesota Court of Appeals distinguished between primary and secondary assumption of risk. Notice how primary assumption of risk focuses upon whether the defendant owed a duty of reasonable care to the plaintiff. Does this simply return to the original question of the defendant's negligence? Is this actually a defense at all?
2. How is the *Thompson* court's definition of secondary assumption of risk similar to the assumption of risk definition discussed in this chapter? How has this defense been changed by the Minnesota comparative negligence statute? Does the statute merely merge the defense into culpability factoring? Explain.
3. Review the *Thompson* jury's comparative negligence percentages, as noted at the beginning of the opinion. Do you agree with the figures, based upon the facts given in the case? Why or why not? What percentages would you have assigned? Explain.

Assumption of risk is somewhat more difficult to establish than contributory or comparative negligence. The following example demonstrates how the elements must be carefully considered.

HYPOTHETICAL

Erving Tanford owns East of Tansmania, a tanning salon. Elizabeth Bundy is one of Tanford's customers. She has been visiting the salon twice a week for ten years. She always uses the same tanning bed. Because of faulty equipment, Elizabeth was exposed during each session to five times more ultraviolet radiation than is normally emitted by tanning equipment. Elizabeth was diagnosed with skin cancer. She sues Tanford for subjecting her to excessively intense ultraviolet light, which is a powerful carcinogen. Tanford was negligent in exposing Elizabeth to such extremely high doses of ultraviolet radiation. Can he offer assumption of risk as a defense?

Did Elizabeth voluntarily assume a known risk with a full appreciation of the dangerous consequences? Clearly, she willfully visited the salon twice weekly for ten years. She chose to use the same bed each time. She knew (or reasonably should have known) that ultraviolet radiation is carcinogenic. But did she fully understand the danger? Did she realize that the equipment emitted five times more radiation than normal? Could she have known about this aspect of the threat? Not likely. Accordingly, she did not assume the risk, and the defense would not protect Tanford from liability.

Suppose a warning were posted above the tanning bed that Elizabeth used, declaring, "DANGER! EMITS EXCESSIVE ULTRAVIOLET LIGHT. USE AT YOUR OWN RISK." Now Elizabeth would have been alerted to the threatening condition. She would have a full appreciation of the dangers involved in using the equipment. Under this version of the facts, Elizabeth would have assumed the risk, and Tanford would not be liable for negligence.

Figure 5-3 outlines the elements of assumption of risk.

§ 5.6 Statutes of Limitations

Statutes of limitations are statutes restricting the time within which a plaintiff may file a lawsuit for particular causes of action against a defendant. (In some jurisdictions, these statutes are called *limitations of*

TERMS

statutes of limitations   Federal and state statutes prescribing the maximum period of time during which various types of civil actions and criminal prosecutions can be brought after the occurrence of the injury or the offense.

Elements of Assumption of Risk
Plaintiff voluntarily assumes a known risk
Plaintiff fully appreciates the dangers involved in facing the risk

FIGURE 5-3
Assumption of risk

actions.) There are also such statutes for negligence actions. Many of these statutes specify that various negligence lawsuits must be filed within two years of the negligent acts giving rise to the plaintiff's claims.

States' statutes of limitations vary in numbers of years and among the different types of negligence. The period for medical malpractice claims, for instance, may be two years in one state and three years in another. Similarly, lawsuits involving premises liability may have one-year statutes of limitations in one state and three-year statutes in another. One should become familiar with the specific statutes of limitations in one's own state for the various types of negligence causes of action.

Note that the statute of limitations is one of the few areas in the practice of law for which there is no remedy if one misses the deadline. Generally, there are provisions throughout the various civil practice acts that allow attorneys to amend, change, supplement pleadings, and remedy oversights in their handling of a case. Should a statute of limitations run out, though—no matter what the reason—judges are powerless to help you. Consequently, this is one of the areas in the practice of law in which malpractice claims most frequently arise.

To obtain malpractice insurance, attorneys must assure the malpractice insurance carrier that they have a reliable calendaring system. In fact, backup systems for recording important dates and deadlines are often required as well. Frequently, a paralegal is called upon to maintain a diary system and keep members of the firm alerted to approaching deadlines and dates. In addition, some firms automatically have all files pulled for review every three months, six months, and yearly to ensure that the cases are not being neglected.

Practical Applications

Figure 5-4 shows two typical statutes of limitations for negligence actions.

Two-Year Statute of Limitations (with three-year absolute limit for injuries not discovered within two years)	*Three-Year Statute of Limitations*
Connecticut General Statutes Annotated § 52-581 (West 1991): No action to recover damages for injury to the person, or to real or personal property, caused by negligence, or by reckless or wanton misconduct, or by malpractice of a physician, surgeon, dentist, podiatrist, chiropractor, hospital or sanatorium, shall be brought but within two years from the date when the injury is first sustained or discovered or in the exercise of reasonable care should have been discovered, and except that no such action may be brought more than three years from the date of the act or omission complained of, except [for counterclaims].	New York Civil Practice Law & Rules § 214 (McKinney 1992): The following actions must be commenced within three years: * * * 5. an action to recover damages for a personal injury except as provided in sections 214-b, 214-c and 215; . . . [providing special rules concerning specific torts and time injury was detected]

Summary

Negligence defenses are used only by the defendant against the plaintiff. The defenses are applied only in response to the plaintiff's allegations that the defendant acted negligently. To determine which party uses negligence defenses, one should ask who is alleging negligence and who is alleged to have been negligent.

Contributory negligence is the plaintiff's negligence that contributed to his or her own injuries. The plaintiff was negligent toward himself or herself and caused (in whole or in part) the harm. This defense exonerates the defendant whose negligence harmed the plaintiff. At common law, any amount of contributory negligence by the plaintiff, however small, would bar the plaintiff's recovery against the negligent defendant. Critics have argued that this defense is unreasonably harsh, in that a defendant who was overwhelmingly responsible for hurting the plaintiff might still avoid liability because of the plaintiff's minuscule contributory negligence. Last clear chance is the plaintiff's response to the contributory negligence defense. Last clear chance means that, although the plaintiff was contributorily negligent, the defendant still had the last opportunity to avoid harming the plaintiff. Last clear chance nullifies the contributory negligence defense.

Comparative negligence is an alternative defense that has largely replaced contributory negligence in both the common law and statute. Comparative negligence measures and compares the negligence of both the plaintiff and the defendant. This allows the trier-of-fact to adjust the plaintiff's recovery to reflect more accurately each party's degree of negligence in causing the harm. The calculation is often in percentages of negligence. This is sometimes called culpability factoring or liability apportionment. These percentages are based entirely upon the trier-of-fact's subjective opinion regarding the specific facts of each case. Critics have criticized the defense for this uncertainty.

Assumption of risk is another negligence defense. It states that the plaintiff voluntarily assumed a known risk with full appreciation of the dangers involved. Like contributory negligence, assumption of risk is a complete defense to negligence. In other words, it totally excuses the defendant's negligence and erases the defendant's liability to the plaintiff.

Most state statutes of limitations restrict the time period within which a plaintiff may file a negligence cause of action against a defendant. In most states, these are two-year statutes, meaning that a plaintiff has two years from the date that the negligent act was committed within which to file a lawsuit against the tortfeasor. It is vital to research the specific statutes of limitations for each particular tort.

Review Questions

1. How are negligence defenses used? Which party uses them? Against whom are the defenses used? What is the purpose of negligence defenses?

2. Define contributory negligence. What are its elements? What is the common law rule? Why is it a particularly effective defense?

3. Explain last clear chance. How is it used? Who uses it against whom? What is its importance to contributory negligence?

4. Why is the contributory negligence defense unfair? What changes have courts and legislatures made to create a more equitable defense? What is this defense called?

5. Define comparative negligence. What are its elements? What is culpability factoring? Liability apportionment? Why are percentages used? Who decides these percentages? Is this defense more fair than contributory negligence? Why or why not?

6. What is assumption of risk? List its elements. Who uses the defense against whom? Must the risk be voluntarily assumed? What is "full appreciation of danger" and why is it significant? How effective is this defense in avoiding the defendant's liability?

7. What are statutes of limitations? What time period is most commonly allowed for negligence causes of action? How can limitations statutes be used as a defense to negligence?

Projects

1. Does your state have one (or more) comparative negligence statutes? Have the courts in your state modified the common law contributory negligence or assumption of risk defenses?

2. In class or study groups, create your own hypotheticals using the negligence defenses discussed in this chapter. Then change the facts to alter the outcomes of the problems.

3. An elevator does not level properly and stops five inches above the floor of a building. A man hurriedly enters the elevator without looking and trips on the threshold. What percentage of liability do you think the jury might apportion between the owner of the elevator and the man who tripped? Explain.

IIII
CHAPTER 6

INTENTIONAL TORTS: INJURIES TO PERSONS

> *When you have the facts on your side, argue the facts. When you have the law on your side, argue the law. When you have neither, holler.*
> — *Albert Gore, Jr.*

§ 6.1 Intentional Torts in General

Generally, a person has a right to be free of threats and actual contact that injures or offends him or her. Therefore, one has a duty not to intentionally injure, offensively touch, or threaten other people.

Intentional torts consist of conduct that is fashioned to harm another person or his or her property. The mischief is directed with the purpose of inflicting injury. All intentional torts include three elements: act, intent, and injurious behavior. **Intent** may be broadly defined as the desire to achieve a particular result. Specifically, the tortfeasor must intend to accomplish the harmful consequences of his or her actions. This does not require malice or ill will, however; the tortfeasor must simply intend to cause the consequences that give rise to the tort or the tortfeasor must know with substantial certainty that certain consequences would result from that act. Commonly, though, those consequences include some type of harm. Then these acts must actually conclude in the injury that was intended.

For certain peculiar intentional torts, intent, strictly speaking, is not required. For example, for reckless infliction of emotional distress, intent is not essential. The tortfeasor need only know (or reasonably

<hr>

TERMS

intentional injury (tort) An injury inflicted by positive, willful, and aggressive conduct, or by design, as opposed to an injury caused by negligence or resulting from an accident.

intent Purpose; the plan, course, or means a person conceives to achieve a certain result. Intent is an essential element of any crime except a strict liability crime or a regulatory offense, and some petty offenses and infractions. Intent is not, however, limited to conscious wrongdoing, and may be inferred or presumed.

should know) that his or her outlandish or outrageous actions will produce emotional injury. This knowledge element acts as a substitute for intent.

Intentional torts involve intentional acts, and as such carry a high degree of risk of injury, and usually a low degree of social benefit. The risk generally greatly outweighs the benefit received. Therefore, the duty not to intentionally injure someone or something is great.

Intent and Action Together

Intent reflects the tortfeasor's state of mind and must occur simultaneously with the misconduct. For example, assume that David and Steven are carpenters. Steven tosses a piece of wood across a room into a pile, but before it lands the wood strikes David in the throat. Steven would not be liable for battery, because, although the board struck David, Steven did not intend this to happen. Suppose David thought about throwing the board back at Steven, but did nothing and walked away. David would not be liable for assault because no action accompanied his desire.

Intentional torts present a relatively black-and-white image of the law, in which it is fairly easy to distinguish the "good" person from the "bad." The victim seems truly exploited, and the tortfeasor is clearly responsible and to blame (from a moral or ethical point of view) for having purposefully injured the victim. Our sense of fair play is rewarded when intentional tortfeasors are held accountable for their mischief.

Crimes versus Torts

It is important to note that a single act can be the basis for both a tort and a criminal action. Both crimes and torts involve wrongs. A *crime* is considered a wrong against the state or society as a whole, in addition to the actual victim. Therefore, the state brings actions against alleged criminals. With tort actions, one person brings suit against another individual; the action is brought by a private attorney on behalf of the injured party. Thus, a tort is considered a civil action.

Suppose that a person is walking down the street at night. Another person comes up to him, aims a gun, and then shoots the pedestrian. In this situation both an assault and a battery have occurred. The pedestrian was first put in fear of harm and then actually harmed. As a result of the same act, the attacker may face both criminal and civil prosecution. The state may seek criminal damages against the attacker. In addition,

---

| | PROFESSIONAL PROFILE | |

Cheryl Katz graduated from her state university with a B.A. in English. Raised in a small town, Katz was anxious to move to New York City to find work. "I was thinking about going to law school, so I wanted to work in the legal field first and learn more about it." She says, "The most interesting positions I had were as a legal assistant handling car accident cases for a two-attorney firm in New York and as a paralegal for a supermarket chain that had its own in-house law department and was self-insured. I learned to be a paralegal through on-the-job training with direct attorney supervision and instruction."

Katz recalls, "I responded to an ad in the *New York Law Journal* for my first job as a legal assistant. They wanted someone without experience who could be trained in their own office procedures. The firm offered tuition reimbursement, which made the position particularly attractive. While the responsibilities and deadlines were similar to those for the attorneys, I was excited to accept the offer."

Initially, the job as a legal assistant in New York was very secretarial. "My duties included typing, filing, and photocopying, as well as making coffee! But my employer was very supportive and anxious to educate his employees to handle car accident cases.

"Many times I made the commute to and from Manhattan while listening to cassettes from a local bar association on the fine points of managing personal injury cases or reading articles on the merits of structured settlements. While working in this office, I developed what I believe is the necessary quality for a paralegal: attention to detail. I learned to be exacting, proofread, keep diaries, and make checklists. This skill has served me well in all my subsequent work. When I finally left the office, my job responsibilities had grown to drafting pleadings, preparing settlement documents, and assisting in preparation for trial," Katz says.

As a paralegal at a large supermarket chain, Katz oversaw all aspects of the law department. She reported directly to the managing attorney and supervised four other paralegals. Typically, the office handled 100 suits per month. Katz says, "My duties included ordering supplies, supervising investigations, reviewing claims and accident reports, plotting trial strategies, and working with the attorneys. I also established a catalog system for closed files, handled releases, produced weekly status reports, and charted the volume of files flowing in and out of the office. I basically dealt exclusively with people who had accident claims."

---

the injured party may proceed with a civil action to be reimbursed for injuries caused as a result of the attack.

§ 6.2 Assault and Battery

The preceding example of the careless carpenters depicts two of the most common intentional torts: assault and battery. Of all torts, these are perhaps the most straightforward.

Assault Defined

Assault is an attempt by one person to make harmful or offensive contact with another individual without consent. Actual physical contact is not necessary; in fact, contact converts an assault to a battery. Assault is distinguishable from battery in that no touching is required.

Freedom from Apprehension

The rights being protected by recognition of this tort involve each person's right to control what touches his or her person. The tort of assault is also intended to protect individuals from the fear or apprehension that unconsented contact will take place. **Apprehension** means that a person reasonably fears for his or her physical safety in anticipation of being struck by the unconsented harmful or distasteful contact. This apprehension must be *reasonable,* meaning that the anxiety must be rational given the perceived threat of contact. For example, if a four-year-old warns that she is going to punch her father's head off, her father probably would not be overly concerned, as it would be unreasonable for an adult to fear a child's threatened battery under such circumstances. Threats at a distance do not present sufficient reason for alarm because it is physically impossible for the threatening party to fulfill the threat. This states the next legal requirement for assault: immediate threat of contact.

Imminent Threat of Contact

Assault involves the imminent or immediate threat that unconsented contact is about to occur. The fear arises from the likelihood that someone or something unwanted is about to strike. For instance, Michelle's threat to hit George while talking to him on the telephone does not present an immediate risk, as the task cannot be completed at the time the threat was made. Therefore, no assault has taken place.

Examples should illustrate these elements. Although assault is a fairly straightforward tort, its elements may best be explored hypothetically.

TERMS

assault   An act of force or threat of force intended to inflict harm upon a person or to put the person in fear that such harm is imminent; an attempt to commit a battery. The perpetrator must have, or appear to have, the present ability to carry out the act.

apprehension   ... Anxiety.

The Case of the Crazy Trucker

Assault involves more than just an errant punch or kick. The imminent threat of battery can occur through an object that the tortfeasor directs at the victim. An example is a thrown rock that misses the victim. An assault occurred if the victim was placed in reasonable apprehension of being struck by the approaching stone.

In the following case, note how the "insane" truck driver commits assault against the plaintiffs through his reckless driving.

ROSENBERG

v.

PACKERLAND PACKING CO.
Appellate Court of Illinois
55 Ill. App. 3d 959, 370 N.E.2d 1235 (1977)
December 13, 1977
Pusateri, Justice

In this consolidated appeal, we are concerned with whether each count of plaintiffs' ... complaint states a cause of action. ... [P]laintiffs-appellants appeal from the dismissal of Counts I and III of their complaint for failure to state a cause of action. ... [P]laintiffs ... alleged that an agent, servant, or lessee of defendant Packerland Packing Co. controlled its tractor and trailer, which defendant owned and operated as an interstate common carrier, in such a manner as to come within two feet of plaintiffs' vehicle at speeds of seventy to eighty miles per hour, and even after signalling by the plaintiffs that said truck should pass them, the unknown operator of defendant's truck continued to make feints at the rear of plaintiffs' vehicle as if he were going

to strike the plaintiffs' vehicle, all of this occurring over a "long span of time." It was alleged that the date of the occurrence was March 9, 1975, that the place of occurrence was I-94 in Lake County, Illinois, and that both vehicles were proceeding in a southerly direction. ... [Plaintiffs alleged that the truck driver] was probably insane.

Count II alleged that the truck driver's conduct constituted the intentional infliction of emotional distress and an intentional assault, and that defendant Packerland was liable ... .

[W]e believe the conduct alleged in Count II may constitute the intentional tort of assault. An assault is a reasonable apprehension of an imminent battery.

* * *

We affirm the trial court's ruling that Count II of the complaint states a valid cause of action and reverse the dismissal of Count III. The cause is remanded for further proceedings.

Affirmed in part, reversed in part, and remanded.

Case Questions

1. What specific actions did the defendant's truck driver engage in that constituted assault?
2. What if the driver's truck had touched the plaintiffs' vehicle? What additional intentional tort would then have occurred?
3. The court's discussion of the intentional infliction of emotional distress claim was omitted here. You may wish to look up the full opinion and compare the Illinois common law elements with those discussed in § 6.4.

HYPOTHETICALS

Palmer and Davis begin arguing in a bar. Palmer balls up his fists and pulls his arm backward as if to swing at Davis. Davis ducks in anticipation of a punch. Has Palmer committed assault?

Applying the legal elements of assault, as previously discussed (which are (1) the tortfeasor's attempt to make unconsented harmful or offensive contact, which (2) makes the victim apprehensive for his or her physical safety, and (3) the threat of contact is imminent), it is clear that Palmer has assaulted Davis. Palmer attempted to touch Davis in a harmful or offensive manner when he drew his arm back to swing. Davis did not consent to this action and feared for his safety, as is obvious because he ducked, expecting to be pelted with Palmer's fist. The danger of contact was immediate, as Palmer could complete his swing and punch within a matter of seconds.

■ ■ ■

Consider another example. Morrison and Fleetly are playing basketball in a gymnasium. Fleetly yells that Morrison stepped out of bounds as he dribbled the ball upcourt. Morrison smiles and fakes a forceful pass to Fleetly's head, causing Fleetly to flinch in anticipation that the ball will hit him in the face. Has Morrison committed assault?

Consent is the key to this hypothetical. Morrison and Fleetly had agreed to play basketball together. It is well known that sports activities such as this involve a certain degree of incidental contact to which participants consent. This could involve being struck by the ball as it is deliberately passed from one player to another. Because Fleetly implicitly agreed in advance to such types of contact while playing the game, Morrison did not assault him.

All elements must exist for assault to occur. If any one feature is absent, then there is no assault. For instance, suppose in the first illustration that Davis had not reacted at all to Palmer's arm gesture. Perhaps Palmer and Davis often indulged in horseplay, such as by pantomiming fist fights, and so Davis assumed that it was just another joking episode. That would remove the apprehension element and thus there would be no assault. Suppose in the second example that Morrison simply threw the ball down and shouted at Fleetly, "Next time you call me a liar, I'll plant this right upside your head!" In that case, the threatened contact would not be imminent, as Morrison warned only of behavior at some unspecified future time, which might in fact never take place. Accordingly, no assault would have happened.

Battery Defined

A completed assault is called a battery. Strictly defined, a **battery** is the intentional, unconsented touching of another person in an offensive or injurious manner. There are three basic elements to this tort:

TERMS

battery   The unconsented-to touching or striking of one person by another, or by an object put in motion by [the first person], with the intention of doing harm or giving offense. Battery is both a crime and a tort.

1. Unconsented physical contact
2. Offensive or harmful contact
3. The tortfeasor's intent to touch another person in an offensive or injurious manner.

Physical Contact Required

Actual touching is necessary for a battery to occur. However, contact need not be made with a person's body. It is sufficient for the tortfeasor to touch the victim's clothing, or an object that the victim is carrying, such as a purse, or an object in which the victim is sitting, such as a chair or automobile. These items are said to become *extensions* of the person which, if touched, translates into touching the person himself or herself.

Lack of Consent

Battery occurs only if the victim did not consent to the physical contact. Consent can be *expressed* or *implied*. Expressed consent is relatively easy to identify. For example, participants in sporting events readily consent to physical contact routinely associated with the activity. Implied consent arises out of particular situations, in which individuals, by being involved, implicitly agree to some types of minor contact. For instance, people walking in crowds impliedly consent to incidental contact as they accidentally bump into passersby. It is reasonable and normal to expect that this will occur in crowded places, and those involved are (or should be) willing to tolerate some minor jostles.

Harmful or Offensive Contact

Battery requires touching that is harmful or offensive. Although harmful contact should be relatively simple to perceive, offensive touching may present some surprises. Often, offensive contact may be intended as positive or complimentary, such as a pat on the back or kiss on the cheek from a co-worker. The recipient, however, may find these actions distasteful. This addresses the consent issue. People do not usually consent to touching that repulses them.

Whether or not the physical contact is offensive is judged by a **reasonable person standard**. Would a reasonable person have been insulted

---

TERMS

reasonable man (person) test (standard) A standard for determining negligence, which asks: "What would a reasonable person have done in the by the contact, given the same or similar circumstances? Reasonableness is often based upon the victim's actions in conjunction with the tortfeasor's. For example, if two co-workers are accustomed to "goofing around" by jokingly touching one another (pats on the back, fake punches, tickling, etc.), then such behavior would not be reasonably offensive. In effect, the participants consented to the activity. In contrast, a male supervisor touching a female employee in a sexually explicit fashion could reasonably be perceived as degrading and offensive.

Intent

Like all intentional torts, battery includes an element of intent. The tortfeasor must have intended to make contact with another individual in a harmful or offensive manner. Thus, accidentally bumping into someone in an elevator as it jerked into motion would not be a battery, because the contact was unintentional. But pinching that person while leaving the elevator would be battery, as the act was purposefully designed to make offensive contact.

Transferred Intent

Sometimes the tortfeasor tries to strike someone but ends up hitting someone else. For instance, if Robert threw a stone at Stuart but struck Mark instead, then Robert has committed battery against Mark. Although Robert intended to strike Stuart, his intent is said to be carried along by the object he set into motion—the stone—and his intent is thus transferred with the stone onto whomever it reaches—in this case, Mark. Note, too, that Robert has assaulted Stuart by throwing the stone and missing, provided that Stuart was placed in reasonable apprehension, and so on.

Transferred intent is an effective tool for protecting persons from misdirected physical contacts. It holds the tortfeasor accountable for the consequences of his or her actions even though, strictly speaking, he or she did not desire to hit the third person involved.

TERMS

same circumstances?" In short, it measures the failure to do that which a person of ordinary intelligence and judgment would have done in the circumstances, or the doing of that which a person of ordinary intelligence and judgment would not have done.

transferred intent The doctrine that if a defendant who intends to injure one person unintentionally harms another, the intent is transferred to the person who is unintentionally harmed. This doctrine permits the defendant to be prosecuted as if he or she had intended to harm the person injured.

The Case of the "Nuked" Plaintiff

Transferred intent is not restricted to objects one can hold in one's hand. Battery can occur if the tortfeasor contacts the victim with any offensive or harmful substance, such as liquids (acids) or toxic gases.

The following case demonstrates how radioactive gases caused a battery. The facts are supplied in great detail so that the reader may fully appreciate the horror of the defendant's alleged behavior and the apparent subsequent cover-up. In this case, the alleged conduct was deliberate, which makes the facts even more chilling.

FIELD
v.
PHILADELPHIA ELECTRIC CO.
Superior Court of Pennsylvania
388 Pa. Super. 400, 565 A.2d 1170 (1989)
September 12, 1989
Hester, Judge

This is an appeal from an April 29, 1988 order which granted appellees' demurrer to five counts of appellants' eight-count complaint. George and Dawn Field (appellants) instituted this action against Philadelphia Electric Co., Bartlett Nuclear, Inc., ... (appellees) to recover for injuries resulting from an alleged intentional exposure to high levels of radiation ... . [T]he trial court dismissed the counts of appellants' complaint which sought damages for intentional exposure to radiation ... and intentional infliction of emotional distress ... .

The trial court determined that: ... there was no common law cause of action for intentional exposure to radiation ... . We reverse and remand for proceedings consistent with this opinion.

Initially, we examine the facts upon which we base this adjudication. ...

Accordingly, for purposes of this appeal, we accept as true the following allegations, which are contained in appellants' complaint. George Field was employed by Bartlett Nuclear, Inc. ("Bartlett") and hired as an independent contractor by the Philadelphia Electric Co. ("PECO") to work at its Peach Bottom Nuclear Plant as a health physics technician. Bartlett is a corporation which provides personnel to manage operational problems at utilities which own and operate nuclear power plants. ...

On February 6, 1985, as a result of a plant shutdown, George Field was directed by PECO personnel to enter an off-gas pipe tunnel in unit three of Peach Bottom. He observed standing water on the floor of the tunnel and radioed to PECO personnel that he thought it unsafe to remain in the water. In response, he was ordered to test for radiation, which he did. After performing the tests, he returned from the tunnel and advised PECO personnel that the standing-water problem should not be resolved while the plant was being operated since it would be dangerous to work in the tunnel while the plant was operational.

Despite these warnings from Field, who was trained and hired in the area of safety control and cleanup, on March 1, 1985, while Peach Bottom was operating, PECO ordered Field and other personnel into the tunnel to resolve the standing-water situation. While Field was in the tunnel, PECO personnel deliberately vented radioactive gases into the tunnel where they knew Field was working. This action was taken in order to keep the reactor operating. The highly radioactive steam triggered a survey meter, a device in Field's possession that measures radiation levels. Field's survey meter went off-scale in the tunnel. As this indicates levels of radiation in excess of that permitted by the Nuclear Regulatory Commission ("NRC"), ... Field immediately directed all personnel to leave the tunnel. He was not aware why the radiation level increased at that time. Two radiation detectors, one located at the tunnel entrance and another located at the control point to the tunnel, both alarmed when Field passed through them. This also indicated radiation exposure in excess of that permitted by

NRC regulations. Field then analyzed air samples at the tunnel entrance with his survey meter, and the meter once again indicated radiation levels in excess of levels permitted by NRC regulations.

Field posted warning signs to the entrances to the contaminated areas, but PECO ordered the signs removed. Later that day, Field asked that his internal exposure to radiation be determined by equipment that was unavailable to him, but PECO refused the request and refused to answer his questions regarding the incident. ...

On March 4, 1985, Field discovered that the reactor operators on March 1, 1985, had deliberately ordered the radioactive steam to be bypassed from the regular system and vented into the tunnel where the operators knew Field was working. This action was taken solely to keep the reactor operational. Field asked three other PECO personnel about the level of his exposure; he was assured that the matter was being investigated, and he was ordered not to discuss the incident with anyone. ... In late July, Field was told by his supervisor that the investigation was complete and documentation regarding the event had been discarded. Field then told his supervisor that he was going to report the incident to the NRC. ...

At one point during Field's inquiries about the incident, PECO personnel made two false statements to Field. They told Field that his field badge indicated that he had not been exposed to radiation on March 1, 1985. They also told him that on March 1, 1985, his survey meter had given an incorrect reading regarding the level of radiation due to moisture in the instrument.

On August 8, 1985, Field again was ordered into the off-gas tunnel at unit three to perform work. He performed tests on the standing water which established that it contained such high levels of radiation that Field believed that he had been misinformed by PECO about the level of his exposure to radiation on March 1st. Later that day, Field demanded that water be retrieved from the tunnel for analysis.

In the meantime, on August 6 and 7, 1985, the NRC conducted an unannounced investigation. ...

On September 25, 1985, Field was terminated for alleged absenteeism. A subsequent NRC investigation of Field's termination led it to conclude that Field had been terminated because he had reported his overexposure to radiation to the NRC. ...

The next issue before us is whether count one of appellants' complaint, entitled tort of intentional exposure to radiation, states a cognizable cause of action. We conclude that it does. In the count, appellants allege that PECO deliberately exposed Field to radiation by operating the reactor knowing that Field would be exposed to dangerous levels of radiation and by deliberately venting radioactive steam on Field knowing his location. We believe this states a cause of action in battery. See Restatement (Second) of Torts § 18 comment c (intent to contact someone with offensive foreign substance constitutes contact for purposes of battery).

Barber v. Pittsburgh Corning Corp., 365 Pa. Super. 247, 529 A.2d 491 (1987), *rev'd on other grounds,* 521 Pa. 29, 555 A.2d 766 (1989), provides a dispositive analysis on whether an "intent" to cause harmful contact is present based on the allegations in appellants' complaint. ... We noted that intent in the context of tort litigation is defined to include the desire to bring about the likely consequences of an intentional act. ...

Instantly, the intent to contact is established by the deliberate venting of steam on Field, with knowledge of his whereabouts. Under *Barber,* the fact that PECO did not intend to harm Field is immaterial. If there is intentional contact, the consequences substantially certain to follow from such contact are within the scope of the tort. ... Accordingly, we conclude that count one states a cause of action in battery under Pennsylvania law.

* * *

In accordance with the foregoing, the order is reversed and the case is remanded for proceedings consistent with this opinion.

Case Questions

1. Although the court did not discuss the point, how does transferred intent apply in *Field?*
2. Did the court determine the defendant's intent to commit battery by exposing Field to radioactive steam? What was the court's rationale?
3. The court's discussion of the plaintiffs' intentional infliction of emotional distress claims was omitted here. You may wish to read the full opinion to compare Pennsylvania common law with the elements discussed in § 6.4.

Battery lends itself to a variety of boisterous hypotheticals. Consider the following examples.

HYPOTHETICALS

Helen is a production analyst for a local investment firm. She is one of only three women in the operation. Another analyst, Calvin, regularly flirts with her. Helen responds politely but coolly to these episodes. One day Calvin, while standing behind Helen, takes hold of her upper arms and leans over her shoulder as if to inspect the file she has before her on her desk. Calvin wisecracks about the "nice view," to which Helen responds by grimacing. Has Calvin committed battery against Helen?

The three basic elements of battery have been satisfied. Helen did not consent to Calvin's touching. Her previous encounters with Calvin did not establish a playful relationship in which she might have encouraged such actions; in fact, she expressly discouraged Calvin's flirting. A reasonable person would have found Calvin's behavior offensive. Helen was insulted by the contact, as evidenced by her expression. Calvin intended to touch Helen in the way she found distasteful. Accordingly, Calvin is liable to Helen for battery. If Calvin's behavior continues to be a problem, it might also be actionable as sexual harassment, which is discussed later in this chapter.

■ ■ ■

Consider another illustration. Shelley is a clerk at a hotdog stand in a football stadium. Phillip, a customer, purchased lunch from another clerk. Shelley thought Phillip unusually rude, so, as Phillip turned to walk away, Shelley threw Phillip a plastic catsup bottle, shouting that he had forgotten his condiments. The bottle brushed Phillip's jacket sleeve and caused him to spill his beverage onto his pants. The bottle then struck Iris in the head, covering her with catsup. Has Shelley committed battery against Phillip and Iris?

Again, the elements unfold clearly. Phillip did not consent to being touched. Shelley's intent to make contact transferred to the catsup bottle that struck Phillip's clothing, which was an extension of his person. Shelley's contact was harmful because it caused Phillip to spill his drink onto himself. Shelley purposefully touched

Phillip in a fashion that injured him. Furthermore, Shelley's intent to strike Phillip was transferred with the bottle, so that in hitting Iris, transferred intent applied. Shelley is liable to both Phillip and Iris for battery.

What if Shelley had been merely another spectator at the football game and, instead of throwing anything, had simply jostled Phillip, causing the spillage onto both Phillip and Iris, as they all were walking down the stairway to their seats? This would be considered incidental contact to which Shelley, Iris, and Phillip impliedly consented. Thus, no battery would have happened.

Figure 6-1 summarizes the elements of assault and battery.

Other intentional torts are less straightforward than assault and battery. False imprisonment poses particular wrinkles and is discussed in the next section.

FIGURE 6-1
Elements of assault and battery

Assault	Battery
Attempt to make harmful or offensive contact with another person without consent	Unconsented physical contact
Placing the victim in reasonable apprehension for physical safety	Offensive or harmful contact
Threat of imminent contact	Intent to touch another person in offensive or injurious manner

§ 6.3 False Imprisonment

False imprisonment occurs when the tortfeasor intentionally confines someone without that person's consent. This tort is meant to protect each individual's right to control his or her own freedom of movement. Essentially, there are four elements to false imprisonment:

1. Confinement without captive's consent
2. Tortfeasor's intent to confine victim

TERMS

false imprisonment The unlawful restraint by one person of the physical liberty of another. Like false arrest, to which it is closely related, it is both a tort and a crime.

3. Confinement for an appreciable length of time
4. No reasonable means of escape.

The Case of the Cruelest Misrepresentation, or Is It a Battery?

In this case, the court was asked to step into the privacy of a couple's bedroom and take the role of a referee of sorts. To protect the privacy of the two unmarried parties, they were assigned the names "Doe" and "Roe." Doe brought this action against Roe for the tortious transmission of genital herpes. The court's job was complicated by the fact that the couple had sexual encounters in two different states. If the disease was contracted in Virginia, there can be no recovery, as Virginia will not allow a tort recovery when a crime was committed. (Both Virginia and the District of Columbia have statutes prohibiting sexual intercourse between unmarried partners.) Doe's only chance for a tort award is to show that the District of Columbia encounter was when she contracted the disease.

DOE v. ROE
United States District Court, District of Columbia
841 F. Supp. 444 (D.D.C. 1994)
January 10, 1994
Pratt, District Judge

In this action, plaintiff seeks to recover for injuries allegedly resulting from the tortious communication of a sexually transmissible disease. Currently before us is defendant's motion for summary judgment under Federal Rule of Civil Procedure (Fed.R.Civ.P.) 56. This Court, sitting by diversity, is required to apply the choice of law rules of the District of Columbia. The sole issue for purposes of this motion is to determine which substantive law applies, *i.e.* the law of the District of Columbia or that of Virginia. For the reasons given herein, we apply the law of each jurisdiction to the events occurring within its respective territory.

Plaintiff and defendant met on March 21, 1990, at a reception in the District of Columbia. At all times relevant to this litigation defendant Roe was a resident of the District of Columbia. Plaintiff Doe resides in Virginia, but was employed in the District of Columbia during 1990. The parties began a social relationship which developed romantically over the course of several contacts, the vast majority of which occurred in the District of Columbia.

On the night of April 26, 1990, the parties returned to plaintiff's home in Virginia after dinner in the District of Columbia. During the course of the evening, the parties engaged in sexual intercourse ("the Virginia encounter"). Complicating the legal scenario, on April 29th, the parties again engaged in sexual intercourse, this time at the Watergate Hotel in the District of Columbia ("the District encounter"). Two days later plaintiff Doe allegedly began to feel the pain associated with Herpes Simplex Type II ("herpes"), commonly known as genital herpes, and human papilloma virus, commonly known as genital warts. Because the incubation period for herpes is somewhere between two to ten days, it is difficult, if not impossible, to determine which encounter resulted in plaintiff's becoming infected.

Plaintiff's complaint alleges that defendant intentionally misrepresented to plaintiff that he was free from sexually transmitted diseases. She seeks relief under theories of negligence, fraud, intentional and negligent infliction of emotional distress, and battery.

Fed.R.Civ.P. 56(c) permits a court to grant summary judgment when the evidence in the record shows that "there is no genuine issue as to any material fact and that the moving party is entitled to a judgment as a matter of law."

* * *

This Court, sitting by diversity, must apply the choice of law rules of the District of Columbia. The law of the forum is presumed to apply unless it is demonstrated that a foreign jurisdiction has a greater interest in the controversy than does the District.

* * *

The choice of law question is central to this action because criminal statutes in both jurisdictions prohibit sexual intercourse between unmarried partners. Therefore, recovery is only possible in a jurisdiction which allows damage awards for tort injuries incurred while committing a crime.

* * *

It is undisputed that recovery is barred under Virginia law. In *Zysk v. Zysk,* 239 Va. 32, 404 S.E.2d 721, 722 (1990), the Virginia Supreme Court held that a plaintiff cannot recover damages for herpes infection when she consented to engage in an immoral or illegal act. Therefore, plaintiff can recover only if District of Columbia law applies.

* * *

District of Columbia substantive law cannot apply to any cause of action arising from the Virginia sexual encounter. Plaintiff is barred from recovery to the extent her cause of action arises from the Virginia encounter. ...

Virginia has a minimal interest in denying recovery to one of its citizens for actions in another jurisdiction if such recovery is available.

* * *

Although the parties' competing experts dispute the normal incubation period for herpes, both agree on the fundamental fact that the period of incubation is at least two to seven days. Plaintiff states that she began experiencing symptoms of the disease "within 48 hours of the sexual encounter with the defendant in Washington, D.C." Declaration of plaintiff, p. 1. Two days after the April 29, 1990, encounter would have been May 1, 1990. This is only five days after the initial sexual encounter in Virginia, and well within the undisputed incubation period of seven days.

Plaintiff also argues that a herpes carrier is contagious during the 24 hour period prior to the appearance of the sores. Because plaintiff did not observe such symptoms during the District encounter, she concludes that defendant could not have been contagious two days earlier in Virginia. Such a theory is a very thin reed on which to rely because it does not recognize the variables inherent in living organisms. Plaintiff's expert noted only that

> [a]n individual with herpes simplex *may* be contageous immediately prior to a visible outbreak ... The contageous period *usually* begins approximately 24 hours prior to the visible outbreak of sores.

Plaintiff then leaps to the conclusion that this 24 hour period is the only time an individual may be contagious. This conclusion cannot be drawn from Dr. Ross' statement. An undisputed second declaration by Dr. Niles states that a person who is asymptomatic may still spread herpes by "shedding" the virus. ... There are no genuine facts in dispute that would preclude summary judgment.

For the foregoing reasons the Court applies Virginia law to the Virginia sexual encounter and District of Columbia law to the District encounter. As a result, recovery would be possible only if plaintiff could trace her injury to the District encounter. Because we conclude that no reasonable trier of fact could determine which encounter resulted in infection, we are forced to grant defendant's motion for summary judgment. We regret this unfortunate result which, if plaintiff's allegations are true, shields from liability conduct which is not only despicable, but at the least is highly irresponsible. We hope plaintiff will appeal our determination that we are unable to grant the relief she seeks.

An order in accordance with this opinion has been issued this date.

Upon consideration of defendant's motion for summary judgment, plaintiff's opposition, the reply thereto, and upon consideration of the entire record herein, it is, this 10th day of January, 1994, hereby

ORDERED that defendant's motion for summary judgment is granted; and it is

ORDERED that this case be dismissed with prejudice.

Case Questions

1. Doe seeks relief under theories of negligence, fraud, intentional and negligent infliction of emotional distress, and battery. On which of these theories is she most successful? Explain.
2. Doe seeks to prove that the District of Columbia encounter was where she contracted herpes, so that she might recover a tort award for damages that occurred while she was committing a crime. Should people be allowed tort recoveries despite the fact that they openly admit they were violating the law? Explain your position.

Confinement

All methods of confinement include (1) a restriction of the victim's freedom of movement, (2) the captive's awareness or fear of the restriction, and (3) the victim's nonconsent to the restriction. The second element prevents the victim from escaping, either because no routes of escape are available, or because the victim is afraid to attempt escape for fear of the tortfeasor's reprisals.

There are several ways in which the tortfeasor may confine his or her captive. These include physical barriers and express or implied threats of force.

Physical Barriers Restricting Movement

Physical barriers are the most common method of falsely imprisoning someone. Placing the captive in a locked room or a moving automobile (while refusing to stop) are common examples. However, the physical barriers need not be so small as a single room or vehicle. A captive may be restricted to the grounds of a series of adjacent buildings. It is even possible for the victim to be penned in by such unexpected blockades as an automobile blocking the victim's access from a driveway to a street. The physical barrier need only restrict the captive's freedom of movement. This essentially traps the victim, either by some actual physical obstruction, such as a locked door, fence, or wall, or by an object which the tortfeasor is using to restrain the captive, such as the automobile blocking the driveway or even the tortfeasor's own body obstructing a doorway.

Express or Implied Threats of Force

Sometimes no locked door or wall is necessary to confine a person. Threats of physical or emotional violence can be quite effective, as are threats against the victim's family or property. In this way, confinement is achieved by expressed intimidation. The victim is afraid to escape for fear of physical or emotional injury. For example, when the tortfeasor warns, "If you leave this room, I will break your legs," the captive is likely to remain as instructed. Similarly, the tortfeasor could threaten, "If you leave this house, I will tell Joe that you wrecked his new car." In this situation, the victim is restrained by the threat of emotional injury, if certain information is revealed that would incriminate the captive.

These types of threats need not be explicit, however. Implied threats also work effectively. For instance, if a store manager tells a shoplifting suspect to wait in a room for questioning "so that nobody has to telephone the police," the threat of arrest and criminal prosecution is clearly implied, and the suspect will probably comply out of fear.

Captive's Consent to Confinement

The intentional tort of false imprisonment cannot occur if the victim consents to the captivity. **Consent** includes awareness and acceptance of the confinement. Thus, if a shoplifting suspect agrees to remain in a room pending questioning by store security, this would constitute consent, because the patron knows and accepts the restriction to the room.

Intent to Confine

The tortfeasor must intend to confine the victim for false imprisonment to happen. Consider the example of an accidental lock-in at a department store, where a customer is inadvertently locked inside the store after closing hours. There would be no false imprisonment, because the store management had no desire to confine the patron.

Intent may be expressed or implied by conduct. The tortfeasor who states his or her intention to confine another person is easiest to identify. Often, however, intent is indicated by conduct. Again, the shoplifting

---

TERMS

consent   Agreement; approval; acquiescence; being of one mind. Consent necessarily involves two or more persons because, without at least two persons, there cannot be a unity of opinion or the possibility of thinking alike ... .

illustration presents a good example. A shoplifting suspect is stopped by store security and is asked to accompany the guard. Without any word of explanation, the guard takes the suspect to a back room, has the suspect enter, closes the door, and departs. There have been no explicit indications of confinement—the door was not locked—but implicitly it is understood, based on the behavior of the guard, that the suspect is to remain in the room. Accordingly, the intent to restrain may be implied.

Confinement for Appreciable Time Period

Although no definite time period is required, false imprisonment occurs only if the confinement has existed for an appreciable length of time. This depends upon the specific facts of each case. Usually, *appreciable confinement* is defined as unreasonable under the circumstances. That could be a matter of seconds, if someone is restrained in an extremely hazardous situation, such as in a burning building; or it could be a question of an hour or two, such as during a shoplifting investigation.

No Reasonable Means of Escape

False imprisonment cannot happen if the captive has a reasonable avenue of escape. In other words, the confinement must be complete. If the victim could simply walk away from the situation, then no false imprisonment transpired. Reasonable means of escape depend upon the facts of each case, but usually they include any route that a reasonable person would use under the circumstances to flee. For example, if Roger makes improper advances upon Betty in his automobile, and Betty has only to open the door to leave, then she has a reasonable avenue of escape, and no false imprisonment has happened. However, if Roger made the same advances on Betty in a fourth-floor apartment, in which the only exits were one door (which Roger blocked) and the windows, then false imprisonment would have occurred. Betty could hardly be expected to escape by leaping from a fourth-story window.

Many false imprisonment cases involve shoplifting or alleged shoplifting. The difficulty in these cases stems from the conflicting interests involved: the patron's freedom to move about freely versus the business's right to protect its property from theft. Notice that there are competing tort interests here. The customer seeks protection from false imprisonment, while the store owner wishes to prevent conversion and trespass to chattel.

The Case of the Overzealous Store Security Officer

Many false imprisonment cases involve shoplifting. All too often, store employees, anxious to curb theft of merchandise, become overzealous in their efforts. Suspected shoplifters, on the flimsiest circumstantial evidence, are occasionally subjected to unreasonable searches, confinements, interrogations, and the accompanying stresses and embarrassment. When the evidence against such suspects is extremely speculative, as in the case reprinted here, the result is often tort litigation. The suspect becomes the plaintiff. The store, as the defendant, suddenly finds itself attempting to justify its employees' outrageous conduct. Depending upon the facts, possible causes of action may include false imprisonment, infliction of emotional distress, assault, battery, invasion of privacy, or defamation. In the following case, false imprisonment and intentional infliction of emotional distress were successfully claimed, although only the issue of punitive damages was being considered on appeal.

ROGERS
v.
T.J.X. COS.
Supreme Court of North Carolina
329 N.C. 226, 404 S.E.2d 664 (1991)
June 12, 1991
Martin, Justice

This action was filed on 12 August 1988 by the plaintiff for compensatory and punitive damages for false imprisonment and intentional infliction of emotional distress. Summary judgment for defendants was granted. The Court of Appeals reversed the trial court on all claims except the punitive damages issue. ... The only issue before this Court is whether there is a genuine issue of material fact on the plaintiff's claim for punitive damages. We hold that the trial court erred in granting summary judgment for the defendants on that issue and therefore reverse the Court of Appeals.

The action arose out of events occurring on 17 July 1988 at the T.J. Maxx department store in Cary, North Carolina, owned by defendant T.J.X. Companies, Inc. Taken in the light most favorable to the plaintiff, as we must for summary judgment purposes, the evidence tends to show the following. Plaintiff entered T.J. Maxx, hereinafter "the store," about 4:30 P.M. shopping for linens. She wore bermuda shorts and a T-shirt and carried a pocketbook, approximately twelve

inches by twelve inches. The purse contained two cosmetic bags, a wallet, two pens, a glasses' case, and a ziploc bag containing material and wallpaper samples. Plaintiff went first to the cosmetics area and then to the linens department. After leaving the linens department, she walked around a counter containing dishes and crystal and then left the store without making a purchase. Plaintiff never entered the lingerie department and never examined any items of lingerie.

As plaintiff exited the store, Michael Nourse stopped her, identified himself as a store security officer, and asked her to return to the store because he wished to talk with her about some merchandise. Nourse carried a badge of his own design and an identification card issued by the company; he showed these items to plaintiff. Plaintiff told him that he was making a mistake, but complied with his request and accompanied Nourse to his office at the back of the store. Plaintiff testified that she did not feel that she had a choice about accompanying Nourse because "he was the law of the store" and she had to obey him. On the way to the office, Nourse asked another store employee, Sheri Steffens, to join them and act as a witness.

Once inside the small office, plaintiff immediately dumped the contents of her purse onto the desk. Nourse told plaintiff to take a seat, but she refused, saying that this would not take long because she was a good customer and had not stolen anything. Nourse responded, "Good customers will steal," and again directed her to have a seat. Telling her he would soon return, he then left the office for five to fifteen minutes. Plaintiff testified that she believed that he might have gone to call the police, and she stepped out of the office to look for them. Seeing no one, she gathered up her belongings, but did not feel free to leave because Nourse had told her he would return. Steffens paged Nourse, who returned momentarily. He said to plaintiff, "Ma'am, all we want is our merchandise. What did you do with it? You were in our lingerie department." Plaintiff denied wrongdoing, again dumped her purse on the desk, and told him that he must have seen her putting the packet of material samples into her purse. As she reached to gather her belongings, Nourse instructed her not to touch anything.

Nourse pulled down a clipboard hanging on the wall and showed her a card which said that the store employees had the right to detain her if they had reason to believe she had been shoplifting. Nourse repeatedly questioned plaintiff about the location of the missing merchandise as she tried to read the card. Plaintiff told him to "shut up" so that she could concentrate. Nourse remarked to Steffens, "Usually the dog that barks the loudest is guilty." Nourse then told plaintiff that he could call the police if she wanted them to settle it; that he could handcuff her to a chair; and that he would call the police and have them put her in jail. Plaintiff continued to deny the allegations and asked if he wanted her to take her clothes off to prove that she had not done anything, even though she was a very modest person. Steffens testified that plaintiff was very upset throughout the incident and that Nourse's attitude and demeanor toward plaintiff was sarcastic.

Nourse instructed plaintiff to sign two forms, one of which was a waiver of Miranda rights. The other form released T.J. Maxx from liability for any claims arising out of the incident. Neither of the papers had been filled out when plaintiff signed. Plaintiff testified that she signed the release form only because she believed that she would not be allowed to leave the store and go home if she did not sign it. Nourse refused to give plaintiff copies of the forms, because it was not company policy. After signing the papers, plaintiff left the store and drove home. She had been in the security office approximately 35 minutes. About one-half hour after plaintiff left the store, Nourse announced to Steffens that he had found the missing merchandise, a beige brassiere.

Plaintiff's evidence showed that she became sick, nervous and upset as a result of the incident. She had difficulty sleeping and took sleeping pills for two weeks as prescribed by her doctor. In addition, she testified that she no longer went shopping, because she felt as if someone was always looking over her shoulder.

False imprisonment is the illegal restraint of the person of any one against his or her will. The tort may be committed by words or acts; therefore, actual force is not required. Restraint of the person is essential, whether by threats, express or implied, or by conduct. The Court of Appeals held that plaintiff had established facts sufficient to support her claim for false imprisonment ... .

[The Court's discussion of punitive damages and intentional infliction of emotional distress is omitted.]

Taken in the light most favorable to the plaintiff, the evidence tends to show that (1) defendant Nourse impersonated a police officer by using a badge of his own design; (2) plaintiff was restrained against her will in the store security office for approximately one-half hour; (3) plaintiff was badgered, insulted and pressured to confess by defendant Nourse despite her efforts to prove her innocence; (4) plaintiff was frightened and upset and asked if she could leave; (5) defendant unlawfully detained plaintiff after [a] determination that no offense had been committed; (6) plaintiff was made to give up personal information including her driver's license number, telephone number, and social security number; and (7) plaintiff was forced to sign a release of liability as a condition to her release from Nourse's custody. ...

We hold that there was sufficient evidence of outrageous conduct, in addition to that conduct constituting the false imprisonment, to survive defendants' motion for summary judgment.

... Accordingly, we reverse in part the decision of the Court of Appeals and remand the case to them for further proceedings not inconsistent with this opinion.

REVERSED IN PART AND REMANDED.

Case Questions

1. Given the facts in *Rogers,* did the plaintiff establish the elements (as discussed in this chapter) for assault, battery, intentional infliction of emotional distress?
2. You might wish to read the complete *Rogers* opinion to compare North Carolina's common law regarding intentional infliction of emotional distress with the elements discussed in § 6.4, as well as in some of the other cases partially reprinted in this chapter.

HYPOTHETICALS

Consider Sophie's predicament. A cashier thought he spotted Sophie taking some merchandise and placing it in her purse without paying for it. As Sophie walked out the exit, store security grabbed her. She violently protested, but the guards, without explanation, bodily forced her into a small, unlit room in the rear of the store. They then locked the door, and Sophie sat for three hours until the store manager, who had been on a delivery errand, returned to question her. She was, in fact, innocent of any wrongdoing. Was there false imprisonment?

The confinement was without Sophie's consent, as evidenced by Sophie's protests of the guards' physical handling of her. The restraint was obvious because the door was locked. The store security guards intended to confine Sophie by locking her in the room. She was restrained there for three hours, which would probably be considered unreasonable, particularly because the room was small and unlit. She had no reasonable means of escape, again because the only door to the room was locked. Therefore, the store would be liable to Sophie for false imprisonment.

■ ■ ■

Consider also the case of Murphy. Murphy drove his automobile into a restricted area of a manufacturing plant. Plant security instructed him to remain parked in his vehicle pending the arrival of the supervisor. Murphy said he had no reason to hang around, as he had done nothing wrong. The security officers then left. There were no barriers preventing Murphy from simply driving off the premises, through an open gate, to the highway. Was there false imprisonment?

The critical element in this hypothetical is the reasonable route of escape. Murphy could easily have slipped away, and the guards made no implied or expressed threats (such as arrest and criminal prosecution if he attempted to leave). Accordingly, no false imprisonment took place.

Figure 6-2 illustrates the elements of false imprisonment.

Confinement without captive's consent
Intent to confine
Confinement for appreciable length of time
No reasonable means of escape

FIGURE 6-2
Elements
of false
imprisonment

§ 6.4 Infliction of Emotional Distress

We have all encountered episodes in our lives in which other persons have intentionally caused us emotional upset. Anyone with a sibling can relate to misconduct designed to annoy and distress. In the law of intentional torts, infliction of emotional distress has developed as a separate cause of action to protect injured parties from other people's efforts to cause shock, fright, or other psychological trauma. One owes a duty to others not to intentionally inflict emotional distress. The breach of that duty is called intentional infliction of emotional distress.

Emotional distress may be broadly defined as mental anguish caused by a tortfeasor. Synonyms such as fright, anxiety, shock, grief, mental suffering, or emotional disturbance are commonly used by the courts to describe this tort. The condition can include shame or embarrassment as well.

The critical aspect of infliction of emotional distress is that the victim suffers from mental anguish rather than from some physical injury caused by the tortfeasor. It is the psychological harm that this tort intends to remedy.

Not just any insult or offensive behavior will result in this tort, however. The misdeed must be so outrageous that a reasonable person would suffer severe emotional injury as a consequence. This is the key element to all infliction of emotional distress cases. Minor annoyances or indignities are part of everyday life, and these are not included in this tort. If it were otherwise, the courts would overflow with lawsuits, based upon the irritations we all encounter from other people almost

─────────── TERMS ───────────

emotional distress[†] Mental anguish. In the intentional torts called intentional and reckless infliction of emotional distress, the mental anguish is caused by the tortfeasor's outrageous conduct.

daily. Obviously, the law cannot reshape the world into the loving, peaceful utopia we might prefer, but it can discourage flagrant actions tailored to cause mental suffering.

In the field of intentional torts, there are two varieties of infliction of emotional distress: intentional and reckless. A third version, negligent infliction, is discussed in Chapter 4.

Intentional Infliction

Intentional infliction of emotional distress contains three elements:

1. Outrageous conduct by the tortfeasor
2. Conduct intended to cause severe mental anguish in the victim
3. The victim's suffering severe mental anguish as a consequence of the tortfeasor's behavior.

Outrageous Conduct

As noted earlier, the tortfeasor's behavior must be sufficiently outrageous. The common test for outrageous conduct is one of reasonableness. Would a reasonable person suffer substantial emotional distress as a result of the tortfeasor's actions? Were these activities so outlandish as to *shock the conscience* of a reasonable person? Or, put another way, would a person of *ordinary sensibilities* suffer mental pain as a consequence? This generally excludes all but the most extreme types of egregious conduct.

Examples of outrageous conduct abound in the legal literature. Tasteless practical jokes often provide fodder for emotional distress litigation. Consider the person who places a dead mouse inside a soda pop bottle from which someone is drinking and then tells the drinker about the mouse. Or the heartless prankster who tells a parent that his or her child has just been struck and killed by an automobile when, in fact, this never occurred, as the joker knew perfectly well. Or the person who places revealing photographs of a nude sunbather all around the sunbather's place of employment for fellow workers to see. Or the individual who repeatedly telephones another at all hours of the day and night

---

TERMS

intentional infliction of emotional distress[†] An intentional tort that occurs when the tortfeasor's outrageous conduct, which is intended to cause severe mental anguish in the victim, actually causes the victim such emotional suffering as a result of the tortfeasor's actions.

over several weeks. These are clear instances of outrageous conduct that most people would agree are highly offensive and would cause intense emotional dismay to the victims.

Intentional Acts

Obviously, intentional infliction cases must include the element of intent. The tortfeasor must purposefully behave so as to create mental anguish in the victim; the tortfeasor desires to cause anguish. This separates intentional infliction from reckless infliction, which does not require that the tortfeasor tailor his or her acts to cause mental suffering, as is discussed later in this section.

Actual Emotional Distress

Naturally, the victim must actually suffer emotionally as a result of the tortfeasor's antics. Again, the test for anguish revolves around the way a reasonable person of ordinary sensibilities would react to the tortfeasor's actions. Courts have often complained that determining genuine emotional suffering from faked distress is extremely difficult, because anyone can pretend to be upset by something. However, physical symptoms usually accompany mental distress, such as loss of sleep, weight, appetite, or vigor; illnesses brought on after the mental shock; or other signs of effect, such as tremors, twitches, or sensitivity to loud or sudden noises. It is important to note, though, that modern courts do *not* require physical manifestations in intentional infliction cases. Mental suffering alone, unaccompanied by physical effects, is sufficient, provided that the trier-of-fact is convinced of the authenticity of the distress.

Reckless Infliction

The elements of **reckless infliction of emotional distress** are the same as for intentional infliction, except that intent is not necessary. Instead, it is adequate that the tortfeasor knew or reasonably should

---

TERMS

reckless infliction of emotional distress [†]   An intentional tort that occurs when the tortfeasor's outrageous conduct causes the victim to suffer severe mental anguish. Intent to produce the emotional suffering is not necessary. Instead, it is sufficient that the tortfeasor knew, or reasonably should have known, that his or her misbehavior would produce emotional distress. Often with this tort, the tortfeasor's conduct is wanton, with no apparent regard for the victim's suffering.

have known that his or her deeds would cause severe emotional distress to the victim. The behavior must still be outrageous, but it is enough that the tortfeasor carelessly or wantonly acted so as to emotionally disturb the victim.

The Case of the Humiliated Newspaper Lady

In this case, the court debated what it was "worth" to ninety-six-year-old Nellie Mitchell to suffer the humiliation, embarrassment, damage to reputation, and mental suffering of having her picture inserted in a supermarket tabloid. This case focused on the tort of intentional infliction of emotional distress.

MITCHELL

v.

GLOBE INTERNATIONAL PUBLISHING, INC.
United States District Court, W.D. Arkansas,
Harrison Division
817 F. Supp. 72 (W.D. Ark. 1993)
March 15, 1993
Waters, Chief Judge

In the October 2, 1990, edition of *The Sun,* a supermarket tabloid published by defendant, Globe International Publishing, Inc., a photograph of Nellie Mitchell, a 96-year-old resident of Mountain Home, Arkansas, was used to illustrate a story about "Paper Gal, Audrey Wiles" in Sterling, Australia, who had become pregnant by one of her customers, a "reclusive millionaire" she met on her newspaper route. In fact, Mrs. Mitchell made her living running a newspaper stand and delivering newspapers in Mountain Home.

She sued Globe for defamation, invasion of privacy, and intentional infliction of emotional distress, and the case was tried to a jury in Harrison, Arkansas, beginning on December 2, 1991. The jury found that the defendant's conduct had invaded Mrs. Mitchell's privacy by placing her in a false light and had amounted to an intentional infliction of emotional distress. She was awarded compensatory damages in the amount of $650,000 and punitive damages of $850,000.

* * *

[I]t is the court's duty, as directed by the Court of Appeals, to reduce the compensatory

damage award by some unspecified amount with the only guideline received from the Court of Appeals being that it should be "substantial."

The Court of Appeals said:

Though we are convinced that sufficient evidence exists to sustain a compensatory award for damage to Mitchell's reputation and her mental suffering, we also conclude the amount of the award is shocking and exaggerated.

Thus, it appears that it is this court's duty to determine, in whatever manner, what it is "worth" to Mrs. Mitchell to suffer the humiliation, embarrassment, mental suffering, and damage to her reputation caused by the egregious conduct by defendant in placing her picture and her very existence in the middle of an odious supermarket tabloid which, among other things, had a "road kill cannibal" describing his preference for human flesh from adults over that of children ... . This court still believes that the Harrison, Arkansas, jury, chosen from all walks of life, was better situated to make that decision than this court is, but, as indicated, that is beside the point, because this court has been directed to do it.

This is an especially difficult task where the damages to be awarded are based upon intangibles such as damage to reputation and mental suffering. ...

Of course, because of the nature of the damages in this case, there are no identifiable amounts that can be deducted, so any remittitur will, by its very nature, have to be somewhat arbitrary and speculative ... .

In short, this court has been directed to order a "substantial remittitur" so it must do so. For reasons stated in the earlier opinion, this court is convinced that Mrs. Mitchell suffered substantial damages to her reputation and was caused mental suffering by being a part, against her will, of a detestable publication issued and sold across the country by the defendant.

Vada Sheid, a friend of Mrs. Mitchell described the humiliation that she suffered beginning at page 156 of Vol. I of the trial transcript as follows:

> And I called Nellie and told her that I had the paper, and she came to the store to see this paper, and she said, where did you get this and how did this get into your store? ... And she says, well, that's me, but you know that I'm not pregnant. And I said, of course not. ... [S]he became so disturbed and so humiliated, and she said, but what will my kids think about this? Do you think they'll believe this, and how will I ever explain it to the people in town? And then she said, I'm going to buy up all the papers there is in this town so people in Mountain Home won't know about this.

> * * *

> [S]he went home, and she did not stir out for a few days. ... [S]he was very depressed and humiliated, and she just didn't deliver her papers even for the following week.

> * * *

> Nellie was hurt. She said, I don't know why they're doing this to me; why it was done to me. She said, I've tried not to hurt anyone ... why did they do it? ... But she was hurt, and after that, she said that people would come in and, they'd—She said they look down at my belly, and they'll say, well, Nellie, haven't you had that baby yet? Nellie, when are you going to have that baby? Nellie, you should have had that baby by now.
> And she said that it bothered her.

What is all that "worth"? A Harrison, Arkansas, jury believed that it was worth $650,000, but this court has been directed to reduce that award by ordering a "substantial remittitur." ...

This court recognizes, and recognized from the very first, that Mrs. Mitchell did not show at the trial a great deal of outward evidence of the humiliation, anger, and disgust that many would express under the same circumstances, but the court attributed a great deal of that to her advanced age. ... Admittedly, the court cannot take the evidence and point to any "specials" as lawyers call them, or any other identifiable dollar figures which can, with any certainty, justify an award of damages satisfactory to those who believe that these matters should be determined by some kind of formula. However, under all of the circumstances, the court is convinced that it is "worth" a minimum of $150,000 for Mrs. Mitchell to have been forced to endure what defendant heaped upon her, and the court, therefore, determines that a "substantial remittitur" in this case, as directed by the Court of Appeals, is $500,000. A reduction of a half million dollars is certainly "substantial", and the court believes that an award of at least $150,000 in compensatory damages is justified by the evidence.

This court will deny the motion for a new trial filed herein in behalf of the defendant on the express condition that plaintiff has, within 14 days of the date of this opinion, accepted a remittitur in the amount of $500,000. If, within such period, plaintiff has not notified the court of acceptance of a remittitur in such amount, the motion for a new trial will be granted, and a new trial ordered.

Case Questions

1. Why was the United States District Court so reluctant to reduce or change the award originally made by the jury?
2. Do you feel the original jury verdict was excessive? Explain.

Many reckless infliction cases include the mishandling of the remains of deceased persons. Consider a common fact pattern: A funeral home cremates the deceased instead of following the family's clear and explicit instructions regarding burial. Even though the funeral home did not intend this error, the conduct could be construed as so reckless as to fall within this tort.

Another type of fact situation involves the unanticipated effect of a practical joke. Consider the pranksters who vandalized someone's automobile by smearing it with manure, knowing that the vehicle owner took enormous pride in the car's appearance. The jokers knew that the owner had a weak heart, but were only expecting to shake up the owner. When the owner saw his prize automobile, he collapsed from a heart attack. This illustrates wanton misconduct. Although the pranksters did not intend the victim to suffer heart failure as a consequence of their deed, the tortfeasors' behavior revealed utter disregard for the health and well-being of the victim, and accordingly they would be liable for reckless infliction of emotional distress.

Claims of reckless infliction of emotional distress are sometimes made regarding unwanted, insulting, and demeaning sexual advances from a supervisor or co-worker at a place of employment. These claims are also known as sexual harassment suits.

Sexual Harassment

Title VII of the Civil Rights Act of 1964 makes it unlawful for an employer to discriminate against an individual because of such individual's race, color, religion, sex, or national origin. 42 U.S.C. § 2000-2(a)(1). In addition to tort actions, sexual harassment claims can be brought under the provisions of Title VII. A claimant must show that the workplace is permeated with discriminatory intimidation, ridicule, and insult that alters the conditions of the victim's employment, thereby creating an abusive and hostile work environment. Tangible psychiatric injuries need not be proven.

It should not be very difficult to imagine other emotional damage infliction scenarios like those previously mentioned. However, there are many instances in which the behavior is more subtle.

HYPOTHETICALS

Phyllis could offer an example. She owed money on a charge account at a local appliance store. Unfortunately, she missed several payments because of financial difficulties. Susan, the store sales manager, began repeatedly telephoning Phyllis at work and late in the evenings at home, demanding that Phyllis pay the balance due. The calls continued over several weeks. Phyllis's supervisor became angry that

Phyllis was wasting company time taking these phone calls. The calls at night woke Phyllis several times and agitated her enough to keep her awake. As a result, Phyllis's job performance slumped. Phyllis lost weight and became irritable because of lack of sleep. Has Susan intentionally inflicted emotional distress upon Phyllis?

Susan's actions were designed to upset Phyllis greatly to coerce Phyllis to pay the overdue debt. Susan acted in an outrageous manner—reasonable persons would find repeated telephone calls late at night and on the job to be highly offensive. Phyllis suffered substantial mental anguish (with physical manifestations) as a result of Susan's conduct. Accordingly, Susan would be liable to Phyllis for intentional infliction of emotional distress.

■ ■ ■

Consider another illustration. Baker and Mortimer are accountants with the same firm. Baker planted a fake letter of termination on Mortimer's desk, in which the office manager accused Mortimer of misappropriation of client funds. Upon reading the letter, Mortimer became distraught, shaking and sweating violently and feeling nauseous. Mortimer burst into the manager's office to deny the allegations, at which time Baker disclosed his gag. Has Baker inflicted emotional distress upon Mortimer?

All the elements are present in this hypothetical, including intent to cause mental anguish. Baker should tally his own personal accounts, because he will be liable to Mortimer for intentional infliction of emotional distress.

Figure 6-3 summarizes the elements of infliction of emotional distress.

§ 6.5 Fraud and Misrepresentation

Fraud, or **deceit** as some states call it, occurs when a tortfeasor makes false statements to entice the victim to give up something of value to the tortfeasor. **Misrepresentation** exists when the tortfeasor knowingly makes false statements or purposefully behaves in such a way as to deceive the victim. The two torts are quite similar. Both involve false statements or actions. Both include deception as the tortfeasor's objective. Yet fraud features the element of underhanded economic gain:

TERMS
---

fraud (deceit)   Deceit, deception, or trickery that is intended to induce, and does induce, another to part with anything of value or surrender some legal right.

misrepresentation   The statement of an untruth; a misstatement of fact designed to lead one to believe that something is other than it is; a false statement of fact designed to deceive.

Intentional Infliction	Reckless Infliction
Outrageous conduct	Outrageous conduct
Conduct intended to cause severe mental anguish	Conduct known (or reasonably should be known) to cause severe mental anguish
Victim suffers severe mental anguish as result	Victim suffers severe mental anguish as result

FIGURE 6-3   Elements of infliction of emotional distress

The Case of the Unfriendly Skies

In this case, an American Airlines employee brought an action against her employer for battery, negligent retention and supervision of employees, and violations of Title VII (sexual harassment). Sometimes, although the facts of a case are sufficient to allege one or more causes of tort actions, other legal issues may surface and bring the case to a halt. Here, the defendant raised issues regarding the effective date of Title VII, and the fact that the majority of incidents claimed occurred after the four-year statute of limitations for tort claims.

CAPRIO

v.

AMERICAN AIRLINES, INC.

United States District Court, M.D. Florida

848 F. Supp. 1528 (M.D. Fla. 1994)

March 25, 1994

Kovachevich, District Judge

Defendant, American Airlines, Inc., hired Lorraine M. Caprio, Plaintiff, as a reservation sales agent on April 24, 1978. Plaintiff alleges that Defendant's employees, John Murray and Roy Braganza, subjected Plaintiff to a hostile working environment and sexually harrassed her in violation of her rights secured by Title VII of the Civil Rights Act of 1964, 42 U.S.C. §§ 2000e, *et seq.* The alleged sexual harrassment began in February, 1985 and continued through July, 1989. Plaintiff further alleges that Defendant discharged her on May 1, 1990 in retaliation for a discrimination charge she filed with the Equal Employment Opportunity Commission. In addition, Plaintiff alleges that Defendant negligently hired and retained John Murray and Roy Braganza and that "Defendant, John Murray" committed battery on Plaintiff when he touched Plaintiff's buttocks in an offensive and unwanted manner.

On October 16, 1992, Plaintiff moved to amend her complaint and requested additional relief pursuant to the Civil Rights Act of 1991, Pub.L. No. 102–166, 105 Stat. 1071 (1991). Specifically, Plaintiff amended her prayer for relief and requested compensatory and punitive damages. Plaintiff's motion to amend her complaint was granted ... .

As to Plaintiff's claim under the 1991 Civil Rights Act, Defendant seeks summary judgment and claims that the applicable provisions of the Act operate prospectively only, and all of Plaintiff's alleged injuries pre-date the effective date of the Act.

On November 22, 1991, Congress passed the Civil Rights Act of 1991, which modified employment discrimination law by allowing compensatory and punitive damages for victims of intentional discrimination and jury trials for Title VII claims. Section 402(a) of the 1991 Civil Rights Act provides: "Except as otherwise specifically provided, this Act and the amendments made by this Act shall take effect upon enactment." This language could be construed to mean either that the Act should be applied to any charge or case pending on or after the date of enactment, or that it should be applied only to conduct occurring after that date.

* * *

Until such review [of the retroactivity of the Civil Rights Act of 1991] occurs, this Court will consider the provisions added by the Act as applicable only to conduct arising after the effective date of the Act. Based on the fact that the alleged discriminatory action occurred between February 1985 and July 1989, more than two years prior to the effective date of the Act, Defendant's Motion for Summary Judgment as to Plaintiff's 1991 Civil Rights Act Claims, and to Strike Prayer for Compensatory and Punitive Damages is GRANTED.

On February 23, 1994, Defendant, American Airlines, Inc., filed a motion to dismiss John D. Murray as a defendant in this case, in the event that he is in fact a defendant pursuant to Federal Rule of Civil Procedure 4(j).

* * *

Because more than 120 days have elapsed since the filing of Plaintiff's complaint on April 29, 1992, and John D. Murray has not been served with a summons or complaint, this Court must dismiss him as a defendant. Accordingly, Defendant's Motion to Dismiss John D. Murray as Defendant is GRANTED.

Plaintiff filed this action alleging violations of Title VII of the Civil Rights Act of 1964, 42 U.S.C. §§ 2000e, *et seq.*, as well as pendent state tort claims for battery and negligent retention and supervision. As relief under the pendent tort claims, Plaintiff seeks compensatory and punitive damages. Plaintiff also requests a jury trial as to these issues. Defendant has moved for summary judgment and requests this Court to dismiss Plaintiff's two state tort claims against American Airlines and her request for a jury trial based on these issues. ...

Plaintiff's claim of battery consists of allegations in her complaint that "Murray repeatedly and consistently slapped and/or grabbed Plaintiff suggestively on her buttocks," and "touched Plaintiff's buttocks in an offensive and unwanted manner." Additional allegations of battery are contained in Plaintiff's affidavit and deposition, and in a letter Plaintiff sent to Barbara Landers, Director of Recruitment and Personnel Services at American Airline's corporate office. In these documents, Plaintiff alleges that John Murray and Roy Braganza touched and grabbed Plaintiff's buttocks and breasts on numerous occasions.

In order to state a battery claim against Defendant based on the conduct of its employees, John Murray and Roy Braganza, Plaintiff must offer evidence creating a genuine issue of material fact that Murray and Braganza were acting within the scope of their employment. ...

It is well established that the question of whether an employee was acting within the scope of his employment is one best submitted to a jury. ...

Defendant also seeks summary judgment as to Plaintiff's battery and negligent retention and supervision claims based on Florida's statute of limitations. The Florida limitations period for filing complaints based on intentional torts is four years. Plaintiff filed the instant action with this Court on April 29, 1992.

The majority of Plaintiff's battery and negligent retention and supervision allegations concern conduct that allegedly occurred prior to April 28, 1988, the applicable state statute of limitations period based on the filing of this action. ...

Plaintiff submitted an affidavit, dated February 28, 1994, as evidence to support her position that there is a material dispute of fact as to whether the Florida statute of limitations bars the present action. ...

The contested paragraphs of Plaintiff's affidavit state:

> 5. In 1985, and again in 1989, Roy Braganza reached into my blouse and tried to touch my breasts. I quickly pulled away, but still felt his fingers touch my chest.
> 6. From 1985 to 1989, John Murray consistently and repeatedly slapped or grabbed my buttocks. He also consistently and repeatedly

reached up my dress and grabbed my legs as he would reach for a bag tag. This slapping and grabbing was the normal procedure with Mr. Murray.

7. John Murray also consistently and repeatedly poked me around the breast area. Sometimes he would come in and start tickling me and his fingers would eventually be poking my breast area. These incidents occurred sporadically from 1985 until 1989.

8. Sometime around June or July 1989, while I was working alone at the departure gate, John Murray made a comment about how sexy I looked in my uniform and how he was getting sexually excited. He also rubbed up against me.

* * *

Although the majority of the alleged conduct clearly occurred in 1985, Plaintiff's deposition testimony indicates that some of the conduct may have occurred subsequent to April 28, 1988. In addition, Plaintiff states in her affidavit that she met with American Airlines' personnel on June 16, 1989 to discuss the sexual harassment and working conditions at the Fort Myers branch. ... Based on these reasons, Defendant's Motion to Strike Portions of the Affidavit of Lorraine M. Caprio is DENIED.

Although Plaintiff has alleged that conduct forming the basis of her complaint occurred subsequent to April 28, 1988, the majority of the conduct occurred prior to that date. ... Thus, any

conduct occurring prior to April 28, 1988 is barred by Florida's four-year statute of limitations. Accordingly, Defendant's Motion for Partial Summary Judgment is GRANTED as to the battery and negligent retention and supervision claims to the extent that they are based upon conduct occurring prior to April 28, 1988.

* * *

In order to submit a claim for punitive damages based upon intentional torts to the jury, Plaintiff must make a threshold showing that Defendant's conduct approaches a level that "transcends the level of simple negligence, and even gross negligence, ... and enters the realm of wanton intentionality, exaggerated recklessness, or such an extreme degree of negligence as to parallel an intentional and reprehensible act."

* * *

[With regard to the plaintiff's claim for punitive damages, the court said:] Although Plaintiff alleges that she was fired in retaliation for filing her claim with the EEOC, she has presented no evidence that Defendant's conduct rose to the level of "wanton misconduct equivalent to criminal manslaughter." Accordingly, Defendant's Motion for Partial Summary Judgment is GRANTED as it relates to Plaintiff's request for punitive damages based on the intentional torts of battery and negligent retention and supervision.

Case Questions

1. The defendant was successful in having most of the plaintiff's claims dismissed. What actions was the plaintiff left to proceed with after the United States District Court heard the case?

2. The plaintiff sought legal action because she was greatly disturbed by the actions of two of her fellow employees. Some of the actions were unwanted touchings and grabbings and others were lewd statements. For some plaintiffs, would not the greatest indignity of all be to have hundreds or thousands of law students and attorneys reading the facts of the case for years to come? Is there any solution to this?

the victim surrenders something valuable to the tortfeasor as a result of the spurious comments. As a practical matter, however, a tortfeasor who commits fraud also commits misrepresentation, although they technically are not the same tort. Still, many courts view them as synonymous.

Definitions and Distinctions

Fraud

For fraud, the following must exist:

1. The defrauder must intend to deceive by making a false representation of material fact
2. The defrauder must know that the statements made are false
3. The purpose of the false statements must be to entice the victim into giving the tortfeasor something of value
4. The innocent party must justifiably rely on the misrepresentation
5. The innocent party must be injured.

Misrepresentation

For misrepresentation, the first two elements of fraud must occur. Some courts, however, also add the other elements to misrepresentation, making it identical to fraud. In such jurisdictions, the two concepts are thus redundant.

False Statements Intended to Deceive

A tortfeasor commits fraud or misrepresentation by making material false statements designed to delude the victim. For example, if Aaron tells Stephanie that he can repair her broken dishwasher for $100, when Aaron knows that he lacks the requisite skill and knowledge to do so, then Aaron has made false statements intended to mislead Stephanie into paying him the money for work he cannot perform.

Knowledge of Falsity of Information

The tortfeasor must know that the information given to the victim is false for fraud or misrepresentation to happen. For instance, if Henry sells Michelle a new computer with a defective floppy disk drive of which Henry is totally unaware, then Henry has not engaged in either fraud or misrepresentation, because he did not know about the product defect when he made the sale.

Tortfeasor's Profit from Deception

For fraud, the defrauder must make false statements tailored to encourage the victim to surrender something of value to the tortfeasor. In the preceding example, Aaron duped Stephanie in order to receive her money. This constitutes fraud.

Innocent Party's Injury

Like all torts, the innocent party must prove actual injury as a consequence of the false statements or misrepresentation.

The Case of the Faked Financing

Fraud and misrepresentation often involve money matters. For a variety of reasons, funds may be promised but not delivered. Sometimes, deceit is the root of the evil. In the following case, a lending institution fails in its loan obligation and commits misrepresentation into the bargain. In Arkansas, this tort is called *deceit*.

FIDELITY MORTGAGE CO.
v.
COOK
Supreme Court of Arkansas
307 Ark. 496, 821 S.W.2d 39 (1991)
December 23, 1991
Brown, Justice

The appellant, Fidelity Mortgage Company of Texas, appeals from a judgment for deceit in favor of the appellee, James Martin Cook, d/b/a Cook Construction Company, in the amount of $35,538.29. The salient issue on appeal is whether the circuit judge, who tried the case without a jury, clearly erred in finding that the elements of deceit existed in this case.

We hold that the circuit judge did not err in his findings, and we affirm his decision.

The facts involve the building of a hunting lodge instigated by two men who had formed a partnership—James Cunningham and John Staggers. The partners had agreed between themselves that Cunningham would put up the land for the lodge and Staggers would arrange the financing for the construction. The original contractor for the job quit, apparently due to a

problem in getting paid. Staggers then approached a second contractor, James Cook. Cook was agreeable to doing the job for $250,000 but only if he could receive assurances that he would be paid.

Staggers had had a previous business relationship with W.R. Parker, a principal with Fidelity Mortgage Company. They discussed the need for financing to build a hunting lodge, and Parker put Staggers in touch with James Trimble, a vice-president of Fidelity. Trimble faxed Staggers a letter on September 23, 1988, which stated that Fidelity "hereby agrees ... to loan up to $250,000 (new loan) at a rate of 12% per annum." A commitment fee of $2,500 was required from Staggers. There was no statement in the letter that Fidelity would act as a broker for the loan or seek participation from other financial institutions. Staggers in turn faxed a copy of the letter to Cook's attorney that same day.

On the following day, September 24, 1988, Cook entered into a construction contract with Staggers and Cunningham to build the hunting lodge. Under that contract, Staggers and Cunningham were to pay Cook $150,000 after a certain part of the project had been completed. Cook began construction on September 26, 1988.

During the first week of construction, Cook's attorney called Fidelity and talked to Trimble and was assured that Fidelity would pay the money to Cook in accordance with the construction contract. Trimble also testified that during the last week in September Staggers asked him to write a letter stating that the Fidelity loan was to be used to build a hunting lodge and that payments would be made to Cook pursuant to the construction contract.

On October 11, 1988, Cook submitted a bill for $150,000 to Staggers after completing the requisite part of the project. Payment was not made on that date, and Cook's attorney advised him to stop work. Due to assurances from Trimble that payment would be forthcoming, Cook continued work on the project.

Three days later, on October 14, Trimble, on behalf of Fidelity, wrote the letter that Staggers had requested in which he specifically stated that the loan was for the hunting lodge property and that payments would be made to Cook in accordance with the construction contract. By letter dated October 18, Trimble wrote Staggers that payment would be delayed because one of the trustees (later identified as W.R. Parker) was needed to approve the check, and he was out of the country.

At some point between October 17 and October 21, 1988, Cook stopped work on the project. The amount of work performed by Cook and the fact that Cook was not paid are not in dispute. Fidelity, through Trimble, finally severed its business relationship with Staggers in November or December. At that time Trimble advised Cook's attorney that Staggers had never paid the $2,500 loan commitment fee.

Cook first sued Staggers and Cunningham for $150,000. He obtained judgment and foreclosed his lien against the hunting lodge property, thereby realizing $50,000. ...

Cook next sued Fidelity for deceit on the basis that Fidelity misrepresented its capacity to make the loan and to pay him and further that it intentionally induced him to rely on these false representations. After the bench trial, the circuit judge found for Cook and assessed damages against Fidelity in the amount of $35,538.29,

which represented Cook's out-of-pocket expenses for the job, less the amounts received by garnishment and foreclosure.

Fidelity urges on appeal that the elements of deceit were not proven in this case and that the circuit judge clearly erred in finding that they were. We have had occasion recently to discuss the five elements of deceit, which are:

1. The defendant makes a false representation—ordinarily, one of fact;
2. The defendant knows that the representation is false or he does not have a sufficient basis of information to make it; that is, scienter;
3. The defendant intends to induce the plaintiff to act or to refrain from acting in reliance upon the misrepresentation;
4. The plaintiff justifiably relies upon the representation;
5. The plaintiff suffers damage as a result of the reliance.

Each element must be proven by a preponderance of the evidence in order to prove deceit.

A. FALSE REPRESENTATION

We have no trouble in sustaining the circuit judge's finding of misrepresentation. Simply stated, Fidelity agreed to loan $250,000 to Staggers when its net worth totalled less than $50,000. Had there been any hint that Fidelity would act as the broker for the loan or would ask for institutions to participate in the loan, our conclusion would be different. But there was no such intimation in the loan commitment letter signed by Trimble on behalf of Fidelity on September 23. There, he stated clearly and unequivocally under a heading entitled "Commitment:"

Fidelity Mortgage Company of Texas hereby agrees to loan up to $250,000 (new loan) at a rate of 12% per annum.

This Fidelity simply did not have the capability to do.

We have noted recently that many courts now construe false representation to include "(1) Concealment of material information and (2) Nondisclosure of certain pertinent information." If

Fidelity did not have sufficient assets of its own as of September 23 to make the loan, Trimble should have arranged for independent financing from other institutions before writing the loan commitment letter. But he did not do this. Rather, he obligated Fidelity to make the loan while concealing insufficient net worth and knowing full well that Fidelity did not have the capability to make good on its promise.

Fidelity argues that it was not obligated to make payments because it never received the $2,500 loan fee from Staggers. In the numerous conversations and letters between Fidelity and Cook during September and October 1988, there was no mention that the fee had not been paid. Yet all during this period Trimble made verbal and written assurances on behalf of Fidelity that Cook would be paid for his work. The trial judge correctly found that this conduct constituted a false representation.

B. SCIENTER

Nor do we agree that Fidelity lacked the intent to misrepresent. Trimble and Parker did not reveal the net worth of Fidelity to Cook or his attorney during the critical period of construction. Nor did they indicate that the loan fee had not been paid. On the contrary, the statements of Trimble were in the nature of assurances that all was well and that the delay in payment was only due to Parker's temporary unavailability. Only much later did the true circumstances concerning Fidelity and its relationship to Staggers come to light.

* * *

D. JUSTIFIABLE RELIANCE

There is no question that Cook relied on the loan commitment. Equally as clear is the fact that Fidelity, through Trimble, knew about the construction contract and gave assurances to Cook and his lawyer that it would be paid. Neither Cook nor his attorney were alerted to the fact that anything was amiss. The trial judge's finding of justifiable reliance is not in error.

* * *

The decision of the trial judge is affirmed.

Case Questions

1. What is *scienter?* What is its importance to misrepresentation?
2. Why did the court say that its decision would have been different if Fidelity had arranged independent financing from other institutions? Would this have negated the first two elements of deceit?

Classic illustrations of fraud or misrepresentation seem to utilize used car sales situations, which have become the brunt of many jokes. Still, the examples profile the elements quite well.

HYPOTHETICALS

Ask Mayfield, for instance, who purchased an automobile from Honest Eddy's Used Car Palace. Honest Eddy himself assured Mayfield that the chosen vehicle had been driven only 5,000 miles by a driving instructor from Ontario, that the brakes had just been replaced, and that the engine had been re-tuned. Honest Eddy knew that none of this was true and merely wanted to make the sale at all costs. Mayfield bought the car and drove away. Much to Mayfield's horror and embarrassment, within a week the automobile began to emit huge plumes of blue smoke from its exhaust. It also shook violently upon acceleration and made grinding noises. Has Honest Eddy committed fraud and misrepresentation against Mayfield?

The elements piece together. Honest Eddy knew that the automobile was defective, but lied about its condition to induce Mayfield to buy it. Mayfield surrendered to Honest Eddy something of value (namely, money—the car's purchase price). Because there was deception, misrepresentation exists. Honest Eddy is liable to Mayfield for fraud and misrepresentation.

■ ■ ■

Richard could supply another illustration. He purchased a home from Quality Construction Company (QCC). QCC's sales director assured Richard that the house had been treated for termites when, in fact, it had not. QCC had paid an exterminator to inspect the house, and the exterminator's report advised of the need for termite treatment. After living in the house for a few months, Richard discovered a serious termite infestation. Did QCC engage in fraud or misrepresentation?

The critical elements here are intent and knowledge. Did QCC's sales director know that no termite treatment had been done? QCC had received the exterminator's report recommending treatment. Thus, the sales director should have known that treatment was necessary and should have known that QCC had not performed this task. Thus, knowledge may be *imputed* under the circumstances. Intent, however, is more difficult to ascertain. Did the sales director purposefully mislead Richard? Since the director should have known that no treatment had been applied, his contrary statement to Richard demonstrated his desire to delude Richard. This equals intentional deception. Thus, misrepresentation can be proven. Also, because QCC's objective was to entice Richard to buy the house, the third element of fraud exists.

Figure 6-4 outlines the elements of fraud and misrepresentation.

Fraud	*Misrepresentation*
False statements intended to deceive	False statements intended to deceive
Knowledge of falsity of statements	Knowledge of falsity of statements
Statements designed to entice victim into surrendering something of value	Innocent party suffers damages
The innocent party is injured	

FIGURE 6-4 Elements of fraud and misrepresentation

§ 6.6 Malicious Prosecution and Abuse of Process

Usually the common law distinguishes malicious prosecution from abuse of process in this way: Malicious prosecution occurs in criminal prosecutions, whereas abuse of process happens in civil litigation. They are similar intentional torts.

Malicious Prosecution

Malicious prosecution arises when a private citizen files with the prosecutor a groundless criminal complaint against another person (who is named as the defendant in the subsequent criminal proceeding). The following elements comprise this tort:

1. Groundless criminal prosecution against the accused without probable cause
2. The complainant's malice in filing the spurious charges
3. The accused's acquittal from, or dismissal of, the criminal charges
4. Injury to the accused as a result of the prosecution.

Groundless Criminal Prosecution

The individual registering a criminal complaint with the police or prosecutor is sometimes called the **complainant**. The complainant's actions are considered bogus if he or she preferred criminal charges without probable cause that the accused was guilty of the crime. **Probable cause** is routinely defined as the reasonable belief that the accused is guilty of the alleged crime. This belief need exist only at the time the

---

TERMS

malicious prosecution A criminal prosecution or civil suit commenced maliciously and without probable cause. After the termination of such a prosecution or suit in the defendant's favor, the defendant has the right to bring an action against the original plaintiff for the tort of "malicious prosecution."

complainant 1. The plaintiff in a lawsuit. 2. A person who files a formal accusation of a crime. 3. A person who makes any formal complaint. 4. The prosecuting witness in a criminal proceeding.

probable cause A reasonable amount of suspicion, supported by circumstances sufficiently strong to justify a prudent and cautious person's belief that certain alleged facts are probably true. ...

criminal charges are initiated for probable cause to exist. However, if it later becomes obvious through investigation that the accused did not commit the alleged crime, then the complainant's insistence on the government's continuing prosecution would be malicious prosecution.

Malice

Malice in filing spurious criminal charges may be inferred from the circumstances surrounding the case. If the complainant knew (or reasonably should have known) that the accused did not commit the alleged crime, then malice is implied. Also, if the complainant is using the criminal prosecution to obtain some improper objective, such as intimidating the accused into settling a disputed civil claim or to extort money from the accused, then this likewise implies malice.

Accused's Acquittal from, or Dismissal of, the Criminal Charges

To recover successfully for malicious prosecution, the accused must have been acquitted of the groundless criminal charges initiated by the complainant, or the prosecution must have been otherwise disposed of in the accused's favor (dismissal of charges, for instance).

Injury to the Accused

Like all torts, the accused must prove actual injury as a consequence of the wrongful prosecution. This is most often accomplished by showing damage to the accused's reputation in the community or financial standing, mental anguish, or legal expenses associated with defending the criminal charges.

================= **TERMS** =================

malice State of mind that causes the intentional doing of a wrongful act without legal excuse or justification; a condition of mind prompting a person to the commission of a dangerous or deadly act in deliberate disregard of the lives or safety of others. The term does not necessarily connote personal ill will. It can and frequently does mean general malice. ...

As an element of malicious prosecution, a prosecution motived either by personal malice or by an unjustifiable purpose.

In the law of defamation, to be actionable malice must be actual malice or express malice, as distinct from implied malice or constructive malice. A privileged communication is conditioned upon an absence of malice.

In the law of damages, additional damages may be awarded if the damage to the plaintiff resulted from an injury inflicted recklessly or with malice.

Abuse of Process

Abuse of process is the civil equivalent of malicious prosecution. It occurs when the tortfeasor misuses a legal proceeding against another person to achieve an unlawful objective. The elements of abuse of process are:

1. Misuse of a legal proceeding, or threat of such misuse
2. Misuse to achieve unlawful objectives
3. Injury to the victim as a result of the misuse.

Misuse of Legal Proceedings to Achieve Unlawful Goals

The tortfeasor must intentionally misuse (or threaten to misuse) a legal proceeding against another person to accomplish an objective to which the process abuser is not legally entitled. The tortfeasor normally threatens frivolous civil litigation in an attempt to frighten the victim into paying a disputed claim. For example, the process abuser might file a groundless lawsuit against an innocent defendant in an attempt to "scare up some quick money." This occasionally occurs in personal injury litigation when fault is difficult to assign and prove; the personal injury plaintiff abuses process by suing a convenient (but innocent) defendant (who usually has assets or insurance but seems unlikely to defend a frivolous lawsuit).

Litigation is not the only legal process that may be misapplied, however. Creditors filing improper mechanic's liens against debtors to collect on disputed debts, or a wife accusing her spouse of sexually abusing their children to gain an advantage in a custody hearing, when there are no grounds for the claim and she knows the claim is false, would also be guilty of abuse of process.

The pivotal aspect of abuse of process is the tortfeasor's misuse of a legal proceeding to gain some indirect benefit to which he or she is not legally entitled. The tortfeasor has an ulterior motive for manipulating the legal proceeding. The following hypotheticals illustrate how legal process may be exploited in this way.

When tortfeasors engage in malicious prosecution and abuse of process, their victims are often left with an unpleasant taste from the experience. The victims develop a cynical bitterness toward the apparent ease with which the legal system was manipulated against them. But tort law strives to restore the balance (and the victims' faith in the system)

────────── **TERMS** ──────────

abuse of process   The use of legal process in a manner not contemplated by the law to achieve a purpose not intended by the law.

by affording remedies against these intentional torts. The following examples demonstrate how the legal system bites back when misused in this fashion.

The Case of Bulldozing Legal Process

Anger causes people to act irrationally. Persons wishing to attack others may, out of exasperation, turn to the legal system to exact revenge, even though no legal rights have been violated. Many abuse of process and malicious prosecution cases arise in this fashion, as the following case illustrates.

POTE
v.
JARRELL
Supreme Court of West Virginia
412 S.E.2d 770 (W. Va. 1991)
December 17, 1991

PER CURIAM:

The appellants, Richard Jarrell and Hollis Jarrell, appeal from a jury verdict entered in the Circuit Court of Lewis County, awarding damages to the appellee, Kenneth Pote ... . Appellee Pote filed a civil action against the appellants primarily on the theories of malicious prosecution and abuse of process ... . The appellants' principal argument on appeal is that the trial court erred in denying their motions for a directed verdict on the grounds that they relied on the advice of counsel in initiating criminal charges against appellee Pote and that they did not willfully or maliciously misuse lawfully issued process. This Court is of the opinion that there is no reversible error, and accordingly, the judgment of the circuit court is affirmed.

* * *

The incident ... occurred in October of 1987. Because of the nature of this case, it is necessary to recite the facts at some length.

Pote, in his capacity as manager of Interstate Drilling, Inc., arranged to have the appellants, Richard and Hollis Jarrell, who, were partners in an independent contracting business known as Rick's Dozer Service, provide a TD-15 bulldozer on Interstate Drilling's site to rework a road to a well location and to assist in moving pipe and equipment to the well site. The appellants provided Pote with a bulldozer and a bulldozer operator, Doyle James. Mr. James operated the bulldozer on the day of the incident for approximately three to four hours. Upon completing his work, Mr. James drove the bulldozer to the bottom of the hill near the well location ... and left for the day. Pote and some other workers, however, continued to work on the well in an effort to remove a "packer." At approximately 5:30 P.M., the well had a sudden release of pressure which caused oil and water to surge to the top of the well rig and spill onto the ground. Pote and the other workers attempted to control the flow with shovels. When their attempts to control the flow were unsuccessful, two of the workers ... suggested to Pote that they go to the bottom of the hill to get the bulldozer and use it to dig a ditch to contain the flow. ... Pote, who asserted he was faced with an emergency situation, authorized [the two workers] ... to use the bulldozer. With the use of the bulldozer, they were successful in digging a ditch to contain the flow and in keeping it from going over the hill onto the landowner's property.

* * *

Pote and Richard Jarrell eventually had a heated confrontation over Pote's use of the bulldozer without authorization. After their argument, however, Pote telephoned Richard Jarrell to apologize and assured him that Interstate Drilling would pay for any damage done to the bulldozer.

* * *

Richard Jarrell followed the recommendation of his attorney and went to the office of the magistrate to inquire about a warrant for Pote's arrest. Upon hearing the facts involved in the incident, the magistrate informed Richard Jarrell that he believed it was a civil matter. He did not issue a warrant. Richard Jarrell then went to the office of the prosecuting attorney [... and] filed a complaint for a warrant charging the appellee with the offense of feloniously and willfully injuring and tampering with a vehicle in violation of [state statutes for felonious or willful vehicular damage].

Pote received an invoice from appellants ... requesting payment in the sum of $3,560.21 for damages to the bulldozer and for lost time and income. ... Pote then met with Hollis Jarrell and advised him that he would only reimburse [Jarrell] for the actual damage to the bulldozer and not for the lost time and income. Pote gave Hollis Jarrell a check for [the bulldozer damage]. Hollis Jarrell advised Pote that if he did not pay the entire amount of the invoice, he would have him arrested. ... Pote [later] mailed the appellants a check covering the amount of lost income and time.

The magistrate sent Pote a summons to appear which was received by Pote the day after he mailed the check to the appellants. Pote did not appear and a warrant was then issued for his arrest. Pote was arrested, photographed and fingerprinted, and then released on his own recognizance.

... At trial, the circuit court directed a verdict of acquittal on the felony charge in favor of Pote and the case was submitted to the jury on the misdemeanor offense. Within minutes, the jury found that Pote was not guilty. ...

It is well established in West Virginia that a cause of action may lie for malicious prosecution or abuse of process. At the outset of our resolution of the issues before us, we shall distinguish between malicious prosecution and abuse of process.

... "In an action for malicious prosecution, plaintiff must show: (1) that the prosecution was set on foot and conducted to its termination, resulting in plaintiff's discharge; (2) that it was caused or procured by defendant; (3) that it was without probable cause; and (4) that it was malicious. If plaintiff fails to prove any of these, he cannot recover."

... "Generally, abuse of process consists of the willful or malicious misuse or misapplication of lawfully issued process to accomplish some purpose not intended or warranted by that process."

It appears from the record before us that Pote presented sufficient evidence from which a jury could find that he established all of the elements of his causes of action. The evidence presented to the jury showed that the appellants procured a felony warrant against Pote and caused him to be prosecuted ... . [T]he case against Pote was prosecuted to its termination, resulting in Pote's discharge. ... With respect to the issue of whether there was probable cause to instigate a criminal prosecution against Pote, there was no evidence presented to the jury indicating that Pote feloniously and willfully damaged the bulldozer. Furthermore, the jury heard testimony from the magistrate that the appellants were informed that this was a civil matter rather than a criminal matter. Moreover, the appellees introduced evidence to the jury attempting to show that the appellants misused the criminal process by initiating criminal proceedings against Pote for the sole purpose of obtaining payment for damages to the bulldozer. Thus, we find that Pote established the elements ... and presented sufficient evidence from which the jury could conclude that they proved those elements by a preponderance of the evidence.

* * *

Thus, for the reasons stated herein, we conclude that the judgment of the Circuit Court of Lewis County should be affirmed.
Affirmed.

Case Questions

1. Did the court find that the Jarrells had committed *both* malicious prosecution and abuse of process? Explain.
2. If the Jarrells had filed a civil action against Pote to recover the bulldozer damages, would that have been abuse of process? Why or why not?

HYPOTHETICALS

Martin was offended when a bookstore that sold provocative literature opened in his neighborhood. He registered with the prosecutor a criminal complaint for pornography against the bookstore in the hope that it would shut down or move away. Nothing that the bookstore sold violated the city's pornography ordinance, as the prosecutor informed Martin. Nonetheless, Martin exerted pressure on the prosecutor (through a contact in the mayor's office) to proceed, and subsequently the court dismissed the charges upon the bookstore's attorney's motion. The bookstore lost substantial business as a result of adverse publicity in the newspapers surrounding the case. Has Martin maliciously prosecuted?

Martin's criminal complaint against the bookstore was frivolous, because its merchandise did not violate any criminal ordinance. The prosecutor had told Martin that the bookstore was not acting illegally, so Martin lacked probable cause to believe in the bookstore's guilt. Martin's malice could be inferred, because he knew of the bookstore's innocence but insisted on pressing the criminal prosecution to coerce the bookstore into closing or moving. The bookstore successfully dismissed the criminal charges. It also suffered financial injury as a result of Martin's actions. Accordingly, Martin is liable to the bookstore for malicious prosecution.

■ ■ ■

Felmore's Shipping Company delivered a shipment of desks to Northern Office Supply Corporation. One of Northern's employees, Tony, damaged several desks while moving them into storage with a fork loader truck. The desks were undamaged previously. Northern's president, Gertrude, filed suit against Felmore's, claiming that the desks had been damaged in shipment by Felmore's employees. Has Northern abused process against Felmore's?

Gertrude knew that Felmore's was not responsible for the marred desks, as she had observed Tony carelessly operate the fork loader and damage the desks. Thus, Northern's lawsuit against Felmore was groundless. Filing frivolous litigation constitutes misuse of legal process. It may be deduced that Gertrude's purpose in filing Northern's lawsuit was to intimidate Felmore's into settling the case out of court through its insurance carrier. Felmore's injury exists in that it must defend against this baseless legal action, incurring attorneys' fees, litigation expenses, and lost time for employees required to testify. The lawsuit could also damage Felmore's reputation if the business community became aware of the action, which could easily occur, as lawsuits are a matter of public record. Northern will therefore be liable to Felmore's for abuse of process.

Figure 6-5 specifies the elements of malicious prosecution and abuse of process.

Malicious Prosecution	*Abuse of Process*
Groundless criminal prosecution	Misuse of legal proceeding (or threat of misuse)
Complainant's malice	Misuse to achieve unlawful objectives
Accused's acquittal or dismissal of charges	
Accused's injury	Injury to victim

FIGURE 6-5   Elements of malicious prosecution and abuse of process

§ 6.7   Invasion of Privacy

Invasion of privacy is largely a twentieth-century concept. In 1888, Judge Cooley of the Michigan Supreme Court, in his famous torts treatise, analyzed a series of nineteenth-century court decisions on defamation, trespass upon a personal property right (such as lectures or publications), and breach of confidence under implied contract law. Cooley surmised that a broader right was being protected and defined the legal interest in the famous phrase *the right to be let alone* (Cooley, *Torts* 29 [2d ed. 1888]). In 1890, a famous *Harvard Law Review* article co-authored by (later United States Supreme Court Justice) Louis Brandeis substantially expanded Cooley's theory, coining the phrase *right to privacy* (Warren & Brandeis, "The Right to Privacy," 4 *Harv. L. Rev.* 193 [1890]). American courts and legislatures throughout the twentieth century have incorporated this tort into their common law and statutes. It may be fairly said that this cause of action arose primarily because of this seminal law review article.

Simply put, **invasion of privacy** exists when someone publicly exploits another person's private affairs in an unreasonably intrusive manner. In tort law, there are four separate types of invasion of privacy:

1. Appropriation
2. Unreasonable intrusion
3. Public disclosure of private facts
4. False light in the public eye.

The United States Supreme Court also recognizes a fifth type of invasion of privacy protected under the United States Constitution. This includes actions by governmental agencies that infringe upon a citizen's life, liberty, or property interests safeguarded by the Constitution. However, this type is not covered by tort law; it is a due process issue.

Appropriation

Appropriation occurs when the tortfeasor uses a person's name or likeness without permission to gain some benefit. For example, if an advertising company used a person's photograph to sell a product without that person's consent, then the firm would be liable to the person for invasion of privacy by appropriation. Most cases involving this variety of invasion of privacy consist of unauthorized use of photographs, artist's sketches, or quotations associated with names to sell someone else's goods or services.

Unreasonable Intrusion

Unreasonable intrusion involves an excessive and highly offensive assault upon one's seclusion or solitude. Several illustrations should clarify. If store security personnel demand that a suspected shoplifter disrobe, or if they rifle through the suspect's personal belongings in an illegal search, this would be considered unreasonable intrusion. Intentional eavesdropping upon a private conversation is another example.

■ TERMS ▶

invasion of privacy   A violation of the right of privacy.

appropriation   A wrongful taking of anything which deprives another person of his or her rightful interest.

unreasonable intrusion †   One type of the intentional tort of invasion of privacy. Occurs when the tortfeasor engages in an excessive and highly offensive invasion upon another person's seclusion or solitude.

Recall the Phyllis/Susan hypothetical discussed in connection with infliction of emotional distress? Susan's incessant telephone calls would also constitute unreasonable intrusion. Searching another's mail to discover private information, or obtaining unauthorized access to someone's bank account or tax records, are yet other instances. Courts have also found that illegal, compulsory blood tests equal unreasonable intrusion. Simple trespassing onto an individual's land to snoop would also violate this version of privacy.

The Case of the Cheap Impostor

Many a company has been tempted to hire a person who looks and sounds like a famous actor when the advertising budget does not allow for the "real thing." In New Jersey's Atlantic City, hundreds of would-be actors and actresses make a living copying the stars. If it is good enough for the casinos, why not for television and radio? In this case, Louisiana's nationally known chef, Paul Prudhomme brought an action for invasion of his right to privacy and publicity and for abuse of his right to advertise. The United States District Court denied the defendants' motion to dismiss Prudhomme's case.

PRUDHOMME
v.
PROCTER & GAMBLE CO.
United States District Court for the Eastern District of Louisiana
800 F. Supp. 390 (E.D. La. 1992)
September 14, 1992
Sear, Chief Judge

Plaintiffs Chef Paul Prudhomme and Tasso Travel, Inc. have brought this civil action claiming multiple violations of trademark infringement, invasion of privacy, and unfair competition resulting from a television commercial aired by defendants Procter & Gamble Company and Folgers Coffee Company. In their amended complaint, plaintiffs claim that the commercial depicts an actor bearing a striking resemblance to Prudhomme advocating defendant's coffee product, that plaintiffs never consented to the commercial, and that the commercial suggests Prudhomme's sponsorship or approval of the product to the detriment of plaintiffs.

Defendants filed a Motion to Dismiss or for a More Definite Statement. They claim that plaintiffs fail to allege a claim upon which relief can be granted for any of the alleged violations. As an alternative to dismissal, defendants ask for a more definite statement by plaintiffs of their claims to enable defendants to adequately address the plaintiffs' allegations.

In considering a defendant's motion to dismiss, the well-pleaded allegations of the plaintiffs' complaint must be taken as true. The complaint's allegations "should be construed favorably to the pleader," and it should not be dismissed for failure to state a claim unless there is no doubt that the plaintiffs can prove no set of facts which would entitle them to relief ... .

Plaintiffs' amended complaint alleges violations of two sections of the Lanham Act: § 43(a) involving false or misleading advertising (15 U.S.C. § 1125(a)(1)); and § 32(1) involving trademark infringement (15 U.S.C. § 1114(1)).

* * *

The plaintiffs in this case have alleged sufficient facts to satisfy the ... "likelihood of confusion" test ... . First, plaintiffs' claim that Prudhomme is famous for popularizing cajun-style cuisine and for his restaurants, cookbooks, and food-related products and services. Second, plaintiffs claim that the "look-alike" actor used in defendants' commercial bears a "strong resemblance" to

Prudhomme, due to the actor's portly build, dark hair and full dark beard, facial features, and apparel including a white cap and bandana. Plaintiffs claim that all these features are generally associated with plaintiff Chef Paul Prudhomme. Third, plaintiffs assert that the area being advertised is one Prudhomme is involved in, because the commercial is one in a series portraying restauranteurs "switching" instant coffee on their patrons, and Prudhomme is a famous restauranteur. Fourth, plaintiffs have alleged actual confusion as to Prudhomme's sponsorship of defendant's coffee. Finally, plaintiffs allege bad faith on defendant's behalf, claiming defendants' were attempting to capitalize on Prudhomme's image without plaintiff's consent.

In opposition to plaintiffs' Lanham Act allegations, defendants first claim that there can be no finding of a "likelihood of confusion," because they state that the commercial "clearly identifies" the chef portrayed in the commercial as someone other than Prudhomme. Plaintiffs dispute this assertion, claiming that the identification is ambiguous ... . The mere existence of a disclaimer will not preclude a finding of consumer confusion. ...

Defendants further claim that any alleged use of Prudhomme's "likeness" by defendants is not actionable under the Lanham Act because it is not a proper protectible image. To be protectible, a mark must be shown either to be "distinctive" or to have derived a "secondary meaning." Defendants claim that a person's "likeness" cannot be shown either to be a distinctive mark, or to have acquired any secondary meaning. Defendants' attack should fail for two reasons. First, all look-alike claims necessarily involve allegations of improper use of one's likeness; the fact that there have been successful look-alike claims argues against the defendants' generalized statement that protection of a "likeness" is improper under the Lanham Act.

Second, plaintiffs have alleged enough facts to support a showing that Prudhomme's likeness may well be a protectible image under traditional trademark law. ... In their complaint, plaintiffs allege facts supporting a finding of secondary meaning, which is sufficient to withstand dismissal of their claim under the Lanham Act.

Defendants' final attack on plaintiffs' Lanham Act allegations involves § 32(1), which defendants' claim requires an allegation of unauthorized use of a *registered* trademark. ... While registration may provide a presumption of protection under the Act, certain marks will be protected by the courts even if they are not registered.

Plaintiffs' allegations in their amended complaint satisfy a showing of both "likelihood of confusion" and protectible image, the necessary elements for both their Lanham Act claims, and withstand defendants' motion for dismissal.

* * *

Plaintiff Prudhomme claims that defendants violated his right to privacy by misappropriating Prudhomme's likeness, placing him in a false light, and infringing upon Prudhomme's right to control the publicity of his likeness. Plaintiffs' complaint sufficiently alleges facts to support the misappropriation and false light claims. Defendants' opposition merely attacks the sufficiency of the allegations, an attack which is premature.

With regard to infringement of the right to publicity, defendants claim that this right has not been recognized in Louisiana. They claim that the right of privacy encompasses only four interests in this state: (1) misappropriation of an individual's name or likeness; (2) intrusion on solitude or seclusion; (3) false light; and (4) unreasonable disclosure of embarrassing private facts. In response, plaintiffs claim that other jurisdictions have recognized this right as a "special branch" of the right to privacy. While Louisiana courts have not explicitly adopted this right, they have not specifically precluded it, either. ...

Finally, defendants have asked the court to grant their motion for a more definite statement against plaintiffs. ... Here defendants have proven ... that the complaint can indeed be responded to.

Accordingly,

The motion to dismiss and for a more definite statement submitted by defendants Proctor & Gamble Company and Folgers Coffee Company is DENIED as to all counts of the complaint.

Case Questions

1. Based on the facts, did the plaintiff state a claim for invasion of right to privacy and publicity?
2. In the court's opinion, how did the defendants prove that the complaint could in fact be responded to without further changes?

The Case of the Truthful Video Camera

Increasingly, our ability to protect our privacy is being eroded. Law enforcement units are now using video cameras to catch speeders in the act. Even employers have begun using video cameras with greater frequency to monitor employee and customer behavior. But what are the bounds? Can an employer turn the video camera on at all times and in all locations? In the following case, an employee who was caught on tape "lock-picking" claimed that such taping was an invasion of his privacy.

MARRS

v.

MARRIOTT CORP.

United States District Court for Maryland

830 F. Supp. 274 (D. Md. 1992)

December 21, 1992

Nickerson, District Judge

This case arises out of the termination of Plaintiff Timothy H. Marrs ["Marrs"] from his position as a security guard for Defendant Marriott Corporation ["Marriott"]. Marrs was hired by Marriott on January 15, 1982 and until the events that immediately led to his termination, consistently received positive evaluations of his job performance. Due to religious beliefs which prohibited his working on Saturdays, Marrs was generally assigned to work the night shift as an accommodation to his request to have Saturdays off.

On the morning of September 7, 1990, Defendant Timothy Spicer ["Spicer"], a security investigator for Marriott, noticed that some papers in the locked file drawer of his desk had been tampered with. After finding on September 10, 1990 that the drawer had again been opened and papers disturbed, Spicer requested and received permission to monitor the desk in question with a hidden video camera. On September

11, Spicer, along with Night Shift Supervisor Ed Capers, reviewed the video tape and observed Marrs picking the lock on the desk drawer with a paper clip and flipping through the files.

Marrs does not deny that he picked the lock on the desk. The essence of Marrs' explanation for his activities is that he was merely "practicing his lock picking skills." Because of Marrs' conduct, he was immediately placed on a three day suspension pending an investigation. After the investigation was completed, Marrs was informed that he would be terminated because of the incident. Plaintiff was given the option of resigning in lieu of termination, which he did.

On October 22, 1990 Marrs filed a charge of discrimination with the Montgomery County Human Relations Commission alleging that he was discriminated against on the basis of his religion. ... The Complaint [contained a count for] Invasion of Employee Privacy—Surveillance ... .

* * *

Summary Judgment is proper if the evidence before the court, consisting of the pleadings, depositions, answers to interrogatories, and admissions of record, establishes that there is no genuine issue as to any material fact and that the moving party is entitled to judgment as a matter of law.

* * *

Finally, in assessing such a motion, the Court must view the evidence and all justifiable inferences in the light most favorable to the party opposing the motion.

* * *

Marrs asserts in Count VI that Defendants' videotaping of his activities on the night in question constitutes an invasion of his privacy. Although Marrs has not specified which branch of the tort of invasion of privacy he is alleging, it is assumed that he is alleging an intrusion upon his seclusion. To prove such an invasion, Marrs is required to show that the employer intentionally

intruded upon his solicitude, seclusion or private affairs in a manner that would be highly offensive to a reasonable person. The Court finds no support for the conclusion that Marrs had a reasonable expectation of privacy in an open office. In fact, Plaintiff admits that the area "was a common area that all of [the security guards] had access to." [T]his type of invasion of privacy [,i.e., surveillance,] generally is inapplicable to most areas of the workplace because there can be no liability for observing an employee at work since he is then not in seclusion.

* * *

For all the above stated reasons, Defendants' Motion for Summary Judgment will be granted for all counts with the exception of Count IV as that count relates to Defendant Spicer.

Case Questions

1. Does an employee have an expectation of privacy at work?
2. What would the employee have had to show for the court to have reached a different result?

Public Disclosure of Private Facts

When a tortfeasor communicates purely private information about a person to the public without permission, and a reasonable person would find this disclosure extremely objectionable, then invasion of privacy by **public disclosure of private facts** has taken place. Truth is *not* a defense against this tort, because it is the unauthorized and offensive public revelation of private facts that is being protected against.

The most common example of such disclosure involves communications by the mass media. For example, if a newspaper article mentions an ordinary citizen by name and discusses in detail his or her drug dependency problems, and the person did not consent, then public disclosure of private facts has occurred. Public figures, however, generally do not succeed in lawsuits against the media when such disclosures are made without malice.

TERMS

public disclosure of private facts[†]   One type of the intentional tort of invasion of privacy. Occurs when the tortfeasor communicates purely private information about a person to the public without permission, and a reasonable person would find this disclosure extremely objectionable.

The Case of the Viewing Room Covered by the Umbrella

In some cases, the statement "truth is stranger than fiction" really rings true. As a paralegal you will be privy to numerous stories—some of which, if you heard them outside the law office, would cause you to burst out laughing in disbelief. As a professional, you must learn to maintain your composure no matter what the client reveals to you. In this example, you get to see a case from an insurance company's perspective.

LINEBERRY

v.

STATE FARM FIRE & CASUALTY CO.
United States District Court, Middle District
of Tennessee
885 F. Supp. 1095 (M.D. Tenn. 1995)
April 4, 1995
Echols, District Judge

Plaintiffs, Dewey Lineberry and Bill Robinson, seek a declaratory judgment requiring State Farm Fire & Casualty Co. ["State Farm"] to defend and indemnify them against actions in state court pursuant to personal liability policies of insurance ... .

Plaintiffs are currently defending four separate actions brought in the Circuit Court of Wilson County, Tennessee by four women. The allegations of all four suits are essentially the same. Lineberry apparently had sexual relationships with the four women over the period of time stated in the lawsuits. In the course of building himself a new office building, Lineberry enlisted the help of Robinson to construct a "secret" viewing room adjoining the recreation room and the restroom of Lineberry's personal office. Two-way mirrors were constructed into the walls of the recreation room and restroom so that anyone in the viewing room could look through the mirrors and observe occupants of the recreation room and bathroom without the occupant's knowledge. The occupants of the recreation room and restroom could see only their own reflections in the mirrors. Lineberry and Robinson set up a video camera in the viewing room so that the persons and activities in the recreation room and restroom could secretly be filmed through the two-way mirrors.

On occasions Lineberry brought the unsuspecting females to his office where Robinson, who was hiding in the viewing room, secretly videotaped their sexual activities. Lineberry contends this scheme was approved or suggested by his attorney as a way to preserve proof of his sexual activities in the event one of his unsuspecting female guests falsely accused him of some impropriety. He maintains that this extraordinary precaution was taken only for his own protection, and that he had no intention of disclosing the video tapes of his sexual escapades to any other person. At some later time, Lineberry and his attorney had a dispute. Subsequently, Lineberry's attorney notified the Wilson County District Attorney of Lineberry's clandestine videotaping activities. After a search warrant was obtained, Lineberry's office was searched, and the tapes were seized by local law enforcement officials. The women depicted in the videotapes were then asked to come to the Sheriff's Department, identify themselves on the videotapes, and explain their actions. All four women deny they were aware they had been filmed.

Each of the four women filed a separate lawsuit in the Circuit Court of Wilson County. The suits charge Lineberry and Robinson with outrageous conduct, intentional infliction of emotional distress, fraud or constructive fraud, misrepresentation, appropriation, and invasion of their rights to privacy. Each of the women seek recovery for humiliation, mental distress, and emotional pain and suffering which resulted from the actions of Lineberry and Robinson.

Both Lineberry and Robinson possess personal liability umbrella insurance policies with State Farm. They contend that pursuant to the provisions of those policies, State Farm must defend and indemnify them against the claims for invasion of privacy in the four lawsuits filed in Wilson County, Tennessee.

* * *

The policies also contain a provision which excludes coverage for intentional acts or acts which are expected. ...

Plaintiffs contend that State Farm, having specifically insured them against losses caused by the invasion of the right to privacy, must both defend them against the claims presented in the four lawsuits and indemnify them for any damages awarded to the four women. State Farm contends it is not required to defend or indemnify against these claims because the losses were not the result of an "accident" and the claims fall within the policy's exclusion for intentional or expected acts.

Plaintiffs counter Defendant's arguments by pointing to the language in the policy which defines "personal injury" by specifically listing a number of intentional torts, including invasion of the right of privacy. In other words, the losses insured against are those resulting in personal injury, which under the policy's definition includes certain types of intentional torts. An intentional tort is a civil wrong or injury which occurs as a result of the intentional act of another person. For example, one cannot commit an act of assault and battery accidentally. ...

Defendant alleges that the insurance policy provisions are not contradictory and the coverage is not illusory, because an invasion of the right to privacy is not necessarily an intentional tort. If that were correct, the policy would not necessarily be ambiguous, as the policy would cover injuries resulting from unintentional invasions of the right of privacy and would exclude those which are intentional.

* * *

In the instant case, the umbrella policy expressly covered injuries resulting from invasion of the right of privacy, an inherently intentional tort, but excluded injuries which were intended or expected. Therefore, the Court finds the coverage is illusory, and the policy is ambiguous and must be interpreted against the insurer and in favor of the insured. Accordingly, State Farm must idemnify Plaintiffs for injuries (humiliation, mental distress, emotional pain and suffering) arising from Plaintiffs' alleged invasion of rights to privacy.

The Court will now turn to State Farm's duty to defend. ... The obligation to defend arises whenever the complaint against the insured alleges a claim upon any ground for which there might be a recovery within the terms of a policy. ... The purpose of such duty ... is for the insured to obtain protection against the expense of defending suits, whether meritorious or groundless, *within the area and scope of liability covered by the policy.*

Because this Court has found that the claims for injuries resulting from the alleged invasion of the right to privacy fall within the coverage of the policies, State Farm has a duty to defend against that portion of the complaints against Lineberry and Robinson.

For the foregoing reasons, Lineberry's Motion for Summary Judgment is GRANTED, Plaintiff Robinson's Motion for Summary Judgment is GRANTED, and Defendant State Farm's Motion for Summary Judgment is DENIED.

Case Questions

1. Why did the court find that the defendant insurance company had an obligation to defend the plaintiffs?
2. Do you think that insurance was designed to cover deliberate and intentional acts of insureds? Explain.

False Light in the Public Eye

Invasion of privacy by placing a person in a **false light in the public eye** happens if the tortfeasor publicly attributes to that individual spurious opinions, statements, or actions. For instance, if a magazine uses without permission someone's photograph and name in an embarrassing fashion, this would place the victim in a false light publicly. One fact pattern repeated in many court cases concerns a plaintiff's photograph and name which appear in a newspaper adjacent to a negative story appearing on the same page, when the story and photograph appear in such a way as to suggest a connection between the two. Another example would be the advertisement mentioned previously regarding appropriation.

Perhaps no other intentional tort excites the public indignation more than invasion of privacy. Almost everyone desires a sanctuary from the daily intrusions that dominate our urbanized, highly technological, and mobile society. However, the popular conception of the right to privacy does not always afford legal remedies. The following hypotheticals illustrate how the tort elements must first be satisfied.

HYPOTHETICALS

Mel rents a house from Mickey. After Mel had lived there for six months, Mickey notified Mel to move out of the house within ten days, because Mickey needed the house for his bedridden mother. Mel refused, pointing out that the lease ran for a full year and that it could not be terminated by either party without thirty days' advance notice. After ten days, Mickey moved into the house with his mother and her two grandchildren. Mel refused to leave the house, and everyone lived in a state of considerable tension for two weeks before Mel finally could not stand it any longer and left. Did Mickey invade Mel's privacy by unreasonable intrusion?

Mickey's actions interfered with Mel's solitude in an excessive and highly offensive manner. Mel had complied with the lease agreement and had a legal right to occupy the premises. Mickey's invasion with his invalid mother and two grandchildren substantially disrupted Mel's domestic tranquility. The stress among the house occupants became so extreme that Mel was at last compelled to abandon his residence. Accordingly, Mickey would be liable to Mel for invasion of privacy by unreasonable intrusion.

■ ■ ■

Herman was aghast when he opened the day's newspaper to see an advertisement with his picture, in which he was holding a can of Bartell's Beenie-Weenies. Under the photograph was the caption, "Bartell's Makes the Best Beenie-Weenies!"

TERMS

false light in the public eye[†] One type of the intentional tort of invasion of privacy. Occurs when the tortfeasor publicly attributes to another individual spurious opinions, statements, or actions.

Herman could not recall ever buying this brand and made no such endorsement to anyone associated with the product. He did not give his permission to use the photograph. Has Bartell's invaded Herman's privacy by appropriation?

Bartell's used Herman's likeness in its photograph without his consent. Bartell's hoped to profit from increased sales as a result of this "customer's" endorsement. Bartell's would thus be liable to Herman for invasion of privacy by appropriation.

Furthermore, Bartell's publicly attributed a spurious opinion to Herman in its photograph caption. This would place Herman in a false light in the public eye. Thus, Bartell's would also be liable to Herman for this type of invasion of privacy.

Figure 6-6 summarizes the elements of the four types of invasion of privacy.

§ 6.8 Defamation: Libel and Slander

Defamation consists of two varieties: libel and slander. **Libel** is a written false and disparaging statement about an individual that the tortfeasor communicates to a third person. **Slander** is an oral false and disparaging statement about a person that the tortfeasor communicates to a third party. Courts often refer to this communication element as **publication**. Publication of the defamatory information must injure the victim's reputation in the community. The elements can be outlined as follows:

1. Written (libel) or oral (slander) statement
2. False and defamatory statement about a person
3. Tortfeasor's communication of the statement to a third party
4. Harm to the victim's reputation in the community.

TERMS

defamation Libel or slander; the written or oral publication, falsely and intentionally, of anything that is injurious to the good name or reputation of another person.

libel A false and malicious publication, expressed either in printing, writing, or by signs and pictures, tending to harm a person's reputation and expose him or her to public hatred, contempt, or ridicule.

slander A false and malicious oral statement tending to blacken a person's reputation or to damage his or her means of livelihood.

publication The act of making something known to the public; the act of publishing. ... In the law of libel and slander, the act of communicating a defamation to a person or persons other than the person defamed. Publication is essential because, without it, there is no defamation.

Appropriation	Unreasonable Intrusion	Public Disclosure of Private Facts	False Light in the Public Eye
Unconsented use of person's name or likeness for profit	Excessive and highly offensive invasion of one's seclusion or solitude	Public communication of private information about person without permission	Publicly attributing spurious opinions, statements, or actions to a person
		Reasonable person finds disclosure extremely objectionable	

FIGURE 6-6   Elements of invasion of privacy

Although the first element is obvious, the others require some elaboration.

Nature of the Statement

For libel, the statement must generally be written in some fashion. This does not necessarily mean writing, such as handwriting, or printed words, such as those appearing on this page. There are many forms of written expression, including such unusual methods as billboards, skywriting with smoke or banners pulled by an airplane, or placing objects such as stones into the shapes of letters. The critical element of writing is whether the information is communicated visually through means of an alphabet.

For slander, the statement must be orally delivered. But it does not have to be words. Gestures, particularly obscene ones, also qualify, provided that the meaning of the gestures is sufficiently clear to onlookers to be defamatory.

Harm to Reputation in the Community

A statement is considered *defamatory* if it causes the fourth element—namely, injury to the victim's reputation in the community. For purposes of libel and slander, **community** is narrowly defined as

TERMS

community   1. People living in the same place (city, town, neighborhood) and subject to the same laws. 2. A place where people live together. 3. Society in general. 4. A group of people sharing common interests.

a significant number of persons acquainted or familiar with the victim. Although some courts have held that "a community of one" is sufficient under certain circumstances, most courts maintain that larger numbers are required. Nevertheless, certain expressions, such as "a handful," "a closely associated group," and "associates in the neighborhood or workplace," suggest small numbers in most instances.

Many courts define the victim's injury in more emotional terms. For example, it has commonly been held that statements are libelous or slanderous if they ridicule, humiliate, or subject the victim to contempt or hatred from among his or her peers.

Publication

The tortfeasor must communicate the false and derogatory statement to a third party. That means that statements made by the tortfeasor directly to the victim are defamatory only if seen or heard by another or others.

Publication takes place through any means by which the false information is disseminated. This includes anything spoken, either in person or over amplification (megaphone or loudspeaker at a ballpark, for instance), radio, television, or telephone; or anything written, including letters, telegrams, scribbled messages, billboards, or printed and published works (such as a letter to the editor in the local newspaper, for instance).

Public Figures

Public figures, such as movie and television celebrities or public officers and employees who exercise substantial governmental power, are treated differently than private individuals. These people are used to being under the public eye and have greater access to the media to refute untrue charges than the ordinary person. Accordingly, not as much protection is afforded to public figures. To be successful in claiming defamation, a public figure must show that a statement was made with actual malice. Because this is very hard to prove, few public figures bring suit to challenge statements about them even when they know the assertions to be totally false.

Slander Per Se

Per se is a term indicating that something is automatic or presumed. Some words in and of themselves are defamatory; therefore, injury and damage need not be proven when slander per se is shown.

For example, words that imply criminal conduct, or words that are harmful to one's business, or words implying that one has a loathsome and communicable disease are all presumed to damage one's reputation, so the victim need not prove damages to be successful in a slander per se claim.

Truth and Privilege as Absolute Defenses

Truth is considered an absolute defense in defamation cases. If the information the tortfeasor communicates is true, then no libel or slander occurred. To successfully use this defense, the tortfeasor must prove the veracity of the statement.

What is true is often a matter of opinion. It always depends upon the nature of the derogatory comments. For example, to call a person born out of wedlock a "bastard" is technically accurate, but in today's society the term is rarely used as defined in the dictionary. Similarly, to refer to a sexually promiscuous individual as a "harlot" or "gigolo" could be deemed factual by reasonable persons, particularly those who are morally opposed to the conduct described. Courts have struggled with the elasticity of truth, and a variety of formulas for pinpointing truth have been posited in court opinions. The most common states that literal truth in every detail is unnecessary. If the statement is substantially true, so that a reasonable person would decide that the accusations were justified given these facts, then truth will operate as a defense to defamation actions.

Privilege is also considered an absolute defense in defamation cases. Statements made by attorneys and judges during trials are privileged and cannot be the grounds for a defamation charge. Likewise, legislators are immune from liability for false statements made during debate, even if the lawmakers deliberately make the untrue statements. Congress members have an absolute privilege while speaking on the floor of Congress. Privilege allows all these persons to do their best jobs without fear of repercussions should a statement they make later prove to be untrue.

Defamation is another intentional tort, like assault and battery, that virtually everyone has experienced, either as victim or tortfeasor (or both). One need only recall a recent imprudent remark to mentally invoke accusations of slander or libel. Nevertheless, the elements determine whether defamation has occurred, as the following illustrations show.

The Case of the Living Dead

Imagine one's horror at opening the daily newspaper and, while glancing quickly at the obituaries, spotting oneself listed as recently deceased! Although this may be a shocking revelation, it is the type of mistake that newspapers easily and promptly correct. As the following case illustrates, an erroneous obituary does not always constitute defamation.

DECKER
v.
PRINCETON PACKET, INC.
Supreme Court of New Jersey
116 N.J. 418, 561 A.2d 1122 (1989)
August 8, 1989
Handler, J

This case involves a tort action brought against a newspaper seeking damages for defamation and emotional distress attributable to the publication of a false obituary. The Court is called on to address whether an obituary that reports a death, this being the only false statement, can possibly have a defamatory interpretation. ... The trial court and Appellate Division held that defamation and emotional-harm claims were without merit as a matter of law. Plaintiffs appeal these rulings arguing that defendant's publication of a false obituary without verifying its accuracy caused damage to reputation and emotional harm that should be compensated under our tort law.

On February 15, 1985, the defendant, a newspaper, The Princeton Packet, Inc. ("The Packet"), which publishes on Tuesday and Friday of each week, reported the following obituary for Marcy Goldberg Decker, the plaintiff:

Marcy Goldberg Decker of Princeton died suddenly Feb. 11. She was 31.

Ms. Goldberg was the fiance of Robert J. Feldman of Princeton.

She was a lifelong resident of Princeton and is survived by a son, Jackson T.; her mother, Charlotte Goldberg of Trenton; and a brother, Ronald Goldberg of California.

Funeral arrangements were incomplete at press time.

This obituary is incorrect because Marcy Decker was not dead.

All other information in the obituary—her age, residence, and family relationships—was accurate ... . Plaintiff notified defendant by a telephone call two days after the publication that she was in fact alive. The Packet printed the following retraction on February 19, 1985:

The Packet erroneously reported in Friday's edition that Marcy Decker of Princeton died Feb. 11. The obituary was false. The Packet regrets the error and any inconvenience this may have caused Ms. Decker or her family.

* * *

Plaintiffs deposed three employees of defendant to establish their claims that The Packet was unaware of who had submitted the obituary, [and] that it took no steps to determine the validity of the notice ... .

* * *

A defamatory statement is one that is false and is " 'injurious to the reputation of another' or exposes another person to 'hatred, contempt or ridicule' or subjects another person to 'a loss of the good will and confidence' in which he or she is held by others." Thus, if the statement of Marcy Decker's death in the false obituary could be interpreted by a reasonable person to expose the plaintiff to "hatred, contempt, ridicule or disgrace or subject ... [her] to loss of the good will and confidence of the community," then her action for defamation could proceed to trial.

The principle generally endorsed by most authority throughout the country is that an obituary in which the only false statement concerns the death of the individual, published without malicious intent, is not defamatory *per se*. These cases suggest that publication of a notice of death is usually not defamatory because it does not injure one's reputation. As one court explained, "one is [not] demeaned or belittled by the report of his or her death."

The general rule, however, does have an exception where the false obituary contains additional false information that may be defamatory. ...

This Court finds that the general rule and its limited exception should govern this case and other similar cases. Here, the only false aspect of the obituary was the death of plaintiff Marcy Decker. Therefore, under the general rule, the obituary is not defamatory *per se* because the reported death of an individual when viewed from the perspective of a reasonable person of ordinary intelligence and experience does not impugn reputation. As the trial court observed, the publication of the death notice did not impute to the plaintiff any wrong and did not hold her up to ridicule. Death is a natural state and demeans no one.

... Moreover, the chance of an obituary being incorrect appears slight, and the newspaper can promptly publish a correction, which occurred in this case. Thus, the plaintiffs did have an adequate remedy to correct any false statement and the published correction should have prevented the false obituary from causing any continuing effects.

... Therefore, we hold that where a newspaper mistakenly prints an obituary for a person who is still alive and then retracts its mistake, there is no defamation *per se*, since announcing the death of someone is not by itself injurious to one's reputation.

* * *

Accordingly, the judgment below is affirmed.

Case Questions

1. Do you believe the facts in *Decker* satisfy an action for intentional or reckless infliction of emotional distress? For invasion of privacy? Explain.
2. If the plaintiff could discover who planted the false obituary at the newspaper's offices, could she recover for any intentional torts discussed in this chapter against this unknown person? Why or why not?

HYPOTHETICALS

Arnold owns an automobile painting service. One of his customers, Ginger, was dissatisfied with Arnold's paint job on her automobile; several spots that had not been polished stood out against the rest of the finish. Rather than complain directly to Arnold, Ginger called in to a live local radio station and said that Arnold was a "con artist" and that he had swindled many other people with sloppy work. Has Ginger slandered Arnold?

Ginger communicated information about Arnold to third persons, and so publication occurred. The information was false, as Ginger's dissatisfaction with a single paint job hardly documented Arnold's dishonesty. The critical issue is whether Ginger's statements were defamatory. It is likely that Ginger's accusations about Arnold's honesty and integrity will substantially injure Arnold's business reputation in the community. This is particularly true because the allegations suggest criminal conduct by an innocent person. Thus, Ginger has slandered Arnold and is liable to him for damages.

■ ■ ■

Consider the hypothetical of Helga. She enjoyed writing letters to the editor and her missives regularly appeared in the newspaper. One day Helga turned to the editorial page and read the following response to one of her letters:

Dear Editor:
    In response to Helga Goldblatt's letter in last week's edition, I must say that this woman is mentally ill and needs psychiatric treatment. She suffers from delusions and cannot be trusted. How can she make those ridiculous statements about the city's snow removal policy? I happen to work for the city street department, and I know that we regularly clear side streets after handling the main streets. It usually only takes a few extra days to get to the side streets, not weeks as she said. Why doesn't she take her medicine and get a grip?
    Jackson Winderson

Has Jackson libeled Helga? Jackson's written communication was published—literally—by appearing in the newspaper. Many people would have been exposed to the letter. Helga's reputation in the community undoubtedly will suffer from Jackson's accusations that she is "mentally ill." Although it may be true that Helga was uninformed about the city's snow removal policy, truth as to these matters is irrelevant—the defamatory remarks pertained to Helga's mental capacity. Jackson would be liable to Helga for libel.

Figure 6-7 lists the elements of libel and slander.

Libel	*Slander*
Written statement	Oral statement
False and defamatory statement	False and defamatory statement
Publication to third party	Publication to third party
Injury to victim's reputation in the community	Injury to victim's reputation in the community

FIGURE 6-7
Elements of libel and slander

The Case of the "Woodchipper Murderer"

In this case, a man's wife—a stewardess—disappeared. A news broadcaster suggested that the pilot-husband had murdered his wife like another pilot had in a similar case. Is mere inference enough, or must defamation be proved by explicit words?

BROWN

v.

HEARST CORP.

United States Court of Appeals, First Circuit
54 F.3d 21 (1st Cir. 1955)
May 11, 1995
Boudin, Circuit Judge

In March 1987, Regina Brown, the then-wife of appellant Willis Brown and mother of three children, disappeared. At the time Regina was employed as a flight attendant, and Willis as a pilot, for American Airlines; the couple had lived together in Newtown, Connecticut, but had been separated for four months and were living apart. The police investigated the disappearance and found Regina's car abandoned in New York but no trace of her. The investigation remains open. It is not known whether Regina is alive or dead.

Later in the same year the Browns were divorced in a Connecticut state court, the contested proceedings being completed in Regina's absence. The state court trial was prolonged and a detailed opinion was written by the trial judge pertaining to custody and support. ...

The trial was widely reported in the press, and publicity continued even after the decree. This was due partly to further litigation and the continuing police investigation, but also to a freakish coincidence. About six months before Regina's disappearance, another woman who lived in Newtown, a Pan Am flight attendant married to an Eastern pilot, had disappeared. Fragments of her bone were found in a nearby river, and her pilot husband was convicted in the so-called woodchipper murder.

In November 1990, appellee Hearst Corporation d/b/a WCVB-TV Channel 5 in Boston ("Channel 5") broadcasted from Massachusetts a segment entitled "The Other Pilot's Wife" as a part of the station's regular "newsmagazine" program. It was prepared by Mary Richardson, a journalist with the station, who conducted a substantial amount of research and a number of interviews in preparing the broadcast.

The broadcast opens with the leitmotif—"Tonight the bizarre story of a small New England town where one stewardess is dead, another is missing"—and then offers a brief reprise of the 1986 murder of the Pan Am flight attendant. Next, turning to the Browns, the broadcast describes and depicts an apparent storybook marriage going sour, the divorce petition, and Regina's disappearance. "In the days following Regina's disappearance," says Richardson, "Willis showed no interest in what had happened to her."

* * *

There is other incriminating information about Willis recounted in the program, and the police are described as having suspected Willis and as believing still that "Mr. Brown knows more about the disappearance of his wife than he is letting on." No evidence even remotely exculpatory of Willis is described. On the other hand, Mary Richardson, the "voice over" throughout the program, never asserts that Willis is guilty or even says that she thinks he is guilty. Formally, the program describes the disappearance as a mystery or, at worst, a possible murder still unsolved.

In February 1993, Willis brought the present action against Channel 5 in state court in Texas. The case was removed to federal court and thereafter transferred to the federal district court in Massachusetts. As subsequently amended, Willis' complaint charged defamation, invasion of privacy under Mass. Gen.L. ch. 214 § 1B, "false light" invasion of privacy, and intentional infliction of emotional distress.

After discovery, Channel 5 moved for summary judgment. In a detailed opinion dated July 21, 1994, the district court granted the motion. As to the defamation claim, the court relied in different respects on lack of falsity, the limited protection available for statements of opinion, the "fair report" privilege, and lack of fault. The privacy and intentional infliction claims were dismissed on grounds described below. Willis has now appealed, asserting that all of his claims should have been submitted to a jury.

On appeal from a grant of summary judgment, we review the decision de novo, drawing inferences in favor of the party opposing the motion. ...

Channel 5 does not appear to dispute that the broadcast charges Willis with murder or at least that a jury would be entitled to find this to be the import of the program. The broadcast never flatly expresses that accusation. Indeed, it says that the murder is unsolved and makes clear that the police have nothing much in the way of direct evidence against Willis. But defamation can occur by innuendo as well as by explicit assertion, and the suggestion here is a fairly strong one.

* * *

The broadcast makes clear that the police suspect Willis, and Regina's parents are filmed making even stronger statements of suspicion. Material from the divorce trial is used to establish or buttress doubts about Willis' character and history. The suggestion of murder runs through the program like a gold thread. The broadcast opens with the dramatic footage relating to the woodchipper murder and closes with Richardson's rhetorical question, could "someone" get away with murder?

A common defense to a charge of defamation is "truth." The Supreme Court tells us that in a suit like this one against the media the burden is upon the defamed plaintiff to show that the statements are not true. Neither side addresses this issue. Perhaps each assumes that to carry his burden of proof, Willis could testify at trial that he did not murder his wife and a jury might believe him. In all events, we take the case as one in which a jury might find that murder had been charged and that the charge was false.

Channel 5's primary response is that "[m]uch of the [b]roadcast, and the entirety of its allegedly defamatory sting, is in essence a 'fair report' of the Brown's divorce trial in Connecticut" and thus falls under the Massachusetts privilege allowed for media coverage of an official proceeding. Such a privilege certainly exists in Massachusetts, and there is little doubt that much of the material in the broadcast is drawn from, and attributed to, the divorce proceeding.

For present purposes, we will assume that the privilege extends to non-contemporaneous reports and that the program—so far as it related to the divorce proceeding and the information developed there—conveyed a fair and accurate report of the proceeding. But only a portion of the broadcast purported to be drawn from the proceeding. And, while that portion may be privileged, we are skeptical of Channel 5's claim that the the entire "sting" of the broadcast is privileged material.

* * *

Where the evidence is thus enlarged and the charge cast in a more lurid light, it is not clear to us that the fair report privilege automatically shields the larger whole.

The problem for Willis, we think, is that the Supreme Court has instructed that a state libel-suit plaintiff must demonstrate fault on the part of the media; and this requirement applies even where the plaintiff is not a public official or public figure. In such cases Massachusetts has imposed a requirement that the newspaper or broadcaster be shown to be negligent or worse. Thus, even if a false charge of murder has been made, it remains to see whether Willis provided evidence of negligence to justify submitting the case to a jury. ...

So far as the murder goes, Willis points to nothing to suggest that Channel 5 was negligent in its mustering of the available evidence. Some might think the broadcast gaudy journalism; certainly the interpolation of the woodchipper murder is largely gratuitous. ...

Willis' brief says tersely that the police admitted that they had no evidence against him; and he reasons that it was thus "negligent disregard for the truth" for Channel 5 to "insinuate" that "[he] murdered his wife and disposed of her body in the same fashion as did [the woodchipper murderer]." ...

A different problem is presented by Willis' suggestion that the broadcast charged him with disposing of his wife's body "in the same fashion" as the woodchipper murder. Patently, the broadcast did not so charge; no reasonable juror could draw such an inference. Willis offers no argument to support such an inference, and it is not surprising that elsewhere in his brief he retreats to a more cautious assertion: that the juxtaposition "conveys the message that Brown also murdered his wife and disposed of her body *in some insidious fashion*" (emphasis added).

* * *

Even if all of these doubts are resolved in Willis' favor, we think this narrow remaining claim is too thin to survive summary judgment. About the most one can get from the woodchipper episode is the suggestion that, if Willis killed his wife, he also took steps to assure that her body would not be found.

* * *

A writing or program is normally viewed as a whole; and that requirement has special force here because the woodchipper episode was assertedly about someone else, and its connection to Willis depended upon the rest of the program. We conclude as a matter of law that the broadcast, taken as a whole, cannot reasonably be taken to charge that Willis brutally disposed of his wife's body.

Willis' non-libel claims do not require much discussion. On appeal, Willis' has narrowed his privacy claim to the contention that the program places him in a false light by leaving the viewer with "a false impression," *i.e.*, that Brown killed Regina and disposed of her body in the same fashion as did the woodchipper murderer. The district court thought it sufficient that Massachusetts has never adopted the false light theory of privacy invasion.

* * *

Lastly, Willis charged Channel 5 with intentional infliction of emotional distress. This is a recognized tort under Massachusetts law requiring intended or foreseeable infliction of such distress, "extreme and outrageous conduct," and causation of distress so severe that no reasonable person could be expected to endure it. The district court said that Channel 5's conduct was not negligent and therefore could hardly be "extreme and outrageous."

In all events, many of the legitimate news stories that appear in the media involve foreseeable distress for the subject of the story, probably severe distress in some cases. Regina's disappearance and the divorce trial were news stories, and so was her continued absence and the failure of the police to solve the case. Willis provides no basis to think that generally accurate coverage in such a case is even remotely close to conduct "beyond all possible bounds of decency" and "utterly intolerable in a civilized community." Affirmed.

Case Questions

1. Which of the parties is described as having a privilege?
2. What was the effect of the privilege?

Summary

Intentional torts include actions designed to injure another person or his or her property. All intentional torts embrace an act, intent, and injurious conduct. These elements must occur together. Intentional torts harming the individual include assault, battery, false imprisonment, infliction of emotional distress, fraud, misrepresentation, malicious prosecution, abuse of process, invasion of privacy, and defamation.

Assault is the tortfeasor's attempt to inflict harmful or offensive contact upon another person without consent. Assault places the victim in fear of his or her physical safety, even if the anticipated contact would produce only a distasteful reaction. The threat of contact must be imminent. Battery is a completed assault. It is the intentional, unconsented touching of another person in a harmful or offensive manner. Physical contact is required, although it may be only with the victim's clothing or objects held. Transferred intent means that the contact directed at one person carries over to another individual who was inadvertently struck, so that battery would have occurred to the unintended victim.

False imprisonment is the confinement of someone without his or her consent. Confinement must exist for an appreciable length of time. The victim must have no reasonable means of escape. The tortfeasor must intend to confine the victim and act to accomplish confinement. Confinement may be achieved either by physical barriers or by threat of force which intimidates the victim into remaining in the restricted area.

Infliction of emotional distress has two versions in the intentional torts field: intentional and reckless. Intentional infliction of emotional distress involves outrageous conduct designed to cause severe mental anguish in the victim. The victim must actually suffer emotional turmoil as a result of the tortfeasor's actions. Reckless infliction of emotional distress includes outrageous conduct that the tortfeasor knew, or reasonably should have known, would produce significant emotional injury to the victim. The conduct is considered outrageous if it shocks the conscience of a reasonable person with normal emotional sensibilities.

Fraud consists of false statements made to entice the victim to surrender something of value to the defrauder. Misrepresentation includes false statements or behavior designed to deceive the victim. In many jurisdictions, the two intentional torts are considered virtually identical and interchangeable. The tortfeasor must know that the statements made are false and intend to deceive the victim.

Malicious prosecution happens when a private citizen files a groundless criminal complaint with the prosecutor against an innocent person who is named as the defendant in a criminal prosecution action. To sue the complainant, the innocent defendant must be either acquitted or otherwise victorious in the criminal lawsuit. The complainant must have filed the frivolous criminal charges out of malice for the innocent defendant, and malice may be implied from the circumstances surrounding the case. The innocent defendant must be injured as a consequence of the baseless prosecution. Abuse of process is the misuse (or threat of misuse) of a legal proceeding against another to obtain an unlawful objective. The victim must be harmed by the frivolous legal action. It is the civil equivalent of malicious prosecution.

Invasion of privacy consists of four independent varieties: appropriation, unreasonable intrusion, public disclosure of private facts, and false light in the public eye. Appropriation is the use of a person's name or likeness, without consent, for profit in some way. Unreasonable intrusion involves excessive and highly offensive interference with an individual's seclusion or solitude. Public disclosure of private facts happens when a tortfeasor publicly communicates purely private information about another person and such a disclosure would offend a reasonable person. False light in the public eye occurs when a tortfeasor publicly attributes to another spurious statements, opinions, or actions.

Defamation includes libel and slander. Libel is written communication of false and disparaging statements about an individual to third parties. Slander involves oral communication that does the same thing. Communication to third persons is called publication. The misinformation disseminated must injure the victim by harming his or her reputation in the community. Community can be narrowly defined as a small number of persons who know the victim. Even one third party is sufficient in some cases for publication to exist. Truth is an absolute defense in defamation actions. Public figures must prove actual malice to succeed in a defamation claim.

Review Questions

1. Define and discuss the specific intentional torts causing injuries to persons. Can you give examples of each? Do all intentional torts share any basic elements?

2. What is assault? What is battery? How are the two distinguishable? Similar? When is apprehension necessary? When is physical contact required? What types of contact are included? Must the threat of contact be imminent? Why are intent and consent important? What is transferred intent?

3. Define false imprisonment. What is confinement? How may it be accomplished? How are intent and consent relevant? Must confinement exist for any length of time? What role does escape play?

4. In the field of intentional torts, what are the two types of infliction of emotional distress? How are they alike? Different? What is mental anguish? Outrageous conduct? When is intent necessary?

5. Define fraud and misrepresentation. How are they similar? Distinguishable? Is intent required? What objectives must the tortfeasor have in giving false information?

6. Describe malicious prosecution and abuse of process. Can you determine why they are separate intentional torts? What makes criminal prosecution groundless? What is malice? Must the victim win in criminal litigation? What injury is required? For abuse of process, how can legal proceedings be misused? To what purpose?

7. What are the four varieties of invasion of privacy in tort law? How is each defined? Do you see any similarities between invasion of privacy and any other intentional torts?

8. What are the two aspects of defamation? How are they comparable? What is publication? What makes a statement false and defamatory? What is the role of truth in defamation?

Projects

1. Which intentional torts discussed in this chapter are included in your state's common law? Are any defined by statute? Does your state have any additional intentional torts that deal with harm to persons?

2. Paralegal students often separate into small study groups to discuss cases and problems. You may wish to meet with several classmates to discuss the theories in this and other chapters of the book. You might wish to create your own hypothetical fact situations utilizing the intentional torts discussed in this chapter.

3. Read the case of *Cinel v. Connick* in Appendix C. Was the plaintiff Cinel successful in pursuing his right-to-privacy claim? Do you agree with the appellate court's reasoning in its decision? Explain.

4. Read the *Pepsico, Inc. v. Redmond* case in Appendix C. Do you think the Quaker Oats Company wanted to hire Redmond solely for the trade secrets and confidential information he had access to, or could there have been any other reason for the job offer? Is it possible, when starting a new job, to totally disregard any information or secrets learned in a prior position?

CHAPTER 7

INTENTIONAL TORTS: INJURIES TO PROPERTY

The good of the people is the greatest law.
_____ *Cicero*

§ 7.1 Introduction

The previous chapter examined intentional torts involving injuries to persons. This chapter deals with injury to the rights of a property owner or possessor. (An owner's duty to others was discussed in Chapter 6.)

This chapter includes:

- Intentional torts dealing with injuries to property rights

- Trespass to land

- Toxic torts

- Trespass to chattel

- Conversion

- Slander of title

- Commercial disparagement

- Defamation by computer.

§ 7.2 Trespass to Land

Trespass is an ancient concept in tort law. In medieval English law, torts originated from trespass and trespass on the case. Under modern American law, trespass is recognized in two varieties: trespass to land and trespass to chattel.

Elements of Trespass to Land

Trespass to land occurs when a tortfeasor enters upon a land owner's real estate without consent. The tortfeasor trespasses when he or she intentionally acts in such a way as to violate the land owner's exclusive right to use the land. The elements of trespass to land are threefold:

1. Unauthorized entry upon another person's real estate
2. Tortfeasor's intent to enter without consent
3. Tortfeasor's actions interfering with the land owner's exclusive right to use the land (possession).

Entry Defined

The tortfeasor must enter upon a land owner's real estate without permission. **Entry** occurs when the tortfeasor acts so as to interfere with the land owner's exclusive right to use the property. For example, walking across someone's front lawn constitutes entry, because the tortfeasor entered the land. Also, entry happens if a person throws trash in a neighbor's back yard, because the trash depositor placed an unwanted substance (trash) on the land. Both these examples include the interference element. The front lawn owner cannot utilize his or her property exclusively if someone is walking across it. The neighbor's use of his or her back yard is severely hampered by the accumulation of another's trash. The tortfeasor's conduct in either case has disrupted the land owner's exclusive use of the real estate. This is the foundation of trespass to land.

Unauthorized Entry

The entry must be without consent. This essentially translates as a permission element. For instance, if a farmer allows a person to cross his fields to reach a lake in which to fish, then that person has not committed trespass—the entry was authorized. Similarly, homeowners may invite visitors onto their premises by extending an implied welcome, such as clearing sidewalks of snow up to a house door or placing doorbells outside the doors. This suggests that people may come upon the property to speak with the land owner. Consequently, door-to-door salespersons would not necessarily be trespassing if they had reason to

---

TERMS

trespass   An unauthorized entry or intrusion on the real property of another.
entry   ... The act of going upon real property.

‖‖‖   PROFESSIONAL PROFILE   ‖‖‖

George Urquiola is reported to have compiled the longest legal memorandum on record, a stack of paper about five feet high regarding the DuPont Plaza hotel fire in Puerto Rico. Urquiola is one of the few paralegals around who manages teams of paralegals in major litigation cases.

Urquiola never intended to be a paralegal. He wanted to be a lawyer but thought he should find out what it would be like to work within a law firm environment. While attending the University of Central Florida, he obtained an administrative assistant position with a local law firm that specialized in real estate and general litigation. There he performed such tasks as general office work, local filings, title searches, and maintenance of the law library. As the firm's attorneys gained confidence in his abilities, Urquiola was given a wider range of responsibilities, including client interviews and research assignments.

Urquiola then joined the Army, where he received intense training in legal studies. He became a staff member of the Judge Advocate General (JAG) Corps, where he worked for both the prosecution and the defense on more than fifty cases.

Upon completion of his military commitment, Urquiola joined a firm that had more than 100 attorneys. He served as a coordinator responsible for overseeing the paralegal program, recruiting, hiring, and continuing education. While in New York, he continued his paralegal studies and received a paralegal diploma from New York University's Department of Law and Taxation.

In 1987, Urquiola joined the law firm of Maguire, Voorhis & Wells, where he works for a senior partner who specializes in mass tort and products liability cases. He assists with discovery and investigation, client interviews, drafting of preliminary pleadings, and preparation of case status reports.

Urquiola is the litigation support manager in charge of organizing complex litigation cases. Good organization and management skills have afforded him the opportunity to work on high-profile cases, including the notorious DuPont Plaza fire. "I thoroughly enjoy being an important part of a very special litigation team," Urquiola says.

---

believe that the homeowner welcomed their presence. However, if the yard were fenced in, with a "no soliciting" sign displayed, then the salespersons would know that they did not have permission to enter the property.

Sometimes persons have a lawful right to enter upon another's land. For example, if the land owner gives an easement to a utility company to install utility lines across his or her property, then the utility company has the legal right to enter the premises to install and maintain the lines. Accordingly, no trespass to land could happen. Also, a process server, such as the county sheriff, generally has the legal right to enter the defendant's land to deliver a plaintiff's complaint and summons. No trespass to land would occur in such an instance.

One's lawful right to be upon another's premises may be withdrawn, however. Consider the example of the patron of a store. Customers are invited to come upon the premises to spend money. Suppose one such individual becomes disruptive, annoying other shoppers and employees. The store manager could demand that the agitator leave immediately. At this point, the customer becomes a trespasser, because remaining means that he or she is present upon another's land without consent. Although the customer was originally invited into the store as a patron, once he or she is ordered to leave, trespass occurs.

No Actual Harm Required

It is important to note that, under trespass law, the unauthorized entry need not cause any damage to the real estate. It is sufficient that the transgression occurred. Trespass law presumes that injury has happened simply because the tortfeasor has interfered with the land owner's use of the realty. Thus, simply walking across someone's front lawn without permission is trespass to land, although no actual harm arises from the conduct. These types of trespasses to land are often called *technical trespasses.* Courts generally award only nominal damages in such cases. **Damages** are dollar amounts that the defendant must pay the plaintiff if the plaintiff wins judgment against the defendant. In technical trespass cases, courts usually award a paltry sum, such as one dollar in **nominal damages**, because no actual injury was due to the trespass. The judgment award is ceremonial or symbolic of the technical invasion of the land owner's property rights.

As a practical matter, few lawsuits involve technical trespasses. It is simply too expensive to litigate a trespass action when no injury has resulted. Litigants frequently speak of suing "as a matter of principle," but plaintiffs are rarely sufficiently affluent to afford it.

TERMS

damages   The sum of money that may be recovered in the courts as financial reparation for an injury or wrong suffered as a result of breach of contract or a tortious act.

nominal damages   Damages awarded to a plaintiff in a very small or merely symbolic amount. Such damages are appropriate in a situation where: (1) although a legal right has been violated, no actual damages have been incurred, but the law recognizes the need to vindicate the plaintiff; or (2) some compensable injury has been shown, but the amount of that injury has not been proven.

Intentional Interference

The tortfeasor must have intended to enter the land owner's real estate without consent. Thus, if Twila is forced to cross a neighbor's front yard to escape a pursuing wild animal, she has not committed trespass to land. Twila did not intend to cross her neighbor's property without permission; rather, she was essentially forced across by the chasing animal. However, if she deliberately strolls across her neighbor's yard, the entry was intentional.

Possession: Land Owner's Exclusive Right to Use

To constitute trespass to land, the tortfeasor's unauthorized entry must interfere with the land owner's exclusive right to use his or her realty. This is sometimes called the **exclusive right of possession**, which entitles the land owner to use the property without anyone else's meddling. Recall the illustrations from the discussion of entry: the neighbor could not use his or her land exclusively if someone else's trash was being dumped on it. Nor could someone use his or her front lawn exclusively if another person walked across it.

This exclusivity requirement may at first appear overly harsh. One might well ask what wrong has been done just by crossing someone's land. Trespass intends to protect one's real estate in much the same way as assault and battery are intended to protect one's person. The objective is protection from undesired interferences. In this respect, trespass seeks merely to protect one's realty from other people encroaching upon it, just as assault and battery are meant to deter unwanted physical contact.

Trespass Above and Below Land: Is the Sky the Limit?

Trespass to land may occur not only upon the surface of the realty, but also above and below it. In property law, a Latin phrase summarizes the extent of one's ownership of land: *cujus est solum ejus est usque ad coelum* ("he who has the soil owns upward unto heaven and downward to

---

TERMS

---

exclusive right   A sole right; a right granted to no one else.
exclusive right of possession [†]   A land owner's right to use his or her property without interference from other persons.

The Case of the Unholy Waters

Many invasions onto one's realty can result in trespass to land. Persons and manmade objects readily come to mind as examples. But what about natural substances, such as rainwater? This, too, can provide an injured land owner with a cause of action, should the water, as it often does, cause structural damage.

In the following case, displaced rainwater created a multitude of problems for the property owners. Although the church believes that rain is an act of God, there are times when even the most pious institutions fall victim to poor drainage and even poorer land use planning.

BURT
v.
BEAUTIFUL SAVIOR LUTHERAN CHURCH
Colorado Court of Appeals
809 P.2d 1064 (Colo. Ct. App. 1990)
October 25, 1990
Davidson, Judge

Defendant, Beautiful Savior Lutheran Church of Broomfield, appeals a judgment entered on a jury verdict in favor of plaintiffs, Wayne Burt, Donna Draper, and Curtis Draper, for water damage to Burt's real property resulting from defendant's negligence and trespass. We affirm in part, reverse in part, and remand with directions.

Defendant and Burt are adjoining landowners. The Drapers are Burt's daughter and son-in-law, and are tenants in the Burt residence. Defendant's property, which is immediately west of Burt's, is markedly sloped downwards directly toward the Burt property. Both properties have been plagued with water drainage problems for many years.

In 1964, Burt's property was flooded by surface water from a heavy rain. At that time, he installed an underground drain from his backyard to his front yard which emptied into the street. Then, in 1979, defendant converted the area immediately west of Burt's property into a paved parking lot.

Approximately four years later, in August 1983, after another heavy rain caused flooding on his property, Burt dug a ditch, in part on defendant's property, to drain water into a storm drain on the street. At the same time, in response to flooding on its property, defendant constructed

a 15-foot manhole with a sump pump at a corner of its foundation wall and installed a drainpipe underground from the sump pump to the street. This drainpipe extended along the boundary between defendant's and Burt's property, emptying into the street just west of the Burt property. According to defendant's evidence, at the time the drainpipe was installed, the church pastor asked Burt if he objected to the removal of certain trees which Burt had planted on defendant's property in 1961. The pastor testified that, although he told Burt there was a danger of roots clogging the new drainpipe, Burt replied he did not want the trees removed.

In 1984, approximately six months after defendant's drainpipe was installed, Burt noticed that water was coming into his basement through cracks in the foundation. Responding to Burt's complaint, defendant constructed a dirt berm on its property to deflect surface water flowing down towards Burt's property. Nevertheless, Burt's foundation continued to crack and deteriorate.

Evidence at trial indicated that defendant had installed a drainpipe which was inadequate in size and had unsealable joints that were virtually certain to leak. The evidence also showed that the drainpipe had been improperly installed and was clogged with tree roots. In June 1987, defendant replaced the drainpipe and the water flow into Burt's basement stopped.

Burt then brought this action seeking damages for the repair of his basement foundation, alleging theories of negligence and trespass. At the close of the evidence, the court instructed the jury, without objection, on both trespass and negligence. The trial court, however, refused defendant's request to instruct the jury on comparative negligence. In its ruling, the trial court reasoned that comparative negligence was not appropriate because "it's just for the jury to decide whether there is ground water that was there historically or whether it was created by the church's actions." The trial court also refused defendant's requested instruction of plaintiffs' failure to mitigate damages.

The jury returned a verdict for plaintiffs on both trespass and negligence, and defendant appeals, alleging the refusal to so instruct the jury, and other actions by the trial court, constituted reversible error. Plaintiffs cross-appeal on the issues of costs and interests. We affirm the judgment and reverse and remand on the issue of costs and interest.

[The court's discussion of comparative negligence issue is omitted. The court concluded that the doctrine was inapplicable to trespass actions.]

In early English law, the writ of "trespass" had a basic criminal character and provided a cause of action for all direct and immediate injuries to person or property. "Trespass on the case," a separate writ which developed later, originally allowed remedies for all indirect injuries. ...

In Colorado, liability for trespass requires only an intent to do the act that itself constitutes, or inevitably causes, the intrusion. Specifically, trespass is the physical intrusion upon property of another without the permission of the person lawfully entitled to the possession of the real estate. "One is subject to liability to another for trespass, irrespective of whether he thereby causes harm to any legally protected interest of the other, if he intentionally ... enters land in the possession of the other, or causes a thing or a third person to do so. ..."

Thus, a landowner who sets in motion a force which, in the usual course of events, will damage property of another, is guilty of trespass on such property. Here, defendant's act of constructing the drainpipe in such a way as to cause water leakage into Burt's property amounted to a trespass.

* * *

Here, defendant does not dispute that the evidence was sufficient to support the jury's verdict for plaintiffs on their trespass claim. Therefore, because the defense of comparative negligence is inapplicable to trespass, the failure of the court to instruct the jury thereon was not error.

[The Court's discussion of the mitigation of damages issue is omitted.]

Compensation for injury resulting from trespass can include (a) the diminution of market value or the costs of restoration, (b) the loss of use of the property, and (c) discomfort and annoyance to the occupant. Since the Drapers were in possession of the property and therefore are entitled to damages for trespass, defendant is liable to the Drapers for the damage to their possessory interests. These damages include the loss of use of their basement and the discomfort and annoyance caused by the smell in their home.

[The Court's discussion on the remaining, tangential issues is omitted.]

Case Questions

1. How does the definition of trespass to land in *Burt* compare with the general description in this chapter?
2. When Burt dug his ditch partially upon the defendant's land in August 1983, was this trespass to land?

perdition"). Thus, it is possible for trespass to occur in the air above one's land. For instance, if a utility company erects wires across one's land without consent, this would constitute trespass to land, because the land owner owns the air above the soil. This could present insurmountable difficulties for aircraft. Fortunately, modern common law implies an exception for aircraft to fly over private property.

Similarly, one owns the resources under the earth. Although this enters into the complex area of oil, gas, and mineral law (within which special legal theories have evolved), it may be said generally that one owns the mineral resources beneath one's real estate. Accordingly, if someone mines under a person's land without permission, trespass to land has occurred. Cave exploration cases provide an interesting aspect of this theory. In a famous Indiana court case, *Marengo Cave Co. v. Ross*, 212 Ind. 624, 10 N.E.2d 917 (1937), the Supreme Court of Indiana stated that it was a trespass for the cave company to charge admission for tourists to explore caves below the surface of a land owner's property.

The sanctity of land is an ancient aspect of the human psyche. For millennia, people have used physical force and, as civilization progressed, force of law to protect against such invasions. Today, trespass to land remains an active intentional tort, as these hypotheticals demonstrate.

HYPOTHETICALS

Burrough Excavating Company was digging a basement for a new home. Burrough's backhoe operator dumped the dirt on a vacant lot next to the construction site. This lot was owned by Mark, who never gave Burrough permission to use his lot. Has Burrough trespassed to land against Mark?

The elements line up nicely. Mark did not consent to Burrough's dirt dumping, and so Burrough engaged in unauthorized entry upon another's realty. Burrough obviously intended this entry, as the backhoe operator dumped the dirt on Mark's lot. This dumping interfered with Mark's exclusive use of his property, because he will now have to contend with the dirt pile if he wishes to use his lot. Therefore, Burrough has committed trespass to land against Mark.

■ ■ ■

Consider another hypothetical. George owns a house next to Elizabeth. Elizabeth planted several oak trees on her property with branches that hang over a fence separating her property from George's. George thought the trees were unsightly and trimmed the limbs that hung over onto his yard. He did not ask Elizabeth for permission to remove the limbs. Has a trespass occurred?

Who has trespassed? By allowing her tree branches to cross over onto George's property, Elizabeth committed unauthorized entry onto another's land without consent. Her trees interfered with George's exclusive right of possession, because the branches obstructed George's use of this part of his property. Recall, too, that George owns to the top of the sky under the *ad coelum* doctrine discussed earlier. Anything encroaching upon his airspace constitutes entry. Intent may be implied, as Elizabeth knew the trees crossed the fence but did nothing to remove the overhanging limbs. Thus, Elizabeth has trespassed upon George's land.

Somewhat more problematic is the inverse inquiry: namely, did George trespass against Elizabeth by pruning the trees? Because the trees grew on Elizabeth's property, George's trimming (without permission) encroached upon Elizabeth's use of her trees. But does this constitute unauthorized entry onto another's land? The branches hung over onto George's property, so he did not actually enter upon Elizabeth's land to cut the limbs. He was simply "defending" his property from the encroaching branches. Accordingly, George did not commit trespass to land against Elizabeth.

Recent trespass actions have involved one of the most complex and dynamic developing areas of tort law—namely, toxic tort litigation. Section 7.3 discusses this type of trespass.

§ 7.3 Toxic Tort Actions

A significant percentage of modern tort litigation is devoted to actions involving toxic chemicals, pollution, hazardous waste disposal and transportation, and other environmentally sensitive issues. These are sometimes referred to as **toxic tort actions**. These lawsuits cover causes of action involving the following: trespass to land, negligence, absolute liability for ultrahazardous substances, products liability, and nuisance. This chapter focuses on the trespass to land aspects of toxic tort litigation.

Nature of the Problem

For much of this century, toxic waste disposal was considered simple. Manufacturers or chemical processors applied a centuries-old approach: "out of sight, out of mind." Hazardous waste was simply buried, dumped into waterways, or burned. Much toxic waste found its way into public and private landfills, rivers, and smoke-belching incinerators. This did not eliminate the noxious nature of the waste products, however; it simply shifted the problem to another location. As the years passed, barrels buried at the underground sites rusted and leaked, sending lethal seepage through the soil, contaminating underground

```
━━━━━━━━━━━━━━━━━━━━  TERMS  ━━━━━━━━━━━━━━━━━━━━
```

toxic tort actions [†] Actions involving toxic chemicals, pollution, hazardous waste disposal and transportation, and other environmentally sensitive issues. This litigation applies many tort theories, including trespass to land, negligence, absolute liability for ultrahazardous substances, products liability, and nuisance.

water supplies, and injuring people who drank contaminated well water. Toxic burial leakage also percolated from underground through springs, exposing innocent bystanders to carcinogenic or otherwise lethal substances in surface waters. Rivers and streams simply carried the sludge to haunt downstream land owners, who came into contact with the poisons through irrigation or otherwise working with the polluted waters. Residents near the incineration plants suffered a variety of lung ailments from poisonous air pollutants.

Traditionally, all these intrusions fell neatly within the intentional tort of trespass to land. Nuisance provided neighboring land owners another cause of action with which to litigate against the industrial toxic polluters. Absolute liability also applied under the ultrahazardous substances theory. Negligence lent further legal aid to plaintiffs seeking relief against injuries from the unwanted and toxic invaders.

The Case of the Toxic Tort: Who Pays for the Mess?

Two sisters brought this toxic tort action against Kerr-McGee Chemical Corporation, alleging that their parents contracted and died of cancer as a result of toxic wastes generated and deposited on the factory site of Kerr-McGee's predecessor company, Welsbach. Although Kerr-McGee acquired Welsbach's business, it did not acquire the land or factory in question. The sisters maintain that Kerr-McGee should still be held liable on a theory of strict liability even though the company did not cause or ever own the polluted land in contovery.

LEO v. KERR-MCGEE
United States Court of Appeals, Third Circuit
37 F.3d 96 (3d Cir. 1994)
September 19, 1994
Greenberg, Circuit Judge

This matter is before the court following entry of our order on November 30, 1993, granting defendant-appellant Kerr-McGee Chemical Corporation permission to appeal pursuant to 28 U.S.C. § 1292(b). We will reverse the order of the district court denying Kerr-McGee's motion for summary judgment entered on September 8, 1993, and we will remand the matter to the district court for entry of a summary judgment in its favor.

The facts are largely not in dispute, and, in any event, we accept the allegations of the plaintiffs-appellees Elaine Leo and Linda Yoder for purposes of this appeal. From prior to the turn of the 20th century continuing until 1940, the Welsbach Incandescent Light Company maintained and operated a factory in Gloucester City, New Jersey, for manufacturing incandescent gas mantles, a process involving extracting thorium from monazite ores. This process generated toxic wastes consisting of thorium by-products which Welsbach deposited on the factory site, thus contaminating the surrounding land. In 1940, Welsbach's Illinois-based competitor, Lindsay Light and Chemical Company, purchased Welsbach's gas mantle business. In the sale, Lindsay acquired Welsbach's outstanding orders, records, formulas, raw materials, inventory, customer lists, gas mantle production line, and the right to use the "Welsbach" name. However, Lindsay did not acquire the Gloucester City land and factory. Rather, it moved the gas mantle business to its own plant in Illinois.

Following a series of acquisitions, Kerr-McGee acquired Lindsay, and it thus concedes that in this litigation it stands in Lindsay's shoes. Accordingly, we will refer to Lindsay and Kerr-McGee simply as Kerr-McGee. ...

In 1961, Leo and Yoder, who are sisters, and their parents, Thomas and Catherine Bekes, moved to a home close to the former site of the Welsbach factory in Gloucester City, though Leo and Yoder now live elsewhere. On December 5, 1988, Thomas Bekes died from bladder cancer. In March 1991, the New Jersey Department of Environmental Protection notified Catherine Bekes of the high levels of gamma radiation and thorium on her property and on June 3, 1991, the New Jersey Spill Compensation Fund acquired her residence, forcing her to relocate. Soon thereafter she also died from bladder cancer. Leo and Yoder allege that their parents contracted their bladder cancer from exposure to thorium and other waste substances deposited on the Welsbach land.

On January 29, 1993, Leo and Yoder filed suit, individually, and on behalf of their parents' estates, in the Superior Court of New Jersey against Kerr-McGee and certain other defendants to recover for death, injuries, and the potential risk of cancer arising from their exposure to thorium and other waste substances generated in the Welsbach gas mantle operation and deposited on the Gloucester City property. As germane here, Leo and Yoder seek to impose liability on Kerr-McGee on a theory of strict liability. While Leo and Yoder do not claim that Kerr-McGee itself generated the waste which caused the deaths and injuries, they assert that it is liable by reason of its acquisition of Welsbach's gas mantle business. On March 4, 1993, one of the other defendants removed the case to the United States District Court for the District of New Jersey on the basis of diversity of citizenship.

Subsequently, Kerr-McGee filed a motion to dismiss under Fed.R.Civ.P. 12(b)(6) on the ground that the complaint did not state a claim on which relief may be granted inasmuch as Kerr-McGee never has owned the Gloucester City land and factory. ...

[T]he court denied Kerr-McGee's motion [which it treated as a summary judgment motion], by the order of September 8, 1993. Kerr-McGee then moved for an amendment of the order to allow an interlocutory appeal, and the district court granted the amendment by an order entered on

November 1, 1993. We then granted Kerr-McGee leave to appeal.

... Thus, we undertake to predict how the Supreme Court of New Jersey would resolve the issues in this case.

We start, of course, with *Ramirez*, 431 A.2d 811, in which the Supreme Court of New Jersey held that:

> where one corporation acquires all or substantially all the manufacturing assets of another corporation, even if exclusively for cash, and undertakes essentially the same manufacturing operation as the selling corporation, the purchasing corporation is strictly liable for the injuries caused by defects in the units of the same product line, even if previously manufactured and distributed by the selling corporation or its predecessor.

431 A.2d at 825. As the district court acknowledged, *Ramirez* is distinguishable from this case. Unlike the injuries in *Ramirez*, the injuries of Leo, Yoder, and their parents were not caused by a unit in the product line manufactured first by Welsbach and then by Kerr-McGee. Instead the injuries in this case were caused by conditions created by Welsbach's operations on land which Welsbach retained at the time of the sale of the gas mantle business to Kerr-McGee and on which Kerr-McGee never conducted any manufacturing activities. ...

The *Ramirez* court predicated its conclusion that the successor corporation could be liable for injuries caused by its predecessor's defective product on three rationales: (1) the sale of the enterprise virtually destroyed the injured party's remedy against the original manufacturer; (2) the successor has the ability to assume the original manufacturer's risk-spreading role; and (3) it is fair to require the successor to assume a responsibility for defective products as that responsibility was a burden necessarily attached to the original manufacturer's good will being enjoyed by the successor in the continued operation of the business. Clearly these rationales do not support the extension of successor liability to Kerr-McGee in this case.

The first factor, the destruction of the injured party's remedy is a *necessary* but not a *sufficient* basis on which to place liability on the successor.

Accordingly, if the selling corporation remains a viable entity able to respond in damages to the injured party, a successor acquiring a product line will not be liable for injuries caused by the predecessor's product after the product's sale as in that circumstance there would be no reason to impose successor liability. This initial rationale for the product-line doctrine of successor liability merely focuses on the need for imposition of successor liability rather than whether it is fair to impose it. ...

The second rationale on which the Supreme Court of New Jersey based its result in *Ramirez* was the successor's ability to assume the predecessor corporation's risk-spreading role. We think that the Supreme Court of New Jersey would recognize that Kerr-McGee does not have the capacity to assume Welsbach's risk-spreading role. ...

The impediment to commercial transactions from such a process is evident. Indeed, inasmuch as a manufacturer might build a product or its component parts at more than one facility, a purchaser of a product line might face daunting obstacles in attempting to assess its risks of successor toxic tort liability for conditions on property to be retained by the seller of the product line. Furthermore, a product-line purchaser not acquiring its predecessor's manufacturing facility probably would not be able to lessen the risks of toxic tort liability associated with the real estate. It is doubtful that such a product-line purchaser would be able to undertake cleanup operations on land it did not own. Moreover, the product-line purchaser might be unwilling to undertake such potentially costly projects. It seems clear, therefore, that if *Ramirez* applies here, a purchaser of a product line will be subject to liabilities for toxic torts of unpredictable scope for a indefinite period. ...

In contrast, a successor to a product line may be able to take steps to reduce its risk of liability for injuries caused by the predecessor's products through recall and educational programs which include those products. Furthermore, successor liability for injuries caused by units manufactured by the predecessor, at least when compared to potential toxic tort liability, is a discrete manageable matter. ...

This constant diminution of exposure to product liability is enhanced by the rule followed in New Jersey and elsewhere that a manufacturer cannot be strictly liable unless there was a defect in the product when it left the manufacturer's control. It seems apparent that, except perhaps in design defect cases, a defect in a product when the manufacturer distributed the product is likely to manifest itself and cause injury within a reasonable time after the product is manufactured. Accordingly, as a practical matter, successor liability under *Ramirez* is likely to be imposed in most cases, if at all, for a limited period. ...

On the other hand toxic tort liability can be imposed for activities in the distant past. This tail on potential toxic tort liability following the disposal of chemical wastes is attributable to the fact that the toxic wastes may remain in the ground for long periods, thus exposing persons and property to injury long after manufacturing has ended. ...

The third *Ramirez* rationale, that it is fair to require a successor to assume a responsibility for defective products as that responsibility is a burden necessarily attached to the successor's acquisition of the predecessor's good will, has no application in this case. The good will that Kerr-McGee acquired from Welsbach was attached to the product line it acquired, gas mantles, rather than to the site at which Welsbach manufactured the product.

* * *

We could allow liability to be imposed in this case on Kerr-McGee only if we stretched *Ramirez* far beyond its original scope ... . [W]e will not do that. While the district court believed that this case could come within the *Ramirez* holding, in large part it reached that conclusion because of what it thought was "the traditional New Jersey view that if you are injured somebody ought to be liable for it." But we reject that approach.

* * *

CONCLUSION

We will reverse the order of September 8, 1993, and will remand the matter to the district court for entry of a summary judgment in favor of Kerr-McGee.

Case Questions

1. Why did the appellate court find that Kerr-McGee should not be held liable for the toxic waste caused by the predecessor corporation?
2. The United States Court of Appeals rejected "the traditional New Jersey view that if you are injured somebody ought to be liable for it." What was the end result of this case to the plaintiffs?

Toxic Trespass

Trespass to land occurs when toxic substances enter upon another's property. The trespass elements remain the same:

1. Unauthorized entry upon another person's real estate
2. Tortfeasor's intent to enter without consent
3. Tortfeasor's actions interfering with the land owner's exclusive right to use the land (possession).

In the case of toxic substances, the unauthorized entry is seepage or accumulation of the hazardous material on the victim's land. Few owners consent to having toxins placed over, upon, or under their realty. Most people want such materials to be taken as far away from them as possible.

The tortfeasor's intent to enter without permission may be implied from the disposal method used. For instance, toxic waste buried in metal barrels will, over time, rust through and seep into the underground soil, unless the material is contained in an isolated fashion, such as an underground concrete crypt. If the tortfeasor failed to take sufficient precautions to prevent subterranean seepage, then the intent to trespass may be implied. Another example of implied intent is dumping toxic fluids into waterways. The tortfeasor desired the river or stream to carry the dangerous substances downstream, which would plainly deposit the gunk on the shores of other people's property.

The tortfeasor's interference with the plaintiff's exclusive possession of his or her land is equally clear. The toxic residues are a highly offensive and potent invasion, making some real estate uninhabitable. A more significant illustration of trespass would be difficult to imagine.

When land owners' underground water supplies are contaminated with buried toxic waste seepage, trespass to land occurs. A quick review of the elements shows that they are readily satisfied. Many cases in the court reports tell sad tales of families irreparably harmed through long-term consumption of chemically contaminated well water, poisoned as a result of improper underground waste disposal.

Importance of Environmental Statutes

Aside from trespass, nuisance, absolute liability, and negligence, there are a variety of federal, state, and local statutes regulating environmental toxins. One important federal statute is the Toxic Substances Control Act. This act regulates the manufacture, distribution, processing, use, and disposal of hazardous materials. Detailed recordkeeping regarding the hazardous materials must be maintained, 15 U.S.C. § 2601 *et seq.* (1992). The Hazardous Materials Transportation Act establishes strict requirements for transporters of hazardous waste. Detailed recordkeeping is required to ensure compliance with the act, 49 U.S.C. §§ 1801–1812 (1992). Another federal statute, the Comprehensive Environmental Response, Compensation and Liability Act (CERCLA), addresses any "imminently hazardous chemical substance or mixture" and allows the federal Environmental Protection Agency (EPA) to file civil lawsuits when the use of such a material will pose imminent risk to health or the environment and the EPA has not issued a final rule to protect against such risk.

Trespass to land is merely one type of trespass action. Trespass to chattel is the other and is discussed next.

§ 7.4 Trespass to Chattel

A tortfeasor commits **trespass to chattel** when he or she possesses someone's personal property without consent. A **chattel** is personal property, as opposed to real property, which is land. An automobile, a textbook, a pet dog or cat, and a desk are examples of chattels. Trespass to chattel has elements similar to those of trespass to land:

1. Unauthorized possession of, or interference with the use of, another individual's personal property
2. Intent to deprive (or interfere with) the owner's possession or exclusive use of his or her chattel.

TERMS

trespass to chattel[†] Occurs when the tortfeasor intentionally deprives or interferes with the chattel owner's possession or exclusive use of personal property. The tortfeasor's possession or interference must be unauthorized, which means that the owner cannot have consented.

chattel Personal property that is visible, tangible, and movable. Animals are included within the definition of chattel.

Unauthorized Possession of Another's Chattel

Suppose Nadene takes a neighbor's textbook during class. Unless Nadene obtained the neighbor's consent before seizing the text, Nadene has engaged in unauthorized possession of another's personal property. The book's owner did not give Nadene permission to possess the chattel. When a tortfeasor takes possession of another's personal property without consent, this is sometimes described as the act of **dispossession**.

Consent may be implied under certain circumstances. For instance, if Alfred gives his car keys to a friend, the implication is that the friend may use Alfred's motor vehicle. Similarly, hotel guests may presume that the management intended them to use the electricity, water, soap, and tissues supplied to the rooms. However, if a patron takes the hotel's pillows, sheets, and towels, this would be unauthorized possession, as staying in a hotel does not implicitly entitle guests to keep such items.

Unauthorized Interference with Use

It is possible to trespass to chattel without actually wrenching possession of the personal property from its rightful owner. Interference with the chattel owner's use of the property is sufficient. For instance, if a tortfeasor purposely fed Reggie's prize hogs a contaminated food, so that the hogs became ill and lost weight, then the tortfeasor engaged in unconsented interference with Reggie's use of the animals. If Cherrie's landlord shuts off the electricity to her apartment without permission, then this would also constitute unauthorized interference with the use of her personal property (provided, of course, that Cherrie had paid her electric bill).

Intent to Deprive or Interfere

To commit trespass to chattel, the tortfeasor must intend to interfere with or deprive the chattel owner of possession or the exclusive use of his or her personal property. Intent may be expressed, as it was when Nadene took her neighbor's book. It may also be implied under the circumstances. For example, assume that Cherrie's landlord changed the locks on her apartment door in order to lock her out, although she had paid her rent and had done nothing to violate her rental agreement.

TERMS

dispossession   A forced or fraudulent changing of possession of land from one person to another; ouster.

This would imply the landlord's intent to deprive Cherrie of possession of her personal property inside the apartment. Her use of the chattels would definitely be hindered.

Similarly, lack of intent may be implied. For example, assume Bud found his neighbor's cow grazing along a public highway and took the animal to his barn for safekeeping until he could telephone the neighbor. Although Bud took possession of the cow without his neighbor's consent, Bud did not intend to interfere with the neighbor's use of the cow. Nor did he wish to deprive his neighbor of possession. Bud simply wished to protect the animal from harm. This is emphasized by his efforts to contact his neighbor to come claim the cow. Thus, Bud lacked intent to trespass to chattel.

Figure 7-1 summarizes the elements of trespass to land and trespass to chattel.

Trespass to Land	*Trespass to Chattel*
Unauthorized entry upon another person's real estate	Unauthorized possession of another individual's personal property *or* unauthorized interference with another's use of his or her chattel
Intent to enter without consent (no harm to land required)	Intent to dispossess or interfere with owner's use of his or her personal property
Interference with land owner's exclusive right to use land (possession)	Similar to conversion, which also requires tortfeasor to put dispossessed chattel to own use

FIGURE 7-1   Elements of trespass to land and trespass to chattel

§ 7.5 Conversion

In the history of tort law, trespass to chattel was frequently involved in litigation, often in cases involving domestic livestock. Court opinions from the nineteenth century abound. More recent cases, however, have tended to focus upon conversion, which is a similar but separate tort.

A Case of Not-So-Gut-Wrenching Conflict

Not every invasion of one's personal property constitutes trespass to chattel. Actual dispossession must occur. A trifling interference, fleeting and momentary, will be tolerated under the law. As the following case demonstrates, the invasion of this plaintiff's chattel was insufficient to give rise to this cause of action.

KOEPNICK

v.

SEARS, ROEBUCK & CO.
Court of Appeals of Arizona
158 Ariz. 322, 762 P.2d 609 (1988)
June 16, 1988
Froeb, Presiding Judge

... The issues presented on appeal are: ... whether the trial court erred in granting Sears' motion for judgment notwithstanding the verdict (judgment n.o.v.) on Koepnick's trespass to chattel claim. ...

FACTS

Koepnick was stopped in the Fiesta Mall parking lot by Sears security guards Lessard and Pollack on December 6, 1982, at approximately 6:15 P.M. Lessard and Pollack suspected Koepnick of shoplifting a wrench and therefore detained him for approximately 15 minutes until the Mesa police arrived. Upon arrival of the police, Koepnick and a police officer became involved in an altercation in which Koepnick was injured. The police officer handcuffed Koepnick, placed a call for a backup, and began investigating the shoplifting allegations. Upon investigation it was discovered that Koepnick had receipts for the wrench and for all the Sears merchandise he had been carrying. Additionally, the store clerk who sold the wrench to Koepnick was located. He verified the sale and informed Lessard that he had put the wrench in a small bag, stapled it shut, and then placed that bag into a large bag containing Koepnick's other purchases. The small bag was not among the items in Koepnick's possession in the security room. To determine whether a second wrench was involved, the police and Lessard searched Koepnick's truck which was in the mall parking lot. No stolen items were found. Having completed their investigation, the police cited Koepnick for disorderly conduct and released him. The entire detention lasted approximately 45 minutes.

Koepnick sued Sears for false arrest, assault, trespass to chattel, invasion of privacy and malicious prosecution. The trial court directed a verdict in favor of Sears on all charges except false arrest and trespass to chattel. After a trial on these claims, a jury awarded Koepnick ... $100 compensatory damages and $25,000 punitive damages for trespass to chattel. Sears timely moved for judgment n.o.v. and alternatively for a new trial. The trial court ... granted Sears' motion for judgment n.o.v. on the trespass to chattel charge. ...

Koepnick appeals, challenging the trial court's order granting Sears ... judgment n.o.v. on his trespass to chattel claim. ...

We find no reversible error and therefore affirm the trial court's order granting ... judgment n.o.v. on the trespass to chattel claim.

* * *

TRESPASS TO CHATTEL

Arizona courts follow the Restatement (Second) of Torts absent authority to the contrary. The Restatement provides that the tort of trespass to a chattel may be committed by intentionally dispossessing another of the chattel or using or intermeddling with a chattel in the possession of another. Restatement (Second) of Torts § 217 (1965).

The Restatement (Second) of Torts § 221 (1965) defines dispossession as follows:

> A dispossession may be committed by intentionally
> (a) taking a chattel from the possession of another without the other's consent, or
> ...
> (c) barring the possessor's access to a chattel ... .

Comment b to § 221 provides that dispossession may occur when someone intentionally assumes physical control over the chattel and deals with the chattel in a way which will be destructive of the possessory interest of the other person. Comment b further provides that "on the other hand, an intermeddling with the chattel is not a dispossession unless the actor intends to exercise a dominion and control over it inconsistent with a possession in any other person other than himself."

The Restatement (Second) of Torts § 218 (1965) provides:

> One who commits a trespass to a chattel is subject to liability to the possessor of the chattel if, but only if,
> (a) he dispossesses the other of the chattel, or
> (b) the chattel is impaired as to its condition, quality, or value, or
> (c) the possessor is deprived of the use of the chattel for a substantial time, or
> (d) bodily harm is caused to the possessor, or harm is caused to some person or thing in which the possessor has a legally protected interest.

Koepnick argued at trial that Lessard's participation in searching his truck constituted an actionable trespass to the truck. He was awarded $100 damages by the jury which he characterizes as damages for a dispossession pursuant to subsection (a) or deprivation of use pursuant to subsection (c) of § 218.

* * *

Sears' actions with respect to the trespass consisted of Steve Lessard accompanying a Mesa police officer out to the parking lot and looking in the truck. There is no evidence in the record of an intent on the part of Sears' employee to claim a possessory interest in the truck contrary to Koepnick's interest. No lien or ownership interest claim of any kind was made. Further, there is no evidence that Sears intentionally denied Koepnick access to his truck.

Koepnick was in the City of Mesa's custody at the time of the search and Sears had no control over how the police department conducted its investigation ... .

... In order that an actor who interferes with another's chattel may be liable, his conduct must affect some other and more important interest of the possessor [than for harmless intermeddlings]. Therefore, one who intentionally intermeddles with another's chattel is subject to liability only if his intermeddling is harmful to the possessor's materially valuable interest in the physical condition, quality, or value of the chattel, or if the possessor is deprived of the use of the chattel for a substantial time ... . Sufficient legal protection of the possessor's interest in the mere inviolability of his chattel is afforded by his privilege to use reasonable force to protect his possession against even harmless interference.

Sidebar: The *Koepnick* court stated that an owner could protect his or her chattel from harmless interference through the defense of property defense, discussed in Chapter 8. The court felt this was sufficient legal protection of the chattel owner's interests. But how could Koepnick protect his truck from intrusion by the police officer and Sears' security guard, as the defense would lawfully permit, when he was handcuffed and held elsewhere?

The search in question took approximately two minutes. Neither the truck nor its contents were damaged in any manner by the police or Sears' employee. As a matter of law, Sears' action did not constitute an actionable trespass under § 218(c).

... For a deprivation of use caused by a trespass to chattel to be actionable, the time must be so substantial that it is possible to estimate the loss that is caused. The record in the present case lacks any evidence to permit a jury to estimate any loss caused to Koepnick [as a result of the police officer and Lessard's search of his truck].

We conclude that there was no dispossession of the vehicle as contemplated under § 218 of the Restatement nor was Koepnick deprived of its use for a substantial period of time. ...

The judgment of the trial court is affirmed ... .

* * *

Case Questions

1. Why do you suppose the jury awarded Koepnick such a large damages award, which prompted the trial court to grant judgment notwithstanding the verdict (judgment n.o.v.)? Do you think the jurors would agree that Koepnick suffered no harm as a result of the defendants' actions? Do you?
2. Do you believe that Koepnick satisfied the elements for assault, invasion of privacy, and malicious prosecution?

History

Conversion occurs when a tortfeasor, without consent, deprives an owner of possession of the owner's chattel and puts or *converts* the property to the tortfeasor's own use. It is essentially a broader version of trespass to chattel, but both torts developed separately.

Conversion evolved from the common law action of *trover*, which appeared in England during the fifteenth century as a specific type of trespass on the case action. In trover lawsuits, the court determined that the plaintiff, the chattel owner, had a legal right to possess the personal property (namely, because of ownership), and that the defendant, the tortfeasor, had taken possession of the chattel for his or her own use. Gradually, this element (taking for one's own use) was described in the English court opinions as "converting the property for one's own use." Thus, the term *conversion* began to replace *trover*, and the modern tort of conversion emerged.

===== TERMS =====

conversion   Control over another person's personal property which is wrongfully exercised; control applied in a manner that violates that person's title to or rights in the property. Conversion is both a tort and a crime.

Elements of Conversion

Under modern tort law, conversion consists of three elements:

1. Depriving the owner of possession of a chattel
2. Intent to deprive possession and convert the property to one's own use
3. The owner's nonconsent to the tortfeasor's possession and use of the chattel.

Depriving of Possession

Under conversion, the tortfeasor must actually deprive the owner of possession of personal property. The common law usually employs the phrase *exercising dominion and control over the chattel which is inconsistent with the owner's right to exclusive use.* This means that the tortfeasor controls another's personal property so as to prevent the owner from using it. For example, suppose Nadene took her neighbor's textbook and refused to return it. Nadene's "dominion and control" over the book prevents the neighbor from using his or her chattel.

Extent of Deprivation

Normally, conversion is differentiated from trespass to chattel based upon the scope of the deprivation. With trespass to chattel, many courts have held that the deprivation need only be minor or temporary. With conversion, several courts have ruled that the deprivation must be so extensive as to suggest a desire to deprive the owner of possession permanently. There is considerable disagreement among different jurisdictions as to this issue, however. The majority of courts maintain that conversion has occurred simply because the tortfeasor deprived the owner of dominion and control over the chattel, regardless of length of time or permanent intent.

Methods of Depriving

Deprivation of possession may occur in a variety of ways. *Physical possession* of the chattel is most common, although deprivation may happen through *damage or destruction* of the personal property. For instance, if someone plows under Kathy's garden to plant grass seed, this amounts to deprivation of possession, because Kathy can no longer use her vegetables. Similarly, if someone opens a window during a thunderstorm, and rain floods Sig's stereo, the injury has deprived Sig of the use of his chattel.

Deprivation may also take place simply through use. Some forms of personal property cannot be picked up and carried away. For instance, electricity, free-flowing liquids, and other intangible items are commonly defined as chattels under state commercial codes. One possesses such things by using them. If Morgan, Colleen's neighbor, plugs his garage heater into her electric outlet without permission, and Colleen's electric bill suddenly soars, Morgan has deprived her of dominion and control over her electricity. This translates as deprivation of possession.

Intent to Deprive and Convert to Own Use

First of all, conversion requires that the tortfeasor intend to deprive the owner of possession of his or her chattel. This is comparable to trespass to chattel. However, unlike trespass to chattel, conversion also requires that the tortfeasor convert the personal property to his or her own use. For example, assume Joey and Lisa are acquaintances at school. Then suppose that Joey found Lisa's earrings on a bench at the mall. Joey might keep the earrings until he saw Lisa at school later in the week. But, because Joey did not intend to use the earrings himself, he is not guilty of conversion. However, if Joey wore the earrings to the school dance, he would have converted them to his own use.

It is important to note that the tortfeasor does not have to injure the chattel to convert it. Conversion occurs simply because the owner has been deprived of the use of the personal property without having given permission. Injury occurs to the owner's property rights to exclusively use the chattel.

Lack of Consent

Naturally, the owner must not have granted permission to someone to use or possess the chattel. If Victoria allows a classmate to borrow her text overnight to study, then the classmate has not converted the book. Consent may be expressed, as in the book-borrowing situation, or it may be implied. For example, suppose that when Bob leaves his automobile at a mechanic's for an oil replacement, the mechanic also repairs a broken valve and pipe. The mechanic did not convert Bob's property, because Bob impliedly gave the mechanic permission to possess the vehicle for repair purposes. Of course, Bob did not authorize the additional work, but that is a breach-of-contract question. However, if the mechanic went joy-riding in Bob's car after changing the oil, this would be conversion, because Bob did not implicitly consent to that use of his car.

Even though the chattel owner may have consented to a tortfeasor's possession, this permission may be revoked. This could result in a conversion. For example, Bob complains that he did not authorize the additional work done on his automobile, but he is willing to pay for the oil change, which he did request. The mechanic insists that Bob also pay for the unauthorized repairs and refuses to return Bob's car until he pays the extra amount. Because Bob did not agree to these additional charges, he insists that his vehicle be returned immediately. Thus, Bob has revoked the permission he originally gave the mechanic to possess the chattel. If the mechanic does not comply with Bob's demand, the mechanic will be liable for conversion.

Conversion as a Crime

Many state statutes define conversion as a criminal offense. Some statutes use the term *theft* instead. Simultaneously, conversion is considered an intentional tort under the common law. This means that the chattel owner may sue in a civil action under the tort theory of conversion and may also contact the county prosecutor (or other local law enforcement authority) to file a criminal complaint for conversion. These separate legal actions are commonly pursued simultaneously in most jurisdictions.

The Case of the Purloined Purse

Money is a cherished chattel. It is never in sufficient abundance for most people. Occasionally, some individuals decide to supplement their cash supplies through somewhat unorthodox and illegal means. The following case appears to fit within this category. Although, as the Alabama Supreme Court notes, money is not usually subject to conversion claims, currency from identifiable sources, if converted, will allow the victim a cause of action against the converter.

GREENE COUNTY BOARD OF EDUCATION
v.
BAILEY
Supreme Court of Alabama
586 So. 2d 893 (Ala. 1991)
August 23, 1991
Houston, Justice

The plaintiff, Greene County Board of Education, appeals from the dismissal of its complaint alleging conversion on the part of the defendants, Roland S. Bailey [and] Sarah N. Bailey ... . We reverse and remand.

* * *

[According to the Plaintiff's complaint, between 1972-84, Paramount High School participated in the U.S.D.A.'s National School Breakfast and Lunch Programs. The school filed monthly claims with the State Department of Education for reimbursement for subsidized meals. Roland S. Bailey, sales manager of Alabama Institutional Foods, Inc. (AIF), was directly involved in food sales to Paramount High School. Between 1972-80, Bailey purchased 84 money orders and cashier's checks drawn on the Paramount lunchroom account. Of these, Bailey negotiated 42 checks through AIF's account at a bank at which his wife, Sarah Bailey, worked as a teller. Sarah processed these checks. The 84 checks were valued at $407,883.50, and only $263,425.65 went toward payment of Paramount's food purchases. $144,457.85 was never credited to Paramount's account nor used in the feeding programs. Bailey allegedly submitted false invoices to Paramount.]

The defendants moved to dismiss the complaint under Rule 12(b)(6) .... Specifically, the defendants argued that the plaintiff had failed to allege that specific money capable of identification had been converted. The trial court granted the defendants' motion, stating, in pertinent part, as follows:

"The plaintiff contends that the defendants converted money; however, the money was not any specific money and [the complaint states] a general claim for relief. The plaintiff's theory is that the defendants wrongfully obtained money from the account of the plaintiff through a scheme of false invoices. No particular identifiable earmarked money is alleged to have been taken. Under these circumstances, this Court is of the opinion that a count for conversion is not appropriate."

We disagree.

* * *

To constitute conversion, there must be a wrongful taking or wrongful detention or interference, or an illegal assumption of ownership, or an illegal use or misuse of another's property. The gist of the action is the wrongful exercise of dominion over property to the exclusion or in defiance of a plaintiff's rights, where the plaintiff has a general or specific title to the property or the immediate right to possession.

Generally, an action will not lie for the conversion of money. However, if the money at issue is capable of identification, then a claim of conversion may be appropriate. In *Lewis v. Fowler,* this Court discussed at length the circumstances under which an action for conversion will lie to recover a sum of money:

"[T]rover lies for the conversion of 'earmarked' money or specific money capable of identification ... .

"Money in any form is generally regarded and treated as property, and it is well settled that an action will lie for the conversion thereof, where there is an obligation to keep intact and deliver the specific money in question, and where such money can be identified.

* * *

"Now, in conversion cases, the courts are not confronted so much with a particular piece of money, i.e., a coin or a bill, but with identified or segregated from which money has come or types of accounts into which money has been deposited.

... [M]oney directly traceable to a special account is sufficiently identifiable to support an action for conversion.["] ...

Applying the applicable standard of review to the present case, we are not persuaded that the plaintiff has failed to state a claim for conversion. The allegations of the complaint suggest that the plaintiff may be able to prove that the defendants, through an intricate scheme involving bogus invoices and checks and money orders, converted to their own use funds that had been specifically deposited in the "[Paramount High School] lunchroom account" to pay for the high school's breakfast and lunch programs. ...

Based on the foregoing, we hold that the plaintiff has stated a claim for conversion and, therefore, that the trial court's order dismissing the plaintiff's complaint is due to be reversed and the case remanded for further proceedings.
REVERSED AND REMANDED.

Case Questions

1. Based on the facts, did the plaintiff also state a claim for trespass to chattel? Explain.
2. Should the defendants in this case have also been subjected to criminal prosecution for conversion, under the applicable Alabama statutes? Why or why not?

Conversion, like trespass to chattel, is a mobile tort, as it is easy in most instances to grab and carry away someone else's personal property. If the personal property can be carried away, it may be converted. Hence, there are an infinite variety of fact situations involving conversion. Both torts also fire the victim's blood. While reading the following examples, imagine that your own chattels have been converted; your emotional response may make clear why so many such cases are brought.

HYPOTHETICALS

Buford is painting his wooden fence in his backyard. His neighbor, Starling, needs some paint for his garage door. He notices that Buford has more than enough paint to finish the fence, and so Starling "borrows" two gallons to paint his door. Has Starling converted Buford's paint?

Starling deprived Buford of possession of the paint. Starling clearly intended to deprive possession and convert the paint to his own use, as he applied the paint to his garage door. Buford did not consent to Starling's use of the paint. Starling has committed conversion.

■ ■ ■

Consider Beatrice, who works at an advertising agency. One of her duties is to telephone clients to discuss accounts. Frequently, however, Beatrice telephones long-distance to relatives to discuss family matters. The company has strict regulations prohibiting use of company phones for personal calls. Has Beatrice engaged in conversion?

Deprivation of possession becomes a perplexing query in this hypothetical. Did Beatrice deprive her employer of possession of the telephone? The actual property right being taken here is the use (and cost) of the telephone for placing long-distance calls. Most courts would agree that this satisfies the deprivation requirement. Beatrice intended to use the company's phones for personal use. The company expressly forbade such activities, and so consent was lacking. Accordingly, Beatrice has converted her employer's rights in the telephone system.

Figure 7-2 outlines the elements of conversion.

FIGURE 7-2 Elements of conversion	Depriving owner of possession of his or her personal property (dispossession)
	Intent to dispossess and convert chattel to tortfeasor's own use
	Chattel owner did not consent to tortfeasor's possession and use of personal property

§ 7.6 Slander of Title, Commercial Disparagement, and Defamation by Computer

The intentional torts of slander of title, commercial disparagement, and defamation by computer involve defamed property interests. The trio has a common ancestry. All arose from the intentional tort of defamation, which concerns personal impugnation.

Slander of Title

Slander of title results when a tortfeasor makes false statements about an individual's ownership of property. The false statements are not designed to defame the owner personally; rather, the purpose of the aspersions is to injure the owner's ability to use the property. Slander of title contains three basic elements:

1. False statements regarding a person's ownership of property
2. Intent to hinder or damage the owner's use of the property
3. Communication (publication) of the falsehoods to third parties.

False Statements Regarding Ownership

A tortfeasor commits slander of title by making false statements about a person's ownership of property. This usually occurs when the tortfeasor falsely impugns the title to another's property. Normally, cases involving this tort include real estate and the filing of spurious liens. Often, businesses that provide services to customers who do not pay will file liens against the customers' real estate. The lien attaches to the title of the land so that the property cannot be leased or sold without the lien. Suppose a business threatens to file a lien against a customer who does not owe the business any money. If the lienholder wrongfully files a lien, then the lien has defamed the integrity of the land owner's title. The improper lien falsely suggests to the world that the land owner has not properly paid his or her debts to the lienholder. Anyone thinking of buying or leasing the property will think twice,

---

TERMS

---

slander of title A false or malicious statement, oral or written, that brings into question a person's right or title to real or personal property, causing him or her damage.

because lien property may be sold under certain circumstances to satisfy the debt. Few buyers or tenants would want to become entangled with property that is encumbered by a lien. Thus, a spurious lien could injure the land owner's ability to use the property, even though in actuality the lienholder has no legal right to file the lien against the land owner. This improper lien filing constitutes making false statements about someone's ownership of property.

Intent to Hinder or Damage Owner's Use of Property

By making the false statements about ownership, the tortfeasor must intend to hamper or injure the owner's use of his or her property. This is visibly demonstrated in the preceding lien example. The lienholder filed the lien to prevent the land owner from selling or using his or her realty without first paying the debt supposedly owed to the lienholder. But, in fact, no money was due, so the lien was falsely filed.

Communication (Publication) to Third Parties

The false statements about another's property ownership must be transmitted to third parties in slander of title actions. The slander in the preceding lien example is communicated to the public when the lien is recorded at the county recorder's office. It then becomes a matter of public record for the world to take notice.

Commercial Disparagement

Another type of slander focuses directly upon the chattel itself: commercial disparagement. **Commercial disparagement** may be defined as false statements communicated (published) to third parties about a person's goods, services, or business enterprise. The intentional tort of commercial disparagement includes three varieties: disparagement of goods, disparagement of services, and disparagement of business. Like slander of title, *disparagement of goods* impedes the chattel owner's ability to use his or her personal property. *Disparagement of services* interferes with a

----

$$\blacksquare\ \text{TERMS}\ \blacksquare$$

commercial disparagement [†] An intentional tort that occurs when a tortfeasor communicates false statements to third parties about a person's goods, services, or business enterprise. The tortfeasor must intend to harm the victim's ability to use goods, furnish services, or conduct business. There are three categories: disparagement of goods, disparagement of services, and disparagement of business.

The Case of the Errant Lot Line

Slander of title is usually limited to cases involving improperly filed liens. However, the intentional tort surfaces in other lawsuits, such as the one excerpted here. In *Hossler* the dispute involved an uncertain property line. In addition to slander of title, the case demonstrates why it is vital to obtain correct surveys before purchasing or selling real estate.

HOSSLER v. HAMMEL
Court of Appeals of Indiana
587 N.E.2d 133 (Ind. Ct. App. 1992)
February 24, 1992
Hoffman, Judge

This appeal arises from a property dispute between Roger and Sandra Hossler (plaintiffs) and Michael Hammel (defendant), owners of adjoining lots in Austin's Addition to the original plat of the town of Etna, Indiana.

The facts relevant to the appeal disclose that the Kecks and the Wheelers, the original owners of the lots, had surveys made in 1953, after which they agreed upon a common boundary line. When plaintiffs purchased their lot in 1970, they agreed to the established boundary line without a survey, and when defendant purchased his lot in 1977, he, too, agreed to the established boundary line without a survey. Plaintiffs rented their lot for several years and had a survey made in 1988 in order to sell the lot. The survey indicated the Addition was 9 feet longer east to west than shown in the original plat, and the surveyor allocated the extra footage equally among 6 lots. When defendant became aware of the survey, he insisted that the entire 9 feet be allocated to his lot due to his previous purchase of property in the original plat. After numerous threats from defendant to demolish 8 feet of their garage, plaintiffs filed an action to quiet title in the disputed strip of land. Following a bench trial, the court entered findings of fact and conclusions of law establishing the property line as that which the parties had originally agreed upon but denying damages to plaintiffs for slander of title.

The sole issue for our review is whether plaintiffs failed to meet their burden of proving the elements necessary to prevail on their slander of title claim.

To prevail in a slander of title action, the plaintiff must prove that the defendant made false statements regarding the plaintiff's ownership of the land in question, that the defendant made the statements with malice, and that the statements caused the plaintiff pecuniary loss. As plaintiffs note [in] their brief, "[t]he bone of contention in this case is whether the Defendant uttered statements with malice." Malicious statements are those made with knowledge of their falsity or with reckless disregard for whether or not they were false.

In *Freiburger v. Fry,* this Court found malice where, despite the description in his deed, the Defendant had actual knowledge of an existing fence separating the property and that the owner of the other side refused to move it. The instant case is similar to *Freiburger* in that, while defendant may have been relying on the results of plaintiffs' survey in making his statements, he had actual knowledge of the boundary line from the realtor who sold him the lot as well as from the survey. Moreover, the evidence was undisputed that the boundary line had been agreed upon for over 30 years, and once a person possesses property for 10 years in a continuous, adverse, notorious and exclusive manner, title vests in that person by operation of law.

As the party with the burden of proof on the slander of title issue, plaintiffs are appealing from a negative judgment. Therefore, to be successful they must establish that the judgment is contrary to law. As both parties note, defendant did not testify at trial, and neither of his two witnesses testified as to any statements he made regarding the boundary line. Plaintiffs, on the other hand, presented evidence that defendant threatened to bulldoze their garage, cut holes in their garage with a chainsaw, and keep livestock in their garage. Because this evidence and the evidence of defendant's actual knowledge of the agreed-upon boundary line was without conflict and led to a conclusion opposite that reached by the trial court, the judgment of the trial court is contrary to law and reversed.

Reversed and remanded for determination of damages.

Case Questions

1. Would the defendant's actions, rather than statements, have been sufficient to constitute slander of title? Assume that the defendant did not communicate with the plaintiffs. What if the defendant had parked a bulldozer next to the plaintiffs' garage? What if the defendant had placed livestock on his property adjoining the plaintiffs'? Would these actions satisfy the Indiana common law elements? Would they satisfy the elements discussed in this chapter?
2. Assuming the hypothetical facts from question one, what additional tort(s) would the defendant have committed through his actions?

service provider's ability to engage in provision of services. *Disparagement of business* occurs when the tortfeasor impugns the integrity of another's business venture. Commercial disparagement may be divided into three elements:

1. False statements about an individual's goods, services, or business
2. Intent to injure the victim's ability to use goods, furnish services, or conduct business
3. Communication (publication) to third parties.

False Statements about Goods, Services, or Business

The tortfeasor must express false statements about another's personal property, services, or business reputation (sometimes called *goodwill*). For example, if someone carries a sign in front of a grocery store declaring, "This store sells spoiled fruit!," when in fact the store carries fresh and wholesome fruit, then the sign carrier has made disparaging remarks about the quality of the grocery's foodstuffs. This impugns the integrity of both the goods themselves and the store's reputation. Similarly, if someone tells his or her friends that a particular dentist uses inferior materials to fill cavities when, in reality, the dentist uses professionally acceptable materials, then the dentist's services and reputation have been wrongfully impaired.

Intent to Harm Victim's Ability to Use Goods, Supply Services, or Conduct Business

Disparagement of goods requires that the tortfeasor intend to injure the victim's capability to use chattels, provide services, or engage in business. Normally, cases involving goods relate to sales. In the preceding illustrations, the sign carrier obviously desired to discourage other shoppers from buying fruit at that particular grocery. The person criticizing the dentist wished to dissuade friends from seeking the dentist's services. The clear underlying objective in both examples is to hamper the ability of these enterprises to conduct business.

Communication (Publication) to Third Parties

Like slander of title, commercial disparagement requires that the false statements be communicated to third parties. In the examples, the sign carrier transmitted the false complaints to anyone reading the sign. The friends of the disgruntled patient heard the falsehoods about the dentist. Like the intentional torts of slander and libel (defamation) discussed in Chapter 6, publication may occur through oral or written means. The preceding examples illustrate both media.

Defamation by Computer

Defamation by computer is a relatively recent intentional tort. Because of the proliferation of computerized databases that can store virtually any information about anyone, the likelihood of mistakes has increased. Further, as access to computerized material expands, the dissemination of inaccurate information can become enormously damaging to the victim.

Computerized Credit Reporting

Customers who are the subjects of credit reports are protected by the stringent guidelines of the Fair Credit Reporting Act (FCRA), 15 U.S.C. § 1681 *et seq.* Defamation by computer most frequently involves cases concerning erroneous credit information entered into a readily accessible computer database. A credit company reports to a national credit reporting agency that a particular individual has become delinquent in

The Case of the Disparaged Disk Jockey

Commercial disparagement most commonly occurs with disgruntled customers attacking businesses. However, businesses can also commit this intentional tort, usually against their employees. In the following case, a radio personality found his livelihood jeopardized allegedly as a result of his former employer's disparagement. Note how the court distinguishes defamation from disparagement.

MENEFEE
v.
COLUMBIA BROADCASTING SYSTEM, INC.
Supreme Court of Pennsylvania
458 Pa. 46, 329 A.2d 216, (1974)
October 16, 1974
O'Brien, J.

Robert Menefee, whose executrix is the appellant here, was for twenty years a radio personality in and around Philadelphia. Since 1960, he was employed by radio station WCAU in Philadelphia, which is wholly owned by the Columbia Broadcasting System, Inc. In the summer of 1967, Menefee, who referred to himself as "opinionated but lovable," conducted a one-man talk show from 7:30 P.M. to 10:00 P.M. daily, in which he discussed topics of public interest or controversy. On August 25, 1967, WCAU, through its general manager, John O. Downey, and its Director, Michael Grant, ... exercised a right to terminate Menefee's employment on thirteen weeks' notice, opting to pay him an additional salary rather than continue him in his position for that period. That same day, Grant informed newsmen that Menefee had been fired "because of poor ratings garnered by his nighttime talk show." Several articles subsequently appeared to the same effect in the Philadelphia magazines and newspapers.

Menefee, on January 16, 1968, filed an action in the Court of Common Pleas of Montgomery County against CBS, Inc., and Grant ... . Menefee died on November 9, 1971, one day before trial was to begin. ...

[Plaintiff alleges] the cause of action for untruthful disparagement. ...

Although an action for untruthful disparagement of a property interest resembles actions for defamation, there are several important differences. As the authors of the Restatement of Torts have explained ... "Liability for disparagement [...] differs in several highly important particulars from the liability for the publication of matter which is defamatory to the personal reputation of another. In defamation, truth is a defense required to be proved by the publisher as defendant. In disparagement, the person whose property in goods or the quality of whose goods has been attacked must prove that the disparaging statement of fact is untrue or that the disparaging expression of opinion is incorrect. [...] In defamation, the publication of all libelous communications and of many types of slanderous communications subjects the publisher to liability even though no pecuniary loss or other harm results therefrom. In disparagement, the publisher is not liable unless the disparaging matter has caused financial loss. [...]"

The question before us is, do the appellant's complaints make out a cause of action for untruthful disparagement?

In the first cause of action, ... it is alleged that the defendants "falsely conveyed ... to the public and the broadcasting industry that plaintiff was unable to draw an adequate listening audience, was incapable of earning satisfactory ratings for his program and was therefore incompetent in the performance of his assigned broadcasting duties."

Section 629 of the Restatement defines "disparagement" to be:

"Matter which is intended by its publisher to be understood or which is reasonably understood to cast doubt upon the existence or extent of another's property in land, chattels or intangible things, or upon their quality, is disparaging thereto, if the matter is so understood by its recipient."

Since the complaint also alleges that Robert Menefee was a successful radio personality, it can fairly be said that he had an intangible property interest in his broadcasting personality and that a statement that his program could no longer attract satisfactory ratings would tend to disparage that property interest.

In order to be able to recover for disparagement of such a property interest, the plaintiff must show that he suffered a direct pecuniary loss as the result of the disparagement. ...

Thus, appellant must allege and prove that her husband's estate suffered pecuniary loss as the direct result of the impairment of her husband's value to radio stations in the area caused by the defendant's untrue statements. However, she need not prove that a specific radio station refused to hire him because of reports that his ratings had declined. ...

Order of the Superior Court ... reversed. ... Insofar as it dismisses appellant's cause of action for conspiracy to disparage Robert Menefee's broadcast personality, order reversed and case remanded to the Court of Common Pleas of Montgomery County for further proceedings consistent with this opinion.

Case Questions

1. How did the court distinguish between defamation and disparagement?
2. Do you believe that the plaintiff would have been successful in a defamation action? Explain.

account payments. This bad credit rating can have alarming negative effects upon the person being reported. If the information reported is false, the injury is especially annoying, as future credit may hang in the balance of good credit reports.

Defamation by computer may be defined as the inclusion of false information about a consumer's credit rating, in a computer recordkeeping system, which harms the consumer's ability to secure credit. The tort includes four elements:

1. False information about a person's credit rating
2. Entering such erroneous data into a computerized recordkeeping system
3. Communication (publication) of the incorrect information to third parties
4. Injuring the victim's ability to obtain credit as a result of the false computerized data.

TERMS

defamation by computer [†] An intentional tort that occurs when the tortfeasor includes false information about a person's credit or credit rating in a computer database. This false information must be communicated to third parties, and it must injure the victim's ability to obtain credit.

The Case of the Rejected Check

Imagine your frustration if, when shopping, you got all the way up to the cashier and realized you had forgotten to bring your checkbook. In this case, a man was shopping with his secretary. Upon discovering that he did not have his checkbook, the man returned to his office with his secretary and then sent the secretary back with a check to pay for the merchandise. Can the store request a consumer report before accepting a check for a transaction, or is this an invasion of privacy?

ESTIVERNE
v.
SAK'S FIFTH AVENUE
United States Court of Appeals, Fifth Circuit
9 F.3d 1171 (5th Cir. 1993)
December 28, 1993
Davis, Jones, and Duhé, Circuit Judges

Appellant, Nicolas Estiverne, appeals from the district court's grant of summary judgment for the Defendants, Sak's Fifth Avenue and JBS, Inc., and the imposition of Rule 11 sanctions. Estiverne sued Defendants for discrimination under 42 U.S.C. § 2000a and invasion of privacy when Sak's declined to honor a check written by Estiverne. ...

On November 26, 1991, Nicolas Estiverne and his secretary went to Sak's Fifth Avenue in New Orleans to purchase a watch. After selecting a watch, Estiverne realized that he had left his checkbook at his office. After returning to his office, Estiverne gave his secretary a signed check, together with a credit card and his driver's license, to return to the store to pay for the watch. After receiving the check, the Sak's salesclerk, in accordance with standard policy, submitted it to JBS for approval. Sak's declined to honor the check after JBS refused to approve it. Estiverne sued both JBS and Sak's alleging that his check was not accepted because he is black. He also alleged that Sak's and JBS's inquiry into his credit information was an invasion of privacy. The district court granted summary judgment for Defendants and imposed Rule 11 sanctions against Estiverne totaling more than $15,000. Estiverne appeals. ...

There is no genuine issue of material fact in dispute in this case. The only issue as to summary judgment Estiverne raises on appeal is whether the district court correctly applied the Fair Credit Reporting Act ("FCRA"), 15 U.S.C. §§ 1681–1681t, specifically §§ 1681a(d) and 1681b(3)(E). The district court held that JBS's reports were consumer reports under § 1681a(d) and that Sak's had a "legitimate business need" under 15 U.S.C. § 1681b(3)(E) for the reports for the purpose of deciding whether to accept or reject Estiverne's check. Estiverne argues that paying by check is not a business transaction that authorizes Sak's to obtain a credit history report under the FCRA because he made no application for credit.

This is an issue of first impression for this Court. Section 161a(d) provides that a consumer report is:

> any written, oral, or other communication of any information by a consumer reporting agency bearing on a consumer's credit worthiness, credit standing, credit capacity, character, general reputation, personal characteristics, or mode of living which is used or expected to be used or collected in whole or in part for the purpose of serving as a factor in establishing the consumer's eligibility for ... (3) other purposes authorized under § 1681b of this title.

Section 1681b(3)(E) states that one of the authorized purposes for disclosure of consumer information is "a legitimate business need for the information in connection with a business transaction involving the consumer."

* * *

The FTC has interpreted the definition of consumer report to include lists devised to inform merchants about consumers who have had checks previously dishonored. The FTC stated in its commentary:

> *Bad check lists.* A report indicating that an individual has issued bad checks, provided by printed list or otherwise, to a business for use

in determining whether to accept consumers' checks tendered in transactions primarily for personal, family or household purposes, is a consumer report. The information furnished bears on consumers' character, general reputation and personal characteristics, and it is used or expected to be used in connection with business transactions involving consumers. ...

We defer to the FTC's interpretation of the statute and hold that JBS's reports fall squarely within the definition of a consumer report and that Sak's obtaining of this report for the purpose of deciding whether to accept or reject a check in payment is a "legitimate business need." This holding is also in accord with results reached by other courts that have addressed this issue. Accordingly, the district court did not err in granting summary judgment for JBS and Sak's.

Estiverne does not contest the imposition of Rule 11 sanctions; rather, he contends that sanctions totaling more than $15,000 are unreasonable. We review a district court's calculation of sanctions for an abuse of discretion.

The district court has broad discretion in imposing sanctions reasonably tailored to further the objectives of Rule 11. ...

The district court adopted the amounts found by the magistrate judge as the proper sanctions in line with the objectives of Rule 11. It represented less than the attorneys fees and expenses incurred by Defendants. Estiverne failed to produce any evidence to support his allegations that his check was refused because of his race. The facts alleged in his complaint were misleading and factually incorrect. ... [W]e find no abuse of discretion in the amount of sanctions imposed against Estiverne.

Invoking Federal Rule of Appellate Procedure 38, Sak's seeks sanctions against Estiverne for filing a frivolous appeal. ... Because the issue regarding the FCRA was novel to this Court, we decline to impose sanctions on appeal.

For the foregoing reasons, the district court's grant of summary judgment for Defendants and imposition of Rule 11 sanctions against Estiverne is AFFIRMED.

Case Questions

1. Why do you think Sak's Fifth Avenue's employee requested a consumer report before accepting Mr. Estiverne's check?
2. Is it an invasion of privacy for a store to request a consumer credit report before deciding whether to accept a customer's check?
3. What kind of facts would Mr. Estiverne have needed to include in his complaint for the court to have considered his claims of racial discrimination?

Creation of a New Tort

Legal commentators occasionally spur the development of tort law through their law review articles and treatises. Perhaps the best example is law professor William L. Prosser's writings, which have had significant and immeasurable influence over courts for decades. Prosser's tort handbook is the bible for legal students and remains the best available dissertation on the subject.

Other commentators have entered onto the tort scene with exciting new ideas that spurred courts and legislatures to change the course of the law. The article excerpted here, first published in 1977, blazed the trail for establishment of the intentional tort of defamation by computer. From

G. Stevens & H. Hoffman, "Tort Liability for Defamation by Computer,"
6 *Rutgers Journal of Computers & the Law* 91 (1977) (footnotes omitted):

Protection of the individual from the misuse of computerized personal information has received considerable scholarly attention, but little has been written on the tort liability of the information processor. Eventually, courts will be faced with questions concerning the processor's legal responsibilities for defamation and invasion of privacy. Actions to recover damages for such injuries are possible not only against recipients of computerized reports who make the information public, but also against information processors and suppliers. ...

Defamation

Under common law, a prima facie case for defamation is established if the plaintiff successfully pleads that he was identified in a defamatory matter through a "publication" of the charge by the defendant. The message need only be communicated to one person other than the defamed to be actionable, and any means through which a third party receives it can be considered a publication. While an oral statement may be classified as slander and a written statement as libel, a defamatory message designed for visual perception will be considered libelous. ... Liability could be extended to a key punch operator or a programmer under the theory that without their neglect of duty a defamatory statement might not have appeared.

* * *

The States should enact uniform guidelines for those in the computer information processing chain. ...

HYPOTHETICALS

Heather moved from her apartment in the city of Shelbydale to a house in the town of Wellington. Heather had a charge account with The Prime Account, a national credit card company. Heather wrote all of her credit card companies to report her address change. The Prime Account failed to change Heather's address in its computer billing system and continued to send its monthly invoices to Heather's Shelbydale address. After 90 days, The Prime Account reported Heather's account as delinquent to a national credit rating service. The service indicated Heather's delinquency in its computerized records, which were included in various credit reports to banks. When Heather applied at the Wellington State Bank for a mortgage loan, the bank refused her request, based upon the bad credit information. Is The Prime Account liable to Heather for defamation by computer?

The Prime Account reported that Heather's account was delinquent, and this was accurate. However, the delinquency was due to Heather's failure to receive her monthly statements. The mailing mistake was The Prime Account's fault. However, this error does not negate the truth of Heather's delinquency. The information reported in the computerized credit systems was correct, and thus defamation by computer has not occurred.

■ ■ ■

Sylvia owns a bowling alley. Marshall is a professional bowler who frequents one of Sylvia's competitors but occasionally bowls at Sylvia's establishment. Marshall's scores were repeatedly lower at Sylvia's than at any other bowling alley in town. One day, after a particularly frustrating series, Marshall lay down to "sight" the levelness of the alleys. To his eyes, the lanes looked uneven. Marshall telephoned the American Bowling Federation (ABF) to report that Sylvia's alleys did not comply with their standards. If such a criticism were true, the ABF could revoke its certification of Sylvia's facility. This could result in lost business if bowling leagues relocated to other alleys. In fact, the alleys complied with ABF standards. Has Marshall disparaged Sylvia's business enterprise?

Marshall's comments about Sylvia's alleys were false. The defamed article was the quality of Sylvia's bowling alleys, which would include the integrity of the business itself. Marshall communicated these falsehoods to a third party by telephoning the ABF. Marshall's intent may be implied by his conduct. What purpose could he have furthered by telephoning the ABF? The reasonable response would be that he hoped that the ABF would remove its certification from Sylvia's and thus discourage patronage. This translates as intent to injure another's ability to conduct business. The damage to Sylvia's goodwill would be substantial if the ABF revoked its certification. Therefore, Marshall has committed commercial disparagement.

Figure 7-3 illustrates the requirements for slander of title, commercial disparagement, and defamation by computer.

Slander of Title	Commercial Disparagement	Defamation by Computer
False statements regarding person's property ownership	False statements about person's goods, services, or business	False information about a person's credit rating
Intent to impede or injure owner's use of property	Intent to harm victim's ability to use goods, furnish services, or conduct business	Inputting false information into computerized database
Communication (publication) of falsehoods to third parties	Communication (publication) of falsehoods to third parties	Communication (publication) of falsehoods to third parties
Usually involves filing of spurious liens against real estate	Includes disparagement of goods, disparagement of services, and disparagement of business	Injury to victim's ability to secure credit, as a result of erroneous credit data

FIGURE 7-3 Elements of slander of title, commercial disparagement, and defamation by computer

Summary

Trespass to land occurs when a tortfeasor enters upon another's real estate without permission. The tortfeasor must intend to invade the premises without consent. Also, the tortfeasor's entry must interfere with the land owner's exclusive right to use the land, which is called possession.

Toxic tort actions involve toxic chemicals, pollution, hazardous waste disposal and transportation, and other environmentally sensitive issues. This litigation applies many tort theories, including trespass to land, negligence, absolute liability for ultrahazardous substances, products liability, and nuisance. The same formula for trespass to land applies in cases involving toxic substances that invade an innocent land owner's property through underwater seepage or surface or air contamination.

Trespass to chattel occurs when the tortfeasor possesses or interferes with the use of another's personal property without permission. The tortfeasor must intend to dispossess the owner of his or her chattel, or to interfere with the owner's exclusive use of the chattel.

Conversion deprives a chattel owner of possession of personal property, which the tortfeasor converts to his or her own use. The tortfeasor must intend to dispossess the owner of the chattel and then use it without consent. Conversion occurs whenever the tortfeasor deprives the owner of dominion and control over the personal property. In many jurisdictions, statutes define conversion as a crime, in addition to the common law intentional tort.

Slander of title occurs when false statements are made about an individual's ownership of property. The tortfeasor's intentions are to handicap or harm the owner's use of the property. Commercial disparagement includes disparagement of goods, of services, and of business. Commercial disparagement involves false statements about a person's goods, services, or business intended to injure the victim's ability to use the property, supply the services, or conduct business. Defamation by computer concerns false information about a person's credit rating that is entered into a computer database. Communication, or publication, of the false information to third parties is required of all three of these intentional torts.

Review Questions

1. What are the intentional torts that involve injuries to property rights? How are these distinguishable from intentional torts in which the harm is focused on persons?

2. Define trespass to land and trespass to chattel. How do the two intentional torts differ? How are they similar? What is entry? What is exclusive use? What is possession? Can trespass occur above or below land? What role does consent play in trespass? Is harm to the property required? Must the trespass be intentional? Why or why not? Must trespass to chattel involve dispossession?

3. What are toxic torts? What causes of action are available for injured persons? What federal statutes exist to regulate hazardous or toxic substances? What are the provisions of these statutes?

4. What is conversion? How is it different from trespass to chattel? How is it similar? To what extent must the chattel owner be deprived of possession? How might such deprivation occur? Must the tortfeasor do more than simply dispossess the chattel owner? What are dominion and control, and why are they important? What are the roles of intent and consent in conversion? Can conversion also be a crime? Why?

5. Explain slander of title. How might false statements be made about one's ownership of property? Provide an example of this intentional tort. What intent is involved? What is publication and why is it necessary?

6. List the different types of commercial disparagement. What are the elements of this category of intentional tort? What intent is involved? Why is communication important?

7. What is defamation by computer? Under what circumstances is this intentional tort most likely to arise? Why is communication significant?

Projects

1. Which intentional torts discussed in this chapter are included in your state's common law? Are any defined by statute? Is conversion considered both an intentional tort and a crime in your state? If so, how are the two types of conversion similar and different?

2. Separate into study groups with several classmates to discuss the theories of intentional torts to property. You might wish to create your own hypothetical fact situations utilizing the intentional torts outlined in this chapter. Use the analytical methods discussed in Chapter 2 to answer your group's questions.

3. Slander of title often involves the filing of frivolous or unlawful mechanic's liens. How are mechanic's liens filed in your state? Examine your state's statutes pertaining to mechanic's liens. You might also wish to contact your county recorder's office to discover the procedures used for filing mechanic's liens.

CHAPTER 8

DEFENSES TO INTENTIONAL TORTS

§ 8.1 Introduction

Sometimes intentional torts are legally justified, so that the person engaging in the intentional tort is not liable to the victim. These are collectively called **defenses** to intentional torts. Conduct that normally would constitute an intentional tort, such as battery, could be excused under the theory of self-defense, for instance. Defenses are commonly used by the defendant in a civil lawsuit to exonerate the defendant from liability to the plaintiff.

A legal defense arises only when one party responds to another party's allegations in a lawsuit. Usually, the defendant answers the plaintiff's complaint with defenses. However, if the defendant counter-claimed against the plaintiff, it would be the plaintiff who replied with defenses. If third parties were involved in the litigation through cross-complaints, these third parties would answer with defenses. This presumes, of course, that defenses are available with which to respond.

This chapter focuses on *justification of intentional tortious conduct through defenses*. The following questions may be helpful: (1) May the tortfeasor use a defense to excuse his or her misconduct? (2) Which defenses apply to which intentional torts?

Intentional torts involve intentional acts. Thus, they carry a high degree of risk of injury to others, and usually there is a low degree of social benefit from the act involved. The risk of injury outweighs the

TERMS

defense In both civil and criminal cases, the facts submitted and the legal arguments offered by a defendant in support of his or her claim that the plaintiff's case, or the prosecution's, should be rejected. The term "defense" may apply to a defendant's entire case or to separate grounds, called *affirmative defenses*, offered by a defendant for rejecting all or a portion of the case against him or her.

benefits received from the act. Therefore, the duty not to intentionally injure someone or something is great.

There are several types of legal defenses to intentional torts. This chapter describes:

- Self-defense (defense against assault, battery, or false imprisonment)
- Defense of persons or property (defense against assault, battery, or false imprisonment)
- Rightful repossession (defense against trespass to land, trespass to chattel, conversion, assault, and battery)
- Consent (defense to all intentional torts)
- Mistake (defense to most intentional torts)
- Privilege (broad category of defense against intentional torts)
- Necessity (defense to various intentional torts)
- Public officer's immunity for legal process enforcement, and law enforcement and private citizen's defense for warrantless arrest
- Reasonable discipline by parents and educators over children (defense to assault, battery, false imprisonment, infliction of emotional distress, invasion of privacy)
- Statutes of limitations (defense to all intentional torts).

§ 8.2 Self-Defense

Self-defense is probably the most familiar legal defense for the average person. It is most commonly applied to the intentional torts of assault and battery, but it may be used in cases involving false imprisonment. **Self-defense** is the exercise of reasonable force to repel an attack upon one's person or to avoid confinement. The nature of the action is simple: the victim of an assault or battery may use that degree of force necessary to prevent bodily injury (or offensive contact) from the attacker.

TERMS

self-defense The use of force to protect oneself from death or imminent bodily harm at the hands of an aggressor. A person may use only that amount of force reasonably necessary to protect ... against the peril with which he or she is threatened; thus, deadly force may be used in self-defense only against an aggressor who ... uses deadly force.

| IIII | PROFESSIONAL PROFILE | IIII |

"The sky is the limit," declares Susan Hock. She believes that a flexible, positive attitude is the most important element of success. "Once the paralegal has been able to establish basic skills, there are many nontraditional jobs available outside the law firm setting," she says. Hock helped establish Paralegals Plus, Inc., a free lance agency.

Hock graduated from the University of Central Florida in 1981, following her internship at the state's attorney's office in Orange County, Florida. Initially Hock's days were spent assisting the attorneys in court, drafting documents, and analyzing records as a paralegal.

Upon relocating to Dallas, Texas, Hock applied to Burleson, Pate and Gibson, where she was hired by Phil Burleson, former president of the Dallas Bar Association. One week before Hock applied for the position, Burleson addressed the Dallas Association of Legal Assistants. Following an embarrassing question-and-answer session, Mr. Burleson promised to learn more

about paralegals and about what they do: he hired Hock.

Currently Hock consults with law firms and corporate legal departments regarding the management of paralegals. Hock says, "Once my client's needs are analyzed, I match paralegals and their skills with the positions available." Paralegals assist employers by making the legal process more cost-effective and efficient. "The most rewarding aspect for paralegals is the ability to help clients solve their problems," Hock says.

Working with attorneys is a team effort. For the legal team to work efficiently, the attorney and paralegal must establish a relationship based on trust and adherence to legal ethics. As a professional, the paralegal must assist the attorney in defining the parameters of responsibility delegated. Paralegals should also demonstrate professionalism to gain the attorneys' confidence and receive more substantive assignments, advises Hock.

Similarly, the victim of false imprisonment may use the force needed to prevent or escape confinement.

Consider this likely scenario. Walter is angry at Milo and throws a punch at Milo's face. Milo responds by blocking Walter's fist and, grabbing Walter's wrist, Milo twists Walter's arm behind his back until Walter agrees to calm down. This illustrates assault and self-defense: by throwing the punch, Walter placed Milo in reasonable apprehension of an unconsented contact that endangered his physical safety. Under self-defense, Milo was entitled to use whatever force was necessary to repel the attack.

The issue of self-defense would only arise if Walter (as plaintiff) sued Milo (as defendant) for battery. Walter would allege that Milo committed battery by grabbing his wrist and twisting his arm. Milo would reply with the legal defense of self-defense, which justified his actions. Remember that the defendant uses legal defenses to avoid liability to the plaintiff. In our hypothetical, Milo's self-defense argument would defeat Walter's complaint for battery. Bear in mind that Milo would have his own cause of action against Walter for assault, and Walter would not be able to use self-defense as a defense, because he initiated the attack upon Milo.

The elements of self-defense are (1) use of reasonable force (2) to counter an attacking or offensive force and (3) necessary to prevent bodily injury, offensive contact, or confinement.

Reasonable Force

The neutralizing force a person uses in self-defense is limited. The force cannot be greater than what is reasonably necessary to dispel the attacking force. This is called **reasonable force**. In the preceding example, Milo applied only as much force as needed to prevent Walter from striking Milo. Had Milo broken Walter's arm in retaliation, this would clearly have been excessive force, because breaking Walter's arm was unnecessary to stop the assault. Thus, Milo could not use self-defense as a legal justification. Instead, Milo would have become the aggressor and have engaged in battery against Walter. Common law maintains that the victim of an assault or battery may not turn aggressive once the assailant is incapacitated. Thus, if Walter collapsed after Milo twisted his arm, Milo could not kick Walter into unconsciousness and then claim self-defense.

What constitutes reasonable force varies depending upon the circumstances of each case. If Walter attacked Milo with an axe, then deadly force would be involved. Milo would therefore be warranted in responding with deadly force to repulse the onslaught. If Walter threw rocks at Milo, his force would threaten severe bodily harm. Thus, Milo could react with similarly powerful force, such as knocking Walter down with a pole.

The reasonableness issue is difficult to reduce to clearly defined, black-and-white terms. Much depends upon the options available to the victim. Many courts hold that, in the face of deadly force, if a victim might reasonably escape from the attack, then this choice must first be selected before deadly force may be used in self-defense. Several courts apply the same rule to situations involving threats of serious bodily injury. However, the majority of jurisdictions maintain that a person is not required to flee his or her home if threatened by an intruder. This is sometimes called the **castle doctrine**, in which a dweller

---

TERMS

reasonable force Force that is appropriate in the circumstances. A person is entitled to use "reasonable force" to defend [his or her person] or ... property.

castle doctrine The doctrine that a person may use whatever force is required to defend his or her home and those in it. The principle derives its name from the maxim that "a man's home is his castle."

is considered "king" or "queen" and may use any amount of force, including deadly force, to resist an intruder, such as a burglar.

Countering an Attacking or Offensive Force

The party exercising self-defense must be opposing an attacking or offensive force. Walter's fist is obviously an attacking force. But suppose Walter spit at Milo. This would be an example of an offensive force, as it is contact by which Milo would probably be offended.

Necessity to Prevent Injury, Offensive Contact, or Confinement

The force used in self-defense must be necessary to prevent bodily injury, offensive contact, or to avoid confinement. **Necessary force** is that which is reasonably perceived as required to rebuff an attack or confinement. When Milo grabbed Walter's wrist and twisted his arm, Milo felt this action was required to prevent Walter from continuing his assault. The question again becomes one of reasonableness: Did Milo respond with reasonable force necessary to allay Walter's attack? Or was Milo's force unnecessary (and thus excessive) given Walter's actions? Suppose Walter had only tapped Milo on the shoulder with his finger. Milo's wrist-and-arm twist in response would then be considered unreasonable, unneeded, and extreme. Thus, Milo could not avail himself of a self-defense argument against Walter's battery claim.

Say that Walter was attempting to lock Milo in a room against Milo's will. In self-defense, Milo could reply with as much force as required to avoid being confined. This means that Milo could use that degree of force necessary to escape Walter.

Self-defense is perhaps the easiest legal justification to illustrate. Almost any child who has engaged in a playground shoving match can explain the fundamental concept. However, the legal elements require a more discerning eye, as shown in the following example.

HYPOTHETICAL

Toby Nesmith sat alone at a table in a local tavern. He was waiting to meet a friend from work when two men standing nearby got into a shoving match. One of

---

TERMS

necessary force[†]   That degree of force reasonably perceived as required to repel an attack or resist confinement. It is an aspect of self-defense.

the men, John, pushed the other man, Bruce, into Toby. Toby shoved Bruce back into John, knocking them both to the floor.

John committed battery against Bruce by pushing him. Under the doctrine of transferred intent, when Bruce bumped into Toby, John transferred his battery onto Toby. By pushing Bruce away, Toby used reasonable force to repel an attacking force to prevent injury to himself. Accordingly, Toby could claim self-defense against John.

There remains a puzzling question, however. Could Toby claim self-defense against Bruce, or did Toby commit battery against Bruce? Bruce was essentially the instrumentality that John put into motion to strike Toby, albeit accidentally. Bruce did not intend to contact Toby. Therefore, Bruce did not commit battery or assault against Toby.

Toby could still claim self-defense against Bruce, however. Toby responded to protect himself against injury from both participants in the shoving match. Thus, self-defense would apply. Further, because Bruce was a voluntary participant in the struggle with John, Bruce consented to physical contact associated with a shoving match. This would include inadvertently bumping into an innocent bystander like Toby. Accordingly, Toby did not commit battery against Bruce, because Bruce impliedly consented to the incidental contact involved, which would include Toby's return shove.

The Case of the Violent Visitation

When parents divorce, the noncustodial parent normally receives visitation rights as part of the court's decree. Sometimes, however, while exercising these rights, the visiting parent may clash with the ex-spouse or his or her new mate or other family. These conflicts occasionally become turbulent, resulting in physical confrontations. People have an unfortunate tendency not to be able to get along peaceably in certain circumstances.

In most cases, the law protects those who protect themselves. That is the essence of self-defense, and of defense of persons or property. But, as this case illustrates, self-defense may not preclude liability when it is unclear exactly who is in the wrong.

WHITE v. MASSENGILL
Court of Appeals of Tennessee
1990 WL 64531 (Tenn. Ct. App. 1990)
May 18, 1990
Crawford, Judge

In this assault and battery case, the trial court entered a judgment on a jury verdict for plaintiff, Carl White, against defendant Donald Jerry Massengill, in the amount of $1,392.73. From the trial court's denial of plaintiff's motion for a new trial, plaintiff appeals to this Court.

Plaintiff alleges in his complaint that on September 16, 1988, he went to the house of his ex-wife and her husband, the defendant, Massengill, to pick up his son for weekend visitation. He avers that defendant physically prevented plaintiff's son from leaving the house and when plaintiff advised defendant that he was going to notify the police, defendant Massengill "suddenly and without warning or provocation, violently attacked plaintiff, striking him in the area of the right eye." Plaintiff alleges that he suffered great pain and suffering, permanent physical injuries, and loss of earnings and earning capacity as a result of the attack.

Defendant's answer ... avers that the conduct of the plaintiff brought on the action of the defendant.

* * *

Plaintiff first answers that defendant did not plead provocation as an affirmative defense and therefore the [trial court's jury] charge [which included this defense] was not properly given. ...

Provocation is not considered a defense to an assault and battery action, but may serve to mitigate plaintiff's damages.

... The testimony is conflicting as to which of the two men threw the first punch. Defendant testified that he struck the plaintiff after plaintiff stepped into the doorway of defendant's house and struck the defendant.

* * *

There is material evidence that plaintiff's actions brought on the defendant's attack. Whether these actions rose to a level of provocation sufficient to mitigate damages is a matter for jury deliberation.

Appellant's first issue is without merit.

The second issue is whether the trial court erred by allowing defendant to testify about his nonverbalized thoughts at the time of the incident as evidence of his "state of mind."

* * *

Plaintiff first argues that defendant's state of mind is not relevant to the issues before the court. We disagree. This is an intentional tort action in which the defendant relies upon provocation in mitigation of damages and self-defense as a bar to recovery. Defendant's beliefs concerning the plaintiff's propensities for violence are pertinent to his motivations in striking the plaintiff.

* * *

This issue is without merit.

* * *

The record reveals a very sharp conflict in the testimony of the parties concerning the events leading up to and including the altercation between them. Plaintiff said that defendant started the fight, and defendant said that plaintiff started the fight. Clearly, the defendant relied upon provocation and any diminution of damages in an assault and battery case due to provocative conduct by the plaintiff is peculiarly a matter for the jury. Under the proof in this record, there is material evidence to support the verdict of the jury. ...

The judgment of the trial court is affirmed ... .

Case Questions

1. Did the jury accept the defendant's self-defense argument at trial? How were you able to make this determination?
2. Self-defense was not an issue on appeal. Provocation was disputed as a mitigation of the plaintiff's damages. Why do you suppose the defendant did not cross-appeal on the self-defense issue?
3. Although this was not an issue in the case, do you believe that the trial court should have granted judgment notwithstanding the verdict (j.n.o.v.) for the defendant on the grounds that self-defense barred the plaintiff's recovery? Explain.

The elements of self-defense are summarized in Figure 8-1.

Assault and battery may be justifiable in the defense of others or of property, as discussed in § 8.3.

FIGURE 8-1
Elements of
self-defense

| Use of reasonable force |
| Countering an attacking or offensive force |
| Actions necessary to prevent bodily injury, offensive contact, or confinement |

§ 8.3 Defense of Persons or Property

As a legal justification for assault or battery, defense of other persons or defense of injury to property is similar to self-defense. A person who would otherwise have committed assault or battery may be excused if the action was taken to protect another individual or property from harm. This would include freeing someone subject to false imprisonment.

Defense of Persons: Elements

Defense of persons as a legal justification for assault or battery has the following elements: (1) use of reasonable force (2) to defend or protect a third party from injury (3) when the third party is threatened by an attacking force. For example, if Marie were about to throw a vase at Marjorie, Simon could use reasonable force to subdue Marie before she could complete the throw. Simon would not have committed battery, because he grabbed Marie to prevent her from harming Marjorie. Simon would be entitled to the legal defense of defense of another person to avoid liability for battery.

The same principles used in self-defense to define reasonable force also apply to defense of persons. Thus, Simon could not use excessive force to repel Marie's attack against Marjorie. For instance, if Simon struck Marie sharply in the head with a two-by-four piece of lumber, this would be unnecessarily brutal force to subdue the vase attack.

Also, like self-defense, the repelling force must be used to counter an attacking force. If Marjorie telephoned Simon to complain that Marie had just thrown a vase at her, Simon could not run over and strike Marie and then claim defense of another as an excuse.

TERMS

defense of persons [†] A defense to the intentional torts of assault, battery, and false imprisonment. Its elements include the use of reasonable force to defend or protect a third party from injury when the third party is threatened by an attacking force.

Defense of Property: Elements

Conduct that otherwise might be assault or battery may be vindicated if the action is taken to defend property from damage or dispossession. A property owner has the right to possess and safeguard his or her property from others. The elements of **defense of property** are (1) use of reasonable force (2) to protect property from damage or dispossession (3) when another person, the *invader,* attempts to injure or wrongfully take possession of the property.

The reasonable force contemplated here is essentially identical to that discussed in regard to self-defense. Many courts, however, restrict the defensive force to the least amount necessary to protect the property from harm or dispossession. This is a narrower definition of *reasonableness,* suggesting that human well-being is more important than the safety of property. Under this theory, most courts would not allow deadly force or extreme force likely to cause serious bodily injury to be used to defend property under any circumstances.

The property owner or possessor uses reasonable force to repulse an attacking force that is attempting to harm or possess the property. For example, if Frederick is in the process of committing trespass to chattel or conversion, then Helen, who owns the personal property in danger, may use reasonable force to dispel Frederick's efforts at dispossession.

The use of reasonable force to expel a trespasser to land is called **ejectment.** Defense of real property cases frequently involve land owners who have placed dangerous traps for trespassers. The trespassers are often seeking to steal personal property and usually violate various criminal statutes involving theft or burglary. Nevertheless, land owners may not set up deadly traps to inflict serious bodily injuries upon such criminals. Spring-loaded guns have been the most common snares litigated. A land owner places a shotgun inside a barn or outbuilding which is triggered by a trip-wire placed across a window or doorway. The thief steps upon the wire while trying to enter and is shot. Courts universally condemn this use of deadly force to defend property.

It should be relatively easy to imagine situations in which reasonable force is used to defend another person from attack. Defense of property, however, may be more difficult to conjure.

TERMS

---

defense of property[†]   A defense to the intentional torts of assault and battery. Its elements include the use of reasonable force to protect property from damage or dispossession when another person, called the *invader,* attempts to injure or wrongfully take possession of the property.

ejectment   An action at common law for the right to possession of land.

The Case of the Defiant Trucker

In 1966 the Bobby Fuller Four recorded a popular rock song in which the refrain declared, "I fought the law, and the law won." As this case demonstrates, this is usually the result. However, note the dissent's approach to defense of property against an arguably unlawful seizure by law enforcement officers. Although this case involved criminal law, the court's discussion of defense of property is relevant to tort law.

JURCO v. STATE
Court of Appeals of Alaska
825 P.2d 909 (Alaska Ct. App. 1992)
February 14, 1992
Mannheimer, Judge

David Jurco was convicted, following a jury trial in district court, of disorderly conduct and resisting arrest. These offenses resulted from a confrontation between Jurco and members of the State Troopers who had come to Jurco's residence to serve a court order directing them to take possession of Jurco's truck; the Kenai District Court had ordered forfeiture of the vehicle because Jurco had used it in furtherance of a violation of the fish and game laws.

Unbeknown to the troopers, Jurco had recently filed for bankruptcy. The federal bankruptcy court had directed Jurco not to sell or transfer any of his property or allow creditors to take any of his property without court order. Jurco believed that the bankruptcy court's directive obliged him to resist the troopers' attempt to seize his truck. At first, Jurco argued with the troopers. Finding he could not dissuade them, Jurco got into the truck and started it. With Trooper Eugene Kallus trying to hang on to the side of the truck, Jurco drove the truck away to a different location on his property. Jurco then got out of the truck, removed the battery from the vehicle, and began to let the air out of the truck's tires.

At this point, Trooper Kallus informed Jurco that he was placing him under arrest for disorderly conduct. ...

But even if we assume for purposes of argument that Jurco's interpretation of bankruptcy law is correct, the question remains whether Jurco was entitled to forcibly resist the troopers when they came to execute the Kenai District Court's warrant. We conclude that Jurco was not entitled to forcibly resist the troopers even if he reasonably believed that the seizure of his truck was illegal.

* * *

[At common law] a property owner was entitled to use force to resist an unlawful taking of his property. "One whose lawful possession of property is threatened by the unlawful conduct of another, and who has no time to resort to the law for its protection, may take reasonable steps, including the use of force, to prevent or terminate such interference with the property." This ... common-law rule has also been codified in Alaska; AS [Alaska Statutes] 11.81.350-(a) provides:

Justification: Use of force in defense of property and premises.
(a) A person may use nondeadly force upon another when and to the extent the person reasonably believes it is necessary to terminate what the person reasonably believes to be the commission or attempted commission by the other of an unlawful taking or damaging of property or services.

For purposes of deciding this appeal, we assume that Jurco reasonably believed that the Kenai District Court's order to seize his truck ran afoul of the federal bankruptcy court's order to keep his property together. [Another Alaska statute, Alaska Stat. § 11.81.420, authorized law enforcement officers to use reasonable force, including deadly force, to enforce a court order to seize property, even if the court decree is later determined to have been unlawful.] In such a situation, the joint operation of Alaska Stat. §§ 11.81.420 and 11.81.350(a) would seemingly allow Jurco to use force against the troopers to resist the taking of his truck while at the same time authorizing the troopers to respond with force of their own against Jurco—creating an escalating confrontation that would end only when the troopers resorted to deadly force against Jurco. ...

Sidebar: Is the Alaska Court of Appeals being just a bit melodramatic when characterizing the "escalating confrontation" between Jurco and the troopers as ending only when the police ultimately kill Jurco? The court concludes that the state legislature could not have intended two conflicting statutes—one governing defense of property and the other concerning law officers' enforcement of court orders—to permit members of the public to wrestle with police over chattel possession. Was the court simply exaggerating to justify its rationale?

This could not have been the legislature's intention. With emotions running high on both sides, a property owner who sees that non-deadly force is not enough to make law enforcement officials back down might well begin (unlawfully) to use deadly force on the officers. Or, in the heat of the moment, the officers might mistakenly conclude that the property owner has begun to use deadly force upon them and respond in kind. Both possibilities could easily lead to the infliction of serious injury or death.

Thus, the question presented by Jurco's case is: which of these two statutes did the legislature intend to take precedence when law enforcement officers attempt to execute a court order calling for a seizure of property?

Sidebar: As the Alaska Court of Appeals has framed the issue, which statute will prevail? Are you surprised by this outcome? Or was it predictable from the outset?

We conclude that a person is not entitled to use force to resist the taking of property by law enforcement officers pursuant to a court order.

* * *

It follows that Jurco was not entitled to forcibly resist the State Troopers' efforts to seize his truck under the order issued by the Kenai District Court.

* * *

The judgment of the district court is AFFIRMED. BRYNER, Chief Judge, dissenting.

I disagree with the court's decision ... . In my view, Jurco was entitled to [a jury instruction] on his theory of defense ... that he was seeking to protect his property from what he reasonably believed to be an unlawful taking.

* * *

The majority of this court effectively amends the defense of property statute by engrafting to it an exception that the legislature evidently chose not to include. The court does so in reliance on its own notions of desirable social policy. It is not this court's prerogative, however, to substitute its political views for those expressed by the legislature in the clear and unrestricted language of [Alaska Stat. §] 11.81.350(a).

Case Questions

1. Do you agree with the majority that the legislature intended the law officer enforcement-of-court-orders statute to override the defense-of-property statute? Explain.
2. Do you agree with the dissent that the majority rewrites the two statutes to suit its own vision of preferred social policy?

HYPOTHETICAL

Consider the case of Isaac, who discovered two teenage hoodlums throwing bricks and stones at his house windows. Isaac crept up behind the duo and leapt from behind some bushes. The delinquents were taken by surprise, and Isaac knocked one to the ground with a kick to the stomach and tackled the other. Although both hoodlums suffered minor abrasions and bruises, neither was injured severely. The two hoodlums claim that Isaac has committed battery against them. Does Isaac have a defense?

Isaac used force against the rowdies to prevent damage to his property. The hoodlums were attempting to injure Isaac's house. The primary question is whether Isaac used reasonable force to prevent the property damage. Because neither of the two teenagers suffered severe harm as a result of Isaac's actions, the force should be deemed reasonable to neutralize the teenagers. Accordingly, Isaac could successfully apply defense of property against the allegation of battery.

The elements of defense of persons or property are listed in Figure 8-2.

Defense of property is often used in situations in which sellers repossess property from defaulting buyers.

Defense of Persons	*Defense of Property*
Use of reasonable force	Use of reasonable force
To defend or protect a third party from harm	To protect property from damage or dispossession
Third person is threatened by attacking force	Someone attempts to harm or wrongfully possess property

FIGURE 8-2 Elements of defense of persons or property

§ 8.4 Rightful Repossession

An owner of personal property generally has the right to repossess, by force if necessary, a chattel that has been wrongfully taken or withheld. This is the defense of **rightful repossession**. The defense is generally

---

TERMS

rightful repossession[†] A defense to trespass to land, trespass to chattel, conversion, assault, and battery. Its elements include the use of reasonable force to retake possession of personal property of which the owner has applied to allegations of trespass to land, assault, battery, and sometimes conversion and trespass to chattel. However, the amount of force that may be used is extremely limited. Generally, the elements of rightful repossession include the following: (1) use of reasonable force (2) to retake possession of personal property (3) of which the owner has been wrongfully dispossessed (or to which the owner is denied possession), (4) provided the efforts to retake the chattel are made promptly after the original dispossession or denial of possession occurs. For this defense, reasonable force is defined along the same lines as defense of property.

Retaking Possession of Personal Property

The chattel owner seeks to repossess personal property to which he or she is entitled. This is the crux of the defense. If someone has wrongfully dispossessed an owner of his or her chattel, then the owner is entitled to enter upon the dispossessor's land to recover the chattel. This provides a defense to trespass to land. Reasonable force may be applied to recover possession of the personal property.

To illustrate, suppose Raymond took Carl's motorcycle without asking permission and drove the cycle back to his own garage. Carl would be entitled to enter Raymond's garage to recover the cycle. If Raymond attempted to prevent Carl from entering, Carl could use reasonable force to vanquish Raymond and recover the cycle. Carl would not be liable for either trespass to land or battery, because he would have the defense of rightful repossession.

Prompt Repossession Efforts

Older common law cases held that a chattel owner's efforts to repossess personal property must occur soon after the chattel had been wrongfully taken away. However, just how promptly this had to occur was not clearly defined. Many nineteenth-century opinions ruled that hot pursuit was necessary. Hot pursuit is usually defined for purposes of criminal law, but its meaning is the same for this tort defense. **Hot pursuit**, in this context, may be described as a rapid chase as soon as possible after the owner has discovered that his or her chattel is missing.

═══════════════ TERMS ═══════════════

been wrongfully dispossessed, or to which the owner has been wrongfully denied possession. Efforts to retake the chattel must be made promptly after the original dispossession (or denial of possession) occurs.

hot (fresh) pursuit ... A person may use reasonable force to recover property from a thief if he or she pursues and apprehends [the thief] immediately.

This presumes, of course, that the personal property owner knows who took the chattel.

Wrongful Denial of Possession

The chattel owner need not be dispossessed of the personal property for this defense to apply. Consider the example of someone who originally took possession of the chattel with the owner's consent, but later wrongfully refuses to return it. If the owner then attempted to retake possession and was accused of trespass to land, assault, or battery, the owner could apply rightful repossession as a defense.

Most cases involving denial of possession deal with bailments, in which the owner has delivered possession of the chattel to someone else for a specific purpose, with the explicit understanding that the chattel is to be returned at a certain time or upon demand. When an automobile is taken to a mechanic for repair, for instance, there is a bailment. The mechanic would have lawful possession of the vehicle, because the owner left it for repairs. Suppose, however, that the mechanic made unauthorized repairs and sought to charge the owner. If the owner demanded return of the car and the mechanic refused, then this refusal would constitute wrongful denial of possession. The owner could use reasonable force to enter the mechanic's premises to retake the chattel. The owner would not be liable to the mechanic for trespass to land because of the rightful repossession defense.

Note that this result would be different if there had been a dispute over authorized repairs. Most state statutes provide mechanics with possessory liens, which empower repair persons to keep possession of vehicles until repair charges have been paid. However, some statutes provide that the amounts due must be undisputed.

Wrongful Dispossession

For the defense of rightful repossession to apply, the owner's chattel must have been unlawfully dispossessed, or its return have been unlawfully denied. This means that the dispossessor or retainer must not have a legal right to possess (or deny return of) the chattel.

In the preceding bailment example, the mechanic did not possess the automobile unlawfully, because the owner had left it for repairs. However, when the mechanic performed unauthorized work and sought payment, and the owner demanded the car's return, then the mechanic wrongfully possessed the vehicle—specifically, the repair person committed trespass to chattel and possibly conversion. Thus, the owner would be entitled to repossess with reasonable force and could use that defense against the mechanic's lawsuit for trespass to land, assault, or battery.

Rightful repossession seems a noble defense, albeit more difficult to conceptualize than self-defense or defense of others and property. One might express the emotional essence of the doctrine as, "It's mine and I'm taking it back now!" The defense appeals to a sense of entitlement. As you read the following hypothetical, with whom do your sympathies lie?

The Case of the Free-Roaming Feline

The following case illustrates an unusual application of rightful repossession. Any pet owner, however, will immediately sympathize with the Blanchards. The court discusses self-defense and defense of property, but the case is a classic rightful repossession scenario.

SHEHYN v. UNITED STATES
District of Columbia Court of Appeals
256 A.2d 404 (D.C. 1969)
August 7, 1969
Fickling, J.

Appellant was convicted by a jury of assault, D.C. Code § 22-504. After the court charged the jury on assault and self-defense, the instruction [on defense of property] ... was given and objected to on the ground that it did not correctly state the law on the defense of one's property. The objection was well taken. However, we hold it was harmless error in the context of the case as a whole.

Mr. Blanchard, the complainant, and his wife, who were next door neighbors of appellant, went upon appellant's parking lot to retrieve their pet cat which had escaped from their house and had hidden in appellant's air shaft. Appellant ordered the Blanchards off his property. After they refused, he went inside his house and got a wooden camera tripod about four feet in length and again ordered them to leave. When they refused to leave until they recovered their cat, appellant pushed Mrs. Blanchard aside and struck Mr. Blanchard with the tripod causing injury to his hand, requiring five stitches, and lacerations to his chest. The testimony is conflicting as to why appellant struck Mr. Blanchard. Appellant testified he went into the house to get the

tripod because Mr. Blanchard picked up a brick. Blanchard testified he picked up a brick after appellant came out of his house with the tripod, and then he dropped the brick as appellant was advancing upon him because he did not want to strike appellant, who is an elderly man.

It is well settled that a person may use as much force as is reasonably necessary to eject a trespasser from his property, and that if he used more force than is necessary, he is guilty of assault. This is true regardless of any actual or threatened injury to the property by the trespasser, although this would be a factor in determining the reasonableness of the force used. However, in the instant case, Blanchard was not a trespasser. He had a privilege to go peaceably upon appellant's property to retrieve his cat. In *Carter v. Thurston*, 59 N.H. 104 (1877), where logs went upon a riparian owner's property because of a flood, the court stated:

> This right of pursuit and reclamation [of logs] rests upon the same natural right as that which permits the owner of cattle to pursue into an adjoining field and recover his beasts straying from the highway; but in the pursuit and recovery of his cattle or his logs, the owner must do no unnecessary damage, and is responsible for any excess or abuse of his right.

In an assault case where the complainant was injured while recovering his carpenter's plane, the court stated in *Stuyvesant v. Wilcox*, 92 Mich. 233, 52 N.W. 465, 467 (1892):

> But it is a rule well settled that one has such a right in personal property that he may recapture it and take it into his own possession whenever and wherever he may peaceably do so.

This principle was also followed in *Pierce v. Finerty*, 76 N.H. 38, 76 A. 194, 196 (1910), which involved reclamation of trees upon the land of another:

> There is a right of recaption or reclamation of personal property upon another's land without fault of the owner. In such cases, under certain circumstances, the owner of personal property has a right to enter to retake his property, and is not a trespasser if he does so. ... But the right does not extend to cases where the situation is created by the fault or wrong of such owner.

The applicable rule, which we adopt, is stated in *Restatement (Second) of Torts* § 198 (1965):

> (1) One is privileged to enter land in the possession of another, at a reasonable time and in a reasonable manner, for the purpose of removing a chattel to the immediate possession of which the actor is entitled, and which has come upon the land otherwise than with the actor's consent or by his tortious conduct or contributory negligence.
>
> (2) The actor is subject to liability for any harm done in the exercise of the privilege stated in Subsection (1) to any legally protected interest of the possessor in the land or connected with it, except where the chattel is on the land through the tortious conduct or contributory negligence of the possessor.

In this case there is no evidence in the record which would indicate that the Blanchards acted in an unreasonable manner or at an unreasonable time when they went upon the parking lot to get their cat. The [jury] instruction, even though erroneous, was actually beneficial to appellant since he had no right to eject the Blanchards while they were exercising a privilege given to them by law, and appellant was not entitled to any defense of property instruction.

Affirmed.

Case Questions

1. Although Shehyn, the appellant, was prosecuted under a criminal statute for assault, the defenses used in the case would be identical to those pleaded in a civil lawsuit involving the tort of assault or battery. Did you notice that the Blanchards were alleged to have committed trespass to land? What were their defenses as discussed in *Shehyn*? What portions of the court's opinion alerted you to these defenses?

2. Although the court in *Shehyn* quoted several persuasive precedents from other jurisdictions, it chose to adopt the rule stated in the *Restatement (Second) of Torts* § 198. Why did the *Shehyn* court quote these other state court opinions? Why do you think it adopted the *Restatement* rule, which is considered secondary legal authority, as opposed to the quoted court cases, which are primary authority?

3. Are there any other intentional tort defenses that were not discussed in *Shehyn* but that would apply? What are these? Why do you think they would succeed or fail?

4. Would the decision in *Shehyn* have been different if the Blanchards' cat had entered the appellant's land as a result of the Blanchards' actions? Suppose Mr. Blanchard threw a cat toy too high into the air, causing it to land on top of the appellant's roof, thereby enticing the cat to climb up onto the roof and become trapped there? Would the Blanchards have been legally justified in entering the appellant's real estate under these circumstances?

HYPOTHETICAL

Ann was buying an automobile from Victor. Ann wrote a check to Victor for the final payment and this check bounced (i.e., the bank did not pay it because there were insufficient funds in Ann's account). Victor angrily went over to Ann's house and drove away in the car. As soon as Ann discovered the check problem, she telephoned Victor's apartment and left a message on his answering machine that she would be over directly to pay cash.

The first issue is whether Victor had the right to repossess the automobile once Ann's check bounced. This would depend upon the terms of their agreement or, if the agreement did not address the problem, then upon creditors' rights statutes. For the sake of example, assume that no statutes address the question and that the parties' contract was silent as well. Although it is true that Ann breached her contract by bouncing her payment check to Victor, she also swiftly corrected the error. Most courts would hold that Victor could not use self-help remedies such as repossession without first contacting Ann to see if she could make good on the check. By repossessing the car without first talking with Ann, and because Ann has paid nearly the entire purchase price (and thus has a substantial equity, meaning property interest, in the vehicle), Victor has committed trespass to chattel. Thus, Ann has been wrongfully dispossessed of her chattel. She could then enter Victor's real estate to recover her automobile without being liable to Victor for trespass to land. Ann would be entitled to the defense of rightful repossession.

It should also be noted that Victor would not be able to claim rightful repossession as a defense to trespass to chattel. Because Victor did not first communicate with Ann regarding the bad check and alternative means of payment, most courts would say that Victor could not defend his retaking of the car on the grounds of rightful repossession. However, if Victor had telephoned Ann about the check, and she had replied that she could or would not make the final payment, then Victor would be legally entitled to repossess the vehicle. Under this set of circumstances, Victor could use rightful repossession as a defense to trespass to chattel.

A synopsis of rightful repossession appears in Figure 8-3.

Use of reasonable force
To repossess personal property
Owner has been wrongfully dispossessed of the chattel or has been improperly denied possession
Owner's efforts to repossess chattel occur promptly after original dispossession or denial of possession

FIGURE 8-3   Elements of rightful repossession

§ 8.5 Consent

Consent is a broad defense applicable to every intentional tort. **Consent** occurs when the victim of an intentional tort voluntarily agrees to the tortfeasor's actions, provided that the victim understands (or reasonably should understand) the consequences of the tortfeasor's deeds. This knowledge factor is sometimes called **informed consent**.

The consent defense contains the following elements: (1) Voluntary acceptance of an intentionally tortious act (2) with full knowledge or understanding of the consequences. Actually, consent is not a legal defense at all. As shown in the previous two chapters, it is a deliberately missing element of intentional torts. If consent existed, then the intentional tort could not have occurred. The ancient common law applied the Latin maxim, *volenti non fit injuria,* which translates as, "No wrong may occur to one who is willing." As a practical matter, courts over the centuries have treated consent as a defense to intentional torts.

Informed Consent: Voluntary Acceptance

Consent will be a successful defense to an intentional tort action only if the victim willingly and knowingly agreed to the tortfeasor's conduct. Accordingly, a victim who is coerced into tolerating an intentional tort cannot consent to it, because the victim was compelled to undergo the tort. Further, the victim must comprehend the implications of the tortfeasor's actions to consent to them.

For instance, suppose Randy agrees to wrestle Ralph. Assume that both Randy and Ralph understand the repercussions of wrestling, including possible inadvertent injury. Randy and Ralph will have mutually consented to battery, and so neither could sue the other for this intentional tort if harm did happen. However, assume Randy did not

---

TERMS

consent   Agreement; approval; acquiescence; being of one mind. Consent necessarily involves two or more persons because, without at least two persons, there cannot be a unity of opinion or the possibility of thinking alike. ...

informed consent   Agreement to permit something to occur ... , after having been given as much information as necessary to make an intelligent and rational ("informed") decision. ...

want to wrestle Ralph, but Ralph ridiculed Randy in front of friends, in effect coercing Randy to wrestle. Randy would not have consented because of duress.

Part of the voluntary, or *volition,* factor of consent is the victim's mental capacity to agree. Some persons simply lack sufficient mental abilities to understand the consequences of a tortfeasor's actions. Severely retarded or mentally incapacitated individuals, for example, might not grasp the implications of a tortfeasor's misbehavior. Intoxicated individuals may also have insufficient mental faculties to comprehend the results of an intentional tort. Children, particularly when very young, may lack cognitive development adequate to grasp the ramifications of intentional torts. For such persons, consent could become virtually impossible.

Implied Consent

Consent may be expressed, either orally or in writing, or it may be implied by conduct or circumstances. For instance, public officials or famous persons are assumed to consent to adverse publicity merely by placing themselves in the public limelight. Consent to publicity is therefore implied, and public officials or celebrities cannot recover for libel or slander, unless malice is proven.

The most common example of implied consent involves emergency medical treatment. If a patient is unconscious and is taken to a hospital emergency room, the medical personnel may presume that the patient consents to treatment, at least to the extent of the emergency condition. Thus, if someone is found unconscious on the pavement, suffering from gastrointestinal bleeding, and an ambulance takes her to the hospital, the patient is presumed to agree to treatment of the emergency condition, in this case a "G.I. bleed," which is often life-threatening. Later, if the patient regains consciousness and protests against the treatment (perhaps upon religious grounds), the patient cannot sue for battery for the unauthorized emergency care. However, once conscious and clear-minded, the patient could insist that further treatment be forgone. Failure to stop treatment would then constitute battery. Suppose, instead, that the medical personnel treated beyond the emergency condition, such as removing a portion of diseased skin while treating the intestinal bleeding. Implied consent does not apply to nonemergency treatment, and thus battery would have occurred.

Consent is sometimes characterized as the "you asked for it" defense. However, as the following hypothetical demonstrates, there can be doubt as to what the "it" was to which the victim consented.

The Case of the More-Than-Touch Football Game

Almost everyone has played contact games. Children delight in games such as "tag," "keep-away," and "hide-and-seek," which usually involve some physical contact. Older children and adults engage in rougher sports in which implied consent accepts incidental contact. Sometimes, however, a player forgets that there are limits to the reasonable force to which participants consent. In the following case, it becomes clear that the plaintiff felt that the defendant went well beyond these acceptable lines. The California Court of Appeal, however, was unimpressed. Perhaps none of the judges had ever played a rough game of touch football.

KNIGHT v. JEWETT
California Court of Appeal
232 Cal. App. 3d 1142,
275 Cal. Rptr. 292 (1990)
November 27, 1990
Review granted, **278 Cal. Rptr. 203,**
804 P.2d 1300 (Cal. 1991)
Todd, Acting Presiding Justice

Kendra Knight appeals a summary judgment granted in favor of Michael Jewett in her lawsuit against Jewett for negligence and assault and battery stemming from a touch football game in which she was injured. Knight contends ... it was error to apply the doctrine of assumption of risk to defeat the assault and battery cause of action and ... there were triable issues of fact that should have precluded the granting of summary judgment.

FACTS

On January 25, 1987, Knight and several other individuals, including Jewett, gathered at the Vista home of Ed McDaniels to observe the Super Bowl football game. Knight and Jewett were among those who decided to play a game of co-ed touch football during half-time using a "pee-wee" football often used by children. Apparently, no explicit rules were written down or discussed before the game, other than the requirement that to stop advancement of the player with the ball it was necessary to touch that player above the waist with two hands. Knight and Jewett were on different teams.

Previously, Knight had played touch football and frequently watched football on television.

Knight voluntarily participated in the Super Bowl half-time game. It was her understanding that this game would not involve forceful pushing, hard hitting or hard shoving during the game. She had never observed anyone being injured in a touch football game before this incident.

About five to ten minutes after the game started, Jewett ran into Knight during a play and afterward Knight asked Jewett not to play so rough. Otherwise, she told him, she would stop playing.

On the next play, Knight suffered her injuries, when she was knocked down by Jewett and he stepped on the little finger of her right hand. Kendra had three surgeries on the finger, but they proved unsuccessful. The finger was amputated during a fourth surgery.

According to Jewett, he had jumped up to intercept a pass and as he came down he knocked Knight over. When he landed, he stepped back and onto Knight's hand.

According to Knight's version, her teammate, Andrea Starr had caught the ball and was proceeding up the field. Knight was headed in the same direction, when Jewett, in pursuit of Starr, came from behind Knight and knocked her down. Knight put her arms out to break the fall and Jewett ran over her, stepping on her hand. Jewett continued to pursue Starr for another 10 to 15 feet before catching up with her and tagging her. Starr said the tag was rough enough to cause her to lose her balance and fall and twist her ankle.

Jewett did not intend to step on Knight's hand and did not intend to hurt her.

* * *

Knight contends her cause of action for assault and battery is viable and she should be allowed to proceed to trial on it.

... Jewett argued it must fail because Knight consented to the physical contact.

Consent is a viable defense to the tort of assault and battery. "A person may, by participating in a game, or by other conduct, consent to an act which might otherwise constitute a battery." Here, however, we need not dwell on whether Jewett can successfully interpose a defense of consent to Knight's assault and battery cause of action.

Inasmuch as this case reaches us on appeal from a summary judgment in favor of Jewett, it is only necessary for us to determine whether there is any possibility Knight may be able to establish her case.

A requisite element of assault and battery is intent. Here, however, there is no evidence that Jewett intended to injure Knight or commit a battery on her. Moreover, the record affirmatively shows Knight does not believe Jewett had the intent to step on her hand or injure her. Without the requisite intent, Knight cannot state a cause of action for assault and battery.

A motion for summary judgment is addressed to the sound discretion of the trial court and, absent a clear showing of abuse, the judgment will not be disturbed on appeal. On this record, we discern no abuse of discretion; the granting of summary judgment was proper. ... Affirmed.

Case Questions

1. *Knight* demonstrates how the defense of consent cannot be reached unless the elements of intentional torts (in this case, assault and battery), are satisfied. Although the evidence suggested that the defendant lacked the necessary intent to cause injury, could you imply such intent from Jewett's rough conduct during the game?
2. Presume that Knight had proven Jewett's intent to harm her, thus making a prima facie case for assault and battery (the other elements being satisfied under the facts of the case as given in the opinion). Would Jewett's consent defense prevail? Did Knight consent to the harsh play that Jewett was engaging in? If so, did Knight withdraw her consent when she told Jewett to stop playing so roughly?
3. Are there any other intentional tort defenses that were not discussed in *Knight* but that would apply? What are they? Why do you think they would succeed or fail?

HYPOTHETICAL

Colleen attended a company banquet in her honor as "sales director of the year." The dinner was a "roast" at which co-workers made humorous remarks about the guest of honor. Several of these comments were loaded with sarcasm and a few were in questionable taste. However, none of the comments was taken seriously by the audience, which understood that it was all in good fun. Under other circumstances, however, some members of the audience might have been offended. Colleen, however, took offense at the more colorful character references. Could she sue her co-employees for slander?

Colleen voluntarily agreed to attend the banquet with a complete understanding that co-workers would use the forum to tease and joke about her. She should have known that some of her fellow employees would push the limits of propriety with a few harsh remarks. Because the audience was not offended (given the "roast" atmosphere), and because Colleen knowingly accepted the potentially slanderous conduct, consent would be a defense to Colleen's slander claim.

The components of consent are listed in Figure 8-4.

Consent is clearly the most pervasive defense to intentional torts. Mistake is also quite extensive, as discussed in the next section.

FIGURE 8-4
Elements of consent

Voluntary acceptance of intentionally tortious act
Full knowledge or understanding of consequences

§ 8.6 Mistake

Sometimes people act based upon inaccurate information or incorrect interpretations of events. The actor intended the result of his or her conduct but behaved under false beliefs. Often, had a person known the true state of affairs, he or she would have behaved differently. Tort law recognizes this tendency toward error, in which everyone has engaged at one time or another. The defense of mistake provides individuals with an escape route from intentional tort liability. As a legal defense, **mistake** is the good faith belief, based upon incorrect information, that one is justified in committing an intentional tort under the circumstances. The elements may be detailed as follows: (1) Good faith conviction that one's actions are justified (2) with the belief based upon faulty information; and (3) the conduct would otherwise be considered tortious but for the erroneous belief.

Good Faith Conviction

The actor must reasonably believe that, under the incorrect facts the actor thinks are true, the actor's conduct will be legally excused. For instance, if Sandra thought Martina was converting Sandra's jacket when, in actuality, Martina was merely picking it off the floor, then Sandra would be justified in using reasonable force to recapture her chattel (as she reasonably believed that Martina was attempting to keep it). Naturally, the question revolves around the reasonableness of Sandra's perception of events. Was it obvious that Martina was simply picking up the jacket?

TERMS

mistake 1. An erroneous mental conception that influences a person to act or to decline to act; an unintentional act, omission, or error arising from ignorance, surprise, imposition, or misplaced confidence. ... 2. An error; a misunderstanding; an inaccuracy.

Did it look as if Martina might have been rifling through the pockets looking for valuables? The good faith conviction, like all elements of mistake, depends heavily upon the specific facts of each case.

Belief Based upon Inaccurate Information

To use mistake as a defense to intentional torts, the actor must base his or her conviction upon erroneous details which, if they had been true, would have justified the conduct. Had Martina actually been trying to take Sandra's jacket (or valuables in its pockets), then Sandra would have been entitled to use reasonable force under the defense of rightful repossession. Assume that Sandra saw Martina looking through the jacket's pockets. Suppose that Martina was simply looking to see if anything had fallen out, but to Sandra it appeared that Martina was searching for valuables. This mistaken perception would be reasonable and would excuse Sandra's repossession efforts (such as grabbing Martina's arm and pulling the jacket out of her hands). Sandra would not be liable to Martina for battery, because of the mistake defense.

Otherwise Tortious Acts

It may seem apparent that the defense of mistake applies only if the actor has engaged in behavior which, except for the defense, would be considered tortious. For example, Sandra would have had to commit an intentional tort against Martina (such as battery) in order to claim the defense of mistake or rightful repossession. Otherwise, Sandra would not need to argue any defenses, because she would not need to justify her actions. This factor is present in all intentional tort defenses.

The Second Restatement of Torts

For decades, the American Law Institute has assembled Restatements of the Law, which summarize the legal principles discussed in common law decisions. These include the *Restatement of Torts* and its successor, the *Restatement (Second) of Torts.*

In the *Restatement (Second)*'s chapter 45, justification and excuse to tort liability are discussed. The following is an excerpt applicable to the mistake defense.

Restatement (Second) of Torts § 890
Comments a & f
American Law Institute (1979)

In some cases the law creates a privilege … . [A] privilege is given although it adversely affects the legally protected interests of another.

This is ordinarily true when the actor is protected although mistaken (see Comment *f*), as when one acts in self-defense against another whom he reasonably but erroneously believes to be an aggressor. ...

f. Mistake. ...

When the privilege is conditional, a person is sometimes protected by his reasonable belief in the existence of facts that would give rise to a privilege, even though the facts do not exist. Thus one is not liable for using reasonable force in the protection of himself or another against what he reasonably believes to be an aggression of another ... ; a policeman is not liable for mistakenly arresting one whom he believes to have committed a felony ... and a private person is similarly protected if a felony has been committed ... ; a parent or teacher is not liable for mistakenly but reasonably disciplining a student.

Copyright © 1979 by The American Law Institute. Reprinted with the permission of the American Law Institute.

HYPOTHETICAL

Diedra was shopping at a local convenience store. The manager thought she saw Diedra put a pack of chewing gum into her purse. When Diedra left the store without stopping at the cashier, the manager asked her to step back inside the store to see the contents of her purse. The manager explained that she thought she had seen her take merchandise without paying. Diedra emptied her purse, but no store items were included. If Diedra claimed that the manager had committed false imprisonment, defamation, or infliction of emotional distress, could the manager use mistake as a defense?

Assume that the manager's acts arguably constituted any one of these intentional torts. Nevertheless, courts would readily rule that, under these circumstances, the manager was justified in detaining Diedra for questioning. So long as the interrogation was conducted reasonably (such as in private for a short time period), then the courts would consider the manager's behavior to be acceptable. The manager had a good faith belief that Diedra had shoplifted (although, in fact, she had not). The manager acted based upon this erroneous conviction, expecting that her conduct would be legally excused under the circumstances.

Mistake is summarized in Figure 8-5.

FIGURE 8-5
Elements of mistake

Good faith conviction that actor's conduct is justified
Belief based upon erroneous information
Behavior would be tortious except for incorrect belief

§ 8.7 Privilege

As an intentional torts defense, **privilege** is a legal justification to engage in otherwise tortious conduct in order to accomplish a compelling social goal. This defense is based upon the right of a person to do what most people are not permitted to do. It is a right conferred on a person by society. For example, as a land owner, one may eject a person from one's own property, but other people may not do this. Only the land owner is thus privileged.

Privilege is most commonly a defense to trespass to land, trespass to chattel, conversion, assault, battery, and false imprisonment, although it may be applied against other intentional torts as well. Privilege includes the following considerations:

1. Do the actor's motives for engaging in an intentional tort outweigh the injury to the victim or his or her property?
2. Was the actor justified in committing the intentional tort to accomplish his or her socially desirable purposes, or could a less damaging action have been taken instead?

This formula shows how courts balance values between the socially acceptable motives of the tortfeasor (actor) and the tort victim's compensation for injury. Privilege presumes that the intentional tort is legally justified because of the higher purposes to be achieved.

Motives and Socially Desirable Goals

Motive describes the goal which a participant wishes to accomplish by taking a particular action. Motive may be discovered by probing the mental state of the actor. This mind-reading occurs in many areas of law. For example, in criminal law, *mens rea* loosely translates from the Latin as "evil thoughts" and suggests a psychological component to

---

TERMS

privilege   An immunity, exemption, right, or advantage possessed by an individual, a group of individuals, or a class of persons, which is not possessed by others and which exists by operation of law or by virtue of a license, franchise, grant, or other permission; an exemption from a burden. ...

motive   The reason that leads the mind to desire a result; that which leads the mind to engage in a criminal act; that which causes the mind to form intent; the reason for an intention.

criminal conduct. In tort law, motive is synonymous with **intent**, which is broadly defined as the desire to attain a certain result. For purposes of the privilege defense, motive must be socially advantageous to a point that excuses intentional harm to another person or his or her property. The example of trespassing to save a drowning child's life sharply illustrates the clearly superior social objective that would give rise to the defense against the land owner's trespass-to-land lawsuit.

Less Injurious Alternatives

With privilege defenses, courts frequently ask whether the tortfeasor's objectives could have been reached through behavior that would have been less harmful to the victim. Suppose Karen discovers an automobile on fire next to a natural gas storage facility. Given the likelihood that the burning car will ignite the gas tanks, which would explode along with a sizeable portion of the surrounding neighborhood, Karen sprays the flaming vehicle with water, irreparably damaging the engine. The car owner would complain against Karen's conversion or trespass to chattel. Karen would defend by arguing privilege. The court would query: Could Karen have saved the storage facility (and surrounding area) through a less damaging act?

The answer to this question depends upon the extent of the fire. If only a small portion of the automobile were burning, such as something in the trunk, Karen could have isolated the danger by concentrating water only into the trunk compartment. If the interior were also ablaze, Karen would be forced to expose more car to the water to put out the fire. Still, she might have spared the engine compartment. However, if the inferno had engulfed the entire vehicle, she would have no choice other than to inundate it with water.

Similarity Between Privilege and Other Defenses

Several distinct intentional tort defenses, such as rightful repossession, self-defense, or defense of others or property, are simply particular types of privilege. Each has a social benefits component that justifies otherwise tortious misconduct. Necessity is another form of privilege

---

TERMS

intent   Purpose; the plan, course, or means a person conceives to achieve a certain result. Intent is an essential element of any crime except a strict liability crime or a regulatory offense, and some petty offenses and infractions. Intent is not, however, limited to conscious wrongdoing, and may be inferred or presumed.

that has also become a separate defense in its own right. The same is true of public officer's immunity for legal process enforcement, warrantless arrest, and reasonable discipline. These defenses to intentional torts are discussed in the remaining sections of this chapter.

The *Restatement (Second)* Position

Restatement (Second) of Torts § 890 focuses on privileges, noting that the term is broadly defined to include many of the specific defenses discussed throughout this chapter. The illustrations in the Comments are particularly helpful in understanding the scope of privilege.

Restatement (Second) of Torts § 890 & Comments
American Law Institute (1979)

§ 890. Privileges
One who otherwise would be liable for a tort is not liable if he acts in pursuance of and within the limits of a privilege of his own or of a privilege of another that was properly delegated to him.
Comment:
   a.   As stated in § 10, the word "privilege" is used throughout this Restatement to denote the fact that conduct that under ordinary circumstances would subject the actor to liability, under particular circumstances does not subject him to the liability.

* * *

   In some cases the law creates a privilege ... as when the owner of land is given a privilege to eject a trespasser upon his land or to enter the land of another to abate a private nuisance, or when a citizen is given the privilege of arresting a felon ... .
   c. Purpose of privilege—Conditional privileges created by rule of law. Most of the privileges that are not based on consent are conditioned upon their being performed for the purpose of protecting the interest for which the privilege was given. This is illustrated in cases in which force is used against another; in self-defense or in defense of a third person ... ; in the defense of the possession of land ... ; in the recapture of land or chattels ... ; in an arrest by a private person or a peace officer ... ; in the prevention of crime ... ; in the disciplining of children ... .
   d. Purpose of privilege—Absolute privileges. In certain cases in which the interests of the public are overwhelming, the purpose of the actor is immaterial. Thus for some or all statements, complete immunity from civil liability exists as to defamatory statements made during the course of judicial proceedings ... , as well as to statements by legislators and certain administrative officers while acting in the performance of their functions.

HYPOTHETICAL

Livingston owns a grocery in town. One of his customers notified him that several cans of Buddy Boy's Baked Beans were bulging, which is a symptom of contamination. Livingston opened these cans and discovered that the food had spoiled. He placed an advertisement in the local newspaper warning his customers to return any can of Buddy Boy's, whether bulging or not, because of spoilage. In fact, only four cans of the product were defective. Buddy Boy's manufacturer, E. I. Wilcott & Company, sued Livingston for disparagement of goods. Livingston claimed privilege, arguing that his motive was to protect the public from food poisoning. Would the defense carry the day?

Truth is an absolute defense in any type of defamation action, including commercial disparagement. In our hypothetical, however, the truth was exaggerated. Only a few cans were tainted. Nonetheless, there was no way of determining this without recalling as many cans as possible from Livingston's customers. A court would rule that Livingston was justified in advertising the warning to his customers, and so Livingston would not be liable to E. I. Wilcott & Company for disparagement of goods.

The elements of privilege are abstracted in Figure 8-6.

FIGURE 8-6
Elements of privilege

Actor's motives in committing intentional tort outweigh injury to victim or property
Actor was justified in engaging in intentional tort to accomplish socially desirable goals
No less damaging alternative action could have been taken
Exception: Absolute privilege of judges, legislators, etc. These actors' motives are immaterial.

§ 8.8 Necessity

Necessity is another variety of privilege that excuses otherwise tortious misconduct. Under this defense, the tortfeasor is justified in engaging in an intentional tort to prevent more serious injury from an external force. **Necessity** contains three elements: (1) Committing an intentional tort (2) to avert more serious injury (3) caused by a force other than the tortfeasor (4) and the tortfeasor's actions were reasonably necessary to avert the greater harm. This defense is based on the theory that the benefit—prevention of a greater harm—outweighs the risk of the intentional injury.

Thwarting a More Substantial Harm

In a necessity situation, the tortfeasor is usually faced with having to choose between the lesser of two evils. On the one hand, the tortfeasor must inflict injury upon a victim or the victim's property. On the other hand, the tortfeasor could do nothing and watch a greater havoc occur. For example, suppose Antonio is aboard a ship that suddenly begins to sink. There are several passengers aboard, including Antonio, as well as valuable cargo. If the cargo were thrown overboard, the boat could stay afloat long enough for help to arrive. So Antonio elects to jettison the cargo and save the passengers' lives. The cargo owner could sue Antonio for trespass to chattel, but the defense of necessity would insulate Antonio from liability. Although Antonio committed an intentional tort, he sought only to prevent greater harm caused by a force beyond his control (namely, the ship's sinking).

External Forces

For necessity to operate as a defense to an intentional tort, the more significant danger being averted must originate from a source other than the tortfeasor. For instance, in the previous illustration, the boat began to sink through no fault of Antonio's. However, suppose he had caused an explosion in the engine room by improper fuel mixing, and thus blew a hole in the hull of the craft. Because Antonio created the greater hazard, he could not claim necessity in discarding the cargo

TERMS

necessity 1. That which is necessary; that which must be done. 2. That which is compelled by natural forces and cannot be resisted. Necessity is a defense in a criminal prosecution if the defendant committed the crime to prevent a more serious harm from occurring.

overboard. Had it not been for his misconduct in the engine room, the extreme peril would never have happened. The necessity defense cannot protect a tortfeasor who creates the catastrophic condition and then must engage in an intentional tort to resolve the crisis.

Reasonably Necessary Action

As is generally true with privilege, necessity requires that the tortfeasor's conduct be reasonably necessary to prevent the more substantial danger. Thus, the tortfeasor must use only that degree of force required to avert the greater risk. Using the sinking ship example, suppose that the leak in the ship's hull occurred not because of Antonio's misbehavior but because of faulty sealing techniques. If Antonio could plug the leak rather than abandon ship, it would not be necessary for him to jettison the cargo to save the passengers.

Fires further illustrate this aspect of reasonably required action; many necessity cases involve burning buildings. Several nineteenth-century court opinions discussed "row" structures, which were many discrete buildings attached in long rows down a street. If one were to catch fire, it was likely that the entire block would burn to the ground. To avoid this calamity, the flaming building was often destroyed. There simply was no less damaging alternative when the building was fully ablaze. If the building owner sued for trespass to land, the courts routinely applied the necessity defense to protect the tortfeasor from liability to the building owner.

The *Restatement (Second)* Position

The *Restatement (Second)* addresses necessity as a defense in emergency situations in which the tortfeasor is compelled to immediate action by a crisis. In such cases, the defense operates to protect the defendant from liability. Note how the *Restatement*'s elements are distinguishable from those previously discussed in the text.

Restatement (Second) of Torts §§ 890, 892D & Comments
American Law Institute (1979)

[§ 890, Comment a.] [The emergency defense exists] when the protection of the public is of overriding importance, as when one is privileged to destroy buildings to avert a public disaster. ...

§ 892D. Emergency Action Without Consent
Conduct that injures another does not make the actor liable to the other, even though the other has not consented to it if
   (a) an emergency makes it necessary or apparently necessary, in order to prevent harm to the other, to act before there is opportunity

to obtain consent from the other or one empowered to consent for him, and

(b) the actor has no reason to believe that the other, if he had the opportunity to consent, would decline.

Comment:

a. The rule stated in this Section covers a group of exceptional situations in which the actor is privileged to proceed without the consent of another and without any manifested or apparent consent, on the assumption that if the other had the opportunity to decide he would certainly consent. This privilege must necessarily be a limited one and can arise only in situations of emergency, when there is no time to consult the other or one empowered to consent for him, or for reasons such as the unconsciousness of the other his consent cannot be obtained. The mere possibility that the other might consent if he were able to do so is not enough; and the conduct must be so clearly and manifestly to the other's advantage that there is no reason to believe that the consent would not be given. If the actor knows or has reason to know, because of past refusals or other circumstances, that the consent would not be given, he is not privileged to act. ...

Copyright 1979 by The American Law Institute. Reprinted with the permission of The American Law Institute.

Necessity can be a puzzling defense. Its elements compel courts to balance competing interests, employing somewhat more value judgment than usual. This hypothetical illustrates.

HYPOTHETICAL

Kenneth owns an exotic pet store, in which he sells, among other wild animals, several species of snake. One day a customer accidentally knocked a cage containing a python onto the floor, causing the door to spring open. The snake slithered out into the aisles searching for food. An infant was strapped in an automobile safety seat which her mother used as a carrier while shopping. The youngster's mother was several feet away looking at some unusual fish. The snake approached the infant and clearly intended to consume the child. Quickly, another patron, Jeffrey, impaled the python with a hunting knife (which was on display on a nearby shelf). Kenneth sued Jeffrey for trespass to chattel. Could necessity excuse Jeffrey's actions?

Reasonably necessary action is the critical element in this hypothetical. Did Jeffrey have to kill the snake to prevent it from attacking the baby? Could Jeffrey have taken other action to protect the child? Jeffrey could have grabbed the infant seat and carried the child to safety. Then Jeffrey could have summoned Kenneth or another store employee to capture the python. Accordingly, necessity would not be a successful defense, and Jeffrey would be liable to Kenneth for trespass to chattel.

A short review of the elements of necessity is provided in Figure 8-7.

FIGURE 8-7
Elements of
necessity

Committing intentional tort
Purpose to avert more harmful injury
Harm threatened by force other than tortfeasor
Tortfeasor's actions were reasonably necessary to prevent danger of greater harm

§ 8.9 Public Officer's Immunity for Legal Process Enforcement

Public officials often engage in activity that normally would be considered intentionally tortious. However, because such persons are authorized by law to engage in such conduct, they are protected from liability. Several types of governmental action fall within this protected class. The most common include: (1) process serving; (2) execution sales; (3) attachment or replevin; (4) arrest by warrant; (5) prosecutors acting in official capacity; and (6) judges acting in official capacity.

Service of Process

Process serving is the method by which a defendant in a lawsuit is notified that a plaintiff has filed suit against the defendant. Service of process is the means used to notify the defendant. Most commonly, the court clerk either mails a copy of the summons and the plaintiff's complaint to the defendant (usually by certified or registered mail), or the sheriff delivers the summons and complaint directly to the defendant, or a private process server does so. It is the latter cases of actual physical

---

TERMS

process ... In a technical sense, the means of compelling a defendant to appear in court in a civil case. ...

process serving[†] The method by which a defendant in a lawsuit is notified that a plaintiff has filed suit against the defendant. Also called *service of process.* Governmental officials engaged in process serving are generally immune from intentional tort liability.

service of process (process serving) Delivery of a summons, writ, complaint, or other process to the opposite party, or other person entitled to receive it, in such manner as the law prescribes, whether by leaving a copy at his or her residence, by mailing a copy to [the opposite party] or his or her attorney, or by publication.

delivery that give rise to litigation. The defendant might sue the sheriff for trespass to land when the sheriff arrived on the defendant's real estate to deliver the summons. However, the sheriff has the power, either by statute or common law, to enter another person's land to serve process. The land owner's lawsuit against the sheriff would fail as a result of this defense.

Execution Sales

When a plaintiff wins judgment against the defendant in a civil action, the defendant usually has a certain period of time, often thirty days, within which to pay the judgment. If the defendant fails to pay, the plaintiff may return to court and file a *writ of execution* requesting the court to order the defendant's property sold to satisfy the judgment. These forced sales are often referred to as **execution sales** or **sheriff's sales**, because the sheriff is frequently the public official responsible for seizing and selling the defendant's property. The defendant might sue the sheriff for trespass to land, trespass to chattel, and conversion after the sheriff comes and gets the defendant's property. However, once again the sheriff is legally protected. Statutes and common law empower law enforcement officials to seize and sell property to satisfy judgments. Therefore, the sheriff would be immune from liability.

Attachment or Replevin

Attachment is a court-ordered remedy in a lawsuit. When a plaintiff is entitled to a remedy against the defendant in a lawsuit, and the defendant is likely to dispose of his or her property to avoid losing it in a subsequent execution action, the plaintiff may ask the court to attach the property on the plaintiff's behalf. The court then orders a law enforcement officer, such as the sheriff, to seize the defendant's property subject to attachment. The defendant might think to sue the sheriff for

---

╾──────────────────╼ **TERMS** ╾──────────────────╼

execution sale A public sale by a sheriff or similar officer of property seized under a writ of execution following a levy of execution.

sheriff's sale A sale of real estate carried out by the sheriff under a foreclosure decree or similar court order. A sheriff's sale is also referred to as an *execution sale, foreclosure sale,* or *judicial sale.*

attachment The process by which a person's property is figuratively brought into court to ensure satisfaction of a judgment that may be rendered against him or her. In the event judgment is rendered, the property may be sold to satisfy the judgment.

conversion or trespass to chattel, but the defendant should think again. The sheriff is authorized by statute or common law to take the defendant's property into custody under attachment, and the defendant's cause of action against the sheriff would fail.

Replevin is another court-ordered remedy. A plaintiff sues a defendant who wrongfully possesses the plaintiff's chattel and refuses to return it. The plaintiff asks the court for replevin, which means that the court would order the defendant to return the personal property to the plaintiff. If the defendant still refuses to comply, the court could instruct the sheriff to seize the chattel. The defendant's lawsuit for conversion or trespass to chattel against the sheriff would again be defeated by the law enforcer's defense of legal authority to act.

Arrest by Warrant

Police officers often arrest suspected criminals under the authority of a court-issued warrant for arrest. Suppose the suspect were innocent of any crimes. Could the suspect sue the police department for false imprisonment, assault, battery, and infliction of emotional distress, for having been arrested? If the law enforcement personnel were acting pursuant to an arrest warrant properly ordered by a judge, and if they acted in good faith to apprehend the suspect named in the warrant, then they would not be liable for any intentional torts as a consequence of taking the suspect into custody.

Prosecutors and Judges

Prosecutors and **judges** acting in the scope of their positions are privileged and immune from liability for their actions. If this were not so, no one would accept such a position. It is inherent in these positions to occasionally intentionally injure someone mentally, emotionally, and by reputation. Prosecutors are charged with the responsibility of proving bad things about bad people. Liability for their mistakes

═══════════ **TERMS** ═══════════

replevin   1. An action by which the owner of personal property taken or detained by another may recover possession of it. 2. The name of the writ issued by a court in an action of replevin authorizing the sheriff to seize the property that is the subject of the action pending the outcome of the litigation.

prosecutor   A public official, elected or appointed, who conducts criminal prosecutions on behalf of his or her jurisdiction.

judge   A public officer who conducts or presides over a court of justice.

would have a chilling effect on their performance; that is, they would be too afraid of making a mistake and thus err against social benefit. Judges must make decisions that intentionally injure persons and property. Again, without privilege and/or immunity, there would be a chilling effect that would render judges afraid to make a decision for fear of being wrong. Therefore, public policy has always been to allow these persons immunity from liability in the honest performance of their positions and the privilege to act accordingly.

As a practical matter, the public officer immunity defense is not commonly litigated. The power of its protection precludes intentional tort recovery in most cases.

Nevertheless, there are exceptions to the privilege and immunity doctrines. 42 U.S.C. § 1983 permits liability of public officers (usually other than prosecutors and judges) if the performance of their duties involves activities that deprive persons of their civil rights. Such an

---

The Case of the Defiant Trucker (Part II)

In *Jurco v. State*, partially reprinted in § 8.3, the Alaska Court of Appeals addressed conflicting defenses: namely, defense of property versus law enforcement officers' immunity for legal process enforcement. Reread the case as it applies to this latter defense and as a refresher for the facts. The court also discussed warrantless arrests, which are discussed in a further analysis of this case in § 8.10.

JURCO v. STATE
Court of Appeals of Alaska
825 P.2d 909 (Alaska Ct. App. 1992)
February 14, 1992
Mannheimer, Judge

At common law, a public officer was authorized to use reasonable force against other persons when executing a court order requiring or authorizing the officer to seize another person's property. This common-law rule has been codified in Alaska; [Alaska Statutes §] 11.81.420 provides:

Justification: Performance of public duty.
(a) Unless inconsistent with AS 11.81.320–11.81.410, conduct which would otherwise constitute an offense is justified when it is required or authorized by law or by a judicial decree, judgment, or order.

(b) The justification afforded by this section also applies when ... the person reasonably believes the conduct to be required or authorized by a decree, judgment, or order of a court of competent jurisdiction or in the lawful execution of legal process, notwithstanding lack of jurisdiction of the court or defect in the legal process[.]

Under this statute, law enforcement officers are empowered to use force to execute court decrees, even if it is later shown that the court had no authority to issue the decree. Thus, in Jurco's case, the State Troopers were authorized to use all reasonable force to execute the Alaska District Court's order to seize Jurco's vehicle, even if Jurco was correct in claiming that the pendency of his bankruptcy petition deprived the state district court of the judicial authority to issue orders affecting his property.

action is called a civil rights action or a "1983" action (*1983* is the section number of the law permitting this action, not the year it was passed). If a police officer arrests someone without a warrant and without probable cause, it is a violation of civil rights and the officer may be liable. If excessive force is used in an arrest, it is a violation of civil rights and the officer may be liable. If any action under color or authority of the government—whether local, state, or federal—violates civil rights, the actor(s) may be liable regardless of immunity.

HYPOTHETICAL

Dawn sued Debra. The sheriff delivered a copy of the summons and Dawn's complaint to Debra's house. Debra did not appear at trial, and Dawn won a default judgment against Debra. After thirty days, Debra had failed to pay the judgment. Dawn filed a writ of execution with the court, which ordered the sheriff to seize Debra's property. The sheriff again returned to Debra's house to garner the chattels that could be sold at an execution sale. The proceeds from the sale went to satisfy Dawn's judgment. Debra sued the sheriff for trespass to land, trespass to chattel, and conversion. The sheriff applied the defense of legal process enforcement.

This hypothetical is probably the easiest to answer of any in the text. The sheriff was acting under court order to enforce legal processes, and so the defense would succeed. Debra's lawsuit would be promptly dismissed.

The elements of the legal process enforcement defense are listed in Figure 8-8.

§ 8.10 Warrantless Arrest by Law Enforcement Officials or Citizens

Police officers, and sometimes even ordinary citizens, engage in *warrantless arrests*. Could they be liable for false imprisonment, battery, assault, trespass to land, and infliction of emotional distress?

Statutes and common law authorize law enforcement personnel to arrest criminal suspects, even without court-issued warrants, under certain circumstances. For example, when a police officer witnesses a felony, he or she may arrest the suspect immediately. This proper enforcement of a legal process would be a defense against the suspect's intentional torts lawsuit.

Private citizens, too, may take suspected criminals into custody under the theory of *citizen's arrest*. Under the common law, a private citizen may take a suspect into custody if the citizen has witnessed the suspect commit a felony or breach of the peace. This would include situations in which the citizen reasonably thinks that the suspect has committed a felony. Historically, this defense was often used to protect store owners who detained suspected shoplifters from liability for false imprisonment actions.

Normally, modern warrantless arrest does not involve private citizen participation to the extent the pre-twentieth-century cases did. However, private police, such as company security, are often involved in today's cases.

HYPOTHETICAL

Carter is a night watchman at a local factory. He noticed someone suspicious lurking in the shadows near a restricted access building containing company records and other valuables. He turned his flashlight on the suspect, whom he did not recognize. He demanded identification and the reason the stranger was present on factory grounds. The stranger said nothing and attempted to flee. Carter tackled the individual, forcibly returned him to the security office, and telephoned the police. The stranger turned out to be an employee of a competitor to Carter's employer. The stranger sued Carter for battery, false imprisonment, and infliction of emotional distress. Would Carter be entitled to a defense under citizen's arrest theory?

Carter witnessed a simple trespass to land, which is not a felony under either statutory or common law. The stranger had merely trespassed onto the factory's property. Further, the stranger had not breached the peace. However, Carter reasonably believed that the suspect was about to engage in a felony (namely, burglary or theft). In his experience as a security guard, Carter had seen many felons behave just as the stranger had acted. Thus, Carter's reasonable belief that the suspect was about to commit a felony was sufficient to justify his behavior. Carter would not be liable to the stranger for any of the intentional torts.

The warrantless arrest defense, together with the defense of legal process enforcement, are both summarized in Figure 8-8.

§ 8.11 Reasonable Discipline

We are all familiar with the concept of discipline. Anyone who has either had or been a parent understands the exercise of authority to maintain order within the household. Students for centuries have exchanged horror stories about strict disciplinarian teachers. Such authority figures have used discipline in both the home and schools, which usually involves inflicting several intentional torts, including assault,

Legal Process Enforcement	Warrantless Arrest
Process serving	Law enforcement officers' power to arrest pursuant to court-ordered arrest warrant
Execution sales	Citizen's arrest (felonies or breaches of peace)
Attachment or replevin	
Arrest by warrant	

FIGURE 8-8 Types of legal process enforcement defenses and elements of warrantless arrest defenses

battery, false imprisonment, and infliction of emotional distress. The defense of reasonable discipline, however, protects the disciplinarian from tort liability. There are three elements of **reasonable discipline**: (1) Use of reasonable force (2) by a parent, guardian, or authorized individual against a child (3) to maintain order or punish unacceptable misconduct.

Reasonable Force

The force a parent or guardian applies against a child must be reasonable under the circumstances. Naturally, reasonableness depends upon the exact facts of each case, but a general principle may be gleaned from the court decisions. For purposes of this defense, *reasonable force* may be defined as that degree of force required to restore decorum or punish misconduct. Force that goes beyond this is deemed excessive.

For example, suppose children are fighting in their home. Their mother or father would have the privilege of applying corporal punishment to stop the conflict, so long as the force was reasonable. The father might physically separate the combatants and spank them. However, if the father hit the children over their heads with a wooden board, this would be excessive force, because order could be restored without such extreme actions.

════════════════ **TERMS** ════════════════

reasonable discipline † An intentional tort defense. Its elements include the use of reasonable force by a parent, guardian, or authorized individual against a child to maintain order or punish unacceptable misconduct.

The Case of the Defiant Trucker (Part III)

Jurco v. State, discussed earlier in §§ 8.3 and 8.6, also involved warrantless arrest. As it had done with Jurco's previous issues on appeal, the Alaska Court of Appeals, with "arresting" analysis, ruled against the appellant. Although the court's discussion did not involve tort liability as a result of a warrantless arrest, it is clear that there could be no such liability, because the arrest was lawful.

JURCO v. STATE
Court of Appeals of Alaska
825 P.2d 909 (Alaska Ct. App. 1992)
February 14, 1992
Mannheimer, Judge

Jurco also argues that his arrest was illegal because the troopers did not have an arrest warrant. Jurco acknowledges that [Alaska Stat. §] 12.25.030 authorizes police officers to arrest without a warrant when a misdemeanor is committed in their presence ... .

Finally, even if some additional justification were needed for the troopers' decision to make an arrest instead of issue a citation, that justification was present. It was clear that Jurco was intent on thwarting the troopers' performance of their duty under the court order directing seizure of Jurco's truck; the troopers could reasonably conclude that Jurco would continue to impede their efforts unless he were physically taken into custody.

Parent, Guardian, or Authorized Individual

When a child attends school, the law implies that the teacher assumes the role of parent or guardian while the child is present at the institution. The teacher is referred to as *in loco parentis*, which translates from Latin as "in place of the parent." This means that the teacher (or school principal) basically enjoys the same right to use reasonable force for discipline as do a child's parents. In recent times, however, courts have become antagonistic to this defense when applied to nonparents or guardians.

In the nineteenth and early twentieth centuries, severe corporal punishment was routine in both public and private schools. The old adage, "spare the rod and spoil the child," was taken rather literally by many firm disciplinarians. Many a student has cringed outside a principal's office awaiting the dreaded paddling or ruler across the knuckles.

In modern education, corporal punishment has been severely discouraged as a disciplinary technique. Teachers and principals today are

TERMS

in loco parentis [Latin for] "in the place of parents." Describes a person who, in the absence of a child's parent or guardian, and without formal legal approval, temporarily assumes a parent's obligations with respect to the child.

The Case of the Brush with Authority

In *Authority Song,* Hoosier rock musician John Cougar Mellencamp sang, "I fight authority, authority always wins." Perhaps he was recalling his days in the secondary schools near Seymour, Indiana. Many middle and high school students have felt the full force of the *in loco parentis* doctrine from a teacher or principal. Sometimes the discipline seemed arbitrary, capricious, and excessive. In the case excerpted here, the Michigan Court of Appeals sided with authority against the student.

WILLOUGHBY v. LEHRBASS
Court of Appeals of Michigan
150 Mich. App. 319,
388 N.W.2d 688 (1986)
April 7, 1986
Allen, Judge

On January 23, 1981, plaintiff Frank Dain Willoughby ... was a student in defendant Roger Lehrbass's fifth hour advertising class at Freesoil Community School. On that date, before Lehrbass's class began, the principal asked plaintiff to assist in replacing some doors which had been removed from their hinges. After completing this task, Willoughby walked into the advertising class a few minutes late. According to Lehrbass, another student was giving an oral presentation for the final examination. Willoughby, nevertheless, walked by Lehrbass's desk and with a sweeping motion of his hand started to brush into the wastebasket a number of folded-up pieces of paper sitting on Lehrbass's desk. Lehrbass was using the slips of paper to select the order in which the students would give their oral preparations.

As Willoughby swept his hand across the desk, Lehrbass grabbed his arm and instructed him not to touch the papers. Willoughby then intentionally or accidentally kicked the wastebasket over, and, according to Lehrbass, mumbled something which sounded disrespectful.

Willoughby then walked to a seat in the front row around where he usually sat. Although the students did not have assigned seats, they normally sat in the same area each day. Willoughby testified that he tried one seat in the front row but found it broken or too low. He then headed for some empty seats in the back. When he was halfway there, Lehrbass came up from behind, grabbed his left arm and twisted it behind his back in a "half nelson." Lehrbass said, "Come on, Frank, let's go." Lehrbass began marching Willoughby to the principal's office.

Lehrbass pushed Willoughby out of the classroom and up the steps. Willoughby said, "Let go, you're hurting me." On the landing, Willoughby squirmed loose and said he could find the office himself. However, according to Lehrbass, Willoughby started toward the steps going down—away from the office. (Willoughby's version was that he turned around to go *up* the steps.) In any event, Lehrbass then grabbed Willoughby in a "full nelson," with his arms underneath Willoughby's armpits and his palms on the back of Willoughby's neck. Willoughby testified that he heard cracking up and down his back and felt pain and soreness as Lehrbass pushed against his neck and back.

* * *

Willoughby testified that he consulted a chiropractor that evening because of continuing soreness in his back, neck, and shoulders. He treated with the chiropractor for some time. Subsequently, he saw an orthopedic surgeon who diagnosed his condition as myofascitis, an inflammation of the back muscles or tissues.

Plaintiffs' complaint, filed July 23, 1981, charged defendants with false imprisonment ... and gross abuse and use of unreasonable force on Willoughby. These latter allegations were apparently based on [Mich. Comp. Laws] § 380.1312, which provides in pertinent part:

"(2) A teacher or superintendent may use reasonable physical force on the person of a pupil necessary for the purpose of maintaining proper discipline over pupils in attendance at school.

"(3) A teacher or superintendent shall not be liable in a civil action for the use of physical force on the person of a pupil for the purposes prescribed in this section, except in case of gross abuse and disregard for the health and safety of the pupil."

... The case proceeded to trial on the intentional tort count, and the jury returned a verdict of no cause of action in favor of defendants.

* * *

On a special verdict form the jury specifically found that Lehrbass had not used anything other than reasonable force in disciplining plaintiff Willoughby. ... [T]he common law rule allowing a teacher to use reasonable force against a student [was codified by Michigan statutes]. ...

Plaintiffs next claim error in the jury instructions on battery and the School Code provision concerning corporal punishment. ...

Here, the trial court read the statute to the jury, clearly informing them that (1) a teacher could use reasonable physical force on a pupil *necessary for the purpose of maintaining proper discipline,* and (2) the teacher would not be liable for using physical force on a pupil *for the purpose prescribed in the statute, i.e.,* maintaining proper discipline. (Emphasis added.) The trial court could hardly define the law better than by reading the statute exactly as written. ...

The judge found that under [Mich. Comp. Laws] § 380.1312, a teacher has the right to willfully and intentionally touch a pupil under certain circumstances. ...

We find no reversible error.

* * *

Although there are no published Michigan opinions dealing with corporal punishment of a student, decisions in other jurisdictions are legion. The general rule is that a teacher is immune from liability for reasonable physical force or punishment used on a pupil to maintain discipline. Factors to consider in assessing the reasonableness of the punishment are the nature of the punishment, the child's age and physical condition, and the teacher's motive in inflicting the punishment.

Courts have held the above principles applicable in actions for assault and battery, where a state statute permits a teacher to use reasonable physical force to maintain order in the classroom. Where punishment is excessive or improper, the teacher may be guilty of assault and battery.

We think that in Michigan, as well, the Legislature intended that a teacher might be guilty of assault and battery when his or her conduct exceeds the parameters of the statute. The statute was ... intended to carve a limited exception into the common-law doctrine in order to provide educators with the necessary means of maintaining discipline in the classroom. Here the trial judge adequately instructed the jury on the tort of battery ... and on the applicable statutory provisions.

... The testimony is clear and convincing that young Willoughby was creating a classroom disturbance and that defendant Lehrbass felt that it was necessary to take Willoughby to the school office to restore order. While there is conflicting testimony as to just how much force was necessary to apply to Willoughby on the stairway leading to the office, even Willoughby's own witness ... testified that Willoughby was arguing with defendant Lehrbass and struggling to get away all the way up the stairs. Based on our review of the record, we find little evidence that defendant Lehrbass's use of force was unprovoked and unreasonable. Indeed, the weight of the evidence establishes the contrary.

* * *

Having found no error mandating reversal, the judgment of the trial court is affirmed. No costs.

Case Questions

1. Do you agree with the court that the teacher's use of force was reasonable? Why or why not?
2. Would the outcome of the case have been any different if the plaintiff had suffered permanent physical impairment as a result of the defendant's actions? Explain.
3. When Lehrbass first grabbed Willoughby in the classroom and pushed him through the halls to the stairway, could Willoughby have justified his struggling as a legitimate exercise of self-defense? Would this have made Lehrbass's continued use of force unreasonable? Explain.

commonly equipped with psychological and sociological training, and thus school discipline has taken a less physical approach. Occasionally, litigation arises after a child is struck by a teacher as punishment. Educators must be much more careful than in days past when inflicting corporal penalties, because courts are increasingly less tolerant of the discipline defense for nonparents or guardians.

Maintaining Order or Punishing Misbehavior

The disciplinarian must be using reasonable force against a child to maintain decorum (such as in a school classroom) or penalize rowdy conduct (such as punishing a child who has angrily and intentionally broken a window). However, these motives do not give the disciplinarian a free hand to inflict punishment beyond that which is reasonable. Courts and legislatures are becoming increasingly aware of the significant problem of child abuse, much of which involves parental misconduct that once was judicially protected under the reasonable discipline defense. As social problems become more public and prominent, courts and legislatures become more sensitive to these issues and the search for solutions. As a result, recent court decisions have upheld a child's right to sue parents in tort for using exorbitant force as punishment.

The reasonable discipline defense frequently appears in intentional tort cases involving schools or day care facilities. This is logical, as children spend a significant portion of their lives in educational environments.

HYPOTHETICAL

Carol is a thirteen-year-old student at the Peddleton Middle School. Her history teacher, Mr. Whitewaul, has a reputation as a strict disciplinarian. Eating or drinking anything during his class was absolutely forbidden. Carol suffered from a low-blood-sugar condition and needed to eat a series of special high-energy foods every two hours. One day, Whitewaul discovered Carol eating what looked like a candy bar. He grabbed the food violently out of Carol's hand and threw it in the general direction of the wastebasket. Then, screaming at the top of his voice about six inches from Carol's face, Whitewaul chastised Carol for eating in class. Carol felt humiliated in front of her fellow students and was considerably upset by Whitewaul's yelling. Whitewaul insisted that Carol stand in the corner at the back of the room for the remainder of the period, much to her chagrin. Because of the stress and embarrassment, Carol's blood sugar plummeted, causing her to pass out and fall to the floor. Carol's parents sued Whitewaul for intentional infliction of emotional distress, battery, assault, and false imprisonment. Whitewaul insisted that he was exercising reasonable discipline.

Does Carol, through her parents, have causes of action for each of the intentional torts mentioned? If so, then the discipline defense becomes relevant. As a teacher, Whitewaul stands *in loco parentis* with regard to Carol. Using the formula previously discussed, were Whitewaul's actions reasonably necessary to maintain order or punish misconduct? The force that Whitewaul exerted to wrench the food out of Carol's hand was excessive. He simply could have demanded that she hand him the food, which would have been more reasonable. Whitewaul's thunderous shouting directly into Carol's face was also excessive force. He could have chastised her in a normal tone of voice and accomplished the same objective—namely, alerting Carol and the class that his rule against eating would be strictly enforced. Compelling Carol to stand in the corner (a false imprisonment claim) is also extreme, as Whitewaul had already taken steps to assure that his rule against eating would be in the forefront of each student's mind. Whitewaul's defense of reasonable discipline would fail, and Carol's parents would recover for all of the intentional torts pleaded.

The defense of reasonable discipline is outlined in Figure 8-9.

| Use of reasonable force |
| Force by parents, guardians, or authorized individuals (e.g., educators) |
| Force used to discipline children or maintain order in groups of children |

FIGURE 8-9
Elements of reasonable discipline

§ 8.12 Statutes of Limitations

Statutes of limitations are statutes restricting the time within which a plaintiff may file his or her lawsuit for particular causes of action against a defendant. All states have statutes of limitations for almost all tort actions, including intentional torts. (Sometimes they are called *limitation of actions*.) The most common tort statutes of limitations are two years. This means that the plaintiff has two years from the date that an intentional tort occurred to file his or her lawsuit against the defendant. If the plaintiff fails to file within this statutory time period, then his or her cause of action against the defendant is barred forever.

Although two years is a common statute of limitations period for many torts, the exact time period varies among states and different types of torts. One should always research the specific statute of limitations for each cause of action, whether in tort or in other areas of law. This is a vital piece of information for both the plaintiff and the defendant. If the statute of limitations has expired, the defendant may respond with this defense and have the plaintiff's case dismissed or otherwise disposed of (usually by summary judgment). The plaintiff's attorney must be aware of the statute of limitations and file the lawsuit in a timely manner, or risk a malpractice suit.

Worker's Compensation

Another defense to an intentional tort action might be that the action is prevented by a state's worker's compensation statute. These statutes cover workers who are injured or killed as a result of incidents occurring during the course and scope of their employment. Worker's compensation statutes bar tort actions against the employer and are considered a worker's sole remedy for on-the-job injuries and death, regardless of fault.

Summary

Self-defense is the exercise of reasonable force to repel an attack upon one's person or to avoid confinement. Self-defense counters an offensive force that threatens bodily injury, repugnant contact, or sequestration. The amount of force a person may use in self-defense is limited to that amount necessary to repel the attacking force. Any greater resistance is excessive and the defense would be ineffective. The defense is used against allegations of assault, battery, or false imprisonment.

Defense of persons or property is another legal justification for assault or battery. Defense of persons involves the use of reasonable force to defend or protect a third party from injury when the third person is threatened by an attacking force. Here, reasonable force is defined identically as for self-defense. Defense of property allows reasonable force to protect property from damage or dispossession when an invader attempts to injure or wrongfully take custody of the property. Reasonable force to protect property is usually defined as less force than would ordinarily be allowed to protect persons. Courts generally do not permit deadly force to be used to protect property, although one may apply deadly force in defense of one's home against intruders, under the castle rule.

Rightful repossession empowers a chattel owner to enter upon another's real estate to legally repossess personal property that has been wrongfully taken or withheld. The chattel owner would not be liable for trespass to land, trespass to chattel, or conversion, because he or she was justified in retaking control of the property. The defense also may protect against claims of assault or battery. Reasonable force may be used to repossess the chattel. Reasonable force is defined along the same lines as for defense of property. The efforts to regain possession must occur promptly after the property is first taken from the owner, or from the time the possessor wrongfully refuses to return the property to the owner. For the defense to succeed, the chattel owner must have been wrongfully dispossessed, or return of the property must have been improperly refused.

Consent may be a defense to all intentional torts. Consent occurs when a victim of an intentional tort voluntarily agrees to endure the tortious actions. Voluntary agreement involves the victim understanding the consequences of the tortfeasor's conduct. This is called informed consent. Consent may be expressed or implied based upon the behavior of the parties.

As a defense to intentional torts, mistake is a good faith belief, based upon incorrect information, that a person is justified in committing an intentional tort under the circumstances. This belief must be reasonable, and reasonableness is determined on a case-by-case basis. This belief must be based on erroneous details which, if they had been true, would have excused the intentional torts committed.

Privilege is sometimes considered a broad category embracing all the other defenses discussed in this chapter. To use the defense, one must ask if the actor's motives for engaging in the intentional tort outweigh the injury to the victim or property. Further, one must ask if the actor was justified in committing the intentional tort to achieve socially desirable goals (which outweigh the injury factor). Could these goals have been accomplished without inflicting the harm to the victim?

The necessity defense allows a tortfeasor to commit an intentional tort to prevent more serious injury from an external force. The tortfeasor's actions must be reasonably necessary to avert the more substantial danger. Necessity is basically a choice between the lesser of two evils. The tortfeasor cannot cause the greater threat of harm if the necessity defense is to insulate him or her from liability.

Public officials are immune from intentional tort liability for the proper enforcement of legal processes, such as service of process, execution sales, attachment, replevin, or arrest by warrant. Both statutes and common law protect governmental employees involved in these activities, as legal process enforcement is necessary to implement the judicial system. Normally, law enforcement officers, such as sheriffs, participate in these processes.

Law enforcement officials are authorized by statutes and common law to make warrantless arrests, usually when a felony is committed or suspected in their presence. Under the defense of citizen's arrest, private persons may restrain suspected felons without liability for assault, battery, false imprisonment, infliction of emotional distress, trespass to land, or other intentional torts.

Parents are permitted to use reasonable force to punish or correct their children. Persons standing in place of parents, such as educators, are said to be *in loco parentis* and may also employ reasonable force to penalize students or maintain order. Modern cases and statutes have become more sensitive to child abuse problems, and so this defense has been substantially narrowed in recent years.

Most state statutes of limitations restrict the time period within which a plaintiff may file his or her intentional tort causes of action against a defendant. In most states, these are two-year statutes, meaning that a plaintiff has two years from the date that the intentional tort was committed within which to file his or her lawsuit against the tortfeasor. It is vital to research specific statutes of limitations for each particular tort.

State worker's compensation statutes bar tort actions against workers' employers regardless of fault.

Review Questions

1. What are defenses? How are they applied against intentional torts? In what type of situation would a defense most likely be raised?

2. Explain self-defense. Against which intentional torts might this defense be used? What is reasonable force? How is it defined? How is it similar to necessary force?

3. Discuss defense of persons or property. How is it similar to self-defense? Different? How is defense of persons different from defense of property? Similar? How is reasonable force defined for this defense?

4. What is rightful repossession? What type of property is involved? Against which intentional torts might this defense be applied? How is reasonable force defined? What is the role of wrongful dispossession or denial of

possession? Must the property owner's efforts to repossess be taken within a certain time frame? What is this called?

5. Describe consent. Is the defense widely applicable to the intentional torts? What is informed consent? Implied consent?

6. Explain mistake. What is the role of the good faith conviction? Why must the information believed be inaccurate? How broad is the defense?

7. Does privilege include all defenses to intentional torts? Why? Against which intentional torts would the defense be utilized? What are its characteristics? What is the role of motive? Of socially acceptable goals? Of less injurious alternatives?

8. What are the elements of necessity? How is it used as an intentional tort defense? What is the significance of external forces? Why must the action be reasonably necessary?

9. Discuss the various types of public official immunity for legal process enforcement. What intentional torts might apply to these cases? How does the defense operate in each such instance?

10. What is warrantless arrest? Citizen's arrest? How are these protected from intentional tort liability?

11. Who may use reasonable discipline? Against whom may it be employed? What are the elements of the defense? What is the modern status of the defense in courts and legislatures?

12. What are statutes of limitations? What is the time period most commonly used for tort causes of action? How can statutes of limitations be used as a defense to intentional torts?

Projects

1. Does the common law of your state recognize all the defenses discussed in this chapter? Is any of the terminology different? Are any defenses defined under statutes?

2. Read the case of *Jordan v. Town of Pratt* in Appendix C. What immunity defense was raised? Was it successful? Explain.

||||

CHAPTER 9

STRICT, OR ABSOLUTE, LIABILITY

§ 9.1 Introduction

Intentional torts and negligence account for the bulk of torts. However, there remain several important torts to study. The remainder primarily consists of strict, or absolute, liability. Products liability is one form of strict liability. The terms *strict liability* and *absolute liability* are interchangeable. Strict liability differs from intentional torts and negligence in that fault is unnecessary to establish liability. From the defendant's standpoint, absolute liability can be serious trouble indeed.

This chapter discusses the following:

- Absolute liability for abnormally dangerous activities

- Wild animal owner absolute liability

- Distinctions between wild and domestic animals

- Toxic tort strict liability

- Proximate cause in strict liability cases.

§ 9.2 Strict Liability Generally

Under intentional torts and negligence, tortfeasors are held accountable for their wrongful actions. Fault is an essential part of the reasoning. What was the defendant's misconduct that hurt the plaintiff? Was it intentional, willful, and wanton, or was it negligent action? Placing the blame is second nature in negligence or intentional torts analysis.

Fault Is Irrelevant

Absolute or **strict liability** holds the tortfeasor responsible for his or her behavior regardless of fault. In other words, the tortfeasor could have used every possible degree of care to protect against injuring the victim, but this would not prevent liability. Fault is irrelevant to absolute liability. The tortfeasor would be strictly liable just because he or she did something specific that hurt the plaintiff.

Limitations to Absolute Liability

One's sense of fair play may rebel against strict liability. One might think that it is unfair to hold a defendant accountable even if he or she did not intentionally or negligently misbehave. This fault concept extends throughout every area of law. This is why absolute liability is restricted to certain types of activities, such as abnormally dangerous tasks and defectively manufactured products, where the risk involved substantially outweighs the benefit.

Public Policy Objectives Behind Strict Liability

Under strict liability, society (through its courts and legislatures) has decided that the person engaged in certain ventures should bear the risk of liability to individuals innocently injured as a consequence of the dangerous or defective item or action. It is society's decision that persons owning wild animals, using fire or explosives, or manufacturing defective products are in the best economic position to pay for plaintiffs' injuries arising from these activities.

Insurance Analogy

Absolute liability resembles insurance. Defendants are insuring, or guaranteeing, the safety of plaintiffs who come into contact with what

---

TERMS

absolute liability   Liability for an injury whether or not there is fault or negligence.

strict liability   Liability for an injury whether or not there is fault or negligence; absolute liability. The law imposes strict liability in product liability cases.

IIII   PROFESSIONAL PROFILE   IIII

On the advice of her parents, Marion Gillerlain applied to the Philadelphia Institute of Paralegal Training. The advice was sound, as her paralegal degree and subsequent experience opened doors to another career.

Gillerlain landed her first paralegal job in the litigation department of a large law firm in her home town of Kansas City, Missouri. Because of the relative newness of the profession, she had several job interviews before actually receiving an offer. Hired to work on a complex, multidistrict products liability case, everything she learned was "baptism by fire." It was great experience for her, and when she rotated off the case, after three and one-half years, she was able to work on a variety of different matters. The most gratifying experience was when Gillerlain had to assume responsibility for preparing the exhibit and witness lists, trial exhibits, and witness files on a matter that had been pending for four years. She had just one month to prepare over 1,300 exhibits! Because she had become so familiar with all those exhibits, the attorneys asked her to sit with them throughout the month-long trial. Gillerlain remained with that firm for more than five years.

Gillerlain's next employer had a reputation for its innovative paralegal program. Once again, her role was as a jurisdictional manager in yet another complex litigation matter. She was responsible for about 300 federal and state cases, dealing with both medical and products liability aspects. The firm computerized the entire project because of the number and complexity of the cases. Between the computer usage and trial preparation, she was able to add to her skill base. Gillerlain remained with that firm for two and one-half years.

Today Gillerlain is an independent paralegal. She enjoys the freedom that independent work offers. Gillerlain has the best of both worlds, especially with her other part-time work; she designed and wrote a six-hour seminar entitled "How to Be a Better Legal Assistant." She is scheduled to do regional tours throughout the country to present this weeklong seminar. The opportunity perfectly meshes her paralegal expertise and her public speaking skills.

---

tort law calls **abnormally dangerous** or **ultrahazardous instrumentalities**. These activities or objects are just plainly dangerous by their very nature. Even if all precautions are taken, an injury might still occur.

Historical Development

Ancient English common law held the owners of animals, slaves, or objects absolutely liable for causing the death of another person.

=========================   **TERMS**   =========================

abnormally dangerous (ultrahazardous) instrumentalities[†] Activities or objects that are, by their very nature, extremely hazardous to persons or property. These are relevant to strict (absolute) liability cases.

For instance, suppose a boat broke its mooring and floated down-stream, colliding with and drowning a swimmer. In medieval England, the boat would be considered a *deodand,* because it killed someone. The term originated from the Latin *Deo dandum,* which translates as "a thing to be given to God." The ecclesiastical courts insisted that the offending, sinful property be seized and placed into God's service. Deodands had to be forfeited to the church or the crown, or sometimes to the injured party's surviving family, to be used in pious pursuits. It was seen as a charitable redemption: the owner would pay for his or her sinful chattel by giving it up. It did not matter that the chattel killed accidentally. This was probably one of the earliest forms of strict liability.

§ 9.3 Abnormally Dangerous Activities

Abnormally dangerous activities are inherently perilous because of the actions and the devices involved. Common examples include the use of explosives, flammable substances, noxious gases, poisons, hazardous wastes (the so-called **toxic torts**), or (in some jurisdictions) electricity, natural gas, and water supplied through unprotected utility lines. Many early twentieth-century cases refer to *ultrahazardous activities.* This is the term used by the original *Restatement of Torts* § 520 (the oft-called *First Restatement*). Although some courts split hairs distinguishing ultrahazardous from abnormally dangerous, the expressions are essentially interchangeable.

Restatement (Second) Rule

Restatement (Second) of Torts § 520 declares that persons engaged in abnormally dangerous activities shall be strictly liable for injuries caused by their actions. The *Restatement* lists several criteria for absolute liability:

1. The abnormally dangerous activity created a high risk of substantial injury to an individual or his or her property.

TERMS

toxic tort actions [†] Claims and suits involving toxic chemicals, pollution, hazardous waste disposal and transportation, and other environmentally sensitive issues. Toxic tort actions apply many tort theories, including trespass to land, negligence, absolute liability for ultrahazardous substances, products liability, and nuisance.

2. This risk could not be removed through the use of reasonable care.

3. The activity is not commonly undertaken (the common usage principle).

4. The activity was inappropriately undertaken in the place in which the victim was harmed.

5. The hazards that the activity creates outweigh the benefits that the activity brings to the community.

High Risk of Substantial Injury

To be abnormally dangerous, the defendant's activity must create a great threat of seriously injuring the plaintiff or the plaintiff's property. For instance, consider a highway construction company that uses dynamite to excavate rock and earth. Dynamite is dangerous stuff. It presents an enormous risk of injuring others nearby if it is not used properly. The threat of harm is significant, as people could be killed or their property destroyed if the dynamite is not used correctly.

Reasonable Care

If the tortfeasor could have eliminated the risk of harm through the use of reasonable care, then the activity is not abnormally dangerous, and absolute liability does not apply. For example, a utility company could exercise reasonable care and protect citizens from the great threat posed by electricity or natural gas simply by using insulated wires or double-sealed underground pipelines. Reasonable care could easily eliminate the risks of electrocution or explosion. If the utility company actually used these (or other) reasonable precautions, but a victim nonetheless was somehow injured, then the activity (supplying electricity or natural gas) would not be ultrahazardous.

Note the hidden implication in this element, though. Failure to use reasonable care to safeguard others from the risks involved in the activity could make it abnormally dangerous. For instance, suppose a utility ran electricity through uninsulated wires. Many courts have held that this would make the activity ultrahazardous, so the utility company would be strictly liable for injuries. However, not all courts interpret the *Second Restatement*'s reasonable care standard in this way.

Common Usage Principle

Abnormally dangerous activities and substances are those not commonly undertaken or used in everyday life. This is sometimes called the

common usage principle. For instance, consider explosives, toxic chemicals, or poisonous gases. How often does the average person use them? Does anyone in the reader's neighborhood? What about the manufacturing plant across town? But, it could be said, that is only one facility, and the vast majority of the public in the community does not use such substances. These, then, would be examples of abnormally dangerous substances, because they are not commonly used.

What about flammable substances? Many courts have included these as ultrahazardous items. But virtually everyone uses gasoline every day. Would gasoline not fall within common usage? Whether gasoline is abnormally dangerous depends upon how it is being used. Suppose SludgeCo Oil Company operates a gasoline refinery, with several massive fuel tanks storing hundreds of thousands of gallons. Few people in the community probably have such facilities in their backyards. Gasoline may be commonly used, but not in the way this storage facility uses it. The gas one keeps in his or her garage for the lawn mower would not be ultrahazardous; however, the huge storage tanks would be abnormally dangerous.

Inappropriate Use in Certain Place

To be ultrahazardous, the activity or substance must have been inappropriately performed or used in the place in which the victim was harmed. For example, suppose a chemical manufacturer opened a plant adjacent to a housing subdivision that uses well water. Suppose that the plant dumped toxic chemicals into holding ponds on its premises. Harmful chemicals could seep into the ground and contaminate the water supplies of nearby residents. Perhaps several of these homeowners became ill as a consequence. The activity (using toxic chemical retention ponds) is abnormally dangerous because it created a serious risk of substantial harm, was not of common usage, and was inappropriately undertaken at the location in which the plaintiffs were harmed (adjacent to residences).

Hazards Outweigh Benefits: Balancing Test

Courts often apply a balancing test to decide if an activity is abnormally dangerous. Such an analysis compares the dangers created by the

TERMS

common use principle [†] Doctrine in strict liability cases that defines abnormally dangerous activities and substances as those not commonly undertaken or used in everyday life.

activity with the benefits that the community derives from the activity. This is similar to the benefits analysis used in many nuisance cases.

For example, suppose a local builder is building a new road to improve access between hospitals and an isolated rural town. The construction crew uses dynamite to clear the area for the road. A nearby homeowner suffers structural damage to her house as a result of the blasting and sues the builder under strict liability theory. Courts following the *Second Restatement* would balance the benefits derived against the risks involved. The road would improve the community's access to hospital facilities. The dangers created by dynamite use, which in this case involved structural damage, are probably outweighed by these benefits.

The Case of the Ultrahazardous Activity

Land owners are becoming increasingly concerned with the safety of their groundwater. In this case, the plaintiffs claimed that the use of certain industrial solvents, which were used as degreasers in preparation for painting, was an ultrahazardous activity, and that defendants should be strictly liable.

CEREGHINO v. BOEING CO.
United States District Court for
the District of Oregon
826 F. Supp. 1243 (D. Or. 1993)
May 10, 1993
Jelderks, United States Magistrate Judge

Plaintiffs Joseph A. Cereghino, on his own behalf and as personal representative of the estate of Angelo Cereghino, and Mario Cereghino (collectively Cereghinos) bring this action, based on the release of certain chemicals, against the Boeing Company (Boeing), International Controls Corporation (ICC), Datron Systems, Inc. (Datron), and Elecspec Corporation (Elecspec). ...

The Cereghinos own farmland in Multnomah County, Oregon, located on the north side of Northeast Sandy Boulevard near the intersection of Northeast 185th Avenue and Sandy Boulevard. Industrial activities giving rise to this action began in 1964 on the south side of Sandy Boulevard, opposite the Cereghinos' land. At that time, Electronic Specialty Company (ESC), which is not a party to this action, began to operate a manufacturing facility on the site.

* * *

In early 1986, Boeing discovered that groundwater on the industrial site contained hazardous industrial solvents. It reported this finding to the United States Environmental Protection Agency, and to the Oregon Department of Environmental Quality. In July 1986, Boeing entered into a Consent Order and Compliance Agreement with those agencies. ...

In August 1986, the Cereghinos were notified that the groundwater in their land was contaminated with trichloroethylene (TCE). They subsequently learned that TCE and trichloroethane (TCA) had migrated into their groundwater from neighboring property. TCE and TCA are industrial solvents used as degreasers and in preparation for painting. These compounds are listed as hazardous wastes under the Federal Resource, Conservation and Recovery Act. 40 C.F.R. § 261.31. Boeing stopped using TCE in 1980. The levels of TCA detected in the groundwater on the Cereghinos' property do not exceed federal drinking water standards. TCE levels do exceed those standards.

Plaintiffs filed this action in January 1992. Their amended complaint, filed in January 1993, asserts that Boeing has owned the industrial site and has operated industrial facilities on that site "from about 1963 to the present, and at all material times thereto … ." They also allege that, from 1968 to 1985, ICC, Datron, and Elecspec operated manufacturing facilities on the land owned by Boeing, and that these defendants "used, handled, stored and disposed of hazardous substances, including but not limited to [TCE] and [TCA], in the course of the operation of the manufacturing and/or industrial facilities located on Boeing's land."

* * *

[The court's discussion of issues other than the ultrahazardous activity claim have been omitted.]

Plaintiffs' ultrahazardous activity claim asserts that defendants' "use, handling, storage and disposal of hazardous substances" constituted an ultrahazardous activity. This claim adds that defendants knew, or in the exercise of reasonable care should have known, that releases resulting from these activities would substantially harm landholders such as themselves.

Strict liability may be imposed on those who engage in "ultrahazardous" activities. An activity is considered ultrahazardous if it is "extraordinary, exceptional, or unusual, considering the locality in which it is carried on; when there is a risk of grave harm from such abnormality; and when the risk cannot be eliminated by the exercise of reasonable care … ." No Oregon court has decided whether the use of solvents such as TCE and TCA constitutes an ultrahazardous activity.

Boeing has submitted the uncontroverted affidavit of an expert who states that TCE and TCA are commonly-used degreasing agents, and opines that "it is entirely feasible to use both TCA and TCE in ways that would prevent any contamination of soil or groundwater." Boeing has also submitted uncontroverted evidence that use of degreasing solvents is common in the area around its property, and that plaintiffs themselves use solvents in maintenance of their farming equipment.

Boeing has shown the absence of material issues of fact as to whether use of the solvents in question here constituted an ultrahazardous activity. Use of solvents cannot be classified as ultrahazardous in this case and the motion for summary judgment on this claim should be granted.

Case Questions

1. Do you agree with the United States District Court's decision?
2. What could a home purchaser do to prevent being surprised about potentially toxic chemicals being found on land years after the purchase?

Many courts have applied the *Second Restatement*'s approach throughout this century. Several jurisdictions, however, have rejected the rule, either in whole or in part. Still, the *Second Restatement* provides a comprehensive, general formula for analyzing abnormally dangerous activities and absolute liability.

Defenses

Many state legislatures have enacted statutes protecting certain abnormally dangerous activities from strict liability. These statutes usually shield public utilities distributing electricity and natural gas, private contractors performing construction (particularly highway) work for

The Case of Asbestos in the Air

John Maiorana, a 40-year-old man, died of cancer. Thirteen years prior to his death, Maiorana was exposed to asbestos on the job. How can his estate show a definite connection between the cancer and the asbestos? In toxic tort actions, plaintiff's counsel has the difficult task of proving causation, when the onset of disease may occur many years after exposure to a potentially harmful substance.

IN RE JOINT EASTERN & SOUTHERN DISTRICTS ASBESTOS LITIGATION
United States District Court of Appeals, Second Circuit
52 F.3d 1124 (2d Cir. 1995)
April 6, 1995
Cabranes, Circuit Judge

This case marks the convergence of epidemiological evidence, probabilistic causation in carcinogenic torts, and the important issue of the extent to which a trial court may assess the sufficiency of scientific evidence, in light of the Supreme Court's recent holding in *Daubert v. Merrell Dow Pharmaceuticals, Inc.,* ___ U.S. ___, 113 S.Ct. 2786, 125 L.Ed.2d 469 (1993). That decision enlarged district courts' "gatekeeping" roles in appraising the admissibility of scientific evidence. The central question before us is the standard governing federal judges' evaluation of the *sufficiency*—as opposed to admissibility—of scientific evidence already admitted.

In 1983, John Maiorana ("Maiorana") died of colon cancer. His widow, plaintiff/appellant Arlene M. Maiorana ("plaintiff"), claimed that her husband's illness was caused by exposure to Cafco D., an asbestos spray manufactured by defendant-appellee United States Mineral Products Co. ("USMP"). This spray was used for insulation on two construction sites—the World Trade Center in New York City and Meadowbrook Hospital in Nassau County, New York—where Maiorana was employed as a sheet metal worker.

The scientific community is divided on whether asbestos exposure significantly increases the risk of contracting colon cancer. At trial in the United States District Court for the Southern District of New York ... , both plaintiff and USMP brought expert witnesses and numerous epidemiological studies to bear on their likely causal factors. After

considering this evidence, the jury on February 10, 1993, returned a verdict in favor of the plaintiff.

In an opinion dated July 23, 1993, the district court granted USMP's motion for judgment as a matter of law, setting aside the jury verdict. We believe that the district court ... inappropriately usurped the role of the jury. ...

Cafco D is a fireproof asbestos spray formerly used for insulating construction sites. In the fall of 1969 and spring of 1970, two major construction projects where Cafco D was used were the World Trade Center ("WTC") in Manhattan and the Meadowbrook Hospital ("Meadowbrook") in Nassau County, New York.

Maiorana was employed as a sheet metal worker for a small company which performed sheet metal work on both the WTC and Meadowbrook projects. Plaintiff contends that Maiorana and the other sheet metal workers—who worked in close proximity to the asbestos sprayers—were exposed to asbestos through contact with Cafco D.

In January 1983, Maiorana was diagnosed with colon cancer. Six months later, on June 16, 1983, Maiorana died from the disease. He was 40.

Plaintiff filed her original complaint on July 28, 1987, in connection with a case brought by sixteen plaintiffs on behalf of themselves and their deceased spouses against a number of manufacturers of asbestos-containing products. These manufacturers included USMP, the producer of Cafco D. By way of several third-party complaints and impleaders, a number of third-party defendants were added to the litigation ... .

In a series of rulings in 1991, the district court awarded summary judgment in favor of defendants, including USMP, on the grounds that the epidemiological and clinical evidence of causation were insufficient to meet the preponderance standard.

On appeal, we reversed the grant of summary judgment and remanded for further proceedings, concluding that the evidence was sufficient to survive summary judgment. We found that plaintiff had presented not only epidemiological studies in support of a causal connection between asbestos exposure and colon cancer, but also clinical evidence—in the form of Maiorana's own medical records and personal history, which plaintiff's experts used to exclude other possible causal factors. We found that the statements of the plaintiff's experts, viewed in the light most favorable to plaintiff, were the "equivalent of stating that asbestos exposure more probably than not caused the colon cancer."

From January 20 to February 10, 1993, the case was tried before a jury. By the time the jury was ready to deliver its verdict, all the original direct defendants but USMP had settled. The jury found in favor of plaintiff in the amount of $4,510,000. After allocating percentages of fault among USMP and third-party defendants, the jury found USMP 50% responsible for plaintiff's damages and found three of the third-party defendants approximately equally negligent (both Tishman and Castagna were assessed to be 14% responsible; subcontractor Mario & DiBono was assessed to be 15% responsible). In addition, the jury absolved the Port Authority of any liability.

On March 10, 1993, USMP moved for judgment as a matter of law ... .

In an extensive and thoughtful opinion dated July 23, 1993, the district court granted USMP's motion for judgment as a matter of law. The district court based its decision on its findings that (1) plaintiff's epidemiological evidence was insufficient to support a causal connection between asbestos exposure and colon cancer, and (2) plaintiff had failed to present affirmative clinical evidence to overcome the paucity of statistically significant epidemiological proof.

Epidemiology is the study of disease patterns in human populations. It "attempts to define a relationship between a disease and a factor suspected of causing it." As the district court observed, epidemiological evidence is indispensable in toxic and carcinogenic tort actions where direct proof of causation is lacking.

Epidemiologists speak in the statistical language of risks and probabilities. ...

In order for plaintiff to present a jury question on the issue of causation, the district court noted that she bore the burden of demonstrating that asbestos exposure was "more likely than not" the cause of Maiorana's colon cancer.

* * *

Plaintiff's expert witnesses—Dr. Steven Markowitz and Dr. Carl Shy—testified at trial that there was a causal relationship between asbestos exposure and colon cancer. The district court, however, conducted an independent and detailed analysis of many of the epidemiological studies and concluded that there was no basis for plaintiff's experts' conclusions. ... The district court criticized the methodologies employed in these studies, however, and found that when considered in the context of all the studies, plaintiff's evidence "establishe[d] only the conclusions that the association between exposure to asbestos and developing colon cancer is, at best, weak, and that the consistency of this purported association across the studies is, at best, poor."

* * *

Given plaintiff's failure to show that any asbestos fibers were found in Maiorana's cancerous tissues, the district court found that the sum total of plaintiff's evidence did not justify the jury's finding of causation, and that "the jury's finding could only have been the result of sheer surmise and conjecture."

* * *

In the present case, the sufficiency inquiry bears on the factual issue of causation—whether the body of plaintiff's evidence was sufficient to persuade a rational jury that Maiorana's exposure to asbestos more likely than not caused his colon cancer. Causation in toxic torts normally comprises two separate inquiries: whether the epidemiological or other scientific evidence establishes a causal link between c (asbestos exposure) and d (colon cancer), and whether plaintiff is within the class of persons to which inferences from the general causation evidence should be applied.

For the reasons stated below, we hold that the district court overstepped the boundaries set forth in *Daubert*. It impermissibly crossed the line from assessing evidentiary reliability to usurping the role of the jury. Accordingly, we reverse the district court's entry of judgment as a matter of law with respect to the jury verdict in favor of plaintiff.

* * *

The issue before the district court in this case, then, was whether the epidemiological and clinical data already in evidence was sufficient to justify the jury's verdict finding causation.

* * *

In rejecting plaintiff's experts' differential diagnosis, the district court gave little weight to Maiorana's relatively young age of death. While conceding it was "uncommon for a 40-year-old man to develop colon cancer," the court emphasized the absence of asbestos fibers in Maiorana's colon cancer tissues and the typical latency period of more than 20 years for colon cancer, compared to only 13 years for Maiorana. The district court's conclusions regarding latency periods, however, ignored Markowitz's testimony

on the study by Seidman which indicated an increased incidence of gastrointestinal cancer among individuals exposed to asbestos 10 years previously. That a latency period of 13 years was too short appeared to constitute an independent medical conclusion by the district court.

For the above reasons, we hold that the district court erred in ruling that plaintiff presented insufficient epidemiological and clinical evidence to support the jury's verdict finding causation. In our view, the district court impermissibly made a number of independent scientific conclusions—without granting plaintiff the requisite favorable inferences—in a manner not authorized by *Daubert*.

* * *

By way of summary:
On the issue of causation, we reverse the district court's entry of judgment as a matter of law, and we reinstate the jury verdict in favor of plaintiff. The district court erred in failing to draw all reasonable inferences in favor of plaintiff ... .

In view of the conditional order for a remittitur, we remand to the district court to provide plaintiff with the requisite opportunity to decide whether to accept the reduced verdict or submit to a new trial.

Case Questions

1. Normally, the statute of limitations for tort actions is just a few years. Is it fair to hold a defendant liable for an incident that may have occurred ten, twenty, or more years ago? Explain.
2. What are some of the potential problems a defendant would face in defending a matter based on an occurrence that transpired many years ago?

the government, and municipal zoos or parks that maintain wild animals. Under these statutes, the protected entities cannot be held absolutely liable for injuries caused by wild animals or ultrahazardous activities. Instead, plaintiffs must prove that the protected defendants were negligent or committed intentional torts, unless the defendants have purchased liability insurance to cover injuries under these circumstances.

Public Policy Objectives Behind Statutory Immunity

Legislatures often justify immunity statutes on the grounds that government (and the private companies that often work under governmental contracts) must be protected from the harshness of strict liability if certain essential activities are to be performed. How, the argument goes, can governments build roads, operate zoos or parks, supply utilities, or enable private industry to satisfy energy demands, if these activities carry the burden of strict liability whenever someone inadvertently gets hurt? This reasoning is similar to the benefits balancing act that courts often apply under the *Second Restatement* approach. Because legislatures enact statutes, and the public can change the legislature (through voting) and thus change the statutes, citizens who disagree with the immunity laws can elect new legislators to modify these provisions.

The Case of the Saturday Night Special

Many Americans recall the 1981 assassination attempt on President Ronald Reagan. Several bystanders were seriously injured when John Hinckley fired his fateful shots. Searching for a deeper pocket than Hinckley's, one injured person sued the manufacturer of Hinckley's gun, commonly called a "Saturday Night Special," under ultrahazardous activity and products liability theories. The D.C. Court of Appeals shot down the appellants' attempt to hold the manufacturer absolutely liable.

DELAHANTY v. HINCKLEY
District of Columbia
Court of Appeals
564 A.2d 758 (D.C. 1989)
October 11, 1989
Ferren, Associate Judge

Thomas and Jean Delahanty, appellants, filed suit in the United States District Court for the District of Columbia against John Hinckley for injuries Thomas suffered when Hinckley attempted to assassinate President Ronald Reagan. The Delahantys also sued the manufacturer of the gun, R.G. Industries, Inc., its foreign parent company, Roehm, and individual officers of Roehm.

Appellants advanced three legal theories for holding the gun manufacturers liable in these circumstances: negligence, strict products liability ... , and a "social utility" claim apparently based on strict liability for abnormally dangerous activities under *Restatement (Second) of Torts* §§ 519, 520 (1977) ... .

The District Court dismissed appellants' complaint against the gun manufacturers and their officers for failure to state a claim upon which relief could be granted. On appeal, the United States Court of Appeals for the District of Columbia Circuit *sua sponte* asked this court ... to decide whether, in the District of Columbia, "manufacturers and distributors of Saturday Night Specials may be strictly liable for injuries arising from these guns' criminal use." On consideration of this question, we conclude that traditional tort theories—negligence and strict liability under the *Restatement (Second) of Torts*—provide no basis for holding the gun manufacturer liable. ...

We reject each of the theories appellants have advanced in the federal courts and in this court. ...

Appellants also present what they call a "social utility claim," arguing that the manufacturer should be held strictly liable because the type of gun in this case is "inherently and abnormally dangerous with no social value." Appellants appear to base this claim ... on liability for abnormally dangerous activities, *Restatement (Second) of Torts* §§ 519, 520, a doctrine not yet explicitly adopted in the District of Columbia ... .

Like other courts that have considered the issue ... we reject application of the "abnormally dangerous activity" doctrine to gun manufacture and sale.

Appellants argue that the marketing of the guns is the abnormally dangerous activity for which the manufacturers should be held liable. We cannot agree. The cause of action under *Restatement* § 519 applies only to activities that are dangerous in themselves and to injuries that result directly from the dangerous activity. "The marketing of a handgun is not dangerous in and of itself, and when injury occurs, it is not the direct result of the sale itself, but rather the result of actions taken by a third party." Furthermore, handgun marketing cannot be classified as abnormally dangerous by applying the factors of *Restatement* § 520 ... . For example, any high degree of risk of harm, or any likelihood that such harm will be great, would result from the use, not the marketing as such, of handguns. ...

In sum, given appellants' proffered theories, we perceive no basis under the facts alleged for holding the gun manufacturers and their officers liable under the law of the District of Columbia for Hinckley's criminal use of the gun.

Case Questions

1. Apart from negligence or strict liability, is there another avenue by which manufacturers and sellers of "Saturday Night Specials" could be held absolutely liable for resulting injuries when the weapons are used in crimes? What governmental agency would have to be involved in this process?
2. What does *sua sponte* mean, as used in the court's opinion?

Cases involving toxic substances often revolve around absolute liability theory, applying the abnormally dangerous activity analysis. Of all the causes of action usually associated with toxic torts (including trespass to land, negligence, nuisance, and strict liability), absolute liability offers the best common law avenue for plaintiffs to recover.

HYPOTHETICAL

Suppose local businesses operated a Fourth of July fireworks celebration, which involved shooting the fireworks into the air high above town. Suppose excessive explosives were used in the fireworks. When they were detonated, flaming debris fell onto nearby houses, causing many fires. Could the homeowners succeed in a strict liability lawsuit against the companies responsible for the fireworks display?

Were the fireworks abnormally dangerous activities? Apply the *Second Restatement*'s criteria for absolute liability. Fireworks exploding in mid-air create a tremendous risk that flaming debris could fall onto buildings' roofs, setting fires. The threat and the harm are substantial. Could reasonable care have avoided the risk? Fireworks that explode in the air are going to fall somewhere, perhaps in flaming pieces. No degree of reasonable care could prevent the danger of resulting fires. Aerial fireworks of the types described in this example are not commonly used by the public. The fireworks were inappropriately used in the area in which the fires occurred, because the power used was excessive and the fireworks detonated above the houses, subjecting them to the severe fire risk. The threat of harm outweighs the benefits to the community, as fireworks displays are conducted only once or twice per year and the benefits are purely aesthetic and momentary. The fireworks promoters will be strictly liable to the homeowners. (This conclusion assumes, of course, that there are no state statutes or local ordinances granting the fireworks promoters immunity from absolute liability.)

Figure 9-1 summarizes absolute liability for abnormally dangerous activities. All absolute liability cases, as discussed in this chapter, must satisfy the requirements of proximate cause, which is discussed in § 9.5.

Definitions and Examples	Restatement (2d) of Torts § 520	Defenses
Abnormally dangerous = Ultrahazardous	Activity creates high risk of substantial harm	Statutory immunities for certain types of ultrahazardous activities
These activities are, by their very nature, perilous	Risk could not be eliminated through exercise of reasonable care	Most often include governmental activities involving uses of explosives, chemicals, or energy service
Examples: use of explosives, flammable substances, noxious gases, or poisons	Activity is not commonly undertaken (common usage principle)	Immunities reflect public policy objectives to balance necessary public services against individual right to compensation for injury
Some courts include unprotected use of utilities (electricity, natural gas, water)	Activity is inappropriate in place where injury happened	
	Hazards created outweigh community benefits from activity	

FIGURE 9-1 Absolute liability for abnormally dangerous activities and defenses

§ 9.4   Animal Owners' Liability

Modern absolute liability first arose in the common law involving private ownership of wild animals and the use of fire or explosives. This section discusses owners' liability for injuries inflicted by their wild animals.

Wild Animals Defined

The ancient common law cases use the Latin term ***ferae naturae***, meaning "wild nature," to refer to wild animals. These are animals that have naturally wild dispositions, as opposed to tame animals, which are called ***domitae naturae***, meaning "domesticated nature." Examples of *ferae naturae* include deer, bison, elk, bear, snakes, bees, stream or ocean fish, coyotes, foxes, wild birds, lions, tigers, gophers, raccoons, opossums, or prairie dogs.

Ownership of Wildlife

Under ancient English common law, the king owned all wildlife in the realm. This is why poachers were often hanged or beheaded for taking the crown's property during medieval times. As English law evolved, an average person could claim ownership of a wild animal—the trick was to catch the beast. Once someone had control over a wild animal, it was considered to be his or her property until it escaped to its natural, free state. The common law cases call this ownership the exercise of **dominion and control** over the wild animal. American common law holds that the state (or the federal government), under its police power, owns wildlife in trust for the benefit of all citizens. This is why one must obtain state or federal hunting or fishing licenses to take wildlife.

TERMS

ferae naturae   Wild animals.
domitae naturae[†]   [Latin for] "domesticated nature" and referring to tame, domestic animals.
dominion   Ownership and control.
control   The power or authority to direct or manage.

For example, suppose Kathleen has an apiary—in other words, she is a beekeeper. The bees are wildlife, *ferae naturae*. However, if Kathleen catches and places them in her apiary hives, they may stay and produce honey for her. Now Kathleen owns the bees. As long as she exercises dominion and control over the insects, they are hers. But once the bees fly away, they are *ferae naturae* again, and Kathleen does not own them (that is, unless she catches them again).

Importance of Wildlife Ownership

Wildlife ownership is important for purposes of absolute liability. If a wild animal injures someone, the victim cannot sue the beast (or, at the very least, cannot easily collect judgment). Instead, the plaintiff looks to the animal's owner for compensation. Owners are strictly liable for the injuries their wildlife inflicts. It does not matter that the owner exercised every precaution to safeguard others from being hurt by the wild animals. If the beast attacks and hurts someone, the owner must compensate the victim for the injuries. Because the common law presumes that wild animals are dangerous by nature, strict liability applies to any injuries they cause.

Suppose Ken's pet bear mauls a visitor to Ken's home. The victim will sue Ken under strict liability. One might argue that premises liability, using negligence theory, should apply instead, because Ken owns the land and the chattels that harmed the plaintiff, but this argument would lose. Because bears are wildlife, Ken is absolutely liable for his pet's mischief.

Comparison with Domesticated Animals

Domitae naturae are animals that the law presumes to be harmless. Examples of domestic animals include dogs, cats, pet birds, or livestock such as pigs, horses, cows, or sheep. When domesticated animals hurt someone, the common law states that the owner is liable if he or she was negligent in handling the animals. Liability would also arise if an owner intentionally used domestic animals to hurt someone. For example, suppose an attack dog's owner ordered the animal to attack a victim. This is a form of battery, as the animal would be considered an extension of the tortfeasor's body.

Practical Applications

Check to find out if your local jurisdiction has an applicable leash law. Many municipalities have local laws requiring pet owners to keep their pets fenced in or on a leash. Should a victim be injured by a stray dog, you should inquire about local leash laws.

Vicious Propensity Rule

Owners may be held absolutely liable for injuries caused by their domestic animals if the animals exhibit vicious tendencies. When a dog growls or snarls, when a bull paws the ground and snorts, or when a cat arches its back and hisses, these are all demonstrations of vicious propensities. When a domestic animal routinely displays these characteristics, so that it gets a reputation for viciousness, it is said to have *vicious propensities.* An owner of such an animal will be held strictly liable for any injuries the beast inflicts, under the so-called **vicious propensity rule**. All states except Indiana have adopted this common law principle. Indiana has a hybrid vicious propensity rule, peculiar to its common law heritage, under which an owner's negligence in handling the animal must be proven, whether or not the animal displays a vicious propensity.

Defenses in Animal Absolute Liability Cases

Normally, negligence or intentional tort defenses are ineffective against strict liability. However, certain exceptions have arisen in the common law for particular types of absolute liability, such as cases involving animals. The following defenses can protect an animal owner from strict liability:

1. Assumption of risk
2. Contributory and comparative negligence
3. Consent
4. Self-defense and defense of others.

Assumption of Risk

If the individual injured by a wild (or vicious-propensity domestic) animal voluntarily assumed a known risk, with full appreciation of the dangers involved, then the owner is not strictly liable for the inflicted injuries. Courts justify this defense on equitable grounds. It would be

---

TERMS

---

vicious propensity rule[†] Doctrine in absolute liability cases involving domestic animals. Normally owners are not strictly liable for injuries caused by their domestic animals. However, if the animals display vicious propensities and hurt someone or their property, then the owner is absolutely liable. Vicious propensities are proven by past episodes of the animal's nasty behavior.

unfair to hold owners absolutely liable for harm their animals caused if the victims chose to subject themselves to the danger. This may colloquially be phrased as the "you got what you asked for" theory.

Contributory and Comparative Negligence

Courts often rule that the plaintiff's contributory or comparative negligence in an animal attack will prevent the owner's absolute liability. Some courts state that a plaintiff's contributory negligence bars strict liability altogether. This means that the plaintiff would have to prove that the defendant (owner) was negligent in keeping the animal that attacked and hurt the plaintiff. Other courts simply ignore absolute liability theory and reshape the case in a negligence mold, in which the plaintiff's and defendant's respective degrees of negligence are compared.

Consent

An injured plaintiff might have consented to exposure to a dangerous animal. Consent is usually based upon a person's employment responsibilities while working around animals. For example, suppose Gordon works for a police-dog-training facility, where he serves as an attack victim. He knows from observation and experience that the dogs are dangerous. Even if Gordon was not wearing his protective padding, and he was bitten by one of the dogs, he has implicitly consented to this danger as part of his job. Basically, this is assumption of risk couched in consent terms. The same reasoning would apply for keepers, trainers, or feeders of wild animals for zoos or circuses.

Self-Defense and Defense of Others

When a wild or vicious domestic animal attacks a victim, but the owner used the animal as a means of self-defense or defense of other persons, then the owner would not be strictly liable for the inflicted injuries. For instance, suppose someone attacks Arthur while he is out walking his dog, which has a vicious reputation around the neighborhood. To repel the danger, Arthur commands his dog to attack. His assailant is knocked to the ground, chewed up a bit, and scared away. Arthur would not be absolutely liable for the injuries caused by his dog. The same scenario would arise if Arthur saw someone attacking a member of his family or a friend and he used the dog to protect that person. However, remember the limitations to these defenses. One may not become the aggressor and still use them to escape liability. Hence, if Arthur's dog had chased the fleeing attacker down the street, Arthur could not use these defenses to avoid liability.

Dog-Bite Statutes

Most jurisdictions have statutes that have changed the common law owner liability (and the available defenses) in dog-bite cases. These statutes can substantially affect a dog owner's liability and defenses.

Dog-bite hypotheticals present interesting applications of absolute liability. In the following example, consider the vicious propensity rule and its effects on the canine owner's liability.

The Case of Bite-Worse-Than-Bark

Postal carriers have an endless series of anecdotes about nasty dogs. Fortunately, most such encounters end without serious harm to either person or pet. However, in a few instances, one or the other suffers serious injury. In this case, the plaintiff was faced with an extremely vicious canine breed, as the expert testimony established. But a dog is a dog, and dogs are presumed harmless, according to the traditional common law, which the Texas Court of Appeals vapidly recites. One wonders if stare decisis leads to cognitive atrophy.

POWERS v. PALACIOS
Court of Appeals of Texas
794 S.W.2d 493 (Tex. Ct. App. 1990),
rev'd on other grounds,
813 S.W.2d 489 (Tex. 1991)
June 29, 1990
Seerden, Justice

Brenda Powers sued Paul Palacios, seeking damages for injuries, including loss of a finger, sustained when a pit bull dog kept at his residence attacked her while she was delivering mail. Following a jury trial, the trial court rendered a take-nothing judgment. We affirm the judgment of the trial court. ...

Appellant's point of error number four complains of the refusal of the trial court to submit her proposed Question 4 to the jury.

The evidence showed that appellant was attacked by a dog which was kept at appellee's residence. The dog was of a breed commonly known as a pit bull.

Appellant presented expert testimony that these dogs have a savage and vicious nature and are dangerous to humans.

Appellant's requested Special Issue 4 would have inquired of the jury:

Did Defendant Paul Palacios allow, either by express consent or implied consent, Jessie Palacios (the dog's owner) to have on Paul Palacios's premises a vicious animal on Feb. 23, 1987, the day of the attack?

Appellant correctly cites *Marshall v. Ranne*, [citation omitted] which is the leading Texas case relating to the law of wild and vicious animals. It holds that suits for damages caused by vicious animals should be governed by the law of strict liability. It also expressly adopts as the correct rule the *Restatement (Second) of Torts* §§ 507, 509 (1938).

These sections provide a distinction between the strict liability of a possessor of a "wild animal" (§ 507) and an "abnormally dangerous domestic animal" (§ 509) by providing that the possessor of the latter must have "reason to know" that the animal has dangerous propensities abnormal to its class, while the only condition for imposing liability on the possessor of a "wild animal" is that the damage result from a dangerous propensity characteristic of wild animals of its class.

Appellant's proposed Question 4, and her argument in support thereof, presupposes that the pit bull is a wild animal. The court refused to submit the request, but submitted Question 5, which inquired whether appellee had reason to know that the dog had dangerous propensities abnormal to its class. This question is consistent with the *Marshall* rule on abnormally dangerous domestic animals. The jury answered Question 5 "No."

We have been cited no cases differentiating between wild and domestic animals. *Black's Law Dictionary* contains these definitions:

Domestic animals. Such as are habituated to live in or about the habitations of men, or such as contribute to the support of a family.

Wild animals. Animals of an untamable disposition; animals in a state of nature.

We hold that the trial court was correct in refusing to submit to the jury the question based on appellant's theory that the dog in question was a wild animal. ...

The judgment of the trial court is affirmed.

Case Questions

1. The plaintiff's expert testimony established that the defendant's pit bull had "a savage and vicious nature" that is "dangerous to humans." Would this not satisfy the *Black's Law Dictionary* definition of *wild animal* as one with "an untamable disposition"? Explain.
2. Does the expert testimony that pit bulls, as a breed, are "dangerous to humans" contradict Black's definition of *domestic animals* as those "habituated to live in or about the habitations of men, or such as contribute to the support of family"? Why or why not?
3. Why do you think the jury did not apply the strict liability rule applicable in vicious propensity cases? How could the defendant not have reason to know of the pit bull's viciousness, given the plaintiff's expert testimony about their inherent malevolence?

HYPOTHETICAL

Toby Jones owns a towing service. He uses Doberman pinscher dogs to guard the parking lot in which he keeps towed vehicles. The area is surrounded by large, barbed-wire fences with "no trespassing" signs attached every few feet. The guard dogs would bark, snarl, bite, and lunge at anyone who came near the fencing. Early one morning, Chet Paisley stopped by to claim an automobile that had been towed for illegal parking. After paying the storage fees, Chet walked back to the holding area. Toby had forgotten to chain the dogs from the night before, and they were running loose in the parking lot. When they saw Chet, they attacked and severely injured him.

The common law presumes that dogs are harmless, domestic creatures. However, there is considerable evidence that Toby's Dobermans displayed vicious propensities. Accordingly, the harmlessness presumption falls aside, and the dogs are viewed as potentially dangerous, like wild animals. Under absolute liability, Toby would be responsible for Chet's injuries. Toby's negligence or intent are irrelevant here. It only matters that the dogs were abnormally dangerous instrumentalities, because of their vicious propensities. Once strict liability applies, the result is easy: the animal owner must compensate the victim for his or her injuries.

Would the result have been different if Toby had posted signs stating, "WARNING! DANGEROUS ATTACK DOGS! DO NOT ENTER WITHOUT AUTHORIZED PERSONNEL TO ACCOMPANY YOU"? If Chet had seen such signs but entered regardless, he would have assumed the risk. Chet would have voluntarily assumed a known risk (the dangerous dogs) with full appreciation of the threat involved (being bitten or mauled). Chet would also have been contributorily negligent in entering the enclosed parking lot without Toby or another employee accompanying him.

Figure 9-2 summarizes animal owner strict liability and the available defenses.

Wildlife (ferae naturae)	Domestic Animals (domitae naturae)	Defenses
Owner strictly liable for injuries caused by wild animals	Owner absolutely liable for injuries caused by domestic animals *only* if such animals display vicious propensities	1. Assumption of risk 2. Contributory negligence 3. Comparative negligence 4. Consent 5. Self-defense 6. Defense of others

FIGURE 9-2   Animal owners' absolute liability and defenses

§ 9.5 Scope of Liability: Proximate Cause

Proximate cause in absolute liability cases is defined similarly to proximate cause in negligence cases. Animals or abnormally dangerous activities must proximately cause the victim's injuries if the tortfeasor is to be held strictly liable. For absolute liability purposes, proximate cause has the following elements:

1. The plaintiff's injuries must have been a reasonably foreseeable consequence of the defendant's actions; and
2. The victim must have been a foreseeable plaintiff (meaning that it must have been reasonably foreseeable that the plaintiff would be injured as a result of the defendant's activities).

These elements are defined the same as in negligence theory.

TERMS

proximate cause   As an element of liability in a tort case, that cause which, unbroken by any intervening cause, produced the injury, and without which the result would not have occurred; the primary cause; the efficient cause. Note that the proximate cause of an injury is not necessarily the final cause or the act or omission nearest in time to the injury.

No Duty of Reasonable Care

When applied to strict liability cases, proximate cause does not include the duty of reasonable care, which is an element of negligence theory. Nevertheless, some courts insist on including the duty while discussing proximate cause in absolute liability cases. But negligence is irrelevant to strict liability; therefore, the duty of reasonable care (as used in negligence's proximate cause analysis) is also irrelevant.

In the hypotheticals discussed throughout this chapter, apply the proximate cause standard to each example. Did the tortfeasor's actions proximately cause the victim's injuries? A variety of answers are possible. As with negligence, proximate cause in absolute liability cases can be a puzzle.

Summary

Fault is irrelevant to strict liability. If the tortfeasor is found to be absolutely liable, his or her negligence or intent does not affect the liability. This may seem harsh and unfair, because a tortfeasor might exercise every degree of care to avoid injuring others and still be held responsible under absolute liability. Strict liability is limited to cases involving abnormally dangerous instrumentalities, such as wild animals, vicious domestic animals, ultrahazardous activities, and products liability. Through its courts and legislatures, the public has established absolute liability as an insurance measure to protect innocent victims from harm caused by particularly perilous pursuits.

Abnormally dangerous, or ultrahazardous, activities are inherently perilous. Use of explosives, flammable substances, noxious gases, poisons, hazardous wastes, and sometimes electricity, natural gas, or water utilities are examples. *Restatement (Second) of Torts* § 520 states that persons engaged in abnormally dangerous activities are strictly liable for injuries caused by these activities. The activity must create a high risk of substantial harm, which risk could not have been eliminated through the exercise of reasonable care; the activity or substance must not be commonly undertaken or used; the activity must have been inappropriately used in the place in which the injury happened; and the activity's hazards must outweigh the activity's benefits to the community. As a defense to strict liability, many legislatures have enacted statutes protecting certain activities from absolute liability.

The common law calls wild animals *ferae naturae* ("wild nature") and domestic animals *domitae naturae* ("domesticated nature"). At common law wild animals are presumed to be naturally dangerous, while domestic animals are assumed to be harmless and docile creatures. Wild animals may be owned by individuals who capture and restrain the beasts. This is called exercising dominion and control. Owners are absolutely liable for injuries their wild animals inflict. However, owners are strictly liable only for injuries caused by their domestic animals if these animals exhibited vicious propensities. The defenses of assumption of risk, contributory and comparative negligence, consent, and self-defense or defense of others apply to animal liability cases.

Absolute liability in animal and abnormally dangerous activity cases is limited by proximate cause. For strict liability to apply, the defendant's actions must have proximately caused the plaintiff's injuries. This means that the plaintiff's injuries must have been reasonably foreseeable as a consequence of the defendant's conduct, and it must have been foreseeable that the plaintiff could be injured as a result of the defendant's actions. This is called the foreseeable plaintiffs theory. There is no duty of reasonable care when proximate cause is applied to strict liability cases, because the duty involves negligence theory, which is irrelevant to absolute liability.

Review Questions

1. How is strict, or absolute, liability different from negligence and intentional torts? What role does fault play in absolute liability? What are the limitations to strict liability? What are the public policy objectives behind absolute liability? How is strict liability like insurance?

2. What are abnormally dangerous activities? Ultrahazardous activities? How does the *Restatement (Second) of Torts* define the term? What elements are required for absolute liability to apply? What is the function of reasonable care? What is the common usage principle? What balancing test do courts apply in abnormally dangerous activity cases?

3. How does the common law define wild animals? Domestic animals? What does the common law presume about each type of animal? How can wildlife be owned? Why is this important to the question of liability? When does strict liability apply to injuries inflicted by wild animals? By domestic animals? What is the vicious propensity rule? What defenses apply to animal owner absolute liability cases?

4. How is proximate cause defined in strict liability cases? Why is it important? How is it different from proximate cause in negligence theory?

Projects

1. Does your state have any statutes concerning dog-bite liability? If so, what defenses are included in the statutes?

2. Does your state have any statutes that limit absolute liability for abnormally dangerous activities? Are there any state statutes pertaining to hazardous waste disposal or transportation?

3. Do your state courts follow the *Second Restatement* approach to strict liability in abnormally dangerous activities?

4. In class or study groups, create your own hypotheticals using the strict liability theories and defenses discussed in this chapter. Then change the facts to affect the outcomes of the problems.

CHAPTER 10

PRODUCTS LIABILITY

Law and order exist for the purpose of establishing justice and ... when they fail in this purpose they become the dangerously structured dams that block the flow of social progress.
— *Martin Luther King, Jr.*

§ 10.1 Introduction

Products liability is another type of strict liability. Generally, under products liability, the manufacturer or seller of a product is absolutely liable for any injuries caused by a defect in the product. Products liability occupies a prominent position in torts study, as it is involved in a sizeable portion of tort litigation. It is probably the most significant development in tort law since the courts accepted negligence theory as a separate tort. This chapter includes:

- The parties in products liability cases

- The elements of products liability

- *Restatement (Second) of Torts* § 402A

- The defenses to products liability

- Comparison of products liability with contract law warranties.

TERMS

product(s) liability The liability of a manufacturer or seller of an article for an injury caused to a person or to property by a defect in the article sold. A product liability suit is a tort action in which strict liability is imposed. The manufacturer or seller of a defective product may be liable to third parties as well as to purchasers, as privity of contract is not a requirement in a product liability case.

§ 10.2 Products Liability Theory and History

Products liability was established as a distinct tort theory in the landmark case of *Greenman v. Yuba Power Products, Inc.,* 59 Cal. 2d 57, 377 P.2d 897, 27 Cal. Rptr. 697 (1962). In this case, the California Supreme Court completed over 100 years of legal evolution that culminated in strict products liability.

Public Policy Objectives Behind Products Liability

Products liability is society's decision, through its courts and legislatures, that businesses manufacturing and selling defective products are in the best economic position to bear the expenses incurred when a faulty product injures an innocent user. The theory may be simply put: Why should the hapless victim shoulder the burdens (medical costs, permanent injuries, etc.) produced by a defectively made product? Instead, should not the manufacturer or seller of that product be liable for the resulting harms? Does that not seem reasonable and ethical? If one has ever been hurt by a defective product, one might answer affirmatively. If one were a manufacturer or seller, however, he or she might feel differently.

Historical Development of Products Liability

In the early nineteenth century, English and American common law held that persons injured by defective products had to sue under contract law rather than tort law. These courts felt that the appropriate cause of action was breach of contract or, more precisely, breach of warranty. A **warranty** is a guarantee that a product or service meets certain quality standards. If a product fails to meet such standards, as is the case when a product is defective, then the warranty has been breached.

Under early nineteenth-century English and American common law, only persons who had made contracts with the manufacturer or seller of a defective product could recover damages for breach of warranty or

===== **TERMS** =====

warranty 1. Generally, an agreement to be responsible for all damages arising from the falsity of a statement or the failure of an assurance. 2. With respect to a contract for sale of goods, a promise, either express or implied by law, with respect to the fitness or merchantability of the article that is the subject of the contract.

IIII   PROFESSIONAL PROFILE   IIII

A resident of Duluth, Minnesota, Yedat Singh received his paralegal certificate ten years ago. He completed his internship at the law firm where he had been working as a process server. Subsequently, Singh convinced the attorneys of that firm to hire him as a full-time paralegal. "I was the first paralegal the law firm ever hired, and when I first started, neither the attorneys nor I had a very clear idea of how my time and skills could best be utilized by the firm. Fortunately, the attorneys I worked for were very busy and willing to delegate any work that could possibly be done by a paralegal," Singh says. Within two years there were two other paralegals working for the firm, and the attorneys were utterly convinced of the benefits of working with paralegals.

The firm Singh worked for specialized in car and motorcycle accidents. Originally he worked in both these areas, but motorcycle incidents became his specialty. Most of his workdays were fast-paced and unpredictable. On a "typical" day he would spend most of his time meeting with several attorneys, calling or meeting with clients, and drafting legal documents and correspondence. Some of the legal documents that he prepared were complaints, bills of particulars, and various responses to discovery

requests. It was also his responsibility to keep track of the clients' medical records, bills, and other documentation.

One of the most interesting and exciting aspects of Singh's job involved reconstructing accidents on videotape with engineers who were retained by the firm. "It was very exciting and rewarding to me to be an integral part of a million-dollar case," Singh says. Although he found working on trial preparation very interesting, it also involved working long hours under a lot of pressure at times. It was not uncommon to work late into the night—and in some instances, early into the next morning—to prepare for a long and complex trial.

The group of attorneys who employed Singh understood the importance of team effort and recognized that every member of the law firm staff is essential: Typically, when the firm was about to undertake a large case, the attorneys would decide on a team to handle the work. Such a team usually consisted of a partner of the firm, an associate attorney, a paralegal or two, and a secretary. The team would meet to discuss how the project would be handled and then work together to see the project through to a successful conclusion.

---

breach of contract. This contractual relationship is called **privity of contract**. Privity exists when parties are directly engaged in an agreement between them. If Joseph enters into a contract with Harris, in which Joseph agrees to sell Harris a product for a certain price, then there is privity of contract between them. The landmark case that announced the privity rule was *Winterbottom v. Wright,* 10 Meeson & Welsby 109, 152 Eng. Rep. 402 (1842). In this case, the plaintiff drove a horse-drawn coach for the Postmaster-General. This coach was manufactured

===== TERMS =====

privity of contract The legal relationship between the parties to a contract. In some circumstances, a party must be in privity of contract with another party in order to assert a claim.

especially for the Postmaster-General by the defendant. The plaintiff was maimed when the vehicle's axle broke and threw him from the carriage seat. The plaintiff sued the defendant for failing to properly maintain the coach under a service contract. The court held that the plaintiff was not a party to either the service agreement or the manufacturing agreement. Thus, the plaintiff lacked privity of contract and therefore could not recover for the injuries caused by the defectively assembled coach. The only party that could sue under such circumstances would be the Postmaster-General, with whom the defendant contracted to make the carriage. But in this case the Postmaster-General was not harmed. The injured plaintiff was left without compensation.

Almost immediately, American courts began to carve out exceptions to the privity-of-contract rule. In *Thomas v. Winchester*, 6 N.Y. 397 (1852), the New York Court of Appeals ruled that a mislabelled medicine (which actually contained poison) was inherently dangerous, and accordingly the injured party did not have to have privity of contract with the manufacturer or seller to recover damages. In this case, the plaintiff's husband had purchased a bottle, labelled "dandelion extract," that in actuality contained belladonna, a deadly poison. The defendant manufacturer who mislabelled the product sold it to a druggist, who resold it to a physician, who prescribed it to the plaintiff. There was no privity of contract between the plaintiff and the defendant. Nonetheless, the court permitted the plaintiff to recover damages for injuries caused when she took the poison from the mislabelled bottle. The court reasoned that poisons are imminently dangerous by their very nature. Accordingly, remote users of a mislabelled drug could be seriously injured. Thus, privity of contract is unnecessary if the defective product (such as a mislabelled poison) is imminently dangerous. Later courts characterized this as the **imminent danger exception** to the privity-of-contract rule.

Throughout the nineteenth century, the New York Court of Appeals, and many courts following its lead, expanded the imminent danger rule to include spoiled food, explosives, improperly assembled scaffolding, an exploding coffee urn, and defectively made automobile wheels. Many courts found liability in contract warranty law, but this still required privity of contract. The landmark case in this century, which is often said to have sparked modern products liability law, is *MacPherson v. Buick Motor Co.*, 217 N.Y. 382, 111 N.E. 1050 (1916). Writing for the majority, Justice Cardozo declared that privity of contract was obsolete. If a product, because of its defective manufacture,

---

TERMS

imminent danger exception † A nineteenth- and early twentieth-century exception to the privity of contract requirement in defective product cases.

became unreasonably dangerous, then the manufacturer or seller would be liable for injuries caused by the defective product. Cardozo applied negligence theory to determine whether the defective product was unreasonably dangerous. The manufacturer had to be negligent in making the faulty product.

MacPherson ushered in a cascade of court opinions following and expanding its precedent. In *Escola v. Coca Cola Bottling Co.*, 24 Cal. 2d 453, 150 P.2d 436 (1944), Justice Traynor of the California Supreme Court, in his concurring opinion, opined that negligence was no longer necessary for defective product manufacturers to be liable. Instead, he proposed strict liability. It took eighteen years before the California Supreme Court adopted this view in *Greenman v. Yuba Power Products*. Many other state courts quickly joined the new common law theory.

The American Law Institute followed *Greenman* with its famous *Restatement (Second) of Torts* § 402A, which virtually every American jurisdiction has adopted (in some form or another) as the definitive rule for strict products liability. The *Restatement*'s position is discussed in greater detail in § 10.4.

The Case of the Sleeping Driver

A car leaves the roadway, travels over the median, crashes over a retaining wall, and then is engulfed in fire. No other vehicles are involved in the accident. From the plaintiff's standpoint, there must be something terribly wrong with the car. From the defendant's perspective, the driver must not have been paying attention to the road. A jury must find the truth. The result of this case hinges on the elements needed to sustain a products liability cause of action.

BOUTTE
v.
NISSAN MOTOR CORP.
Court of Appeal of Louisiana, Third Circuit
663 So. 2d 154 (La. Ct. of App. 1995)
September 13, 1995
Cooks, Judge

Defendant in this products liability case appeals and seeks reversal of an adverse judgment. Plaintiff also appeals assigning as sole error that the jury's award is inadequate. For the following reasons, we amend and affirm as amended.

On July 23, 1989 John Boutte (plaintiff) was returning to his home in Grand Marais, near New Iberia, when involved in a one-car accident. Boutte was travelling on Highway 90 when his

1987 Nissan Maxima left the roadway, travelled through the median, crashed over the concrete retaining wall of a culvert in the median knocking out a large piece of the wall, and stopped approximately 210 feet from the point where it left the roadway. As the car drove over the wall, the underbody of the automobile was damaged. After Boutte escaped from the vehicle, it was engulfed by fire. Boutte's ankles were severely fractured during the accident.

The day before the accident, Boutte woke up at 5:00 A.M. and reported to work at 7:00 A.M. After working an eight-hour day, he returned home to eat, showered and dressed for a party. He drove to Lafayette to pick up his girlfriend. While at her home, Boutte consumed one straight drink of Crown Royal. Boutte and his girlfriend rode to New Iberia together for a Hawaiian luau where he consumed two more drinks of Crown Royal and coke. After the party, he dropped his girlfriend off at her home in Lafayette and began the return trip to Grand Marais. When his vehicle left the road at 2:10 A.M., Boutte had been awake for 21 hours.

Boutte filed suit against Nissan Motor Corporation (Nissan) alleging a defect in the brakes or steering of his automobile caused it to travel off the roadway. He later amended his petition alleging a defect existed in the passive restraint system of the automobile. Nissan argued there were no defects existing in Boutte's automobile. It asserted the automobile left the roadway because Boutte fell asleep while driving. Nissan further asserted Boutte's injuries were not caused by the restraint system.

* * *

Nissan argues Boutte failed to establish by competent expert testimony there was a defect in the 1987 Maxima because he did not: (1) Prove a defect existed by way of competent expert testimony; (2) prove he sustained enhanced injuries as a result of an alleged defect; and (3) prove any design alternative would have prevented or lessened his injuries. Nissan also asserts it should not have been assessed any fault for Boutte's injuries.

It is well-settled that an appellate court may not set aside a trial court's or a jury's finding of fact in the absence of "manifest error" or unless it is "clearly wrong."

* * *

Nissan acknowledges that the United States Supreme Court recently, in *Daubert v. Merrell Dow Pharmaceuticals, Inc.,* ___ U.S. ___, 113 S.Ct. 2786, 125 L.Ed.2d 469 (1993), rejected the rigid "general acceptance" test first memorialized, 72 years past, in *Frye v. United States,* 54 App.D.C. 46, 47, 293 F. 1013, 1014 (1923). The *Frye* test found life in "a short and citation-free 1923 decision concerning the admissibility of evidence derived from a systolic blood pressure deception test, a crude precursor to the polygraph machine."

Ruling inadmissible expert testimony relating to blood pressure as a "truth" indicator on test results, the *Frye* court stated: "... *the thing from which the deduction is made must be sufficiently established to have gained general acceptance in the particular field in which it belongs."*

We must presume that the trial judge performed his "gatekeeping function" in ruling admissible the expert testimony Nissan now complains should have been excluded. ...

Boutte presented the testimony of William H. Muzzy III, as an expert in mechanical engineering with expertise in injury mechanics, occupant motion and restraint systems. ... Muzzy's testimony concerned the relationship between Boutte's injuries and the restraint system. We find Muzzy's testimony had a reliable foundation; and, it was relevant.

Nissan presented the testimony of Dr. Charles Hatsell, a medical doctor who also obtained a Ph.D. in electrical engineering. ... Dr. Hatsell, however, acknowledged he never tested restraint systems.

Muzzy testified the lap belt anchor point of Nissan's restraint system did not meet the requirements of Motor Vehicle Safety Standard 209, which provides the lap belt must stay on the occupant's pelvis in all cases including crashes and rollovers. When Boutte fastened the lap belt, it was positioned over his thighs. In Muzzy's opinion Boutte's legs slid forward during the accident and became entrapped by the knee bolsters located on the lower portion of the dashboard because the lap belt was not properly positioned on his pelvis. ...

On the contrary, Nissan's expert concluded Boutte's injuries were not caused by his knees becoming entrapped in the knee bolsters. Hatsell postulated Boutte's right ankle broke because it was on the brakes when the accident occurred. ... In Dr. Hatsell's opinion Boutte would have sustained the same injuries to his ankles even if the restraint system suggested by his expert was installed. As a consequence, Nissan urges the alleged defective restraint system was not a *cause in fact* of Boutte's injury; and it should not have been assigned any fault in causing his injuries. ... We cannot say the trial judge manifestly erred in admitting Boutte's expert's testimony; and we are prevented from second-guessing the jury's findings based on this evidence.

* * *

The jury assessed Boutte with 84% fault. Boutte complains he should not have been assessed any fault. He argues his injuries would have been minor but for Nissan's defective lap belt.

* * *

It appears the jury accepted Nissan's evidence suggesting Boutte fell asleep while driving his vehicle after being awake for 21 hours, which caused him to travel off the road. On this record, we cannot say the jury manifestly erred in finding Boutte at fault for *causing the accident*. However, under our comparative fault system, Boutte's fault in *causing the accident* does not relieve Nissan of liability for the harm occasioned by the defect existing in the vehicle's restraint system.

When apportioning fault, the trier of fact shall consider the nature of the conduct of each party at fault and the extent of the causal relation between the conduct and the damages claimed. After considering the fault of the parties in causing Boutte's *harm,* we find Nissan has a greater degree of fault. ... When Boutte's vehicle left the roadway, he could not take any steps to prevent the risk of harm occasioned by the vehicle's impact with the concrete retaining wall and the ground below. Once the jury found the vehicle's restraint system was defective in design and this defect contributed to the injury Boutte sustained, Nissan's fault should have been assessed in relation to the *injury sustained* by Boutte rather than the *cause of the accident.* The record evidence convinces us that Nissan's fault was substantially greater than Boutte's in *causing injury* to his knee. Boutte's expert testified the injury he sustained would not have occurred or would have been reduced significantly if the vehicle's restraint system was not defective. The jury obviously found Boutte's expert's testimony on this issue more credible. Its factual findings, thus, compel that we reallocate fault in this case and assign Nissan 75% fault in causing Boutte's injury. Therefore, we amend the judgment to reduce Boutte's liability to 25% and increase Nissan's liability to 75%.

Boutte complains his lump sum award of $450,000 is inadequate to compensate him for the injuries he sustained. He argues after totalling the stipulated past medical expenses ($32,118.48), estimated possible future medical expenses ($15,000), estimated lost past earnings ($136,150), and estimated lost future earnings ($521,423), he has not been compensated for all of his estimated lost future earnings as well as pain and suffering.

* * *

Because we find the jury did not abuse its vast discretion in awarding damages, we are prevented from comparing the awards in the referenced cases with the present. Accordingly, we affirm the jury's lump sum damages award.

Case Questions

1. Apparently, the jury accepted Nissan's evidence that the plaintiff fell asleep at the wheel after twenty-one hours without sleep. Under these facts, because it was the plaintiff's negligence that set the accident in motion, is it fair to hold the defendant liable for any portion of the accident? Explain.
2. How did the court of appeal apportion fault? How would you have allocated fault if you were on the jury? Explain.

§ 10.3 Parties

Three classes of parties are involved in products liability cases: the product manufacturer, the seller, and the ultimate user.

Manufacturers and Sellers

The **product manufacturer** makes the defective product that gives rise to the entire products liability lawsuit. **Seller** includes anyone who is in the business of selling goods such as the one that is faulty. This includes the manufacturer as well as wholesalers and retailers. **Wholesalers** are businesses that buy and sell goods to **retailers**, which in turn sell the products to customers, usually individual persons.

The Ultimate User

When we buy a product, we are **purchasers**. In products liability law, however, the party injured by flawed merchandise need not be the original buyer. Instead, a member of the purchaser's family, or a friend of the buyer, could recover damages if hurt by a defective product. The key is whether it is reasonably foreseeable that the user would have utilized the product. This individual is called the **ultimate user**, because that person eventually used the product that caused an injury.

In products liability litigation, the ultimate user becomes the plaintiff who sues various defendants: the retailer, the wholesaler(s), and the manufacturer. The plaintiff uses a shotgun approach to products liability—namely, sue all the sellers. This may seem excessive, but the plaintiff has a logical explanation. The plaintiff sues all the sellers along the product distribution chain to ensure that one of them (probably the manufacturer)

TERMS

product manufacturer [†] The maker of a product which, if defective, gives rise to products liability.

seller A person who sells property he or she owns; a person who contracts for the sale of property, real or personal; a vendor.

wholesaler A person who sells goods at wholesale, as opposed to retail.

retailer A person engaged in the business of making retail sales of goods or merchandise.

purchaser A person who acquires property by purchase.

ultimate user [†] In products liability law, a person who is injured by a defective product. It must have been reasonably foreseeable that the injured party would use the defective product.

will have sufficient monies to pay a judgment. In tort law, this is called "going for the **deep pocket**." In other words, the plaintiff tries to sue defendants that have money and could satisfy a damages award. Figure 10-1 shows the product distribution chain between manufacturers, sellers, purchasers, and ultimate users. The deficient product passes through many hands before reaching its unfortunate victim.

Now that we have met the parties to products liability actions, it is time to investigate the elements of products liability.

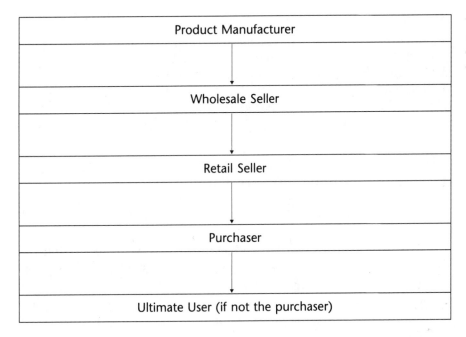

FIGURE 10-1
Product distribution chain

§ 10.4 Elements

Products liability is defined as strict, or absolute, liability for the seller or manufacturer of a defectively made product that injures a user of the item.

No Privity of Contract Requirement

Privity of contract is not required in products liability. The ultimate user need not have purchased the merchandise directly from the seller or manufacturer, although some states require that a sale of the product have occurred somewhere between the manufacturer and the ultimate user. However, it need not be a direct transaction between the two.

Negligence Is Irrelevant

Remember that the seller or manufacturer's negligence is irrelevant to strict liability. It does not matter how much care the seller or manufacturer used in making or maintaining the product. Every possible precaution could have been utilized, but that simply makes no difference. If the product was defective, and a user was harmed as a result, absolute liability applies—period.

A Typical Products Liability Formula

There are five elements of products liability, as defined by most state courts or statutes:

1. The defect must render the product unreasonably dangerous to use.
2. The seller or manufacturer must be in the business of selling products such as the flawed one(s).
3. The product cannot have been substantially changed between the time it left the seller or manufacturer's hands and the time it reached the ultimate user.
4. The defect must have proximately caused the ultimate user's injuries.
5. The ultimate user must have used the product properly, that is, in a way that the product was designed to be used.

In some jurisdictions, several additional elements are required:

6. The ultimate user must have been foreseeable (foreseeable plaintiffs theory).
7. The seller or manufacturer must have been responsible for the condition in which the product was maintained.
8. In a few states a sale of the product must have occurred. This could be a sale between the manufacturer and a wholesaler, or a wholesaler to a retailer, or a retailer to a customer. Basically, someone at some point had to buy the defective thing.

Restatement (Second) **Rule**

Section 402A of the *Restatement (Second) of Torts* contains fewer elements than those just discussed. It states:

> (1) One who sells any product in a defective condition unreasonably dangerous to the user or consumer or to his property is subject to liability for physical harm thereby caused to the ultimate user or consumer, or to his property, if
> (a) the seller is engaged in the business of selling such a product, and
> (b) it is expected to and does reach the user or consumer without substantial change in the condition in which it is sold.
> (2) The rule stated in Subsection (1) applies though
> (a) the seller has exercised all possible care in the preparation and sale of this product, and
> (b) the user or consumer has not bought the product from or entered into any contractual relation with the seller.

Subsection (2)(a) of § 402A indicates that the seller is liable regardless of the degree of care used to safeguard the public from injury by the defective product. Subsection (2)(b) states that privity of contract is unnecessary for strict liability to apply.

Unreasonably Dangerous Products

The product must be unreasonably dangerous as a result of its defect. Courts look to see if the product has become unreasonably threatening because of its defect. There are four types of unreasonably dangerous defects: (1) fault in product design; (2) error in product manufacturer or assembly; (3) improper product maintenance; and (4) manufacturer/seller's failure to warn.

Faulty Product Design

Products can be unreasonably dangerous if they have a defective design. Courts look to see whether the product is inherently dangerous because of a poor design but for which (that is, if such a defect did not exist) the product would have been safe to use. For instance, suppose a manufacturer assembles a toy with small, removable parts that can be swallowed by an infant, and thereby cause serious injury or death. The toy would be inherently dangerous, because the removable parts design would expose small children to the dangers of choking. This design defect makes the product unreasonably dangerous.

Courts decide faulty design (which make products unreasonably dangerous) in terms of three tests: the consumer contemplation test, the danger/utility test, and the state-of-the-art discoverability test.

Consumer Contemplation Test   In its Comments, *Restatement* § 402A states that a product is unreasonably dangerous if the consumer ordinarily would not appreciate the threat inherent in its design. This assumes that the ultimate user, like most people, understands that some products have dangers built in to their uses. The defect becomes unreasonably hazardous because the reasonable person would not be expected to anticipate the danger created by the faulty design. Legal commentators and courts have labelled this the **consumer contemplation test**.

For example, suppose that Nicholas bought a top-loading washing machine. He had to lean across the control panel to load his clothing inside. In doing so, he might accidentally press the start button with his body. This might start the machine while his hands were inside the washing drum. Nicholas could get his fingers caught, which would probably produce some nasty injuries.

Under the consumer contemplation test, would a reasonable person have anticipated this situation? Nicholas should have seen where the start button was located as he began loading his laundry into the machine. He knew that the machine could begin operating once this button was pushed. He should have known that his body could press against the switch and start the washer. In other words, he should have contemplated the risk inherent in the product's poor design. Thus, the product was not unreasonably dangerous under the consumer contemplation test.

Danger/Utility Test   Many courts and legal scholars have formulated another test to determine if a product is unreasonably dangerous by its design. This is called the **danger/utility test**. Under this standard, a product is unreasonably hazardous if the danger created by its design outweighs the benefits derived from its use. Consider the previous

---

TERMS

consumer contemplation test[†]   A theory in products liability concerning faulty product design that makes a product unreasonably dangerous. If a reasonable person would not have anticipated the danger created by the fault in the product, then the product is unreasonably dangerous.

danger/utility test[†]   A theory in products liability concerning faulty product design that makes a product unreasonably dangerous. Under this test, a product is unreasonably hazardous if the danger created by its design outweighs the benefits derived from its use.

washing machine example. The danger created by the poorly located button arises only if Nicholas happens inadvertently to press it with his body while his arms are inside the machine. Normally, he derives tremendous benefits from the device—he gets clean clothes. If he is cautious where he stands while loading, Nicholas should be able to avoid the accidental start risk. Using the danger/utility test, the washer is not unreasonably dangerous.

State-of-the-Art Discoverability Test If manufacturers could have discovered hazards created by defective product designs, using current, state-of-the-art technologies, then failure to do so makes a design-flawed product unreasonably dangerous. For example, suppose an automobile manufacturer installed ordinary glass in the small vent windows in a vehicle's doors. State-of-the-art crash testing would quickly indicate that this glass shatters into sharp, pointed fragments during a collision. This glass could seriously harm a driver or passenger. If the car maker did not discover this defect through modern testing procedures, then it would be strictly liable for any injuries caused by the fragile windows.

Error in Product Manufacture or Assembly

Safely designed products may become unreasonably dangerous as a result of improper assembly or manufacture. For instance, suppose a lawn-mower manufacturer failed to tighten the bolt holding the blade with sufficient torque. This could result in the blade flying off during use. Suppose this happened to a purchaser, who was severely cut by the blade. The lawn mower, although designed properly, became unreasonably dangerous because it was not suitably assembled. This is sometimes called an **assembly defect**.

Improper Product Maintenance

Sellers occasionally fail to maintain merchandise properly. When a buyer purchases the product, it might not function correctly because of a **maintenance defect**. For example, suppose a lawn and garden shop

TERMS

assembly defect [†] A theory in products liability concerning whether a defective product is unreasonably dangerous. Errors in product manufacture or assembly may render a product unreasonably hazardous despite a safe design.

maintenance defect [†] A theory in products liability concerning whether a defective product is unreasonably dangerous. If a seller fails to maintain a product properly, and the product later causes injury to the ultimate user, then the product was unreasonably dangerous.

sells chain saws. The chain on such a saw must be oiled frequently to operate appropriately. Oil is stored inside the saw in a special reservoir. Suppose the seller forgot to keep oil in its chain saws. While displaying one model to a customer, one of the seller's employees started a saw. Without oil, the saw froze up and the chain snapped, sailing through the air into the face of the surprised customer. The product was unreasonably dangerous because the seller did not properly maintain it.

The seller was negligent in forgetting to keep oil in the saw. Using the negligence formula, the seller would also be liable under negligence theory, as well as products liability.

Seller or Manufacturer's Failure to Warn

Sometimes products are unreasonably dangerous by their very nature. Lawn mowers, chain saws, poisons, and chemicals can be lethal if not cautiously used. However, purchasers may not always spot the obvious dangers in a product. Accordingly, manufacturers and sellers have an obligation to warn the ultimate user about inherent product dangers. Failure to warn could result in strict liability. For instance, look at almost any household appliance. Each one warns not to place hands or feet here or there, because of rotating knives, extremely hot surfaces, or the presence of scalding liquids. If one uses rat poison or insect sprays, the containers warn not to ingest the contents or get them in one's eyes. These are common examples of warnings that manufacturers and sellers use to avoid absolute liability. If the user is warned, then the user knows the risks. To apply, the warning must be in an obvious and noticeable place.

Business Requirement

Section 402A of the *Restatement (Second) of Torts,* and most common law and statutory versions of products liability, insist that the manufacturer or seller be engaged in the business of selling products such as the defective item(s) that injured the ultimate user. This requirement is easily met in most cases involving manufacturers, wholesalers, or retailers. Its purpose is to exclude products liability for people who are not in the business of selling such goods. For example, suppose Laurie sold Micron a vacuum cleaner, which she had bought from a department store. Because of a design defect, it exploded and injured Micron. Products liability is not intended to hold Laurie liable for this mishap, because she neither manufactured nor was in the business of selling such merchandise. Laurie, like Micron, is essentially an innocent bystander. Under products liability theory, she would not be liable for the defective product. Instead, Micron would sue the department store and manufacturer.

Substantially Unchanged Condition Requirement

For products liability to apply, the product must reach the ultimate user without any substantial changes in its condition from the time it left the manufacturer or seller. This is a crucial requirement. If something happened along the product distribution chain to alter the product (perhaps creating the unreasonably dangerous condition), then it would be unfair to hold manufacturers or sellers accountable for something they did not cause.

For instance, suppose Rachel purchased milk at a nearby grocery. The milk was fresh when she bought it. However, during the drive home, Rachel gets caught in traffic tangled because of an automobile accident. As a result, it takes her over an hour to arrive home. The temperature outside was 100 degrees, and her vehicle had no air conditioning. During this period, the milk spoiled. A visiting relative later drank the milk and suffered food poisoning. The relative wishes to sue the grocery. However, products liability would not apply, because the milk did not reach the ultimate user (Rachel's relative) in a substantially unchanged condition.

In some states, products liability common law or statutes require that, for strict liability to exist, the manufacturer or seller must be responsible for how the defective product was maintained. This seems logical. If the seller were not in any way responsible for how the product was assembled or stored (until it was sold or used), then that seller would have no control over the products it distributes. Products liability attempts to place the blame on the party responsible for the defect, so this requirement seems sensible to protect innocent sellers from absolute liability for product defects caused by someone else.

Proximate Cause

Recall the discussion of proximate cause in strict liability cases. That analysis also applies in products liability cases: the defective product must have been the proximate cause of the plaintiff's injury if liability is to attach.

Proper Use Requirement

The ultimate user must use the defective product properly in order for products liability to apply. In other words, the user must use the product for some function for which it was designed or intended to be used. For example, if Cliff wanted to climb onto his roof, he would probably use a ladder. If one of the ladder's rungs broke (because of the manufacturer's failure to use proper glues), and Cliff fell to the ground and broke various bones, he would be entitled to sue the manufacturer and seller under products liability. However, if he had used stacked vegetable crates to climb upon instead of a ladder, and these collapsed under his weight, Cliff could not sue under products liability. Vegetable crates are neither designed nor intended for people to climb on. They are supposed to be used to store produce.

Foreseeable Plaintiffs Theory

In some jurisdictions, it must have been reasonably foreseeable that the ultimate user would use the defective product. This is called the zone of danger (or foreseeable plaintiffs) theory in negligence. Some ultimate users are not reasonably foreseeable. For example, it is highly improbable that a one-year-old infant would come into contact with industrial cleaners used in manufacturing processes. Such a person could not be a reasonably foreseeable ultimate user of such a product. However, members of a product purchaser's family, or the buyer's neighbors, could be foreseeable users of defective goods. How many times in one's family has more than one individual used an appliance or tool? Have you ever borrowed products from your neighbors?

Consider Diana, who borrowed a pen from a classmate with which to take notes during the lecture. The pen had a manufacturing defect that made the plastic casing unusually brittle. While writing, the pen shatters in Diana's hand, and she is cut by the many tiny fragments. Was Diana a reasonably foreseeable ultimate user? Yes. Classmates often share pens, pencils, notebooks, and many other products during classes. It was reasonably foreseeable that someone might borrow a pen to take notes in class. Diana could sue the pen manufacturer under products liability as a foreseeable plaintiff.

Having analyzed the various elements of products liability, we may now proceed to apply the theory to hypotheticals.

HYPOTHETICALS

Burgess Primer Corporation manufactures paint. Eleanor bought Burgess's "Supreme Ease" paint at Painter Place, a local retailer that carried Burgess products. Eleanor selected various colors, which store employees mixed together. While applying the paint indoors, Eleanor noticed that the paint stung her skin as it splattered from her roller. Apparently, Eleanor was allergic to certain oils that had been mixed into the paint. When she showered later that day, she noticed that the paint had left her arms and face mottled with burn marks. Many of these became infected. Medical tests indicated that a significant percentage of the population suffered this allergic reaction to the paint mix.

Are Burgess Primer Corporation (as manufacturer) and Painter Place (as seller) strictly liable for an unreasonably dangerous product? Applying the generic formula, first ask if the defect made the product unreasonably dangerous. The fault here is product assembly (i.e., how the paint was mixed). Using the consumer contemplation test, would a reasonable person anticipate that he or she might be allergic to paint oils? This is not an obvious hazard that an ordinary person would detect from a can of paint. Thus, the product's dangerous condition rendered it unreasonably dangerous to the ultimate user, Eleanor. Under the danger/utility test, the hazard in using the product outweighed the benefits, as many people were allergic to the particular mix.

Both Burgess and Painter Place were engaged in the business of selling paint. The product reached the ultimate user, Eleanor, in the same condition as it left the retailer. Also, Eleanor used the paint properly, in a way in which paint is intended to be used. It was reasonably foreseeable that Eleanor would use the paint she bought at a retail store, so she is a foreseeable plaintiff. Both Burgess and the retailer were responsible for how the paint was maintained. Further, a sale occurred (for those jurisdictions requiring it). So far, even with the extra elements, it seems as though strict liability will favor Eleanor.

But who was the proximate cause of Eleanor's injuries? Burgess manufactured the paint base and the various colors. However, the paint did not become unreasonably dangerous until Painter Place's employees mixed it. Therefore, Burgess, as manufacturer, did not proximately cause Eleanor's injuries. Painter Place was clearly the proximate cause of the harm. Proximate cause is a crucial determination, because it absolves Burgess from strict products liability. Painter Place is absolutely liable for Eleanor's injuries under products liability theory.

■ ■ ■

Consider another hypothetical. Fairfield Seed Company sold sweet corn seeds to retail variety stores. Fairfield had erroneously treated the seeds with a toxic insecticide used for field corn seeds. As the corn grew, this chemical was absorbed into the ears of sweet corn. When the gardeners (who had bought the seed from the retailers) ate the corn, they became ill.

Would the retail variety stores and Fairfield be strictly liable for the gardeners' injuries from an unreasonably dangerous product? Apply either the consumer contemplation test or the danger/utility test. The reasonable gardener would not expect sweet corn seeds to be treated with a poison harmful to humans. The risks far outweigh the benefits. Both Fairfield and the retailers were in the business of selling garden seeds. Fairfield improperly prepared the seeds, which would be a manufacturing defect. The dangerous seeds reached the ultimate users in the same condition as when they left the manufacturer. Fairfield was responsible for the condition of the product. Fairfield's insecticide coating proximately caused the gardeners' injuries, because the ultimate users ate the contaminated ears of corn grown from the poisoned seed. The gardeners used the product as it was designed (i.e., to grow corn to eat) and were foreseeable plaintiffs. All the elements of products liability have been met; thus, Fairfield is strictly liable for the gardeners' injuries caused by the poison corn.

What about the retailers' liability, however? There are two critical queries here. First, did the retailers proximately cause the ultimate users' injuries? Second, were the retailers responsible for the condition in which the defective product was maintained?

The retailers did not contaminate the seeds. The seeds came in sealed packages, which the retailers simply stocked on shelves for customers to pick up and purchase. Thus, the retailers did nothing to proximately cause the gardeners' injuries. Furthermore, the retailers had no control over the manufacturing processes that contaminated the seeds. They were not responsible for how the seeds were prepared. The retailers maintained the condition of the seeds just as they were supposed to, namely, by stocking their shelves with sealed packages. Under this analysis, the retailers would not be strictly liable for the harm to the gardeners.

The Case of the Saturday Night Special (The Sequel)

In the last discussion of this case, the D.C. Court of Appeals ruled that the sale of a "Saturday Night Special" handgun was not an ultrahazardous activity for purposes of absolute liability. The appellants also argued products liability theory, but as in the first round, the court once again guns down this proposition, exempting the manufacturer from strict liability. Reread the earlier excerpt in Chapter 9 for the facts and procedural history.

DELAHANTY

v.

HINCKLEY

District of Columbia Court of Appeals
564 A.2d 758 (D.C. 1989)
October 11, 1989
Ferren, Associate Judge

Appellants advanced three legal theories for holding the gun manufacturers liable in these circumstances: negligence, strict products liability under the *Restatement (Second) of Torts* § 402A (1965), and a "social utility" claim apparently based on strict liability for abnormally dangerous activities ... . Appellants alleged in their complaint that: Hinckley needed an easily concealable weapon for his assassination attempt; the gun manufactured by [the defendant] is an easily concealable, inexpensive handgun; the gun is poorly constructed, unreliable, and therefore not useful for legitimate purposes such as military use, target practice, or self-defense; as a result of the gun's low price, it is used for criminal

purposes; and the manufacturers knew of the gun's criminal uses.

* * *

Appellants first claim the manufacturers of the gun used by Hinckley are strictly liable for sale of a defective product. They rely on *Restatement (Second) of Torts* § 402A, which imposes liability for the sale of "any product in a defective condition unreasonably dangerous to the user or consumer ... ". We join the other courts which have rejected the application of this theory in circumstances such as these. Appellants point to no malfunction of the gun caused by improper design or manufacture that led to Thomas Delahanty's injuries. Instead, appellants argue that the manufacturers had a duty to warn of the dangers of criminal misuse of the gun. There is no duty to warn, however, "when the danger, or potentiality of danger, is generally known and recognized." *Restatement (Second) of Torts*, § 402A comment j. Because hazards of firearms are obvious, the manufacturer had no duty to warn.

Case Questions

1. Suppose that, when Hinckley fired at the president, the handgun had exploded because of a defective firing pin. Suppose also that Delahanty had been injured by the flying shrapnel. Would Delahanty's products liability claim against the manufacturer have succeeded under these facts? Would Delahanty have been the ultimate user under these facts? Explain.
2. What if the bullets that struck Delahanty had been defectively manufactured, so that they exploded upon impact. Would Delahanty then have had a products liability claim against the bullet manufacturer? Would Delahanty have been the ultimate user under these facts? Explain.

Figure 10-2 summarizes the elements of products liability, under both the generic, common law formula and the *Second Restatement* § 402A.

§ 10.5 Defenses

There are several defenses to absolute liability. Some of those defenses also apply to products liability.

Contributory or Comparative Negligence Not a Defense

Courts have generally held that contributory negligence is not a defense in products liability cases. This seems logical, because contributory negligence is a defense to negligence and negligence has no place in strict liability cases. Allowing the ultimate user's contributory negligence to bar absolute liability for a defective product would be the legal equivalent of mixing apples and oranges.

Ultimate User's Misuse of Product

Saying that contributory or comparative negligence is not a defense is not to say, however, that the plaintiff (the ultimate user) can use a defective product irresponsibly or wantonly. The ultimate user is expected to use the product properly, as it was intended to be used. This is an element of products liability, although some courts consider product misuse to be a defense. If the ultimate user misuses a defective product and is injured as a consequence, his or her products liability claim against the manufacturer or seller will be denied, because the harm resulted

Typical Common Law or Statutory Formula	Comparison with Restatement (2d) of Torts § 402A	Additional Elements (in Some States)
Defect makes product unreasonably dangerous	Same	Ultimate user must be reasonably foreseeable (foreseeable plaintiffs theory)
Manufacturer or seller must be in business of selling products such as the defective one(s)	Same	Manufacturer or seller must be responsible for condition in which defective product was maintained
Defective product cannot have been substantially changed from time it left manufacturer or seller until it was used by ultimate user	Same	A sale of the defective product must have occurred
Defect must have proximately caused the ultimate user's injuries	Not included	
Ultimate user must have used the product properly (in a way in which it was designed or intended to be used)	Not included	
Implicit	Degree of care that manufacturer or seller used in making or maintaining the defective product is immaterial; also, no contractual relationship or sale is required	Some states, by statute or common law, require a sale

from the plaintiff's misuse of the product. This defense is effective even though the misused product was defective.

Some product uses may be unusual, but are not actually misuses. For example, chairs are designed to be sat on. Yet how often have you used a chair as a stepping stool to reach something stored on a high shelf? Using a chair as a ladder is not a misuse of the product, because it is reasonably foreseeable that one might use a chair for such a purpose. In other words, reasonably foreseeable uses, even though the product may not originally have been intended or designed for such functions, are acceptable uses. A products liability claim would not be barred if the ultimate user used the product in a reasonably foreseeable fashion.

Removal of Safety Devices

Adult smokers commonly remove the "childproof" safety devices on butane lighters, increasing the risk of injury.

Employees who are under great pressure to produce a lot while working on an assembly line or in a factory may deliberately dismantle the very safety device that is there to protect them. If the safety device is removed, a machine might run faster than was intended, or it may become easier to get to the interior of the machine when it jams or needs cleaning. For these injured parties, a products liability cause of action will not be available, because the product was misused and altered.

Unfortunately, you will frequently see misuse of products by injured parties who will tell you that they removed the guard or safety device from a machine at work.

Practical Applications

Assumption of Risk

Assumption of risk, however, is usually accepted as a defense. The ultimate user assumes the risk of being injured by a hazardous product in three ways: (1) by discovering the defect but disregarding it and using the product anyway; (2) by failing to properly maintain the product; and (3) by failing to follow instructions or heed warnings for safe product use.

Ignoring a Discovered Defect

Recall the basic definition of assumption of risk. **Assumption of risk** is the plaintiff's voluntary assumption of a known risk with a full appreciation of the dangers involved in facing that risk. In products liability cases, the plaintiff is the ultimate user. The ultimate user assumes the risk by discovering a product defect and then ignoring the risks involved and using the product anyway. For example, suppose Steve discovers that his circular saw blade is bent. The warp would cause the blade to rub against the saw's protective sheathing when it rotated. This would create sparks, which could burn him. Steve decides that the risk is worth taking and he uses the saw. Sparks fly into his eyes (because he does not wear protective eyewear). Steve assumed a known risk with a full comprehension of the possible hazardous consequences.

Failure to Properly Maintain Product

Ultimate users cannot recover in products liability if they failed to properly maintain the product for safe uses. Courts often characterize this as an assumption-of-risk defense. The circular saw example illustrates this type of assumption of risk. Steve did not maintain the saw so that it could be safely used. The blade was bent. Before using it, he should have replaced the damaged blade with a new blade, or at least had the bad blade repaired. It is the ultimate user's responsibility to maintain the merchandise for safe uses.

Consider another illustration. Suppose Gil failed to put motor oil in his automobile. If he proceeded to drive for hundreds of miles, his motor would undoubtedly burn out. He failed to properly maintain the vehicle by putting in the suitable amount of lubrication. Gil could not recover under products liability from the manufacturer or seller. He assumed the risk of ruining his car by not properly maintaining it.

Failure to Follow Instructions or Heed Warnings

How often have you used a product without first reading the instructions? Surely everyone has done this. Most of the time the products we use are sufficiently simple that we can use them properly after a quick glance. With a complex product, however, following instructions could

---

TERMS

assumption of risk   The legal principle that a person who knows and deliberately exposes himself or herself to a danger assumes responsibility for the risk, rather than the person who actually created the danger. Assumption of risk is often referred to as voluntary assumption of risk. It is a defense to negligence.

prevent injuries. Products liability plaintiffs often argue that defectively designed products are unreasonably dangerous. However, sometimes these plaintiffs did not follow the manufacturer's instructions for product use and as a consequence were hurt. Also, an ultimate user occasionally disregards manufacturer's warnings that specifically point out the dangers inherent in the product design. Both of these actions are types of assumption of risk.

Assume, in the saw example, that the manufacturer printed on the side of the saw, "WARNING! DO NOT USE IF BLADE IS BENT!" If Steve disregarded this warning and were hurt from the bent saw, he could not recover damages for a defectively designed product. Steve assumed the risk by ignoring the warning.

Suppose, instead of a bent blade, that the blade was merely loose. The instructions included directions for blade tightening. If Steve did not read or follow these directions, and he was hurt because the blade flew off while he was using the saw, he could not recover damages under products liability. Steve assumed the risk by failing to follow instructions to properly maintain the product.

The Case of the Toxic Fire Paint

Product misuse does not always require an unusual use of an item. Sometimes the product may be applied to achieve the results for which it was intended, but the actual operation of the item is inappropriate and causes the user's injuries. As the following case illustrates, the paint was used as paint is ordinarily intended. However, the way in which the paint was applied was the misuse. Nor were the firefighters reasonably foreseeable plaintiffs. Although one cannot help but sympathize with the plaintiffs, the Fourth Circuit's analysis of products liability theory reaches the correct result.

HIGGINS
v.
E.I. DUPONT DE NEMOURS & CO.
U.S. Court of Appeals, Fourth Circuit
863 F.2d 1162 (4th Cir. 1988)
December 23, 1988
Murnaghan, Circuit Judge

Plaintiffs Higgins and Jones appeal from the district court's order granting summary judgment in favor of defendant, E.I. DuPont de Nemours & Co., Inc. ("DuPont"), regarding their survival actions. Plaintiffs also appeal the dismissal of their wrongful death actions ... .

Plaintiffs brought the actions to recover for the deaths of their children and fetuses who allegedly died from the teratogenic effect of chemicals contained in Imron paint. Each of the husbands had worked for the Baltimore City Fire Department in the same fire house, where they used Imron paint to "touch up" the fire engines. Plaintiffs claimed that the deaths were caused by glycol ether acetates and lead supplied by Dow and contained in Imron paint which was developed, manufactured and distributed by DuPont. DuPont advertised Imron paint for sale through distributors for use by industrial professionals, such as fleet truck and transit systems, body shops, marinas, car dealers and manufacturers of aircraft, fire engines, heavy duty construction equipment, and utility vans. Imron was sold and delivered by DuPont to C & R Paint Supply, Inc.

("C & R"), which in turn, sold and delivered the product to the Key Highway repair yard of the Baltimore City Fire Department, where fire apparatus was regularly painted and repainted. C & R never sold or delivered Imron paint directly to the City firehouses nor did it directly solicit business from the Fire Department through sales representatives. Furthermore, it is undisputed that C & R understood that the City's fire vehicles were repaired and painted only at the Key Highway repair shop. Nothing suggests that C & R even suspected that Imron paint was sent out to the individual fire houses until 1985 when it received an unusual request from the City Fire Department for some empty quart containers.

However, from 1979 to 1985, the City Fire Department's Key Highway facility redistributed quantities of Imron in both marked (i.e., with DuPont's labels affixed) and unmarked one-gallon paint cans, coffee cans, or glass jars to the plaintiffs for their use in touching up fire apparatus in the firehouse. The city did not provide the plaintiffs with separate instructions or warnings as to the use of Imron, or with protective clothes to wear while applying the Imron paint.

Each of the labels affixed to the Imron paint products which C & R sold to the City Fire Department stated in clear lettering on the front of the cans:

> FOR INDUSTRIAL USE ONLY by professional, trained personnel. Not for sale to or use by the general public.

This warning was accompanied by instruction on the back of the label which required the use of a supplied-air respirator, eye protection, gloves, protective clothing and adequate ventilation. Furthermore, C & R supplied Material Safety Data Sheets ("MSDS") to the City Fire Department which repeated the safety precautions … . However, none of the information constituting a warning specifically warned of the possible teratogenic effects of the product.

* * *

The district court found that the firefighters were not "professional, trained personnel" for the obvious use of Imron products, i.e., painting. That they were professional firefighters and not professional painters was evidence from the manner in which they mixed and applied the paint. The evidence shows that the firefighters painted in their fire department work uniforms, mixed the paint in cups and sometimes with their fingers and did not heed any of the label precautions which a professional painter would have taken seriously. We agree with the district court that the labels were adequate enough to warn plaintiffs that they were not sufficiently well-trained to use Imron paint. Therefore, DuPont did not distribute a product which was unreasonably dangerous when used for a purpose and in a manner that is reasonably foreseeable, i.e., for industrial use by trained painters. Imron paint was not defective.

Because plaintiffs did not fall into the class of foreseeable users of Imron paint which DuPont had specifically circumscribed to limit its potential liability, the district court held that had the City heeded the warning and not redistributed Imron paint in unlabeled cans to the firehouse, plaintiffs would not have been injured. Likewise, plaintiffs could not complain when they failed to observe the warnings on the Imron paint cans which the City redistributed to them in the original, labeled cans. The district court held that such a misuse of the product barred recovery as a matter of law. Although our sympathy rests with the plaintiffs who have suffered unspeakable losses, we must agree with the district court that plaintiffs' real complaint lies with the City Fire Department and not DuPont.

* * *

Misuse of a product may bar recovery against the manufacturer where the misuse is the sole proximate cause of damage, or where it is the intervening or superseding cause. Product misuse is defined as use of a product in a manner that could not reasonably be foreseen by the defendant. Reasonably foreseeable uses include " 'the incidental and attendant consequences that accompany normal use.' " The district court found that the normal use of Imron paint was restricted to industrial purposes for which professional painters, who appreciated the attendant risks, were required. The district court held that DuPont could not reasonably foresee that either the City would redistribute Imron paint in either labeled or unlabeled containers or that plaintiffs, who were amateur painters, would use Imron paint after reading the various conspicuous warnings contained on the labeled cannisters [*sic*] which did reach them. … [W]e still agree with the basic reasoning of the district court, … that the firefighters were not professional, trained personnel. Plaintiffs failed to provide any contradictory evidence. DuPont had a right to rely on its warning to cut off the chain of causation and to insulate it from becoming a virtual insurer against all injuries arising from its product.

Affirmed.

Case Questions

1. Was it not reasonably foreseeable that Imron paint might be shifted into unmarked containers for easier use? Why or why not? What is the significance of DuPont's labeling for this issue?
2. Two of the multiple defendants in this case were the mayor and city council of Baltimore, Maryland. Do you believe the plaintiffs would succeed against them, under respondeat superior, for the torts of the Baltimore City Fire Department? Explain the tort theories that the plaintiffs could successfully apply.

Defenses are a defective product manufacturer's best friend. Even if every products liability element is satisfied, defenses can spare the seller from the wrath of strict liability, as the following hypotheticals illustrate.

HYPOTHETICALS

Douglas owns a tire repair shop. He sells new tires from all the national brands and repairs old tires. Marjorie came into the shop one day with a punctured tire. Douglas agreed that it could be patched and repaired, but he instructed Marjorie to use the tire only as a spare for emergencies. He recommended that she purchase a reconditioned tire for regular use. Marjorie insisted that Douglas put her patched tire back onto her car. Douglas warned that the patch might not hold up over long-term, constant use. Nevertheless, he had the repaired tire re-mounted on her car. Later the following month, while Marjorie was driving to work, the patch failed and the tire blew out. Marjorie's car ran off the road, collided with a telephone pole, and injured her.

Marjorie's products liability claim against Douglas would fail. Marjorie assumed the risk of using the patched tire contrary to Douglas's specific instructions and warnings. She voluntarily assumed a known risk with a full appreciation of the hazards involved. The defense of assumption of risk would protect Douglas from strict products liability.

■ ■ ■

The Oasis Sprinkler Company manufactures underground lawn sprinkler systems. Oasis offers a do-it-yourself kit for handy customers. Josephine purchased one of these kits. The detailed assembly instructions directed her to attach the sprinkler heads to the underground pipe using a special copper clamp. "Be certain to crimp the clamp with pliers to ensure a snug connection," read the instructions. Josephine did not crimp the clamps, although she did put them in place. Later, while the sprinkler system was in use, one of the sprinkler heads flew into the air under the force of the water pressure. It struck Josephine's daughter, Janice, in the forehead, causing a wound that required several stitches to close the cut.

Could Janice and Josephine win a products liability lawsuit against Oasis? Not if the assumption-of-risk defense can be successfully applied. Josephine disregarded the manufacturer's specific instructions for assembling the product. However, Oasis failed to warn about the possible dangers that could occur if the clamps were not crimped. So we have a manufacturer's failure to warn situation versus a user's failure to follow instructions defense. Which wins? Is the manufacturer's failure to warn sufficient to hold Oasis liable for an unreasonably dangerous product? Or is Josephine's failure to obey instructions a complete defense under assumption of risk?

The key to this problem is whether a reasonable ultimate user (i.e., a reasonable person) would have anticipated that the sprinkler heads might fly off under high water pressure if the clamps were not crimped. Most people know that water carried through pipes is under great pressure, which makes the water a powerful, focused force. A loose connection could easily give way and send a sprinkler head flying in any direction. Reasonable persons know this from everyday experience with garden hoses or plumbing. Josephine should have anticipated this risk; therefore, it is considered a known risk that she voluntarily assumed, despite a full appreciation of the dangers involved. Assumption of risk will overpower the manufacturer's failure to warn of this particular hazard. Accordingly, the defense of assumption of risk will protect Oasis from strict products liability.

■ ■ ■

One last hypothetical illuminates the misuse situation. The Comfort King Corporation manufactures recliner chairs. When Herbert visited a friend, who owned such a recliner, Herbert noticed that a light bulb was burned out in his friend's hallway. He used the recliner as a ladder to reach the light fixture. As he stood on the chair, it reclined, sending him sprawling across the hall and smashing his head into a closet doorknob. Herbert thought the chair was unreasonably dangerous, so he sued Comfort King under products liability.

Comfort King, however, shrugged off the lawsuit. The product misuse defense was there to protect the company from strict liability. Recliner chairs are not designed or intended to be used as ladders or stoops. After all, recliners *recline*. They cannot be safely stood upon for that reason. Herbert should have reasonably anticipated the danger created by misusing the chair in this fashion. Herbert's misuse of the product is a solid products liability defense for Comfort King.

Figure 10-3 lists the defenses to products liability.

Contributory Negligence	Assumption of Risk	Product Misuse by Ultimate User
Not considered a defense in products liability cases	Ultimate user's voluntary assumption of known risk with full appreciation of dangers involved	If ultimate user misuses the product, then he or she cannot recover under products liability
	Occurs when ultimate user ignores a discovered defect and uses the product while knowing of its dangerous condition	Reasonably foreseeable uses are *not* misuses of products
	Occurs when ultimate user fails to properly maintain product	
	Occurs when ultimate user fails to follow instructions or heed warnings for safe product use	

FIGURE 10-3
Defenses of products liability

§ 10.6 Comparison to Contract Law Warranties

Products liability has roots in contract law warranties. A *warranty* is a guarantee that a product seller gives a buyer. The guarantee states that the product will perform to certain standards or will not break down over a period of time. This warranty is part of the contract between the buyer and the seller.

If the products fails to comply with the guarantee, the warranty is *breached*. This **breach of warranty** is also a violation of the parties' agreement that the product shall remain in a particular condition while used.

TERMS

breach of warranty   The violation of an express warranty or implied warranty.

The Uniform Commercial Code (UCC) is a model (suggested) statute concerning the sale of goods that has been adopted by all states. One of its provisions, § 2-314, concerns implied warranties that all sellers of goods provide with their goods as to the goods being "merchantable," which means that all goods must be of fair average quality and fit for their ordinary purpose. This warranty protects the buyer against defective goods.

Another provision of the UCC, § 2-315, provides that if the seller knows of a particular purpose for which the buyer is buying, then the goods must be fit for that purpose.

These two provisions have allowed liability for injuries sustained as a result of defects in products. Because the UCC has been adopted by all states, decisions on these points tend to be congruent nationwide.

Similarities Between Products Liability and Breach of Warranty

Breach of warranty is similar to products liability in that both involve strict liability. For some reason, many contract law textbooks fail to notice this. If the product fails to comply with the seller's warranty, then that is breach of warranty. The seller is liable for this breach—period ... just like absolute liability. If the seller breaches the warranty, then the seller is liable to the buyer for damages for breach of warranty (i.e., breach of contract).

Products liability and breach of warranty are also similar in that both typically involve defective and unreasonably dangerous products. In almost every products liability lawsuit, the plaintiff's complaint will plead both causes of action, assuming that the defendant warranted the product to the plaintiff.

Like products liability, many product warranty statutes or modern common law cases permit the reasonably foreseeable ultimate user (other than the purchaser) to recover damages for breach of warranty. In contract law, this is intended to extend the agreement to include (most often) the buyer's family. So, even under contract law, the ancient privity-of-contract requirement has been loosened.

Difference Between Products Liability and Breach of Warranty

The obvious difference between breach of warranty and products liability is the *contract requirement*. For breach of warranty, there must be an agreement between the seller and the buyer which includes the warranty, either explicitly or implicitly. Under products liability, no contract is required. This is clearly set forth in *Restatement (Second) of Torts* § 402A, and the *MacPherson* case. Without a contract requirement, products liability can apply in many more cases than can breach of warranty, which is usually limited to litigation between product buyers and sellers.

A detailed discussion of warranty law is beyond the scope of this text, but the reader will probably study breach of warranty in business law courses. It is an important part of contract law and deserves close attention.

Summary

Products liability became a distinct tort theory in the early 1960s. For more than 100 years, American and English courts combined contract law and negligence to hold manufacturers and sellers liable for injuries caused by defective products. Finally, in 1962, strict liability was applied to such cases. As a matter of public policy, products liability places the risk of harm created by unreasonably dangerous products upon those who make and sell them. The law presumes that the innocent user should not be forced to bear the costs associated with harmful products.

The parties in products liability cases include the manufacturer, other sellers (such as retailers or wholesalers), and the consumers, or ultimate users, of the product. Often the ultimate user is a member of the product buyer's family or a neighbor or friend. By looking at a product's distribution chain, it becomes clear how the product leaves the manufacturer and reaches the ultimate user.

Products liability is strict, or absolute, liability. No privity of contract is required between the manufacturer or seller and the ultimate user. The manufacturer or seller's negligence is irrelevant. The product must contain a defect rendering it unreasonably dangerous to use. This fault may arise in a design defect, by improper product maintenance, or by the manufacturer or seller's failure to warn the buyer of hazards in using the product. The manufacturer or seller must be engaged in the business of selling products like the defective one. The product cannot be substantially changed from the time it left the manufacturer or seller and reached the ultimate user. The defect must proximately cause the ultimate user's injuries. The ultimate user must use the product in a way in which it was designed or intended.

Contributory negligence is not a defense to products liability. Product misuse is a defense, although it is often included as an element in the products liability formula. If the ultimate user misuses the product, even though the product is defective, the manufacturer and seller will not be strictly liable for the harm. Assumption of risk is another defense to products liability. If the ultimate user ignores a discovered defect and, by using the product, is hurt, the user has assumed the risk, and the manufacturer or seller would not be strictly liable. The same is true if the ultimate user fails to properly maintain a product, follow instructions, or heed warnings for safe use.

Products liability is similar to contract law warranties. First, both involve absolute liability. Second, both involve defective or unreasonably dangerous products. Third, under many warranty statutes and common law, the ultimate user is protected even if he or she was not the original product purchaser. Products liability is different from warranty law because, for breach of warranty, there must be a contract between the manufacturer or seller and the buyer.

Review Questions

1. What are the public policy objectives behind products liability? How are they similar to the public policy objectives mentioned in Chapter 9 for "regular" strict liability?

2. How did modern products liability evolve? What were some of the landmark cases during the nineteenth and early twentieth centuries that led these developments? What was the imminent danger exception? It was an exception to what rule?

3. How is negligence relevant to products liability? Is privity of contract required? Who are the parties in products liability cases? Who is the ultimate user?

4. Discuss the elements of a typical products liability formula. How are these different from the elements in *Restatement (Second) of Torts* § 402A? How are they similar?

5. How would you define an unreasonably dangerous product? What is faulty product design? Explain the consumer contemplation test, the danger/utility test, and the state-of-the-art discoverability test. Why are these tests important?

6. Explain how errors in product manufacture or assembly make a product unreasonably dangerous for products liability purposes.

7. In products liability, what role does improper product maintenance play? Manufacturer or seller's failure to warn of product hazards?

8. Define (a) the business requirement, (b) the substantially unchanged condition requirement, and (c) the proper use requirement. Why are they relevant to products liability? Does proximate cause play any role? What about foreseeable plaintiffs theory?

9. Is contributory negligence a defense to products liability? Why or why not? What about product misuse?

10. Explain how assumption of risk operates as a defense to products liability. Identify the three ways in which the ultimate user assumes the risk of using a defective product.

Projects

1. Which version of products liability do your state courts follow? Is it different from, or identical to, the *Second Restatement*'s § 402A?

2. Has your state legislature enacted any products liability statutes? If so, how are they similar to the elements discussed in this chapter? How are they different?

3. How does a products liability case differ from a negligence case?

IIII
CHAPTER 11

SPECIAL TORT ACTIONS

All that makes existence valuable to any one depends on the enforcement of restraints upon the actions of other people.

— *John Stuart Mill*

§ 11.1 Introduction

You have now reached an area of torts that is often overlooked in paralegal education. These forgotten torts are just as important as the major torts of negligence and strict liability.

Special tort actions include nuisance, which involves issues of both tort and property law, and negligence per se, which is often a statutory tort. Tort litigation also often includes wrongful death actions, which are usually associated with negligence claims. Within the past thirty years, a new, related tort, *wrongful life,* has emerged in the appellate courts. Another rapidly developing area of modern tort law is so-called toxic torts, which involve hazardous substances, toxic waste disposal, and other environmental issues.

This chapter investigates these special tort actions. Much of our discussion will incorporate negligence and absolute liability theories. Specifically, the following torts and issues are discussed:

- Private nuisances

- "Coming to the nuisance" defense

- Public nuisances

- Nuisances per se

- Nuisance remedies: abatement, damages, and injunctions

- Negligence per se

- Wrongful death statutes

- Wrongful life actions.

§ 11.2 Nuisances

A **nuisance** is an unreasonable or unlawful use of one's real property that injures another person or interferes with another person's use of his or her real property. Nuisances are defined by common law and by statute. There are two types of nuisances: private and public. Occasionally, the same activity constitutes both a private and a public nuisance. These are sometimes called *mixed nuisances*.

Private Nuisance Defined

A **private nuisance** occurs when someone (1) uses his or her land in such a way as to (2) unreasonably and substantially interfere with (3) another person's use and enjoyment of his or her land. The tortfeasor (defendant) is the land user whose activities offend his or her neighbors. The neighboring land user(s) (plaintiff[s]) sue the tortfeasor for engaging in a private nuisance. The second element in commission of a private nuisance, unreasonable and substantial interference, is the most susceptible of interpretation.

Unreasonable and Substantial Defined

Whether the tortfeasor's use of real estate is unreasonable and substantially interferes with another's land use is usually defined in terms of offensiveness. The critical question is: How offensive is the tortfeasor's land use? Offensiveness is determined by applying the reasonable person standard. Would a reasonable person with ordinary sensitivities find the tortfeasor's land use unreasonably offensive? If so, then the tortfeasor has unreasonably and substantially interfered with the plaintiff's

---

TERMS

nuisance Anything a person does that annoys or disturbs another person in his or her use, possession, or enjoyment of his or her property, or which renders the ordinary use or possession of the property uncomfortable. What constitutes a nuisance in a particular case depends upon numerous factors, including the type of neighborhood in which the property is located, the nature of the act or acts complained of, their proximity to the persons alleging injury or damage, their frequency or continuity, and the nature and extent of the resulting injury, damage, or annoyance.

private nuisance A nuisance that threatens injury to one or just a few persons; a nuisance that violates only private rights and produces damages to one or no more than a few persons.

|||| PROFESSIONAL PROFILE ||||

"Winning toxic tort cases!," says Kina Jackson, is the most rewarding aspect of her work as a paralegal at the Environmental Protection Bureau of her state's Department of Law. She obtained her position five years ago after scoring well on a civil service examination. Her chief responsibilities include drafting pleadings and performing legal research. "On a typical day," Jackson says, "I am asked by attorneys to find cases that support arguments they will make."

Born in Salt Lake City, Utah, Jackson is married with two children. She attended college where she received her A.A.S.—paralegal degree. She has served on the paralegal advisory committee at the college for years.

Jackson says a good educational background includes developing organizational skills, writing proficiency, and research skills. "In addition, it is very helpful to be able to narrow a question of law and avoid wasting time researching outside the scope of inquiry," she says. However, she emphasizes, "It should be well understood by prospective paralegals that the most valuable training you will receive is the training you give yourself."

Jackson wishes that she had had more exposure to basic research skills other than merely legal research. "I wish I had learned more about legislative intent and how inflexible judicial schedules can be. The latter is responsible for many late hours of working, long after others go home."

"Choose a field of law that you enjoy and agree with philosophically," Jackson says. She admonishes paralegals to avoid jobs where they must work with people who hold ideals, values, morals, or politics that are contrary to the goals of your company or agency. "You won't be happy," she says. "Learn to be good at what you do because once you land the job, the learning has just begun."

use and enjoyment of his or her land. Therefore, the tortfeasor has committed a private nuisance.

Community Standard

The reasonable person standard is normally a community standard. In other words, it asks how people living in the community in which the alleged nuisance is taking place would react to the activity. This *reasonable community* reaction supposedly evaluates whether the tortfeasor's land use is unreasonable and a substantial interference with neighboring land uses. The finder of fact, usually a jury, makes this determination.

Use and Enjoyment

Use and enjoyment is a term of art in nuisance law. The two are always used together. The term *use* would be sufficient, but *enjoyment* imparts an emotional aspect to nuisance law. The alleged nuisance activity ruins the pleasure neighbors gain through the ways in which they use their real estate. This seems to make the tortfeasor's activities more blameworthy.

Classic Examples

There are many common examples of private nuisances to which to apply the elements just explained. These situations can be classified in broad categories: (1) physical effects on land; (2) health hazards or offending sensibilities; and (3) unwanted associations with neighboring uses.

Physical Effects on Land

Neighboring land users often complain if a tortfeasor's use of realty creates constant vibrations, pollution of water or soil, destruction of crops, flooding, excessive clutter, or unwanted excavations.

Ground Vibrations   For example, suppose a manufacturing plant next door to Jenny's house operates twenty-four hours a day. This plant uses heavy machinery that produces powerful vibrations. These vibrations can be felt for hundreds of feet in all directions. The ground actually shakes slightly from the effect. Over several years, this phenomenon has caused Jenny's house foundation to crack. She would argue that these constant vibrations were an unreasonable and substantial interference with her use and enjoyment of her home. In short, the manufacturing plant would be creating a private nuisance.

Pollution of Water or Soil   Consider another example. Suppose a chemical processing plant dumped its waste waters onto vacant land behind its buildings. These wastes seeped into the soil and polluted underground water supplies. The chemicals also spread across the soil surface onto neighboring lands, making them sterile. These are unreasonable and substantial interferences with the neighboring land owners' use and enjoyment of their realty. The chemical plant has produced a private nuisance.

Crop Destruction   Take another hypothetical. The Blackout Power Company burns coal to produce electricity. Thick, black smoke belches from its tall smokestacks. As the wind disperses the smoke, coal dust settles on the neighbors' land, upon which grow corn and soybeans. The neighbors' crops grow poorly because of the coal dust on their leaves. Blackout's activity is an unreasonable and substantial interference with the neighboring farmers' use and enjoyment of their crop land. A private nuisance exists.

Flooding Flooding can also be a private nuisance. Suppose Deatra lives along a small creek. Several miles downstream, another land owner erects a dam to create a small lake for fishermen. However, the lake extends beyond the downstream user's land and floods Deatra's property, including her home. Although this case could involve issues of *riparian* (water) law, in terms of nuisance law, the downstream land owner has unreasonably and substantially interfered with Deatra's use and enjoyment of her real estate by flooding her out.

Excessive Clutter Few individuals would ever want to live adjacent to a junkyard or trash dump. Most people find such land uses to be offensive to many senses, one of which is sight. Having to look at junk or trash piled high next door can be aesthetically depressing. Many courts have found such uses to be private nuisances for this reason, although, more commonly, neighbors are also offended by refuse odors.

Unwanted Excavations Excavation companies sometimes purchase soil from vacant lot owners to haul away and use in construction projects. These excavations leave deep and, for some people, unsightly holes in the vacant lots. Suppose Andy's house is next to several vacant lots that have been excavated in this fashion. A quick search of the case law reveals that several courts would find this to be a private nuisance.

Health Hazards or Offending Sensibilities

People's **sensibilities** are ways in which their physical senses (sight, hearing, smell, taste, and touch) and their emotional senses (what they find disgusting, repulsive, threatening, etc.) are affected. Private nuisances offend a person's sensibilities. They can also create health hazards.

Noxious Odors Land uses that produce harmful, obnoxious odors are frequent candidates as private nuisances, as in the previous trash dump

---

TERMS

sensibilities [†] In nuisance law, ways in which people's physical and emotional sense are affected.

example. Suppose Nicki lives next to a livestock farm, a chemical processing plant, or a paper mill. These may not create any bad smells at all, but sometimes they emit a powerful and dreadful stink. Much nuisance litigation has involved offensive odors produced by activities such as these.

Smoke and Dust   Smoke and dust emissions can produce serious health hazards for neighbors. Consider the Blackout Power Company example. Neighbors who breathe the coal-dust-laden air could suffer severe respiratory injury. If this happened, the courts would probably rule that Blackout was involved in creating a private nuisance.

Excessive Noise and Temperatures   Land uses that produce excessive noise can harm neighbors' health. In nuisance litigation, many plaintiffs have complained of sleep loss, nervousness, and associated physical and emotional symptoms because of a neighbor's excessive noise. Imagine how Eric might be affected if he lived next to a motor vehicle race track that ran late-night races on week nights.

Factories producing extreme heat might also pose health problems for neighbors. Persons living adjacent to steel mills have sued for nuisance because of the high temperatures produced by the blast furnaces. The heat from these operations can raise air temperatures to uncomfortable levels. When the heat becomes unreasonable, the courts may find private nuisances.

Toxic Tort Nuisances   The disposal or transportation of hazardous wastes or toxic chemicals are frequently the ground for private nuisance actions. Underground or surface water supplies that are contaminated by leaking toxic chemical dumps, or air that is filled with poisonous dusts (such as uranium dust vented from a nuclear power plant) are excellent examples of private nuisances. Much of the toxic tort litigation brought today involves nuisance actions.

Incessant Telephone Calls   Creditors occasionally use intimidation tactics to coerce customers to pay delinquent accounts. A favorite technique is the late-night telephone call. The creditor might telephone a delinquent customer several times late at night, every day for weeks or even months, to try to persuade the patron to pay the overdue amounts. Customers subjected to such harassment often suffer emotional distress and related physical manifestations.

Courts routinely determine that such activity constitutes a private nuisance. It is an unreasonable interference with the customer's use and enjoyment of the privacy of his or her home life. In fact, plaintiffs besieged with incessant phone calling often sue the culprit under several causes of action—namely, the intentional torts of invasion of privacy or intentional infliction of emotional distress—along with nuisance.

Unwanted Associations with Neighboring Uses

For decades, land owners have rushed to the courthouse to file private nuisance actions against the owners of houses of ill repute, X-rated movie theatres, adult bookstores, and liquor or gambling establishments. These cases illustrate clearly the personal nature of offensiveness. Some persons simply cánnot abide living in the vicinity of these types of activities. They do not wish to be associated with these land uses. These persons typically become plaintiffs in nuisance lawsuits in an attempt to drive out activities that they find repugnant.

In cases such as these, courts often struggle with community standards to decide if the activities are private nuisances. Are the plaintiffs overreacting, or are their objections reasonable? Would reasonable persons agree that having to live adjacent to establishments engaged in these pursuits is an unreasonable and substantial interference with the use and enjoyment of the realty? This is not an easy question to answer, as can be seen by reading some of the hundreds of appellate court opinions discussing the subject.

"Coming to the Nuisance" Defense

Often, a person will move into a neighborhood in which one of the activities previously described is already situated. In many cases, the manufacturer, trash dump, junkyard, or adult bookstore has been doing business in the same location for years. The plaintiff came to the area after the alleged nuisance was already there. When this happens, and the plaintiff then sues for private nuisance, the defendant may plead the "coming to the nuisance" defense. The **coming to the nuisance** defense involves the plaintiff who owns or uses land at a location in which the alleged nuisance activity was already occurring. If the plaintiff came to the nuisance, then he or she cannot recover against the defendant. The defense is similar to the defense of assumption of risk, in that the plaintiff knew (or reasonably should have known) that the

---

TERMS

coming to the nuisance defense [†] A defense to private nuisance lawsuits that may be used successfully when a plaintiff owns or uses land at a location in which the alleged nuisance activity was previously occurring. The plaintiff is said to have "come to the nuisance" and thus cannot recover against the defendant.

preexisting activity would offend him or her. Consequently, a reasonable person would not have chosen to buy or use land adjacent to a known, present, and distasteful land use next door. In essence, the plaintiff assumes the risk of obnoxiousness from the nuisance activity by coming to the place while knowing that the nuisance is already there, waiting to offend the plaintiff.

The Case of Intrusion on Hog Heaven

Incompatible land uses often make unhappy neighbors. Unfortunately, it is not always apparent that such incompatibilities will exist until after the activities have cohabited for some time. Then one of the land owners usually is harmed by the other, and a nuisance action enters the picture. As the case here illustrates, a business can create a nuisance through its own actions or those of its customers.

SHERK

v.

INDIANA WASTE SYSTEMS, INC.
Court of Appeals of Indiana
495 N.E.2d 815 (Ind. Ct. App. 1986)
July 31, 1986
Conover, Judge

Plaintiff-Appellant Dale J. Sherk (Sherk) appeals a negative judgment in his nuisance action against Defendants-Appellees Indiana Waste Systems, Inc. (IWS) and Prairie View Farms, Inc.

We reverse.

ISSUES

Sherk presents three issues for review. Because we reverse we consider only two issues. Restated, they are

1. whether the trial court erred in finding IWS and Prairie View were not responsible for noise generated by others, and
2. whether the trial court erred in finding IWS's use of the land was reasonable and thus a good defense to this action.

FACTS

Sherk raises hogs. IWS operates a landfill on land adjacent to Sherk's former hog breeding facility. IWS leases its land from Prairie View. Sherk's hogs suffered a 50% reduction in conception rates from the time IWS started its operation

there. Eventually, Sherk had to close down his hog breeding facility at that location because of such losses.

Sherk, attributing that reduction to noise from the landfill operation, sued IWS and Prairie View Farms, Inc. (hereinafter collectively IWS). Sherk alleged IWS operated its landfill in such a noisy manner it constituted a nuisance and damaged him.

The case was tried by the court. ...

The trial court found *inter alia* (1) noise generated by IWS's operation of its landfill did not cause Sherk's problem, (2) truck traffic increased as a result of the opening of the landfill, (3) noise emanating from the increased truck traffic caused the reduction in conception rates, and (4) IWS's operation of the landfill was reasonable. The trial court entered judgment against Sherk. He appeals.

* * *

Sherk contends the trial court erred when it concluded IWS was not responsible for the noise and vibration generated by the trash hauling trucks entering and leaving its landfill. Sherk also contends the trial court erred when it decided reasonableness of use is a defense to an action for a nuisance and IWS's use of its land is reasonable. ...

When deciding whether one's use of his property is a nuisance to his neighbors it is necessary to balance the competing interests of the land-owners. In so doing we use a common sense approach. Mere annoyance or inconvenience will not support an action for a nuisance because the damages resulting therefrom are deemed *damnum absque injuria* in recognition of the fact life is not perfect. Thus, "reasonable use" of one's property may be a defense to a nuisance action where the use merely causes *incidental* injury to another. Where, however, one uses his property for his profit so as to practically confiscate or destroy his neighbor's property he should be compelled to respond in damages, for it can hardly be said such use is reasonable. Whether one's use of property is reasonable is determined by the effect such use has on neighboring property. Liability is imposed in those cases where the harm or risk thereto is greater than the owner of such property should be required to bear under the circumstances.

Sherk argues but for the landfill operation there would have been no noise obstructing the free use of his property as a hog breeding facility. Thus, he opines, IWS should be liable for the noise generated by the trash hauling trucks. IWS in turn argues because the trial court found its use of its property was reasonable IWS is absolved of any responsibility for its customers' noisy trucks.

... [A] business may be liable for the acts of its customers or others if acts by them upon the business property or in going to or leaving it obstruct a neighbor's use of his property.

The facts found by the trial court here show (1) the conception rate of Sherk's pigs ranged between 70% and 90% before the landfill began its operations; (2) the rate was reduced to 30% following the opening of the landfill; (3) the reduction in rate of conception was due to the noise generated by the trash hauling trucks traveling to and from the landfill.

It is apparent but for the landfill there substantially would have been no noisy truck traffic in the vicinity of Sherk's pigs, and they would have continued breeding successfully in the peace and tranquility which they apparently require. The interference here is more than a mere annoyance or incidental harm. The use of IWS's property has destroyed the usefulness of Sherk's property as a hog breeding facility. The evidence and all reasonable inferences from it leads inescapably to the conclusion IWS's use of its property was unreasonable in relation to Sherk's use of his property as a hog breeding facility.

Because the trial court found no liability, it made no findings as to damages. While a proper remedy for nuisance may consist of damages or injunction or some combination of the two ... , Sherk seeks no injunction, only damages.

Reversed, and remanded for hearing and determination as to Sherk's damages only.

Case Questions

1. Do you agree with the court that IWS's use of its property was unreasonable? Why or why not?
2. Suppose that IWS had begun operating its landfill before Sherk established his hog breeding facility. Would the outcome of the case be different? Explain.

Private nuisance hypotheticals provide the reader with some of the earthiest factual situations in tort law. Students can easily relate to intrusions upon their senses or values. However, one must guard against identifying too strongly with the offended individual over the business allegedly creating the nuisance. As the following examples illustrate, each party in the nuisance story has its side to tell.

HYPOTHETICALS

Harvey Foreman bought a house in a residential subdivision in 1989. His real estate is adjacent to seventy acres of pasture land. In 1990, the pasture was sold to the Waste Away Company, which erected a trash processing plant and landfill in 1991. This plant began compacting trash for landfill use as well as incinerating trash. Early in 1992 Harvey began smelling unpleasant odors and smoke from the trash piles and smokestacks. In warm weather, the smell was extremely nasty. Fumes seemed to hover all around the neighborhood. Does Harvey have a cause of action for private nuisance?

When Harvey bought his home in 1989, he assumed that he would be living next door to pasture land, which is free from odors and has a clear, natural view. He probably anticipated that wildlife or livestock would graze the realty next door. This rustic expectation was shattered in 1990 when Waste Away transformed the land into a trash processing facility and landfill.

Using the private nuisance formula, first ask whether Waste Away's use of its real estate unreasonably and substantially interfered with Harvey's use and enjoyment of his property. Every day, odors and smoke floated across Harvey's land from the trash facility. The neighborhood became inundated with the foul smell of piled or burning trash. Reasonable persons with ordinary sensibilities (or, as it is sometimes called, sensitivities) would find such odors and smoke to be offensive. Most subdivision residents in Harvey's community could reasonably be expected to react adversely to the invading stench. Waste Away has created a private nuisance.

■ ■ ■

Consider another hypothetical. The Sanctified Brethren Church purchased a building site for a new cathedral in July 1991. Across the street, one block away, were several taverns, an X-rated movie theatre, and an adult bookstore. Once construction began, members of the church filed suit against the owners of these businesses, claiming private nuisance. Would the church's lawsuit be successful?

No. Assuming that the church could first prove that these businesses constituted a private nuisance, the businesses could avail themselves of the coming to the nuisance defense. The church knew that these businesses were already located in the neighborhood when it purchased its building site. The church voluntarily decided to situate its cathedral within close proximity of activities that church members found offensive. Therefore, the church would fail in its lawsuit.

There are literally thousands of different factual patterns involving private nuisance to be found in the court reporters. This tort can be quite interesting to study, given the variety and peculiarity of the fact scenarios that allegedly produce nuisances. One might wish to consult the index to the *American Law Reports* series, published by The Lawyers' Cooperative Publishing Company. (These are abbreviated as ALR, ALR2d, ALR3d, ALR4th, ALR5th, and ALR Fed.) Each series contains many annotations involving different examples of nuisances. These are often entertaining as well as enlightening—one reason that nuisance is frequently regarded as a "fun" tort subject in law study. Figure 11-1 lists the elements to private nuisance.

Elements	Examples	Defense
Activity that unreasonably and substantially interferes with use and enjoyment of another's land	Physical effects on land (vibrations, pollution, crop destruction, flooding, junk clutter, or excavations)	Coming to the nuisance
Unreasonable and *substantial* defined by community standard (reasonable person standard) regarding offensiveness of activity	Health hazards and offending sensibilities (noxious odors, smoke, dust, extreme noise or temperature, incessant telephone calling)	Plaintiff arrives to use land after nuisance activity already exists
Defendant's activity must proximately cause plaintiff's injuries	Unwanted associations with neighboring uses (prostitution houses, distributors of explicit sexual material, gambling institutions)	

FIGURE 11-1
Elements of private nuisance

§ 11.3 Public Nuisances

In addition to private nuisances, there are also public nuisances. A **public nuisance** is a land use that injures the public at large rather than just a single individual. A public nuisance unreasonably interferes with the public's enjoyment of legal rights common to the public. The elements of public nuisance may be broken down as: (1) The tortfeasor's

TERMS

public nuisance An act or omission that adversely affects the safety, health, or morals of the public, or causes some substantial annoyance, inconvenience, or injury to the public.

activity that (2) unreasonably and substantially interferes with (3) the public's use and enjoyment of legal rights common to the public.

Unlike private nuisances, which can adversely affect a single person, a public nuisance must harm the general public. More than one person must always be affected (or, at least, potentially affected) by the alleged nuisance activity. This does not require a multitude of angry citizens. Residents of a single neighborhood would suffice.

The standard of unreasonable and substantial interference is identical to that used in private nuisances, except that the interference must be to the public rather than a sole plaintiff.

Use and Enjoyment of Common Legal Rights

The use and enjoyment element in public nuisance is significantly different from the one discussed in private nuisances. With public nuisances, the tortfeasor's obnoxious land use interferes with the public's common legal rights, such as the right to peaceably assemble in public places, the right to use public streets and sidewalks without being subjected to offensive activities, or the right to safe and healthy conditions in one's neighborhood.

Governments as Plaintiffs

Although citizens often file public nuisance complaints with their local governmental agencies, it is the government, through its municipal governing bodies (e.g., city council, county commissioners) or its prosecuting attorneys, that sues defendants alleged to be committing public nuisances. This is because the government represents the public at large and must enforce its citizens' legal rights against tortfeasors. At common law, or by statute or, in some states, by state constitutional provision, state and local governments have the authority to protect their citizens from public nuisances. The source of this power is the states' **police powers**, which give governments authority to file lawsuits or enact legislation to protect the public's health, welfare, safety, or morals. These are usually very broad powers that give governments considerable flexibility to forbid certain so-called offensive activities.

███ TERMS ███
---

police power   The power of government to make and enforce laws and regulations necessary to maintain and enhance the public welfare and to prevent individuals from violating the rights of others.

Types of Public Nuisances

Almost all public nuisances are defined by statute or ordinance. Many such laws focus on land uses *which legislators believe* a majority of the population would find offensive, unhealthy, or immoral. The reader may know from personal experience that this belief may be unfounded or exaggerated. That, of course, depends upon whether one agrees or disagrees with what the government has labelled a public nuisance. Common targets of public nuisance laws include institutions devoted to (1) gambling, (2) prostitution, (3) distribution of sexually explicit materials, (4) sale of alcohol, or (5) toxic waste management. Other typical public nuisances include (1) allowing certain weeds or poisonous plants to grow on one's land; (2) failing to comply with health code provisions by keeping one's residence clean and vermin-free; and (3) keeping unrestrained wild or vicious animals on one's property. However, public nuisances may also include many of the same activities discussed in the private nuisances section.

Mixed Nuisances

Often, the same activity can constitute both a private and a public nuisance. These are sometimes called **mixed nuisances.** Apply this rule of thumb in such cases: The greater the number of persons adversely affected by an allegedly offensive land use, the more likely it will be considered a public, as well as a private, nuisance.

Nuisances Per Se

Courts often consider activities violating public nuisance statutes to be **nuisances per se.** *Per se* is Latin meaning "by itself." In tort law, it usually means that some behavior has violated a statute, and therefore the defendant is automatically liable. Sometimes courts, in the common law, decree that certain conduct is per se tortious. Negligence per se is an example. Per se nuisances have also been established by common law court decisions.

A public nuisance per se is an activity that violates the statute and is automatically considered a public nuisance. The tortfeasor thus loses

TERMS

mixed nuisance A nuisance that is both public and private in its effects.

nuisance per se An act, occupation, or structure that is considered a nuisance at all times and under any circumstances, regardless of location or surroundings.

from the start of litigation, simply by violating the statute. Statutes (and, rarely, common law) may also declare certain private nuisances to be per se nuisances.

"Coming to the Nuisance" Not a Defense

Generally, courts do not recognize the coming to the nuisance defense in public nuisance cases. This defense focuses on the individual plaintiff who purchases or uses land next to a preexisting, private nuisance activity. Public nuisances, by definition, affect the public at large, and the very existence or continuation of the public nuisance activity is considered harmful, whether it was preexisting or not.

As *Jacobs* demonstrates, what constitutes a public nuisance or a nuisance per se is generally a question of common law interpretation and statutory construction. But underlying questions of substance and form are the value judgments implicit in all nuisance per se or public nuisance cases. The following examples present such choices. Despite the temptation to become caught up in "good" versus "bad," one must concentrate on the legal elements and their application to the facts.

HYPOTHETICALS

Armstrong McCarter has an apiary in his backyard. He lives in a suburban neighborhood. Several hundred honeybees congregate in Armstrong's hives. The bees produce honey which Armstrong sells at local groceries. Frequently, children in the area have been stung by honeybees. Parents complained to Armstrong, but he simply shrugged off each incident, stating that there was no proof that his bees were responsible. However, there were no other honeybee colonies in the neighborhood. A town ordinance prohibits the keeping of wildlife within the city limits. Has Armstrong committed a public nuisance or a nuisance per se?

Armstrong's use of his land (maintaining an apiary) substantially and unreasonably interfered with his neighbors' use and enjoyment of the public streets and sidewalks in the area, as well as their own realty. Children were often stung by honeybees, and the only large honeybee colony in the neighborhood was Armstrong's. A trier-of-fact could reasonably infer that Armstrong's bees were responsible for the attacks. Of course, a local governmental agency would first have to sue Armstrong for public nuisance, and the case would have to go to trial. Reasonable persons would find these bee encounters to be offensive and dangerous. The public at large was threatened by Armstrong's *ferae naturae*. The bees unreasonably and substantially interfered with citizens' use of public streets and sidewalks. Under its police power, the local government would have authority to sue Armstrong for public nuisance.

Armstrong also violated the local ordinance prohibiting the keeping of wildlife within the city limits. This constitutes a nuisance per se, giving the town government another cause of action against Armstrong.

■ ■ ■

Consider another hypothetical. Darling Davis operates a massage parlor across from the local public high school. Although there is no evidence of prostitution at the establishment, Davis offers nude massages, during which both customers and masseurs disrobe. From across the street, high-school students can see clearly through the windows of Davis's building. Is Davis engaged in a public nuisance?

Davis's use of her land could adversely affect the students. The erotic views could disrupt school activities as children (and adults) cluster around windows to catch the revealing sights next door. Arguably, this is an unreasonable and substantial interference with a public right—namely, the right to use the public school for educational pursuits. Under its police powers, the municipal government could sue Davis for public nuisance.

The Case of the Door-to-Door Solicitation

Many people commonly think of door-to-door salespersons as nuisances, but the law does not automatically define them as such. As the following case suggests, not all forms of solicitation are included in public nuisance ordinances, such as the Florida example in this case.

JACOBS v. CITY OF JACKSONVILLE
U.S. District Court, Middle District of Florida
762 F. Supp. 327 (M.D. Fla. 1991)
April 8, 1991
Moore, II, District Judge

This cause was tried before the Court on March 11, 1990. ... [T]he Court now issues the following findings of fact and conclusions of law.

* * *

Plaintiff, Jerry L. Jacobs, does business under the fictitious name of Youth Opportunities Unlimited (hereinafter "Y.O.U."), and is a person who, personally and through his employees, sells or offers for sale merchandise by traveling from door-to-door, while carrying such merchandise. Y.O.U. is a for-profit organization which derives income through the sale of cookies, candy, and other items. These sales are conducted primarily by teenagers who are Y.O.U. members. Plaintiff holds a city permit to operate as a peddler of merchandise.

* * *

Plaintiff and the Y.O.U. salespersons conduct the door-to-door activities in various neighborhoods in Jacksonville on a rotating basis; as a result, sales in any particular neighborhood are

made no more than a few times per year. Each individual Y.O.U. product item is sold to the consumer for $4.00. ... No evidence was introduced to show that a large number of the residences solicited found Y.O.U.'s sales activities to be annoying or injurious, although the evidence did show that Y.O.U. salespersons are occasionally unwelcome at a few residences.

* * *

The City of Jacksonville, through Officer J.P. Baptist of the Jacksonville Sheriff's Office, has threatened Plaintiff with arrest under [Jacksonville ordinance] § 250.303, for engaging in residential door-to-door peddling activities without invitation. ...

In most instances, Plaintiff has not been expressly "requested or invited" by the owner or occupant of the private residence before engaging in door-to-door sales activity. Plaintiff does not solicit at any private residence where a "No Solicitation" sign is visible.

... The Court finds that Plaintiff is a "peddler" as defined in the Code, ... subject to the prohibition on door-to-door peddling set forth in J.O.C. § 250.303.

* * *

Under Florida law, unless a homeowner manifests externally in some manner his or her wish to remain unmolested by the visits of solicitors or peddlers, a solicitor or peddler may take ... an implied invitation to call upon residences ... . *Prior v. White*, 132 Fla. 1, 180 So. 347, 355 (1938). In *Prior*, the Florida Supreme Court invalidated an anti-peddling ordinance of New Smyrna Beach, Florida, as applied to the door-to-door sales activities of a Fuller Brush Company salesman. The New Smyrna ordinance was virtually identical to the Jacksonville ordinance now at issue. The court held that peddling and soliciting in New Smyrna was not a public nuisance because custom and usage established an implied invitation to solicit sales at private residences, and therefore could not be punished as a crime or misdemeanor. The court further held that a municipality cannot, through an attempted exercise of its police powers, declare by ordinance or otherwise that an activity is a public nuisance, when in fact such activity is not proved to be a public nuisance.

Prior v. White is still good law in Florida, never having been overruled by the Florida Supreme Court. Recent cases also have held that a municipality may not declare an activity to be a public nuisance unless that activity does in fact constitute a public nuisance. In addition, Florida courts continue to recognize the implied invitation theory. Since the principles set forth in *Prior* remain part of the law of Florida, *Prior* is binding upon this Court in its interpretation of Florida law. ... Thus, the facts of each case must be examined carefully to determine whether the type of door-to-door peddling engaged in by the parties in that case constitutes a public nuisance.

A public nuisance is defined as an activity that "violates public rights, subverts public order, decency or morals, or causes inconvenience or damage to the public generally." It is not completely clear under *Prior* which party bears the burden of proving that peddling is or is not a public nuisance. ...

In this case, door-to-door peddling in Jacksonville, Florida has not been proved to be a public nuisance. The Defendants have introduced virtually no evidence that proves peddling in Jacksonville by Y.O.U. or by others is a public nuisance, and have made little attempt to make such a showing. ...

Even assuming the Plaintiff bears the burden of proving that door-to-door peddling ... is not a public nuisance, the Court finds that Plaintiff has met this burden. The evidence introduced at trial showed that Y.O.U. sold 90,000 items in Jacksonville in 1990, an average of roughly one item per residence solicited. The evidence showed that a sizeable number, approximately one-half, of the residences solicited made a purchase from Y.O.U. Thus, thousands of customers in Jacksonville evidently did not find Plaintiff's organization materially annoying to them personally, which demonstrates that Y.O.U.'s activities do not materially inconvenience the public at large or subvert public order. ... Thus, Plaintiff has affirmatively proved, in the absence of any effective rebuttal evidence by the Defendants, that Y.O.U.'s activities do not inconvenience the public in a manner that amounts to a public nuisance. Accordingly, under the authority of *Prior v. White*, the ordinance is unreasonable and an invalid exercise of the police power as applied to the Plaintiff and the Y.O.U. organization.

* * *

ORDERED AND ADJUDGED:

... Defendants are permanently enjoined from arresting or prosecuting Plaintiff or any members of Youth Opportunities Unlimited under color of Jacksonville Ordinance Code § 250.303.

Case Questions

1. How does the court's definition of a public nuisance differ from that discussed in this chapter?
2. Do you agree with the court that the plaintiff's activities did not violate the ordinance? Explain.

Admittedly, cases such as Davis's involve value judgments and presume a threat to the public morals. One may agree or disagree with the alleged public threat produced by a massage parlor next to a school. However, many cases have involved exactly these fact situations, and courts promptly conclude that public nuisances have occurred.

Figure 11-2 lists the elements of public nuisances and nuisances per se.

Elements	Examples	Defense
Activity that unreasonably and substantially interferes with public's use and enjoyment of legal rights common to public at large	Prostitution establishments Pornography distributors	Coming to the nuisance *not* a defense to public nuisances
Plaintiff is governmental agency responsible for protecting public interest harmed by public nuisance activity	Historically, gambling and alcohol establishments were often considered public nuisances, although not normally at the present time	
State and local governments have authority to litigate public nuisances under general police powers to protect public health, safety, morals, and welfare	Allowing noxious weeds to grow on one's land Failing to comply with public health statutes Keeping unrestrained wild animals on one's land	
Mixed nuisances include public and private nuisances		Coming to the nuisance defense effective against private nuisance portion of mixed nuisance actions
Nuisances per se are nuisance activities that violate statutes or ordinances		Coming to the nuisance defense not usually effective against nuisance per se actions

FIGURE 11-2 Elements of public nuisances, mixed nuisances, and nuisances per se

§ 11.4 Remedies for Nuisances

When one has identified a private or public nuisance, what does one do about it? In other words, what remedies are available to plaintiffs against defendants? **Remedies** are the relief that plaintiffs receive against defendants in lawsuits. The most common remedy in tort actions is *money* **damages**, in which the defendant must pay the plaintiff a sum of money to satisfy the judgment. The trier-of-fact sets the amount owed after a trial has been held.

Other, nonmonetary remedies are also available for torts such as nuisance. These are called equitable remedies. **Equitable remedies** do not involve money damages; instead, the court orders the defendant to do (or, more commonly, *not* to do) something. When the court orders a defendant to do something, it is called a **mandamus order**. When the court orders a defendant not to do something, it is called an **injunction** or *restraining order*.

For centuries, money damages were considered inappropriate in nuisance cases. Courts would apply only equitable remedies. In nuisance law, the most common equitable remedies include (1) abatement and (2) injunction, although now money damages are occasionally permitted in nuisance cases.

TERMS

remedy The means by which a right is enforced, an injury is redressed, and relief is obtained.

damages The sum of money that may be recovered in the courts as financial reparation for an injury or wrong suffered as a result of breach of contract or a tortious act.

equitable relief (remedy) A remedy available in equity rather than at law; generally relief other than money damages.

mandamus [Latin for] "we command." A writ issuing from a court of competent jurisdiction, directed to an inferior court, board, or corporation, or to an officer of a branch of government (judicial, executive, or legislative), requiring the performance of some ministerial act. A writ of mandamus is an extraordinary remedy.

injunction A court order that commands or prohibits some act or course of conduct. It is preventive in nature and designed to protect a plaintiff from irreparable injury to his or her property or property rights by prohibiting or commanding the doing of certain acts. An injunction is a form of equitable relief.

Abatement

In nuisance cases, abatement is the most common remedy plaintiffs seek. With **abatement**, the defendant is ordered to cease, or *abate*, the nuisance activity. Abatement is often permanent. The defendant must desist from conducting the nuisance activity after a judgment for abatement is entered. This provides complete relief for the plaintiff, because the nuisance activity will be discontinued. Abatement can create harsh economic consequences for defendants, but the public policy behind abatement is clear: Nuisance tortfeasors have injured someone (or, if the public, many people). As long as the nuisance continues, the plaintiff(s) will continue to be hurt. The only certain solution is to stop the nuisance altogether.

Money Damages

When abatement could impose an unreasonably severe economic burden upon the nuisance tortfeasor, courts have broken with the ancient common law tradition and awarded plaintiffs money damages instead of abatement. This way, the plaintiffs can be compensated for their injuries produced by the nuisance activities, and the defendant can survive (economically) by staying in business, even though the nuisance also continues. Courts using this alternative are usually attempting to balance interests between conflicting land uses.

Injunctions

Courts enforce abatement through injunctive relief. *Injunctions* are court orders to defendants to cease and desist from engaging in nuisance activities. There are two types of injunctions: (1) temporary injunctions, including temporary restraining orders (T.R.O.s); and (2) permanent injunctions.

Temporary Injunctions

Temporary injunctions are often used from the time a plaintiff files suit until the first court hearing. The plaintiff, in his or her complaint,

---

TERMS

abatement A lessening or elimination.

asks the court to issue a **temporary restraining order** (T.R.O.), forbidding the defendant from conducting an alleged nuisance activity until a court hearing can be held to determine if the activity constitutes a nuisance. Under most rules of civil procedure, T.R.O.s may be issued for up to ten days, while the court convenes a hearing to decide if a nuisance has occurred. After the hearing, if the evidence convinces the judge that a nuisance is happening, the court may order further temporary injunctive relief, banning the defendant's nuisance activity until a trial on the merits may be held.

The purpose of temporary injunctions is to protect the plaintiff from further harm if a nuisance is in fact occurring. Plaintiffs often must post bonds to compensate the defendant if the court or jury later decides that the defendant did not engage in a nuisance. This is to protect the defendant from economic losses suffered while the injunctions were in effect and the defendant was not permitted to conduct the nuisance activity (which could mean lost profits or extra expenses).

Permanent Injunctions

Permanent injunctions are abatement orders instructing the defendant to permanently stop doing the nuisance activity. They are usually issued after a trial on the merits, once the trier-of-fact has concluded that a nuisance exists. If the defendant fails to obey a permanent injunction by continuing the nuisance, the court can punish the defendant by holding him or her in **contempt**. This punishment may involve monetary fines or even imprisonment.

Review of Hypotheticals

Review the hypotheticals from the previous sections of this chapter. Consider which remedies are suitable. In class or study groups, one may

---

TERMS

temporary restraining order (TRO)   Under the Federal Rules of Civil Procedure, injunctive relief that the court is empowered to grant, without notice to the opposite party and pending a hearing on the merits, upon a showing that failure to do so will result in "immediate and irreparable injury, loss, or damage." TROs are similarly available under state rules of civil procedure.

permanent injunction   An injunction granted after a final hearing on the merits, as distinguished from a temporary injunction granted to provide temporary relief.

contempt   An act of disrespect toward a court or legislative body; deliberate disobedience of a court order.

The Case of the Great Texas Dust-Off

State statutes often provide private citizens and public agencies with authority to litigate against private or public nuisances. As the following case indicates, private citizens may enforce nuisance actions against tortfeasors under the Texas Clean Air Act. The Texas Court of Appeals, in an excellently reasoned and articulate opinion, explains the applicable nuisance remedies.

MANCHESTER TERMINAL CORP.
v.
TEXAS TX TX MARINE TRANSPORTATION., INC.
Court of Appeals of Texas
781 S.W.2d 646 (Tex. Ct. App. 1989)
October 26, 1989
Evans, Chief Justice

Manchester Terminal Corporation (Manchester) appeals from an order of the trial court granting a plea of abatement and dismissing Manchester's cause of action for lack of subject matter jurisdiction. Manchester, the owner and operator of a marine terminal storage facility on the Houston Ship Channel, initiated this action against appellees, Texas TX TX Marine Transportation, Inc. (Texas Marine), the operator of a petroleum coke facility, Atlantic Richfield Company d/b/a [doing business as] Lyondell Petrochemical Company (Lyondell), the owner and operator of a petroleum coke refinery, and the Port of Houston Authority (Port of Houston), the owner of the land on which the petroleum coke facility is located.

Manchester alleged that the activities of Texas Marine and Lyondell in transporting and storing petroleum coke on the Port of Houston property generated large amounts of petroleum coke dust, which settled on Manchester's property and contaminated its facilities and stored goods. Manchester alleged that this pollution significantly impaired its ability to solicit and accept goods for storage, resulting in substantial economic injury and posing a significant health hazard to its employees and the employees of other companies working at its terminal. Manchester characterized these actions as constituting trespass and nuisance, and asserted that they violated Tex. Const. art. I, sec. 17. Manchester

sought a permanent injunction to prevent the transportation and storage of petroleum coke at the Texas Marine facility, as well as more than $12.5 million in damages.

Texas Marine and Lyondell filed a plea to the jurisdiction and a plea in abatement, in which they asserted that Manchester's cause of action was already the subject of proceedings before the Texas Air Control Board (TACB) … .

In Manchester's first three points of error, it asserts that the trial court erred in … dismissing its cause of action because (1) the Texas Clean Air Act explicitly recognizes the right of private persons to bring common-law actions to abate or recover for nuisances or conditions of pollution … .

We sustain these points of error.

* * *

["]The Texas Clean Air Act (the Act) was enacted to safeguard the air resources of the State from pollution by controlling or abating air pollution or emissions of air contaminants, consistent with the protection of health, general welfare and physical property of the people, including the aesthetic enjoyment of the air resources by the people and the maintenance of adequate visibility." The Act provides that its provisions are to be vigorously enforced.

… [S]ection 1.06 [of the Act] expressly provides:
  Sec. 1.06. Nothing in this Act affects the right of any private person to pursue all common law remedies available to abate a condition of pollution or other nuisance or recover damages therefor, or both.

Section 1.06, which has been a part of the Act since its inception, clearly and directly expresses the legislature's intent to preserve *the right of any private person to pursue all common-law remedies available to abate a condition of pollution or other nuisance, or to recover damages therefor or both.* Manchester's pleadings allege both trespass and nuisance, which are well-recognized common-law remedies to abate or recover damages for pollution.

* * *

Texas Marine and Lyondell also argue that a court decree granting injunctive relief to Manchester would, in effect, nullify and set aside the statutory permits issued by the TACB. We disagree. Although Texas Marine may hold a valid permit from the TACB authorizing the emission of specified amounts of pollutants into the air, neither the permit nor the underlying legislation gives Texas Marine the right to conduct its business in a manner which, under the law, constitutes a trespass or a nuisance.

It has long been the law in this state that proof of negligence is not essential to imposition of liability for creation or maintenance of a nuisance. A nuisance does not rest on the degree of care used, but on the degree of danger or annoyance existing even with the best of care. When a commercial enterprise causes or permits the escape of noxious things such as smoke, soot, or odor, so as to substantially impair the comfort or enjoyment of those occupying neighboring property, such activity may be judicially declared a nuisance, justifying equitable relief or an award of damages.

Unless a particular commercial enterprise constitutes a nuisance per se, courts are reluctant to enter an injunctive order that will absolutely prohibit the operation of a lawful business. The courts will intervene, however, if a business is being conducted in such a manner as to constitute a nuisance to particular individuals. In such a case, a court, in the exercise of its equitable powers, may frame its decree to permit the continuation of the enterprise, and also protect the aggrieved individual against further loss.

Under the pleading in this case, it would be possible for the trial court to fashion a decree that would allow Texas Marine to continue its business operations under the TACB permit, and at the same time, require that Texas Marine refrain from operating its business in a manner that would cause further loss or damage to Manchester. The trial court could also award damages to Manchester without adversely affecting Texas Marine's ability to conduct its lawful business operations pursuant to the TACB permit. We therefore overrule the contentions that any relief granted to Manchester under its pleadings would have the effect of nullifying the permit issued by the TACB. ...

* * *

The order of the trial court is reversed and the cause remanded for further proceedings.

Case Questions

1. How did the Texas Court of Appeals define nuisance in *Manchester*?
2. What remedies did the court of appeals consider appropriate in this case?
3. Given the facts reported in the court's opinion, could the defendant's petroleum coke dust emissions have been considered a public nuisance or a nuisance per se, discussed in § 11.3? Explain your analysis. Did the *Manchester* court think that a nuisance per se occurred in this case?

wish to discuss whether money damages is an appropriate alternative to abatement. Figure 11-3 restates the remedies available in nuisance lawsuits.

Equitable Remedies	Money Damages
Abatement (permanent prohibition against nuisance activity)	Money damages may be awarded if abatement would put unreasonable economic burdens on the defendant
Temporary injunctions (forbidding nuisance activity during litigation process)	
Permanent injunctions (used for abatement)	

FIGURE 11-3
Remedies for nuisances

It is time to investigate another special tort action, negligence per se, which is examined in § 11.5.

§ 11.5 Negligence Per Se

Negligence per se is behavior that is automatically negligent as a matter of law. When a statute defines certain conduct as negligent, and a tortfeasor violates the statute by engaging in that activity, then the tortfeasor is presumed to have been negligent by violating the statute. To meet the burden of proof, a plaintiff need only show that the defendant's actions violated the negligence statute. The defendant is then presumed negligent. This shifts the proof burden to the defendant, who must then present effective negligence defenses to avoid liability. A per se negligent defendant might also avoid liability by showing that he or she was not the proximate cause of the plaintiff's injuries. In other words, the defendant would have to prove that his or her violation of the statute did not proximately cause the plaintiff's harm.

TERMS

negligence per se Negligence that is beyond debate because the law, usually a statute or ordinance, has established a duty or standard of care that the defendant has violated, as a result of which he has caused injury to the plaintiff.

Defenses to Negligence Per Se

The negligence defenses of contributory negligence, comparative negligence, and assumption of risk also apply to negligence per se cases.

Plaintiff Within Class of Persons Protected by Statute

Not every statutory violation constitutes negligence per se. To recover under negligence per se theory, the plaintiff must be within the class of persons protected by the statute or ordinance. For example, suppose a restaurant serves maggot-infested meat to its customers. This violates several state and local health statutes. Suppose Kent ate at the restaurant and became ill. He would fall within the class of persons protected by the health statutes that require restaurants to serve wholesome food to patrons. The restaurant's violation of the statutes would be considered negligence per se, and Kent would have an excellent cause of action against the establishment.

Absolute Liability Mislabelled as Negligence Per Se

Courts occasionally equate negligence per se with strict, or absolute, liability. However, the two tort theories are distinct. Negligence per se simply presumes negligence because of the tortfeasor's violation of a statute. Negligence is based upon the tortfeasor's failure to exercise reasonable care. Absolute liability holds the tortfeasor accountable, regardless of fault, for doing an abnormally dangerous activity. No degree of care is sufficient to avoid strict liability.

This confusion between absolute liability and negligence per se occurs because of the outcomes in each type of case. If the defendant violates a negligence statute, he or she is presumed automatically negligent. Liability is almost as certain as in strict liability cases. Thus, the two concepts are often equated, although they are substantially different.

Toxic Torts as Negligence Per Se

Statutes sometimes declare that violations of regulations regarding the transportation, disposal, or management of hazardous or toxic substances create a presumption of negligence as a matter of law. These statutory provisions boost plaintiffs' causes of action against tortfeasors who carelessly control abnormally dangerous materials.

Not every statutory violation is negligence per se. All elements must be satisfied for the doctrine to apply. The following hypotheticals further demonstrate this principle.

The Case of the Statutory Hangover

In *Ohio Casualty,* partially reprinted in Chapter 6, the reader faced an intriguing negligence issue: Did a tavern owner violate a duty of care by serving alcohol to an intoxicated customer who subsequently injured himself? The Oklahoma Supreme Court said no. Review the earlier reprint for the relevant facts. In the portion of its opinion reprinted here, the court rules on the negligence per se issue. After the court's decision, the inebriated driver must have felt a severe case of statutory hangover.

**OHIO CASUALTY
INSURANCE CO.
v.
TODD
Supreme Court of Oklahoma
813 P.2d 508 (Okla. 1991)
June 11, 1991
Summers, Justice**

... Section 537(A)(2) [Oklahoma Statutes] states in relevant part that no person shall "[s]ell, deliver or knowingly furnish alcoholic beverages to an intoxicated person."

A. NEGLIGENCE PER SE

Robertson [the intoxicated driver/customer] urges that Todd [the tavern owner] violated Section 537(A)(2) and that the violation amounted to negligence per se. In *Hampton v. Hammons,* we explained the elements which must be found before the violation of a statute is negligence per se. ... [W]e pointed out that (1) the injury must have been caused by the violation, (2) the injury must be of a type intended to be prevented by the ordinance, and (3) the injured party must be one of the class intended to be protected by the statute.

Because we find the third element to be missing, we do not address the first two. In *Brigance,* we stated that the purpose behind Section 537(A)(2) was to protect innocent third parties who were injured by intoxicated persons. In *Cuevas v. Royal D'Iberville Hotel,* the Mississippi Supreme Court construed a statute similar to Section 537(A)(2), and found that the intoxicated person was excluded from the class of persons meant to be protected by the statute. In making this determination, the court pointed out the class to be protected was the general public, and that this class, while broad in range, could not be said to include "an adult individual ... who voluntarily consumes intoxicants and then, by reason of his inebriated condition, injures himself." We agree.

We find nothing in Section 537(A)(2), or in any of the statutes regulating the sale of alcohol, which indicate[s] that the legislature intended to protect the intoxicated adult who, by his own actions, causes injury to himself. Instead, it appears that the legislature intended to protect the "unsuspecting public"—in effect all of the populace except the willing imbiber. Thus, a violation of Section 537(A)(2) does not amount to negligence per se under the facts of this case.

Case Questions

1. What if a passenger riding in Robertson's vehicle had been injured? Would the passenger then have a cause of action against the tavern owner for violating § 537(A)(2), under negligence per se theory? Explain.
2. Do you agree with the court that Robertson does not fall within the scope of the class protected by § 537(A)(2)? Explain.

HYPOTHETICALS

Woodrow Smelter was driving his automobile at night along the Old River Road. Although it was pitch black, he did not have his headlights on. This violated a local county ordinance and state statute requiring headlight use at all times beginning an hour before sundown and ending an hour after sunrise. Woodrow collided with Bertha Godfrey, a pedestrian walking along the side of the road. Bertha sues Woodrow for negligence per se. Was he?

By driving without headlights, Woodrow violated an ordinance and statute that required motor vehicles to use lights at night. This was intended to protect other drivers and pedestrians from "invisible" vehicles hitting them in the dark. Bertha falls within the classification of persons protected by the statute and ordinance. Therefore, she could successfully sue Woodrow for negligence per se.

■ ■ ■

Consider another hypothetical. Barfly Beer Company sells "Brewster's Choice," a "light" beer low in calories. One of its distributors, the Barley Brothers Emporium, sells the product in town. A state health statute requires any manufacturer or seller of items for human consumption to distribute them in containers free from foreign substances. Barley collected empty bottles to send back to Barfly to be cleaned and reused. Sometimes, drinkers would put cigarette butts into the bottles. Neither Barley nor Barfly checked the bottles for foreign substances; they were simply sent back to the Barfly plant, refilled, and redistributed. Leigh Ann drank one of the beers from a bottle with a cigarette butt floating in the bottom. As one might imagine, Leigh Ann became physically ill as a result. Aside from the clear products liability issue, has Barfly or Barley been negligent per se?

The health statute was intended to protect consumers like Leigh Ann from injuries caused by foreign objects floating inside beverage bottles. Barfly and Barley each violated the statute. Their negligence may be presumed.

Figure 11-4 summarizes negligence per se.

Defendant's actions are automatically considered negligent because they violated a negligence statute or ordinance
Plaintiff must fall within class of persons protected by statute
Defendant's statutory violation must proximately cause plaintiff's injuries
Negligence defenses apply to negligence per se

FIGURE 11-4 Elements of negligence per se

§ 11.6 Wrongful Death

Wrongful death statutes give the surviving family members of a deceased tort victim a cause of action against the tortfeasor whose negligence or intentional torts resulted in the victim's death.

Typical Facts in Wrongful Death Cases

The factual pattern in wrongful death actions may be summarized as follows: (1) a tortfeasor commits a tort against the victim; (2) the victim dies as a result of the tortfeasor's actions; (3) the victim's spouse, children, estate, or person who relied on the deceased person for economic support, or all of them, sue the tortfeasor for wrongfully causing the victim's death.

Plaintiffs in Wrongful Death Actions

Under wrongful death statutes, the surviving family members, usually the victim's spouse or children, become the plaintiffs. However, some statutes allow the victim's parents or siblings to become plaintiffs. The victim's estate may also be permitted to sue the defendant for wrongful death damages under some statutes.

Damages

Wrongful death statutes usually define the types of damages that plaintiffs may recover against defendants. These damages include lost lifetime earnings potential and loss of consortium.

TERMS

wrongful death statutes State statutes that allow the personal representative of the decedent to bring an action on behalf of the decedent's statutory beneficiaries if the decedent's death was the result of the defendant's wrongful act.

*Practical
Applications*

Be sure to check the precise wording of the wrongful death statute in your jurisdiction. In some states, such as California, the statute of limitations for wrongful death runs from the date of death, not the date of the accident.

Lost Lifetime Earnings Potential

A tort victim's surviving family members may recover damages for the lost income that the victim would likely have earned had he or she not been killed by the tortfeasor. Wrongful death statutes usually define these damages in terms of the decedent's lost earnings potential based upon income at the time of death. This income base is projected over time. The future time period used is normally the victim's life expectancy, which is calculated from insurance actuarial tables. The projected earnings potential is usually adjusted for the victim's projected living expenses, had he or she survived. An economist is usually hired as an expert witness to introduce this evidence at trial.

Loss of Consortium

Wrongful death statutes often permit a tort victim's surviving family to recover damages for the lost love and companionship of the decedent. This is similar to pain and suffering damages. However, many statutes do not allow recovery of such damages. Wrongful death statutes (or courts interpreting them) often label this type of damages **loss of consortium**. Many statutes define *consortium* as both economic and intangible benefits lost to a victim's surviving family because of the victim's death. The intangible element could include lost love, companionship, and even the survivors' mental anguish upon losing a loved one.

Defenses

In wrongful death actions, the tortfeasor may use any defense applicable to the specific tort that produced the victim's injury. For example, suppose the victim had been contributorily or comparatively negligent, or assumed the risk, of the defendant's actions that killed the victim.

TERMS

loss of consortium   The loss of a spouse's assistance or companionship, or the loss of a spouse's ability or willingness to have sexual relations. If such loss results from a tort, it gives rise to a cause of action in favor of the partner of the spouse injured by the tort.

Suppose the tortfeasor killed the victim while acting in self-defense or defense of others. The tortfeasor may escape liability for wrongfully causing the victim's death if any of the suitable tort defenses apply in the case. Defenses are available in a wrongful death action just as if the victim were still alive and, as plaintiff, were suing the defendant.

A Case of "Death-Before-Litigation"

Some issues that come before appellate courts seem to have obvious answers. Some are so obvious, in fact, that one wonders why an appeal was necessary to answer them. The Montana Supreme Court may have been thinking this very question as it wrote the following straightfaced opinion, in response to a perfectly serious Ninth Circuit Court of Appeals query. Note Justice Gray's remarkable judicial restraint in avoiding humorous gibes that a lesser jurist might have felt compelled to include in the opinion. (Case questions are omitted following the case, as there is nothing left to ask.)

CARROLL v. W.R. GRACE & CO.
Supreme Court of Montana
830 P.2d 1253 (Mont. 1992)
January 14, 1992
Gray, Justice

This case is before us on certified questions from the Ninth Circuit Court of Appeals concerning the point at which a Montana wrongful death action accrues. ...

Appellant (and defendant), W.R. Grace and Company, claims that the action accrues at the date of injury. Respondent (and plaintiff), Edith Carroll, claims that a wrongful death action accrues at the death of the injured person. We conclude that a wrongful death action does not accrue until the death of the injured person.

Charles Carroll (decedent) was employed by W.R. Grace and Company (Grace) at its vermiculite mine located in Libby, Montana, from 1958 until 1976; he underwent yearly chest x-rays provided by Grace from 1967 until 1976. Decedent retired in 1976, but continued to seek medical help regarding shortness of breath and a heart condition.

Mr. Carroll died in 1989, thirteen years after retirement. His autopsy report listed the cause of death as "severe interstitial fibrosis with pulmonary failure, apparently due to 'asbestosis.'"

Decedent's medical records show that he had been diagnosed as suffering from asbestosis as early as 1972.

Edith Carroll, wife of decedent, filed a survival claim and a wrongful death claim against Grace, her husband's former employer, asserting that her husband's asbestosis was related to his employment at Grace's mine. She contends that she did not know his death was related to his employment until she read the autopsy report. She filed her suit as a diversity action in the United States District Court within two months of her husband's death.

Grace moved for summary judgment based on the running of the statutes of limitations for both survival and wrongful death claims. The U.S. District Court granted summary judgment, holding that the statute of limitations had run on both claims. Edith Carroll appealed to the United States Court of Appeals for the Ninth Circuit. The Ninth Circuit affirmed the District Court's holding that the survival claim was barred by the applicable three-year statute of limitations, but stated that Montana law was not definitive on the issue of when a wrongful death action accrues. ...

Wrongful death claims are creatures of statute in Montana. As such, the question of when a wrongful death claim accrues requires an analysis of the general accrual statute and the wrongful death statute itself.

The general accrual statute for all actions in Montana provides:

> [A] claim or cause of action accrues when all elements of the claim or cause exist or have occurred, [and] the right to maintain an action on the claim or cause is complete ... .

The wrongful death statute reads:

> Action for wrongful death. When injuries to and the death of one person are caused by the wrongful act or neglect of another, the personal representative of the decedent's estate may maintain an action for damages against the person causing the death ... .

The language of Montana's general accrual statute is plain and straightforward: "all elements" of a claim must exist before the claim can accrue. The meaning is equally clear and not susceptible to differing interpretations: only when all elements exist is a claim complete. [The general accrual statute] applies, by its terms, to all claims and causes of action. Thus, a wrongful death claim, like any other cause of action, accrues only when all elements of the claim have occurred; the claim simply does not exist until that time. The question, then, is whether death is an element of a wrongful death claim.

The wrongful death statute references "... injuries to *and the death* of one person ... ". (Emphasis added.) When these occurrences are caused by the "wrongful act or neglect of another," a wrongful death action may be maintained against the person who caused the death of the injured person. It is clear from the legislature's use of the conjunctive "and" that the death of the injured person is an element of a wrongful death claim.

The wrongful death statute contains additional language mandating the conclusion that death is an element of the claim. "[T]he personal representative of the decedent's estate ..." files a wrongful death action. A "decedent" is indisputably a person who has died and a personal representative of an estate cannot be appointed until there is a decedent. Thus, the death itself is a critical element in a wrongful death action.

To summarize, no claim exists until all elements of a cause of action occur pursuant to [the general accrual statute], and death is an element of a wrongful death claim under ... Montana's wrongful death statute. Therefore, we hold that a wrongful death action in Montana accrues at the time of decedent's death.

The following example illustrates how a wrongful death action might arise under a hypothetical statute.

HYPOTHETICAL

Jordan Vic Orthmell owns a cement manufacturing plant. One of his employees, Toby Noogle, drives a cement truck. One of Jordan's customers is Sally Sinchim, who was installing a swimming pool at her home. Toby came to pour cement for the pool. Sally's husband, Abraham, stood beneath the truck inside the excavated pool area. Without first checking to see if anyone was in the way, Toby dumped the entire truckload of cement on top of Abraham, who suffocated and died. Assume that this jurisdiction's wrongful death statute permits family survivors to sue tortfeasors for "negligently, wantonly, or intentionally" causing a victim's death. What is the likely result?

Sally could sue Toby (and, by respondeat superior, Toby's employer, Jordan) for causing the wrongful death of her husband, Abraham. Toby was negligent in pouring the cement without first seeing if anyone was inside the dangerous dumping area. Because Abraham died, Sally has a cause of action for wrongful death.

The family survivors' specific legal rights are entirely dependent upon the language of each wrongful death statute. It is important to become familiar with the wrongful death statutes in one's state, if one intends to work with plaintiffs for this special tort action. Figure 11-5 summarizes the standard ingredients of wrongful death statutes.

Tortfeasor commits tort against victim, causing victim's death
Victim's surviving spouse and children (or victim's estate) may sue tortfeasor to recover damages under wrongful death statute
Most statutes or courts allow damages for victim's lost lifetime earnings potential and for loss of consortium
Same tort defenses apply in wrongful death actions, depending upon the specific tort tortfeasor committed against deceased victim

FIGURE 11-5 Elements of wrongful death statutes

§ 11.7 Wrongful Life

Wrongful life actions are lawsuits for the wrongful birth of a child. These are also called *wrongful birth* or *wrongful pregnancy* actions. The plaintiffs are usually the surprised parents, and the defendant is normally the physician who performed ineffective sterilization surgery upon either the mother or the father. Wrongful life, then, can be considered another form of medical malpractice, which is negligence.

TERMS

wrongful birth (life, pregnancy)   When an unsound child is born to parents who decided not to prevent or terminate the pregnancy because of erroneous medical advice, or because of medical advice not offered that should have been, the birth may, in some jurisdictions, be the basis for a wrongful birth action.

Typical Fact Pattern: Unwanted Pregnancy

The typical situation involving unwanted pregnancy is as follows: A couple visit a physician, wishing a vasectomy or tubal ligation to prevent future conceptions. The doctor performs the surgery. However, because of the surgeon's negligence, the operation fails. The couple end up conceiving a child and then end up litigating against the physician whose negligence "caused" the unexpected (or unwanted) birth of a child.

Birth Defects

In certain cases, the plaintiffs (parents) sue the physician for the unwanted birth of a child born with birth defects or other congenital problems. The parents would seek to be reimbursed for the added expenses of raising a handicapped child. This may occur when a doctor assures a couple that an unborn child will not be harmed by a disease the mother contracted during pregnancy, but when born, the child does in fact have substantial birth defects caused by the mother's infection. Another such situation involves a child who is born with genetic defects that a doctor assured the parents were not present or inheritable.

Wrongful Life: The New Tort

Wrongful life actions are a recent tort invention, having arisen within the last twenty-five to thirty years. This new tort has received mixed reviews from appellate courts across the United States. Some jurisdictions reject the tort altogether; others permit it in circumstances involving birth deformities; and still others allow the action even for healthy but unwanted children when sterilization has failed. Wrongful life litigation demonstrates the ingenuity of attorneys and legal scholars searching for new sources of recovery for harmed plaintiffs. Depending upon one's point of view, one may consider this tort just another form of "chiseling" against the medical profession, or one may find it a perfectly acceptable compensation for innocent parents who might be unprepared (or unable to afford) family additions. Certainly, the cases have involved much emotion and moral judgment.

Damages

In addition to the expenses incurred during pregnancy and delivery of the "wrongful life" child, plaintiffs seek (and sometimes recover) damages from the responsible physician(s) for the cost of raising the child until he or she reaches the age of majority, most often defined by modern statutes as eighteen years of age. Note that this is the minority view. In the majority of states, the cost of raising a healthy child is not recoverable. One can imagine the enormous judgments such plaintiffs might receive under circumstances in which wrongful life suits are allowed.

The Cases of Wrongful Life and Wrongful Birth Pregnancies

In two separate actions, which were combined, a physician, a hospital, and the manufacturer of a surgical instrument were sued as a result of eighteen unsuccessful tubal ligations. Instead of the desired goal of prevention of pregnancy, normal healthy children were born. One action was labeled a *"wrongful birth"* action. (In some other jurisdictions it is referred to as a *wrongful pregnancy* action.) The other action was called a "wrongful life" action. Both lawsuits were brought against the defendants for the negligent acts that caused the particular children to be born. Can acts leading to the birth of healthy children be termed negligence? Can parents who give birth to a healthy child successfully claim they have been damaged?

BEARDSLEY v. WIERDSMA
Supreme Court of Wyoming
650 P.2d 288 (Wyo. 1982)
September 3, 1982
Brown, Justice

This case involves two separate actions which were consolidated for review. Appellants filed suit against the appellees seeking damages resulting from unsuccessful tubal ligations. ...

Eighteen appellants had tubal ligations so that they would become sterile, but instead became pregnant. They were plaintiffs below. At the time of the suits eleven of these appellants had given birth to healthy, normal children; three of the appellants were pregnant; and four of the appellants had terminated their pregnancies.

＊ ＊ ＊

Appellees here are Dr. Weirdsma, who performed the tubal ligations; Memorial Hospital of Sweetwater County, where the operations were performed; and Davol, Inc., which manufactured the cauterization instrument used in the surgery.

＊ ＊ ＊

The "wrongful life" action asserted by the parents on behalf of their children is an action for

damages based on appellees' negligence which caused a particular child to be born. We hold that a cause of action for "wrongful life" under the circumstances here does not exist.

The vast majority of cases have refused to recognize a cause of action for "wrongful life" on behalf of a child based on the rationale that there is no legal right not to be born.

＊ ＊ ＊

The few courts which have acknowledged a cause of action for wrongful life have done so only for impaired children, and then usually because there was a causal connection between the alleged negligence and the impairment. In *Tarpin v. Sortini*, the question was whether a child born with a hereditary affliction could maintain a tort action against a physician who negligently failed to advise the child's parents before the child's conception of the possibility of the hereditary condition, thereby depriving them of the opportunity to choose not to conceive the child. The California Supreme Court stated:

"In sum, we conclude that while a plaintiff-child in a wrongful life action may not recover general damages for being born impaired as opposed to not being born at all, the child—like his or her parents—may recover special damages for the extraordinary expenses necessary to treat the hereditary ailment."

* * *

The principal issue in this case is whether the parents have a cause of action in their own right for "wrongful birth" against appellees, assuming that fault on appellees' part led to the birth of an unplanned, yet normal and healthy child.

Appellants seek damages against appellees as follows:

"1. For actual expenses to be incurred in the future which have been occasioned by the birth of minor children in question including medical and hospital care during delivery, actual costs of raising such children including medical expenses, expenses for general care and maintenance and other similar expenses.

"2. For the reasonable value of the mental anguish sustained by appellants by reason of wrongful conduct of appellees including interference with the lifestyle decisions made by appellants and for the emotional distress occasioned by changes in the future plans of the appellants and in the case of the appellants who have had abortions the reasonable value of such emotional distress.

"3. For punitive damages against Dr. Wierdsma in a reasonable sum.

"4. For such other and further relief as the court deems proper in the premises together with appellants' costs incurred herein."

Courts which have considered "wrongful birth" cases have reached four different positions concerning damages when a normal, healthy child is born. Because this is a relatively new area of medical malpractice law, we will discuss each of these four positions on damages.

The first view is that the parents have no right to recover any damages or expenses for the performance of unsuccessful sterilization operations. Some earlier cases held that despite any finding of negligence, breach of contract, or misrepresentation on the part of a physician or surgeon, no damages resulted from the birth of a normal child through normal delivery with no permanent harm to the mother. One case was based on the grounds that the gift of a normal child could not be considered an injury to the parents and that in any event, the granting of damages on such grounds would be against public policy.

* * *

The second view is that the parents have a right to recover all damages and expenses, including the cost of rearing the child. Some courts which have allowed damages for the cost of rearing a healthy child seem to have based their decisions on the fact that the right to limit procreation through contraception and through a limited right to abortion is within a constitutionally protected "zone of privacy." ... The court in allowing damages, including rearing and education expenses, said:

* * * That right is legally protectible and need not be justified or explained. The allowance of rearing costs is not an aspersion upon the value of the child's life. It is instead a recognition of the importance of the parent's fundamental right to control their reproductivity.

The third view is that parents have a right to recover all expenses and damages incurred or to be incurred resulting from the birth of an unplanned child, subject to an offset for the benefits that will be enjoyed by the parents. This concept is sometimes called the "benefit-rule." In adopting the "benefit-rule," some courts have applied Restatement, Second, Torts, § 920, p. 509 (1979).

"When the defendant's tortious conduct has caused harm to the plaintiff or to his property and in so doing has conferred a special benefit to the interest of the plaintiff that was harmed, the value of the benefit conferred is considered in mitigation of damages, to the extent that this is equitable."

In applying the "benefit-rule," if fault is found, the trier of fact determines all expenses and damages incurred and to be incurred by the parents, including costs of rearing the child, and then makes a deduction for benefits the child brings to the parents.

The fourth view is that parents have a right to recover all damages and expenses occurring because of the pregnancy and birth, but that they have no right to recover the costs of rearing the child. The courts which do not allow recovery for the expense of rearing an unplanned child do so for a number of policy reasons, any one of which is sufficient to deny recovery: 1) The injury is too remote from the negligence; or 2) the injury is wholly out of proportion to the culpability of the tortfeasor; or 3) allowance of recovery would enter a field that has no just or sensible stopping point; or 4) that the benefits of having a child outweigh any economic loss which parents might incur in rearing and educating a healthy child.

* * *

Consistent with the majority of recent cases, we hold that parents who find themselves in the situation that appellants do here are entitled to recover some items of damages, provided they are able to prove negligence, causation, and damages. Our problem is in determining what items of damages are proper. A ruling denying any damages to appellants would render the medical profession immune from liability for negligent treatment of patients seeking to limit the size of their families.

* * *

We hold that provided appellants prove fault, they are entitled to submit to the trier of fact expenses and damages for 1) recovery of any medical expenses associated with the unsuccessful ligation, such as surgical expense, hospital expense, physicians' fees, and expense of medication, 2) medical and hospital expenses for the birth of the unplanned child, 3) wages necessarily lost by the woman because of pregnancy and childbirth or because of an abortion, 4) pain and suffering of the mother in connection with pregnancy, and 5) cost of abortion, together with pain and suffering of the women who elected to have their pregnancies terminated.

We reject any claim for damages or expenses after the birth of the child. We believe that these latter expenses and damages are too speculative; that the injury is too remote from the negligence; that the injury is out of proportion to the culpability of the tortfeasors; and that the allowance of recovery would place too unreasonable a burden on appellees, since it would likely open the way for fraudulent claims, and since it would enter a field that has no sensible or just stopping point.

We specifically reject the "benefit-rule" or offset concept. " * * * The preciousness of human life should not be held to vary with the circumstances surrounding birth. ..."

We believe that the benefits of the birth of a healthy, normal child outweigh the expense of rearing a child. The bond of affection between child and parent, the pride in a child's achievement, and the comfort, counsel and society of a child are incalculable benefits, which should not be measured by some misplaced attempt to put a specific dollar value on a child's life.

... If the concept of benefit or offset were applied to "wrongful birth" actions, we can conceive of the ridiculous result that benefits could be greater than damages, in which event someone could argue that the parents would owe something to the tortfeasors. We think that a child should not be viewed as a piece of property, with fact finders first assessing the expense and damage incurred because of a child's life, then deducting the value of that child's life. For that reason, we think Restatement, Second, Torts § 920, supra, has no application to "wrongful birth" actions.

* * *

We affirm the trial court's dismissal of the "wrongful life" action. We reverse the trial court's dismissal of the "wrongful birth" or "wrongful pregnancy" action, and remand the cases to the trial court for further proceedings consistent with this opinion.

Case Questions

1. The Wyoming Supreme Court dismissed the "wrongful life" action. How does a wrongful life action differ from a wrongful birth or wrongful pregnancy action?
2. Since the Wyoming Supreme Court found negligence, and sustained the wrongful birth action, how can it justify having the defendants pay for some but not all of the alleged expenses? Explain.
3. Which of the four views regarding "wrongful birth" cases do you think is most fair? Explain.

Wrongful life cases often carry powerful emotional implications, but the temptation to become lost in value judgments must be resisted. Once again, focusing upon the legal elements carries the reader to the appropriate conclusions, as the following example demonstrates.

HYPOTHETICAL

Paul and Vicky Jonson visited Dr. Fritz Halpner, M.D., to see if Paul could get a vasectomy. Paul was concerned that he could transmit a genetic disease to his unborn child. Several members of Paul's family had been afflicted with the congenital disease. Dr. Halpner performed the sterilization surgery. A few months later, Vicky discovered that she was pregnant. Paul's operation did not "take." The Jonsons refused abortion on religious grounds. The Jonsons' baby daughter was born deformed as a result of the genetic disease transmitted from Paul. The Jonsons sued Dr. Halpner for medical malpractice, specifically alleging wrongful life.

Dr. Halpner's vasectomy operation did not prevent Vicky from becoming pregnant. Worse yet, the Jonson child was afflicted with congenital deformities because of Paul's genetically defective sperm. This child would not have been born in this unfortunate condition but for the doctor's negligence in performing the faulty operation. The Jonsons would appear to have a valid claim against Dr. Halpner for the tort of wrongful life.

Figure 11-6 lists the elements of wrongful life.

Also called *wrongful birth* or *wrongful pregnancy* actions
Usually a form of medical malpractice in which physician has negligently performed an ineffective sterilization operation
May include cases involving children born with birth defects
Damages include parents' medical expenses for unwanted birth and, in some jurisdictions, the costs of raising the child

FIGURE 11-6 Elements of wrongful life actions

Summary

A private nuisance is an unreasonable and substantial interference with another person's use and enjoyment of his or her land. Whether a nuisance activity is unreasonable and substantial depends upon its degree of offensiveness. The reasonable person standard is applied to test offensiveness and is based upon the community standard for persons living in the vicinity of the nuisance activity. Private nuisances often involve physical effects on the land, such as vibrations, pollution, and flooding. Private nuisance may also produce health hazards, such as poison gases, hazardous wastes, smoke, or dust, or effects offending the plaintiffs' sensibilities, such as odors or even incessant telephone calling. Private nuisances also include unwanted associations with neighboring uses, such as prostitution houses or gambling emporiums. "Coming to the nuisance" is the primary defense in private nuisance actions.

Public nuisances are activities that harm the public at large rather than a single individual. These nuisances unreasonably and substantially interfere with the public's use and enjoyment of legal rights common to the public. Governmental agencies litigate against public nuisance tortfeasors to enforce the general public's legal rights. State and local governments have the authority to litigate public nuisances under the police powers of the states. Public nuisances often involve so-called immoral activities, such as gambling, prostitution, distribution of sexually explicit materials, or sale of alcohol. Others include permitting noxious weeds to grow on one's property, carelessly disposing of toxic substances, or violating public health laws. Often, nuisances may be both private and public. These are called mixed nuisances. Nuisances per se are activities that violate statutes or ordinances. Public nuisances are often per se nuisances. "Coming to the nuisance" is usually not a defense in public nuisance cases.

Equitable remedies are usually awarded in nuisance litigation instead of money damages. Money damages are sometimes given when equitable remedies would be excessively harsh to the defendant. The relief most often granted involves abatement and injunctions. In abatement, the court orders the defendant to cease and desist the nuisance activity. Normally, the activity must be permanently discontinued. Courts enforce abatement by injunctions. Permanent injunctions forbid the activity forever. Temporary injunctions, such as temporary restraining orders (T.R.O.s), merely halt the defendant's nuisance activity until the court can conduct hearings or a trial on the merits. Defendants who disregard injunctions may find themselves in contempt of court, for which they can be fined or imprisoned.

Negligence per se is any activity that violates a negligence statute. It is considered automatic negligence simply because the defendant's conduct violated the statutory provisions. To recover damages, the plaintiff must fall within the class of persons that the statute was intended to protect. The same defenses apply to negligence per se that apply to ordinary negligence cases. Furthermore, the defendant's statutory violation must have proximately caused the plaintiff's injuries.

Wrongful death statutes provide surviving family members of a deceased tort victim with the right to sue the tortfeasor for wrongfully causing the victim's death. The statutes often grant the deceased victim's estate the right to pursue this cause of action. The tortfeasor's wrong may include negligence or intentional torts. Wrongful death damages usually consist of the victim's lost lifetime earnings potential and loss of consortium. Consortium includes the lost love and companionship between the dead victim and his or her family. The tortfeasor may use any defenses applicable for the alleged tort that caused the wrongful death. If the tortfeasor were accused of negligently causing the victim's death, then negligence defenses would apply. If the tortfeasor's intentional tort killed the victim, then intentional tort defenses would apply.

Wrongful life actions are lawsuits for the wrongful birth of a child. Usually, parents sue a physician for malpractice for negligently performing a sterilization operation. These cases often involve children born with birth defects. The tort has developed within the past quarter-century. Damages include the medical costs associated with pregnancy and birth, as well as the costs of raising the unwanted child. Court reactions to the tort have been mixed. Some jurisdictions reject the tort altogether, while others embrace it in whole or in part.

Review Questions

1. Define private nuisance. Who are the parties to this litigation? What is unreasonable and substantial interference? How is it determined? What is the role of the community standard? What is use and enjoyment?

2. Name the common types of private nuisance. Can you provide hypotheticals to illustrate each? What is "coming to the nuisance"?

3. What is a public nuisance? How is it distinguishable from a private nuisance? Who is affected by a public nuisance? Who acts as plaintiff? What

are some common examples of public nuisance? Does "coming to the nuisance" apply? What are common legal rights? What are mixed nuisances? What is a nuisance per se?

4. What remedies are used in nuisance cases? What about money damages? What is abatement? What are injunctions? Explain the difference between temporary and permanent injunctions. When is a T.R.O. used? What is contempt?

5. Explain negligence per se. When does it occur? What role do statutes play in this special tort? What defenses apply?

6. What are wrongful death statutes? Who are the plaintiffs in wrongful death litigation? What types of torts can be involved? What damages are awarded? What defenses apply?

7. What is wrongful life? What are the usual fact situations involving this special tort? What damages may be awarded?

Projects

1. Read the case of *Fishman v. Beach* in Appendix C. What is the purpose of dram shop acts? Why did the Supreme Court limit liability to just a certain area?

2. Read the case of *Girdley v. Coats* in Appendix C. Should this case be treated as any other malpractice case should be treated? Explain.

||||
CHAPTER 12

TORT IMMUNITIES

We may not all break the Ten Commandments, but we are certainly all capable of it. Within us lurks the breaker of laws, ready to spring out at the first opportunity.

— *Isadora Duncan*

§ 12.1 Introduction

Up to now, something has been missing from the torts analysis. That something is **tort immunities**—absolute defenses against a plaintiff's tort claims. If the defendant successfully invokes an immunity defense, he or she cannot be held liable for any torts committed. It is the reverse of absolute liability. Tort immunities absolutely protect the defendant from tort liability. There are many types of tort immunity, but the most common include sovereign (governmental) immunity and legal infirmities such as infancy or insanity. Tort immunities are similar to **privileges** and the terms are often used interchangeably.

This chapter includes:

- Sovereign (governmental) immunity

- Public officials' immunity

- Young children's immunity

- Statutes of limitation.

TERMS

immunity   An exemption granted by law, contrary to the general rule; a privilege. Immunity may be granted to a class of persons or to an individual.

privilege   An immunity, exemption, right, or advantage possessed by an individual, a group of individuals, or a class of persons, which is not possessed by others and which exists by operation of law or by virtue of a license, franchise, grant, or other permission; an exemption from a burden ... .

§ 12.2 Governmental, or Sovereign, Immunity

Sovereign (governmental) immunity has a long and storied history throughout the annals of tort law. To understand modern applications of this doctrine, one must trace its roots and development.

History

In the history of tort law, governments have held an enviable position. Until the twentieth century, governments were immune from liability for torts committed by their employees. This immunity was called **sovereign immunity**, or (in modern times) **governmental immunity**. It stemmed from the ancient English (and Western European) legal tradition that the king could not be sued by his subjects unless he consented. Official tortfeasors thus enjoyed an enviable immunity from liability unless they agreed to be sued, which one would naturally not if one had committed any torts.

Courts applied the legal maxim *The king can do no wrong.* This maxim traces its origins to pre-Roman times when the emperor was considered divine and, thus, incapable of errors that the law could remedy.

Modern Applications

For centuries, sovereign immunity protected the Crown and all its subordinates. Later, English and American common law spoke of governmental bodies (and their employees) as enjoying sovereign immunity. The term *king* was replaced with *government* in the American system, because our sovereigns are elected officials serving as presidents, governors, mayors, legislators, or (at the state and local level) judges.

Beginning in the early twentieth century, American courts began to whittle away at the governmental immunity doctrine. Many state courts have abolished sovereign immunity as an absolute defense to governmental liability. Legislatures have enacted statutes, such as the Federal Tort Claims Act, that specifically authorize lawsuits against torts

---

TERMS

sovereign (governmental) immunity   The principle that the government—specifically, the United States or any state of the United States—is immune from suit except when it consents to be sued.

IIII   PROFESSIONAL PROFILE   IIII

"I suppose my career as an insurance investigator is indicative that paralegal experience is a good springboard to other exciting opportunities," Michael Murphy says. For years he worked as a law clerk at a tort and family law firm. Murphy was also the law office administrator in charge of complete case management and staff. "One year we filed hundreds of claims after a major airplane crash." One of his duties included accompanying a client as she identified the body of an estranged spouse. The husband had simply dropped out of sight following the fatal flight.

"The best part of the job was helping people who were truly appreciative of my efforts, while the worst part was constantly dealing with death or severe disability," Murphy says. "But, as distasteful as that may have been, I think it makes one somewhat fearless and willing to take on nearly anything without hesitation."

Murphy joined a major insurance company in 1992. "I think I am one of many who started as a paralegal in a law firm—researching the law, drafting pleadings, communicating with clients, and then making the switch to the insurance industry." He believes his experience allows him the unique perspective in knowing which cases will ultimately settle and which will end up being tried.

His advice to students is simple: "Listen and you will learn what you don't know." When asked how he likes working for an insurance company, Murphy was enthusiastic. "I still get to use my legal knowledge and skills, and I get all the benefits of working for a large corporation."

committed by governmental employees (for which governmental agencies could be responsible under respondeat superior).

Early Twentieth-Century Cases

Many courts found the absolute defense of sovereign immunity to be unreasonably harsh on the plaintiffs. To avoid the full force of the immunity, early in the century American courts began distinguishing the different types of governmental activities that were or were not exempt from tort liability. There were two categories: governmental and proprietary. This is sometimes called the *governmental/proprietary distinction*.

Governmental Actions

When governmental bodies perform certain public protection activities, such as providing fire, police, or ambulance services, they are considered to be undertaking **governmental functions**. Persons performing

TERMS

governmental functions The activities engaged in by a government in carrying out its governmental duties.

governmental functions are immune from tort liability, under the early twentieth-century court decisions. Even if the fire, police, or ambulance departments committed torts against a citizen while performing their duties, the old case law would define these as governmental actions immune from liability.

Proprietary Actions

Governmental bodies also perform certain business-like activities (usually associated with the private sector). These are defined as **proprietary actions** and do not carry immunity from tort liability. For example, a municipality may provide utility services to its residents, such as water, sewer, electric, or natural gas, but this activity more closely resembles a private business enterprise than a public, governmental function. If the governmental agency providing such services committed torts, the government would be liable, and the immunity defense would not prevent liability.

Difficulty with the Governmental/Proprietary Distinction

Courts have struggled with the governmental/proprietary distinction for decades. What about cities that provide garbage collection? What about public parks? Are these governmental or proprietary functions? Courts often decide based upon whether a fee is assessed to users of these services. If a fee is charged, then the activity is considered proprietary. If not, then it is governmental. This may be called the **fee standard**.

Similar to the fee standard is the *pecuniary benefit test*. When governments provide services for profit, then the activities are proprietary. If governments offer services for the common public good, without economic benefit to the governmental units themselves, then the activities are governmental.

TERMS

proprietary function A function of local government that it may or may not perform, at its discretion, as opposed to its governmental duties.

fee standard[†] A test courts use in applying the governmental/proprietary distinction. If a governmental agency assesses a fee for an activity, the activity is considered proprietary. If not, it is considered governmental.

Modern Steps to Eliminate the Distinction

Within the past twenty years, many state courts have abolished the governmental/proprietary distinction and with it the defense of sovereign immunity. These courts now focus upon whether the governments committed any torts—just as courts would handle any other tort lawsuit. Many state legislatures and Congress have enacted statutes eliminating or restricting sovereign immunity to particular types of services, such as public parks or utilities.

Encyclopedia Illustrations

57 AMERICAN JURISPRUDENCE 2D *Municipal, County,*
School, and State Tort Liability
§§ 1–2, 5, 19, 61–62, 71, 87, 92, 94–97 (1988)
[All footnotes omitted.]

Generally, where there is tortious injury there is liability. Sovereign or governmental tort immunity is an exception to the rule … .

Sovereign or governmental tort immunity avoids tort liability to the extent of the immunity conferred. Often described as a bar to liability, immunity creates freedom from tort liability in the form of an exemption based on the nature or status of the defendant and denies the courts' jurisdiction to consider the plaintiff's claim. Its effect is not to deny the tort, only the resulting liability.

The roots of sovereign immunity from tort liability extend to medieval England. The doctrine flows from the concept that one could not sue the king in his own courts, hence the phrase "the king can do no wrong." The doctrine, as it developed at common law, had its origins in the English feudal system, and is firmly set in traditional concepts of state sovereignty, as is evident from the fact that the Eleventh Amendment to the United States Constitution broadly grants states immunity from suit in federal courts.

The early English case of *Russell v. The Men of Devon* is credited as initially applying the doctrine of sovereign tort immunity to local governments … .

Most jurisdictions generally adhere to the view that municipal corporations, counties, and other political subdivisions of the state are only generally subject to liability in tort under the express provisions of a state tort claims act or other statute, or a judicial limitation or abrogation of immunity, and hold that they specifically retain immunity from liability for certain functions and activities, based on distinctions as to the nature of particular acts or functions as governmental or proprietary and discretionary or ministerial. In these jurisdictions, municipalities and counties may be held liable in tort as any private person or corporation, subject to exceptions whereby immunity is retained to the extent expressly provided by statute or determined by judicial decision and subject to limitations on the amount and nature of damages recoverable. For this purpose, a local public entity would generally include counties, municipalities, and all other local governmental bodies. ...

In many jurisdictions, the courts have deemed the doctrine of governmental tort immunity for municipal corporations, counties, and political subdivisions of the state a court-made rule, subject to judicial abrogation or abolition without legislative action, and have expressly declared that the doctrine would no longer be recognized ... . In most jurisdictions, judicial abrogation or limitation of local governmental immunity has been quickly followed by legislative reinstatement of the doctrine in varying degrees and subject to similar limitations for particular functions, causes of action, and recoverable damages.

* * *

The state, as sovereign, is generally regarded as immune from liability and suit in its own courts or in any other court without its consent and permission. Accordingly, when the state's acts or omissions, or those of its officers, agents, employees, departments, agencies, and other instrumentalities, give rise to potential tort liability, a tort action may not be maintained against the state in its own courts, whether the action is brought by its own citizens, the citizens of another state, or the citizens or subjects of a foreign state, unless the state by statute has consented to be sued in tort, has otherwise waived its immunity or been estopped to raise the defense, has lost its immunity by judicial abrogation of the doctrine, or has engaged in activities or functions beyond the scope of its tort immunity. ... However, the doctrine of sovereign immunity from suit for torts is disfavored, and subject to a steady movement away from immunity.

* * *

Traditionally, sovereign immunity from tort liability was viewed as a rule of social policy serving to protect the state from burdensome interference in the performance of its governmental functions and to protect the state's control over its funds, property, and instrumentalities. Among the multitude of purposes purportedly served were those of protecting the public purse, providing for smooth operation of government, eliminating public inconvenience and danger that might spring from officials being fearful to act, assuring that citizens would be willing to take public jobs, and preventing citizens from improperly influencing the conduct of government through the threat or use of vexatious litigation. It served to protect and preserve public funds and to ensure that the state provided its citizenry appropriate services while holding taxes at reasonable levels.

* * *

The courts of some states have abrogated or limited the otherwise applicable common-law doctrine of state sovereign immunity from tort liability, finding the doctrine to have been originally a court-made rule and therefore subject to judicial repudiation or modification, although such judicial action is usually followed by quick legislative action to reinstate immunity, at least in part, and may be accompanied by limitations based on the nature of the particular act or function alleged as giving rise to liability.

* * *

A common test for the applicability of governmental tort immunity is whether the act or function giving rise to potential liability can be characterized as governmental or proprietary in nature. Immunity is retained for governmental or public acts or functions but liability may be imposed if the act or function is deemed merely proprietary or private in nature. The basis of the governmental/proprietary distinction in the law of governmental tort immunity and liability has been described as difficult to state. It originated with the courts ... . However, the application of the rule is fraught with difficulties, inconsistencies, uncertainties, and illogical results to the extent that there is a clear trend away from the rule by judicial abrogation or legislative action.

* * *

The governmental/proprietary distinction often applicable in determining the tort immunity or liability of municipalities, counties, and schools, whereby liability may be imposed for proprietary acts or functions while immunity is retained for governmental ones, is not as widely applied in actions against the state or its agencies. ...

Under the rule distinguishing between governmental and proprietary acts or functions ... , there is no clear line between acts or functions that are proprietary, ... and those that are governmental ... . Powers and functions considered governmental or public in one jurisdiction are often viewed as proprietary or private in another, making it impossible to state a rule sufficiently exact to be of much practical value in applying the test, as courts have noted frequently in their decisions abandoning or abrogating the governmental/proprietary test as a measure of state or local tort immunity or liability.

* * *

The underlying test for distinguishing between governmental and proprietary acts or functions, and thereby determining whether a state or local governmental entity is immune from or subject to tort liability, is whether the act performed is for the common good of all, as for the use and benefit of the general public, or whether it is for the special benefit or profit of the [governmental] corporate entity. ...

[L]ocal governmental entities are not immune from tort liability for proprietary functions exercised in an enterprise of a commercial character or usually carried on by private individuals or for the profit, benefit, or the advantage of the governmental unit conducting it, or conducted primarily for pecuniary benefit ... . Thus when a municipal corporation undertakes to furnish a service of a commercial character to individuals for a price, or engages in an undertaking the object of which is profit to itself, liability attaches for negligence in the performance of such compensated service, although such enterprises may ultimately subserve a public need. ...

Suits Against States

Even though many courts have abolished sovereign immunity and allow tort suits, not all states permit all kinds of tort suits to be brought against them. The individual state can decide just what suits it will or will not allow. In fact, in some states there is a special court just for tort claims against the state. In New York, it is called the Court of Claims.

Practical
Applications

The paralegal must be careful when preparing a tort claim against a state to see if there are any special rules. Your jurisdiction might require special procedures for bringing tort claims against the state. The pleadings might be different and have different or shorter time limits than usual. Because suits against the state were not always allowed, there may not be a provision for jury trial when the state is sued.

§ 12.3   Public Officers

Somewhat different from sovereign immunity is the individual tort immunity granted to certain public employees engaged in their official capacities. Certain governmental officials are immune from personal liability for any torts committed while they were performing their public duties.

Exceptions

There are exceptions to the privilege and immunity doctrines. 42 U.S.C. § 1983 permits liability of public officers (usually other than prosecutors and judges) if the performance of their duties involves activities that deprive persons of their civil rights. Such an action is called a civil rights action or a "1983" action; 1983 is the section number of the law permitting this action, not the year it was passed. If a police officer arrests someone without a warrant and without probable cause, the arrest is in violation of the detainee's civil rights and the officer may be liable. If excessive force is used in an arrest, it is a violation of civil rights and the officer may be liable. If any action under color or authority of the government—whether local, state, or federal—violates civil rights, the actor(s) may be liable regardless of immunity.

Who Is Protected

Legislators and judges enjoy an absolute immunity from tort liability for acts in their official governmental capacities. In performing legislative or judicial functions, it is possible that these public officials might commit torts against individual citizens. The common law protects judges and legislators from any liability whatsoever for having committed such torts. Executive branch officials, however, do not receive this blanket immunity, although administrative officers serving judicial or legislative functions do receive absolute immunity. For example, an agency adjudication officer, prosecutor, or county council legislator would be protected completely from tort liability.

Rationale for Immunity

Governmental official immunity is intended to ensure that legislators and judges may pursue their public duties without the chilling effect that fear of tort liability might create. Imagine how cautious legislators or judges would have to be in decision making if, with each sensitive topic, they had to worry about tort liability. These officials might become paralyzed by second-guessing, and the liability spectre could influence their public policy decisions. This rationale for the immunity is often repeated in the common law. To encourage maximum public benefit from the services of the public's judges and legislators, the law must totally protect these officials from tort liability.

§ 12.4 Children of Tender Years

For centuries, the common law has held that young children, often referred to as "children of tender years" in the court opinions, may be immune, or are subject to limited, tort liability.

Definition

Children of **tender years** are usually defined as young children under the age of seven years. Under traditional common law, any person under the age of twenty-one (and in the past twenty-five or so years, eighteen) is classed as a **minor**. However, only very young children normally

---

TERMS

tender years A term used to describe minors, particularly when they are very young.
minor A person who has not yet attained his or her majority; a person who has not reached legal age; a person who has not acquired the capacity to contract.

The Case of the Really Bad Coffee

Judicial immunity is an ancient English and American legal principle. It is a common law norm. However, it is not applied mindlessly by the appellate courts. In appropriate circumstances, the immunity is ineffective. One expects judges to act in a professional, dignified, restrained, and impartial fashion. Ninety-nine percent of the time, judges are somber, firm, stately, formal, and equitable. The other 1 percent act like the trial judge in the following case.

ZARCONE v. PERRY
U.S. Circuit Court of Appeals, Second Circuit
572 F.2d 52 (2d Cir. 1978)
March 3, 1978
Feinberg, Circuit Judge

In this unusual civil rights case, William M. Perry, a former judge of the District Court of Suffolk County, appeals from a verdict in favor of plaintiff Thomas Zarcone, after a jury trial in the United States District Court for the Eastern District of New York ... . The basis of Zarcone's suit was that Perry and other defendants had deprived plaintiff of his constitutional rights in violation of 42 U.S.C. § 1983. The jury awarded plaintiff $80,000 compensatory damages ... [and] $60,000 punitive damages against Perry ... . Only Perry appeals, and on the sole ground that the punitive damages award against him was excessive. We affirm. ...

The incident that gave rise to the lawsuit occurred on April 30, 1975. On that night, then Judge Perry was in his chambers during a break in an evening session of traffic court in Suffolk County, Long Island. Zarcone was operating a mobile food vending truck outside the courthouse. Perry asked Deputy Sheriff Windsor to get some coffee, which he did. Both Perry and Windsor thought the coffee tasted "putrid," and Perry told Windsor to get the coffee vendor and bring him "in front of me in cuffs." Perry directed two plainclothes officers, who happened to be nearby, to accompany Windsor. Wearing his sheriff's uniform equipped with badge, gun and handcuffs, Windsor went to Zarcone and told him that the judge said the coffee was terrible and that Zarcone had to go inside to see the judge. Windsor handcuffed Zarcone, despite the vendor's protestations that it was not necessary. When Zarcone said he was too embarrassed to go into the

courthouse that way, one of the officers suggested that Zarcone walk between them with Zarcone's jacket over his hands.

The group then marched through the hallway of the courthouse, in full view of dozens of people. Zarcone heard someone yell that they were locking up the frankfurter man. When they arrived at Perry's chambers, the judge asked if the Sheriff had "the coffee vending man there in handcuffs." Upon entering the chambers, Perry ordered Zarcone to be left "in handcuffs until I get finished with him." A pseudoofficial inquisition then began. Zarcone stood in front of the judge's desk, behind which the judge sat. A court reporter was present, along with Windsor and the two police officers. Perry told Zarcone that "I have the two cups of coffee here for evidence." According to Zarcone, whom the jury must have believed, Perry then started screaming at him, threatening him and his "livelihood" for about 20 minutes, and thoroughly scaring him. Just before Zarcone was allowed to leave, Perry commanded Windsor to note Zarcone's vehicle and vending license numbers and told Zarcone, "Mister, you are going to be sorrier before I get through with you."

After Zarcone left, he resumed his mobile truck route and came back to the night traffic courthouse about 45 minutes later. Shortly thereafter, Windsor returned and told Zarcone they were to go back to the judge. Zarcone asked if he had to be handcuffed again, but Windsor said no. When they reappeared before Perry, he told Zarcone that he was going to have the two cups of coffee analyzed. Perry also said that if Zarcone would admit he did something wrong, then Perry would drop the charges. Zarcone consistently denied that anything was amiss with the coffee, and no charges were filed.

We have described the night's events in such detail to impart some of the flavor that must have so impressed the jury. The unfortunate occurrence was publicized at the time, and ultimately led to the removal of Judge Perry from the bench. There were unpleasant consequences for Zarcone, as well: He testified that he was very upset by the incident, that he could not sleep, and that he started to stutter and get headaches. Zarcone also required treatment at the Coney Island Hospital, he could not work, and his wife asked him to move out of the house. We need not dwell on this any further, except to note that Perry does not complain here about the jury's award to Zarcone of $80,000 compensatory damages. However, Perry does challenge the amount of punitive damages, and we now turn to this issue.

... [G]iven Perry's position, his relationship of power and authority to plaintiff, who was a simple coffee vendor, the handcuffing, threats and intimidation inflicted upon plaintiff, and Perry's outrageous conduct, we are not compelled to conclude that the jury acted out of "passion and prejudice." In short, we do not find that the verdict of $60,000 shocks our conscience. Perhaps to some the award might seem high and the incident exaggerated out of proportion. But the abuse of official power here was intolerable, and when a jury has dealt with it severely, as it should, we will not draw fine lines to restrain its dispensation of justice.

Judgment affirmed.

Case Questions

1. What do you suppose Judge Perry would have done to Zarcone if he had also sold Perry a frankfurter?
2. Under traditional common law, judges are absolutely immune from tort liability for all judicial actions, regardless of malice or extremity. Why did the Second Circuit deviate from this long-standing rule, repeatedly espoused by the United States Supreme Court? Was Judge Perry's action a judicial act? You might wish to read *Stump v. Sparkman*, 435 U.S. 349, 98 S. Ct. 1099 (1978) for an applicable definition.

enjoy the tender-years immunity. Although many opinions, particularly older cases, have granted immunity to teenagers, most cases limit tender years to below age seven. A significant number of cases, however, include the eight-to-twelve age group within the immunity.

Absolute Immunity for Intentional Torts

Most states still follow the ancient common law rule that children of tender years are incapable of committing intentional torts. They are immune from intentional tort liability. This immunity is based upon the concept that young children are mentally and emotionally incapable of having the proper intent to commit an intentional tort. Because they are so young, they lack the experience and development to appreciate fully the significance of their actions, which sometimes are tortious in nature.

For instance, suppose a four-year-old child tosses a sharpened pencil to get another child's attention. This pencil strikes the other child in the eye, causing injury. Had adults been involved, this would be a clear case of battery. However, most states would rule that the pencil-thrower was immune from liability for this intentional tort. Children of tender years are presumed to be incapable of the intent element in intentional torts.

Immunity from Negligence

Most courts do not grant absolute negligence immunity to young children. Instead, the child tortfeasor's age is merely one factor to be considered in determining the standard of reasonable care which the reasonable child of tender years would have used in a particular case. A minority of states have held that children below a certain age (usually seven years) cannot commit negligence and are therefore immune from liability. Most states, however, would agree that only extremely young children, often less than three or four years of age, are incapable of negligence and would be immune.

Children's immunity is never easy to determine. For example, suppose a five-year-old child swings a golf club backwards, planning to reverse the stroke and hit a golf ball. While doing the backswing, the club accidentally hits another child in the forehead, opening a nasty gash. Was the golfer negligent? Most states would apply a reasonable five-year-old child standard to gauge negligence. Some others follow the under-seven absolute immunity rule. This immunity varies widely among, or even within, jurisdictions.

§ 12.5 Statutes of Limitations

Statutes of limitations are statutes establishing time limits within which plaintiffs may file tort actions against defendants. These time frames vary for different torts and between states.

TERMS

statutes of limitations Federal and state statutes prescribing the maximum period of time during which various types of civil actions and criminal prosecutions can be brought after the occurrence of the injury or the offense.

The Case of Parental Control

As the two-wage-earner family becomes more and more common, a question frequently asked is "Who is minding the children?" When a minor kills another minor, can the killer's mother and grandparents be sued for negligent failure to control a minor? This case presents a threat to all grandparents who take on the role of babysitter to their grandchildren.

WELLS v. HICKMAN
Court of Appeals of Indiana
657 N.E.2d 172 (Ind. Ct. App. 1995)
November 8, 1995
Najam, Judge

Cheryl Wells ("Wells") filed a complaint for the wrongful death of her son, D.E., at the hands of L.H., the son of Gloria Hickman ("Hickman") and the grandson of Albert and Geneva Hickman (the "Grandparents"). L.H. beat D.E. to death while the two boys were in the woods behind the Grandparents' home. Wells alleged that Hickman and the Grandparents failed to control L.H. when they were aware or should have been aware that injury to D.E. was possible and that their negligence resulted in D.E.'s death. Wells brings an interlocutory appeal from the trial court's entry of summary judgment in favor of Hickman. The trial court denied Wells' common law negligence claim against Hickman and entered summary judgment based upon a determination that Wells' recovery was limited by statute to $3,000.00 in damages. The Grandparents bring an interlocutory appeal from the trial court's denial of their motion for summary judgment. The trial court declined to find as a matter of law that the Grandparents had no duty to prevent the death of D.E. and permitted Wells to maintain her action against them. The two interlocutory appeals were consolidated by order of this court on June 8, 1995.

We affirm in part, reverse in part and remand.

Several issues are presented on appeal which we restate as follows:

1. Whether Indiana Code § 34-4-31-1 precludes the recovery of damages in a common law action for parental negligence by limiting parental liability for the wrongful acts of the parent's child.

2. Whether Hickman had a parental duty to exercise reasonable care to control L.H. for the safety of D.E.

3. Whether the Grandparents had a duty to protect D.E. from harm.

D.E. and his mother, Cheryl Wells, were neighbors to L.H. and his mother, Gloria Hickman. L.H. and Hickman lived in a trailer located on land owned by L.H.'s grandparents, Albert and Geneva Hickman. The trailer was parked within 100 feet of the Grandparents' house and L.H. was often at their home. Hickman worked the night shift and usually left for work at 10:00 P.M. The Grandparents cared for L.H. while Hickman was at work, and L.H. often ate his meals and snacks at the Grandparents' home. Either Hickman or the Grandparents always knew L.H.'s whereabouts.

Between the Fall of 1990 and October 15, 1991, L.H. killed a pet dog by beating it to death, and he killed a pet hamster. L.H. had also expressed his desire to commit suicide. L.H. often exhibited anger and, on one occasion, he came home from school with a black eye, cuts and bruises. Upon the recommendation of his school principal, L.H. attended counseling sessions at Southern Hills Counseling Center.

On October 15, 1991, D.E. was celebrating his twelfth birthday. After school, fifteen year old L.H. invited D.E. over to play video games. Wells, D.E.'s mother, agreed. The boys did not play video games and neither Hickman nor the Grandparents were aware that D.E. and L.H. were together. Around 6:30 P.M., L.H. returned home and appeared to be very nervous. Later, L.H. told his mother that he thought he had killed D.E. After a search, D.E.'s body was found lying beside a fallen tree on the Grandparents' property.

* * *

When reviewing a motion for summary judgment, we apply the same standard as the trial court, and we resolve any doubt as to a fact, or an inference to be drawn therefrom, in favor of the party opposing summary judgment. ...

A negligence action is rarely an appropriate case for summary judgment. ... To be liable the parent must know that her child "had a habit of engaging in the particular act or course of conduct which led to the plaintiff's injury." The duty to control one's child is described in the Restatement (Second) of Torts as follows:

> A parent is under a duty to exercise reasonable care so to control his minor child as to prevent it from intentionally harming others or from so conducting itself as to create an unreasonable risk of bodily harm to them, if the parent
>
> (a) knows or has reason to know that he has the ability to control his child, and
>
> (b) knows or should know of the necessity and opportunity for exercising such control.

* * *

The critical issue in this case is foreseeability and we must determine whether Hickman knew or with due care should have known that L.H. would injure D.E. ...

The record indicates Hickman knew that L.H. was a troubled child and she could anticipate the same type of conduct that he had exhibited in the past. Upon the advice of a school principal and from her personal observations, Hickman was aware that L.H. needed professional help. Nevertheless, we cannot conclude, based upon L.H.'s cruelty to animals and his comment about committing suicide, that it was reasonably foreseeable he would kill a neighborhood friend. The boys apparently had played together previously without incident and Hickman could not have seen L.H.'s behavior as a precursor to homicide or even that L.H. would harm D.E. Neither the type of harm inflicted nor the victim in this case was foreseeable and, thus, cannot support the imposition of a duty upon Hickman.

Public policy supports the imposition of a duty to control on a parent under the proper circumstances, but it does not in this case. Parents are in a unique position in society because they have a special power to observe and control the conduct of their minor children. ... Parents have a duty to exercise this power reasonably, especially when they have notice of a child's dangerous tendencies. ...

We hold that a cause of action for parental negligence in the failure to control may be maintained in Indiana, but we decline to find a duty in this case. A duty may be imposed upon a parent for her failure to control her child when the parent knows or should know that the child has engaged in a particular act or course of conduct and it is reasonably foreseeable that this conduct would lead to the plaintiff's injuries. We conclude, as a matter of law, that Hickman had no duty to exercise control over L.H. because the harm and the victim were not reasonably foreseeable. Therefore, summary judgment in favor of Hickman is appropriate.

Wells next contends that the failure to control exception may be extended to the Grandparents in this case because they assumed a parental role over L.H., their grandson. We cannot agree.

As we have already stated, imposition of a duty under this exception requires that the parent knew or should have known that injury to another was reasonably foreseeable. ... [W]e concluded that Hickman could not have reasonably foreseen that L.H. would kill or even harm D.E. and, likewise, we conclude that the Grandparents could not have foreseen this occurrence. Therefore, the trial court erred by failing to enter summary judgment in favor of Albert and Geneva Hickman.

Wells also asserts that the Grandparents are liable based on a negligent entrustment theory and claims that because L.H. was entrusted to their care, they are responsible for the death of D.E. Again, we must disagree.

There is a well recognized duty in tort law that persons entrusted with children have a duty to supervise their charges. ... The duty exists whether or not the supervising party has agreed to watch over the child for some form of compensation.

* * *

[T]he Grandparents were unaware of D.E.'s presence on their property. There was no relationship between the Grandparents and D.E. that would give rise to a duty under a negligent entrustment theory.

Finally, Wells contends that the Grandparents owed D.E. a duty to protect him from harm because he was a social guest upon their premises. A landowner owes a social guest the same duty of care as an invitee. That duty is to exercise reasonable care for a person's protection while he is on the landowner's premises. ...

Assuming that D.E. was a social guest upon the Grandparents' property, he would be owed a duty of reasonable care. This duty requires:

> A person to anticipate and guard against what usually happens or is likely to happen and that a failure to do this is negligence; but that reasonable care does not require him to foresee and guard against that which is unusual and not likely to occur, and a failure to do this is not negligence.

Although the Grandparents were aware that L.H. had emotional problems, they could not have foreseen and guarded against the death of D.E. Because this event was unlikely to occur, they were not negligent. Further, D.E. was not injured by a condition or activity conducted on the land. We do not find the presence of a troubled child to be equivalent to a dangerous condition or activity on the premises. The trial court erred when it denied the Grandparents' motion for summary judgment as they did not have a duty under the circumstances to exercise control over their grandson, they were not entrusted with D.E.'s care and, finally, they were not responsible for D.E.'s death based on premises liability.

The judgment of the trial court is affirmed in part, reversed in part, and remanded with instructions to enter judgment for Albert and Geneva Hickman and against Cheryl Wells, and for Cheryl Wells and against Gloria Hickman in the amount of $3,000.00

Case Questions

1. Based on the facts presented, do you feel that the death of D.E. was foreseeable? Explain.
2. What kind of facts would have had to be present for the court to have sustained an action for negligent failure to control?
3. What is needed to bring a negligent entrustment case?

There are statutes of limitations for tort lawsuits against governmental units. These often establish an elaborate written notification procedure that the plaintiff must follow to notify all the relevant governmental agencies (and their directors) that a lawsuit has been filed against them.

§ 12.6 Worker's Compensation

Workers who are injured or killed as a result of incidents occurring during the course and scope of their employment are covered for their injuries by state worker's compensation statutes. An employee is covered regardless of the employer's fault. Recovery is limited to the amount set forth in statutory tables. This is generally much less than would be awarded for similar injuries in a common law tort claim. As a result of these worker's compensation statutes, employers are immune from employee suits. Worker's compensation is considered the employee's sole remedy. Note also that there are some federal worker's compensation statutes, which apply to certain employees of the United States government.

The Case of the Exclusive Worker's Compensation

Worker's compensation acts are generally considered an employee's exclusive remedy for on-the-job injuries. In this case, an employee alleges both negligent infliction of emotional distress and intentional infliction of emotional distress against her supervisor and employer. Are these the kinds of acts that worker's compensation statutes were designed to cover?

VORVIS
v.
SOUTHERN NEW ENGLAND TELEPHONE CO.
United States District Court for the District of Connecticut
821 F. Supp. 851 (D. Conn. 1993)
May 25, 1993
Edginton, Senior District Judge

This action was removed to this court based on diversity of citizenship and federal question jurisdiction. Defendant has moved to dismiss the complaint, which contains state law claims arising out of her alleged mistreatment in the workplace. For the reasons stated below, the motion to dismiss will be granted in part and denied in part.

Plaintiff, Joyce Vorvis, was employed by defendant, Southern New England Telephone Company ("SNET"), from July 13, 1981 to June 2, 1989, under the terms and conditions of an employment contract. Frank Kulaga was her direct supervisor beginning September 1, 1988. From this time until the end of her employment, plaintiff alleges that she was subjected to extreme and outrageous harassment by Kulaga. She claims he continually subjected her to verbal abuse and caused her to work extra hours without compensation. She alleges that Kulaga made at least one

false verbal statement about her job performance, which, along with the harassment, damaged her reputation. She alleges that Kulaga unfairly disciplined her for certain incompleted work assignments. As a result, she claims she suffered physical and emotional harm and was forced to leave her job on June 2, 1989. Defendants benefited from her departure, she contends, because SNET was in the process of reducing its workforce.

* * *

In Counts I and II, plaintiff alleges intentional infliction of emotional distress against Kulaga and SNET. She claims that from September 1, 1988 through June 2, 1989, SNET intentionally directed Kulaga to treat her in such a way as to cause severe emotional distress which would lead to her departure from SNET. This treatment began after she returned from foot surgery and while she was coping with the illness and death of her sister. The treatment allegedly took place almost every day for a period of over one year, and included chastising, criticism, humiliation in front of coworkers, threats to fire her, extra work assignments for the purpose of causing anxiety, uncompensated work on weekends and evenings, unwarranted vulgar remarks, and disciplinary actions for matters beyond her control. As a result, plaintiff allegedly suffered various physical and psychological injuries, including: tachycardia, fear, crying spells, insomnia, nervousness, headaches, nausea, depression, fear of future injuries, mental pain and anguish, loss of her job, inability to function with coworkers, and loss of work and personal relationships with coworkers.

The exclusivity provision of the Connecticut Worker's Compensation Act provides that:

> An employer shall not be liable to any action for damages on account of personal injury sustained by a employee arising out of and in the course of his employment or on account of death resulting from personal injury so sustained, but an employer shall secure compensation for his employees as follows, except that compensation shall not be paid when the personal injury has been caused by the wilful and serious misconduct between employer and employees ...

Conn.Gen.Stat. § 31-284(a). Under the Workers' Compensation Act, an employee surrenders his or her right to bring common-law action against employer. Intentional tort claims are not barred if the actor is acting with the knowing authorization of the employer. Thus, a claim will not be barred by the Workers' Compensation Act where the tort is intentional and where the defendant employer directed the supervisor to commit the tort.

Here, the exception for "personal injury ... caused by the wilful and serious misconduct between employer and employees" applies as to plaintiff's claims of intentional infliction of emotional distress. Plaintiff alleges an intentional tort that was knowingly authorized by the actor's employer. Thus, the Worker's Compensation Act does not bar this cause of action.

The next step is to determine whether plaintiff has made a claim for intentional infliction of emotional distress. Viewing the allegations in the complaint in the light most favorable to the plaintiff, the court finds that she does. Plaintiff has alleged in the complaint that: (1) defendant intended or knew that emotional distress would likely result from defendant's conduct; (2) defendant's conduct was extreme or outrageous; (3) defendant's conduct caused plaintiff's distress; and (4) plaintiff's emotional distress was severe.

Accordingly, the motion to dismiss must be denied as to Counts I and II.

Plaintiff alleges negligent infliction of emotional distress against Kulaga in Count III, and against SNET in Counts IV and V.

* * *

Under Connecticut law, the issue of compensability under the Workers' Compensation Act is determined by whether or not the worker's injury is one "arising out of and in the course of employment." ...

In the instant case, plaintiff's claim for negligent infliction of emotional distress is barred by the Connecticut Worker's Compensation Act because her alleged injuries arose out of and in the course of her employment, and because the exception for intentional torts does not apply.

Therefore, the motion to dismiss Counts III, IV, and V alleging negligent infliction of emotional distress must be granted.

Case Questions

1. The plaintiff's claims of negligent infliction of emotional distress and intentional infliction of emotional distress were treated differently by the United States District Court. Explain which of the claims, if any, were covered under worker's compensation, and which were permitted as separate claims.

Summary

Tort immunities are absolute defenses against a plaintiff's tort claims. Sovereign, or governmental, immunity is an ancient common law defense that protected governments from tort liability. The doctrine was based on the presumption that "the king could do no wrong," which, in America, translated that the government could not be sued without its consent. American courts have drastically reduced or eliminated sovereign immunity during the twentieth century. In the early decades of this century, courts avoided the immunity by distinguishing between governmental and proprietary actions in which government agencies were engaged. Many states have abolished sovereign immunity altogether as an absolute defense.

Public officers, such as judges or legislators, are immune from personal liability for any torts committed while they are performing their official duties. This ensures that governmental officials may act independently and freely to perform their civil responsibilities, without fear of constant tort liability for their every public action that might tortiously affect individual citizens in some way.

"Children of tender years" are very young children, often under the age of seven years, although many courts have defined the term as including children to age twelve or even through the teenage years. Children of tender years are immune from intentional tort liability in most jurisdictions. Often, a specific age boundary is used. Many courts state that children under seven years are absolutely immune. Others do not rigidly follow any age barrier. For negligence, most courts apply a reasonable child-of-tender-years standard to decide whether negligence has occurred. A minority of states use definite age limits, such as the seven-year-old rule, for negligence cases.

Statutes of limitations restrict the time period within which a plaintiff may file tort causes of action against a defendant. There are statutes of limitations for tort lawsuits against governmental units. These often establish written notification procedures that the plaintiff must follow to notify all the relevant governmental agencies (and their directors) that a lawsuit has been filed against them.

State worker's compensation statutes prevent suits by injured employees against employers.

Review Questions

1. What are tort immunities? What is their function in tort litigation? Who do they protect?

2. Define sovereign, or governmental, immunity. What is the historical rationale behind the defense? How have modern American courts applied the doctrine?

3. What is the governmental/proprietary distinction? How it is used? How are governmental actions defined? Proprietary actions? What is the significance of these distinctions?

4. What is the modern trend among American courts toward sovereign immunity? How has the defense changed during this century?

5. What are public officers' immunities? Who do they protect? Why are these governmental officials granted immunity?

6. Define children of tender years. Who is protected by this defense? How does the immunity differ for intentional torts and negligence?

7. What are statutes of limitations? How do they apply to governmental tort liability?

Project

Read the *Doe v. Cutter Biological* case in Appendix C. The plaintiff seeks to hold two defendants liable, although the plaintiff admits it is not possible to prove which defendant caused the plaintiff's injuries. Is the joint and several liability doctrine fair? Explain. Which particular immunity was involved in this case? What is the enterprise theory? Define the concert-of-action theory.

CHAPTER 13

PARALEGAL ETHICS

§ 13.1 Introduction

Cynics say that legal ethics is a contradiction in terms. They scoff that lawyers and their staffs, like used car dealers or politicians, are universally suspect as underhanded manipulators vying for innocent victims' money. Honest attorneys, paralegals, and legal secretaries rankle at this false, misleading stereotype. Ethical and unethical behavior exists in every profession. There are always rotten apples whose odor taints the wholesomeness of the whole bushel. But, conversely, there are lots of good-quality apples ready for market amongst the handful of rancid produce. The bad apples can easily be identified and removed from the lot.

This is the role of legal ethics: to identify and remove inappropriate conduct from the legal profession. Honest legal practitioners strive to avoid ethical dilemmas—to keep the fruit from spoiling, so to speak. Unscrupulous persons are culled and expelled through disciplinary sanction from state supreme courts or disciplinary agencies.

This final chapter discusses this extremely important aspect of paralegal work, namely, the real-world ethical concerns one encounters daily as a legal assistant. It is no exaggeration to say that legal ethics may be the most important area of study in the paralegal field. This chapter includes:

- NALA's ethics rules applicable to paralegals

- The ABA's ethics standards applicable to paralegals.

§ 13.2 NALA Ethics Codes

The National Association of Legal Assistants, Inc. (NALA) has promulgated two sets of ethics codes designed specifically for paralegals. The Code of Ethics and Professional Responsibility was issued in 1977. NALA updated and improved this code in 1984 with its Model Standards and Guidelines for Utilization of Legal Assistants. For purposes of comparison, the first will be called the *Code* and the latter the *Model Standards.*

Restricted Duties

Canon I of the Code states that paralegals shall not perform any duties that only lawyers may fulfill, nor shall paralegals perform activities that attorneys are prohibited from doing. For instance, paralegals may not engage in the unauthorized practice of law. This is expressly forbidden in Code Canons III and VI. Only attorneys licensed and in good standing with a state's bar licensing authority (usually the state bar or the state supreme court) may practice law. As explained in the Model Standards, this includes providing legal advice to clients, representing clients in court proceedings, contacting adverse parties on a client's behalf, establishing legal fees, accepting clients' cases on behalf of attorneys or the law firm, and preparing legal documents without attorney supervision.

Paralegal Representation Before Administrative Agencies

Many state and federal administrative agencies permit nonlawyers, including paralegals, to represent parties appearing before the agencies in adjudicatory or rulemaking hearings. Such representation is not the unauthorized practice of law, because it is expressly permitted by administrative rules and regulations.

Some state courts refuse to recognize such administrative authorization, and there are common law decisions declaring nonlawyer client representation before administrative agencies to constitute unauthorized legal practice. These courts argue that only the judicial branch has authority to regulate the practice of law. State constitutions or, more often, state statutes vest this regulatory power most frequently in the state supreme court, which might delegate supervisory authority to a state bar agency. In the case of legislative declarations, the state legislature may simply amend its statutes excluding administrative agency

PROFESSIONAL PROFILE

Attorney Bill Wright describes how conferencing software improved his law firm's communications.

Our Bellmawr, New Jersey law office houses 40 people—6 attorneys, 12 paralegals, and 22 support staff. Farr, Burke, Gambacorta & Wright isn't large enough to employ a full-time MIS director, so my partners and I share that role, maintaining 20 PCs on a DEC Pathworks network and a VAX minicomputer. Until about a year ago, the closest we came to groupware, aside from DEC Mail e-mail, was a conference room and a whiteboard.

Then, in September 1994, one of the firm's partners unexpectedly resigned, taking 3 associates, 3 paralegals, 11 support staff, and dozens of clients' files with him. Four days later, he had the audacity to sue us. We promptly filed a counterclaim.

So, in addition to being left short-staffed, we had to deal with a lawsuit. Keeping everyone up-to-date on developments in the case meant impromptu meetings, quick hallway confabs, and a flurry of e-mail. The rest of the time we were in each others' offices commiserating. (There's nothing like a common foe to bring colleagues together.) We spent so much time telling each other what we were doing that we had little time to actually do anything.

Obviously we needed a way to distribute our information more efficiently. E-mail discussions were better than offline meetings, but they were difficult to track. Crucial information was easily lost among all the replies. On the other hand, we didn't have the resources or the time for an expensive and complicated client/server application like Lotus Notes.

While looking for a solution between these two extremes, I read a review of several conferencing packages and was struck by the description of Trax Softworks' TeamTalk. It had everything we needed—threaded discussions within topics, cross-topic searching, and easy installation—at a relatively low price. And it would

run on our existing PCs. We bought it, installed it, and started using it immediately to help in the litigation with our former partner.

TeamTalk paid for itself in a week. We could get more information reading a TeamTalk discussion for 5 to 10 minutes than meeting in the conference room for 2 hours. We now spend less time in meetings and more time in billable work.

Instead of calling a meeting to apprise colleagues of new developments in a case, I find the appropriate discussion in TeamTalk, add a comment or reply, then click Send to notify everyone in the group. We still have meetings, but they're much more focused. Participants review the online discussions beforehand and come to the meeting ready to get down to business.

What started as one discussion on the suit and countersuit with our former partner has grown into 32 discussions covering every part of the firm's operations, from legal procedures to marketing to warehousing information for an attorney on leave.

TeamTalk cuts down on information overload by letting us specify membership for each discussion. TeamTalk also lets us assign varying levels of participation, letting certain members follow a discussion but not add comments or replies to it.

The Management discussion, which disseminates confidential information about managing the firm's business, is limited to the four shareholders. But discussions about the firm's clients and about competing firms are open to everyone in the office.

In the Procedure and Law discussion, attorneys and paralegals share information about the law, courtroom strategies, and particular judges. In the New Time and Billing discussion, administrative staff discuss plans to upgrade current procedures.

In the most novel use of TeamTalk, one of our attorneys created a topic in which coworkers could store information related to her cases while she was on maternity leave. Before leaving, she placed status reports and task lists in the discussion for those covering for her. While she was on leave, coworkers recorded developments so she would be up to speed when she returned.

Though none of us had any trouble learning TeamTalk, there's still some confusion about when to use TeamTalk and when to send e-mail. Some people broadcast messages via e-mail that should be TeamTalk discussions, and vice versa.

Another problem stems from DEC Mail: Though TeamTalk discussions can be accessed from any MAPI- or VIM-compliant e-mail system, our version of DEC Mail doesn't support those standards. Staff who are only on VAX terminals are left out.

In the near future, we may migrate to Novell's Groupwise, one of the few messaging systems that directly supports both VAX systems and PCs.

For the distant future, we're evaluating a more complete groupware solution that would allow us to exchange information with clients around the country.

Our firm represents large financial institutions—including banks, credit card companies, mortgage firms, and automobile finance companies—many of which use Notes. These clients increasingly expect us to link with their networks so they can send us files and receive up-to-the-minute progress reports electronically. Right now, we're handling this exchange by fax—about 300 per day. It should be easier to accommodate all this in Notes.

Reprinted with permission from *PC WORLD*, "Group Problems, Group Solutions: Do Meetings Clog Your Day?," edited by Ann Kremers. Volume 14, Number 2, February 1996.

party representation regulations from the courts' authority. However, when a state constitution plainly roots regulatory power over law practice in the courts, the legislature must pursue constitutional amendment procedures. This is a cumbersome process.

In most instances, however, the courts simply look the other way, allowing nonattorneys to represent clients before administrative agencies that have expressed a willingness to accept such circumstances.

Lay Representation in Justice or Small Claims Courts

Many state statutes permit nonlawyers to represent litigants before justices of the peace (commonly called justice courts) or small claims courts. The common law in most states narrowly construes such statutes, indicating that such lay representation is intended for (1) "one-time" appearances, (2) family or business employee representation, or (3) civil cases only. Thus, paralegals who attempt to carve a niche by representing clients in justice or small claims courts on a regular basis would, under these courts' interpretations, engage in unauthorized law practice.

Supervised Duties

Canon II of the Code declares that paralegals may perform any delegated tasks supervised by a licensed attorney. The supervising lawyer must remain directly responsible to the client, maintaining or establishing the attorney-client relationship and assuming full accountability for the legal services supplied. This provision permits paralegals to conduct initial consultations with clients, in which they gather factual information from the client. It also allows paralegals to complete legal research and writing tasks, investigate cases, compile evidence, arrange (but not conduct) discovery, and prepare materials for trial. However, at each phase, the attorney must guide and direct the paralegal's efforts.

The Model Standards reiterate Code Canon II, adding that a paralegal should disclose his or her status as a paralegal (rather than a lawyer) at the outset of any professional relationship with clients, or when dealing with other attorneys, courts, administrative agencies, or the general public. The Model Standards also emphasize the supervising attorneys' duty to monitor and train paralegals.

No Independent Legal Judgment

Code Canon IV forbids paralegals from exercising independent, professional legal judgment in place of an attorney's. The Model Standards are comparable, stating that a paralegal may perform services for a lawyer, provided that they do not require the exercise of independent legal judgment, and provided that the attorney supervises the paralegal's efforts. Canon V also reminds paralegals to act prudently so that they can determine the extent to which they may assist a client without an attorney's presence. This is especially important during fact-gathering client consultations or when discussing details with clients on the telephone.

Protecting Client Confidences

Paralegals must protect client confidences under Code Canon VII and the Model Standards. It is unethical for a paralegal to violate any statute controlling privileged communications. Examples of privileged communications include discussions between attorney and client, physician and patient, husband and wife, clergy and parishioner, and counsellor and patient.

Clearly, when clients speak with attorneys and their staff, there is an expectation that confidences and disclosures shall remain inside the office. The rule of thumb for paralegals, like all law office staff, is simply not to discuss sensitive client information with anyone. One should always consult with the supervising attorney to see if particular client information is privileged.

Avoiding the Appearance of Impropriety

Code Canon VIII warns paralegals to avoid conduct that would be considered, or even simply appear to be, unethical.

Integrity and Competency

Similarly, Code Canon IX states that paralegals shall maintain their integrity and a high degree of competency. This may require paralegals to complete continuing legal education, as most states now require of attorneys. In fact, Code Canon X encourages paralegals to "strive for perfection through education" to better assist the legal profession and the public.

Catchall Provision

The Code includes a catchall provision declaring that paralegals shall do everything "incidental, necessary, or expedient" to maintain the ethics and responsibility required by statutes or court rules of legal professionals.

Lawyer Ethics Rule Application

Code Canon XII and the Model Standards includes paralegals within the coverage of the American Bar Association's ethics codes. The current version of the ABA regulations is the Model Rules of Professional Conduct, which replaced the Code of Professional Responsibility. All states have their own versions of these attorney ethics provisions, many of which are modeled directly upon the ABA versions.

Model Standards' List of Permissible Activities

To clarify ambiguities in the Code, NALA's Model Standards list permissible activities for paralegals to perform, provided that such items do not conflict with or contradict statutes, court rules, administrative rules and regulations, or the attorneys' ethics codes. Under this list of permissible activities, paralegals may do the following, under the attorney's supervision and guidance:

1. Conduct client interviews and maintain general contact with clients.
2. Locate and interview witnesses.
3. Conduct investigations and legal research for an attorney's review.
4. Draft legal documents for a lawyer's review.
5. Draft correspondence and pleadings for an attorney's review and signature.
6. Summarize depositions, interrogatories, and testimony for a lawyer's review.
7. Attend will executions, real estate closings, depositions, court or administrative hearings, and trials, along with an attorney.
8. Write and sign letters, provided that the paralegal's status is plainly indicated and the correspondence does not contain independent legal opinions or advice.

Legal Effect of NALA Rules

It is important for the reader to note that NALA's ethics provisions have no force of law, in and of themselves. NALA is a private organization, and accordingly its promulgations are advisory. However, courts are likely to give considerable credence to NALA's rules, as historically courts have accepted the ABA's ethics codes as definitive statements of the law.

An Example of Court-Ordered Ethics

Some courts have promulgated rules addressing the ethical use of paralegals, as the following illustration shows. Note the similarities and distinctions between the Rhode Island regulations and NALA's Code.

PROVISIONAL ORDER NO. 18
Supreme Court of Rhode Island
454 A.2d 1222 (R.I. 1983)
February 1, 1983

GUIDELINES FOR USE OF LEGAL ASSISTANTS

These guidelines shall apply to the use of legal assistants by members of the Rhode Island Bar Association. A legal assistant is one who under the supervision of a lawyer, shall apply knowledge of law and legal procedures in rendering direct assistance to lawyers, clients and courts; design, develop and modify procedures, techniques, services and processes; prepare and interpret legal documents; detail procedures for practicing in certain fields of law; research, select, assess, compile and use information from the law library and other references; and analyze and handle procedural problems that involve independent decisions. More specifically, a Legal Assistant is one who engages in the functions set forth in Guideline II. Nothing contained in these guidelines shall be construed as a determination of the competence of any person performing the function of a legal assistant, or as conferring status upon any such person serving as a legal assistant.

GUIDELINE I

A lawyer shall not permit a legal assistant to engage in the unauthorized practice of law. Pursuant to Canon 3 of the Rhode Island Supreme Court Code of Professional Responsibility, the lawyer shares in the ultimate accountability for a violation of this guideline. The legal assistant remains individually accountable for engaging in the unauthorized practice of law.

GUIDELINE II

A legal assistant may perform the following functions, together with other related duties, to assist lawyers in their representation of clients: attend client conferences; correspond with and obtain information from clients; draft legal documents; assist at closings and similar meetings between parties and lawyers; witness execution of documents; prepare transmittal letters; maintain estate/guardianship trust accounts; transfer securities and other assets; assist in the day-to-day administration of trusts and estates; index and organize documents; conduct research; check citations in briefs and memoranda; draft interrogatories and answers thereto, deposition notices and requests for production; prepare summaries of depositions and trial transcripts; interview witnesses; obtain records from doctors, hospitals, police departments, other agencies and institutions; and obtain information from courts. Legal documents, including but not limited to, contract deeds, leases, mortgages, wills, trusts, probate forms, pleadings, pension plans and tax returns, shall be reviewed by a lawyer before being submitted to a client or another party.

In addition, except where otherwise prohibited by statute, court rule or decision, administrative rule or regulation, or by the Code of Professional Responsibility, a lawyer may permit a legal assistant to perform specific services in representation of a client. Thus, a legal assistant may represent clients before administrative agencies or courts where such representation is permitted by statute or agency or court rules.

Notwithstanding any other part of this Guideline,

1) Services requiring the exercise of independent professional legal judgment shall be performed by lawyers and shall not be performed by legal assistants.

2) Legal assistants shall work under the direction and supervision of a lawyer, who shall be ultimately responsible for services and duties performed by legal assistants.

3) The lawyer maintains direct responsibility for all aspects of the lawyer-client relationship, including responsibility for all actions taken by and errors of omission by the legal assistant.

GUIDELINE III

A lawyer shall direct a legal assistant to avoid any conduct which if engaged in by a lawyer would violate the Code of Professional Responsibility. In particular, the lawyer shall instruct the legal assistant regarding the confidential nature of the attorney/client relationship, and shall direct the legal assistant to refrain from disclosing any confidential information obtained from a client or in connection with representation of a client.

GUIDELINE IV

A lawyer shall direct a legal assistant to disclose that he or she is not a lawyer at the outset in contacts with clients, courts, administrative agencies, attorneys, or, when acting in a professional capacity, the public.

GUIDELINE V

A lawyer may permit a legal assistant to sign correspondence relating to the legal assistant's work, provided the legal assistant's non-lawyer status is clear and the contents of the letter do not constitute legal advice. Correspondence containing substantive instructions or legal advice to a client shall be signed by an attorney.

GUIDELINE VI

Except where permitted by statute, court rule or decision, a lawyer shall not permit a legal assistant to appear in court as a legal advocate on behalf of a client. Nothing in this Guideline shall be construed to bar or limit a legal assistant's right or obligation to appear in any forum as a witness on behalf of a client.

GUIDELINE VII

A lawyer may permit a legal assistant to use a business card, with the employer's name indicated, provided the card is approved by the employer and the legal assistant's non-lawyer status is clearly indicated.

GUIDELINE VIII

A lawyer shall not form a partnership with a legal assistant if any part of the partnership's activity involves the practice of law.

GUIDELINE IX

Compensation of legal assistants shall not be in the manner of sharing legal fees, nor shall the legal assistant receive any remuneration for referring legal matters to a lawyer.

GUIDELINE X

A lawyer shall not use or employ as a legal assistant any attorney who has been suspended or disbarred pursuant to an order of this court, or an attorney who has resigned in this or any other jurisdiction for reasons related to a breach of ethical conduct.

Entered as an order of this court this 1st day of February, 1983.

Case Questions

1. Under the Rhode Island Rules, paralegals are liable for engaging in the unauthorized practice of law. Assume that these rules applied in your state. What sanctions could be imposed under your state statutes or court rules?
2. Has your state supreme court enacted paralegal ethics rules? If so, how are they different from Rhode Island's? The NALA rules?

§ 13.3 NFPA Ethics Rules

The National Federation of Paralegal Associations (NFPA) has also established ethical rules for appropriate paralegal conduct. NFPA's Affirmation of Responsibility lists six categories, which are outlined in Figure 13-1. Like NALA's codes, these rules alone have no legal effect upon paralegals. However, courts and bar authorities may incorporate them in their decisions, thus incorporating them into the common law or administrative law.

The ABA's ethics rules also apply to paralegals. These standards are discussed in § 13.4.

1. A paralegal shall take initiative in the expansion of the paralegal's role in the legal profession within the parameters of the unauthorized practice of law statutes.

2. A paralegal shall maintain the highest level of ethical conduct.

3. A paralegal shall maintain a high level of competence and shall contribute to the integrity of the paralegal profession.

4. A paralegal shall preserve client confidences and privileged communications.

5. A paralegal shall serve the public interests by contributing to the availability and delivery of quality legal services.

6. A paralegal shall promote the development of the paralegal profession.

FIGURE 13-1   NFPA Affirmation of Responsibility

§ 13.4 ABA Ethics Standards

The American Bar Association (ABA) has promulgated its own sets of ethical regulations for attorneys. Currently it follows the Model Rules of Professional Conduct (Model Rules), which replaced its older Code of Professional Responsibility (CPR). Many state bars and courts have adopted the ABA's Model Rules and Code as legally binding and enforceable regulations against attorneys and their employees. Courts have ruled that the ABA's standards apply to paralegals. Thus, paralegals should become familiar with the provisions of the ABA Model Rules and the CPR.

ABA Code of Professional Responsibility

The CPR is divided into nine Canons, all of which broadly prescribe ethical conduct for lawyers. Figure 13-2 summarizes the Canons. Within the Canons are Disciplinary Rules (DRs) and Ethical Considerations (ECs) which provide more detailed guidance on ethical issues. The DRs and ECs carefully discuss permissible attorney conduct in advertising; soliciting clients; contacting clients, adverse parties, or the public; protecting client confidences; establishing and sharing legal fees; withdrawing from representation; undertaking unauthorized practice of law; maintaining prohibited interactions with client's interests; providing competent and zealous representation; and other ethical questions. The ABA Model Rules, although they use different phraseology, address identical concerns.

Ethics codes tend to be cut-and-dried when presented abstractly. It is more helpful to explore their application in real-world settings.

CANON 1: A Lawyer Should Assist in Maintaining the Integrity and Competence of the Legal Profession.

CANON 2: A Lawyer Should Assist the Legal Profession in Fulfilling Its Duty to Make Legal Counsel Available.

CANON 3: A Lawyer Should Assist in Preventing the Unauthorized Practice of Law.

CANON 4: A Lawyer Should Preserve the Confidences and Secrets of a Client.

CANON 5: A Lawyer Should Exercise Independent Professional Judgment on Behalf of a Client.

CANON 6: A Lawyer Should Represent a Client Competently.

CANON 7: A Lawyer Should Represent a Client Zealously Within the Bounds of the Law.

CANON 8: A Lawyer Should Assist in Improving the Legal System.

CANON 9: A Lawyer Should Avoid Even the Appearance of Professional Impropriety.

FIGURE 13-2 ABA Code of Professional Responsibility Canons

A Case of Unauthorized Practice

Several states have statutes permitting nonattorneys to represent clients in certain specialized courts (e.g., justice-of-the-peace, small claims, city, traffic). These statutes are often written plainly and clearly. The legislature's intentions should be sufficiently obvious, even to the courts. But as the following case illustrates, courts may be unwilling to permit uninitiated "outsiders" into the client representation arena. After reading the Montana Supreme Court's opinion, one might wonder if this is just another boost to the lawyers' practice monopoly.

SPARKS v. JOHNSON
Supreme Court of Montana
826 P.2d 928 (Mont. 1992)
February 6, 1992
Per curiam

This is an original proceeding arising out of a criminal theft prosecution in the City Court of Whitefish, Montana. Petitioners Karen Sparks, the defendant in that proceeding, and Jerry O'Neil, seek declaratory and injunctive relief, including a writ of mandamus. They request this Court's declaration that O'Neil and other non-attorneys similarly situated have the right, pursuant to §§ 25-31-601 and 37-61-210, MCA [Montana Code Annotated], to act as attorneys in Montana courts of limited jurisdiction on a regular and recurring basis. The Office of the Attorney General responded, as did Whitefish City Judge Brad Johnson.

The petition before us raises the question of lay representation in Montana's courts of limited jurisdiction. While it is clear that Article VII, § 2(3) of the 1972 Montana Constitution vests exclusive jurisdiction in this Court to make rules governing practice in all Montana courts, we have not heretofore comprehensively addressed this issue which now is arising with increasing frequency. Because of the statewide importance and implications of the issue, we accept original jurisdiction of this petition ... in order to provide guidance on the question of lay representation to the courts of limited jurisdiction throughout the state.

The underlying facts upon which this proceeding is based are not in dispute. The Whitefish City Attorney filed a complaint against Karen Sparks in Whitefish City Court for misdemeanor theft pursuant to § 45-6-301, MCA. At her initial appearance on September 18, 1991, Sparks appeared and acknowledged that she possessed a copy of the complaint and that she was aware an arrest warrant had been issued. Sparks was informed of her right to counsel and her right to a continuance so she could obtain counsel. Sparks pled not guilty and requested a court-appointed attorney. The court explained that it was not seeking confinement for Sparks and, therefore, would not provide her with a court-appointed attorney. Sparks persisted, prompting the court to provide defendant with an Affidavit/Request for Court Appointed Counsel form.

After Sparks' repeated attempts to secure court-appointed counsel, the court issued a Memorandum on Oct. 17, 1991, concluding again that she was not entitled to court-appointed counsel but could obtain private counsel. On or about Oct. 21, 1991, Jerry O'Neil filed a notice of appearance in the Whitefish City Court indicating that he would appear on behalf of defendant Sparks. The court subsequently denied O'Neil the right to represent Sparks in City Court and a jury trial was set for Nov. 7, 1991.

The present petition was filed with this Court on Nov. 8, 1991, seeking a stay of pending proceedings in the Whitefish City Court, a declaratory judgment that O'Neil has the right under §§ 25-31-601, MCA, and 37-61-210, MCA, to act as an attorney in the justice and city courts of Montana, and related injunctive and mandamus relief. This Court stayed the underlying proceedings. ...

Standing is a threshold issue. Thus, we must determine at the outset whether Jerry O'Neil has standing in the action before us. We conclude that he does not.

Although included as a "petitioner" in the caption of the petition to this Court, O'Neil essentially seeks to come before us as a legal representative of Sparks. O'Neil, an acknowledged lay person and not an attorney of record, possesses no legally recognized relationship to Sparks; therefore, he will not be recognized by this Court in the conduct or disposition of the case. We construe this action to be a pro se action by Karen Sparks seeking representation by the person of her choice in the city court criminal proceeding in which she is a defendant.

Sparks contends that § 25-31-601, MCA, authorizes lay representation in criminal cases in Montana justices' courts. She argues further that § 37-61-210, MCA, extends that right to lay representation in criminal cases to city courts. We disagree.

Section 25-31-601, MCA, provides that "[p]arties in justice's court may appear and act in person or by attorney; and any person, except the constable by whom the summons or jury process was served, may act as attorney." The statute is found in Title 25 of the Montana Code Annotated, entitled "Civil Procedure." Chapter 31 of that Title is "Procedure in Justices' Courts."

Section 25-31-601, MCA, is limited, by its plain language and placement in the Montana codes, to civil litigation in justices' courts. It does not apply to criminal proceedings in those courts or in other courts of limited jurisdiction. The criminal procedure statutes applicable to courts of limited jurisdiction, set forth in title 46, Chapter 17, parts 1 through 4, do not contain language permitting representation by "any person."

Sparks' further contention that lay representation in criminal proceedings is extended to city courts by virtue of § 37-61-210, MCA, is also incorrect, even aside from our conclusion above that Montana law does not authorize lay representation in criminal proceedings in justices' courts.

Section 37-61-210, MCA, is entitled "penalty for practicing without license" and provides that "[i]f any person practices law in any court, except a justice's court or a city court, without having received a license as attorney and counselor, he is guilty of a contempt of court." Sparks' reliance on § 37-61-210, MCA, as authority for legal representation by "any person" in a criminal proceeding in city court, is erroneous. Both the plain language and the placement of § 37-61-210, MCA, in the Licensing part of Title 37 (entitled "Professions and Occupations"), Chapter 61 (entitled "Attorneys at Law") of the Montana Code Annotated make it clear that it is a licensing and penalty statute. It does not, by its terms, authorize practice in either justices' or city courts; it merely alludes to, and exempts from penalty, such practice as may be authorized by other statutes. Therefore, we conclude that only such practice before courts of limited jurisdiction as is specifically authorized by existing statute or Court rule can be undertaken by lay people.

Sparks' reliance on a past Order of this Court in a case to which she was not a party is also to no avail. Orders without accompanying opinions have no precedential value from case to case, but pertain only to the circumstances of the action involved.

Sparks' final contention is that § 25-31-601, MCA, authorizes lay representation of parties in courts of limited jurisdiction on a regular and recurring basis. While this is a case of first impression in Montana, statutes similar to § 25-31-601, MCA, have been addressed in other states and held applicable only to a "one time" representation of a party in a justice or magistrate court.

State ex rel. Freison v. Isner (W. Va. 1981), 285 S.E.2d 641, involved a collection agency appearing in magistrate court on behalf of petitioner's creditors through its nonlawyer manager. The court found that the statute authorizing appearances by lay persons in civil litigation did not permit the unauthorized practice of law, but anticipated the representation of a party by a nonlawyer on a "casual, nonrecurring, non-pay basis as a means of assisting the party pro se." The *Freison* court concluded that the West Virginia law, similar to Montana's, provides only for "an isolated or casual appearance by a non-lawyer friend or relative of a party to proceedings in magistrate court ... ."

Similarly, the Supreme Court of Iowa held that a bill collector who attempted to bring suit in justice court as an assignee of his various clients was prohibited from doing so. *Bump v. Barnett* (Iowa 1944), 16 N.W.2d 579. The Iowa court, in referring to a statute much like § 25-31-601, MCA, stated that:

> "The salutary purpose of the statute may not thus be perverted to encourage the growth of a class of 'justice court lawyers,' unfettered by the rules that bind licensed attorneys and without training in law and ethics."

The Iowa court concluded that the bill collector was engaged in the illegal practice of law by his repeated representations in justice court.

We agree with the reasoning of the West Virginia and Iowa courts. Section 25-31-601, MCA, was not intended to permit the unauthorized practice of law; the intent is to enable a friend or relative to assist and speak on behalf of a party at one proceeding. We hold that the statute is a "one-time only" grant of a privilege in justices' court civil proceedings. Further, we extend this specific privilege to civil proceedings in city courts pursuant to our constitutional authority to make rules governing practice for all Montana courts.

Finally, even if the underlying proceeding in Whitefish City Court were a civil one, it is clear that O'Neil's representation of Sparks would not be permissible. We take judicial notice that O'Neil attempted to represent at least one other person in a criminal action in a court of limited jurisdiction. We also note that petitioner's brief herein provides a list of O'Neil's "clients." Neither O'Neil nor any other lay person has authority to represent "clients" on a recurring basis in courts of limited jurisdiction. Such recurring representation constitutes the unauthorized practice of law.

Nothing herein impacts on the "student practice rule" at the University of Montana School of Law. Under this rule, students who have completed two years of law school are supervised by a licensed attorney and perform legal activities in Montana courts.

IT IS THEREFORE ORDERED that the Petition herein, and all relief requested therein, is denied and dismissed.

IT IS FURTHER ORDERED that the stay of further proceedings in *City of Whitefish v. Karen Sparks* is hereby lifted.

DATED this 6th day of February, 1992.
Chief Justice Turnage and Justices Harrison, Gray, Trieweiler, McDonough, Hunt, and Weber concur.

Case Questions

1. Under the Montana statute, "any person" other than the constable who delivered service of process is permitted to act as attorney for a litigant in justice court. How did the Montana Supreme Court discover, in this plain, unambiguous language, that the rule only applies to a litigant's "friend or relative to assist and speak on behalf of a party at one proceeding" on a "one-time only" basis? Do you agree with the court's interpretation?
2. Paralegals would be considered lay persons under *Sparks*. Thus, despite the Montana legislature's broad statutory authorization, paralegals would be engaging in the unauthorized practice of law by appearing in justice court to represent a litigant in more than a single case. Do you believe that this is simply the court's attempt to protect the state bar from nonattorney competition? Or do you believe the court was primarily motivated to protect the public from inexperienced lay legal representation? Explain.
3. The *Sparks* court notes that the Montana Constitution vests it with exclusive authority to regulate law practice before the state's courts. Why, then, did the court not rule Mont. Code Ann. §§ 25-31-601 and 37-61-210 unconstitutional, as an impermissible legislative encroachment upon judicial functions?

§ 13.5 Hypothetical Problems

Consider the following hypotheticals, which illustrate the various ethical precepts discussed in the first section. For convenience, assume that the courts would accept the NALA provisions as part of the common law pertaining to unethical conduct by legal professionals. Although these problems are hypothetical, they are captioned according to the format used in attorney disciplinary complaints or court contempt proceedings.

HYPOTHETICALS

1. *In re* Piper

Leslie Piper is a paralegal in the law firm of Hawker, Hillary, Iscoff, & Prill. The firm represents Carl "Bump" Ostrem in a matter involving fraud and misrepresentation. Ulysses Masterdam had sold Ostrem a hot tub, indicating that it was brand new when, in fact, it had been previously used and repossessed. Piper telephoned Masterdam, requesting a complete refund of Ostrem's payment as well as "damages" for misrepresentation. When Masterdam became angry and offensive, Piper threatened criminal prosecution against Masterdam under the criminal fraud statute. Under the ABA's Model Rules and CPR, it is impermissible for lawyers to coerce payment of civil obligations by threatening criminal action.

Has Piper acted unethically? Yes. Piper engaged in behavior prohibited by the ABA CPR and Model Rules by threatening criminal prosecution to settle Ostrem's civil claims. An attorney could not have ethically made such statements; neither could Piper.

■ ■ ■

2. *In re* Nover

Bradley Nover is a paralegal working for the mortgage department of First National City State Bank. One of Nover's duties is to file liens and mortgages at the county recorder's office. The department employs one attorney who is supposed to supervise its six paralegals, including Nover. However, because of the heavy workload, Nover often finds himself working solo. Nover left a draft of a mortgage release on the lawyer's desk for review. It was returned the next day with no changes. Nover notified Lester Arnold, against whose land the mortgage had been filed. Arnold had just paid the full balance due on the mortgage. Nover told Arnold that the mortgage release would be mailed within the next few days. However, Nover failed to follow through, and the release was never filed. Several months later, when Arnold attempted to sell his realty, he discovered Nover's error. Arnold sued the bank for slander of title.

Has Nover acted unethically? Yes. Nover should have filed the mortgage release after consulting with his supervising attorney and communicating with Arnold. Nover's failure to do so resulted in tortious injury to Arnold. This demonstrates incompetent and improper professional conduct.

■ ■ ■

3. *In re* Quentlen

Sandra Quentlen is a paralegal employed at the law firm of Bingham, Dingham, & Clingham. She works for three personal injury (P.I.) attorneys in the firm. During the first few months of her training, Quentlen spent much time discussing procedural and substantive legal questions with her supervising attorneys, particularly when she had questions concerning the appropriate discovery forms to use in different circumstances. After six months, however, Quentlen became sufficiently adept at handling discovery that the attorneys simply turned over the client files to her after the initial consultation. Quentlen then proceeded to handle each P.I. file herself, with the attorneys simply signing the appropriate documents. Quentlen met with clients and witnesses; she drafted and filed all interrogatories and motions for discovery; and she handled all witness interviews.

Has Quentlen acted unethically? Yes. Without her lawyers' active supervision, Quentlen has engaged in the unauthorized practice of law by single-handedly coordinating discovery. She has exercised independent legal judgment in preparing and filing discovery documents. She may also have used independent legal judgment in advising clients or discussing legal questions with witnesses. She met with litigants without disclosing her status as a legal assistant.

■ ■ ■

4. *In re* Madisson

Oscar Madisson is a paralegal in the insurance department of Indemnicorp, a large insurance corporation. His duties consist of researching recent developments in tort law pertaining to insurance. He has been employed by Indemnicorp for five years performing these tasks. However, he has not enrolled in any paralegal courses at the local university (which has a legal administration program) since he graduated from the institution six years ago. Unknown to Madisson, the state legislature enacted new legislation substantially revising tort liability for municipal employees. Madisson advised one of the corporation's officers to settle an insurance claim, based upon the old municipal tort liability statute. As a consequence, the insured sued the company for negligence.

Has Madisson committed an ethical faux pas? Clearly. Madisson failed to remain abreast of current developments in the law. His carelessness would also render Indemnicorp liable, under respondeat superior, for his negligence.

■ ■ ■

5. *In re* Walkinski

Donna Walkinski is a paralegal working at the law firm of Cedar, Pine, Maple & Elm. One of her tasks is to handle initial client consultations. Walkinski met with John and Beverly Parker, both of whom wished to file an action against Michael Denton for cutting down several trees on the Parkers' land without permission. The following conversation excerpts transpired between Walkinski and the Parkers:

> WALKINSKI: "Hello, my name is Donna Walkinski. I'll be meeting with you today to discuss that lawsuit you want to file against Denton."
>
> [Walkinski then took the Parkers to the conference room.]
>
> WALKINSKI: "Now let me explain what we'll be doing today. I need to obtain some factual information to use when I prepare your court complaint."
>
> [Walkinski then proceeds to ask various factual questions.]
>
> J. PARKER: "After we complained to Denton about cutting down the trees, he offered to give us the wood for our fireplace. We took it. Does that affect our legal rights?"
>
> WALKINSKI: "No. Denton committed trespass to land by cutting the trees. You can still recover damages for the value of the trees."
>
> B. PARKER: "We sold the cut wood. Would we have to deduct that from what we ask for in court?"
>
> WALKINSKI: "No. Getting the wood doesn't matter at all, as a matter of law."
>
> [At the end of the meeting, Walkinski mentioned the following.]
>
> WALKINSKI: "Now it will take me several days to prepare these pleadings. I will give you a call when they're ready, so you can come back and we will review them and sign them."
>
> PARKERS: "Thank you. We'll make an appointment for next week as we leave."

Walkinski engaged in the unauthorized practice of law. She made no mention of her status as a paralegal to the Parkers. In fact, the Parkers may easily have believed Walkinski to be a licensed attorney, given her conduct during the consultation.

Furthermore, Walkinski provided the clients with independent legal advice which, incidentally, was incorrect.

■ ■ ■

6. *In re* Larken

Edith Larken is a paralegal employed at the law firm of Tried, True, Tested & Tempered. One day she telephoned Simms O'Connor, a dishwasher employed at The Living End, a restaurant against which one of Tried's clients, Amanda Marcia, had several tort claims, including negligence, negligent infliction of emotional distress, and battery. Marcia had contracted food poisoning after eating at the restaurant. Larken telephoned O'Connor to see if he would be willing to make a statement in the case. The following conversation ensued:

LARKEN: "Do you remember anything about the food they were serving that night?"

O'CONNOR: "Yeah, well, the boss wouldn't like me saying this, but there was an awful stench back there [in the kitchen] when they were cooking something."

LARKEN: "Was it the pork? Did anyone say anything to the manager or the cook about it?"

O'CONNOR: "I don't rightly know if it was pork or not. I don't remember anyone talking about it. But the smell was pretty bad. Everybody back there must have noticed it."

LARKEN: "The doctors weren't sure whether the pork made our client sick or something else, so it's important that we know for sure whether the smell came from spoiled pork."

O'CONNOR: "I really don't know for sure. I'm the dishwasher, so I don't work much with the food before it's cooked and eaten. After some folks get done with a meal, it's hard to tell what was on the plate."

LARKEN: "Thanks for your help. I'll be in touch if I need any more information."

O'CONNOR: "Sure, glad to help out."

Larken disclosed client confidences when she told O'Connor about the physicians' uncertainty as to the cause of Marcia's ailment. This admission could be fatal to Marcia's case, in the event O'Connor related the statement to the restaurant management.

■ ■ ■

7. *In re* Dennison

Paul Dennison is a paralegal employed by Bartram J. Hollingsworth III, attorney at law. One of Hollingsworth's clients is Aslo, Simon & Conley, an investment firm. Hollingsworth instructed Dennison to telephone Doubleday Savings Bank to discuss a computer inaccuracy on one of Aslo's commercial investment accounts. Hollingsworth feared that Aslo might possibly be liable for defamation by computer. Dennison spoke with Ernest Duley, commercial investment coordinator, who himself was a paralegal with whom Dennison attended college. Dennison mentioned the error to Duley. Duley inquired about the high frequency of withdrawals and deposits in the account. Dennison replied that Aslo had to cover "unexpected exigencies." Duley asked Dennison to elaborate. Dennison mentioned that Aslo had been the primary financing partner in the recent Southside Mall fiasco, in which both Aslo and several of their investment clients "lost a bundle." Dennison told Duley that, as a result, funds from Aslo's client investment accounts had had to be temporarily diverted. Duley warned that this "revenue dunking" was illegal commingling of client and nonclient funds. Dennison laughed, saying, "I guess we can't slip things past you, can we?" Later, Duley recommended to the bank's executive vice president to report Aslo's conduct to the attorney general's office.

Dennison acted unethically. Like Larken in the previous hypothetical, Dennison disclosed confidential client information (i.e., the Southside Mall losses, the commingling of funds). Furthermore, Dennison's involvement in illegal commingling violated the NALA and ABA rules precluding legal professionals from engaging in unlawful or inappropriate activities.

§ 13.6 Further Ethics Information

The American Bar Association, as well as some state bars, issues ethics opinions to attorneys advising them of appropriate or inappropriate conduct under certain factual circumstances. State courts also report opinions involving attorney discipline which discuss ethical considerations. Although these cases involve attorneys, many also address legal ethics involving paralegals or legal secretaries. NALA and NFPA have also collected ethics opinions and court cases directly involving paralegal ethics problems. State paralegal associations may also have researched such cases. One is encouraged to contact these sources for additional ethics information pertinent to one's jurisdiction.

Summary

NALA has issued two ethics codes applicable to paralegals. These rules broadly summarize the activities in which paralegals may ethically engage. NALA's Code and Model Standards declare that paralegals may not engage in the unauthorized practice of law, shall perform delegated duties under attorneys' supervision, shall not apply independent legal judgment, shall protect client confidences, shall maintain professional integrity and educational competence, and shall comply with the various rules and statutes regulating attorneys' conduct.

The NFPA, another national paralegal organization, has also issued ethical rules applying to paralegals. They emphasize the paralegal's role in working to provide legal services to the highest standards of ethics and professional integrity.

The ABA's Code of Professional Responsibility and Model Rules of Professional Conduct apply to paralegals. These rules provide both broad and particular guidance to attorneys and their staff regarding unethical behavior.

Hypothetical problems provide the best illustrations of unethical versus ethical conduct among paralegals. One should consult the state bar, the ABA, and paralegal associations, as well as NALA, for further information concerning paralegal ethics practices.

Review Questions

1. Who has designed ethics provisions specifically addressing paralegals?

2. In such ethics codes, what activities are specifically authorized? Under which ethics code are these listed?

3. What is the unauthorized practice of law? What types of actions can it include?

4. Under what circumstances are paralegals permitted to represent clients? What are some courts' reactions?

5. When can paralegals perform legal tasks? What restrictions apply under the ethics codes?

6. What must paralegals recall when dealing with clients, adverse parties, witnesses, or the general public?

Projects

1. How is "unauthorized practice of law" defined in your state statutes? What are the penalties for violations?

2. Does your state have a statute that permits lay representation of clients in certain courts? If so, how does it compare to the Montana statute discussed in the *Sparks* case, reprinted in this chapter?

APPENDIX A

CONFIDENTIAL CLIENT INFORMATION FORM

CONFIDENTIAL CLIENT INFORMATION FORM

This questionnaire is a *confidential* questionnaire for the use of our office only in preparing your claim for personal injuries. The information you furnish us will not be released and will be held strictly confidential. When your claim has been concluded, we will return this questionnaire to you if you wish. Please answer every question fully and accurately because, as your attorneys, we must know all about you and your case. One surprise because of an incorrect or incomplete answer could cause you to lose your case. All of the questions are important even though they may not appear to have anything to do with your case.

Please type or print all answers. Use additional sheets of paper or reverse side of this form if needed.

Your name: _____

Your address: _____

Your telephone number: _____

Date of accident: _____

Insurance company: _____

Workers' Compensation number, if any: _____

Birthplace: _____

Social Security number: _____

Age: _____ Birth date: _____

Married: _____ Single: _____ Divorced: _____ Separated: _____

Widower: _____ Widow: _____

If divorced, date and place: _____

Names, ages, and addresses of all those (including children) who are dependent upon you for support, and your relationship to each:

Name	Address	Age	Relationship

List the addresses where you have resided during the past ten years and give the period of time at each residence, including dates:

Residence	From	To

Have you ever used any other name? _____
Where? _____ Why? _____
Are you married at the present time? _____
Date of marriage: _____ Place: _____

WORK BACKGROUND

Present job: _____
Name and address of employer: _____

_____

Present job title and duties: _____
How long have you worked at this job? _____
Phone: _____ Your present pay: _____
When you first began working for this employer: _____
List prior employment for past five years:

Name	Address	Date Employed	Job

EDUCATION

How many years did you complete in school? _____
College? _____
Is your spouse employed? _____ Employer's name and address:

_____

Average income entire
Wages: $ _____ per _____ year for spouse: $ _____
How long employed? _____ Prior employment: _____
Are you living in your employer's household or premises? _____
If related to employer, state relationship: _____
Occupation when injured: _____
Were you doing your regular work? _____
On whose payroll when injured? _____
Wages when injured (per day, per week): _____
Work days per week: _____
Were you a temporary or steady employee? _____
If under 18 years of age, give name and address of your guardian or parent:

_____

ACCIDENT

Date of the injury (hour): _____
Date you were forced to leave work because of your injury (hour): _____

_____

Place where injury was sustained (no., street, city or town): _____

_____

Were you on employer's premises? _____
Was injury caused by another person? _____

Name of other person: _____

Who is he/she employed by? _____

Have you claimed or received settlement for this injury? _____

_____

From whom? _____

Name and address of eyewitnesses: _____

_____

When did you first report your injury? _____

To whom did you first report your injury? _____

Have you returned to work? _____

If so, what date? _____

Describe your injury and how the accident happened: _____

_____

MEDICAL HISTORY BEFORE ACCIDENT

Were you hospitalized at any time before the accident in this case? If so, list below all hospitalizations:

Date	Hospital	Doctor	Duration	Nature of Illness

Have you had any physical examinations before this accident? If so, list all physical examinations for five years before the accident:

Date	Place	Name of Doctor	Purpose

Have you had any accidents or injuries before this accident? If so, list every such accident or injury, whether there was a claim for damages or not:

Date	Place	Nature of Accident or Injury	Treated By

Have you had any illnesses or diseases before this accident? If so, list every such illness or disease suffered in the five years before this accident:

Date	Nature of Illness	Duration	Treated By

Have you had any chronic health problems? If so, list them below:

_____

Did you use any drugs regularly before the accident? If so, list the type and reason why you used them below:

_____

Have you ever had any insurance of any kind declined or cancelled? If so, give reason:

_____

Have you ever had any broken bones? If so, give date and circumstances:

_____

List below what normal activities, including sports, hobbies, or other activities, you enjoyed before this accident:

_____

STATEMENTS MADE

Have you told any police officer, investigator, insurance adjustor, or any other person about the accident? _____

Have you given any written statement to any person about the accident? _____ If so, answer the following:

Name of person to whom statement was given: _____

Date given: _____

If written, do you have a copy? _____

Persons present at time: _____

Did you sign the statement? _____

Please give us any statement you know the employer made about the accident, or that you understand he/she may have made: _____

_____

When and where made: _____

Name and address of person who heard it: _____

_____

DAMAGES FROM ACCIDENT

State in full detail, all injuries you received as a result of this accident:

_____

_____

State your physical condition—scars, deformities, headaches, pains, etc.—due to injuries received in this accident: _____

_____

Have you missed any time from work as a result of your injury?_____

If so, list the inclusive dates you were unable to work:

From: _____ To: _____

From: _____ To: _____

Did you lose wages for the periods of time missed from work due to this accident? _____ If so, state the total wages lost to date and the dates:

_____

Have you had any increases or decreases in your pay since the accident? _____ If so, explain: _____

_____

List all hospitals in which you were examined or treated, or to which you were admitted as a patient as a result of the injuries sustained in the accident and the dates:

Hospital   Address   Dates

List the full name, address, and telephone number of each physician or surgeon who has examined or treated you for your injuries as a result of the accident:

Name   Address   Telephone No.

Have you used any of the following in connection with treatment?

Back or neck brace? _____ Dates: _____
Crutches? _____ Dates: _____
Traction? _____ Dates: _____
Physiotherapy? _____ Dates: _____
Other? _____ Dates: _____

List here all of your usual employment activities which you have NOT been able to perform, or can perform only with difficulty, since the accident: _____

Time lost from school (if you are a pupil): _____

Please summarize your out-of-pocket expenses, and if you have not previously given us the name and address, indicate to whom they are owed, as well as the amounts and whether they have been paid.

_____
_____

CONCLUSION

In completing this questionnaire, have you thought of any information which we have not asked which MAY be of some assistance to us in serving you? If so, please state it here, no matter how silly, trivial, or embarrassing it may seem.

_____

Dated this _____ day of _____ , 19___.

I have read the above statement and the statements contained therein are true and correct.

_____
Client

APPENDIX B

UNDERSTANDING APPELLATE COURT OPINIONS

Legal analysis consists of understanding appellate court opinions and applying rules of law to different factual situations. This section addresses legal analysis, a critical aspect of legal study.

Briefing Cases

Many of the chapters of this book include reprinted portions of appellate court opinions to illustrate various tort principles. At first glance, court decisions may appear garbled or unfocused. A structured formula applied to each case helps organize the ideas that the courts express. There are several such methods, but the most popular is explained here.

Structured Analysis

A structured analysis breaks an opinion into several components: facts, procedural history, issues on appeal, rationale, and ruling(s). This approach represents the standard analytical framework used by law school and paralegal students.

Facts   From the court opinion, the reader gleans the *facts* that underlie or are necessary to the appellate court's final determination of the case. These are sometimes called the *legally significant facts*. Many facts in the case provide mere background information; these are called *background facts*. Although background facts are not critical to the court's decision, they must be noted to comprehend the complete circumstances involved in the litigation. Sometimes appellate opinions include irrelevant facts that have no real bearing on the outcome of the appeal.

Procedural History   The *procedural history*, or *judicial history* as it is sometimes called, is the appellate court's summary of the previous events in the lawsuit: who sued whom, what legal claims were involved, and (most importantly) how the trial court decided the case (if a bench trial) or in whose favor the jury returned its verdict. Procedural history may include a summary of a lower appellate court's decision rendered before the case was appealed to the court that wrote the opinion being studied. Procedural information is critical to grasp the importance of the appellate court's ruling.

Issues   The *issues* include the questions appealed from the trial court's judgment. Every appeal has at least one issue being reviewed by the appellate court, although more often several issues are involved. Issues are normally phrased in terms of a question: Did the trial court err in admitting certain evidence? Given the facts proven during trial, did the defendant commit a certain tort against the plaintiff?

Rationale   The *rationale* is the appellate court's reasoning to explain its ruling. It is the process through which the court applies the rules of law to the facts of the case. This application is accomplished by linking a series of arguments that appear to lead to a single logical conclusion (which, conveniently, happens to be the court's decision). Consider the following example. Suppose a state statute requires owners of agricultural vehicles used to haul grain to obtain a special commercial license. Charles sells his old twin-axle grain truck to Donny, who plans to use it in a furniture delivery business. Donny purchases ordinary truck license plates. Has Donny violated the statute? In its rationale, an appellate court would first explain the statutory language (i.e., rule of law) and then apply it to the facts of the case. Thus, although Donny bought a vehicle formerly used to haul grain, its present function is entirely non-agricultural (i.e., conveying furniture). Because the truck is not being used to carry grain, Donny would not be required to purchase the special licenses and thus has not violated the statute.

Ruling   The *ruling* is the appellate court's decision in the case. This decree is directed toward the trial (or lower appellate) court's ruling. If the appellate court agrees that the trial court was correct in deciding the issue on appeal, then the appellate court *affirms* the trial court's judgment. If the appellate court disagrees with the trial court's determination of the appealed issue, then the appellate court *reverses* or *vacates* the trial court's decree. Often reversal or vacation is accompanied by a *remand*, or return, of the case to the trial court with instructions from the appellate court. These instructions may be simply that judgment should be entered for the plaintiff or the defendant (depending, of course, upon which side the appellate court thinks should prevail), or they may include directions that certain factual questions be retried by the trial court.

Briefing an Appellate Court Opinion

As mentioned previously, law school and paralegal students most often use this briefing formula to analyze appellate court opinions. To illustrate how this is done in practice, an actual appellate court opinion has been reproduced here, followed by a suggested case brief that summarizes the elements of the opinion using the briefing formula. To assist in reading opinions reprinted in this book, certain tangential matters and terminology are summarized or explained in brackets: "[ ]." Any parts of the original opinion that have been omitted are indicated in bracketed comments or by bracketed ellipses: "[...]."

Edwards v. Terryville Meat Co.
N.Y. Supreme Court, Appellate Division
577 N.Y.S.2d 477 (App. Div. 1991)
December 23, 1991

Before MANGANO, P.J., and KUNZEMAN, EIBER and BALLETTA, JJ.

MEMORANDUM BY THE COURT.

In a negligence action to recover damages for personal injuries, the plaintiffs appeal [...] from [...] an order and judgment [...] of the Supreme Court, Suffolk County (Cannavo, J.), entered September 11, 1989, as granted the defendant's motion for summary judgment dismissing the complaint [...].

ORDERED that the order and judgment entered September 11, 1989, is affirmed [...].

In this slip-and-fall case, it was incumbent upon the plaintiffs to come forth with evidence showing that the defendant had either created the allegedly dangerous condition or that it had actual or constructive notice of the condition (*see, Eddy v. Tops Friendly Markets*, 91 A.D.2d 1203, 459 N.Y.S.2d 196, *aff'd*, 59 N.Y.2d 692, 463 N.Y.S.2d 437, 450 N.E.2d 243[1983]). "To constitute constructive notice, a defect must be visible and apparent and it must exist for a sufficient length of time prior to the accident to permit defendant's employees to discover and remedy it" (*Gordon v. American Museum of Natural History*, 67 N.Y.2d 836, 837, 501 N.Y.S.2d 646, 492 N.E.2d 774 [1986]). The injured plaintiff was in the defendant's store for only about 10 minutes before she allegedly slipped and fell on an unknown milky-colored substance which she concededly did not see until after she fell. There is no evidence that the defendant caused the substance to be on the floor, nor is there sufficient evidence to establish that the defendant had either actual or constructive notice of the substance [citations omitted]. Accordingly, the Supreme Court properly granted the defendant's motion for summary judgment.

A Suggested Case Brief

Citation: *Edwards v. Terryville Meat Co.*, 577 N.Y.S.2d 477 (App. Div. 1991).

Facts: Injured plaintiff was in defendant's store 10 minutes when she slipped and fell on unknown milky substance on floor. Plaintiff did not see substance until after falling. No evidence that defendant caused substance to be on floor.

Proc.: Injured plaintiff and spouse sued defendant for negligence. Supreme Court of Suffolk County granted defendant's motion for summary judgment dismissing plaintiffs' complaint.

Issue: Did trial court err in granting defendant's motion for summary judgment?

(*Implied Issue*) Did plaintiffs present sufficient evidence to establish defendant's liability for negligently causing plaintiff's injuries?

Rationale: This is a slip-and-fall negligence case. To establish defendant's negligence, plaintiffs must prove either that (1) defendant caused slippery substance to be on floor, or (2) defendant knew (or had constructive notice) that substance was on floor. Constructive notice requires that substance be present on floor for sufficient length of time prior to accident to permit defendant's employees to discover and remedy it. In this case, there was no evidence that defendant had created the hazard that befell plaintiff. Further, there was insufficient evidence that defendant had actual or constructive notice of the substance, given the short time (10 minutes) that plaintiff was in store until she slipped and fell. Thus, trial court correctly granted defendant's motion for summary judgment.

Ruling: Appellate Division affirmed supreme court's decision.

APPENDIX C

SUPPLEMENTARY CASES

Stander v. Orentreich

Russell v. Archer Building Centers, Inc.

Fishman v. Beach

Frankel v. Warwick Hotel

Cinel v. Connick

Pepsico, Inc. v. Redmond

Doe v. Cutter Biological, a Division of Miles, Inc.

Girdley v. Coats

Jordan v. Town of Pratt

STANDER v. ORENTREICH
Supreme Court, New York County
627 N.Y.S.2d 879 (Sup. Ct. 1995)
May 16, 1995
Sklar, Justice
[See Chapters 3, 6, 11.]

The essential question raised by the present motion and cross motion in this action for medical malpractice and related claims is whether plaintiffs' causes of action are barred by the statute of limitations.

Plaintiff Bella Stander and her husband plaintiff Robert Mason move to dismiss the first affirmative defense of defendant dermatologist, Norman Orentreich, MD, which raises the statute of limitations defense. ...

Plaintiff visited Dr Orentreich in July and August 1979 for treatment of linear scleroderma, a skin condition, on her face. Dr Orentreich recommended injections of liquid silicone as the sole treatment for this condition. Silicone is considered a medical device under FDA regulations, not a drug. Based on his recommendation

Stander received two sets of injections into her cheek and forehead. She discontinued treatment because the injections were painful and caused discoloration of the skin.

Stander alleges that she noticed no other adverse reactions until somewhere between February and April 1986 when small pink lumps appeared on her forehead. She had these removed by a different doctor—a plastic surgeon—who initially hypothesized that the lumps resulted from factors unrelated to her 1979 treatment by Dr Orentreich. Shortly thereafter more lumps appeared which she had removed in 1987. After pathology analysis and a conversation in February 1988 with a representative from Dow Corning, the manufacturer of the liquid silicone, Stander suspected that the cause of the painful pink lumps emerging on her forehead was the silicone which defendant injected in 1979.

Plaintiff asserts that after learning the purported cause of the lumps, she also learned that Dr Orentreich had injected her with a nonmedical grade of silicone which was not, as manufactured, suitable for injection into humans, but which defendant reprocessed to cause it to become medical grade. The parties dispute whether or not the liquid silicone which defendant injected was or was not suitable for that use. Plaintiffs allege that defendant negligently processed or manufactured the purportedly reprocessed silicone.

... Plaintiffs have alleged four causes of action against Dr Orentreich: first, for medical malpractice based on departures from accepted standards of medical care; second, for failure to obtain the plaintiff's informed consent to the treatment administered; third, a derivative action for loss of services, society and consortium suffered by plaintiff's spouse, Robert Mason; and fourth, for injury resulting from defendant's alleged negligent manufacture, processing and administration of the injectable liquid silicone.

The statute of limitations requires an action for medical malpractice to be commenced "within two years and six months of the date of the act, omission or failure complained of. ... " The alleged malpractice occurred in July and August of 1979. Plaintiffs have not alleged that the continuous treatment doctrine applies to toll the statute of limitations. Another exception that can extend the time to commence a medical malpractice action is the "foreign object" exception. The statute, however, specifically excludes chemical compounds from the scope of the exception. Stander alleges that the cause of her injury was liquid silicone injected into her body, which defendant alleges is a chemical compound.

Whether the silicone constitutes a chemical compound within the meaning of the statute, and/or a medical device, plaintiffs cannot invoke the benefit of the foreign object exception. This discovery rule is available to delay the running of the statute of limitations "only in circumstances where a foreign object is negligently

'left' in the patient's body without any intended continuing treatment purpose ... ."

Dr Orentreich intentionally injected the silicone into Bella Stander precisely as a treatment designed to ameliorate plaintiff's skin condition. This places plantiffs' allegations outside the narrow scope of an exception which the Court of Appeals has consistently refused to broaden. These cases indicate, that the exception as interpreted does not apply. Accordingly, plaintiffs' first cause of action is time barred.

The failure to obtain a patient's informed consent sounds in medical malpractice and is subject to the same two and one half year statute of limitations. Accordingly, plaintiffs' second cause of action for lack of informed consent is also time barred.

... Here, plaintiffs specifically disavow any claim sounding in warranty and strict products liability and assert that the fourth cause of action is premised "on a theory of simple negligence."

"An action to recover for personal injuries or wrongful death against a medical practitioner or a medical facility or hospital may be based *either* on negligence principles or on the more particularized medical malpractice standard." When the duty owing to the plaintiff by the defendant arises from the physician-patient relationship or is substantially related to medical treatment, the breach thereof gives rise to an action sounding in medical malpractice as opposed to simple negligence. Where the issue relating to due care may be easily discernible by a jury on common knowledge, simple negligence rules apply.

Plaintiff's fourth cause of action somewhat inartfully asserts that Dr Orentreich negligently manufactured or processed the silicone into what was supposed to be "medical grade" silicone, and that Dr Orentreich negligently administered it to Bella Stander. To the extent that this claim is based on Dr Orentreich's "administration" of the silicone injections into Stander, plaintiffs are asserting a claim for medical malpractice and accordingly that claim is time barred for the reasons discussed above.

To the extent that plaintiffs are claiming that Dr Orentreich used his skills as a chemist to transform nonmedical grade liquid silicone, which was unacceptable for injection into humans, and attempted chemically to reprocess it into a medical grade silicone, but failed to do so due to his negligence, plaintiffs have alleged an action outside the scope of medical malpractice. Plaintiffs' allegation does not directly bear upon the doctor-patient relationship, or the doctor's instructions to or treatment of plaintiff. Rather than implicating as faulty Dr Orentreich's skills as a medical practitioner, plaintiffs are implicating Dr Orentreich's conduct as a chemist and manufacturer. The expert testimony that might be needed would bear on defendant's conduct in these capacities rather than as a medical doctor treating a patient. Such an allegation is cognizable as an action sounding in simple negligence.

Plaintiffs' claim, that since the fourth cause of action sounds in negligence the statute of limitations set forth in CPLR § 214-c applies, is without merit. CPLR § 214-c does not apply to acts or omissions which occurred before July 1, 1986, and which caused an injury that was discovered or should have been discovered before July 1, 1986 and "an action for which was or would have been barred because the applicable period of limitations had expired prior to such date." ... Thus CPLR § 214-c is unavailing.

Plaintiffs also claim that the fourth cause of action is timely under the revival statute. Laws of 1993, chap. 419. "An Act to authorize extension of the statute of limitations for commencing a cause of action for personal injury or death caused by silicone." ... This section shall not be applicable to any action for medical malpractice.

This unconsolidated statute was enacted primarily to revive previously time barred causes of action of women injured by silicone breast implants. However, the purpose is broader than to protect only such women. ... It was designed "[t]o allow the hundreds of injured people, almost all women, who suffered physical injuries more than four years ago as a result of the implantation of silicone in their bodies, to file lawsuits for those injuries even though their cases are time barred under present law."

* * *

To the extent that plaintiffs allege a claim of negligent manufacture or processing of silicone, it is distinguishable from other recent similar actions against defendant which resulted in the dismissal of claims for strict products liability, breach of warranty, and negligent administration (i.e., medical malpractice). Accordingly, plaintiffs' fourth cause of action for negligent manufacture or processing of silicone liquid which was ultimately injected into Bella Stander is timely, pursuant to L. 1993, ch. 419.

Loss of consortium is a derivative action dependent upon inter alia a viable cause of action for negligence. Accordingly, because plaintiffs have timely commenced a viable claim for simple negligence in their fourth cause of action, Stander's spouse's derivative cause of action for loss of consortium stated in the third cause of action is also viable.

RUSSELL v. ARCHER BUILDING CENTERS, INC.
New York Supreme Court, Appellate Division, Third Department
631 N.Y.S.2d 102 (App. Div. 1995)
September 14, 1995
Crew, Justice

[See Chapter 4.]

Appeal from an order of the Supreme Court (Ingraham, J.), entered December 15, 1994 in Otsego County, which denied defendant's motion for summary judgment dismissing the complaint.

On March 22, 1993, plaintiff Frances Russell (hereinafter Russell) was shopping with her husband, plaintiff John Russell, in a hardware/lumber store owned by defendant in the City of Oneonta, Otsego County. Plaintiffs sought out the tile display and as Russell stepped back to view a sheet of tile, she tripped over the bottom rail of a steel display rack forming one side of the aisle in which she was standing and broke her wrist. The rack in question, which was designed to hold doors and was only partially filled at the time of the accident, appears to have been the only rack in the area where Russell fell.

Plaintiffs commenced this action alleging that the empty segment of the display rack constituted a hazard to the shopping public and caused Russell's injury. Defendant answered and after examinations before trial, moved for summary judgment dismissing the complaint contending that the display rack was in open and plain view. Defendant further contended that the rack did not constitute a hidden or concealed danger and that it was not liable for the obvious condition which, with the exercise of reasonable care, was readily observable. Supreme Court, finding an issue of fact as to whether the rack was open and obvious when placed in an location where a customer might back into it to view other merchandise, denied the motion. This appeal by defendant followed.

There must be a reversal. While a landowner who holds property open to the public has a general duty to maintain the property in a reasonably safe condition to prevent foreseeable injuries, this duty extends only to conditions that are not readily observable. There is no duty to warn of conditions that can be readily observed with the normal use of one's senses.

Searching the record in the light most favorable to plaintiffs, we find no basis for finding an issue of fact as to whether the rack was open and obvious. Here, a photograph of the display rack with its offending bottom rail reveals that the rack did not protrude into the plainly discernible and uncluttered aisle, but rather formed a readily apparent part of the merchandise display area. Had Russell exercised ordinary care, she would have observed the self-evident boundaries of the aisle as she walked down it before stopping immediately adjacent to the rack to examine the tile display. Accordingly, the order should be reversed and summary judgment granted to defendant.

ORDERED that the order is reversed, on the law, with costs, motion granted, summary judgment awarded to defendant and complaint dismissed.

FISHMAN v. BEACH
New York Supreme Court, Appellate Division, Third Department
625 N.Y.S.2d 730 (App. Div. 1995)
April 27, 1995
Peters, Justice

[See Chapter 4.]

Appeal from an order of the Supreme Court (Teresi, J.), entered June 29, 1994 in Albany County, which denied a motion by defendant HAJ Entertainment Inc. for summary judgment dismissing the complaint against it.

This action arises as a result of personal injuries sustained by plaintiff after he left a restaurant/bar owned by defendant HAJ Entertainment Inc., doing business as Quintessence (hereinafter Quintessence), on the evening of May 18, 1991. Plaintiff contends that after a verbal confrontation with defendant Christopher Beach and his companion on or about the outdoor steps of Quintessence, plaintiff and Beach became involved in a altercation occurring approximately 60 to 100 feet from the entrance to the restaurant/bar. During such altercation, plaintiff contends that he was caused to enter Madison Avenue and was struck by a car driven by defendant Gino M. Masciotra.

Plaintiff thereafter commenced the instant action against Beach, Masciotra and Quintessence alleging, *inter alia*, a violation of General Obligations Law § 11-101 (the Dram Shop Act) and common-law negligence. Supreme Court denied the motion of Quintessence for summary judgment seeking dismissal of all claims against it.

To sustain a claim under the Dram Shop Act, plaintiff must establish that the vendor unlawfully sold alcohol to an intoxicated person. At the time of the instant accident, an unlawful sale was defined as the sale of alcohol to a "visibly intoxicated person." Hence, on a motion for summary judgment, Quintessence bore the initial burden of establishing entitlement to judgment as a matter of law and, once satisfied, the burden thereby shifted to plaintiff to produce evidentiary proof in admissible form to establish the existence of a triable issue of fact.

In support of the instant motion, Quintessence offered the deposition transcript of its bartender to establish that there was a policy in existence at the time which dictated the procedures to be followed when a patron was either becoming intoxicated or was already intoxicated. The bartender testified that he was not aware of any incidents which occurred in Quintessence on the night of May 17, 1991 or during the early morning hours of May 18, 1991. He further testified that no complaints regarding the presence of an intoxicated person on Quintessence's premises were brought to the attention of himself or other staff employed by Quintessence. Quintessence further annexed the deposition testimony of both David Dolowich and Cynthia Markowitz, patrons accompanying Beach, which indicated that Beach was not acting visibly intoxicated at any time during that evening. Portions of plaintiff's deposition testimony further indicated that plaintiff did not encounter Beach until he left the restaurant. We find that such evidence clearly satisfied Quintessence's initial burden on the motion for summary judgment.

In opposition thereto, plaintiff set forth his own affidavit detailing that Beach was in a visibly intoxicated condition while standing on the outdoor steps of Quintessence and annexed portions of the deposition transcript of Dolowich, which indicated that Beach was present at Quintessence for approximately 1½ hours during which time he consumed between four and five

alcoholic beverages. Plaintiff further submitted an affidavit by a neurologist, Sheldon Staunton, who opined that based upon an affidavit of service describing Beach to be approximately 5 feet 8 inches tall, weighing approximately 145 pounds, his consumption of four or five alcoholic beverages within this undisputed time period would result in actual intoxication.

Viewed in the light most favorable to plaintiff, we find that in the absence of any testimony from Beach, plaintiff has sustained his burden of establishing the existence of a triable issue of fact as to whether Beach was intoxicated at the time of the altercation and if so, whether he had been served alcoholic beverages at Quintessence while he was in a "visibly intoxicated" condition. Accordingly, we reject the contentions raised by Quintessence that on this motion for summary judgment, plaintiff was required to present direct evidence on the actual amount of alcohol consumed by Beach and that one of its employees had to have actually observed Beach to be in a "visibly intoxicated" condition when served with such beverages.

As to the cause of action alleging common-law negligence, we reverse. While clearly Quintessence had a duty to act in a reasonable manner to control the conduct of persons on its premises such as to prevent harm to its patrons, "[d]efendant's duty * * * was limited to conduct on its premises which it had the opportunity to control and of which it was reasonably aware."

The evidence submitted by both parties established that there was no incident which arose while the parties were inside of the premises and, therefore, defendants' duty to control the conduct of Beach was limited only to that conduct of which it was reasonably aware. The facts show that while there was a verbal exchange on the outdoor steps of such premises while music played inside, the record does not reflect that a doorman was stationed there at that time or that Quintessence personnel were informed of any need for assistance. Moreover, the physical altercation which ultimately resulted in plaintiff's injuries indisputably occurred no less than 60 to 100 feet from such premises in a city street. We therefore find that Quintessence cannot be held to a duty "to control the conduct of patrons in consuming alcoholic beverages * * * beyond the area where supervision and control may reasonably be exercised." Accordingly, we dismiss plaintiff's common-law negligence cause of action against Quintessence.

ORDERED that the order is modified, on the law, without costs, by reversing so much thereof as denied the motion by defendant HAJ Entertainment Inc. for summary judgment on the common-law negligence claim; motion granted to that extent, summary judgment awarded to said defendant and the common-law negligence claim is dismissed; and, as so modified, affirmed.

FRANKEL v. WARWICK HOTEL
United States District Court, E.D. Pennsylvania
881 F. Supp. 183 (E.D. Pa. 1995)
March 31, 1995
Joyner, District Judge

[See Chapter 6.]

This diversity case, involving a dispute between a father and his son, has been brought before the Court by motion of the defendants, who seek dismissal of the amended complaint pursuant to Fed.R.Civ.P. 12(b)(6). For the reasons that follow, the defendants' motion to dismiss will be granted.

The issue for the Court is whether Plaintiff has stated a claim on which relief can be granted; thus, we must take as true all of the factual allegations made in the amended complaint. *ALA, Inc. v. CCAIR, Inc.,* 29 F.3d 855, 859 (3d Cir.1994). Accordingly, the facts giving rise to this lawsuit are as follows. In the fall of 1989, Plaintiff Adam Frankel accepted a job offer from his father, Defendant William Frankel, to work as a restaurant manager at the Warwick Hotel in Philadelphia. Adam Frankel's status was that of an at-will employee. The elder Mr. Frankel is a partner in the Warwick Hotel and an officer of the Frankel Management Company of Philadelphia, Inc. ... On June 8, 1991, the younger Mr. Frankel married Annika Moriarity, a Roman Catholic. On October 16, 1992, William Frankel because of his antipathy toward Ms. Moriarity and her religion, informed his son that he would be fired unless he divorced his wife. The son refused to leave his wife, and as a result, he was fired on October 24, 1992.

Adam Frankel's amended complaint, filed against the Warwick Hotel, Frankel Management, and William Frankel, contains four counts. In the first two counts, Adam Frankel alleges that he was wrongfully discharged. The third count is brought against William Frankel under an intentional infliction of emotional distress theory. In the fourth count, Adam Frankel alleges that the defendants are liable under the tort theory of invasion of privacy by intentionally interfering with his marriage. In support of their motion, the defendants assert that the amended complaint must be dismissed because the allegations fail to state a claim upon which relief can be granted.

In considering a motion to dismiss pursuant to Rule 12(b)(6), the complaint's allegations must be construed favorably to the pleader. The court must accept as true all of the plaintiff's factual allegations and draw from them all reasonable inferences. *Schrob v. Catterson,* 948 F.2d 1402, 1405 (3d Cir.1991) (citations omitted). Thus, the court will grant a Rule 12(b)(6) motion only if the non-moving party cannot prevail legally under the set of facts alleged. *Markowitz v. Northeast Land Co.,* 906 F.2d 100, 103 (3d Cir.1990). In deciding this motion, this Court will apply these standards to each of the four counts raised in Adam Frankel's amended complaint.

Under Pennsylvania law, employees may be discharged at any time, for any reason or for no reason at all. As a general rule, there is no common law cause of action against an employer for termination of an at-will employment relationship.

* * *

Generally, the recognized exceptions concern an employee's discharge after he or she refused to violate the law, *see Woodson v. AMF Leisureland Ctrs., Inc.*, 842 F.2d 699 (3d Cir.1988) (dismissal for refusal to serve liquor to intoxicated person); *McNulty v. Borden, Inc.*, 474 F.Supp. 1111 (E.D. Pa.1979) (dismissal for refusal to participate in antitrust violations); *Field v. Philadelphia Elec. Co.*, 388 Pa.Super. 400, 565 A.2d 1170 (1989) (employee fired for making statutorily required report to NRC), or an employee's right of political participation, *see Novosel* (dismissal for refusal to participate in political lobbying); *Reuther v. Fowler & Williams Inc.*, 255 Pa.Super. 28, 386 A.2d 119 (1978) (employee fired for absence due to jury duty), or employer conduct in violation of a specific statute, as in *Perks v. Firestone Tire & Rubber Co.*, 611 F.2d 1363 (3d Cir. 1979) (employment terminated for individual's refusal to take polygraph test).

* * *

Since Adam Frankel concedes that he was an at-will employee, the issue here is whether the case falls within that limited exception allowing recovery for a termination that has violated public policy. The younger Mr. Frankel points to three areas of the law as potential sources of public policy justifying a cause of action, all of which relate to policy favoring family cohesiveness. These sources include the Pennsylvania Divorce Code, 23 Pa.Cons.Stat.Ann. § 3101, *et seq.*, legislative findings supporting the general policy that the family deserves protection and preservation, and the Commonwealth's prevention of testamentary attempts to destroy the family. Adam Frankel's contention that these pronouncements amount to the sort of clearly mandated articulations of public policy which justify the creation of an exception to the at-will doctrine, however, is without merit. Like the provisions relied upon by the *McGonagle* plaintiff, the statements relating to the preservation of the family are too vague to be used as a basis for an exception to the employee-at-will doctrine. Typical of

the language relied upon is the policy statement contained in the Pennsylvania Divorce Code, which notes that "the protection and preservation of the family is of paramount public concern." 23 Pa.Cons.Stat.Ann. § 3102(a). As is apparent, the provision does not specifically prohibit or mandate any particular conduct; it is instead a vague and general expression of the legislature's view concerning the importance of family unity. As such, it is an inappropriate basis for the creation of an exception to the general rule. Thus, we hold that the case arising from the facts alleged is governed by the general rule regarding termination of an at-will employee. As a result, we must grant the defendants' motion to dismiss as it relates to the first two counts of the amended complaint.

Pennsylvania courts recognize the tort of intentional infliction of emotional distress, but have been cautious in permitting recovery. *Williams v. Guzzardi*, 875 F.2d 46, 52 (3d Cir.1989). Thus, in order for a plaintiff to recover under this theory of liability, the defendant must have acted in a manner "so outrageous in character and so extreme in degree as to go beyond all possible bounds of decency and to be regarded as atrocious and utterly intolerable in a civilized society."

To recover, a plaintiff must establish the following four elements: (1) defendant's conduct must be intentional or reckless, (2) the conduct must be extreme and outrageous, (3) it must cause emotional distress, and (4) the emotional distress must be severe. *Williams*, 875 F.2d at 52. Further, under Pennsylvania law, to state such a claim in a situation where the plaintiff has allegedly suffered emotional distress as a result of outrageous conduct directed at the plaintiff, as is the case here, there must be an allegation of physical injury. We further note that such a cause of action rarely lies in the context of the employee-employer relationship. As the Third Circuit has noted, "it is extremely rare to find conduct in the employment context that will rise to the level of outrageousness necessary to provide a basis for recovery for the tort of intentional infliction of emotional distress."

Applying these principles to the instant matter, this Court concludes that the intentional infliction of emotional distress claim must be dismissed. The pertinent conduct is William Frankel's alleged threat to discharge his son unless he divorced his wife. While we do not endorse the elder Mr. Frankel's alleged conduct, we cannot conclude that it was so outrageous as to be "utterly intolerable in a civilized society." Moreover, we note that the younger Mr. Frankel has not alleged that he suffered physical injury, as is required under Pennsylvania law. Accordingly, plaintiff's claim for damages under the theory of intentional infliction of emotional distress must be dismissed.

An invasion of privacy is actionable under Pennsylvania law, *Harris v. Easton Publishing Co.*, 335 Pa.Super. 141, 483 A.2d 1377, 1383 (1984), and consists of four distinct torts, including (1) intrusion upon seclusion, (2) appropriation of name or likeness, (3) publicity given to one's private life, and (4) publicity placing one in a false light. *Id.* Here, Adam Frankel alleges that the defendants are liable under the intrusion upon seclusion tort. Intrusion upon seclusion occurs when a person "intentionally intrudes, physically or otherwise, upon the solitude or seclusion of another or his private affairs or concerns ... if the intrusion would be highly offensive to the reasonable person." *Borse v. Piece Goods Shop, Inc.*, 963 F.2d 611, 620 (3d Cir.1992) (quoting Restatement (Second) of Torts § 652B). Further, a defendant will not be liable unless the invasion is substantial. *Id.* at 621. The intrusion may be (1) a physical intrusion into a place where the plaintiff has secluded himself or herself,

(2) the use of defendant's senses to oversee or overhear plaintiff's private affairs, (3) or some other form of investigation or examination into plaintiff's private concerns. *Id.; Harris*, 483 A.2d at 1383.

Turning to the instant matter, we conclude that Adam Frankel has failed to state a cause of action for invasion of privacy. As the cases make clear, this tort encompasses the physical or sensory penetration of a person's zone of seclusion in an attempt to collect private information concerning that person's affairs. The facts alleged here, that William Frankel terminated his son's employment because the son refused to divorce his wife, do not amount to the type of harm compensable under this theory. Further, to the extent that the intrusion alleged by Adam Frankel is an intentional interference with his marriage, we note that the Restatement specifically excludes marriage contracts from the tort of intentional interference with contract. *See* Restatement (Second) of Torts § 766 (1977) ("One who intentionally and improperly interferes with the performance of a contract (except a contract to marry) between another and a third person by inducing or otherwise causing the third person not to perform the contract, is subject to liability ..."). Thus, we must conclude that Adam Frankel has failed to state a claim for invasion of privacy in his amended complaint.

For the foregoing reasons, the defendants' motion to dismiss plaintiff's amended complaint is granted.

CINEL v. CONNICK
United States Court of Appeals, Fifth Circuit
15 F.3d 1338 (5th Cir. 1994)
March 11, 1994
Duhé, Circuit Judge

[See Chapter 6.]

Appellant, Dino Cinel, appeals from the district court's grant of Appellees' motions to dismiss under Federal Rule of Civil Procedure 12(b)(6). We modify and affirm.

Appellant sued numerous state actors and private persons, contending that they conspired together over a period of years to deprive him of his civil rights by making public certain allegedly confidential information gathered during a criminal investigation of him. He also asserts state law claims for negligence, state constitutional violations, and invasion of his privacy.

BACKGROUND

In 1988 Dino Cinel was a Roman Catholic priest at St. Rita's Catholic Church in New Orleans, Louisiana. While Cinel was away, another priest at the rectory where Cinel lived, accidentally discovered a variety of sexually oriented materials in Cinel's room including a homemade video tape of Cinel engaged in homosexual activity, primarily with two young men, Christopher Fontaine and Ronald Tichenor. Church officials turned the materials over to the Orleans Parish District Attorney's Office. Cinel alleges that in exchange for transactional immunity and under a confidentiality agreement, he provided the names and addresses of the other men depicted in the film to the DA's office. Upon verifying that they were consenting adults at the time of their sexual involvement with Cinel, the DA's office decided not to prosecute Cinel.

Cinel further alleges that George Tolar, while an investigator for the DA's office, during the investigation gave the names and addresses of Fontaine and Tichenor, and certain unidentified documents in the DA's file, to Gary Raymond. Raymond was a private investigator working for two lawyers, David Paddison and Darryl Tschirn. Cinel contends that Raymond used the information given him by Tolar to solicit the two men as clients for attorneys. One of the men, Fontaine, represented by Paddison and Tschirn, then sued Cinel and the Church in state court in 1989. The other, Tichenor, represented by the same counsel, sued Cinel in 1991.

In 1990, in connection with the Fontaine state civil suit, the state court, at the request of the Church, issued a subpoena duces tecum directing the DA's office to release the materials found in Cinel's room to the litigants in the Fontaine suit. Pursuant to a consent judgment drafted in response to the subpoena, by an assistant district attorney, Raymond Bigelow, the DA's office released the materials to Paddison and Tschirn as custodians, and Raymond was authorized to make copies of the materials "upon the request of any party to this [the Fontaine] litigation." Cinel alleges in his complaint that the allegedly confidential materials were released "under the pretext of a subpoena and consent judgment." However no facts support that conclusion.

Cinel also alleges that a year later Raymond gave copies of the materials to Richard Angelico, a local television investigative reporter, and that Angelico and his employer, WDSU Television, Inc., broadcast excerpts of the materials. Cinel also contends that in February 1992, Raymond sold some of the materials to Geraldo Rivera and his employer, Tribune Entertainment Company, which broadcast excerpts of the material on the national syndicated television program "Now It Can Be Told." Cinel brought § 1983 claims, together with pendent state law claims, against Harry Connick, the district attorney, Raymond Bigelow, and George Tolar in their individual and official capacities. He also sued Gary Raymond, David Paddison, Darryl Tschirn, Richard Angelico, WDSU Television Inc., Geraldo Rivera, and Tribune Entertainment. After the filing of several motions, the district court granted Appellees' motions to dismiss under Federal Rules of civil Procedure 12(b)(6). Cinel appeals.

* * *

Appellant asserts claims against all Appellees under 42 U.S.C. § 1983 for a violation of his rights to privacy and due process. To state a cause of action under § 1983, Appellant must allege that some person, acting under state or territorial law, has deprived him of a federal right.

* * *

… Appellant's allegations involving Tolar's release to Raymond of the names and addresses of the men depicted in the video do not implicate any constitutional privacy interests. The release of this information alone does not involve intimate details of Appellant's life. Thus, these facts alleged by Appellant are insufficient to state a claim for a deprivation of his constitutional right of privacy.

Appellant also fails to state a claim for relief against Tolar, Bigelow, and Connick in their individual and official capacities for the release of the sexually oriented materials found in Cinel's room to the private litigants, the Church and Fontaine, pursuant to a subpoena. Because the

Church had viewed the materials before giving them to the DA's office, and Fontaine had participated in making the video, the information disclosed was not private as to these parties. In other words, Appellant cannot claim that his privacy has been invaded when allegedly private materials have been disclosed to those who already know the details of that material. Nonetheless, assuming that Appellant had a privacy interest in some of the materials requested by the subpoena, the government officials had a legitimate interest in complying with a validly issued subpoena. Moreover, the government officials drafted the consent judgment to ensure that Appellant's rights were protected by allowing the material to be copied only for the civil litigants.

Appellant fails to state a claim that the state actors denied him his procedural due process rights by not notifying him of the subpoena duces tecum. Appellant has submitted no legal authority to this Court, and we have found none in our independent research, that creates an affirmative duty of a non-party or a governmental official in possession of documents to notify the owner of the subpoenaed documents. ...

Finally, Appellant does not have any claim under the Due Process Clause for damage to his reputation against any Appellees as a result of the publication of the materials. The Supreme Court held in *Paul v. Davis*, 424 U.S. 693, 712, 96 S.Ct. 1155, 1165, 47 L.Ed.2d 405 (1976), that an interest in reputation alone does not implicate a "liberty" or "property" interest sufficient to invoke due process protection.

The remainder of Appellant's § 1983 claims involve an alleged conspiracy between the state and private actors to publish allegedly privileged information from the DA's file and the sexually oriented materials released under the pretext of a civil subpoena. A private party may be held liable under § 1983 if he or she is a "willful participant in joint activity with the State or its agents."...

Appellant has failed to allege facts that suggest that Tolar's release of information from the DA's file to Raymond rises to the level of a conspiracy to deprive Appellant of his constitutional rights. Appellant contends that Tolar released the information "for the purpose of aiding and abetting [Raymond, Paddison, and Tschirn] and prejudicing Cinel in the civil litigation." Appellant avers that Raymond, Paddison, and Tschirn used the information "to solicit and procure Fontaine and Tichenor as clients in violation of Rule 7.3 of the Louisiana Rules of Professional Conduct." Perhaps, as Appellant alleges, this was improper client solicitation; however, nothing in his complaint implies or states that these Appellees agreed to undertake a scheme to deprive Appellant of his constitutional rights. A lapse of ethics by the Appellees is insufficient by itself to rise to the level of a conspiracy to deprive Appellant of his federal constitutional or statutory rights. Moreover, the subsequent allegation that Angelico and WDSU published the documents cannot be linked back to a state actor. Nothing in Appellant's complaint intimates that Tolar's intention in releasing the information to Raymond was to make it available for future publication.

Likewise, Appellant has failed to aver facts that suggest an agreement between the state actors and the private actors to publish the materials released pursuant to the subpoena. ... Without an agreement between private and state actors, any possible joint action involving only private parties is not actionable under § 1983.

* * *

Appellant's only discussion of his negligence claims against Paddison and Tschirn is in his reply brief. An appellant abandons all issues not raised and argued in its *initial* brief on appeal.

* * *

Appellant alleges that Raymond, Paddison, Tschirn, Angelico, WDSU, Rivera and Tribune invaded his right of privacy under Louisiana Civil Code article 2315. Under Louisiana law, one can be held liable for invasion of privacy for making an "unreasonable disclosure of embarrassing private facts." To recover for this tort, a plaintiff must prove that 1) the defendant publicized information concerning the plaintiff's private life, 2) the publicized matter would be highly offensive to the reasonable person, and 3) the information is not of legitimate public concern. Whether a matter is of public concern is a question of law for the court.

The district court held that the materials were a matter of legitimate public concern. It explained that the material related to Appellant's guilt or innocence of criminal conduct. Also, the material implicated the public's concern with the performance of its elected DA, especially because the DA's decision cannot be reviewed by a court. *See State v. Perez,* 464 So.2d 737, 744 (La. 1985) (explaining that the district attorney is given absolute discretion in the institution of criminal charges). Finally, the materials concerned Appellant's activities while an ordained Catholic priest and the Church's response to those activities.

At oral argument, Appellant conceded the newsworthiness of the details surrounding his story. Appellant contends, however, that the broadcast portions of the homemade videotape and allegedly confidential deposition added nothing to this topic and were what constituted the invasion of his privacy. We disagree. The materials broadcast by the Appellees were substantially related to Appellant's story. Perhaps the use of the materials reflected the media's insensitivity, and no doubt Appellant was embarrassed, but we are not prepared to make editorial decisions for the media regarding information directly related to matters of public concern. *See e.g., Ross v. Midwest Communications, Inc.,* 870 F.2d 271, 275 (5th Cir.) ("judges, acting with the benefit of hindsight, must resist the temptation to edit journalists aggressively"), *cert. denied,* 493 U.S. 935, 110 S.Ct. 326, 107 L.Ed.2d 316 (1989); *Neff v. Time, Inc.,* 406 F.Supp. 858, 860 (W.D.Pa. 1976) (noting that "the courts are not concerned with establishing canons of good taste for the press or the public") (internal quotations omitted); *Cape Publications, Inc. v. Bridges,* 423 So.2d 426, 427–28 (Fla.Dist.Ct.App.1982) (concluding that when plaintiff's nude picture was relevant to a story of public interest, there is no invasion of privacy, even though picture may be embarrassing or distressful to the plaintiff), *cert. denied,* 464 U.S. 893, 104 S.Ct. 239, 78 L.Ed.2d 229 (1983).

Appellant argues that the district court erred in dismissing his complaint without leave to amend. ... Appellant did not ask the district court for leave to amend; his brief to this Court is his first such request. ...

We hereby modify the district court's judgment insofar as it dismisses with prejudice Appellant's claims for due process on the issue of transactional immunity and for fair trial under the state and federal constitutions to dismiss those claims for lack of subject matter jurisdiction. The district court's judgment is affirmed as modified.

MODIFIED IN PART and AFFIRMED.

PEPSICO, INC. v. REDMOND
United States Court of Appeals, Seventh Circuit
54 F.3d 1262 (7th Cir. 1995)
May 11, 1995
Flaum, Circuit Judge
[See Chapter 7.]

Plaintiff PepsiCo, Inc., sought a preliminary injunction against defendants William Redmond and the Quaker Oats Company to prevent Redmond, a former PepsiCo employee, from divulging PepsiCo trade secrets and confidential information in his new job with Quaker and from assuming any duties with Quaker relating to beverage pricing, marketing, and distribution. The district court agreed with PepsiCo and granted the injunction. We now affirm that decision.

The facts of this case lay against a backdrop of fierce beverage-industry competition between Quaker and PepsiCo, especially in "sports drinks" and "new age drinks." Quaker's sports drink,

"Gatorade," is the dominant brand in its market niche. PepsiCo introduced its Gatorade rival, "All Sport," in March and April of 1994, but sales of All Sport lag far behind those of Gatorade. Quaker also has the lead in the new-age-drink category. Although PepsiCo has entered the market through joint ventures with the Thomas J. Lipton Company and Ocean Spray Cranberries, Inc., Quaker purchased Snapple Beverage Corp., a large new-age-drink maker, in late 1994. PepsiCo's products have about half of Snapple's market share. ... Meanwhile, PepsiCo and Quaker each face strong competition from Coca Cola Co., which has its own sports drink, "PowerAde," and which introduced its own Snapple-rival, "Fruitopia," in 1994, as well as from independent beverage producers.

William Redmond, Jr., worked for PepsiCo in its Pepsi-Cola North America division ("PCNA") from 1984 to 1994. ...

Redmond's relatively high-level position at PCNA gave him access to inside information and trade secrets. Redmond, like other PepsiCo management employees, had signed a confidentiality agreement with PepsiCo. That agreement stated in relevant part that he

> w[ould] not disclose at any time, to anyone other than officers or employees of [PepsiCo], or make use of, confidential information relating to the business of [PepsiCo] ... obtained while in the employ of [PepsiCo], which shall not be generally known or available to the public or recognized as standard practices.

Donald Uzzi, who had left PepsiCo in the beginning of 1994 to become the head of Quaker's Gatorade division, began courting Redmond for Quaker in May, 1994. ...

On November 8, 1994, Uzzi extended Redmond a written offer for the position of Vice President–Field Operations for Gatorade and Redmond accepted.

* * *

On November 10, 1994, Redmond met with Barnes and told her that he had decided to accept the Quaker offer and was resigning from PCNA. Barnes immediately took Redmond to

Bensyl, who told Redmond that PepsiCo was considering legal action against him.

* * *

From November 23, 1994, to December 1, 1994, the district court conducted a preliminary injunction hearing on the same matter. At the hearing, PepsiCo offered evidence of a number of trade secrets and confidential information it desired protected and to which Redmond was privy. First, it identified PCNA's "Strategic Plan," an annually revised document that contains PCNA's plans to compete, its financial goals, and its strategies for manufacturing, production, marketing, packaging, and distribution for the coming three years. ...

Second, PepsiCo pointed to PCNA's Annual Operating Plan ("AOP") as a trade secret. The AOP is a national plan for a given year and guides PCNA's financial goals, marketing plans, promotional event calendars, growth expectations, and operational changes in that year.

* * *

PepsiCo also showed that Redmond had intimate knowledge of PCNA "attack plans" for specific markets. ...

Finally, PepsiCo offered evidence of PCNA trade secrets regarding innovations in its selling and delivery systems. Under this plan, PCNA is testing a new delivery system that could give PCNA an advantage over its competitors in negotiations with retailers over shelf space and merchandising.

* * *

On December 15, 1994, the district court issued an order enjoining Redmond from assuming his position at Quaker through May, 1995, and permanently from using or disclosing any PCNA trade secrets or confidential information. ...

Both parties agree that the primary issue on appeal is whether the district court correctly concluded that PepsiCo had a reasonable likelihood of succes's on its various claims for trade secret misappropriation and breach of a confidentiality agreement. ...

The Illinois Trade Secrets Act ("ITSA"), which governs the trade secret issues in this case, provides that a court may enjoin the "actual or threatened misappropriation" of a trade secret. ...

The question of threatened or inevitable misappropriation in this case lies at the heart of a basic tension in trade secret law. Trade secret law serves to protect "standards of commercial morality" and "encourage[ ] invention and innovation" while maintaining "the public interest in having free and open competition in the manufacture and sale of unpatented goods."

* * *

PepsiCo presented substantial evidence at the preliminary injunction hearing that Redmond possessed extensive and intimate knowledge about PCNA's strategic goals for 1995 in sports drinks and new age drinks.

* * *

Thus, when we couple the demonstrated inevitability that Redmond would rely on PCNA trade secrets in his new job at Quaker with the district court's reluctance to believe that Redmond would refrain from disclosing these secrets in his new position (or that Quaker would ensure Redmond did not disclose them), we conclude that the district court correctly decided

that PepsiCo demonstrated a likelihood of success on its statutory claim of trade secret misappropriation.

* * *

[W]e conclude that the district court did not abuse its discretion in granting the preliminary injunction on the issue of trade secret misappropriation.

* * *

Finally, Redmond and Quaker have contended in the alternative that the injunction issued against them is overbroad.

* * *

However, the injunction against Redmond's immediate employment at Quaker extends no further than necessary and was well within the district court's discretion.

For the foregoing reasons, we affirm the district court's order enjoining Redmond from assuming his responsibilities at Quaker through May, 1995, and preventing him forever from disclosing PCNA trade secrets and confidential information.

Affirmed.

DOE v. CUTTER BIOLOGICAL, A DIVISION OF MILES, INC.
United States District Court, D. Idaho
852 F. Supp. 909 (D. Idaho 1994)
May 12, 1994
Ryan, Senior District Judge

[See Chapter 10.]

Plaintiff John Doe is a hemophiliac. Because of his condition, John Doe received a clotting agent known as Factor VIII which facilitates the clotting of blood in hemophiliacs. In December of 1991, John Doe tested positive for the HIV virus.

On October 30, 1992, John Doe commenced this federal action naming those providers of Factor VIII products which were administered to him by the Pocatello Regional Medical Center between 1979 and 1985. At this juncture, the

named defendants include: Miles Inc. (Miles), and Armour Pharmaceutical Corporation (Armour).

[T]his court respectfully requested the Idaho Supreme Court to exercise its discretionary authority under Idaho Appellate Rule 12.1(c) to accept and decide the following questions:

Assuming plaintiff is able to prove that more than one defendant breached a duty of care to the plaintiff, would Idaho allow recovery when it is not possible for plaintiff to prove which defendant caused plaintiff's injury; and, if so, under what theory?

* * *

Based on traditional theories of causation under Idaho law and John Doe's admitted inability to prove which dose of Factor VIII caused him to contract the HIV virus and, ultimately, to develop AIDS, defendants filed motions for summary judgment as to the issue of causation. ...

In support of their position, defendants note the absence of judicial decisions on the issue of alternative liability and, from a legislative standpoint, emphasize the advent of tort reform, the limitations placed on the common law doctrine of joint and several liability under Idaho Code §§ 6-803(3)-(7) ... .

* * *

As stated earlier, the concept of alternate liability was first developed in the case of *Summers v. Tice,* 33 Cal.2d 80, 199 P.2d 1 (1948). In *Summers,* the plaintiff was injured while hunting quail with the two defendants. Both defendants carried identical shotguns and ammunition. During the hunt, defendants shot simultaneously at the same bird, and plaintiff was struck by bird shot from one of the defendants' guns. Both defendants were found to have acted negligently, but it could not be determined which of them had fired the shot that injured the plaintiff. The California court held that the burden of proof should be shifted to the defendants on the issue of causation. In justifying such a shift, the court said that the defendants were "both wrongdoers—both negligent toward plaintiff. They brought about a situation where the negligence of one of them injured the plaintiff, hence it should rest with them each to absolve himself if he can."

In the absence of any direct pronouncement by the Idaho Supreme Court on the issue of alternate liability, plaintiff relies heavily on the decision of *Hackworth,* wherein the Idaho Supreme Court included the *Summers* case in a string of citations. From this, plaintiff contends that the Idaho Supreme Court would find "one or more of the following alternative theories of

liability ... applicable to the question of causation in this case: (a) Alternative liability, Section 433B(3), Restatement (Second) of Torts; (b) Market share liability; (c) Enterprise liability; and/or (d) Concert of action, Section 876 of the Restatement (Second) of Torts."

Mere citation to *Summers* certainly does not compel the conclusion that the Idaho Supreme Court would adopt *any* theory of alternative liability. And, had the Idaho Supreme Court expressly adopted the holding from *Summers* in a case where a plaintiff was unable to prove which of two or more negligent defendants caused his injury, such would not compel the conclusion that any or all of the alternative theories of liability should be applied to the suppliers of the Factor VIII concentrates in this case.

On the contrary, unlike the defendants in *Summers,* Miles and Armour point out that their actions in providing Factor VIII concentrates to the plaintiff were not identical and that such actions were certainly not simultaneous in time. Also, when it comes to determining which dose of Factor VIII caused plaintiff's infliction with the HIV virus, Miles and Armour contend that they have no better access to information—which would assist in that determination—than the plaintiff.

In Idaho, and under the circumstances herein, this court finds the viability of the theory of alternate liability originated in *Summers* to be questionable. At this point, ... the court finds it useful to discuss each of the other three theories of alternative liability advanced by the plaintiff.

The concept of market share liability was first developed by the California Supreme Court in *Sindell v. Abbott Laboratories,* to address unique causation problems raised by diethylstilbesterol (DES) litigation. In *Sindell,* the plaintiff alleged that she was injured by DES which her mother ingested while pregnant with the plaintiff. Although the plaintiff could not identify the manufacturer responsible for making the DES taken by her mother, the court held that if the plaintiff joined the manufacturers of a substantial share of the DES that her mother might have taken, the burden of proof would shift to the defendants to prove that they could not have supplied the DES which caused the plaintiff's injuries. The court ruled further that each defendant failing to make such a showing would be held liable for the proportion of the judgment represented by its share of the drug market.

In *Sindell,* to support application of the market share theory of liability, the California Supreme Court emphasized two factors—neither of which apply in the case at bar.

First, the court determined that DES was fungible or interchangeable because all DES companies produced the drug from an identical formula. In fact, DES was usually manufactured as a "generic" drug without regard to the actual manufacturer. Thus, each DES manufacturer's product posed the same risk of harm to its users.

Factor VIII concentrates are not akin to DES. On the contrary, as summarized in another proceeding:

Unlike DES, Factor VIII is not a generic, fungible drug. Each processor prepares its Factor VIII concentrate by its own proprietary processes using plasma collected from its own sources. Each firm's Factor VIII concentrate is clearly distinguishable by brand name, package color, lot number, and number of units of Factor VIII per vial; each firm's Factor VIII concentrate is separately licensed by the Food and Drug Administration. There is no evidence that all Factor VIII products caused or were equally capable of causing HIV infection. Thus, *the risk posed by the different brands of Factor VIII is not identical.*

In other words, one of the bases for the *Sindell* court applying the market share theory of liability was that *each* DES pill was inherently dangerous and potentially harmful, whereas, in this case, it cannot be said that the Factor VIII concentrates at issue were inherently harmful. Rather, such concentrates would only have been harmful if particular plasma donors had been infected with the HIV virus.

The second factor which contributed to the *Sindell* court's application of the market share theory of liability was that the DES product could not be traced to any specific producer. Unlike DES, however, with Factor VIII, it would have been possible—had plaintiff kept such records—

to identify the source and lot number for each dose of Factor VIII used by the plaintiff and provided by Defendant Miles, as opposed to Defendant Armour.

In summary, while the market share theory of liability may have been appropriate to apply in the context of DES litigation, *even if* the Idaho Supreme Court had ever sanctioned the use of such a theory—and it has not—it is not clear that the market share theory should be applied to the context of Factor VIII litigation.

As summarized by the New York Court of Appeals:

"Enterprise liability," *also joint and several,* derives from the opinion in *Hall v. DuPont de Nemours & Co.* In that case, plaintiffs were unable to identify the manufacturers of allegedly unsafe blasting caps for the simple reason that the caps had been obliterated by explosion. Since the six defendants in that case did, however, comprise virtually the entire American blasting cap industry and since it appeared that their blasting caps were *manufactured to meet industry-wide safety standards set by their own trade association,* the court held that *defendants could be liable for the joint control of the risk of accidental explosion.*

This court is not aware of any case in which the enterprise theory has been applied to manufacturers of Factor VIII concentrates. ...

Unlike members of the blasting caps industry in *Hall* who were found to have exercised joint control of the risks involved in that case, the actions of Miles and Armour in producing Factor VIII concentrates were closely controlled and/or regulated by the FDA. ...

"[T]he concert of action theory derives from a criminal law concept ... . 'If plaintiffs can establish that all defendants acted tortiously pursuant to a common design, they will all be held liable for the entire result.' "

... Idaho Code § 6-803(3) essentially abolished joint and several liability in Idaho. Thus, it does not appear that the concert of action theory of alternative liability would be viable in Idaho.

* * *

Prior to 1987, Idaho's Supreme Court adhered to the common law rule of joint and several liability, as it recognized:

> [E]ach tortfeasor whose negligence is a proximate cause of an *indivisible* injury should remain individually liable for *all* compensable damages attributable to that injury. Such is the underlying basis for the rule of joint and several liability.

* * *

However, in 1987, the Idaho legislature enacted Idaho Code § 6-803(3), which limited the doctrine of joint and several liability, and thereby *superseded all previous Idaho court decisions.*

* * *

Thus, given the recognition that the theory of alternative liability set forth in *Summers v. Tice* involves joint and several liability, and given that the Idaho Supreme Court fully acknowledges that the Idaho legislature abolished joint and several liability when it enacted Idaho Code § 6-803(3), existing Idaho law precludes the endorsement of alternative liability theories.

In addition to the operation of Idaho Code § 6-803(3), which limits the operation of joint and several liability in Idaho, the plain language of Idaho's blood shield statute expressly precludes providers of "blood products" or "blood derivatives" from being held liable for anything other than their own negligence. In the face of this clear statement of public policy by Idaho's legislature, it is difficult to imagine how any theory of alternative liability could be endorsed in this type of case.

* * *

Because plaintiff concedes that "at trial it will be difficult, if not impossible, to determine which of the Defendants processed the Factor VIII which caused [him] to be stricken with AIDS," defendants' motions for summary judgment on

the issue of causation are well taken and must be granted.

* * *

In addition to precluding recovery based on implied warranties, blood shield statutes also preclude actions based on strict liability in tort.

* * *

... Notwithstanding the possibility for change in Idaho's statute, as currently worded, and under the circumstances in this case, the Idaho blood shield statute does not permit an action based on strict liability or implied warranties against suppliers of Factor VIII concentrates such as Miles and Armour. Rather, against these defendants Idaho Code § 39-3702 only permits actions based on negligence.

* * *

Neither the Idaho legislature nor the highest court of this state has declared that, without proof of causation, a plaintiff, such as John Doe, should be able to recover against providers of Factor VIII concentrates, such as Miles and Armour. Accordingly, to avoid summary judgment on his negligence claims, plaintiff contends that this court "should *predict* which alternate theory of causation the Idaho Supreme Court would adopt in this case." This court is not empowered to make such a prediction.

* * *

Thus, it is this court's conclusion that plaintiff's motion for partial summary judgment requesting the adoption of one or more alternative liability theories should be denied; that defendants' motions for summary judgment on the issue of causation should be granted; and that plaintiff's attempt to assert products liability claims based on strict liability or implied warranties of merchantability and fitness for a particular purpose should be denied.

GIRDLEY v. COATS
Supreme Court of Missouri
825 S.W.2d 295 (Mo. 1992)
February 25, 1992
Benton, Judge

[See Chapter 11.]

Plaintiffs, Karen and Jeffrey Girdley, filed a four-count petition against Stephen H. Coats, D.O., and Stephen H. Coats, D.O., Inc., for a negligently performed bilateral tubal ligation. Count III of the Girdleys' petition sought "the reasonable cost of raising and educating the child" because of the negligence of Dr. Coats. Count IV sought the same expenses based on a breach of contract theory. The trial court dismissed Counts III and IV and pursuant to Rule 74.01(b) determined that the order was final for purposes of appeal.

On appeal, the Court of Appeals, Southern District, reversed and remanded the decision of the trial judge with directions to deny the motion to dismiss Counts III and IV. Transfer was granted by this Court. The judgment of the trial judge dismissing Counts III and IV is affirmed.

In reviewing the dismissal, an appellate court assumes all pleaded facts to be true and makes every favorable inference in favor of plaintiffs that may reasonably be drawn from those facts; if any ground is shown that would entitle the plaintiff to relief, the dismissal is improper.

Plaintiffs allege they were unable to afford the expense of any more children. Mrs. Girdley thus consulted with Dr. Coats who recommended bilateral tubal ligation. On March 24, 1988, she underwent surgery and was informed by Dr. Coats that he had ligated the right fallopian tube but that her left ovary and corresponding fallopian tube were congenitally absent. After the sterilization procedure, Dr. Coats advised that she was sterile with no risk of conception. On April 29, 1989, Mrs. Girdley delivered the couple's third child.

Various causes of action arise involving the birth of a child. Although some confusion exists, a consensus has developed labeling the various actions: (1) "wrongful conception" or "wrongful pregnancy"—a medical malpractice action brought by the parents of a child born after a physician negligently performed a sterilization procedure; (2) "wrongful birth"—a claim brought by parents of a child born with defects; and (3) "wrongful life"—a claim brought by the child suffering from such defects. *Wilson v. Kuenzi,* 751 S.W.2d 741, 743 (Mo. banc 1988), *cert. denied,* 488 U.S. 893, 109 S.Ct. 229, 102 L.Ed.2d 219 (1989), declines to recognize causes of action for wrongful birth and wrongful life in this state.

In Missouri, the cause of action for the tort of wrongful conception was specifically recognized in *Miller v. Duhart,* 637 S.W.2d 183 (Mo.App. 1982), which noted that such an action has strong support in the law and is "merely a descriptive label for a form of malpractice." Traditionally, Missouri does not analyze malpractice in terms of contract law.

Clearly, there is a legally cognizable cause of action. However, the parties are sharply divided as to the appropriate measure of damages. The issue may be framed: If a negligently performed sterilization procedure results in the birth of a healthy child, may the plaintiff recover the expenses of raising and educating that child?

Numerous courts have wrestled with this issue, advancing several theories of recovery, along with a plethora of supporting reasons.

A review of the cases establishes that there are four possibilities: (1) no recovery rule; (2) full recovery rule; (3) limited damages rule; and (4) benefits rule. An overwhelming majority of jurisdictions has adopted the limited damages rule whereby recovery of the expenses of raising and educating a child is denied as an element of damages.

Contrary to this majority position, appellants urge that Missouri adopt the full recovery rule claiming that such a rule would protect a constitutional right not to procreate and would allegedly promote sound social policies. Further, appellants assert that the full recovery rule is more in keeping with traditional tort principles. Appellants' position enjoys support in, at most, only three jurisdictions. *Custodio v. Bauer,* 251 Cal.App.2d 303, 59 Cal. Rptr. 463 (1967); *Marciniak v. Lundborg,* 153 Wis.2d 59, 450 N.W.2d 243 (1990); *Lovelace Medical Center v. Mendez,* 111 N.M. 336, 805 P.2d 603 (1991) (emphasizing that wrongful conception invaded the family's financial security).

Several courts have persuasively articulated the various rationales supporting the limited damages rule—most being variations on themes of public policy. The Kansas Supreme Court concluded that a parent cannot be damaged by the birth of a healthy child:

> As a matter of public policy, the birth of a normal and healthy child does not constitute a legal harm for which damages are recoverable. We recognize wrongful death actions because of the great value we place on human life. ... The birth of a normal, healthy child may be one of the consequences of a negligently performed sterilization, but we hold that it is not a legal wrong for which damages should or may be awarded. *Byrd v. Wesley Medical Center,* 699 P.2d at 468.

The Arkansas Supreme Court reasoned:

> We are persuaded for several reasons to follow those courts which have declined to grant damages for the expense of raising a child. It is a question which meddles with the concept of life and the stability of the family unit. Litigation cannot answer every question; every question cannot be answered in terms of dollars

and cents. We are also convinced that the damage to the child will be significant; that being an unwanted or "emotional bastard," who will some day learn that its parents did not want it and, in fact, went to court to force someone else to pay for its raising, will be harmful to that child. It will undermine society's need for a strong and healthy family relationship. We have not become so sophisticated a society to dismiss that emotional trauma as nonsense. *Wilbur v. Kerr,* 628 S.W.2d at 571.

The Illinois Supreme Court analyzed the issues:

> One can, of course, in mechanical logic reach a different conclusion, but only on the ground that human life and the state of parenthood are compensable losses. In a proper hierarchy of values the benefit of life should not be outweighed by the expense of supporting it. Respect for life and the rights proceeding from it are at the heart of our legal system and, broader still, our civilization. *Cockrum v. Baumgartner,* 69 Ill.Dec. at 172, 447 N.E.2d at 389.

Though arguing that the full recovery rule is a natural extension of general principles of tort law, appellants necessarily ignore some of those general principles. The issue of mitigation of damages demonstrates the fallacy of applying strict tort principles in cases where the alleged injury is the birth of a normal, healthy child. It is generally recognized that one injured by the tort of another is required to mitigate damages. *Phegley v. Graham,* 358 Mo. 551, 215 S.W.2d 499, 505 (1948). In the case of a pregnancy caused by a negligent sterilization procedure, either adoption or abortion would clearly mitigate the expense of raising the child. These options illustrate the difficulty in applying strict tort principles to damages from wrongful conception.

> Yet courts recognizing this cause of action have rejected the argument that parents should choose among the various methods of mitigation ...

Speculative results are not a proper element of damages. The costs of child rearing—and especially education—are necessarily speculative.

Who can divine, soon after birth, whether the child will be a financial boon or burden to the parents, what level of education will be required or what unique expenses could arise? These determinations are beyond the scope of probative proof. Likewise, an attempt to quantify the expense of raising a child and offsetting that expense by the "benefits" conferred on the family is neither workable nor desirable.

> Perhaps the costs of rearing and educating the child could be determined through use of actuarial tables or similar economic information. But whether these costs are outweighed by the emotional benefits which will be conferred by that child cannot be calculated. The child may turn out to be loving, obedient and attentive, or hostile, unruly and callous. The child may grow up to be President of the United States, or to be an infamous criminal. In short, it is impossible to tell, at an early stage in the child's life, whether its parents have sustained a net loss or net gain.

Judge Turnage's eloquent dissent proposes the "benefits rule," offsetting the "pecuniary and non-pecuniary" benefits to parents from having the child *against* the costs of rearing a child. However, Restatement (Second) of Torts § 920 cmt. b (1977) provides:

> Damages resulting from an invasion of one interest are not diminished by showing that another interest has been benefited.

The dissent thus demonstrates that principles of tort law cannot strictly be applied to this issue.

To the extent that general tort principles militate against application of the full recovery rule, appellants shift into a policy analysis. This Court declines the invitation to waft between strict application of tort principles and application of public policy, in order to achieve the result of shifting the responsibility of supporting a child from its parents to a third party.

The question remains which specific damages are recoverable. Although the issue of damages was not directly before the court in *Miller v.*

Duhart, the court of appeals summarized the type of damages:

> As a form of malpractice, "wrongful conception" gives rise to compensatory damages that are measurable. Such damages might include prenatal and postnatal medical expenses, the mother's pain and suffering during the pregnancy and delivery, loss of consortium, and the cost of a second, corrective sterilization procedure. *Miller v. Duhart*, 637 S.W.2d at 188.

The measure of damages in a wrongful conception case shall not include the expenses of raising and educating a healthy, normal child. However, in addition to the damages listed in *Miller v. Duhart*, plaintiffs are entitled to recover, subject to appropriate proof, emotional distress, loss of wages, pain and suffering associated with the second corrective procedure, and any permanent impairment suffered by the parents as a result of the pregnancy, the delivery, or the second corrective procedure.

The judgment of the trial court is affirmed.

* * *

WILLIAM E. TURNAGE, Special Judge, concurring in part and dissenting in part.

I concur in the holding that there is a cause of action for a so-called "wrongful conception" or "wrongful pregnancy." To me these terms are complete misnomers because I believe the cause of action to be simply one of medical malpractice which happens to involve the birth of a child.

I respectfully dissent from the holding that the cost of rearing a healthy child born as the result of a physician's malpractice in the performance of a sterilization procedure is not recoverable. ... I believe this case is about medical malpractice and whether or not an exception will be carved out to exonerate physicians from liability for the bulk of the damages which flow from malpractice in performing sterilization procedures.

The principal reason given by the states which deny recovery for the costs of rearing a healthy child is the fact that society places such a high value on human life that the birth of a healthy child cannot be a legal wrong for which damages may be recovered. ...

In *Jones v. Malinowski,* 299 Md. 257, 473 A.2d 429, 435[3] (1984), the court answered the above argument in two ways. The court stated:

> To adopt such a policy and rule of law would be to subject a physician to liability for the direct, foreseeable and natural consequences of all negligently performed operations except those involving sterilization—a result, we think, completely at odds with reason. That the public policy of Maryland may foster the development and preservation of the family relationship does not, in our view, compel the adoption of a per se rule denying recovery by parents of child rearing costs from the physician whose negligence has caused their expenditure. In other words, it is not to disparage the value of human life and the societal need for harmonious family units to protect the parents' choice not to have children by recognizing child rearing costs as a compensable element of damages in negligent sterilization cases.

In *University of Arizona Health Sciences Center v. Superior Court,* 136 Ariz. 579, 584, 667 P.2d 1294, 1299 (1983), the court stated that even though a family can adjust to the birth of an unplanned child it must be recognized that there are cases where such birth can cause emotional or economic problems to the parents. In Note, *Judicial Limitations on Damages Recoverable for the Wrongful Birth of a Healthy Infant,* 68 Va.L.Rev. 1311, 1316–17 (1982), the author considered this argument and stated:

> Although they may well have realized that they would love a child if one were born to them, they may also have realized that their affection would not provide the money to feed the child or the time for the working mother to resume her interrupted career. To disallow the parents' recovery because they love their child is to leave uncompensated the significant emotional and economic harms that may accompany a wrongful birth. In a family of limited means, the application of an overriding-benefit theory injures the child as well as the parents,

since the exclusion of all damages denies the family a fund from which to provide for the unplanned child.

* * *

To award damages to the parents for the rearing of an unplanned child does not disparage the worth of the child or indicate a disregard on the part of the court for the worth of a human being. The awarding of such damages is simply the recognition that in today's world it is costly to rear a child and, in fact, the presence of an unplanned child in a family of limited means or in a family with a working mother can prove to be a disruptive factor which will damage the family unit if the child does not bring with it some financial help.

The majority does not suggest, nor is there reason that it should, that the decision of the Girdleys for the wife to undergo a sterilization procedure was in any way illegal or improper. Having elected to undergo a proper procedure to limit the size of their family, this court should not ignore the reality of the hardship which the arrival of an unplanned child can create. To do so is simply to take a "head in the sand" approach to the problem.

* * *

No one could argue persuasively that it would be reasonable to require a mother to undergo an abortion or place her child for adoption in order to minimize the damages which could be assessed against the negligent physician who performed the sterilization on her. This rule has no application in the manner suggested by the majority.

The majority holds that the costs of child rearing are speculative. It should first be noted that this court by Rule 88.01 has adopted Civil Procedure Form No. 14 for the amount of child support to be awarded in actions involving child support. Courts have long awarded reasonable amounts necessary for the support of children.

JORDAN v. TOWN OF PRATT
United States District Court, S.D. West Virginia
886 F. Supp. 555 (S.D. W. Va. 1995)
May 24, 1995
Haden, Chief Judge

[See Chapter 12.]

Charles Jordan contends Mark March, a police officer for the Town of Pratt, West Virginia, violated his civil rights by arresting him June 21, 1993 on a charge of impersonating a police officer. He contends he "was employed as [sic] by the Air National Guard ... to function as a military police officer one weekend per month, two weeks of the year and any other occasions when [he] was on active duty, and [he] served as a police/security guard for the Adjutant General of West Virginia the remainder of [his] employment." He asserts March and defendant Williams came to his home on June 19, 1993 in response to a complaint concerning a neighbor's dog. Mr. Jordan contends March inquired where he was employed, and when informed Jordan was employed by the Air National Guard, March began "rudely interrogating" him, accused him of lying, and unsuccessfully attempted to take his badge. Mr. Jordan further contends March informed him he was going to check his credentials as a police officer and if he determined they were not legitimate, he would return and arrest Jordan. Mr. Jordan asserts March telephoned a Lieutenant Colonel Johnson of the Air National Guard to determine whether Jordan was a police officer and Johnson informed March that Jordan was a police officer.

Mr. Jordan contends that despite knowing Jordan was a police officer, Officer March, with the approval of Chief of Police Williams, swore out a false complaint and warrant for Jordan's arrest on a charge of impersonating a police officer. Thereafter, Officer March arrested Jordan. Jordan spent approximately four hours in custody. The charge was dropped six weeks later.

The Court must examine whether defendants are protected from suit by the doctrine of qualified immunity. In *Wiley v. Doory,* 14 F.3d 993, 995 (4th Cir.1994) our Court of Appeals discussed generally the application of qualified immunity as follows:

> Qualified immunity shields a governmental official from liability for civil monetary damages if the officer's "conduct does not violate clearly established statutory or constitutional rights of which a reasonable person would have known." "In determining whether the specific right allegedly violated was 'clearly established,' the proper focus is not upon the right at its most general or abstract level, but at the level of its application to the specific conduct being challenged." Moreover, "the manner in which this [clearly established] right applies to the actions of the official must also be apparent." As such, if there is a "legitimate question" as to whether an official's conduct constitutes a constitutional violation, the official is entitled to qualified immunity.

The test for determining whether qualified immunity is available for a particular defendant is an objectively reasonable one. *Shaw v. Stroud,* 13 F.3d 791, 801 (4th Cir.), *cert. denied,* ___ U.S. ___ , 115 S.Ct. 67, 130 L.Ed.2d 24, *and cert. denied,* ___ U.S. ___ , 115 S.Ct. 68, 130 L.Ed.2d 24 (1994). Describing application of the "objectively reasonable" qualified immunity test to actions of police officers, our Court of Appeals has observed:

> "[O]fficers are entitled to qualified immunity when they rely on standard operating procedures, if that reliance is reasonable. A police officer is entitled to prevail on an assertion of qualified immunity if a reasonable officer possessing the same information would have believed his conduct was lawful."

"[T]he basic purpose of qualified immunity ... is to spare individual officials the burdens and uncertainties of standing trial in those instances where their conduct would strike an objective observer as falling within the range of reasonable judgment. ... '[T]he determination whether a reasonable person in the officer's position would have known that his conduct would violate the right at issue must be made ... in light of any exigencies of time and circumstance that reasonably may have affected the officer's perception.' "

The express purpose of the test of objective reasonableness is to accord "police officers latitude in exercising what are inescapably discretionary functions replete with close judgment calls." ... Moreover, "[b]ecause qualified immunity is designed to shield officers not only from liability but from the burdens of litigation, its establishment at the pleading or summary judgment stage has been specifically encouraged."

* * *

The right in issue is the Fourth Amendment right "not to be arrested except upon probable cause to believe" Jordan had violated West Virgina's law against impersonating a law enforcement officer pursuant to *W.V.Code* § 61-1-9 (1990). In order to defeat the motion for summary judgment, Jordan bears the burden of presenting sufficient evidence supporting his contention he was arrested without probable cause.

* * *

The offense contours are thus straightforward: whenever one falsely represents himself to be a law enforcement officer with the intent to deceive another, that person has violated the statute. The parties dispute whether Jordan's particular employment met the definition of law enforcement officer.

Jordan contends he was clearly a law enforcement officer under the statute because he was commissioned as a police officer for the adjutant general of West Virginia. ...

Defendants argue, in essence, that Jordan's position as security guard with the West Virginia National Guard does not qualify as a law enforcement officer for the purposes of *W.Va.Code* § 61-1-9. The legal question for the Court is whether it was clearly established at the time of the incident that a security guard with the West

Virginia National Guard qualifies as a law enforcement officer for the purposes of *W.Va.Code* § 61-1-9.

... It is not incumbent for this Court to determine definitively whether adjutant general security guards are the law enforcement officers referred to in § 61-1-9 because it appears, even if they are, such was not clearly established or known at the time of Mr. Jordan's arrest. ... Moreover, although they are "deemed to have met all the requirements for certification as a law enforcement officer," they are not deemed to be law enforcement officers as that term is used in *W.Va.Code* § 61-1-9. Their status appears to be more accurately described as that of quasi-law enforcement officers. Therefore, the Court concludes the law was not *clearly* established that Mr. Jordan's employment as an adjutant general's security guard constituted employment as a law enforcement officer, as that term is used in § 61-1-9.

Defendants have presented evidence Officer March received a complaint from a neighbor of Mr. Jordan who asserted Mr. Jordan had represented himself to be a police officer with authority in the Town of Pratt. Although Jordan challenges the some of the facts asserted by the neighbor, it is undisputed Officer March relied upon those facts in seeking a warrant for the arrest. Based upon those facts known to Officer March, the Court concludes a prudent police officer of reasonable caution could determine appropriately Mr. Jordan was in violation of the statute. The complaint information supports a finding of probable cause to make the arrest.

Because the Court determines probable cause existed to make the arrest, Defendants' motion for summary judgment on Mr. Jordan's § 1983 claim is GRANTED.

... Because Mr. Jordan failed to do more than assert bald allegations of state law violations, those state law claims will be dismissed and summary judgment on those issues will be GRANTED in favor of Defendants.

Mrs. Jordan has asserted a claim of invasion of privacy under West Virginia state law. She contends, "[a]s a result of his position as Chief of

Police, Defendant Williams came into information regarding the sexual assault of the daughter of the Plaintiff," and he "intentionally and negligently failed to keep this information confidential as required by state law and the dictates of his position, and did communicate the same in order to embarrass Plaintiff[.]" Defendants contend Mrs. Jordan has not established sufficiently an invasion of privacy claim. The Court agrees.

* * *

By her deposition testimony Mrs. Jordan stated Chief Williams told his daughter of the assault incident involving Mrs. Jordan's daughter in order to ascertain whether his own daughter had been similarly victimized. According to Mrs. Jordan, Chief Williams was concerned for his daughter because the two girls were playmates. Significantly, Mrs. Jordan stated she could understand Chief Williams concern. In such a situation, it is apparent to the Court Chief Williams conversation with his daughter was not unreasonable, although perhaps a poor exercise in judgment. Therefore, defendants' motion for summary judgment in regard to Mrs. Jordan's invasion of privacy claim is GRANTED.

Based upon the foregoing, Defendants' motion for summary judgment is GRANTED, and this action is dismissed.

GLOSSARY

abatement   A lessening or elimination.

abnormally dangerous (ultrahazardous) instrumentalities [†]   Activities or objects that are, by their very nature, extremely hazardous to persons or property. These are relevant to strict (absolute) liability cases.

absolute liability   Liability for an injury whether or not there is fault or negligence.

abuse of process   The use of legal process in a manner not contemplated by the law to achieve a purpose not intended by the law.

apprehension   Anxiety.

appropriation   A wrongful taking of anything which deprives another person of his or her rightful interest.

assault   An act of force or threat of force intended to inflict harm upon a person or to put the person in fear that such harm is imminent; an attempt to commit a battery. The perpetrator must have, or appear to have, the present ability to carry out the act.

assembly defect [†]   A theory in products liability concerning whether a defective product is unreasonably dangerous. Errors in product manufacture or assembly may render a product unreasonably hazardous despite a safe design.

assumption of risk   The legal principle that a person who knows and deliberately exposes himself or herself to a danger assumes responsibility for the risk, rather than the person who actually created the danger. Assumption of risk is often referred to as *voluntary assumption of risk*. It is a defense to negligence.

attachment   The process by which a person's property is figuratively brought into court to ensure satisfaction of a judgment that may be

rendered against him or her. In the event judgment is rendered, the property may be sold to satisfy the judgment.

attractive nuisance   An unusual mechanism, apparatus, or condition that is dangerous to young children but is so interesting and alluring as to attract them to the premises on which it is kept.

attractive nuisance doctrine (attraction theory)   The principle in the law of negligence that a person who maintains an attractive nuisance on his or her property must exercise reasonable care to protect young children against its dangers, or be held responsible for any injury that occurs, even though the injured child trespassed upon [the] property or was otherwise at fault.

bailee   The person to whom property is entrusted in a bailment.

bailment   The entrusting of personal property by one person (the bailor) to another (the bailee) for a specific purpose, with the understanding that the property will be returned when the purpose is accomplished, the stated duration of the bailment is over, or the bailor reclaims it.

bailor   The person who entrusts property to another in a bailment.

battery   The unconsented-to touching or striking of one person by another, or by an object put in motion by [the first person], with the intention of doing harm or giving offense. Battery is both a crime and a tort.

breach of warranty   The violation of an express warranty or implied warranty.

burden of rejoinder (rebuttal) [†]   The defendant's burden of proof to refute the plaintiff's evidence in a lawsuit.

business directory A listing (whether print or online) of corporations and other business organizations according to name, geographic location, product or service, brand name, advertising, and the like.

castle doctrine The doctrine that a person may use whatever force is required to defend his or her home and those in it. The principle derives its name from the maxim that "a man's home is his castle."

cause-in-fact † Cause of injury in negligence cases. If the tortfeasor's actions resulted in the victim's injuries, then the tortfeasor was the cause-in-fact of the victim's harm. Cause-in-fact includes direct, or but-for, causation as well as indirect causation.

chattel Personal property that is visible, tangible, and movable. Animals are included within the definition of chattel.

coming and going rule † Rule used when employees commit torts while coming to or going from work. In respondeat superior cases, this rule helps decide whether an employee's actions fall outside the scope of employment.

coming to the nuisance defense † A defense to private nuisance lawsuits that may be used successfully when a plaintiff owns or uses land at a location in which the alleged nuisance activity was previously occurring. The plaintiff is said to have "come to the nuisance" and thus cannot recover against the defendant.

commercial disparagement When one makes a false or misleading statement about a business to discourage the public from patronizing the business.

commercial disparagement † An intentional tort that occurs when a tortfeasor communicates false statements to third parties about a person's goods, services, or business enterprise. The tortfeasor must intend to harm the victim's ability to use goods, furnish services, or conduct business. There are three categories: disparagement of goods, disparagement of services, and disparagement of business.

common use principle † Doctrine in strict liability cases that defines abnormally dangerous activities and substances as those not commonly undertaken or used in everyday life.

community 1. People living in the same place (city, town, neighborhood) and subject to the same laws. 2. A place where people live together. 3. Society in general. 4. A group of people sharing common interests.

comparative negligence The doctrine adopted by most states that requires a comparison of the negligence of the defendant with the negligence of the plaintiff: the greater the negligence of the defendant, the lesser the level of care required of the plaintiff to permit him or her to recover. In other words, the plaintiff's negligence does not defeat his or her cause of action, but it does reduce the damages he or she is entitled to recover. Also called *comparative fault.*

compensatory damages Damages recoverable in a lawsuit for loss or injury suffered by the plaintiff as a result of the defendant's conduct. Also called actual damages, they may include expenses, loss of time, reduced earning capacity, bodily injury, and mental anguish.

complainant 1. The plaintiff in a lawsuit. 2. A person who files a formal accusation of a crime. 3. A person who makes any formal complaint. 4. The prosecuting witness in a criminal proceeding.

consent Agreement; approval; acquiescence; being of one mind. Consent necessarily involves two or more persons because, without at least two persons, there cannot be a unity of opinion or the possibility of thinking alike .

consumer contemplation test † A theory in products liability concerning faulty product design that makes a product unreasonably dangerous. If a reasonable person would not have anticipated the danger created by the fault in the product, then the product is unreasonably dangerous.

contempt   An act of disrespect toward a court or legislative body; deliberate disobedience of a court order.

contribution   1. A payment of his share of a debt or judgment by a person who is jointly liable.   2. The right of a person who has satisfied a shared indebtedness to have those with whom she shared it contribute in defraying its cost.

contributory negligence   In the law of negligence, a failure by the plaintiff to exercise reasonable care which, in part at least, is the cause of an injury. Contributory negligence defeats a plaintiff's cause of action for negligence in states that have not adopted the doctrine of comparative negligence.

control   The power or authority to direct or manage.

conversion   Control over another person's personal property which is wrongfully exercised; control applied in a manner that violates that person's title to or rights in the property. Conversion is both a tort and a crime.

culpability factoring (liability apportionment) †   A defense to negligence. When the plaintiff's negligence contributed to his or her injuries, comparative negligence calculates the percentages of the defendant's and the plaintiff's negligence and adjusts the plaintiff's damages according to the numbers. The trier-of-fact decides the percentages.

damages   The sum of money that may be recovered in the courts as financial reparation for an injury or wrong suffered as a result of breach of contract or a tortious act.

danger/utility test †   A theory in products liability concerning faulty product design that makes a product unreasonably dangerous. Under this test, a product is unreasonably hazardous if the danger created by its design outweighs the benefits derived from its use.

deep pocket   A term applied to a defendant or potential defendant who is viewed as having assets sufficient to satisfy a judgment in a lawsuit or a potential lawsuit.

defamation   Libel or slander; the written or oral publication, falsely and intentionally, of anything that is injurious to the good name or reputation of another person.

defamation by computer   When personal information about an individual that is kept in a computer system is misused or is incorrect and results in injury to that person's reputation or ability to obtain credit.

defamation by computer †   An intentional tort that occurs when the tortfeasor includes false information about a person's credit or credit rating in a computer database. This false information must be communicated to third parties, and it must injure the victim's ability to obtain credit.

defense   In both civil and criminal cases, the facts submitted and the legal arguments offered by a defendant in support of his or her claim that the plaintiff's case, or the prosecution's, should be rejected. The term "defense" may apply to a defendant's entire case or to separate grounds, called *affirmative defenses,* offered by a defendant for rejecting all or a portion of the case against him or her.

defense of persons †   A defense to the intentional torts of assault, battery, and false imprisonment. Its elements include the use of reasonable force to defend or protect a third party from injury when the third party is threatened by an attacking force.

defense of property †   A defense to the intentional torts of assault and battery. Its elements include the use of reasonable force to protect property from damage or dispossession when another person, called the *invader,* attempts to injure or wrongfully take possession of the property.

direct (but-for) causation †   A form of causation of injury in negligence cases. The formula is applied as a question: But for the defendant's actions, would the plaintiff have been harmed? If not, then the defendant directly caused the plaintiff's injuries.

discovery   A means for providing a party, in advance of trial, with access to facts that are within the knowledge of the other side, to enable the party to better try his or her case. A motion to compel discovery is the procedural means for compelling the adverse party to reveal such facts or to produce documents, books, and other things within his or her possession or control.

dispossession   A forced or fraudulent changing of possession of land from one person to another; ouster.

dominion   Ownership and control.

domitae naturae [†]   [Latin for] "domesticated nature" and referring to tame, domestic animals.

due (reasonable) care   That degree of care which a person of ordinary prudence would exercise in similar circumstances. Same as ordinary care or reasonable care.

duty   1. A legal obligation, whether imposed by the common law, statute, court order, or contract. A tort is committed only when there has been a breach of duty resulting in injury.   2. Any obligation or responsibility.

ejectment   An action at common law for the right to possession of land.

emotional distress [†]   Mental anguish. In the intentional torts called *intentional* and *reckless infliction of emotional distress,* the mental anguish is caused by the tortfeasor's outrageous conduct.

entry   The act of going upon real property.

equitable relief (remedy)   A remedy available in equity rather than at law; generally relief other than money damages.

exclusive right   A sole right; a right granted to no one else.

exclusive right of possession [†]   A land owner's right to use his or her property without interference from other persons.

execution sale   A public sale by a sheriff or similar officer of property seized under a writ of execution following a levy of execution.

false imprisonment   The unlawful restraint by one person of the physical liberty of another. Like false arrest, to which it is closely related, it is both a tort and a crime.

false light in the public eye [†]   One type of the intentional tort of invasion of privacy. Occurs when the tortfeasor publicly attributes to another individual spurious opinions, statements, or actions.

family relationships rule [†]   Doctrine used in negligent infliction of emotional distress cases. Under this rule, a bystander may recover damages if he or she witnesses a tortfeasor injuring one or more of the bystander's relatives.

fee standard [†]   A test courts use in applying the governmental/proprietary distinction. If a governmental agency assesses a fee for an activity, the activity is considered proprietary. If not, it is considered governmental.

ferae naturae   Wild animals.

fictitious name   An artificial name that a person or a corporation adopts for business or professional purposes.

foreseeability [†]   The notion that a specific action, under particular circumstances, would produce an anticipated result. In negligence law, if it were reasonably foreseeable that the plaintiff would be harmed by the defendant's actions, then the scope of duty includes the plaintiff. Foreseeability of injury is another aspect of negligence theory, which falls within proximate cause. Foreseeability is defined in terms of reasonableness.

foreseeable plaintiffs theory [†]   A theory used in analyzing negligence cases. Under this theory, if it were reasonably foreseeable that the injured victim would be harmed as a consequence of the tortfeasor's actions, then the tortfeasor's scope of duty includes the victim. The victim is said to be a *foreseeable plaintiff.* Unforeseeable plaintiffs fall outside the defendant's scope of duty, because their injuries could not have been reasonably anticipated as a result of the defendant's conduct. The theory is also used in products liability analysis.

fraud (deceit) Deceit, deception, or trickery that is intended to induce, and does induce, another to part with anything of value or surrender some legal right.

frolic of his own (frolic and detour rule) The conduct of an employee or agent who has departed from the scope of employment (that is, from doing [the] employer's or principal's business) to do something for himself or herself. The principal or employer is not liable for injury to a third party caused by the negligence of an agent or employee who is on a "frolic of his own."

governmental functions The activities engaged in by a government in carrying out its governmental duties.

great care The degree of care a prudent person usually exercises concerning his or her own affairs of great importance.

gross negligence Willfully and intentionally acting, or failing to act, with a deliberate indifference to how others may be affected.

hearsay The testimony of a witness as to a statement made to him or her outside of court, or made to someone else who told him or her what was said, that is offered in court to prove the truth of the matter contained in the statement.

hot (fresh) pursuit A person may use reasonable force to recover property from a thief if he or she pursues and apprehends [the thief] immediately.

imminent danger exception [†] A nineteenth- and early twentieth-century exception to the privity of contract requirement in defective product cases.

immunity An exemption granted by law, contrary to the general rule; a privilege. Immunity may be granted to a class of persons or to an individual.

impact rule The rule, existing in only a few states, that for a plaintiff to recover damages for mental anguish in a negligence action, impact must have occurred, or at a minimum, there must have been physical contact.

impleader A defendant's action in bringing into a lawsuit, as an additional defendant, a party whom the defendant asserts is responsible to the plaintiff for the damages or other remedy the plaintiff seeks.

in loco parentis [Latin for] "in the place of parents." Describes a person who, in the absence of a child's parent or guardian, and without formal legal approval, temporarily assumes a parent's obligations with respect to the child.

independent contractor As distinguished from an employee, a person who contracts to do work for another person in his or her own way, controlling the means and method by which the work is done but not the end product. An independent contractor is the agent of the person with whom he or she contracts.

indirect causation [†] A form of causation of injury in negligence cases. The most common test is substantial factor analysis.

infliction of emotional distress Results from someone's outrageous conduct which is designed to cause another to suffer anxiety, fright, or anguish.

informed consent Agreement to permit something to occur ... , after having been given as much information as necessary to make an intelligent and rational ("informed") decision.

injunction A court order that commands or prohibits some act or course of conduct. It is preventive in nature and designed to protect a plaintiff from irreparable injury to his or her property or property rights by prohibiting or commanding the doing of certain acts. An injunction is a form of equitable relief.

intent   Purpose; the plan, course, or means a person conceives to achieve a certain result. Intent is an essential element of any crime except a strict liability crime or a regulatory offense, and some petty offenses and infractions. Intent is not, however, limited to conscious wrongdoing, and may be inferred or presumed.

intentional infliction of emotional distress †   An intentional tort that occurs when the tortfeasor's outrageous conduct, which is intended to cause severe mental anguish in the victim, actually causes the victim such emotional suffering as a result of the tortfeasor's actions.

intentional injury (tort)   An injury inflicted by positive, willful, and aggressive conduct, or by design, as opposed to an injury caused by negligence or resulting from an accident.

invasion of privacy   A violation of the right of privacy.

investigation   1. An inquiry, either judicial, legislative, or administrative, for the discovery and collection of facts concerning a particular matter or matters.   2. Inquiry; looking into something; research.

invitee   A person who enters the premises of another at the latter's invitation, or for business purposes, or for their mutual advantage. [N]ote that the distinction between invitee and licensee has been abandoned in some jurisdictions.

joint and several liability   The liability of two or more persons who jointly commit a tort (joint tortfeasors).

judge   A public officer who conducts or presides over a court of justice.

last clear chance doctrine   A rule of negligence law by which a negligent defendant is held liable to a plaintiff who has negligently placed himself or herself in peril, if the defendant had a later opportunity than the plaintiff to avoid the occurrence that resulted in injury. In some jurisdictions, the doctrine is referred to as the *discovered peril doctrine* and in others as the *humanitarian doctrine.*

libel   A false and malicious publication, expressed either in printing, writing, or by signs and pictures, tending to harm a person's reputation and expose him or her to public hatred, contempt, or ridicule.

licensee   A person who enters upon the property of another for his own convenience, pleasure, or benefit, uninvited but tolerated by the owner. [N]ote that the distinction between a licensee and an invitee has been abandoned in some jurisdictions.

loss of consortium   The loss of a spouse's assistance or companionship, or the loss of a spouse's ability or willingness to have sexual relations. If such loss results from a tort, it gives rise to a cause of action in favor of the partner of the spouse injured by the tort.

maintenance defect †   A theory in products liability concerning whether a defective product is unreasonably dangerous. If a seller fails to maintain a product properly, and the product later causes injury to the ultimate user, then the product was unreasonably dangerous.

malice   State of mind that causes the intentional doing of a wrongful act without legal excuse or justification; a condition of mind prompting a person to the commission of a dangerous or deadly act in deliberate disregard of the lives or safety of others. The term does not necessarily connote personal ill will. It can and frequently does mean general malice. ...

As an element of malicious prosecution, a prosecution motived either by personal malice or by an unjustifiable purpose.

In the law of defamation, to be actionable malice must be actual malice or express malice, as distinct from implied malice or constructive malice. A privileged communication is conditioned upon an absence of malice.

In the law of damages, additional damages may be awarded if the damage to the plaintiff resulted from an injury inflicted recklessly or with malice.

malicious prosecution A criminal prosecution or civil suit commenced maliciously and without probable cause. After the termination of such a prosecution or suit in the defendant's favor, the defendant has the right to bring an action against the original plaintiff for the tort of "malicious prosecution."

mandamus [Latin for] "we command." A writ issuing from a court of competent jurisdiction, directed to an inferior court, board, or corporation, or to an officer of a branch of government (judicial, executive, or legislative), requiring the performance of some ministerial act. A writ of mandamus is an extraordinary remedy.

minor A person who has not yet attained his or her majority; a person who has not reached legal age; a person who has not acquired the capacity to contract.

misrepresentation The statement of an untruth; a misstatement of fact designed to lead one to believe that something is other than it is; a false statement of fact designed to deceive.

mistake 1. An erroneous mental conception that influences a person to act or to decline to act; an unintentional act, omission, or error arising from ignorance, surprise, imposition, or misplaced confidence. ... 2. An error; a misunderstanding; an inaccuracy.

mixed nuisance A nuisance that is both public and private in its effects.

motive The reason that leads the mind to desire a result; that which leads the mind to engage in a criminal act; that which causes the mind to form intent; the reason for an intention.

necessary force † That degree of force reasonably perceived as required to repel an attack or resist confinement. It is an aspect of self-defense.

necessity 1. That which is necessary; that which must be done. 2. That which is compelled by natural forces and cannot be resisted. Necessity is a defense in a criminal prosecution if the defendant committed the crime to prevent a more serious harm from occurring.

negligence The failure to do something that a reasonable person would do in the same circumstances, or the doing of something a reasonable person would not do. Negligence is a wrong generally characterized by carelessness, inattentiveness, and neglectfulness rather than by a positive intent to cause injury.

negligence per se Negligence that is beyond debate because the law, usually a statute or ordinance, has established a duty or standard of care that the defendant has violated, as a result of which he has caused injury to the plaintiff.

negligent infliction of emotional distress † Outrageous conduct by the tortfeasor which the tortfeasor reasonably should have anticipated would produce significant and reasonably foreseeable emotional injury to the victim. By his or her actions, the tortfeasor must breach the duty of reasonable care, and the victim must be a reasonably foreseeable plaintiff.

nominal damages Damages awarded to a plaintiff in a very small or merely symbolic amount. Such damages are appropriate in a situation where: (1) although a legal right has been violated, no actual damages have been incurred, but the law recognizes the need to vindicate the plaintiff; or (2) some compensable injury has been shown, but the amount of that injury has not been proven.

nuisance Anything a person does that annoys or disturbs another person in his or her use, possession, or enjoyment of his or her property, or which renders the ordinary use or possession of the property uncomfortable. What constitutes a nuisance in a particular case depends upon numerous factors, including the type of neighborhood in which the property is located, the nature of the act or acts complained of, their proximity to the persons alleging injury or damage, their frequency or continuity, and the nature and extent of the resulting injury, damage, or annoyance.

nuisance per se An act, occupation, or structure that is considered a nuisance at all times and under any circumstances, regardless of location or surroundings.

occupier † An individual who does not own, but who uses, real estate, including tenants (lessees).

permanent injunction An injunction granted after a final hearing on the merits, as distinguished from a temporary injunction granted to provide temporary relief.

physical manifestations rule † Doctrine applied in negligent infliction of emotional distress cases. Under this rule, the plaintiff may recover damages if he or she suffered physical symptoms accompanying the mental anguish.

piercing the corporate veil Ignoring the corporate entity to reach or to proceed legally against the corporation's directors, officers, or managers directly and personally. Although a corporation's officers and directors are not normally liable for the acts of the corporation, the courts will hold them responsible for corporate acts if the purpose of organizing the corporation was to perpetrate fraud or if the corporation was a mere shell without substantial assets or capital. This judicial process is known as "piercing the corporate veil."

police power The power of government to make and enforce laws and regulations necessary to maintain and enhance the public welfare and to prevent individuals from violating the rights of others.

preponderance of the evidence The degree of proof required in most civil actions. It means "more likely than not"; that the greater weight and value of the credible evidence, taken as a whole, belongs to one side in a lawsuit rather than to the other side. In other words, the party whose evidence is more convincing has a "preponderance of the evidence" on its side and must, as a matter of law, prevail in the lawsuit because it has met its burden of proof. The expression "preponderance of the evidence" has nothing to do with the number of witnesses a party presents, only with the credibility and value of their testimony.

prima facie case A cause of action or defense that is sufficiently established by a party's evidence to justify a verdict in his or her favor, provided the other party does not rebut that evidence; a case supported by sufficient evidence to justify its submission to the trier of fact and the rendition of a compatible verdict.

private nuisance A nuisance that threatens injury to one or just a few persons; a nuisance that violates only private rights and produces damages to one or no more than a few persons.

privilege An immunity, exemption, right, or advantage possessed by an individual, a group of individuals, or a class of persons, which is not possessed by others and which exists by operation of law or by virtue of a license, franchise, grant, or other permission; an exemption from a burden.

privity of contract The legal relationship between the parties to a contract. In some circumstances, a party must be in privity of contract with another party in order to assert a claim.

probable cause A reasonable amount of suspicion, supported by circumstances sufficiently strong to justify a prudent and cautious person's belief that certain alleged facts are probably true.

process In a technical sense, the means of compelling a defendant to appear in court in a civil case.

process serving † The method by which a defendant in a lawsuit is notified that a plaintiff has filed suit against the defendant. Also called *service of process*. Governmental officials engaged in process serving are generally immune from intentional tort liability.

product manufacturer † The maker of a product which, if defective, gives rise to products liability.

product(s) liability The liability of a manufacturer or seller of an article for an injury caused to a person or to property by a defect in the article sold. A product liability suit is a tort action in which strict liability is imposed. The manufacturer or seller of a defective product may be liable to third parties as well as to purchasers, as privity of contract is not a requirement in a product liability case.

professional community standard of care † The standard of reasonable care used in negligence cases involving defendants with special skills and knowledge.

proprietary function A function of local government that it may or may not perform, at its discretion, as opposed to its governmental duties.

prosecutor A public official, elected or appointed, who conducts criminal prosecutions on behalf of his or her jurisdiction.

proximate cause As an element of liability in a tort case, that cause which, unbroken by any intervening cause, produced the injury, and without which the result would not have occurred; the primary cause; the efficient cause. Note that the proximate cause of an injury is not necessarily the final cause or the act or omission nearest in time to the injury.

public disclosure of private facts † One type of the intentional tort of invasion of privacy. Occurs when the tortfeasor communicates purely private information about a person to the public without permission, and a reasonable person would find this disclosure extremely objectionable.

public nuisance An act or omission that adversely affects the safety, health, or morals of the public, or causes some substantial annoyance, inconvenience, or injury to the public.

publication The act of making something known to the public; the act of publishing. ... In the law of libel and slander, the act of communicating a defamation to a person or persons other than the person defamed. Publication is essential because, without it, there is no defamation.

punitive damages Damages that are awarded over and above compensatory damages or actual damages because of the wanton, reckless, or malicious nature of the wrong done by the plaintiff. Such damages bear no relation to the plaintiff's actual loss and are often called exemplary damages, because their purpose is to make an example of the plaintiff to discourage others from engaging in the same kind of conduct in the future.

purchaser A person who acquires property by purchase.

reasonable discipline † An intentional tort defense. Its elements include the use of reasonable force by a parent, guardian, or authorized individual against a child to maintain order or punish unacceptable misconduct.

reasonable force Force that is appropriate in the circumstances. A person is entitled to use "reasonable force" to defend [his or her person] or ... property.

reasonable man (person) test (standard) A standard for determining negligence, which asks: "What would a reasonable person have done in the same circumstances?" In short, it measures the failure to do that which a person of ordinary intelligence and judgment would have done in the circumstances, or the doing of that which a person of ordinary intelligence and judgment would not have done.

reckless infliction of emotional distress † An intentional tort that occurs when the tortfeasor's outrageous conduct causes the victim to suffer severe mental anguish. Intent to produce the emotional suffering is not necessary. Instead, it is sufficient that the tortfeasor knew, or reasonably should have known, that his or her misbehavior would produce emotional distress. Often with this tort, the tortfeasor's conduct is wanton, with no apparent regard for the victim's suffering.

remedy The means by which a right is enforced, an injury is redressed, and relief is obtained.

replevin 1. An action by which the owner of personal property taken or detained by another may recover possession of it. 2. The name of the writ issued by a court in an action of replevin authorizing the sheriff to seize the property that is the subject of the action pending the outcome of the litigation.

res ipsa loquitur   [Latin for] "the thing speaks for itself." When an instrumentality (i.e., a thing) causes injury, an inference or rebuttable presumption arises that the injury was caused by the defendant's negligence, if the thing or instrumentality was under the exclusive control or management of the defendant and the occurrence was such as in the ordinary course of events would not have happened if the defendant had used reasonable care.

respondeat superior   [Latin for] "let the master respond." The doctrine under which liability is imposed upon an employer for the acts of its employees committed in the course and scope of their employment. Similarly, respondeat superior makes a principal liable for a tort committed by his or her agent, and a master responsible for the negligence of his or her servant.

retailer   A person engaged in the business of making retail sales of goods or merchandise.

rightful repossession †   A defense to trespass to land, trespass to chattel, conversion, assault, and battery. Its elements include the use of reasonable force to retake possession of personal property of which the owner has been wrongfully dispossessed, or to which the owner has been wrongfully denied possession. Efforts to retake the chattel must be made promptly after the original dispossession (or denial of possession) occurs.

scope of duty †   In negligence law, defined in terms of those individuals who might foreseeably be injured as a result of the tortfeasor's actions. This is called *reasonable foreseeability.* The scope of duty includes all those foreseeable plaintiffs who could have been hurt because of the tortfeasor's conduct. This is called *foreseeability of the victim.*

scope of employment   A phrase referring to activities carried out by an employee in doing the work assigned to him or her by his or her employer. Under the doctrine of respondeat superior, an employer is not liable for injury inflicted by an employee acting outside of the "scope of his employment." However, an employee's acts which are merely incidental to his or her regular duties, but are of benefit to the employer, are generally deemed to fall within the scope of his or her employment.

self-defense   The use of force to protect oneself from death or imminent bodily harm at the hands of an aggressor. A person may use only that amount of force reasonably necessary to protect ... against the peril with which he or she is threatened; thus, deadly force may be used in self-defense only against an aggressor who ... uses deadly force.

seller   A person who sells property he or she owns; a person who contracts for the sale of property, real or personal; a vendor.

sensibilities †   In nuisance law, ways in which people's physical and emotional sense are affected.

sensory perception rule †   Doctrine used in negligent infliction of emotional distress cases. Under this rule, a bystander may recover damages if he or she witnesses a tortfeasor injuring another person, so long as the bystander perceives the event directly through his or her own senses.

service of process (process serving)   Delivery of a summons, writ, complaint, or other process to the opposite party, or other person entitled to receive it, in such manner as the law prescribes, whether by leaving a copy at his or her residence, by mailing a copy to [the opposite party] or his or her attorney, or by publication.

sheriff's sale   A sale of real estate carried out by the sheriff under a foreclosure decree or similar court order. A sheriff's sale is also referred to as an *execution sale, foreclosure sale,* or *judicial sale.*

slander   A false and malicious oral statement tending to blacken a person's reputation or to damage his or her means of livelihood.

slander of title   A false or malicious statement, oral or written, that brings into question a person's right or title to real or personal property, causing him or her damage.

slight care   A very minimal degree of care; the least degree of care.

sovereign (governmental) immunity   The principle that the government—specifically, the United States or any state of the United States—is immune from suit except when it consents to be sued.

statutes of limitations   Federal and state statutes prescribing the maximum period of time during which various types of civil actions and criminal prosecutions can be brought after the occurrence of the injury or the offense.

strict (absolute) liability   Liability for an injury whether or not there is fault or negligence; absolute liability. The law imposes strict liability in product liability cases.

substantial factor analysis [†]   A test for indirect causation in negligence cases. The tortfeasor is liable for injuries to the victim when the tortfeasor's conduct was a substantial factor in producing the harm.

sunshine law   State and federal statutes requiring that meetings of administrative agencies be open to the public.

"taking the victim as you find him" [†]   A theory of negligence cases which states that the victim's injuries were reasonably foreseeable even if the tortfeasor was unaware of the victim's peculiar physical, health, or other preexisting conditions. In effect, the tortfeasor takes the victim as the tortfeasor finds him, and thus proximately causes the harm.

temporary restraining order (TRO)   Under the Federal Rules of Civil Procedure, injunctive relief that the court is empowered to grant, without notice to the opposite party and pending a hearing on the merits, upon a showing that failure to do so will result in "immediate and irreparable injury, loss, or damage." TROs are similarly available under state rules of civil procedure.

tender years   A term used to describe minors, particularly when they are very young.

tort   A wrong involving a breach of duty and resulting in an injury to the person or property of another. A tort is distinguished from a breach of contract in that a tort is a violation of a duty established by law, whereas a breach of contract results from a failure to meet an obligation created by the agreement of the parties. Although the same act may be both a crime and a tort, the crime is an offense against the public which is prosecuted by the state in a criminal action; the tort is a private wrong that must be pursued by the injured party in a civil action.

tortfeasor   A person who commits a tort.

toxic tort actions [†]   Claims and suits involving toxic chemicals, pollution, hazardous waste disposal and transportation, and other environmentally sensitive issues. Toxic tort actions apply many tort theories, including trespass to land, negligence, absolute liability for ultrahazardous substances, products liability, and nuisance.

transferred intent   The doctrine that if a defendant who intends to injure one person unintentionally harms another, the intent is transferred to the person who is unintentionally harmed. This doctrine permits the defendant to be prosecuted as if he or she had intended to harm the person injured.

trespass   An unauthorized entry or intrusion on the real property of another.

trespass to chattel [†]   Occurs when the tortfeasor intentionally deprives or interferes with the chattel owner's possession or exclusive use of personal property. The tortfeasor's possession or interference must be unauthorized, which means that the owner cannot have consented.

ultimate user [†]   In products liability law, a person who is injured by a defective product. It must have been reasonably foreseeable that the injured party would use the defective product.

unforeseeable plaintiffs [†] Persons whose injuries the tort feasor could not reasonably have anticipated as a result of the tortfeasor's actions.

unreasonable intrusion [†] One type of the intentional tort of invasion of privacy. Occurs when the tortfeasor engages in an excessive and highly offensive invasion upon another person's seclusion or solitude.

vicarious liability Liability imposed upon a person because of the act or omission of another.

vicious propensity rule [†] Doctrine in absolute liability cases involving domestic animals. Normally owners are not strictly liable for injuries caused by their domestic animals. However, if the animals display vicious propensities and hurt someone or their property, then the owner is absolutely liable. Vicious propensities are proven by past episodes of the animal's nasty behavior.

warranty 1. Generally, an agreement to be responsible for all damages arising from the falsity of a statement or the failure of an assurance. 2. With respect to a contract for sale of goods, a promise, either express or implied by law, with respect to the fitness or merchantability of the article that is the subject of the contract.

wholesaler A person who sells goods at wholesale, as opposed to retail.

wrongful birth (life, pregnancy) When an unsound child is born to parents who decided not to prevent or terminate the pregnancy because of erroneous medical advice, or because of medical advice not offered that should have been, the birth may, in some jurisdictions, be the basis for a wrongful birth action.

wrongful death statutes State statutes that allow the personal representative of the decedent to bring an action on behalf of the decedent's statutory beneficiaries if the decedent's death was the result of the defendant's wrongful act.

zone of danger rule [†] Doctrine used in negligent infliction of emotional distress cases. Under this rule, if a bystander witnesses substantial injury to another person, often a relative, then the bystander may recover damages for negligent infliction of emotional distress if he or she fell within the zone of danger created by the tortfeasor's conduct that hurt the other person.

INDEX